TRIAL PRACTICE SERIES

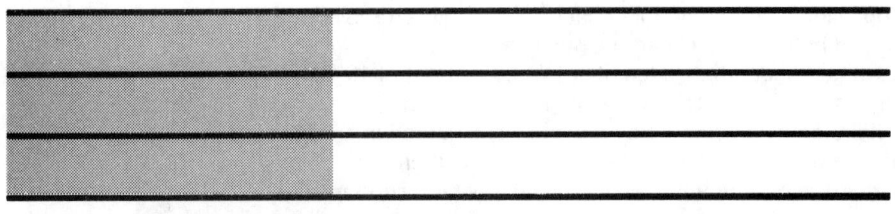

Determining Economic Loss in Injury and Death Cases
Second Edition

Wm. Gary Baker, Ph.D.
Professor of Finance
School of Business
Washburn University of
  Topeka

Michael K. Seck, J.D., M.B.A.
Partner: Fisher, Patterson,
  Sayler & Smith
Overland Park, Kansas
Member of the Kansas Bar

Shepard's/McGraw-Hill, Inc.
P.O. Box 35300
Colorado Springs, Colorado 80935-3530

McGraw-Hill, Inc.
New York ● St. Louis ● San Francisco ● Auckland ● Bogotá ● Caracas
Colorado Springs ● Hamburg ● Lisbon ● London ● Madrid ● Mexico
Milan ● Montreal ● New Delhi ● Panama ● Paris ● San Juan ● São Paulo
Singapore ● Sydney ● Tokyo ● Toronto

Revised edition of *Determining Economic Loss in Injury and
Death Cases*, by Wm. Gary Baker and Michael K. Seck
(Shepard's/McGraw-Hill 1987).

12345678910 SHLB 932109876543

Library of Congress Cataloging-in-Publication Data

Baker, Wm. Gary.
    Determining economic loss in injury and death cases / Wm. Gary
Baker, Michael K. Seck. — 2nd ed.
        p. cm. — (Trial practice series)
    Includes index.
    ISBN 0-07-172565-2
    1. Damages—Unites States. 2. Lost earnings damages—United
States. 3. Personal injuries—United States. 4. Wrongful death—United
States. 5. Forensic economics—United States. I. Seck, Michael K. II. Title.   III.
Series.
KF1250.B35 1993
346.7303'23—dc20
[347.306323]   93-36089
                                                                                      CIP

ISBN 0-07-172565-2

DEL3

The Publisher for this book was Mary Kay LaRue, the Sponsoring Editor was Patrick
McCahill, and the Legal Editor was Catherine Gasteazoro.

Shepard's Trial Practice Series

This book is dedicated to Dr. Oliver Guinn, a friend, colleague and mentor and to my children, Bill, Matt, Jeff and Anne. And to Jeff's wife, Lori, and their daughter, Kimberly.

Preface

This book is designed to assist attorneys in their understanding of the present value of future streams of money. Hopefully the book will serve as a practical guide to aid in the understanding of the methods employed by economists when they calculate present values.

As with any undertaking of this magnitude there are many people who make the completion of the project possible. The group most responsible for the completion of this project are the attorneys, both plaintiff and defense, who have asked me to be involved in economic evaluations, and who have examined and cross-examined me.

Mike Seck, the co-author, has been more than understanding and for that I am grateful. Thank you, Mike.

And finally, the one who takes the garbled work and performs magic and does it in a most patient manner, our editor, Catherine Gasteazoro. You have been truly marvelous. Thank you.

Contents

Detailed

2   Historic Loss

5   Discount Rates: The Present Value Calculation

8   Modifications and the Vocational Expert

1 The Economist's Role and Overview

§1.01   The Role of the Economist

More and more economists and actuaries are being asked by attorneys to assist in the economic evaluation of loss resulting from an injury. Economists and actuaries are being retained by the plaintiff's attorney to assist in the calculation of (1) historic loss, (2) future income, and (3) future expenses. Defense attorneys are retaining economists to review the plaintiff's economist's report and to assist the defense attorney in his or her preparation for trial cross-examination of plaintiff's economist.

§1.02   Plaintiff's Economist's Role

The plaintiff's economist performs three different functions. First, the economist calculates the loss suffered by the plaintiff as a result of an injury caused by the actions of the defendant. Second, if the case goes to trial, the economist must educate the jury on what *present value* is and how it is calculated. Finally, after explaining what present value is, the economist must give his or her opinion on past and future losses.

§1.03   —Types of Losses Economist Can Estimate

Economists calculate dollar losses, in-kind losses, and increases in expenses. The economic analysis involves *dollar losses* from wages, fringe benefits, retirement programs, dividend income, rental income, royalty income, lost income from having put a spouse through school and then divorcing, increases in asset values during a marriage, and lost profits from a business. *In-kind losses* are the result of someone receiving a benefit for which dollars were not actually paid. Examples of in-kind benefits would include the lost output from a garden, or the value of household services provided by a husband, a wife, or a child.

Other calculations the economist can make include the estimate of future *expenses* that may be incurred as a result of an injury. These expenses may be nursing home care, therapy, additional personal equipment such as vehicle modification for the handicapped, modifications to the home, drugs, future surgery, and the like.

Today economists are estimating the value of life. This area is referred to as *hedonics*.

§1.04   —Calculating Plaintiff's Loss

Plaintiff's loss may consist of lost income, as a result of the injury, or additional expenses resulting from the injury, and the loss in the value of life. The economist makes an estimate of past losses and future losses.

Typically, the *historic loss* is from the date of the injury until the assumed date of the trial. The *future loss* is from the date of the trial forward. The future loss of wages may run to age 65, or some other assumed termination date, while additional expenses may run throughout the injured party's life.

In the calculation of the present value of future income and future medical expenses, the economist must determine the basis for the dollar forecast, and appropriate growth rate for future income and expenses, and, finally, an appropriate discount rate, or interest rate.

§1.05   —Types of Losses Economists Cannot Estimate

Economists cannot estimate losses which do not have a dollar basis. Economists do not estimate pain and suffering, the joy of having a child. The economic loss is a loss which can have a dollar amount assigned to it. In §1.03, the in-kind value of a garden was mentioned. The economists could estimate the dollar value of the produce from the garden but not the joy from having a garden and raising one's own vegetables. In a similar fashion, the economist may use studies to estimate a *value for life* but the economist does not attempt to estimate the *joy of living*.

§1.06   Defendant's Economist's Role

The primary role of the defendant's economist is to review the written report of the plaintiff's economist and assist the defense attorney in preparation for trial. Typically, a defense attorney who retains an economist does not list the economist as a witness, since an economist testifying for the defense would establish the minimum loss. On summation, plaintiff's attorney would argue that the loss is between the dollar amount estimated by the plaintiff's economist and the dollar amount estimated by the defendant's economist.

§1.07   Overview of the Book

In estimating the present value of future income and the present value of future expenses, the following basic formula is used:

$$\text{Present Value of Future Income} = \$ \sum_{t=0}^{n} * [(1+g)^t / (1+d)^t]$$

Where:

$\$$ represents the beginning earnings or expenses
g represents the annual growth rate of the dollars
d represents the annual interest rate, or discount rate, used to reduce the future dollar stream to present value
t represents the number of years into the future the analysis occurs

This formula can be modified to take into account partial disability of an injured party, adjustments for participating in the labor force, adjustments for seeking employment, consumption, household services, and taxes. When these other variables are entered into the analysis, the formula is expanded and referred to as an extended analysis. The formula for the extended analysis is:

$$\text{Present Value of Future Income} = \$ \sum_{t=0}^{n} * M * [(1+g)^t / (1+d)^t] * P_L * P_S * P_F * C * HS * Tx$$

Where:

$\$$ represents the beginning earnings or expenses

M represents the modification to lost income due to a disability

g represents the annual growth rate of the dollars

d represents the annual interest rate, or discount rate, used to reduce the future dollar stream to present value

t represents the number of years into the future the analysis occurs

P_L represents the probability an individual will live each successive year (mortality adjustment)

P_S represents the probability an individual will seek employment

P_F represents the probability an individual will find employment

C represents individual consumption

HS represents household services

Tx represents taxes

The extended formula will appear at the beginning of each of the chapters that addresses one of the variables. The variable being addressed will be underlined. How each of the variables affects the size of the present value figure will be explained in the chapter.

A brief overview of each chapter appears below. The overview will indicate what variable is being examined and how that variable affects the present value. That is, does the variable, when included in the analysis, cause the present value to become larger, or does the variable cause the present value to become smaller? The basic formula, or basic analysis, uses the 4 variable—dollars, growth rate, discount rate, and the number of years—to calculate the present value of a future income stream or the present value of a future stream of expenses. The extended analysis uses all 11 variables to calculate the present value of the income or expense stream.

There are only two approaches that should properly be considered. Either the analysis uses 4 variables, or it uses all 11. One should not pick and choose which variables should be included.

§1.08 —Chapter 2: Historic Loss

Chapter 2 is concerned with the historic loss. This is the dollars lost between the date of the accident and the present value date. The losses identified as historic losses will typically be future losses also.

For example, the historic losses may consist of wages, medical expenses, and household services. The losses began on the date of the accident and continue until the present value date.

The present value of the future losses will begin on the present value date and continue in to the future. The future losses will also consist of wages, medical expenses, and household services.

§1.09   Chapter 3: Base Dollars

$$\text{Present Value of Future Income} = \underline{\$} \sum_{t=0}^{n} * \text{M} * [(1+g)^t / (1+d)^t] * P_L * P_S * P_F * C * HS * Tx$$

Chapter 3 is concerned with the base dollar amount ("$") used in the present value calculation. The economist can address three types of calculations.

The first type of calculation is designed to estimate the present value of the future income stream. The income stream in a broad sense can include wages or salary, overtime compensation, rental income, dividend income, medical expenses, nursing home care, domestic services, fringe benefits, health insurance costs, and retirement benefits.

The second type of calculation is designed to estimate the present value of future in-kind benefits. An example of in-kind services is household services. A death or injury can result in the loss of these services. Although there is no actual cash involved in the providing of the services, there can be a cash loss if the services must be hired to replace the loss. It is in this area that the value of life, or hedonics, is calculated.

The third type of calculation is designed to estimate the present value of future medical expenses. The medical expenses include doctor's fees, hospital charges, prescription drugs, therapy, and any expenses connected with environmental modification.

Determining the base dollar amount used in the calculation of the present value is the purpose of Chapter 3. The higher the base dollar amount, the larger the present value will be.

§1.10   —Chapter 4: The Growth Rate

$$\text{Present Value of Future Income} = \$ \sum_{t=0}^{n} * \text{M} * [\underline{(1+g)}^t / (1+d)^t] * P_L * P_S * P_F * C * \underline{HS} * Tx$$

The growth rate applied to earnings and to current expenses is critical to the calculation of the present value. Different growth rates may be applicable to different losses. For example, the growth rate used to calculate the present value of a future income stream may be different form the growth rate used to calculate the present value of future medical expenses.

Chapter 4 discusses the concept of growth rates, how growth rates may be calculated from existing data, and how the growth rates are applied in the present value analysis. The impact of various growth assumptions is also demonstrated. The higher the growth rate, the larger the present value of the future income and future expenses will be.

§1.11   —Chapter 5: Discount Rates: The Present Value Calculation

$$\text{Present Value of Future Income} = \$ \sum_{t=0}^{n} * M * [(1+g)^t / \underline{(1+d)}^t] * P_L * P_S * P_F * C * HS * Tx$$

The *discount rate* is synonymous with the term *interest rate*. The terms refer to the rate at which funds invested in an asset earn a return. Chapter 5 addresses what *discounting to present value* means, how different discount rates are calculated, and how the size of the discount rate affects the present value calculation. The larger the discount rate, the lower the present value will be.

§1.12   —Chapter 6: Combining Growth and Discount

$$\text{Present Value of Future Income} = \$ \sum_{t=0}^{n} * M * \underline{[(1+g)^t / (1+d)^t]} * P_L * P_S * P_F * C * HS * Tx$$

Chapter 6 combines the concept of a *growth rate* with the concept of a *discount rate*. The two methods of calculating the present value of a future income stream are presented. A worksheet is developed that permits the calculation of the present value of future income streams given assumed growth and discount rates.

§1.13   —Chapter 7: Wages, Salaries, and Fringes

$$\text{Present Value of Future Income} = \$ \sum_{t=0}^{n} * M * [(\underline{1+g})^t / (1+d)^t] * P_L * P_S * P_F * C * HS * Tx$$

Chapter 7 addresses the losses associated with employment. The losses include the wages, salary, overtime payments, and fringe benefits. The source of wage and salary information is presented. These sources include employee, employer, federal, and state sources.

§1.14   —Chapter 8: Modifications and the Vocational Expert

$$\text{Present Value of Future Income} = \$ \sum_{t=0}^{n} * \underline{M} * [(1+g)^t / (1+d)^t] * P_L * P_S * P_F * C * HS * Tx$$

The basic formula for calculating the present value of future income can be modified to reflect disability. If a person is disabled, the ability to earn may be reduced but not eliminated. "M" represents the degree to which an individual's earning capacity has been diminished or modified. The chapter also addresses sources of information used to modify the loss. The larger reduction in earning capacity, the larger the present figure will be.

§1.15   —Chapter 9: Household Services

$$\text{Present Value of Future Income} = \underline{\$} \sum_{t=0}^{n} * M * [(1+g)^t / (1+d)^t] * P_L * P_S * P_F * C * HS * Tx$$

The value of household services has become an item of economic study. The value of household services has significant value to a family. Chapter 9 presents results of different studies addressing the value of household services.

§1.16   —Chapter 10: Life Care Plans

$$\text{Present Value of Future Income} = \underline{\$} \sum_{t=0}^{n} * M * [(1+g)^t / (1+d)^t] * P_L * P_S * P_F * C * HS * Tx$$

Life care plans are constructed by persons specially trained to identify the needs of a person who is disabled. Chapter 10 presents a life care plan prepared by such a specialist. The construction of the present value of the life care plan is explained. The present value of the life care plan is presented.

§1.17   —Chapter 11: Hedonic Loss

$$\text{Present Value of Future Income} = \underline{\$} \sum_{t=0}^{n} * M * [(1+g)^t / (1+d)^t] * P_L * P_S * P_F * C * HS * Tx$$

Hedonics is thought to evaluate the "joy of living." Chapter 11 attempts to put the concept of hedonics in perspective and to explain how the concept of hedonics is now being used in the courtroom.

§1.18 —Chapter 12: Mortality Adjustment

$$\text{Present Value of Future Income} = \$ \sum_{t=0}^{n} * M * [(1+g)^t / (1+d)^t] * \underline{P_L} * P_S * P_F * C * HS * T_X$$

The *probability of living* refers to the mortality adjustment. Mortality tables are presented for men and women by race. The adjustment of mortality is made by adjusting each year's present value calculation by the probability of living. Chapter 12 shows how the annual adjustments are made. Mortality adjustments lower the present value of the future income stream.

§1.19 —Chapter 13: Probability of Seeking and Finding Employment

$$\text{Present Value of Future Income} = \$ \sum_{t=0}^{n} * M * [(1+g)^t / (1+d)^t] * P_L * \underline{P_S} * \underline{P_F} * C * HS * T_X$$

The *probability of seeking employment* shows how likely it is an individual will seek or try to find employment. This figure is combined with the *probability of finding employment*. The two should be used together and combined with the probability of living when calculating the present value of the income stream. The adjustment for seeking and finding employment reduces the present value of the income stream.

§1.20 —Chapter 14: Consumption

$$\text{Present Value of Future Income} = \$ \sum_{t=0}^{n} * M * [(1+g)^t / (1+d)^t] * P_L * P_S * P_F * \underline{C} * HS * T_X$$

Personal consumption refers to the proportion of one's income that is used to benefit the individual directly. Usually, the question of personal consumption arises only in a wrongful death action, since consumption would continue if the individual were disabled. Adjustments for personal consumption would cause the present value of the income stream to be diminished.

§1.21 —Chapter 15: Taxes

$$\text{Present Value of Future Income} = \$ \sum_{t=0}^{n} * M * [(1+g)^t / (1+d)^t] * P_L * P_S * P_F * C * HS * \underline{T_x}$$

If federal income taxes are to be included, then the economist must estimate the tax rates for each of the future years for which the analysis is being done. Additionally, the economist must estimate the tax deductible items for the individual for each future year in order to estimate the appropriate marginal tax rate to apply to the estimate. Studies indicate that inclusion of the individual tax rate causes the present value of the future stream of money to increase.

§1.22 —Chapter 16: Worklife Expectancy

Work life expectancy tables are government publications showing how long a person of a certain age is likely to remain in the labor force. Work life tables for men and women are presented. The work life table is incorporated into the extended formula by using the probability of being employed.

§1.23 —Chapter 17: Age Earnings Profile

The *age earnings profile* is cross-sectional economic data showing that highest earnings accrue to those in their mid-fifties. Many attorneys improperly use the earnings profile to argue that an individual's earnings will peak prior to retirement. The argument is that, after some age, earnings will decline for the full-time worker. The issue is presented in Chapter 17.

§1.24 —Chapter 18: A Quick Method to Evaluate Present Value

Chapter 18 demonstrates the *Alaska* plan. This method permits the growth rate used by the economist to be exactly equal to the discount rate employed by the economist. All that is required to calculate the present value is to multiply the annual dollar amount by the number of years the analysis covers.

§1.25 —Chapter 19: Judging the Economist's Estimate of Present Value

Although the *Alaska* plan has shortcomings, it can be used as a quick and easy method for estimating an economic loss. However, the method is limited to certainty. That is, the method does not work for the extended analysis.

§1.26   —Chapter 20: Selecting an Economist

Basic criteria for the selection of an economist are presented in Chapter 20. Recognizing there are not right economists for any case, the critical characteristics are integrity and the ability to communicate a difficult area clearly to the jury.

§1.27   —Chapter 21: Case Studies

Case studies are presented along with a sample of direct examination and cross-examination.

§1.28   —Chapter 22: Evaluating Structured Settlements

Chapter 22 presents worksheets to permit the attorney to estimate the present value of future income and expenses. In addition to making present value calculations the worksheets can be used to estimate the present value of settlement offers. Examples are presented.

§1.29   —Chapter 23: Sample Testimony

Chapter 23 presents sample testimony, or questions, which can be used to qualify the expert witness. Questions are presented to assist in the cross-examination of the expert as well.

2 Historic Loss

§2.01   Introduction

This chapter will explain what *historic loss* is, what values are included in historic loss, and how historic loss is calculated. Some economists include, whether by design or by accident, prejudgment interest in the calculation of the historic loss. Section 2.11 demonstrates how prejudgment interest may be included in the calculation of the historic loss.

§2.02   What Is Meant by *Historic Loss*

Historic loss is the economic loss that occurs between the date of the injury and some arbitrarily assumed date following the accident. The assumed date utilized by the economist is usually the plaintiff's birthday or the date of trial. The historic losses may consist of different types of losses: lost income, lost household services, incurred medical expenses, and the lost pleasure of living.

Lost income occurs when an injury leaves the plaintiff in a position where he or she is unable to continue to work or continues to work but at a reduced level. In either case, the plaintiff has a lower income than before the injury. The difference of income before and after the accident is the basis for determining lost income.

Lost household services represent the plaintiff's inability to perform household chores after the injury. Again, the loss does not mean the plaintiff is unable to perform any household services, only that he or she is unable to perform them at the same level as before the accident.

There are cases where an injury may leave the plaintiff without employment but some of the damages are mitigated because the value of household services increases after the accident. Suppose a female grade school teacher and mother of two grade school children suffers an injury to the larynx, rendering her unable to continue in the classroom. The loss to the family may be the income the woman is unable to earn since she cannot continue in the classroom, but some of the loss may be mitigated since the value of her household services may increase if she is unable to find alternative employment outside the home.

The historical medical expenses are the sum of what has been spent on medical care from the date of the injury to the date of the trial. The term *medical care* takes on the broadest of terms when the historic expenses are being calculated. The expenses include hospital care, physicians' fees, prescription drugs, therapy of all types, transportation expenses to and from medical facilities, possibly dental care, and whatever other costs may be attributed to the injury.

The hedonic losses address the value of life. While all economists would agree that there is value to life and that an injury may reduce the joy of living, some economists attempt to quantify the loss and attach a dollar value to the loss of joy.

§2.03   Comparing Disability to Death

Economically, the size of the historic lost income and lost household services is the same for the totally, permanently disabled person as it is for the person who has died. In both cases the ability to replace income or household services is absent. However, in the cases where the plaintiff is partially disabled, the reduced ability to earn or provide household services must be considered. The historic loss experienced by a partially disabled plaintiff depends on the degree of disability suffered. In order to assess the degree of economic disability a vocational rehabilitation specialist may be utilized. The specialist attempts to determine the decline in ability to earn experienced by the injured person.

§2.04   Calculating the Historic Wage Loss When Specific Wage Increases Are Known

Assume the plaintiff was injured three years ago today, on the tenth anniversary of his employment. At the time of the injury the annual earnings were $10,400, based on a wage of $5 per hour. Since the injury, the plaintiff has been unable to return to work. The historic loss from wages is what the plaintiff could have earned had the injury not occurred.

The basis for estimating the historic lost income is dependent on the information available to the economist. If employer records indicate that wage increases occurred on the employment anniversary, then the date of wage increases is established. How much the wage increased may be determined by asking the employer or by looking at the record of employees holding the same or similar positions.

If the employer testifies that the wage scale of $5 per hour went into effect on the day of the injury and the employer further testified that the injured party would have received $5.50 and $6 per hour on the successive two anniversaries of employment, the historic loss is calculated based on this record. The first year following the injury the plaintiff would have earned $10,400 ($5 per hour times 2,080 hours per year); the second year following the injury the annual income would have been $11,440 ($5.50 per hour times 2,080 hours per year); the third year following the injury the annual income would have been $12,480 ($6 per hour times 2,080 hours per year). The total historic loss would be the sum of these three amounts, $34,320.

In this case the basis for estimating the historic loss of income is the testimony of the employer. Had the employer been unable or unwilling to testify, the economist would have to turn to other sources to estimate historic wage increases.

§2.05   Calculating the Historic Wage Loss When Specific Wage Increases Are Not Known

When the wage increases are unavailable from the employer, the economist must turn to other sources to establish how the wage "may have" increased. Sources used to increase historic wages include the wages reported in the Standard Industrial Classification Tables, wages reported for the total private nonagricultural sector of the economy, and the Consumer Price Index. See the following three sections for further discussion.

When using the Consumer Price Index as a measure of how historic wages increased, the economist is no longer estimating historic lost income, but rather is estimating lost purchasing power. Here the economist is estimating how much money it would have taken to maintain plaintiff's purchasing power had the injury not occurred.

§2.06   —Using the Rate of Growth in Wages Paid in the Total Private Nonagricultural Sector

There are two problems faced by the economist. First, the employer was unable or unwilling to provide information concerning wage rates that would have prevailed since the accident. Second, the data available through government statistics is not current enough. That is, there is no estimate for the current year's wage rate.

Table 2-1   Total Private Nonagricultural Hourly Wages 1987 - 1991

Year	Hourly Wage Rate	Percentage Change
1987	$8.98	
1988	9.28	3.34
1989	9.66	4.09
1990	10.02	3.73
1991	10.33	3.09
1992	10.59	2.52

Source: Economic Report of the President, Table B-42 (1993).

Table 2-1 shows the total private nonagricultural hourly wages for the period 1987 through 1992. The economist may use this type of data to estimate how wages grew in the private nonagricultural sector of the economy. In 1989 the hourly rate was $9.66, an increase of 4.09 per cent from the 1988 hourly wage of $9.28. The 1990 wage of $10.02 is 3.73 per cent more than the 1989 wage of $9.66. The growth rates are also presented on Table 2-1. The concept of growth rates and how growth rates are calculated is examined in Chapter 4.

Working under the assumption that the injury occurred in 1989 when the plaintiff was earning $5 per hour, the economist would permit the 1990 wage to increase by 3.73 per cent, as indicated by the growth rate of the private nonagricultural sector of the economy, to $5.19 per hour. The $5.19 per hour represents the plaintiff's wage in 1990. Multiplying the hourly wage by 2,080 hours of work per year, the economist estimates the 1990 lost income to be $10,795.

The 1991 hourly wage is estimated by multiplying the 1990 hourly rate of $5.19 by the growth rate of wages for 1991. The increase was 3.09 per cent and the 1991 hourly wage is $5.35 resulting in an annual income of $11,128. The historic losses are presented in Table 2-2.

Table 2-2   Historic Lost Income Using Rate of Change of Wages in the Private Nonagricultural Sector as the Basis for Wage Increases

Year	Hourly Rate	Total Hours Worked	Total Annual Wages
1989	$5.00	2,080	$10,400
1990	5.19	2,080	10,795
1991	5.35	2,080	11,128
1992	5.49	2,080	11,419
	Total Historic Lost Income		$43,742

Using this approach, the economist has established a historic loss of $43,742.

§2.07   —Using the Consumer Price Index

Table 2-3 presents the historic rates of inflation from 1989 through 1992. The rate of inflation would indicate how the wage should have increased if the purchasing power of the individual was to be maintained.

Table 2-3   Consumer Price Index 1989 - 1992

Year	Consumer Price Index	Percentage Change
1989	124.00	
1990	130.70	5.40
1991	136.20	4.21
1992	140.30	3.01

Source: Economic Report of the President, Table B-55 (1993).

At the time of the injury in 1989, the plaintiff was earning $5 per hour. If the wage increased at the same rate as inflation, then the wage in 1990 would have been $5.27 per hour, which is 5.40 per cent more than the 1989 wage. The 1991 hourly wage would have been $5.49, or 4.21 per cent higher than the 1991 wage. The 1992 Consumer Price Index was 3.01 per cent higher than the 1991 Index.

Table 2-4 shows the historic loss of income if the Consumer Price Index had been used to increase the past wages.

Table 2-4   Historic Lost Income Using the Consumer Price Index as the Wage Inflator

Year	Hourly Rate	Total Hours Worked	Total Annual Wages
1989	$5.00	2,080	$10,400
1990	5.27	2,080	10,962
1991	5.49	2,080	11,419
1992	5.66	2,080	11,773
		Total Historic Loss	$44,554

Using the Consumer Price Index to estimate the historic loss of purchasing power, the economist established a historic loss of $44,554.

§2.08   —Using the Industrial Production Index

As Table 2-5 shows, the Industrial Production Index registered a slight increase for 1990 and 1992.

Table 2-5   Industrial Production Index 1989 - 1992

Year	Industrial Production Index	Percentage Change
1989	108.1	
1990	109.2	1.02
1991	107.1	.98
1992	108.7	1.49

Source: Economic Report of the President (1993) and Industrial Production, Federal Reserve Bulletin, Table 2.13 (Apr 1993).

If the economist were to use the Industrial Production Index as a basis for calculating the historic lost wages, then the $5 per hour wage in 1989 would be estimated to increase to $5.051 per hour. As before, the wage rate is increased and decreased to reflect changes in the Industrial Production Index.

Table 2-6   Historic Lost Income Using Rate of Change Indicated by the Change in the Industrial Production Index as the Basis for Wage Increases

Year	Hourly Rate	Total Hours Worked	Total Annual Wages
1989	$5.00	2,080	$10,400
1990	5.05	2,080	10,504
1991	4.95	2,080	10,296
1992	5.02	2,080	10,442
		Total Loss	$41,642

Using the Industrial Production Index as the basis of the historic wage changes, the historic loss of income is $41,642. This is lower than either of the other two estimates of lost income.

§2.09   Calculating the Historic Medical Expense

Historic medical expenses represent bills already incurred. The inclusion of historic medical expenses in an economist's report should only be done for convenience or clarity. There should be no need for analysis other than possibly summing the total of the already incurred expenses.

§2.10   Calculating the Historic Value of Lost House-hold Services

Calculating the value of lost household services requires establishing the amount of time the plaintiff spent in performing this type of service. In the absence of specific information, the value of household services may be estimated from different sources. One such study is *Household Work: What's it Worth and Why?*[1] Another study addressing household services is found in Sylvia Porter's *New Money Book for the 80's.*[2] The Sylvia Porter book addresses only the value of a

---

[1] This study is authored by W. Keith Bryant, Cathleen D. Zick, and Hysohin Kim and is published by Media Services at Cornell University (1992).

[2] S. Porter, New Money Book for the 80's 621 (1980).

housewife-mother not employed outside the home. As with wages, the economist will increase the value of household services from the date of the accident to the date of the trial to reflect the increased value of services caused by inflation.

Suppose an injury occurred January 2, 1989, leaving a 30-year-old housewife and mother of two children totally disabled. The case goes to trial January 2, 1993. The economist is to testify regarding the value of the household services. The value of household services appears in Table 2-7.

Table 2-7   1988 Dollar Value of Household Services

Age of Youngest Child	Nonblack Females			
	Not Emp	0-34 hrs	35-40 hrs	40+ hrs
1	14,833	16,997	11,295	11,489
2-5	15,920	11,551	10,349	11,489
6-14	13,739	11,383	8,418	7,809
15-17	12,283	9,726	6,344	7,809
18+	12,924	9,097	6,948	5,802

Age of Youngest Child	Nonblack Males			
	Not Emp	0-34 hrs	35-40 hrs	40+ hrs
1			7,871	7,808
2-5			9,291	5,958
6-14			9,409	7,903
15-17			6,586	6,341
18+	11,155	9,650	6,724	6,284

Source: W. Keith Bryant, Cathleen D. Zick & Hyoshin Kim, *Household Work: What's It Worth and Why?*, Cornell Univ Bulletin 322 IB228 (1992).

The Bryant, Zick, Kim study does not provide as much detail as to the value of household services provided by black parents as by nonblack parents. However, the study does provide a comparison of hours spent in household services. Table 2-8 presents the comparison.

Table 2-8

Median Hours Per Week Spent in
Household Work by Married Men and Women

Sex	Black	Nonblack	Black as % of Nonblack
Males	9.94	12.75	77.96
Females	30.3	34.85	86.94

To establish the value of household services, the economist must know the age of the youngest child. Assume the youngest child is six years old and has nonblack parents, and the mother is not employed outside the home. The 1988 value of household services provided by the mother is $13,739.

In order to determine the future value of the household services, the economist will increase the value from the 1988 values to the inflation adjusted values that would reflect the economic loss each successive year.

The 1988 value of household services was $13,739 and the Consumer Price Index (CPI) had a value of 118.3. In order to estimate the 1989 value of the household services the 1988 value is also increased by 4.82%, the rate of increase in the CPI. Thus, the 1989 value of household services is estimated to have increased from $13,739 to $14,401 in 1989. By using the CPI the value of household services each year is computed. Table 2-9 presents the value of household services.

Table 2-9   Value of Household Services

Year	CPI	Value of Services
1988	118.3	$13,739
1989	124.0	14,401
1990	130.7	15,179
1991	136.2	15,818
1992	140.3	16,294

This approach gives a value for household services for the four years 1989 through 1992. The historic value of the lost household services would be the sum of the values for those years, and totals $61,692.

Had the Sylvia Porter information been used as the basis for estimating the value of the household services, the procedure would have been the same. However, the value of the lost services would total $138,669. This is the $18,862 dollar value of household services established in 1979 inflated to the 1989, 1990, 1991, and 1992 values.

§2.11   Incorporating Prejudgment Interest into the Analysis

Some states permit the inclusion of prejudgment interest as part of the historic loss.[3] *Prejudgment interest* is the interest that could have been earned on the wage or household services had the plaintiff been compensated for the loss at the time the loss occurred. The lost interest would be calculated by establishing a fair rate of return and calculating the interest that could have been earned had the money been received and invested.

Using the value of household services developed in §2.10, $61,692, the interest is calculated on an average annual figure. Table 2-10 shows the value of household services in 1989 to be $14,401. The figure assumes that the value is paid in a lump sum to the plaintiff. The forgone interest to be calculated requires knowledge of when the payment was to be made. If the full amount of the annual service is paid on January 2, 1989, the date of the injury, then interest would accrue on the entire principal. If the principal was paid at the end of the year, then no interest would accrue through 1989. A third alternative is to permit the principal to be paid in 12 equal payments, meaning the value of the service is provided on a monthly basis.

Allowing an acceptable interest rate to be 8 per cent per year throughout the historic loss, the three different methods of "paying" for the services result in three different prejudgment interest calculations. These are discussed in the next three sections.

§2.12   —Calculating Prejudgment Interest When Payment for Services Occurs at the Beginning of the Year

The first year, 1989, the value of the household services was $14,401. Since the money is paid at the beginning of the year, interest is paid on the full principal at the annual rate of 8 per cent. Interest during the first year would total $1,152 ($14,401 × 8%).

When interest is added to the principal, the sum at the end of the first year would equal $15,553. This is the beginning principal for the second year. To the $15,553, the value of the second year's household services is added ($15,179). This increases the principal at the beginning of 1990 to $30,732. During the second year, interest at 8 per cent would be earned on the full $30,732. Interest would equal $2,459 ($30,732 × 8%), and the ending principal would be $31,191.

The same occurs in the third and fourth years. The value of the third year's household services, $15,818, raises the principal to $47,764. During the third year, interest at 8 per cent earns an additional $3,921. The same process increases the principal and interest to $74,761 by the end of 1992. Thus, on January 2, 1993, at the time of the trial, the historic loss totals $74,761. This figure includes the value of household services plus interest that could have been earned on the

---

[3] Annotation, *Validity and Construction of State Statute or Rule Allowing Changing Rate Prejudgment Interest in Tort Actions*, 40 ALR4th 147 (1985).

money. The value of the household services was being computed at the beginning of the year so the loss as of January 2, 1993 must include the value of 1993 household services, an additional $16,294. The total historic loss for household services is $91,055. The principal is $77,985, and interest is an additional $13,070. Table 2-10 presents the calculation of the interest payments when payment for services occurs at the beginning of the year. No money is added to the $91,055 in 1993 since the present value is being calculated as of the beginning of 1993.

Table 2-10   Interest Calculations When Payment Occurs at the Beginning of the Year

Year	Value of Household Services	Beginning Principal	Interest Earned (8%)	Ending Principal
1989	14,401	14,401	1,152	15,553
1990	15,179	30,732	2,459	33,191
1991	15,818	49,009	3,921	52,929
1992	16,294	69,223	5,538	74,761
1993	16,294	91,055		

§2.13   —Calculating Prejudgment Interest When Payment for Services Occurs at the End of the Year

Table 2-11 shows that the ending balance, when payment of services occurs at the end of the year, is $85,517, or $5,538 less than when the payments are made at the beginning of the year. The difference in the balance at the end of 1992 is due solely to different interest income, a result of the timing of the payments for services.

Table 2-11   Interest Calculations When Payment Occurs at the End of the Year

Year	Value of Household Services	Beginning Principal	Interest Earned (8%)	Ending Principal
1989	14,401	0	0	14,401
1990	15,179	14,401	1,152	30,732
1991	15,818	30,732	2,459	49,009
1992	16,294	49,009	3,921	69,223
1993	16,294	85,517		

§2.14 —Calculating Prejudgment Interest When Payment for Services Occurs at the End of Each Month

When payment for household services occurs monthly rather than annually, the ending principal plus interest will be more than when payments occur at the end of the year and be less than when payments occur at the beginning of the year. Annual payments represent the two extreme values for principal plus interest.

To calculate the principal plus interest for monthly payments, it is assumed that one-half the annual principal is at interest throughout the entire year. Table 2-12 shows the calculation of the principal plus interest.

Table 2-12   Interest Calculations When Payment Occurs Monthly

Year	Value of Household Services	Earning Principal	Interest Earned (8%)	Ending Principal
1989	14,401	14,401	576	14,977
1990	15,179	14,977	1,805	31,961
1991	15,818	31,961	3,190	50,969
1992	16,294	50,969	4,729	71,992
1993	16,294			88,286

§2.15   Moving Historic Losses to Current Dollars

Some economists will not apply forgone interest calculations to the historic loss. Rather, the economist will argue that historic losses should be stated in terms of current dollars. This means that the economic loss occurring in 1989 of $9,900 must be converted to current dollars in order to maintain the lost purchasing power. This is accomplished by increasing the historic value of household services to reflect increases in the Consumer Price Index (CPI). This permits the plaintiff to recover the same purchasing power that was lost as a result of the injury. Table 2-13 shows the historic loss increased to 1992 dollars. The value of the household services in 1989 was $9,900 but to replace them in 1992 dollars would take $11,201. The value of household services is converted to 1992 dollars. The total loss in 1992 dollars is $45,005.

Table 2-13 Value of Household Services Inflation Adjusted to 1992

Year	Value in 1989	Change in CPI	Value in 1992 Dollars
Value in 1989	$9,900	From 124.0 to 140.3	$11,201*
Value in 1990	10,377	From 130.7 to 140.3	11,139
Value in 1991	10,938	From 136.2 to 140.3	11,267
Value in 1992	11,398	In 1992 dollars	11,398
		Total	$45,005

*This value is obtained by dividing 140.3 by 124.0 and multiplying by $9,900.

§2.16 A Question on Using Current Dollars When Prejudgment Interest Is Not Permitted

When household services were adjusted for inflation (Table 2-13), the present value of the loss was $45,005.

There is the argument that if the state does not permit the inclusion of prejudgment interest, then it should not permit the adjustment to current purchasing power. The line of reasoning is that part of the interest rate is payment for anticipated inflation. That is, the nominal rate of interest includes a real return plus an inflation premium. Thus, to permit the increase of the historic loss to current dollars permits the inclusion of part of the historic interest.

§2.17 Including Both Prejudgment Interest and Adjustment to Current Purchasing Power

If both prejudgment interest and adjustment to current purchasing power are included, the analysis requires knowledge of the base wage, the historic rate of inflation, and the appropriate interest rate earned on investments. The analysis must be done year by year.

Care must be taken not to doublecount inflation. Interest rates are composed of two parts: the real rate of interest plus the inflation premium.[4] If interest has been computed after values have been inflated, a double counting of inflation has occurred.

§2.18 Summary

Historic loss refers to the loss of income, the value of the household services which the plaintiff was unable to perform as a result of an injury, and the accumulated

---

[4] P. Rose & D. Fraser, Financial Institutions (2d ed 1985).

medical expenses. The historic loss includes a time period from the date of the injury to the date of the trial.

If a significant period of time has elapsed between the time of the injury and the date of the trial, the economist will permit annual increases in historic wages and the value of the household services. Historic medical expenses should be a summation of past bills.

Wage increases may be determined from employer records or, if those are not available, from government statistics. Household services may also be increased to reflect the increased value of the services. The increase in value is usually accomplished by permitting growth in the value of services to occur at the annual rate of change in the Consumer Price Index.

If prejudgment interest is included in the analysis, the economist will calculate the amount of interest that would have been earned had the dollar value of the wages, services, or medical expenses been invested at the time the loss occurred.

If the economist converts the historic loss of wages, services, and medical expenses to current dollars, then he or she is repaying past dollars without a loss of purchasing power.

§2.19   Direct Examination of the Economist

The plaintiff's attorney wants the jury to understand what the *historic loss* is. The time frame must be clearly identified as from the date of the injury to the date of trial.

Having established the time frame, it is necessary to establish what losses the plaintiff experienced. Is the analysis of historical loss going to include lost wages, lost household services, or both? The plaintiff's attorney also wants to point out to the jury how conservative the economist was in the analysis. In examining the economist on wages, the attorney may wish to focus on the point that the plaintiff never "advanced" in position. That is, throughout the entire analysis the economist was attempting to determine the wages that would have been earned at the same job, not at a "better" job.

Likewise, with household services, the plaintiff's attorney wishes to point out how conservative the analysis was. For example, if the economist employed a more conservative study for household services than some other less conservative study, this should be brought to the attention of the jury.

§2.20   Cross-Examination of the Economist

The goal of cross-examination of the economist is to call into question the assumptions which he or she made in arriving at the value of the plaintiff's historic loss. By showing that the assumptions are arbitrary, it can be argued that the historic loss is overstated. If the historic loss is overstated, there is no reason to believe that the estimates of the present value of future income are any more accurate. Questions that may be asked of the economist include:

Q.   Isn't it true that the plaintiff was injured in 1989?

Q.   Isn't it true that you forecast a wage for 1990 which the plaintiff did not earn?

Q.   Isn't it true that your calculation of the historic loss includes wages which plaintiff never earned?

Q.   Isn't it true that you let the value of household services increase at the historical rate of inflation?

Q.   Isn't it true that you have no evidence that this would be an appropriate rate?

Q.   Did you base your analysis on the Gauger and Walker Study?

Q.   Isn't it true that you did not determine whether the value of household services in that study was appropriate for this part of the country?

Q.   Isn't is true that you did not determine whether the plaintiff would have worked about the house as specified in the study?

There are many questions which can be asked the economist which will elicit a negative response, or "I did not consider that." By showing the factors that the economist did not consider or the information he or she did not obtain prior to rendering an opinion, it can be shown that there is little basis for the economist's opinion and, therefore, little value to the estimate of, for example, the value of household services.

3

The Base Dollars

$$\text{Present Value of Future Income} = \sum_{t=0}^{n} \underline{\$} * M * (1+g)^{t} / (1+d)^{t} * P_L * P_S * P_F * C * HS * Tx$$

§3.01   Introduction

The base dollar amount in the present value equation is "$" and represents the current dollar amount of what is being forecast. When estimating a present value figure, the economist will be forecasting the present value of a future cash inflow, like income, or the present value of future cash outflows, like medical expenses. In some cases the economist will be estimating both.

The critical point is that *base dollars* represent current dollars or today's dollars. The base dollars may be historic data which have been obtained from a source, like the employer, and "moved" to current dollars. "Moving to current dollars" means taking a historic value and increasing or projecting the dollars to today's value. The higher the base dollars used in the present value equation, the greater will be the present value of the cash inflow or outflow.

It is in the base dollar amount that most disagreement between the plaintiff's attorney/economist and defense attorney/economist should occur. The reason is twofold.

First, assume a person's earnings are estimated to be $10,000 per year and the present value of the future income is $300,000. The argument may be that the appropriate income should have been $5,000 instead of $10,000 per year. The jury will clearly see that the present value of an income of $5,000 is one-half of the present value of $10,000. If it is possible to show that the economist should have used an income level of $5,000 instead of $10,000, the present value is halved.

The second reason to focus attention on the base dollar amount is clarity. No other variable is as clearly understood by the jury, and no other variable has such a direct impact on the present value of the money stream.

This chapter is an overview of where the economist may obtain the data used to make the forecast and how the economist uses the data.

§3.02   What Economists Estimate

Economists attempt to estimate different types of dollar values. The most common types of estimates are the estimates of *cash inflows* and *cash outflows*. Economists are also asked to estimate losses that represent in-kind losses or have no associated cash flows.

The most common type of estimates are the inflow that represents income[1] and household services.[2]

Economists are also asked to estimate the present value of future medical expenses[3] and hedonic losses.[4]

§3.03   —Income Losses

Income losses experienced by the plaintiff may be cash losses or in-kind losses. Cash losses are the result of reduced earnings capacity or earnings potential and are reflected in lower wages and or salaries. Since fringe benefits are usually a percentage of wages and salaries, lower wages and salaries will result in lower fringe benefits. Other cash losses the plaintiff may experience include reduced rental income, reduced interest income, reduced dividend income, reduced capital gains, and reduced business or farm income.

§3.04   —Medical Expenses

The most common types of expenses that economists estimate include ongoing medical expenses and expenses incurred as a result of an injury. Medical expenses would include doctors' fees, hospital care, surgery, therapy, prescription drugs, transportation to and from medical services, and nursing care. It is not uncommon

---

[1] *See* ch 7 (Wages, Salaries, and Fringe Benefits).

[2] *See* ch 9.

[3] Ch 10.

[4] Ch 11.

to have the present value of future medical expenses exceed the present value of the future income stream. If the medical requirements are serious and expected to be life-time in duration a life care plan is often presented. The life care plan would also present the frequency of the need. For example, the life care plan might say a motorized wheel chair costing $5,400 today needs to be replaced every fifth year.

§3.05   —Household Services

In addition to the loss of cash income, the economist may calculate the in-kind loss. An in-kind income is a nonmonetary income. The most common example of in-kind income is the value to a family of household services. If an accident leaves a family member unable to perform housework, then the rest of the family experiences a loss of in-kind services.

§3.06   —Hedonic Loss

Hedonic is defined as pertaining to or marked by pleasure. Thus hedonic loss is the loss, or decrease in the pleasure of living. However, the estimation of the hedonic loss has come to mean the value of life and not the joy associated with living the life.

An accident may leave a person permanently disabled and unable to continue his or her hobby of piano playing. This represents a loss in the pleasure associated with life. Another example of hedonic loss might be the loss of sight that results in never being able to see a child, or grandchild. Hedonic analysis does not attempt to measure the value of joy, but does attempt to measure the value attributed to life itself.

§3.07   Summary

The base dollar amount "$" used in the present value formula represents the current value of what is being estimated. It is the current income, medical expense, value of household service, or the hedonic values. The larger the base dollar amount, the higher will be the present value, and the smaller the base dollar amount the lower will be the present value.

The base dollar amount offers the defense attorney the easiest inroad for decreasing the plaintiff's economist's economic forecast. The base dollar amount has a direct relationship with the present value. If the base dollars are doubled, the present value is doubled, if the base dollar amount is halved, the present value is halved.

4

The Growth Rate

$$\text{Present Value of Future Income} = \sum_{t=0}^{n} \$ * M * (1+g)^t / (1+d)^t * P_L * P_S * P_F * C * HS * Tx$$

§4.01   Introduction

The understanding of the concepts of growth and growth rates is critical to understanding the calculation of the present value of an income or expense stream. There are two important items to consider when evaluating growth rates: (1) how the growth rate is established, i.e., the methodology, and (2) how the growth rate is applied in the analysis.

The major purposes of this chapter are to demonstrate what growth rates are, how growth rates are used to forecast future values, and how the different methods used to estimate growth rates lead to different conclusions. In addition, the distinction between real growth rates and nominal growth rates will be made.

§4.02   The Concept of Growth

Growth, or *rate of growth*, refers to how quickly something increases in size. This growth rate may refer to how the market value of one's home or the value of a common stock investment has increased over time.

If a person purchased a house for $24,000 and sold the house 33 years later for $120,000, the value of the house has increased five times. The question which might be asked is: What is the annual rate of growth of the investment in the house? Did the value of the house grow at an annual rate of 3 per cent, or at some other rate of growth?

In cases of wrongful death or disability, the same concept can be applied to the injured party's income or wages. For example, suppose the injured party went to work for a construction firm nine years ago at $5.00 per hour. Last year the individual was injured. At the time of the injury the individual was earning $18.00 per hour. Over the course of employment, the annual rate of increase in the individual's hourly wage can be calculated. This growth rate can be used as the estimate of the future growth of wages.

In a similar manner, if an injury results in ongoing medical expenses, it is necessary to estimate the rate of growth associated with the future recurring medical expenses. This may be done by using the historic rate of growth of medical costs as a guide to the future rate of growth of medical costs.

§4.03   Methods Used to Calculate Growth Rates

The concept of growth is neither difficult to grasp nor difficult to calculate. There are different methods which can be employed to calculate growth rates. The rate of growth may be calculated by using the exponential growth formula, the average percentage change formula, or the linear regression formula. The two most common methods employed, and the ones that will be discussed here, are the exponential growth formula and the average percentage change formula.

§4.04   Calculating Growth Rates Using Exponential Growth

If $1,000 of principal was deposited in an interest-bearing account for one year, how much would be in the account at the end of the year? The answer, of course, depends on what interest rate is being paid on the account. The interest rate in this case represents the growth rate. If the interest rate paid is 4 per cent, then the account would earn $40 during the year. The ending amount in the account would be $1,000 in principal plus the $40 earned in interest, or $1,040.

$$\$1,040 = \$1,000 + \$40$$

The $1,040, the amount in the account at the end of one year, is called the *ending value*, or *future value*. The $1,000 deposited in the account at the beginning of the year is called the *beginning value*, or *present value*. The difference between the two will reflect the growth rate or interest earned on the funds. The relationship can be written in the following form:

Present Value * (1 + Growth Rate) = Future Value

or

Beginning Value * (1 + Growth Rate) = Ending Value

The expression (1 + Growth Rate) shows how large the future value, or ending value, of the invested principal will be in one year. Since the growth rate is 4 per cent, the expression becomes (1 + .04), or 1.04. This means that in one year the future value, or ending value, will be 1.04 times the present value.

Suppose the $1,000, known as the *principal*, *present value*, or *beginning value*, was to be invested for two years earning 4 per cent each year, and the interest was to be compounded. *Compounded* means that interest during the second year will be paid on the $40 interest earned in the first year.

The $1,040 in the account at the end of the first year would be invested for another year, earning 4 per cent. At the end of the second year, the account would be worth $1,081.60.

Present Value * (1 + Growth Rate) = Future Value
$1,040 * (1 + .04) = $1,081.60

During the second year interest amounted to $41.60 (the ending amount of $1,081.60 less the beginning amount of $1,040). The effect of compounding can be seen when the amount of interest earned in the first year is compared to the amount of interest earned in the second year. During the first year $40 was earned in interest. During the second year $41.60 was earned in interest. The $1.60 more in interest in the second year is the result of the first year's interest of $40 earning 4 per cent in year two.

The future value, or ending value, of the $1,000 invested for two years at 4 per cent can be calculated in the following manner:

Future Value = $1,000 * (1 + Growth Rate) *(1 + Growth Rate)

or

Future Value = $1,000 * (1 + .04) *(1 + .04)
Future Value = $1,081.60

The expression (1 + .04) represents the annual rate of growth of the principal. There will be one such expression for every year the funds are invested. If the funds are invested for three years, then the expression (1 + .04) would appear three times. If the funds were invested for nine years, then the expression would appear nine times.

Instead of writing out the expression (1 + Growth Rate) for each year being considered, an exponent is used to state the number of years being considered, or the number of times the expression should be written. The formula was:

$$\text{Future Value} = \$1,000 * (1 + .04) * (1 + .04)$$

and now becomes:

$$\text{Future Value} = \$1,000 * (1 + .04)^2$$

where 2, the exponent, represents the number of years the funds will be invested. One might note in passing that this is the source of the term *exponential growth*.

If the funds were invested for nine years, then the exponent would be 9 and the formula would be:

$$\text{Future Value} = \$1,000 * (1 + .04)^9$$

Using the exponential growth formula, the general expression for calculating the future value of a sum of money is:

$$\text{Future Value} = \text{Present Value} * (1 + \text{Growth Rate})^t$$

Where:

"g" represents the growth rate

"t" represents the number of periods compounding occurs

"Present Value" represents the investment made today, or the "base dollar" amount

A table can be constructed to facilitate the calculation of the future value of an investment. The table is used to establish what is called a *growth factor*. A growth factor determines the future value of $1 and is calculated by using the following formula:

$$(1 + g)^t$$

Consider an investment earning 4 per cent per year for one year. To find the growth factor, use Table 4-1 and find the value where the row for one period intersects with the column headed 4 per cent. The value, or growth factor, is 1.04. The growth factor is then multiplied by the present value to determine the future value.

$$\text{Future Value} = \text{Present Value} * (1 + \text{Growth Rate})^t$$
$$\text{Future Value} = \text{Present Value} * \text{Growth Factor}$$
$$\text{Future Value} = \text{Present Value} * 1.04$$

Table 4-1 Growth Table

Growth Rates

Period	0.020	0.030	0.040	0.050	0.060	0.070
0	1.000	1.000	1.000	1.000	1.000	1.000
1	1.020	1.030	1.040	1.050	1.060	1.070
2	1.040	1.061	1.082	1.103	1.124	1.145
3	1.061	1.093	1.125	1.158	1.191	1.225
4	1.082	1.126	1.170	1.216	1.262	1.311
5	1.104	1.159	1.217	1.276	1.338	1.403
6	1.126	1.194	1.265	1.340	1.419	1.501
7	1.149	1.230	1.316	1.407	1.504	1.606
8	1.172	1.267	1.369	1.477	1.594	1.718
9	1.195	1.305	1.423	1.551	1.689	1.838

Thus, the future value of $1 received one year from now earning 4 per cent annually would be $1 times the growth factor of 1.04, or $1.04. Had the present value been $100, then the future value would have been $100 times the growth factor of 1.04, or $104.

Had $800 (present value) been invested for seven years at 7 per cent per year, the growth factor would be 1.606 (*see* Table 4-1). Stated differently, the future value would become 1.060 times larger than the initial investment.

$$\text{Future Value} = \text{Present Value} * (1 + \text{Growth Rate})^t$$
$$\text{Future Value} = \$800 * (1 + .07)^7$$
$$\text{Future Value} = \$800 * 1.606$$
$$\text{Future Value} = \$1,284.63$$

A more complete growth table is present in Appendix A.

Example One. What is the future value of $600 invested for five years at 6 per cent? From Table 4-1, the growth factor is found by reading down the column headed 6 per cent until it intersects with the row corresponding to year five. The growth factor is 1.338 and is multiplied by $600 to arrive at the future value of $802.80.

Example Two. What is the future value of $10 invested at 4 per cent for three years? The growth factor is 1.125 and, when multiplied by the present value of $10, yields a future value of $11.25.

Many of the calculators in use today have the key y^x, called a power function key. It is read, "Raise the value of y to the power of x." Using the previous example of investing $600 for five years at 6 per cent the expression would be: "Raise the value of 1.06 to the 5th power." This would be accomplished by entering 1.06 into the calculator, pressing the "y to the x" key, (y^x), 5, and "=". The resulting display should be 1.338, the same factor that appears in Table 4-1.

To determine the future value, the factor displayed on the calculator is multiplied by the present value to determine the future value.

Step One: Enter 1 plus the growth rate (1 + .06)
Step Two: Press the key "y to the x" (y^x)
Step Three: Enter the number of periods growth will occur (5)
Step Four: Press "=" (The growth factor of 1.338 is displayed)
Step Five: To calculate the future value press "times" (x) and enter the present value of $600
Step Six: Press "=" The future value is $802.94

§4.05   Solving for Growth Using Exponential Growth Rates

To this point, the growth rate has been known and the future value had to be calculated. In some cases what is unknown is the growth rate. By using Table 4-1, or a calculator, the growth rate may be calculated.

Recall that there are four variables involved in the growth calculation. Three variables are known and the fourth is to be calculated. Up to this point what is known is the present value, the growth rate, and the number of periods growth is to occur. What is being calculated is the future value.

When calculating a growth rate, what is known is the present value, the future value, and the number of periods growth occurs; that is, the number of periods between the future value and the present value. What is not known is the growth rate earned by the investment.

Returning to the question posed in §4.02, if a house was purchased for $24,000 and sold 33 years later for $120,000, what was the rate of growth of the investment? The answer to the question can be determined by using the exponential growth formula. What is known is the present value of the house, the future value of the house, and the number of years (growth periods) the house was owned.

$$\text{Future Value} = \text{Present Value} * (1 + \text{Growth Rate})^t$$

The ending value, or future value, is $120,000. The beginning value, or present value is $24,000. This means the initial investment of $24,000 has grown at some rate (g), to become $120,000. Since growth has occurred over a 33-year period, "t" equals 33. What must be calculated is the growth rate.

$$\text{Future Value} = \text{Present Value} * (1 + \text{Growth Rate})^t$$

$$\$120,000 = \$24,000 * (1 + \text{Growth Rate})^{33}$$

The formula can be rearranged as follows:

$$\frac{\$120,000}{\$24,000} = (1 + \text{Growth Rate})^{33}$$

or

$$5 = (1 + \text{Growth Rate})^{33}$$

Recall that $(1 + \text{Growth Rate})^{33}$ is the growth factor. By referring to the growth table in Appendix A, the growth rate can be determined. The relevant portion of that table is presented in Table 4-2. Since "t" is the number of periods growth occurred, and the value is known to be 5, look across row 33 until the growth factor of 5 is found. Read up to the top of the column to find out the rate of growth. The column is for 5 per cent annual growth. Or, $24,000 invested at 5.003 per cent annually for 33 years will grow to $120,000.

Table 4-2

Growth Rates

Periods	.020	.030	.040	.050	.060	.070
26	1.673	2.157	2.772	3.556	4.549	5.807
27	1.707	2.221	2.883	3.733	4.822	6.214
28	1.741	2.288	2.999	3.920	5.112	6.649
29	1.776	2.357	3.119	4.116	5.418	7.114
30	1.811	2.427	3.243	4.322	5.743	7.612
31	1.848	2.500	3.373	4.538	6.088	8.145
32	1.885	2.575	3.508	4.765	6.453	8.715
33	1.922	2.652	3.648	5.003	6.841	9.325
34	1.961	2.732	3.794	5.253	7.251	9.978
35	2.000	2.814	3.946	5.516	7.686	10.677

Rather than referring to a table to find the annual growth rate, a calculator having the "power key" (y^x) can be used to find the growth rate. Returning to the above example recall:

$$5 = (1 + \text{Growth Rate})^{33}$$

This can be rewritten as:

$$33\sqrt{5} = (1 + \text{Growth Rate})$$

This is read as the 33rd root of 5 equals 1 plus the growth rate. Using the calculator with the "y to the x" key:

Step One: Enter "5," (the growth factor)
Step Two: Press the "y to the x" key, (y^x)
Step Three: Enter the number of periods that growth occurred, 33
Step Four: Press the key: "1/X", called reciprocal
Step Five: Press "=". The factor 1.049979 should appear on the display
Step Six: Press minus 1, (-1), and "=". The display should show a value of .049979, which is the annual growth rate using the exponential growth formula

§4.06   Calculating Growth Rates Using Average Percentage Change

When a growth rate is calculated using the method of *average percentage change*, the economist is striking the average of a series of one-year exponential growth rates. Consider the following values for a $100 investment:

Table 4-3

Year	Investment
1988	$100.00
1989	104.30
1989	107.74
1990	114.25
1991	127.00
1992	138.01

To find the annual rate of increase in the investment from one year to the next, the difference between the two values is divided by the earlier value. In this case, the difference between the 1988 and 1989 values is divided by the 1988 value. The annual rate of increase in the investment is:

$$\frac{\text{1989 Investment minus the 1988 Investment}}{\text{1988 Investment}}$$

$$\frac{104.30 - 100.00}{100.00}$$

$$\frac{4.30}{100.00}$$

$$4.30\%$$

In this manner the annual rate of return on the investment is computed for each year. The results are presented in Table 4-4.

Table 4-4

Year	Investment	Percentage Return on Investment
1988	$100.00	
1989	104.30	4.30
1989	107.74	3.30
1990	114.25	6.23
1991	127.00	10.97
1992	138.01	8.67
	Sum	33.47
	Average	6.69

The average percentage change is calculated by adding up the column "Percentage Return on Investment" and dividing by the number of observations, in this case five. The sum of the column is 33.47 and the average percentage change, or growth rate, is 6.69 per cent annually. The calculation of the average percentage change requires the calculation of the percentage change from year to year and then determining the average of the annual changes.

§4.07   —Strengths and Weakness of the Methods

Two methods used to calculate growth rates have been examined: the *exponential growth* and the *average percentage change*. There are certain characteristics each method possesses that need to be explored.

The *exponential growth* rate, while easy to calculate, ignores all values between the beginning number and the ending number. Consider the purchase of a share of stock in XYZ Corporation on January 2, 1987. If the stock is sold on January 2, 1993, the rate of growth in the investment is determined by comparing the beginning and ending value of the stock. That is to say, all values between the beginning and ending values are ignored. Suppose two stocks, XYZ and ABC, were both purchased on January 2, 1987. Table 4-5 shows the price of each stock on January 2 of each of the following years.

Table 4-5

Year	XYZ	ABC
1987	$20.00	$20.00
1988	20.00	35.00
1989	20.00	45.00
1990	20.00	55.00
1991	20.00	65.00
1992	20.00	100.00
1993	42.00	42.00

Both stocks opened in 1987 at a price of $20.00 per share and ended at $42.00 per share. Using the exponential growth rate, both would have the same growth rate. The $20 invested at the beginning of 1987 has grown at some rate and reached $42 by 1993. The growth rate is 13.16 per cent. But the exponential growth process ignores all the price activity that occurred between the beginning and ending period. Note the difference in the price behavior of the two stocks. The shortcoming is that all activity between the first and last years is ignored. This can result in a biased growth rate being used in the analysis.

The shortcomings of the *average percentage change* should also be examined. Average percentage change takes into consideration each year's change in values. Consider the following example of changes in salary:

Table 4-6

Year	Salary	Percentage Change
1990	$10,000	
1991	20,000	+100%
1992	10,000	-50%

There are two years where the average percentage changed was calculated. From 1990 to 1991 the salary increased from $10,000 to $20,000, for an increase of 100 per cent. From 1991 to 1992 the salary decreased from $20,000 to $10,000, for a 50 per cent decrease in salary. On the average the salary had an average increase of 25 per cent ((100% - 50%)/2), yet the beginning and ending salary are the same.

§4.08   The Effect of Growth Rates on Future Earnings

The larger the growth rate employed by the economist, the larger will be the present value of the future earnings. Typically, the plaintiff's attorney will argue for a higher growth rate, and the defendant's attorney will argue for a lower growth rate. The plaintiff's attorney usually argues for a higher growth rate by asking the economist whether the growth rate employed was conservative. The defendant's attorney in turn will ask the economist: "Isn't it true that if a lower growth rate had been employed, then the present value of the future earnings would have been lower?" The answer to both questions is *yes*.

§4.09   The Effect of Mathematical Rounding on the Calculated Value of Future Earnings

When examining the growth rate employed to estimate future values, do not ignore the effect that mathematical rounding can have on the future values. For example, assume that the following annual salaries have been gathered from an employer's records:

Table 4-7

Year	Salary
1987	$10,000
1988	11,000
1989	12,300
1990	13,900
1991	15,200
1992	16,700
1993	19,400

By using the exponential growth method to calculate the historic rate of growth of wages, an annual growth rate of 11.677 per cent is established. This growth rate may be rounded to 12 per cent. If the future wage is to be projected over a long period of time, the rounding may lead to significant differences in the future wage. The further into the future the forecast is being made, the more significant the rounding becomes.

Suppose that the $19,400 is the basis for the forecast and a 30-year projection is being made. The growth formula to determine the wages 30 years from today is:

$$\text{Future Value} = \$19,400 * (1 + \text{Growth Rate})^{30}$$

The growth rate may take on the value of 11.677 per cent or be rounded to 12 per cent. The future value using 11.677 per cent is calculated to be $532,983. Using a growth rate of 12 per cent, the future salary is calculated to be $581,222, or 9 per cent higher. This difference is due strictly to rounding 11.677 per cent to 12 per cent.

Had the forecast been only for five years, then the projected salary at the 11.677 per cent annual growth rate is $33,699. An annual growth rate of 12 per cent projects earnings in five years to be $34,189, only 1.5 per cent more than the unrounded value.

§4.10 Sources of Growth Information

In order to determine a growth rate of moneys to be received in the future, the economist must establish a basis for the growth rate. Often this is done by examining historic data. The historic growth rate established is then used as the growth rate for future wage or cost projections. The following sections, §§4.11-4.20, present sources of information from which the growth rate may be calculated. Each section shows what the growth rate is, using exponential growth rates and, when possible, the average percentage change. A summary of the data is in §4.21. Sections 4.11 through 4.20 may be omitted without loss of continuity.

§4.11 —Client or Spouse Information

The client and spouse are often the least reliable sources of information available. Usually, the client can give information regarding the income level or how helpful an individual was about the home. The client cannot usually provide adequate information on which to base decisions concerning rates of growth of wages. One of the losses considered in a wrongful death or disability case can be that of household services. Often, after the death of a spouse, the deceased partner's worth is substantially altered in the eyes of the survivor.

§4.12 —Employer Records

The following table presents the employer's records and shows the individual's hourly wages. Both the average annual percentage change in wages and the exponential growth rate in the wages are calculated. The growth rate in wages using average percentage change averages 7.42 per cent annually, while growth was 7.40 per cent using exponential change.

Table 4-8

January 1 Each Year	Hourly Wages	Annual Percentage Change
1977	$3.46	
1978	3.75	8.38

January 1 Each Year	Hourly Wages	Annual Percentage Change
1979	3.96	5.60
1980	4.27	7.83
1981	4.55	6.56
1982	4.80	5.49
1983	5.05	5.21
1984	5.38	6.53
1985	6.05	12.45
1986	6.70	10.74
1987	7.23	7.91
1988	7.57	7.19
1989	8.35	7.74
1990	8.99	7.66
1991	9.65	7.34
1992	10.10	4.66
Average Percentage Change		7.42%
Exponential Growth Rate		7.40%

§4.13   —Individual Tax Returns

When using the tax returns as a source of information, the economist must be careful to take the amount listed as wages and salaries. If the spouse of the injured party works, then care must be exercised to deduct that portion which was earned by the spouse. Likewise, care must be taken not to include income which would continue. For example, rental income could continue regardless of the condition of the plaintiff or injured party. This could also be true of dividend income, interest income, and perhaps royalty income.

For the growth rate of wages to be determined, at least two tax returns or, preferably, W-2 forms, would be necessary. If the 1985 and 1992 W-2 forms were the only two forms available, the exponential growth formula could be used to show the growth rate of wages. For example, if the 1985 wage shown on the W-2 form is $11,190 and the 1992 wage is shown as $20,072, then the growth rate would be 8.71 per cent compounded annually.

§4.14   —Total Private Nonagricultural Hourly Wages

The average hourly wage paid in the total private nonagricultural sector of the United States economy is presented in Table 4-9. The wages were $1.52 per hour in 1952 and have increased steadily each year to the 1992 wage of $10.59 per hour. The average annual percentage increase in wages from 1952 through 1992 inclusive was 4.99 per cent, while the exponential rate of growth of wages for the same period of time was 4.91 per cent.

Table 4-9   Total Private Nonagricultural Hourly Wages

Year	Private Nonagricultural Hourly Wages	Percentage Change
1952	1.52	
1953	1.61	5.92
1954	1.65	2.48
1955	1.71	3.64
1956	1.80	5.26
1957	1.89	5.00
1958	1.95	3.59
1959	2.02	3.47
1960	2.09	2.39
1961	2.14	3.74
1962	2.22	2.70
1963	2.28	3.51
1964	2.36	4.24
1965	2.46	4.07
1966	2.56	4.69
1967	2.68	6.34
1968	2.85	6.67
1969	3.04	6.25
1970	3.23	6.81
1971	3.45	7.25
1972	3.70	6.49
1973	3.94	7.61
1974	4.24	6.84
1975	4.53	7.28
1976	4.86	8.02
1977	5.25	8.38
1978	5.69	8.26
1979	6.16	8.12
1980	6.66	8.86
1981	7.25	5.93
1982	7.68	4.43
1983	8.02	3.87
1984	8.33	2.88
1985	8.57	2.22
1986	8.76	2.51
1987	8.98	3.34
1988	9.28	3.34
1989	9.66	4.09

Year	Private Nonagricultural Hourly Wages	Percentage Change
1990	10.01	3.73
1991	10.33	3.19
1992	10.59	2.52
Average Percentage Change		4.99%
Exponential Growth Rate		4.97%

Table 4-10 shows the average percentage change from the beginning year (the top row) to any year through 1992. For example, the wage paid in the private nonagricultural sector of the economy in 1959 was $2.02 per hour (*see* Table 4-9). By 1980 the wage had grown to $6.66 per hour. Table 4-10 shows the average percentage increase in wages from 1959 to 1980 to be 5.86 per cent. If the economist is using a time frame of 1975 to 1986, then Table 4-10 indicates the average growth in wages for that period of time to be 6.20 per cent.

Table 4-10   Private Nonagricultural Wage Average Percentage Change

Table 4-10A

Year	1952	1953	1954	1955	1956	1957	1958	1959	1960
1952									
1953	5.92								
1954	4.20	2.48							
1955	4.01	3.06	3.64						
1956	4.33	3.79	4.45	5.26					
1957	4.46	4.10	4.63	5.13	5.00				
1958	4.25	3.91	4.27	4.48	4.09	3.17			
1959	4.15	3.86	4.13	4.26	3.92	3.38	3.59		
1960	4.07	3.80	4.02	4.10	3.81	3.41	3.53	3.47	
1961	3.88	3.63	3.79	3.81	3.52	3.16	3.15	2.93	2.39
1962	3.87	3.64	3.78	3.80	3.56	3.27	3.30	3.20	3.07
1963	3.76	3.54	3.66	3.67	3.44	3.18	3.18	3.07	2.94
1964	3.74	3.54	3.65	3.65	3.45	3.22	3.23	3.16	3.09
1965	3.78	3.60	3.70	3.71	3.53	3.35	3.38	3.34	3.32
1966	3.80	3.64	3.73	3.74	3.59	3.43	3.46	3.44	3.44
1967	3.86	3.71	3.80	3.82	3.69	3.56	3.60	3.60	3.62
1968	4.01	3.89	3.99	4.01	3.91	3.81	3.87	3.90	3.96
1969	4.17	4.06	4.16	4.20	4.12	4.05	4.13	4.18	4.26
1970	4.28	4.19	4.30	4.34	4.27	4.22	4.30	4.37	4.46
1971	4.42	4.33	4.44	4.49	4.44	4.40	4.50	4.57	4.67
1972	4.56	4.49	4.60	4.66	4.62	4.59	4.69	4.78	4.89
1973	4.65	4.59	4.70	4.76	4.73	4.71	4.81	4.90	5.01

Year	1952	1953	1954	1955	1956	1957	1958	1959	1960
1974	4.79	4.73	4.84	4.91	4.89	4.88	4.99	5.08	5.20
1975	4.87	4.83	4.94	5.00	4.99	4.99	5.10	5.19	5.31
1976	4.98	4.93	5.05	5.11	5.11	5.11	5.22	5.31	5.43
1977	5.10	5.06	5.18	5.25	5.24	5.26	5.37	5.46	5.58
1978	5.22	5.20	5.31	5.38	5.39	5.41	5.52	5.62	5.74
1979	5.34	5.31	5.43	5.50	5.51	5.53	5.65	5.75	5.87
1980	5.44	5.42	5.53	5.61	5.62	5.65	5.76	5.86	5.98
1981	5.55	5.54	5.65	5.73	5.75	5.78	5.89	6.00	6.12
1982	5.57	5.55	5.66	5.74	5.76	5.79	5.90	6.00	6.11
1983	5.53	5.52	5.62	5.69	5.71	5.73	5.84	5.93	6.04
1984	5.47	5.46	5.56	5.62	5.64	5.66	5.76	5.84	5.94
1985	5.40	5.38	5.48	5.54	5.55	5.57	5.65	5.73	5.82
1986	5.31	5.29	5.37	5.43	5.44	5.45	5.53	5.60	5.69
1987	5.23	5.20	5.29	5.34	5.34	5.35	5.43	5.49	5.57
1988	5.17	5.15	5.23	5.28	5.28	5.29	5.36	5.42	5.49
1989	5.14	5.12	5.20	5.24	5.24	5.25	5.32	5.37	5.44
1990	5.10	5.08	5.15	5.20	5.20	5.20	5.26	5.32	5.38
1991	5.05	5.03	5.10	5.14	5.14	5.14	5.20	5.25	5.31
1992	4.99	4.97	5.03	5.07	5.07	5.07	5.12	5.17	5.22

Table 4-10B

Year	1961	1962	1963	1964	1965	1966	1967	1968	1969
1961									
1962	3.74								
1963	3.22	2.70							
1964	3.32	3.11	3.51						
1965	3.55	3.48	3.87	4.24					
1966	3.65	3.63	3.94	4.15	4.07				
1967	3.82	3.84	4.12	4.33	4.38	4.69			
1968	4.18	4.26	4.57	4.83	5.03	5.52	6.34		
1969	4.49	4.60	4.92	5.20	5.44	5.90	6.50	6.67	
1970	4.69	4.81	5.11	5.37	5.60	5.99	6.42	6.46	6.25
1971	4.90	5.03	5.32	5.58	5.80	6.15	6.52	6.58	6.53
1972	5.11	5.25	5.54	5.79	6.01	6.33	6.66	6.74	6.77
1973	5.23	5.36	5.63	5.87	6.07	6.36	6.63	6.69	6.70
1974	5.41	5.55	5.81	6.04	6.24	6.51	6.77	6.85	6.88
1975	5.51	5.65	5.90	6.11	6.30	6.55	6.78	6.84	6.87
1976	5.63	5.77	6.00	6.21	6.39	6.62	6.84	6.90	6.93
1977	5.78	5.92	6.15	6.35	6.53	6.75	6.96	7.02	7.07
1978	5.93	6.07	6.30	6.50	6.67	6.89	7.09	7.16	7.22
1979	6.06	6.20	6.42	6.61	6.78	6.99	7.18	7.26	7.32
1980	6.17	6.31	6.52	6.71	6.87	7.07	7.26	7.33	7.39
1981	6.31	6.44	6.65	6.83	7.00	7.19	7.37	7.45	7.51
1982	6.29	6.42	6.61	6.78	6.93	7.11	7.27	7.34	7.39
1983	6.20	6.32	6.50	6.66	6.79	6.95	7.10	7.15	7.18

Year	1961	1962	1963	1964	1965	1966	1967	1968	1969
1984	6.10	6.20	6.37	6.51	6.63	6.78	6.90	6.93	6.95
1985	5.97	6.06	6.22	6.35	6.45	6.58	6.68	6.70	6.70
1986	5.82	5.90	6.04	6.16	6.25	6.36	6.45	6.45	6.44
1987	5.69	5.77	5.90	6.00	6.08	6.18	6.25	6.25	6.22
1988	5.60	5.68	5.79	5.89	5.96	6.05	6.11	6.10	6.07
1989	5.55	5.62	5.73	5.82	5.88	5.96	6.02	6.01	5.97
1990	5.48	5.55	5.65	5.73	5.79	5.87	5.92	5.90	5.86
1991	5.41	5.46	5.56	5.64	5.69	5.76	5.80	5.78	5.74
1992	5.31	5.37	5.46	5.53	5.58	5.63	5.67	5.64	5.60

Table 4-10C

Year	1970	1971	1972	1973	1974	1975	1976	1977	1978
1970									
1971	6.81								
1972	7.03	7.25							
1973	6.85	6.87	6.49						
1974	7.04	7.12	7.05	7.61					
1975	7.00	7.05	6.98	7.23	6.84				
1976	7.05	7.09	7.06	7.25	7.06	7.28			
1977	7.19	7.25	7.25	7.44	7.38	7.65	8.02		
1978	7.34	7.41	7.44	7.63	7.63	7.90	8.20	8.38	
1979	7.44	7.52	7.56	7.73	7.76	7.99	8.22	8.32	8.26
1980	7.51	7.58	7.63	7.79	7.82	8.01	8.20	8.25	8.19
1981	7.63	7.71	7.76	7.92	7.97	8.15	8.33	8.40	8.41
1982	7.49	7.55	7.58	7.70	7.71	7.84	7.93	7.91	7.79
1983	7.25	7.29	7.29	7.37	7.35	7.41	7.43	7.33	7.12
1984	7.00	7.02	7.00	7.04	6.99	7.00	6.97	6.82	6.56
1985	6.74	6.73	6.69	6.71	6.62	6.60	6.53	6.34	6.05
1986	6.45	6.43	6.37	6.36	6.26	6.20	6.10	5.88	5.57
1987	6.22	6.18	6.11	6.09	5.97	5.90	5.77	5.54	5.23
1988	6.06	6.02	5.94	5.90	5.78	5.70	5.57	5.34	5.04
1989	5.96	5.91	5.83	5.79	5.67	5.59	5.45	5.24	4.95
1990	5.84	5.79	5.71	5.66	5.54	5.45	5.32	5.12	4.84
1991	5.71	5.66	5.58	5.53	5.40	5.31	5.18	4.98	4.72
1992	5.57	5.51	5.42	5.37	5.24	5.15	5.02	4.81	4.56

Table 4-10D

Year	1979	1980	1981	1982	1983	1984	1985	1986	1987
1979									
1980	8.12								
1981	8.49	8.86							
1982	7.64	7.39	5.93						
1983	6.83	6.41	5.18	4.43					
1984	6.21	5.74	4.70	4.08	3.74				
1985	5.68	5.19	4.28	3.72	3.37	3.00			

Year	1979	1980	1981	1982	1983	1984	1985	1986	1987
1986	5.19	4.70	3.86	3.35	2.99	2.61	2.22		
1987	4.85	4.38	3.64	3.18	2.87	2.58	2.36	2.51	
1988	4.68	4.25	3.60	3.21	2.96	2.77	2.69	2.93	3.34
1989	4.62	4.24	3.66	3.33	3.15	3.03	3.04	3.32	3.72
1990	4.53	4.17	3.65	3.37	3.22	3.13	3.16	3.39	3.69
1991	4.42	4.09	3.61	3.35	3.22	3.14	3.16	3.35	3.56
1992	4.28	3.96	3.51	3.27	3.14	3.06	3.07	3.21	3.35

Table 4-10E

Year	1988	1989	1990	1991
1988				
1989	4.09			
1990	3.86	3.62		
1991	3.64	3.41	3.20	
1992	3.36	3.11	2.86	2.52

§4.15 —Standard Industrial Classification Tables

When the individual has no earnings history, or a very limited earnings history, the economist will turn to other sources in order to establish a growth rate for wages. Usually the sources used will be government publications. One such publication is the Standard Industrial Classification (SIC) Tables. The Standard Industrial Classification Tables are used to facilitate the collection and analysis of economic data. Since the SIC Tables present hourly wages, the data may be used to establish growth rates for annual wages. The average hourly wage paid in the Medical Instruments and Supplies Sector of the economy, SIC number 384, is presented in Table 4-11. The wages of $1.54 per hour in 1952 had increased steadily each year to the wage in 1983 of $7.38 per hour.

At some point in time the SIC classification of 384, Medical Instruments and Supplies, was divided into two parts, SIC 3841 and SIC 3842. These are Surgical and Medical Instruments and Surgical Appliances and Supplies respectively.

The Government now reports hourly compensation in all three categories. However, the most recent publication[1] gives hourly compensation for Medical instruments and Supplies, SIC 384, for the years 1988 and 1989, while the other hourly compensation for the other two categories is reported from 1972 through 1989. Table 4-11 presents the hourly earnings and growth rates for SIC 3841 and 3842.

---

[1] US Dept of Labor, Bureau of Labor Statistics, Employment Hours and Earnings, United States, 1909-90, 2 volumes (Washington, DC Mar 1991).

Table 4-11   Hourly Wages SIC Codes 3841 and 3842

Year	SIC	3841	SIC	3842
1972	3.04		3.25	
1973	3.23	6.25	3.45	6.15
1974	3.54	9.60	3.73	8.12
1975	3.93	11.02	4.06	8.85
1976	4.11	4.58	4.40	8.37
1977	4.36	6.08	4.72	7.27
1978	4.70	7.80	5.12	8.47
1979	5.03	7.02	5.54	8.20
1980	5.57	10.74	6.00	8.30
1981	6.32	13.46	6.54	9.00
1982	7.05	11.55	6.98	6.73
1983	7.41	5.11	7.38	5.73
1984	7.84	5.80	7.69	4.20
1985	8.28	5.61	8.05	4.68
1986	8.62	4.11	8.33	3.48
1987	8.76	1.62	8.53	2.40
1988	9.18	4.79	8.68	1.76
1989	9.43	2.72	9.15	5.41

Average Percentage Change		6.93		6.30
Exponential Growth		6.49		5.92

§4.16   —Statistical Abstracts of the United States

Table 4-12 shows the median money income for men and women, respectively. These sources of information permit the economist to estimate historic growth rates for the employee based on the number of years of education completed by the individual. When using this source, the growth rate must be calculated using the exponential growth method since not all years are presented. The tables indicate that the mean money income for men who are high school graduates increased from $24,745 in 1987 to $28,043 in 1990. This is an increase of 4.26 per cent per year. During the same period of time, the income of women in the same category has increased 5.32 per cent annually, from $16,223 to $18,954.

**Table 4-12   Mean Money Earnings of Persons by
Educational Attainment and Sex**

	Male		Female	
	1987	1990	1987	1990
Elementary				
Less than 8 Yrs	16,863	NA	10,163	NA
8 Years	18,946	19,188	12,655	13,222
Secondary				
1-3 years	21,327	22,564	13,136	15,381
4 Years	24,745	28,043	16,223	18,954
College				
1-3 years	29,253	34,188	19,336	22,654
4 years	38,117	44,554	23,506	28,911
5+ Years	47,903	55,831	30,255	35,827

Source: Statistical Abstracts of the United States Table 713 (1992) and Table 737
(1990).

§4.17 —Consumer Price Index

The Consumer Price Index (CPI), published each month by the Bureau of
Labor Statistics, is a measure of changes in prices of a fixed "market basket" of
goods and services purchased as a normal party of daily life. The CPI considers
sales tax but considers neither income tax nor money withheld for Social Security.
Price information is collected in 85 areas from nearly 32,400 business enterprises,
24,000 tenants, and 18,000 housing units. "The CPI is the most representative
measure of prices paid by the 'average' American."[2] It is sometimes referred to as
the *cost of living index*.[3]

The historical increase in the CPI can be used as an estimate for the future
growth rate of wages. The rationale is that increases in future wages is an attempt
to maintain purchasing power. Or stated another way, in calculating the present
value of the future income stream, the economist is attempting to leave the injured
party no worse off than had the injury not occurred, by maintaining the
purchasing power of the salary to be received in future periods.

---

[2] Chapmen, *The Consumer Price Index: A History and Source List*, 13, No 4 Reference Servs
Rev 47, 47-51 (Winter 1985).

[3] "When the CPI was first instituted in 1917, it was called the Cost-of-Living Index for the
United States, and was used by the Shipbuilding Labor Adjustment Board to increase a fair wage
scale for workers in the shipbuilding yards." *Id.*

Using the average percentage change, the CPI has increased 4.30 per cent annually from 1952 to 1992 inclusively, while the exponential growth rate indicates an average increase of 4.25 per cent annually.

Table 4-13   Consumer Price Index 1952 to 1992

Year	Consumer Price Index	Average Percentage Change
1952	26.50	
1953	26.70	.75
1954	26.90	.75
1955	26.80	.37
1956	27.20	1.49
1957	28.10	3.31
1958	28.90	2.85
1959	29.10	.69
1960	29.60	1.72
1961	29.90	1.01
1962	30.20	1.12
1963	30.60	1.32
1964	31.00	1.31
1965	31.50	1.61
1966	32.40	2.86
1967	33.40	3.09
1968	34.80	4.19
1969	36.70	5.46
1970	38.80	5.72
1971	40.50	4.38
1972	41.80	3.21
1973	44.40	6.22
1974	49.30	11.04
1975	53.80	9.13
1976	56.90	5.76
1977	60.60	6.50
1978	65.20	7.59
1979	72.60	11.35
1980	82.40	13.50
1981	90.90	10.37
1982	96.50	6.16
1983	99.60	3.21
1984	103.90	4.32
1985	107.60	3.56
1986	109.60	1.86

Year	Consumer Price Index	Average Percentage Change
1987	113.60	3.65
1988	118.30	4.14
1989	124.00	4.82
1990	130.70	5.40
1991	136.20	4.21
1992	140.30	3.01
		4.30
Average Percentage Change Exponential Growth Rate		4.25

Table 4-14 shows the rate of inflation from any year to any year. For example, the average rate of inflation for the period 1975 to 1980 is 7.80 per cent. By reading across the bottom line, 1992, the highest average rate of inflation ending in 1992 was 6.29 from 1972 to 1992. The same average occurred between 1973 and 1992.

Table 4-14 Consumer Price Index Average Rate of Change

Table 4-14A

Year	1952	1953	1954	1955	1956	1957	1958	1959	1960
1952									
1953	0.75								
1954	0.75	0.75							
1955	0.38	0.19	-0.37						
1956	0.66	0.62	0.56	1.49					
1957	1.19	1.29	1.48	2.40	3.31				
1958	1.46	1.61	1.82	2.55	3.08	2.85			
1959	1.35	1.45	1.59	2.09	2.28	1.77	0.69		
1960	1.40	1.49	1.61	2.01	2.14	1.75	1.21	1.72	
1961	1.36	1.43	1.53	1.85	1.92	1.57	1.14	1.37	1.01
1962	1.32	1.38	1.46	1.73	1.76	1.45	1.11	1.25	1.01
1963	1.32	1.38	1.45	1.67	1.70	1.43	1.15	1.26	1.11
1964	1.32	1.37	1.43	1.63	1.65	1.42	1.18	1.27	1.16
1965	1.34	1.39	1.45	1.63	1.65	1.44	1.24	1.33	1.25
1966	1.45	1.50	1.57	1.74	1.77	1.60	1.44	1.55	1.52
1967	1.56	1.62	1.68	1.86	1.89	1.75	1.62	1.74	1.74
1968	1.72	1.79	1.86	2.04	2.08	1.97	1.88	2.01	2.05
1969	1.94	2.02	2.10	2.28	2.34	2.26	2.21	2.36	2.43
1970	2.15	2.24	2.33	2.51	2.58	2.53	2.50	2.66	2.76
1971	2.27	2.36	2.45	2.63	2.70	2.66	2.64	2.81	2.91
1972	2.32	2.40	2.49	2.66	2.73	2.70	2.68	2.84	2.93

Year	1952	1953	1954	1955	1956	1957	1958	1959	1960
1973	2.50	2.59	2.69	2.86	2.94	2.92	2.92	3.08	3.18
1974	2.89	2.99	3.11	3.29	3.39	3.39	3.43	3.61	3.74
1975	3.16	3.27	3.39	3.58	3.69	3.71	3.76	3.95	4.10
1976	3.27	3.38	3.50	3.68	3.79	3.82	3.87	4.06	4.21
1977	3.40	3.51	3.63	3.81	3.92	3.95	4.01	4.20	4.34
1978	3.56	3.67	3.80	3.98	4.09	4.13	4.19	4.38	4.52
1979	3.85	3.97	4.10	4.28	4.41	4.46	4.53	4.72	4.88
1980	4.19	4.32	4.46	4.65	4.78	4.85	4.94	5.14	5.31
1981	4.41	4.54	4.68	4.87	5.01	5.08	5.17	5.38	5.55
1982	4.46	4.59	4.73	4.92	5.05	5.12	5.21	5.41	5.58
1983	4.42	4.55	4.68	4.86	4.98	5.05	5.13	5.32	5.48
1984	4.42	4.54	4.67	4.84	4.96	5.02	5.10	5.28	5.43
1985	4.39	4.51	4.63	4.80	4.91	4.97	5.05	5.21	5.35
1986	4.32	4.43	4.54	4.70	4.81	4.86	4.93	5.09	5.22
1987	4.30	4.40	4.52	4.67	4.77	4.82	4.89	5.04	5.16
1988	4.30	4.40	4.50	4.65	4.75	4.80	4.86	5.01	5.12
1989	4.31	4.41	4.51	4.66	4.75	4.80	4.86	5.00	5.11
1990	4.34	4.44	4.54	4.68	4.77	4.82	4.88	5.01	5.12
1991	4.34	4.43	4.53	4.67	4.76	4.80	4.86	4.99	5.09
1992	4.30	4.39	4.49	4.62	4.71	4.75	4.80	4.93	5.03

Table 4-14B

Year	1961	1962	1963	1964	1965	1966	1967	1968	1969
1961									
1962	1.00								
1963	1.16	1.32							
1964	1.21	1.32	1.31						
1965	1.31	1.41	1.46	1.61					
1966	1.62	1.78	1.93	2.24	2.86				
1967	1.87	2.04	2.22	2.52	2.97	3.09			
1968	2.20	2.40	2.61	2.94	3.38	3.64	4.19		
1969	2.61	2.83	3.09	3.44	3.90	4.25	4.83	5.46	
1970	2.95	3.20	3.46	3.82	4.26	4.61	5.12	5.59	5.72
1971	3.09	3.33	3.58	3.90	4.28	4.57	4.94	5.19	5.05
1972	3.11	3.32	3.54	3.82	4.13	4.34	4.59	4.69	4.44
1973	3.36	3.58	3.80	4.08	4.39	4.61	4.86	5.00	4.88
1974	3.95	4.20	4.46	4.78	5.13	5.41	5.75	6.00	6.11
1975	4.32	4.58	4.85	5.17	5.53	5.83	6.17	6.45	6.62
1976	4.42	4.66	4.92	5.22	5.55	5.82	6.12	6.36	6.49
1977	4.55	4.79	5.03	5.32	5.63	5.88	6.16	6.38	6.50
1978	4.73	4.96	5.20	5.48	5.78	6.02	6.29	6.50	6.62
1979	5.10	5.34	5.59	5.87	6.18	6.43	6.71	6.94	7.09
1980	5.54	5.79	6.05	6.35	6.67	6.94	7.23	7.49	7.67
1981	5.78	6.03	6.29	6.58	6.89	7.16	7.45	7.71	7.89

Year	1961	1962	1963	1964	1965	1966	1967	1968	1969
1982	5.80	6.04	6.28	6.56	6.85	7.10	7.37	7.60	7.76
1983	5.68	5.90	6.13	6.38	6.65	6.87	7.11	7.30	7.43
1984	5.62	5.83	6.04	6.28	6.53	6.73	6.94	7.12	7.23
1985	5.53	5.73	5.93	6.15	6.38	6.56	6.76	6.91	7.00
1986	5.39	5.57	5.75	5.96	6.16	6.33	6.50	6.63	6.70
1987	5.32	5.49	5.67	5.86	6.05	6.20	6.36	6.47	6.53
1988	5.28	5.44	5.61	5.78	5.97	6.11	6.25	6.35	6.40
1989	5.26	5.42	5.57	5.75	5.92	6.05	6.19	6.28	6.32
1990	5.26	5.42	5.57	5.73	5.90	6.02	6.15	6.24	6.28
1991	5.23	5.38	5.52	5.68	5.83	5.95	6.07	6.15	6.18
1992	5.16	5.30	5.43	5.58	5.73	5.84	5.95	6.02	6.05

Table 4-14C

Year	1970	1971	1972	1973	1974	1975	1976	1977	1978
1970									
1971	4.38								
1972	3.80	3.21							
1973	4.60	4.71	6.22						
1974	6.21	6.82	8.63	11.04					
1975	6.80	7.40	8.79	10.08	9.13				
1976	6.62	7.07	8.04	8.64	7.44	5.76			
1977	6.61	6.98	7.73	8.11	7.13	6.13	6.50		
1978	6.73	7.06	7.71	8.00	7.25	6.62	7.05	7.59	
1979	7.24	7.60	8.23	8.56	8.07	7.80	8.48	9.47	11.35
1980	7.87	8.26	8.89	9.27	8.97	8.94	9.74	10.81	12.42
1981	8.09	8.46	9.04	9.40	9.16	9.17	9.85	10.69	11.72
1982	7.93	8.25	8.76	9.04	8.79	8.74	9.24	9.78	10.33
1983	7.57	7.83	8.25	8.46	8.17	8.05	8.38	8.69	8.91
1984	7.33	7.56	7.92	8.08	7.78	7.63	7.87	8.06	8.14
1985	7.08	7.28	7.59	7.70	7.40	7.23	7.39	7.50	7.49
1986	6.76	6.91	7.18	7.25	6.94	6.74	6.84	6.87	6.78
1987	6.57	6.71	6.94	7.00	6.69	6.48	6.55	6.55	6.44
1988	6.44	6.56	6.77	6.81	6.50	6.30	6.35	6.33	6.21
1989	6.35	6.46	6.65	6.68	6.39	6.20	6.23	6.21	6.08
1990	6.31	6.41	6.58	6.61	6.33	6.14	6.17	6.14	6.02
1991	6.21	6.30	6.46	6.47	6.20	6.02	6.04	6.01	5.88
1992	6.06	6.14	6.29	6.29	6.03	5.84	5.85	5.81	5.68

Table 4-14D

Year	1979	1980	1981	1982	1983	1984	1985	1986	1987
1979									
1980	13.50								
1981	11.91	10.32							
1982	9.99	8.24	6.16						
1983	8.30	6.56	4.69	3.21					
1984	7.50	6.00	4.56	3.76	4.32				
1985	6.84	5.51	4.31	3.70	3.94	3.56			
1986	6.13	4.90	3.82	3.24	3.25	2.71	1.86		
1987	5.82	4.73	3.79	3.32	3.35	3.02	2.75	3.65	
1988	5.63	4.65	3.84	3.46	3.50	3.30	3.22	3.89	4.14
1989	5.55	4.67	3.96	3.65	3.72	3.61	3.62	4.20	4.48
1990	5.54	4.74	4.12	3.87	3.96	3.90	3.97	4.50	4.79
1991	5.43	4.69	4.13	3.91	3.99	3.95	4.01	4.44	4.64
1992	5.24	4.55	4.03	3.82	3.88	3.83	3.87	4.20	4.32

Table 4-14E

Year	1988	1989	1990	1991
1988				
1989	4.82			
1990	5.11	5.40		
1991	4.81	4.81	4.21	
1992	4.36	4.21	3.61	3.01

§4.18 —Census Data

The United States Department of Commerce, Bureau of Census, publishes population and income data by state. As an example, Table 4-15 presents income data for the state of Colorado by education and age of worker. If the economist can obtain the 1970 census data, then the rate of growth of wages could be calculated using the exponential growth formula.

Table 4-15   Income Based on 1980 Census Data, State of Colorado, 35 to 44 years old

	Education		
	8th Grade	High School Graduate	College Graduate
Mean Annual Income	$13,338	$17,406	$27,813
Mean Annual Earnings	13,011	16,503	26,333
Mean Weekly Earnings	383	339	542

The census data for the state of Colorado breaks the income data down into rural Colorado, the Colorado Springs Standard Metropolitan Statistical Area, and the Denver-Boulder Standard Metropolitan Statistical Area. The income data is also presented by sex and race. The category of race includes white, black, Asian and Pacific Islander, and Spanish origin. Incomes in each of these categories are presented by age category: 18-24, 25-34, 35-44, 45-54, 55-64, and over 65. To date the 1990 is not available.

§4.19   —Professional Publications

Many professional organizations publish salary data. If the data can be obtained, the growth rates may be estimated.

For example, the American Assembly of Collegiate Schools of Business Statistical Service publishes annual salary data for university faculty members employed by schools of business. Table 4-16 shows the salaries for the 1981-1982, 1985-1986, and 1992-1993 academic years. Also shown on the table are the growth rates of salaries between those two points in time as calculated by the exponential growth rate.

Table 4-16   Median Salaries, School of Business Faculty by Rank

Rank	1981-82	1985-86	1992-93	Growth Rate 81-82 to 92-93
Professor	$36,500	47,500	$61,900	4.92%
Associate Professor	29,500	39,500	52,300	5.34
Assistant Professor	25,500	35,500	49,000	6.12
Instructor	18,500	23,500	33,100	5.43

Other professional publications which would contain income levels would be the American Institute of Certified Public Accountants, trade magazines, and union publications. The *Occupational Outlook Handbook*, published by the United States Department of Labor, Bureau of Labor Statistics, describes various jobs and gives salary ranges.

§4.20   —Medical Price Index

When medical expenses are being estimated, the Medical Price Index may be used to establish the appropriate growth rate. Table 4-17 shows the Medical Price Index from 1952 through 1992 inclusive. As the table indicates, the average percentage increase in the index is 6.33 per cent, while the exponential growth rate is 6.30 per cent.

Table 4-17   Medical Price Index 1952 to 1992

Year	Index	Percentage Change
1952	16.70	
1953	17.30	3.59
1954	17.80	2.89
1955	18.20	2.25
1956	18.90	3.85
1957	19.70	4.23
1958	20.60	4.57
1959	21.50	4.37
1960	22.30	3.72
1961	22.90	2.69
1962	23.50	2.62
1963	24.10	2.55
1964	24.60	2.07
1965	25.20	2.44
1966	26.30	4.37
1967	28.20	7.22
1968	29.90	6.03
1969	31.90	6.69
1970	34.00	6.58
1971	36.10	6.18
1972	37.30	3.32
1973	38.80	4.02
1974	42.40	9.28
1975	47.50	12.03
1976	52.00	9.47
1977	57.00	9.62
1978	61.80	8.42
1979	67.50	9.22
1980	74.90	10.96
1981	82.90	10.68
1982	92.50	11.58
1983	100.60	8.76
1984	106.80	6.16
1985	113.50	6.27
1986	122.00	7.49
1987	130.10	6.64
1988	138.60	6.53
1989	149.30	7.72
1990	162.80	9.04

Year	Index	Percentage Change
1991	177.00	8.72
1992	192.00	8.47

Average Percentage Change	6.33%
Exponential Growth Rate	6.30%

Source: Economic Report of the President Table B-56 (1992).

Table 4-18   Average Rate of Change in the Medical Price Index

Table 4-18A

Year	1952	1953	1954	1955	1956	1957	1958	1959	1960
1952									
1953	3.59								
1954	3.24	2.89							
1955	2.91	2.57	2.25						
1956	3.14	2.99	3.05	3.85					
1957	3.36	3.30	3.44	4.04	4.23				
1958	3.56	3.56	3.72	4.22	4.40	4.57			
1959	3.68	3.69	3.85	4.25	4.39	4.47	4.37		
1960	3.68	3.70	3.83	4.15	4.22	4.22	4.04	3.72	
1961	3.57	3.57	3.67	3.90	3.92	3.84	3.59	3.21	2.69
1962	3.48	3.47	3.54	3.72	3.70	3.59	3.35	3.01	2.66
1963	3.39	3.37	3.43	3.58	3.54	3.42	3.19	2.90	2.62
1964	3.28	3.26	3.29	3.41	3.35	3.23	3.00	2.73	2.48
1965	3.22	3.19	3.21	3.31	3.25	3.13	2.92	2.68	2.48
1966	3.30	3.28	3.31	3.41	3.36	3.27	3.10	2.92	2.79
1967	3.56	3.56	3.61	3.73	3.71	3.66	3.56	3.46	3.42
1968	3.72	3.72	3.78	3.90	3.91	3.88	3.81	3.75	3.75
1969	3.89	3.91	3.98	4.10	4.12	4.11	4.07	4.04	4.08
1970	4.04	4.07	4.14	4.27	4.30	4.30	4.28	4.27	4.33
1971	4.15	4.18	4.26	4.39	4.42	4.44	4.43	4.43	4.49
1972	4.11	4.14	4.21	4.32	4.35	4.36	4.35	4.35	4.40
1973	4.11	4.13	4.20	4.31	4.33	4.34	4.33	4.32	4.37
1974	4.34	4.38	4.45	4.57	4.61	4.63	4.63	4.65	4.72
1975	4.68	4.73	4.81	4.94	5.00	5.04	5.07	5.11	5.21
1976	4.88	4.93	5.03	5.16	5.22	5.28	5.31	5.37	5.47
1977	5.07	5.13	5.22	5.36	5.43	5.49	5.54	5.61	5.72
1978	5.20	5.26	5.36	5.49	5.57	5.63	5.68	5.75	5.87
1979	5.34	5.41	5.51	5.65	5.73	5.79	5.85	5.93	6.04
1980	5.54	5.62	5.72	5.86	5.95	6.02	6.09	6.17	6.29
1981	5.72	5.80	5.91	6.05	6.13	6.21	6.29	6.37	6.50
1982	5.92	6.00	6.11	6.25	6.34	6.43	6.51	6.60	6.73

Year	1952	1953	1954	1955	1956	1957	1958	1959	1960
1983	6.01	6.09	6.20	6.34	6.43	6.52	6.60	6.69	6.82
1984	6.01	6.09	6.20	6.33	6.42	6.50	6.58	6.67	6.79
1985	6.02	6.10	6.20	6.33	6.42	6.50	6.57	6.65	6.77
1986	6.06	6.14	6.24	6.37	6.45	6.53	6.60	6.68	6.80
1987	6.08	6.15	6.25	6.38	6.46	6.53	6.60	6.68	6.79
1988	6.09	6.17	6.26	6.38	6.46	6.53	6.60	6.68	6.78
1989	6.14	6.21	6.30	6.42	6.50	6.57	6.64	6.71	6.81
1990	6.21	6.29	6.38	6.50	6.58	6.65	6.71	6.79	6.89
1991	6.28	6.35	6.44	6.56	6.64	6.71	6.77	6.85	6.95
1992	6.33	6.40	6.50	6.61	6.69	6.76	6.82	6.90	7.00

Table 4-18B

Year	1961	1962	1963	1964	1965	1966	1967	1968	1969
1961									
1962	2.62								
1963	2.59	2.55							
1964	2.42	2.31	2.07						
1965	2.42	2.36	2.26	2.44					
1966	2.81	2.86	2.96	3.40	4.37				
1967	3.55	3.73	4.03	4.68	5.79	7.22			
1968	3.90	4.11	4.43	5.01	5.87	6.63	6.03		
1969	4.25	4.48	4.80	5.35	6.08	6.65	6.36	6.69	
1970	4.51	4.74	5.06	5.55	6.18	6.63	6.43	6.64	6.58
1971	4.68	4.90	5.20	5.64	6.18	6.54	6.37	6.48	6.38
1972	4.55	4.75	4.99	5.35	5.77	6.00	5.76	5.69	5.36
1973	4.51	4.68	4.89	5.21	5.55	5.72	5.47	5.36	5.03
1974	4.88	5.06	5.29	5.61	5.97	6.17	6.01	6.01	5.88
1975	5.39	5.60	5.85	6.20	6.57	6.82	6.77	6.87	6.90
1976	5.66	5.88	6.13	6.47	6.84	7.08	7.07	7.20	7.27
1977	5.91	6.12	6.38	6.71	7.07	7.31	7.32	7.47	7.56
1978	6.05	6.27	6.52	6.83	7.17	7.41	7.42	7.56	7.66
1979	6.23	6.44	6.69	6.99	7.32	7.55	7.57	7.71	7.81
1980	6.48	6.69	6.94	7.24	7.56	7.79	7.83	7.98	8.10
1981	6.69	6.90	7.14	7.44	7.76	7.98	8.04	8.19	8.32
1982	6.92	7.14	7.38	7.67	7.98	8.21	8.27	8.43	8.57
1983	7.01	7.21	7.45	7.73	8.02	8.24	8.30	8.45	8.58
1984	6.97	7.17	7.39	7.65	7.93	8.12	8.18	8.31	8.42
1985	6.94	7.13	7.34	7.59	7.84	8.03	8.07	8.19	8.29
1986	6.96	7.14	7.34	7.58	7.83	8.00	8.04	8.15	8.24
1987	6.95	7.12	7.31	7.54	7.77	7.93	7.97	8.07	8.15
1988	6.93	7.10	7.28	7.50	7.72	7.87	7.90	8.00	8.06
1989	6.96	7.12	7.30	7.51	7.72	7.86	7.89	7.98	8.05
1990	7.03	7.19	7.36	7.57	7.77	7.91	7.94	8.03	8.09
1991	7.09	7.24	7.41	7.61	7.81	7.95	7.98	8.06	8.12
1992	7.13	7.29	7.45	7.64	7.83	7.97	8.00	8.08	8.14

Table 4-18C

Year	1970	1971	1972	1973	1974	1975	1976	1977	1978
1970									
1971	6.18								
1972	4.75	3.32							
1973	4.51	3.67	4.02						
1974	5.70	5.54	6.65	9.28					
1975	6.97	7.16	8.44	10.65	12.03				
1976	7.38	7.63	8.70	10.26	10.75	9.47			
1977	7.70	7.96	8.88	10.10	10.37	9.54	9.62		
1978	7.79	8.02	8.81	9.76	9.88	9.17	9.02	8.42	
1979	7.95	8.17	8.87	9.67	9.75	9.18	9.09	8.82	9.22
1980	8.25	8.48	9.13	9.86	9.95	9.54	9.56	9.54	10.09
1981	8.47	8.70	9.30	9.96	10.06	9.73	9.78	9.82	10.29
1982	8.73	8.96	9.53	10.14	10.25	9.99	10.08	10.17	10.61
1983	8.73	8.95	9.46	10.00	10.08	9.84	9.89	9.94	10.24
1984	8.55	8.73	9.18	9.65	9.69	9.43	9.43	9.40	9.56
1985	8.40	8.56	8.96	9.37	9.38	9.12	9.08	9.01	9.09
1986	8.34	8.49	8.85	9.23	9.22	8.97	8.92	8.84	8.89
1987	8.24	8.37	8.71	9.04	9.02	8.77	8.71	8.62	8.64
1988	8.15	8.26	8.57	8.87	8.85	8.60	8.53	8.43	8.43
1989	8.12	8.23	8.52	8.80	8.77	8.54	8.47	8.37	8.37
1990	8.17	8.28	8.55	8.82	8.79	8.57	8.51	8.42	8.42
1991	8.20	8.30	8.56	8.81	8.78	8.58	8.52	8.44	8.45
1992	8.21	8.31	8.55	8.79	8.77	8.57	8.52	8.45	8.45

Table 4-18D

Year	1979	1980	1981	1982	1983	1984	1985	1986	1987
1979									
1980	10.96								
1981	10.82	10.68							
1982	11.07	11.13	11.58						
1983	10.50	10.34	10.17	8.76					
1984	9.63	9.30	8.83	7.46	6.16				
1985	9.07	8.69	8.19	7.06	6.22	6.27			
1986	8.84	8.49	8.05	7.17	6.64	6.88	7.49		
1987	8.57	8.23	7.82	7.06	6.64	6.80	7.06	6.64	
1988	8.34	8.01	7.63	6.98	6.62	6.73	6.89	6.59	6.53
1989	8.28	7.98	7.64	7.08	6.80	6.93	7.10	6.96	7.13
1990	8.35	8.09	7.80	7.33	7.12	7.28	7.48	7.48	7.77
1991	8.38	8.15	7.89	7.48	7.32	7.49	7.69	7.73	8.00
1992	8.39	8.17	7.94	7.58	7.45	7.61	7.80	7.86	8.10

Table 4-18E

Year	1988	1989	1990	1991
1989	7.72			
1990	8.38	9.04		
1991	8.49	8.88	8.72	
1992	8.49	8.75	8.60	8.47

§4.21   Comparing the Growth Rates

The present value of the future stream of money is directly affected by the growth rate. The larger the growth rate the larger the present value. Table 4-19 shows the impact that the various growth rates have on future income level and the present value of the future income level.

The following example assumes a current salary of $20,000. The analysis is for 30 years and utilizes a growth rate of zero. The only variable is the growth rate of wages.

Table 4-19   Present Value of Future Wages

	Growth Rate	Salary in 30 Years	Present Value of Future Income
Employer Records			
Average % Change	7.42	$171,232	$2,038,164
Exponential Growth	7.40	170,278	2,030,078
Private Nonagricultural			
Average % Change	4.99	86,192	1,326,497
Exponential Growth	4.91	84,244	1,308,422
SIC Code 3841			
Average % Change	6.93	149,285	1,865,885
Exponential Growth	6.49	131,915	1,742,425
SIC Code 3842			
Average % Change	6.30	125,034	1,667,205
Exponential Growth	5.92	112,297	1,559,075
Consumer Price Index			
Average % Change	4.30	70,723	1,179,599
Exponential Growth	4.25	69,713	1,169,711

The present salary is $20,000 and depending on the growth rate employed, the future salary will range from a low of $69,713 to a high of $171,232. In a similar manner the present values will also have a wide range of values. Tables 4-20 and 4-21 have the present value of the future income levels when the growth rate of wages is based on Employer Records and when the growth rate is based on the Consumer Price Index.

Table 4-20   Present Value of Future Income Stream Using the Employer Records to Determine the Growth Rate of Wages

Period	Future Income Growth Rate 7.42%	Total Income	Future Income Growth Rate 7.4%	Total Income
0	$ 20,000	$ 20,000	$ 20,000	$ 20,000
1	21,484	41,484	21,480	41,480
2	23,078	64,562	23,070	64,550
3	24,791	89,353	24,777	89,326
4	26,630	115,983	26,610	115,936
5	28,606	144,588	28,579	144,516
6	30,728	175,317	30,694	175,210
7	33,009	208,325	32,966	208,175
8	35,458	243,783	35,405	243,580
9	38,089	281,872	38,025	281,605
10	40,915	322,787	40,839	322,444
11	43,951	366,738	43,861	366,305
12	47,212	413,950	47,107	13,411
13	50,715	464,665	50,592	464,004
14	54,478	519,143	54,336	518,340
15	58,520	577,663	58,357	576,697
16	62,863	640,526	62,676	639,373
17	67,527	708,053	67,314	706,686
18	72,538	780,590	72,295	778,981
19	77,920	858,510	77,645	856,626
20	83,701	942,211	83,390	940,016
21	89,912	1,032,124	89,561	1,029,577
22	96,584	1,128,707	96,189	1,125,766
23	103,750	1,232,457	103,307	1,229,073
24	111,448	1,343,906	110,951	1,340,024
25	119,718	1,463,623	119,162	1,459,186
26	128,601	1,592,224	127,980	1,587,166
27	138,143	1,730,367	137,450	1,724,616
28	148,393	1,878,760	147,622	1,872,238
29	159,404	2,038,164	158,546	2,030,783

Table 4-21   Present Value of Future Income Stream Using the Consumer Price Index to Determine the Growth Rate of Wages

Period	Future Income Growth Rate 4.30%	Total Income	Future Income Growth Rate 4.25%	Total Income
0	$ 20,000	$ 20,000	$ 20,000	$ 20,000
1	20,860	40,860	20,850	40,850
2	21,757	62,617	21,736	62,586
3	22,693	85,310	22,660	85,246
4	23,668	108,978	23,623	108,869
5	24,686	133,664	24,627	133,496
6	25,748	159,411	25,674	159,170
7	26,855	186,266	26,765	185,934
8	28,009	214,276	27,902	213,836
9	29,214	243,489	29,088	242,924
10	30,470	273,959	30,324	273,249
11	31,780	305,740	31,613	304,862
12	33,147	338,886	32,957	337,818
13	34,572	373,459	34,357	372,176
14	36,059	409,517	35,817	407,993
15	37,609	447,127	37,340	445,333
16	39,226	486,353	38,927	484,260
17	40,913	527,266	40,581	524,841
18	42,672	569,939	42,306	567,146
19	44,507	614,446	44,104	611,250
20	46,421	660,867	45,978	657,228
21	48,417	709,284	47,932	705,160
22	50,499	759,784	49,969	755,130
23	52,671	812,454	52,093	807,223
24	54,936	867,390	54,307	861,530
25	57,298	924,688	56,615	918,145
26	59,762	984,449	59,021	977,166
27	62,331	1,046,781	61,530	1,038,695
28	65,012	1,111,792	64,145	1,102,840
29	67,807	1,179,599	66,871	1,169,711

The attorney should make sure the proper growth rate is employed by the economist. For example, it would be improper for the economist to use the rate of growth indicated by the Medical Price Index when calculating the present value of a future wage stream. Likewise, growth rates based on wages would be inappropriate when calculating future medical expenses.

§4.22   Summary

Growth rates are critical to the present value calculation. The higher the growth rate, the greater the present value of the future income stream. Growth rates are typically calculated using the average percentage change method or the exponential rate of growth method. Care should be taken to insure that the growth rate employed by the economist is a relevant growth rate. Finally, the attorney should make sure that mathematical rounding has not added an unusually large amount of money to the economist's figures.

§4.23   Direct Examination

The purpose of the direct examination is to educate the jury in the economic principles needed to establish the economic loss. The economist, while in the courtroom, is primarily an educator. The economist is to explain what the present value concept is, how it is done mathematically, and how it is relevant in this case. Since the growth rate is employed, it is necessary for the economist to explain why growth is important, how it is incorporated into the analysis, and why the particular growth rate was chosen.

§4.24   Cross-Examination

The cross-examination is to establish two things. First, it is essential that the cross-examination establish that the figures used as the growth rates are historically accurate. This means that the source and the numbers should be examined for accuracy. The second thing the defense attorney wishes to do is to introduce the thought to the jury that the economist has used a growth rate that purposefully increases the size of the economic loss.

For example, if the economist has relied upon data published by the Bureau of Labor Statistics, check to make sure that data available for the specific city or region might not result in a lower growth rate than that for the nation as a whole. The national statistics may tend to ignore geographic differences in certain job categories.

The tables showing the growth rates over the different time periods can also be used to show that the economist could have picked a different time frame and thus used a different growth rate, i.e., a lower growth rate.

5

Discount Rates: The Present Value Calculation

$$\text{Present Value of Future Income} = \sum_{t=0}^{n} \$ * M * (1+g)^t / (1+d)^{\underline{t}} * P_L * P_S * P_F * C * HS * Tx$$

§5.01   Introduction

This chapter will explain what *present value* is and how *present value* is calculated. Since the present value is determined by the rate of earnings on invested funds, returns on alternative investments will be explored, and the impact that alternative investments have on present value will be evaluated. This chapter also contains the return each year for several types of investments. The average annual return by year from 1952 through 1992 is presented for investments in three-month Treasury Bills, six-month Treasury Bills, one-year Treasury Bills, long-term government securities with 10-year maturities, Moody's Aaa Bonds, Moody's Baa Bonds, and high grade municipal bonds.

§5.02   What Is Meant by *Discounting* and *Present Value*

When the economist calculates the present value of a future stream of dollars, be it income, medical expenses, household services, or dividends, it is necessary to reduce future dollars to present dollars called *present value*. The reducing of future dollars to present dollars is *discounting*. Stated another way, discounting determines the present value of future dollars.

Although discussed in the context of the Employer's Liability Act of April 22, 1908,[1] as amended by the Act of April 5, 1910,[2] the United States Supreme Court in *Chesapeake & Ohio Railroad v Kelly*[3] mandated that awards for future damages be discounted to present value at some appropriate discount rate. The appropriate rate of interest was recognized as that which would be earned on "the best and safest investments."[4] As a result, both state and federal courts have developed varying approaches.[5]

An example of discounting occurs when a family plans to pay $5,000 college tuition for a child five years from today. It is not necessary to place $5,000 in an investment account today. Money invested will earn a return each year. What must be placed in the account today is an amount of money which, when combined with the interest earned, will be equal to $5,000 in five years. The amount of money placed in the account today is the present value of $5,000. How much

---

[1] Ch 149, 35 Stat 65.

[2] Ch 143, 36 Stat 291.

[3] 241 US 485 (1916).

[4] *Id* 491.

[5] Baulieu v Elliot, 434 P2d 665 (Alaska 1967); Kuczkowski v Bolubasz, 491 Pa 561, 421 A2d 1027 (1980).

should be placed in the account depends on the interest rate, or earnings rate. The amount of money earned in interest will depend on what type of investment is made.

§5.03 The Present Value Formula for One Future Payment

In order to determine the present value of one dollar received in the future, the following formula is employed:

Present Value $= 1/(1 +i)^t$

Where "i" is the interest or discount rate
"t" is the number of periods until the dollar is received

If the interest or discount rate is assumed to be 6 per cent and "t" is assumed to be 12 years, then the expression asks: "What is the present value of $1 received in 12 years if the investment earns 6 per cent per year?"

Table 5-1 can be used to determine the present value of one dollar received some time in the future. A more complete table is presented in Appendix B.

Table 5-1 Present Value of $1 Payment Received in "t" Periods

Discount Rate in Per Cent

Period	2%	4%	6%	8%	10%
1	.980	.962	.943	.926	.909
2	.961	.925	.890	.857	.826
3	.942	.889	.840	.794	.751
4	.924	.855	.792	.735	.683
5	.906	.822	.747	.681	.621
6	.888	.790	.705	.630	.564
7	.871	.760	.665	.583	.513
8	.853	.731	.627	.540	.467
9	.837	.703	.592	.500	.424
10	.820	.676	.558	.463	.386
11	.804	.650	.527	.429	.350
12	.788	.625	.497	.397	.319
13	.773	.601	.469	.368	.290
14	.758	.577	.442	.340	.263
15	.743	.555	.417	.315	.239

To find the present value of $1 received in 12 years earning 6 per cent per period, read across the row labeled "12" until it intersects with the column headed "6%." Where they intersect the factor is .497. The present value of $1 received in 12 periods earning at 6 per cent is 49.7 cents. The .497 is also called the *present value factor*.

In order to find the present value of more than $1, the present value factor is multiplied by the number of dollars to be received in the future.

Returning to the earlier question of the tuition payment of $5,000 in five years (§5.02) the amount of money that must be set aside now depends on the amount of interest the investment can earn. Suppose current investments earn 10 per cent per year. The discount factor from Table 5-1 would be .621. The discount factor is found where the row headed "5" intersects with the column headed "10%." This means that for every one dollar needed in five years, 62.1 cents must be invested now. The present value of the tuition payment is $3,105, or $5,000 times the factor of .621.

§5.04   The Present Value Formula When Payments Occur in More Than One Future Period

Many times the payments made, or income received, occurs more than once. Such is the case with mortgage payments, car payments, and tuition payments. Likewise, income is not received once in a lifetime but rather each month of employment.

Suppose $5,000 in annual tuition were to be paid each year for four years with the first payment starting one year from today. What is the present value of the tuition payments? The present value will depend on the interest which can be earned on the investment. Assume the current earnings on passbook savings is 6 per cent per year.

The present value of the four tuition payments would be calculated by multiplying the annual payment of $5,000 by the discount factor found in Table 5-1.

Table 5-2   The Present Value of Tuition Payments

Year	Tuition		Factor	Present Value
1	$5,000	X	.943 =	$4,715
2	5,000	X	.890 =	4,450
3	5,000	X	.840 =	4,200
4	5,000	X	.792 =	3,960
			Present Value	$17,325

The present value of the tuition payment for each year is shown in Table 5-2. The present value of the payment due in one year is $4,715, for year two the present value is $4,450, and so on. The present value of all the tuition payments is $17,325.

Since all future payments are the same, the present value factors could have been summed and multiplied by the future value $5,000. The sum of the factors is 3.465 and, when multiplied by $5,000, yields the same present value of $17,325.

The following formula can be used to determine the present value factor, or present value of $1, when there are "t" future payments.

Present Value $= \dfrac{1[1/(1+i)^t]}{i}$

Where "i" is the interest or discount rate
"t" is the number of periods payments are received

The formula may be used to calculate the present value of a stream of future payments. For example, what is the present value of $1 received each year for the next five years if the investment earns 6 per cent per year. Table 5-3 presents the present value factors.

All Table 5-3 does is add. Any factor on the table is the summation from Table 5-1. In the tuition example, the sum of discount factors from Table 5-1 was 3.465. This factor can be found in Table 5-3 where the row "4" intersects with the column headed "6%."

Table 5-1 is used when one future payment occurs; Table 5-3 is used when more than one future payment occurs. When using Table 5-3 the payments must be equal.

Table 5-3   Present Value of $1 Payment Received Each Period for "t" Periods

Discount Rate in Per Cent

Period	2%	4%	6%	8%	10%
1	.980	.962	.943	.926	.909
2	1.942	1.886	1.833	1.783	1.736
3	2.884	2.775	2.673	2.577	2.487
4	3.808	3.630	3.465	3.312	3.170
5	4.713	4.452	4.212	3.993	3.791
6	5.601	5.242	4.917	4.623	4.355
7	6.472	6.002	5.582	5.206	4.868
8	7.325	6.733	6.210	5.747	5.335
9	8.162	7.435	6.802	6.247	5.759
10	8.983	8.111	7.360	6.710	6.145
11	9.787	8.760	7.887	7.139	6.495
12	10.575	9.385	8.384	7.536	6.814

Period	2%	4%	6%	8%	10%
13	11.348	9.986	8.853	7.904	7.103
14	12.106	10.563	9.295	8.244	7.367
15	12.849	11.118	9.712	8.559	7.606

§5.05 —Calculating Present Value When Payments Do Not Start Immediately

Tuition payments for a younger child may not start for six years. When the tuition payments do start they will be $6,000 each year for four years. The present value of the payments will depend on the interest which can be earned on the investment. Assume an 8 per cent yield on the investment.

There are two methods for calculating the present value of the future tuition payments. The first method is to treat each payment separately using Table 5-1. The other method is to treat them as identical future payments and use Table 5-3. In either case the answers should be the same.

Using Table 5-1 the future value of $6,000 is multiplied by the appropriate discount factor in order to determine the present value of each individual payment. The entire present value is then determined by summing the present value of the individual payments.

Table 5-4   Present Value of Tuition Payments

Period	Tuition Payment		Discount Factor	Present Value
6	$6,000	X	.630	= $3,780
7	6,000	X	.583	= 3,498
8	6,000	X	.540	= 3,240
9	6,000	X	.500	= 3,000
		Total Present Value		$13,518

The present value of the future tuition payments is $13,518. The same results can be achieved using Table 5-3. A stream of tuition payments starting in one year ending nine years from today has a present value factor of 6.247. But the first five years are not to be paid, thus they may be deducted. The present value factor for the first five years is 3.993. The difference between 6.247 and 3.993 is 2.254, which is the present value factor of $1 received in years six through nine. The present value of the tuition payments is $6,000 times the factor 2.254 which equals $13,524. The differences in the two answers is due to rounding in the tables.

§5.06 —Calculating Present Value When Payments Are Not the Same Size

If the future payments are not the same size, then Tables 5-1 and 5-3 are combined to find the present value. Suppose an individual were to receive from a trust fund the following payments: $10,000 in five years, $12,000 in six years, and $12,000 in ten years, and $3,000 each year for ten years with payments starting in three years.

Again, it is necessary to make an interest assumption. Suppose the funds can be invested to earn 10 per cent annually. Once the interest rate is known, the present value can be determined. The present value of the three payments of $10,000, $12,000, and $15,000 can be calculated using Table 5-1. The annual payment of $3,000 for ten years can be calculated from either table, but it is faster to use Table 5-3.

From Table 5-1:

Year	Amount to Be Received	Discount Factor	Present Value
5	$ 5,000	.621	$ 3,105
6	10,000	.564	5,640
10	12,000	.386	4,632
		Present Value	$13,377

From Table 5-3:
Discount factor for 12 years at 10% = 6.814
Discount factor for 2 years at 10% = 1.736
The difference   5.078

The annual payment of $3,000 times the factor of 5.078 gives a present value of the annuity of $15,234. This added to the present value of the lump sum payments gives a total present value of $28,611.

§5.07   A Primer on Evaluating Structured Settlements

The process presented in §§5.03-5.06 can be used in evaluating basic structured settlement offers.[6] The defendant or the defendant's insurance carrier makes an offer to the plaintiff or plaintiff's attorney. The offer may appear in the following form:

---

[6] N. Jacob & R. Pettit, Investments 504 (1984).

The plaintiff will be paid $5,000 on the fifth, tenth, and fifteenth anniversaries of the settlement. In addition, the plaintiff will receive $12,000 per year for 15 years, the first payment to be on the first anniversary of the settlement.

In order to estimate the present value of the offer, it would be necessary to determine the interest being assumed by the defendant or the defendant's insurance carrier. If the interest rate can be determined, the present value can be calculated using Tables 5-1 and 5-3.

If the interest rate is 8 per cent, the $5,000 payments received on the fifth, tenth, and fifteenth anniversaries have a present value of $3,405, $2,315, and $1,575, respectively. The 15-year annuity is $12,000 times the present value factor 8.559 (from Table 5-3). The present value of the annuity is $102,708. The offer is $110,003, which is the sum of the present value of the 15-year annuity and the three payments of $5,000 each.

§5.08 How the Discount or Interest Rate Affects Present Value

It is extremely important to choose an appropriate discount rate. The higher the interest rate, the smaller will be the present value of the future stream of dollars. For example, suppose that the present value of $10,000 received each year for the next 15 years is to be calculated. If the appropriate interest rate is 2 per cent annually, then the discount factor is 12.849 (from Table 5-3) and the present value is $128,490. However, if the appropriate discount rate is 10 per cent annually, then the discount factor declines to 7.606 and the present value of the stream of income is only $76,060. The difference between the two figures, $52,430, is due strictly to the difference in the interest rate assumed. The defendant's attorney will argue that the economist's discount rate is too low, while the plaintiff's attorney will argue that the economist has been very conservative by using such a high interest assumption.

§5.09 Types of Investments

There is much debate over what is an appropriate type of investment to consider when discounting to present value. Sections 5.11 through 5.19 will present different types of investments and calculate the yields on the various investments. These sections may be skipped without loss of continuity. The investments which will be considered are: three-month Treasury Bills; six-month Treasury Bills; one-year Treasury Bills; long-term government bonds; corporate bonds; municipal bonds; common stock; and finally, combinations of the various investments.

§5.10   Returns

The following sections show the historical returns which could have been earned on alternative investments. The tables show the average annual return on the investments starting in any year from 1952 and running through 1992. These tables may be used as a quick reference to determine the approximate yield from various investments. These sections can be skipped without loss of continuity.

§5.11   —Three-Month Treasury Bills

A Treasury Bill (T-Bill) is a short-term obligation of the United States government. The bills mature in 13, 26, or 52 weeks. The 13-week and 26-week bills are auctioned each week by the Treasury Department and the 52-week bills are auctioned once a month.[7] T-Bills are sold in increments of $5,000, starting at $10,000. The bills pay no interest; rather, they are sold at discount. This means that, if the purchase of a $10,000 T-Bill maturing in one year is made today, the purchase price will be less than $10,000. The difference between the purchase price and the $10,000 maturity value is the return, or interest, paid on the investment. As Table 5-5 shows, an investment in three-month Treasury Bills has averaged a return of 5.51 per cent since 1952.

Table 5-5   Yield on Three-Month Treasury Bills

Year	Yield
1952	1.77
1953	1.93
1954	0.95
1955	1.75
1956	2.69
1957	3.27
1958	1.84
1959	3.41
1960	2.93
1961	2.38
1962	2.78
1963	3.16
1964	3.55
1965	3.95
1966	4.88

---

[7] There are other types of bonds, such as the low-coupon bond and the zero-rate bond. In the case of the low-coupon bond, the semiannual interest payments are less than the market would dictate. Consequently, the bonds' selling price is below par value. This means that some of the return to the investor is being returned through a capital gain. Zero rate bonds pay no interest. The return is the difference between the current price and the maturity value.

Year	Yield
1967	4.32
1968	5.34
1969	6.68
1970	6.55
1971	4.35
1972	4.07
1973	7.04
1974	7.89
1975	5.84
1976	4.99
1977	5.27
1978	7.22
1979	10.04
1980	11.51
1981	14.03
1982	10.69
1983	8.63
1984	9.58
1985	7.48
1986	5.98
1987	5.82
1988	6.69
1989	8.12
1990	7.51
1991	5.42
1992	3.45
Average Yield	5.51

Table 5-6   Average Return on Three-Month Treasury Bills

Table 5-6A

Year	1952	1953	1954	1955	1956	1957	1958	1959	1960
1952	1.77								
1953	1.85	1.93							
1954	1.55	1.44	0.95						
1955	1.60	1.55	1.35	1.75					
1956	1.82	1.83	1.80	2.22	2.69				
1957	2.06	2.12	2.16	2.57	2.98	3.27			
1958	2.03	2.07	2.10	2.39	2.60	2.55	1.84		
1959	2.20	2.26	2.32	2.59	2.80	2.84	2.62	3.41	
1960	2.28	2.35	2.40	2.65	2.82	2.86	2.72	3.17	2.93
1961	2.29	2.35	2.40	2.61	2.75	2.76	2.64	2.90	2.65
1962	2.33	2.39	2.44	2.63	2.75	2.77	2.67	2.87	2.69
1963	2.40	2.46	2.51	2.69	2.80	2.82	2.75	2.93	2.81
1964	2.49	2.55	2.61	2.77	2.89	2.91	2.86	3.03	2.96
1965	2.60	2.66	2.72	2.88	2.99	3.03	3.00	3.16	3.12
1966	2.75	2.82	2.89	3.05	3.17	3.21	3.21	3.38	3.38
1967	2.85	2.92	2.99	3.15	3.26	3.31	3.32	3.48	3.49
1968	2.99	3.07	3.15	3.30	3.42	3.48	3.50	3.67	3.70
1969	3.20	3.28	3.37	3.53	3.65	3.73	3.77	3.94	4.00
1970	3.37	3.46	3.55	3.72	3.85	3.93	3.98	4.16	4.23
1971	3.42	3.51	3.60	3.75	3.88	3.96	4.01	4.17	4.24
1972	3.45	3.54	3.62	3.77	3.89	3.97	4.01	4.17	4.23
1973	3.62	3.70	3.79	3.94	4.06	4.15	4.20	4.36	4.43
1974	3.80	3.89	3.99	4.14	4.27	4.35	4.42	4.58	4.66
1975	3.89	3.98	4.07	4.22	4.34	4.43	4.50	4.65	4.73
1976	3.93	4.02	4.11	4.26	4.38	4.46	4.52	4.67	4.75
1977	3.98	4.07	4.16	4.30	4.42	4.50	4.56	4.70	4.77
1978	4.10	4.19	4.28	4.42	4.54	4.62	4.69	4.83	4.90
1979	4.31	4.41	4.50	4.65	4.77	4.86	4.93	5.08	5.16
1980	4.56	4.66	4.76	4.91	5.04	5.13	5.22	5.37	5.46
1981	4.88	4.99	5.09	5.25	5.38	5.49	5.58	5.75	5.85
1982	5.07	5.18	5.29	5.44	5.58	5.69	5.79	5.95	6.06
1983	5.18	5.29	5.40	5.55	5.69	5.80	5.90	6.06	6.17
1984	5.31	5.42	5.53	5.69	5.82	5.93	6.03	6.19	6.31
1985	5.37	5.48	5.59	5.74	5.88	5.99	6.08	6.24	6.35
1986	5.39	5.50	5.61	5.75	5.88	5.99	6.08	6.23	6.34
1987	5.40	5.51	5.61	5.75	5.88	5.98	6.07	6.22	6.32
1988	5.44	5.54	5.64	5.78	5.90	6.00	6.09	6.23	6.33
1989	5.51	5.61	5.71	5.85	5.97	6.07	6.16	6.29	6.39
1990	5.56	5.66	5.76	5.89	6.01	6.11	6.20	6.33	6.43
1991	5.56	5.65	5.75	5.88	6.00	6.09	6.17	6.31	6.40
1992	5.51	5.60	5.69	5.82	5.93	6.02	6.10	6.22	6.31

Table 5-6B

Year	1961	1962	1963	1964	1965	1966	1967	1968	1969
1961	2.38								
1962	2.58	2.78							
1963	2.77	2.97	3.16						
1964	2.97	3.16	3.35	3.55					
1965	3.16	3.36	3.55	3.75	3.95				
1966	3.45	3.66	3.89	4.13	4.42	4.88			
1967	3.57	3.77	3.97	4.18	4.39	4.60	4.32		
1968	3.79	4.00	4.20	4.41	4.62	4.85	4.83	5.34	
1969	4.11	4.33	4.55	4.79	5.03	5.30	5.45	6.01	6.68
1970	4.36	4.58	4.80	5.04	5.29	5.55	5.72	6.19	6.61
1971	4.36	4.56	4.75	4.95	5.15	5.35	5.45	5.73	5.86
1972	4.33	4.51	4.68	4.85	5.02	5.17	5.22	5.40	5.41
1973	4.54	4.72	4.90	5.07	5.24	5.40	5.48	5.67	5.74
1974	4.78	4.97	5.15	5.33	5.51	5.68	5.78	5.99	6.10
1975	4.85	5.03	5.20	5.37	5.54	5.70	5.79	5.97	6.06
1976	4.86	5.03	5.19	5.34	5.49	5.63	5.71	5.86	5.92
1977	4.88	5.04	5.19	5.34	5.47	5.60	5.67	5.80	5.85
1978	5.01	5.17	5.32	5.46	5.60	5.73	5.80	5.93	5.99
1979	5.28	5.44	5.60	5.75	5.89	6.03	6.12	6.27	6.36
1980	5.59	5.76	5.92	6.09	6.25	6.40	6.51	6.67	6.79
1981	5.99	6.17	6.35	6.53	6.70	6.88	7.01	7.20	7.34
1982	6.20	6.39	6.57	6.75	6.92	7.10	7.24	7.43	7.58
1983	6.31	6.49	6.67	6.84	7.01	7.18	7.32	7.51	7.65
1984	6.45	6.62	6.80	6.97	7.14	7.31	7.45	7.63	7.77
1985	6.49	6.66	6.83	6.99	7.16	7.32	7.45	7.62	7.76
1986	6.47	6.63	6.79	6.95	7.11	7.26	7.37	7.53	7.66
1987	6.44	6.60	6.75	6.90	7.05	7.19	7.30	7.45	7.56
1988	6.45	6.60	6.75	6.89	7.03	7.17	7.27	7.41	7.52
1989	6.51	6.66	6.80	6.94	7.08	7.21	7.31	7.44	7.55
1990	6.54	6.69	6.83	6.96	7.09	7.22	7.32	7.45	7.54
1991	6.51	6.65	6.78	6.91	7.03	7.15	7.24	7.36	7.45
1992	6.41	6.54	6.67	6.79	6.90	7.01	7.10	7.21	7.28

Table 5-6C

Year	1970	1971	1972	1973	1974	1975	1976	1977	1978
1970	6.55								
1971	5.45	4.35							
1972	4.99	4.21	4.07						
1973	5.50	5.15	5.56	7.04					
1974	5.98	5.84	6.33	7.46	7.89				
1975	5.96	5.84	6.21	6.92	6.86	5.84			
1976	5.82	5.70	5.97	6.44	6.24	5.41	4.99		
1977	5.75	5.63	5.85	6.20	5.99	5.36	5.13	5.27	
1978	5.91	5.83	6.04	6.37	6.24	5.83	5.83	6.24	7.22
1979	6.32	6.30	6.54	6.90	6.87	6.67	6.88	7.51	8.63
1980	6.80	6.82	7.10	7.47	7.54	7.48	7.80	8.51	9.59
1981	7.40	7.48	7.79	8.20	8.35	8.41	8.84	9.61	10.70
1982	7.65	7.74	8.05	8.45	8.61	8.70	9.11	9.79	10.70
1983	7.72	7.81	8.10	8.47	8.61	8.69	9.05	9.63	10.35
1984	7.85	7.94	8.21	8.56	8.70	8.78	9.11	9.62	10.24
1985	7.82	7.91	8.16	8.48	8.60	8.66	8.94	9.38	9.90
1986	7.71	7.79	8.02	8.30	8.39	8.44	8.67	9.04	9.46
1987	7.61	7.67	7.88	8.13	8.21	8.24	8.44	8.75	9.10
1988	7.56	7.62	7.81	8.04	8.11	8.13	8.30	8.58	8.88
1989	7.59	7.64	7.83	8.05	8.11	8.13	8.29	8.54	8.82
1990	7.58	7.64	7.81	8.02	8.07	8.09	8.24	8.47	8.71
1991	7.49	7.53	7.69	7.88	7.93	7.93	8.06	8.27	8.48
1992	7.31	7.35	7.49	7.66	7.69	7.68	7.79	7.96	8.14

Table 5-6D

Year	1979	1980	1981	1982	1983	1984	1985	1986	1987
1979	10.04								
1980	10.77	11.51							
1981	11.86	12.77	14.03						
1982	11.57	12.07	12.36	10.69					
1983	10.98	11.21	11.12	9.66	8.63				
1984	10.75	10.89	10.73	9.63	9.11	9.58			
1985	10.28	10.32	10.08	9.09	8.56	7.48	7.48		
1986	9.74	9.70	9.40	8.47	7.92	7.68	6.73	5.98	
1987	9.31	9.21	8.89	8.03	7.50	7.22	6.43	5.90	5.82
1988	9.04	8.93	8.61	7.84	7.36	7.11	6.49	6.16	6.26
1989	8.96	8.85	8.56	7.87	7.47	7.28	6.82	6.65	6.88
1990	8.84	8.73	8.45	7.83	7.48	7.31	6.93	6.82	7.04
1991	8.58	8.45	8.18	7.59	7.25	7.08	6.72	6.59	6.71
1992	8.21	8.07	7.78	7.22	6.87	6.67	6.31	6.14	6.17

Table 5-6E

Year	1988	1989	1990	1991	1992
1988	6.69				
1989	7.41	8.12			
1990	7.44	7.82	7.51		
1991	6.94	7.02	6.47	5.42	
1992	6.24	6.13	5.46	4.44	3.45

Source: Economic Report of the President Table B-69 (1993).

§5.12 —Six-Month Treasury Bills

The six-month Treasury Bill was first offered in 1960. Since that time the six-month bill has had an average return of 6.38 per cent.

Table 5-7 Yield on Six-Month Treasury Bills

Year	Yield
1959	3.83
1960	3.25
1961	2.60
1962	2.91
1963	3.25
1964	3.69
1965	4.06
1966	5.08
1967	4.63
1968	5.47
1969	6.85
1970	6.56
1971	4.51
1972	4.47
1973	7.18
1974	7.93
1975	6.12
1976	5.27
1977	5.51
1978	7.57
1979	10.02
1980	11.37
1981	13.78
1982	11.08
1983	8.75

Year	Yield
1984	9.80
1985	7.66
1986	6.03
1987	6.05
1988	6.92
1989	8.04
1990	7.47
1991	5.49
1992	3.57
Average Yield	6.38

Economic Report of the President Table B-69 (1993).

Table 5-8   Average Return on Six-Month Treasury Bills

Table 5-8A

Year	1959	1960	1961	1962	1963	1964	1965	1966	1967
1959	3.83								
1960	3.54	3.25							
1961	3.23	2.93	2.60						
1962	3.15	2.92	2.76	2.91					
1963	3.17	3.00	2.92	3.08	3.25				
1964	3.26	3.14	3.11	3.28	3.47	3.69			
1965	3.37	3.29	3.30	3.48	3.67	3.88	4.06		
1966	3.58	3.55	3.60	3.80	4.02	4.28	4.57	5.08	
1967	3.70	3.68	3.75	3.94	4.14	4.37	4.59	4.86	4.63
1968	3.88	3.88	3.96	4.16	4.36	4.59	4.81	5.06	5.05
1969	4.15	4.18	4.28	4.49	4.72	4.96	5.22	5.51	5.65
1970	4.35	4.40	4.51	4.72	4.95	5.19	5.44	5.72	5.88
1971	4.36	4.41	4.51	4.70	4.90	5.11	5.31	5.52	5.60
1972	4.37	4.41	4.51	4.68	4.86	5.04	5.20	5.37	5.42
1973	4.56	4.61	4.71	4.89	5.07	5.25	5.42	5.59	5.67
1974	4.77	4.83	4.94	5.12	5.31	5.49	5.67	5.85	5.95
1975	4.85	4.91	5.02	5.19	5.37	5.55	5.71	5.88	5.97
1976	4.87	4.93	5.04	5.20	5.36	5.52	5.68	5.82	5.90
1977	4.90	4.96	5.06	5.22	5.37	5.52	5.66	5.80	5.86
1978	5.04	5.10	5.20	5.36	5.51	5.66	5.80	5.93	6.01
1979	5.27	5.35	5.46	5.62	5.77	5.93	6.08	6.23	6.31
1980	5.55	5.63	5.75	5.92	6.09	6.25	6.41	6.57	6.68
1981	5.91	6.00	6.13	6.31	6.49	6.67	6.85	7.02	7.15
1982	6.12	6.22	6.36	6.54	6.72	6.90	7.08	7.26	7.40
1983	6.23	6.33	6.46	6.64	6.82	7.00	7.17	7.34	7.47
1984	6.37	6.47	6.60	6.78	6.95	7.13	7.30	7.47	7.60
1985	6.41	6.51	6.64	6.81	6.98	7.15	7.32	7.48	7.61

Year	1959	1960	1961	1962	1963	1964	1965	1966	1967
1986	6.40	6.50	6.62	6.78	6.94	7.10	7.26	7.41	7.53
1987	6.39	6.48	6.60	6.75	6.91	7.06	7.21	7.35	7.46
1988	6.41	6.50	6.61	6.76	6.91	7.05	7.19	7.33	7.43
1989	6.46	6.55	6.66	6.81	6.95	7.09	7.23	7.36	7.46
1990	6.49	6.58	6.69	6.83	6.97	7.11	7.24	7.36	7.46
1991	6.46	6.54	6.65	6.78	6.92	7.05	7.17	7.29	7.38
1992	6.38	6.45	6.55	6.68	6.81	6.93	7.04	7.15	7.23

Table 5-8B

Year	1968	1969	1970	1971	1972	1973	1974	1975	1976
1968	5.47								
1969	6.16	6.85							
1970	6.29	6.71	6.56						
1971	5.85	5.97	5.54	4.51					
1972	5.57	5.60	5.18	4.49	4.47				
1973	5.84	5.91	5.68	5.39	5.83	7.18			
1974	6.14	6.25	6.13	6.02	6.53	7.56	7.93		
1975	6.14	6.23	6.13	6.04	6.43	7.08	7.03	6.12	
1976	6.04	6.11	6.01	5.91	6.19	6.63	6.44	5.70	5.27
1977	5.99	6.04	5.94	5.86	6.08	6.40	6.21	5.63	5.39
1978	6.13	6.20	6.12	6.07	6.29	6.60	6.48	6.12	6.12
1979	6.46	6.54	6.51	6.51	6.76	7.09	7.07	6.90	7.09
1980	6.83	6.95	6.96	7.00	7.27	7.62	7.68	7.64	7.95
1981	7.33	7.47	7.52	7.61	7.92	8.31	8.45	8.52	8.92
1982	7.58	7.73	7.80	7.90	8.21	8.58	8.74	8.84	9.23
1983	7.65	7.80	7.87	7.97	8.25	8.60	8.74	8.83	9.17
1984	7.78	7.92	7.99	8.10	8.37	8.70	8.84	8.93	9.24
1985	7.77	7.91	7.97	8.07	8.32	8.62	8.74	8.81	9.08
1986	7.68	7.80	7.86	7.94	8.17	8.43	8.53	8.58	8.80
1987	7.60	7.71	7.76	7.83	8.04	8.27	8.35	8.39	8.57
1988	7.57	7.67	7.71	7.78	7.97	8.19	8.26	8.28	8.45
1989	7.59	7.69	7.73	7.79	7.98	8.18	8.24	8.26	8.42
1990	7.58	7.68	7.72	7.78	7.95	8.14	8.20	8.22	8.35
1991	7.50	7.58	7.62	7.67	7.83	8.00	8.05	8.05	8.18
1992	7.34	7.42	7.44	7.48	7.62	7.78	7.81	7.81	7.90

Table 5-8C

Year	1977	1978	1979	1980	1981	1982	1983	1984	1985
1977	5.51								
1978	6.54	7.57							
1979	7.70	8.80	10.02						
1980	8.62	9.65	10.70	11.37					
1981	9.65	10.69	11.72	12.58	13.78				
1982	9.89	10.76	11.56	12.08	12.43	11.08			
1983	9.73	10.43	11.00	11.25	11.20	9.92	8.75		
1984	9.74	10.34	10.80	10.96	10.85	9.88	9.28	9.80	
1985	9.50	10.00	10.35	10.41	10.21	9.32	8.74	8.73	7.66
1986	9.16	9.56	9.81	9.78	9.52	8.66	8.06	7.83	6.85
1987	8.87	9.21	9.39	9.32	9.02	8.23	7.66	7.39	6.58
1988	8.71	9.00	9.15	9.05	8.76	8.04	7.54	7.29	6.67
1989	8.66	8.92	9.05	8.95	8.68	8.04	7.61	7.42	6.94
1990	8.58	8.81	8.91	8.81	8.56	7.98	7.59	7.42	7.03
1991	8.37	8.57	8.65	8.54	8.28	7.73	7.36	7.18	6.81
1992	8.07	8.24	8.29	8.15	7.89	7.35	6.98	6.78	6.40

Table 5-8D

Year	1986	1987	1988	1989	1990	1991	1992
1986	6.03						
1987	6.04	6.05					
1988	6.33	6.49	6.92				
1989	6.76	7.00	7.48	8.04			
1990	6.90	7.12	7.48	7.76	7.47		
1991	6.67	6.79	6.98	7.00	6.48	5.49	
1992	6.22	6.26	6.30	6.14	5.51	3.57	3.57

§5.13   —One-Year Treasury Bills

The annual return has averaged 6.05 per cent from 1952 through 1992 inclusive.

Table 5-9   Yield on One-Year Treasury Bills

Year	Yield
1952	1.84
1953	2.11
1954	0.93
1955	1.93
1956	2.91
1957	3.66
1958	2.13

Year	Yield
1959	4.29
1960	3.66
1961	2.89
1962	3.10
1963	3.41
1964	3.89
1965	4.23
1966	5.34
1967	4.94
1968	5.76
1969	7.28
1970	6.94
1971	4.90
1972	5.01
1973	7.54
1974	8.35
1975	6.72
1976	5.84
1977	6.06
1978	8.39
1979	10.80
1980	12.22
1981	15.13
1982	12.45
1983	9.65
1984	11.01
1985	8.47
1986	6.07
1987	6.33
1988	7.17
1989	7.91
1990	7.36
1991	5.54
1992	3.75
Average Yield	6.05

Source: Federal Reserve Bulletins.

Table 5-10   Average Return on One-Year Treasury Bills 1952-1992

Table 5-10A

Year	1952	1953	1954	1955	1956	1957	1958	1959	1960
1952	1.84								
1953	1.98	2.11							
1954	1.63	1.52	0.93						
1955	1.70	1.66	1.43	1.93					
1956	1.94	1.97	1.92	2.42	2.91				
1957	2.23	2.31	2.36	2.83	3.29	3.66			
1958	2.22	2.28	2.31	2.66	2.90	2.90	2.13		
1959	2.48	2.57	2.64	2.98	3.25	3.36	3.21	4.29	
1960	2.61	2.70	2.79	3.10	3.33	3.44	3.36	3.98	3.66
1961	2.64	2.72	2.80	3.07	3.26	3.33	3.24	3.61	3.28
1962	2.68	2.76	2.83	3.07	3.23	3.29	3.21	3.49	3.22
1963	2.74	2.82	2.89	3.11	3.26	3.31	3.25	3.47	3.27
1964	2.83	2.91	2.98	3.19	3.33	3.38	3.34	3.54	3.39
1965	2.93	3.01	3.09	3.28	3.42	3.47	3.45	3.64	3.53
1966	3.09	3.18	3.26	3.45	3.59	3.66	3.66	3.85	3.79
1967	3.20	3.29	3.38	3.57	3.70	3.78	3.79	3.97	3.93
1968	3.35	3.45	3.54	3.72	3.86	3.94	3.97	4.15	4.14
1969	3.57	3.67	3.77	3.96	4.11	4.20	4.24	4.44	4.45
1970	3.75	3.86	3.96	4.15	4.30	4.39	4.45	4.64	4.68
1971	3.81	3.91	4.01	4.19	4.33	4.43	4.48	4.66	4.70
1972	3.86	3.97	4.06	4.24	4.37	4.46	4.52	4.69	4.72
1973	4.03	4.14	4.24	4.41	4.55	4.65	4.71	4.88	4.92
1974	4.22	4.33	4.43	4.61	4.75	4.85	4.92	5.10	5.15
1975	4.32	4.43	4.54	4.71	4.85	4.95	5.02	5.19	5.25
1976	4.38	4.49	4.59	4.76	4.89	4.99	5.06	5.23	5.28
1977	4.45	4.55	4.65	4.82	4.95	5.04	5.11	5.27	5.33
1978	4.59	4.70	4.80	4.97	5.10	5.20	5.27	5.43	5.49
1979	4.82	4.93	5.03	5.20	5.34	5.44	5.52	5.68	5.75
1980	5.07	5.19	5.30	5.47	5.61	5.72	5.81	5.98	6.06
1981	5.41	5.53	5.65	5.83	5.98	6.10	6.20	6.38	6.47
1982	5.63	5.76	5.89	6.06	6.22	6.34	6.45	6.63	6.73
1983	5.76	5.89	6.01	6.19	6.34	6.47	6.57	6.75	6.85
1984	5.92	6.05	6.17	6.35	6.50	6.63	6.74	6.92	7.02
1985	5.99	6.12	6.24	6.42	6.57	6.69	6.80	6.97	7.08
1986	6.00	6.12	6.24	6.41	6.55	6.67	6.77	6.94	7.04
1987	6.01	6.12	6.24	6.40	6.54	6.66	6.76	6.92	7.01
1988	6.04	6.15	6.27	6.43	6.56	6.68	6.77	6.93	7.02
1989	6.09	6.20	6.31	6.47	6.60	6.71	6.81	6.96	7.05
1990	6.12	6.23	6.34	6.49	6.62	6.73	6.83	6.97	7.06
1991	6.10	6.21	6.32	6.47	6.59	6.70	6.79	6.93	7.01
1992	6.05	6.15	6.26	6.40	6.52	6.62	6.70	6.84	6.91

Table 5-10B

Year	1961	1962	1963	1964	1965	1966	1967	1968	1969
1961	2.89								
1962	3.00	3.10							
1963	3.13	3.26	3.41						
1964	3.32	3.47	3.65	3.89					
1965	3.50	3.66	3.84	4.06	4.23				
1966	3.81	3.99	4.22	4.49	4.79	5.34			
1967	3.97	4.15	4.36	4.60	4.84	5.14	4.94		
1968	4.20	4.38	4.60	4.83	5.07	5.35	5.35	5.76	
1969	4.54	4.74	4.98	5.24	5.51	5.83	5.99	6.52	7.28
1970	4.78	4.99	5.22	5.48	5.75	6.05	6.23	6.66	7.11
1971	4.79	4.98	5.19	5.41	5.63	5.86	5.96	6.22	6.37
1972	4.81	4.98	5.17	5.37	5.55	5.74	5.81	5.98	6.03
1973	5.02	5.20	5.39	5.58	5.77	5.96	6.05	6.24	6.33
1974	5.26	5.44	5.63	5.83	6.03	6.23	6.34	6.54	6.67
1975	5.35	5.53	5.72	5.91	6.09	6.28	6.38	6.56	6.68
1976	5.38	5.55	5.73	5.90	6.07	6.24	6.33	6.48	6.57
1977	5.42	5.58	5.75	5.91	6.07	6.22	6.30	6.44	6.52
1978	5.59	5.75	5.91	6.08	6.24	6.39	6.48	6.62	6.70
1979	5.86	6.03	6.20	6.37	6.54	6.71	6.81	6.97	7.08
1980	6.18	6.35	6.53	6.72	6.90	7.07	7.20	7.37	7.50
1981	6.61	6.79	6.99	7.19	7.38	7.58	7.73	7.92	8.09
1982	6.87	7.06	7.26	7.46	7.66	7.86	8.02	8.23	8.40
1983	6.99	7.18	7.37	7.57	7.77	7.96	8.12	8.32	8.49
1984	7.16	7.35	7.54	7.74	7.93	8.12	8.28	8.47	8.64
1985	7.21	7.39	7.58	7.77	7.95	8.14	8.29	8.47	8.63
1986	7.17	7.34	7.52	7.70	7.87	8.04	8.18	8.35	8.49
1987	7.14	7.30	7.47	7.64	7.80	7.96	8.09	8.25	8.38
1988	7.14	7.30	7.46	7.62	7.78	7.93	8.05	8.19	8.32
1989	7.17	7.32	7.47	7.63	7.78	7.93	8.04	8.18	8.30
1990	7.17	7.32	7.47	7.62	7.76	7.91	8.01	8.15	8.25
1991	7.12	7.26	7.40	7.55	7.68	7.81	7.91	8.04	8.14
1992	7.01	7.15	7.28	7.42	7.54	7.66	7.75	7.87	7.95

Table 5-10C

Year	1970	1971	1972	1973	1974	1975	1976	1977	1978
1970	6.94								
1971	5.92	4.90							
1972	5.62	4.96	5.01						
1973	6.10	5.82	6.28	7.54					
1974	6.55	6.45	6.97	7.95	8.35				
1975	6.58	6.50	6.91	7.54	7.54	6.72			
1976	6.47	6.39	6.69	7.11	6.97	6.28	5.84		
1977	6.42	6.35	6.59	6.90	6.74	6.21	5.95	6.06	
1978	6.64	6.60	6.84	7.15	7.07	6.75	6.76	7.23	8.39
1979	7.06	7.07	7.34	7.67	7.69	7.56	7.77	8.42	9.60
1980	7.52	7.58	7.88	8.24	8.34	8.34	8.66	9.37	10.47
1981	8.16	8.27	8.61	9.01	9.19	9.31	9.74	10.52	11.64
1982	8.49	8.62	8.96	9.35	9.55	9.70	10.13	10.84	11.80
1983	8.57	8.70	9.01	9.38	9.56	9.70	10.07	10.67	11.44
1984	8.73	8.86	9.17	9.51	9.69	9.83	10.17	10.71	11.38
1985	8.72	8.84	9.12	9.43	9.59	9.70	10.00	10.46	11.02
1986	8.56	8.66	8.91	9.19	9.32	9.40	9.64	10.03	10.47
1987	8.44	8.53	8.75	9.00	9.11	9.16	9.37	9.69	10.05
1988	8.37	8.45	8.66	8.89	8.98	9.02	9.20	9.48	9.79
1989	8.35	8.42	8.62	8.83	8.91	8.95	9.11	9.36	9.63
1990	8.30	8.37	8.55	8.75	8.82	8.85	8.99	9.22	9.46
1991	8.18	8.23	8.40	8.58	8.64	8.65	8.78	8.97	9.18
1992	7.98	8.03	8.18	8.34	8.38	8.38	8.48	8.64	8.82

Table 5-10D

Year	1979	1980	1981	1982	1983	1984	1985	1986	1987
1979	10.80								
1980	11.51	12.22							
1981	12.72	13.68	15.13						
1982	12.65	13.27	13.79	12.45					
1983	12.05	12.36	12.41	11.05	9.65				
1984	11.88	12.09	12.06	11.04	10.33	11.01			
1985	11.39	11.49	11.34	10.40	9.71	8.47	8.47		
1986	10.73	10.71	10.46	9.53	8.80	8.52	7.27	6.07	
1987	10.24	10.17	9.87	9.00	8.31	7.97	6.96	6.20	6.33
1988	9.93	9.83	9.54	8.74	8.12	7.81	7.01	6.52	6.75
1989	9.75	9.64	9.35	8.63	8.09	7.83	7.19	6.87	7.14
1990	9.55	9.43	9.16	8.49	8.00	7.76	7.22	6.97	7.19
1991	9.24	9.11	8.83	8.20	7.72	7.48	6.98	6.73	6.86
1992	8.85	8.70	8.40	7.79	7.33	7.07	6.58	6.30	6.34

Table 5-10E

Year	1988	1989	1990	1991	1992
1988	7.17				
1989	7.54	7.91			
1990	7.48	7.64	7.36		
1991	7.00	6.94	6.45	5.54	
1992	6.35	6.14	5.55	4.65	3.75

§5.14 —Long-Term Government Securities, Composite of Over Ten-Year Maturities

Long-term government securities are those which do not mature for at least 10 years. Table 5-11 shows the 1952-1992 returns for long-term government securities with an over 10-year composite maturity. The average return was 6.84 per cent.

Table 5-11 Yield on Bonds with 10-Year Constant Maturity

Year	Yield
1952	
1953	2.85
1954	2.40
1955	2.82
1956	3.18
1957	3.65
1958	3.32
1959	4.33
1960	4.12
1961	3.88
1962	3.95
1963	4.00
1964	4.19
1965	4.28
1966	4.92
1967	5.07
1968	5.65
1969	6.67
1970	7.35
1971	6.16
1972	6.21
1973	6.84
1974	7.56
1975	7.99

Year	Yield
1976	7.61
1977	7.42
1978	8.41
1979	9.44
1980	11.46
1981	13.91
1982	13.00
1983	11.10
1984	12.44
1985	10.62
1986	7.68
1987	8.39
1988	8.85
1989	8.49
1990	8.55
1991	7.86
1992	7.01
Average Yield	6.84

Table 5-12   Average Yield on Bonds with 10-Year Constant Maturity

Table 5-12A

Year	1952	1953	1954	1955	1956	1957	1958	1959	1960
1952									
1953		2.85							
1954		2.63	2.40						
1955		2.69	2.61	2.82					
1956		2.81	2.80	3.00	3.18				
1957		2.98	3.01	3.22	3.42	3.65			
1958		3.04	3.07	3.24	3.38	3.49	3.32		
1959		3.22	3.28	3.46	3.62	3.77	3.83	4.33	
1960		3.33	3.40	3.57	3.72	3.86	3.92	4.23	4.12
1961		3.39	3.46	3.61	3.75	3.86	3.91	4.11	4.00
1962		3.45	3.52	3.66	3.78	3.88	3.92	4.07	3.98
1963		3.50	3.57	3.69	3.80	3.89	3.93	4.06	3.99
1964		3.56	3.62	3.74	3.85	3.93	3.97	4.08	4.03
1965		3.61	3.68	3.79	3.89	3.97	4.01	4.11	4.07
1966		3.71	3.77	3.89	3.98	4.06	4.11	4.21	4.19
1967		3.80	3.87	3.98	4.07	4.16	4.21	4.30	4.30
1968		3.91	3.98	4.10	4.20	4.28	4.34	4.44	4.45
1969		4.08	4.15	4.27	4.37	4.46	4.53	4.64	4.67
1970		4.26	4.34	4.46	4.57	4.67	4.75	4.87	4.92
1971		4.36	4.44	4.56	4.67	4.77	4.85	4.97	5.02
1972		4.45	4.53	4.65	4.76	4.86	4.94	5.06	5.11
1973		4.56	4.65	4.77	4.88	4.98	5.06	5.17	5.24
1974		4.70	4.79	4.91	5.02	5.12	5.21	5.32	5.39
1975		4.84	4.93	5.05	5.17	5.27	5.36	5.48	5.55
1976		4.96	5.05	5.17	5.28	5.39	5.48	5.60	5.67
1977		5.06	5.15	5.27	5.38	5.48	5.58	5.69	5.77
1978		5.19	5.28	5.40	5.51	5.62	5.71	5.83	5.91
1979		5.34	5.44	5.56	5.68	5.78	5.88	6.00	6.09
1980		5.56	5.66	5.79	5.91	6.02	6.12	6.25	6.34
1981		5.85	5.96	6.09	6.21	6.34	6.45	6.58	6.69
1982		6.09	6.20	6.34	6.47	6.59	6.71	6.85	6.96
1983		6.25	6.36	6.50	6.63	6.76	6.88	7.02	7.13
1984		6.44	6.56	6.70	6.83	6.96	7.08	7.23	7.35
1985		6.57	6.69	6.82	6.96	7.09	7.21	7.35	7.47
1986		6.60	6.72	6.85	6.98	7.11	7.23	7.37	7.48
1987		6.65	6.77	6.90	7.03	7.15	7.27	7.40	7.51
1988		6.71	6.82	6.96	7.08	7.20	7.32	7.45	7.56
1989		6.76	6.87	7.00	7.12	7.24	7.35	7.48	7.59
1990		6.81	6.92	7.04	7.16	7.28	7.39	7.52	7.62
1991		6.84	6.94	7.06	7.18	7.30	7.40	7.53	7.63
1992		6.84	6.94	7.06	7.18	7.29	7.39	7.51	7.61

Table 5-12B

Year	1961	1962	1963	1964	1965	1966	1967	1968	1969
1961	3.88								
1962	3.92	3.95							
1963	3.94	3.98	4.00						
1964	4.01	4.05	4.10	4.19					
1965	4.06	4.11	4.16	4.24	4.28				
1966	4.20	4.27	4.35	4.46	4.60	4.92			
1967	4.33	4.40	4.49	4.62	4.76	5.00	5.07		
1968	4.49	4.58	4.69	4.82	4.98	5.21	5.36	5.65	
1969	4.73	4.84	4.97	5.13	5.32	5.58	5.80	6.16	6.67
1970	5.00	5.12	5.27	5.45	5.66	5.93	6.19	6.56	7.01
1971	5.10	5.22	5.37	5.54	5.73	5.97	6.18	6.46	6.73
1972	5.19	5.31	5.45	5.61	5.79	6.00	6.19	6.41	6.60
1973	5.32	5.44	5.58	5.73	5.91	6.11	6.28	6.48	6.65
1974	5.48	5.60	5.74	5.90	6.07	6.27	6.44	6.63	6.80
1975	5.65	5.77	5.91	6.07	6.25	6.44	6.61	6.80	6.97
1976	5.77	5.90	6.04	6.19	6.36	6.55	6.71	6.89	7.05
1977	5.87	5.99	6.13	6.28	6.44	6.62	6.78	6.95	7.09
1978	6.01	6.13	6.27	6.42	6.58	6.76	6.91	7.08	7.22
1979	6.19	6.32	6.46	6.61	6.77	6.95	7.11	7.28	7.42
1980	6.45	6.59	6.74	6.90	7.07	7.25	7.42	7.60	7.76
1981	6.81	6.95	7.11	7.29	7.47	7.67	7.85	8.05	8.23
1982	7.09	7.24	7.41	7.59	7.78	7.98	8.17	8.38	8.57
1983	7.26	7.42	7.58	7.76	7.95	8.15	8.34	8.55	8.74
1984	7.48	7.64	7.80	7.98	8.17	8.38	8.57	8.78	8.97
1985	7.61	7.76	7.93	8.10	8.29	8.49	8.68	8.88	9.07
1986	7.61	7.76	7.92	8.09	8.26	8.45	8.63	8.82	8.99
1987	7.64	7.78	7.93	8.10	8.27	8.45	8.62	8.80	8.96
1988	7.68	7.82	7.97	8.13	8.29	8.47	8.63	8.80	8.96
1989	7.71	7.85	7.99	8.14	8.30	8.47	8.62	8.78	8.93
1990	7.74	7.87	8.01	8.16	8.31	8.47	8.62	8.77	8.92
1991	7.74	7.87	8.00	8.15	8.29	8.45	8.59	8.74	8.87
1992	7.72	7.84	7.97	8.11	8.25	8.39	8.53	8.67	8.79

Table 5-12C

Year	1970	1971	1972	1973	1974	1975	1976	1977	1978
1970	7.35								
1971	6.76	6.16							
1972	6.57	6.19	6.21						
1973	6.64	6.40	6.53	6.84					
1974	6.82	6.69	6.87	7.20	7.56				
1975	7.02	6.95	7.15	7.46	7.78	7.99			
1976	7.10	7.06	7.24	7.50	7.72	7.80	7.61		
1977	7.14	7.11	7.27	7.48	7.65	7.67	7.52	7.42	
1978	7.28	7.28	7.43	7.64	7.80	7.86	7.81	7.92	8.41
1979	7.50	7.52	7.69	7.90	8.07	8.17	8.22	8.42	8.93
1980	7.86	7.91	8.10	8.34	8.56	8.72	8.87	9.18	9.77
1981	8.36	8.46	8.69	8.96	9.23	9.46	9.71	10.13	10.81
1982	8.72	8.83	9.08	9.36	9.64	9.91	10.18	10.61	11.24
1983	8.89	9.01	9.25	9.52	9.79	10.04	10.29	10.68	11.22
1984	9.13	9.25	9.49	9.77	10.03	10.28	10.53	10.90	11.39
1985	9.22	9.34	9.57	9.83	10.08	10.31	10.54	10.87	11.30
1986	9.13	9.24	9.45	9.68	9.90	10.09	10.28	10.55	10.90
1987	9.09	9.19	9.38	9.59	9.79	9.96	10.12	10.35	10.65
1988	9.08	9.17	9.35	9.55	9.73	9.88	10.03	10.23	10.48
1989	9.05	9.14	9.30	9.48	9.65	9.79	9.92	10.09	10.32
1990	9.02	9.11	9.26	9.43	9.58	9.71	9.82	9.98	10.18
1991	8.97	9.05	9.19	9.35	9.49	9.60	9.70	9.84	10.01
1992	8.88	8.95	9.09	9.23	9.36	9.46	9.54	9.66	9.80

Table 5-12D

Year	1979	1980	1981	1982	1983	1984	1985	1986	1987
1979	9.44								
1980	10.45	11.46							
1981	11.60	12.69	13.91						
1982	11.95	12.79	13.46	13.00					
1983	11.78	12.37	12.67	12.05	11.10				
1984	11.89	12.38	12.61	12.18	11.77	12.44			
1985	11.71	12.09	12.21	11.79	11.39	10.62	10.62		
1986	11.21	11.46	11.46	10.97	10.46	10.25	9.15	7.68	
1987	10.89	11.08	11.02	10.54	10.05	9.78	8.90	8.04	8.39
1988	10.69	10.83	10.75	10.30	9.85	9.60	8.89	8.31	8.62
1989	10.49	10.59	10.50	10.07	9.65	9.41	8.81	8.35	8.58
1990	10.33	10.41	10.30	9.90	9.52	9.29	8.76	8.39	8.57
1991	10.14	10.20	10.08	9.70	9.33	9.11	8.63	8.30	8.43
1992	9.91	9.95	9.83	9.45	9.10	8.88	8.43	8.12	8.19

Table 5-12E

Year	1988	1989	1990	1991	1992
1988	8.85				
1989	8.67	8.49			
1990	8.63	8.52	8.55		
1991	8.44	8.30	8.21	7.86	
1992	8.15	7.98	7.81	7.44	7.01

§5.15   —Mood's Aaa Corporate Bonds

Corporate bonds are debt instruments issued by United States corporations. Bonds make two promises to the purchaser of the bond: (1) to pay interest semiannually, and (2) to repay the amount borrowed, or principal, at some future date.[8] Bond rating services have developed categories to assist the investor in evaluating the bond's ability to pay interest and to repay the principal. Two such rating services are Moody's and Standard and Poor's.

The ratings, running from the highest and most secure bond, to the lowest, or least secure bond, are "AAA" to "DDD-D" for Standard and Poor's and "Aaa" to "C" for Moody's.

Bonds rated "Aaa" "Have extremely strong capacity to pay interest and repay principal.[9] Table 5-13 presents the return on Moody's Aaa rated corporate bond from 1952 to 1992. The average return is 7.31 per cent.

Table 5-13   Yield on Aaa Corporate Bonds

Year	Yield
1952	2.96
1953	3.20
1954	2.90
1955	3.06
1956	3.36
1957	3.89
1958	3.79
1959	4.36
1960	4.41
1961	4.35
1962	4.33
1963	4.26
1964	4.40
1965	4.49

[8] Standard & Poors Corp, Bond Guide 10 (Mar 1985).
[9] *Id.*

Year	Yield
1966	5.13
1967	5.51
1968	6.18
1969	7.03
1970	8.04
1971	7.39
1972	7.21
1973	7.44
1974	8.57
1975	8.83
1976	8.43
1977	8.02
1978	8.73
1979	9.63
1980	11.94
1981	14.17
1982	13.79
1983	12.04
1984	12.71
1985	11.37
1986	9.02
1987	9.38
1988	9.71
1989	9.26
1990	9.32
1991	8.77
1992	8.14
Average Yield	7.31

Source: Economic Report of the President Table B-69 (1993).

Table 5-14   Average Return on Aaa Corporate Bonds (Moody's)

Table 5-14A

Year	1952	1953	1954	1955	1956	1957	1958	1959	1960
1952	2.96								
1953	3.08	3.20							
1954	3.02	3.05	2.90						
1955	3.03	3.05	2.98	3.06					
1956	3.10	3.13	3.11	3.21	3.36				
1957	3.23	3.28	3.30	3.44	3.63	3.89			
1958	3.31	3.37	3.40	3.53	3.68	3.84	3.79		
1959	3.44	3.51	3.56	3.69	3.85	4.01	4.08	4.36	
1960	3.55	3.62	3.68	3.81	3.96	4.11	4.19	4.39	4.41
1961	3.63	3.70	3.77	3.89	4.03	4.16	4.23	4.37	4.38
1962	3.69	3.77	3.83	3.94	4.07	4.19	4.25	4.36	4.36
1963	3.74	3.81	3.87	3.98	4.09	4.20	4.25	4.34	4.34
1964	3.79	3.86	3.92	4.02	4.13	4.22	4.27	4.35	4.35
1965	3.84	3.91	3.97	4.06	4.16	4.25	4.30	4.37	4.37
1966	3.93	4.00	4.06	4.15	4.25	4.34	4.39	4.47	4.48
1967	4.03	4.10	4.16	4.26	4.36	4.45	4.50	4.58	4.61
1968	4.15	4.23	4.29	4.39	4.50	4.59	4.66	4.74	4.78
1969	4.31	4.39	4.47	4.57	4.68	4.78	4.85	4.95	5.01
1970	4.51	4.59	4.68	4.79	4.90	5.01	5.10	5.21	5.28
1971	4.65	4.74	4.83	4.94	5.06	5.17	5.26	5.38	5.46
1972	4.77	4.86	4.95	5.07	5.18	5.30	5.39	5.51	5.59
1973	4.90	4.99	5.08	5.19	5.31	5.42	5.52	5.64	5.73
1974	5.05	5.15	5.24	5.36	5.48	5.60	5.70	5.82	5.92
1975	5.21	5.31	5.41	5.53	5.65	5.77	5.87	6.00	6.10
1976	5.34	5.44	5.54	5.66	5.78	5.90	6.01	6.13	6.24
1977	5.44	5.54	5.64	5.76	5.88	6.00	6.11	6.23	6.33
1978	5.57	5.67	5.76	5.88	6.01	6.13	6.23	6.36	6.46
1979	5.71	5.81	5.91	6.03	6.16	6.28	6.39	6.51	6.62
1980	5.93	6.03	6.14	6.26	6.39	6.52	6.63	6.76	6.87
1981	6.20	6.31	6.42	6.55	6.69	6.82	6.94	7.08	7.20
1982	6.45	6.56	6.68	6.81	6.95	7.09	7.22	7.36	7.49
1983	6.62	6.74	6.86	6.99	7.13	7.27	7.40	7.55	7.68
1984	6.80	6.92	7.04	7.18	7.33	7.47	7.60	7.75	7.88
1985	6.94	7.06	7.18	7.32	7.46	7.60	7.73	7.88	8.02
1986	7.00	7.12	7.24	7.37	7.51	7.65	7.78	7.92	8.05
1987	7.06	7.18	7.30	7.43	7.57	7.70	7.83	7.97	8.10
1988	7.14	7.25	7.37	7.50	7.63	7.77	7.89	8.03	8.16
1989	7.19	7.31	7.42	7.55	7.68	7.81	7.94	8.07	8.19
1990	7.25	7.36	7.47	7.60	7.73	7.86	7.98	8.11	8.23
1991	7.28	7.40	7.51	7.63	7.76	7.88	8.00	8.13	8.25
1992	7.31	7.41	7.52	7.64	7.77	7.89	8.00	8.13	8.24

Table 5-14B

Year	1961	1962	1963	1964	1965	1966	1967	1968	1969
1961	4.35								
1962	4.34	4.33							
1963	4.31	4.30	4.26						
1964	4.34	4.33	4.33	4.40					
1965	4.37	4.37	4.38	4.45	4.49				
1966	4.49	4.52	4.57	4.67	4.81	5.13			
1967	4.64	4.69	4.76	4.88	5.04	5.32	5.51		
1968	4.83	4.90	5.00	5.14	5.33	5.61	5.85	6.18	
1969	5.08	5.17	5.29	5.46	5.67	5.96	6.24	6.61	7.03
1970	5.37	5.49	5.63	5.83	6.06	6.38	6.69	7.08	7.54
1971	5.56	5.68	5.83	6.02	6.25	6.55	6.83	7.16	7.49
1972	5.69	5.82	5.96	6.15	6.37	6.64	6.89	7.17	7.42
1973	5.83	5.95	6.10	6.28	6.49	6.74	6.97	7.22	7.42
1974	6.02	6.15	6.30	6.49	6.70	6.94	7.17	7.41	7.61
1975	6.21	6.34	6.50	6.69	6.89	7.13	7.36	7.59	7.79
1976	6.35	6.48	6.64	6.82	7.02	7.25	7.46	7.68	7.87
1977	6.45	6.58	6.73	6.91	7.10	7.32	7.51	7.71	7.88
1978	6.57	6.71	6.85	7.03	7.21	7.42	7.62	7.81	7.97
1979	6.74	6.87	7.02	7.19	7.38	7.58	7.77	7.96	8.12
1980	7.00	7.13	7.29	7.47	7.66	7.87	8.07	8.26	8.44
1981	7.34	7.49	7.65	7.84	8.04	8.27	8.47	8.69	8.88
1982	7.63	7.79	7.96	8.15	8.36	8.59	8.81	9.03	9.23
1983	7.82	7.98	8.15	8.35	8.56	8.78	9.00	9.22	9.42
1984	8.03	8.19	8.36	8.56	8.76	8.99	9.20	9.42	9.62
1985	8.16	8.32	8.49	8.68	8.89	9.11	9.32	9.53	9.73
1986	8.19	8.35	8.51	8.70	8.89	9.10	9.30	9.50	9.69
1987	8.24	8.39	8.55	8.73	8.92	9.12	9.31	9.50	9.67
1988	8.29	8.44	8.59	8.77	8.95	9.14	9.32	9.51	9.67
1989	8.32	8.46	8.62	8.79	8.96	9.15	9.32	9.50	9.65
1990	8.36	8.49	8.64	8.81	8.97	9.15	9.32	9.49	9.64
1991	8.37	8.50	8.65	8.80	8.97	9.14	9.30	9.46	9.60
1992	8.36	8.49	8.63	8.78	8.94	9.10	9.26	9.40	9.54

Table 5-14C

Year	1970	1971	1972	1973	1974	1975	1976	1977	1978
1970	8.04								
1971	7.72	7.39							
1972	7.55	7.30	7.21						
1973	7.52	7.35	7.33	7.44					
1974	7.73	7.65	7.74	8.01	8.57				
1975	7.91	7.89	8.01	8.28	8.70	8.83			
1976	7.99	7.98	8.10	8.32	8.61	8.63	8.43		
1977	7.99	7.98	8.08	8.26	8.46	8.43	8.23	8.02	
1978	8.07	8.08	8.18	8.34	8.52	8.50	8.39	8.38	8.73
1979	8.23	8.25	8.36	8.52	8.70	8.73	8.70	8.79	9.18
1980	8.57	8.62	8.76	8.95	9.16	9.26	9.35	9.58	10.10
1981	9.03	9.12	9.30	9.53	9.79	9.96	10.15	10.50	11.12
1982	9.40	9.51	9.71	9.96	10.23	10.44	10.67	11.05	11.65
1983	9.59	9.71	9.90	10.14	10.42	10.62	10.84	11.19	11.72
1984	9.80	9.92	10.12	10.36	10.62	10.83	11.05	11.38	11.86
1985	9.89	10.02	10.21	10.44	10.69	10.88	11.08	11.38	11.80
1986	9.84	9.96	10.13	10.34	10.56	10.72	10.90	11.14	11.49
1987	9.82	9.92	10.08	10.27	10.47	10.62	10.77	10.98	11.28
1988	9.81	9.91	10.06	10.24	10.42	10.56	10.69	10.88	11.14
1989	9.78	9.88	10.01	10.18	10.35	10.47	10.59	10.75	10.98
1990	9.76	9.85	9.98	10.13	10.29	10.40	10.50	10.65	10.85
1991	9.72	9.80	9.92	10.06	10.21	10.30	10.39	10.52	10.70
1992	9.65	9.72	9.83	9.96	10.10	10.18	10.26	10.38	10.53

Table 5-14D

Year	1979	1980	1981	1982	1983	1984	1985	1986	1987
1979	9.63								
1980	10.79	11.94							
1981	11.91	13.06	14.17						
1982	12.38	13.30	13.98	13.79					
1983	12.31	12.99	13.33	12.92	12.04				
1984	12.38	12.93	13.18	12.85	12.38	12.71			
1985	12.24	12.67	12.82	12.48	12.04	11.37	11.37		
1986	11.83	12.15	12.18	11.79	11.29	11.03	10.20	9.02	
1987	11.56	11.80	11.78	11.39	10.90	10.62	9.92	9.20	9.38
1988	11.38	11.57	11.52	11.15	10.71	10.44	9.87	9.37	9.55
1989	11.18	11.34	11.27	10.91	10.50	10.24	9.75	9.34	9.45
1990	11.03	11.16	11.08	10.73	10.35	10.11	9.68	9.34	9.42
1991	10.85	10.96	10.87	10.54	10.18	9.94	9.55	9.24	9.29
1992	10.66	10.74	10.64	10.32	9.97	9.74	9.37	9.09	9.10

Table 5-14E

Year	1988	1989	1990	1991	1992
1988	9.71				
1989	9.49	9.26			
1990	9.43	9.29	9.32		
1991	9.27	9.12	9.05	8.77	
1992	9.04	8.87	8.74	8.46	8.14

Source: Economic Report of the President Table B69 (1993).

§5.16   —Moody's Baa Corporate Bonds

Bonds rated "Baa" are considered more risky than bonds rated "Aaa." Corporations with debt rated "Baa" are considered as having earnings adequate to pay interest and repay principal.[10] Table 5-15 shows the average annual return for "Baa" bonds for the period 1952-1992. Returns averaged 8.28 per cent.

Table 5-15   Annual Return on Baa Corporate Bonds

Year	Yield	Year	Yield
1952	3.52	1973	8.24
1953	3.74	1974	9.50
1954	3.51	1975	10.61
1955	3.53	1976	9.75
1956	3.88	1977	8.97
1957	4.71	1978	9.49
1958	4.73	1979	10.69
1959	5.05	1980	13.67
1960	5.19	1981	16.04
1961	5.08	1982	16.11
1962	5.02	1983	13.55
1963	4.86	1984	14.19
1964	4.83	1985	12.72
1965	4.87	1986	10.39
1966	5.67	1987	10.58
1967	6.23	1988	10.83
1968	6.94	1989	10.18
1969	7.81	1990	10.36
1970	9.11	1991	9.80
1971	8.56	1992	8.98
1972	8.16	Average Yield	8.28

Source: Economic Report of the President Table B-69 (1993).

---

[10] R. Kolb, Investments 44 (1986).

Table 5-16   Average Returns on Baa Corporate Bonds (Moody's)

Table 5-16A

Year	1952	1953	1954	1955	1956	1957	1958	1959	1960
1952	3.52								
1953	3.63	3.74							
1954	3.59	3.63	3.51						
1955	3.58	3.59	3.52	3.53					
1956	3.64	3.67	3.64	3.71	3.88				
1957	3.82	3.87	3.91	4.04	4.30	4.71			
1958	3.95	4.02	4.07	4.21	4.44	4.72	4.73		
1959	4.08	4.16	4.24	4.38	4.59	4.83	4.89	5.05	
1960	4.21	4.29	4.37	4.52	4.71	4.92	4.99	5.12	5.19
1961	4.29	4.38	4.46	4.60	4.77	4.95	5.01	5.11	5.14
1962	4.36	4.44	4.52	4.65	4.81	4.96	5.01	5.09	5.10
1963	4.40	4.48	4.56	4.67	4.82	4.95	4.99	5.04	5.04
1964	4.43	4.51	4.58	4.69	4.82	4.93	4.97	5.01	5.00
1965	4.47	4.54	4.61	4.70	4.82	4.93	4.95	4.99	4.98
1966	4.55	4.62	4.69	4.79	4.90	5.00	5.03	5.07	5.07
1967	4.65	4.73	4.80	4.90	5.01	5.11	5.15	5.20	5.22
1968	4.79	4.87	4.94	5.04	5.16	5.27	5.32	5.37	5.41
1969	4.95	5.04	5.12	5.23	5.35	5.46	5.52	5.60	5.65
1970	5.17	5.26	5.35	5.47	5.60	5.72	5.80	5.89	5.96
1971	5.34	5.44	5.53	5.65	5.78	5.91	6.00	6.09	6.18
1972	5.48	5.57	5.67	5.79	5.92	6.05	6.14	6.24	6.33
1973	5.60	5.70	5.80	5.92	6.05	6.18	6.27	6.37	6.47
1974	5.77	5.87	5.98	6.10	6.23	6.36	6.46	6.57	6.67
1975	5.97	6.08	6.19	6.31	6.45	6.59	6.69	6.81	6.92
1976	6.12	6.23	6.34	6.47	6.61	6.75	6.85	6.97	7.08
1977	6.23	6.34	6.45	6.58	6.72	6.85	6.96	7.08	7.19
1978	6.35	6.46	6.57	6.70	6.84	6.97	7.08	7.20	7.31
1979	6.51	6.62	6.73	6.86	7.00	7.13	7.24	7.36	7.48
1980	6.76	6.87	6.99	7.12	7.26	7.41	7.52	7.65	7.77
1981	7.07	7.19	7.31	7.45	7.60	7.75	7.88	8.01	8.15
1982	7.36	7.49	7.61	7.76	7.92	8.07	8.21	8.35	8.50
1983	7.55	7.68	7.81	7.96	8.12	8.28	8.41	8.56	8.71
1984	7.75	7.88	8.02	8.17	8.33	8.49	8.63	8.78	8.93
1985	7.90	8.03	8.16	8.31	8.47	8.63	8.77	8.92	9.07
1986	7.97	8.10	8.23	8.38	8.54	8.69	8.83	8.98	9.12
1987	8.04	8.17	8.30	8.45	8.60	8.75	8.89	9.03	9.17
1988	8.12	8.24	8.37	8.52	8.67	8.82	8.95	9.09	9.23
1989	8.17	8.30	8.42	8.56	8.71	8.86	8.99	9.13	9.26
1990	8.23	8.35	8.48	8.61	8.76	8.90	9.03	9.16	9.30
1991	8.27	8.39	8.51	8.65	8.79	8.93	9.05	9.18	9.31
1992	8.28	8.40	8.52	8.65	8.79	8.93	9.05	9.18	9.30

Table 5-16B

Year	1961	1962	1963	1964	1965	1966	1967	1968	1969
1961	5.08								
1962	5.05	5.02							
1963	4.99	4.94	4.86						
1964	4.95	4.90	4.85	4.83					
1965	4.93	4.90	4.85	4.85	4.87				
1966	5.06	5.05	5.06	5.12	5.27	5.67			
1967	5.22	5.25	5.29	5.40	5.59	5.95	6.23		
1968	5.44	5.49	5.57	5.71	5.93	6.28	6.59	6.94	
1969	5.70	5.78	5.89	6.06	6.30	6.66	6.99	7.38	7.81
1970	6.04	6.15	6.29	6.49	6.77	7.15	7.52	7.95	8.46
1971	6.27	6.39	6.54	6.75	7.03	7.39	7.73	8.11	8.49
1972	6.43	6.55	6.70	6.91	7.17	7.50	7.80	8.12	8.41
1973	6.57	6.69	6.84	7.04	7.29	7.59	7.86	8.14	8.38
1974	6.78	6.91	7.07	7.27	7.51	7.80	8.07	8.33	8.56
1975	7.03	7.17	7.34	7.54	7.79	8.08	8.35	8.62	8.86
1976	7.20	7.34	7.51	7.71	7.95	8.23	8.49	8.74	8.97
1977	7.31	7.45	7.61	7.80	8.03	8.30	8.53	8.77	8.97
1978	7.43	7.57	7.73	7.92	8.14	8.39	8.61	8.83	9.02
1979	7.60	7.74	7.90	8.09	8.31	8.55	8.77	8.99	9.17
1980	7.90	8.05	8.22	8.42	8.64	8.89	9.12	9.35	9.55
1981	8.29	8.45	8.63	8.84	9.08	9.34	9.58	9.82	10.05
1982	8.65	8.82	9.01	9.22	9.47	9.74	9.99	10.24	10.48
1983	8.86	9.03	9.22	9.44	9.68	9.95	10.20	10.45	10.68
1984	9.08	9.26	9.45	9.67	9.91	10.17	10.42	10.67	10.90
1985	9.23	9.40	9.59	9.81	10.04	10.30	10.54	10.78	11.01
1986	9.27	9.44	9.62	9.83	10.06	10.30	10.54	10.76	10.98
1987	9.32	9.48	9.66	9.86	10.08	10.32	10.54	10.75	10.95
1988	9.37	9.53	9.71	9.90	10.11	10.34	10.55	10.76	10.95
1989	9.40	9.56	9.72	9.91	10.11	10.33	10.54	10.73	10.91
1990	9.43	9.58	9.75	9.93	10.12	10.33	10.53	10.72	10.89
1991	9.45	9.59	9.75	9.92	10.11	10.31	10.50	10.68	10.84
1992	9.43	9.57	9.72	9.89	10.07	10.26	10.44	10.61	10.76

Table 5-16C

Year	1970	1971	1972	1973	1974	1975	1976	1977	1978
1970	9.11								
1971	8.84	8.56							
1972	8.61	8.36	8.16						
1973	8.52	8.32	8.20	8.24					
1974	8.71	8.62	8.63	8.87	9.50				
1975	9.03	9.01	9.13	9.45	10.06	10.61			
1976	9.13	9.14	9.25	9.53	9.95	10.18	9.75		
1977	9.11	9.11	9.21	9.41	9.71	9.78	9.36	8.97	
1978	9.15	9.16	9.25	9.43	9.66	9.71	9.40	9.23	9.49
1979	9.31	9.33	9.43	9.61	9.84	9.90	9.73	9.72	10.09
1980	9.70	9.76	9.90	10.12	10.38	10.53	10.51	10.71	11.28
1981	10.23	10.33	10.51	10.77	11.09	11.32	11.44	11.77	12.47
1982	10.68	10.82	11.02	11.31	11.65	11.92	12.10	12.50	13.20
1983	10.89	11.03	11.23	11.51	11.84	12.10	12.28	12.65	13.26
1984	11.11	11.25	11.46	11.73	12.05	12.31	12.50	12.84	13.39
1985	11.21	11.35	11.55	11.81	12.11	12.34	12.52	12.83	13.31
1986	11.16	11.29	11.47	11.71	11.98	12.18	12.32	12.58	12.98
1987	11.13	11.25	11.42	11.63	11.88	12.06	12.18	12.40	12.74
1988	11.11	11.23	11.38	11.58	11.81	11.97	12.08	12.27	12.57
1989	11.07	11.17	11.32	11.50	11.70	11.85	11.94	12.11	12.37
1990	11.03	11.13	11.26	11.44	11.63	11.76	11.83	11.98	12.22
1991	10.98	11.07	11.19	11.35	11.52	11.64	11.71	11.84	12.04
1992	10.89	10.97	11.09	11.23	11.39	11.50	11.55	11.66	11.84

Table 5-16D

Year	1979	1980	1981	1982	1983	1984	1985	1986	1987
1979	10.69								
1980	12.18	13.67							
1981	13.47	14.86	16.04						
1982	14.13	15.27	16.08	16.11					
1983	14.01	14.84	15.23	14.83	13.55				
1984	14.04	14.71	14.97	14.62	13.87	14.19			
1985	13.85	14.38	14.52	14.14	13.49	12.72	12.72		
1986	13.42	13.81	13.83	13.39	12.71	12.43	11.56	10.39	
1987	13.10	13.41	13.37	12.92	12.29	11.97	11.23	10.49	10.58
1988	12.88	13.12	13.05	12.62	12.04	11.74	11.13	10.60	10.71
1989	12.63	12.83	12.73	12.32	11.78	11.48	10.94	10.50	10.53
1990	12.44	12.60	12.50	12.10	11.60	11.32	10.84	10.47	10.49
1991	12.24	12.37	12.25	11.87	11.40	11.13	10.69	10.36	10.35
1992	12.01	12.11	11.98	11.61	11.16	10.89	10.48	10.16	10.12

Table 5-16E

Year	1988	1989	1990	1991	1992
1988	10.83				
1989	10.51	10.18			
1990	10.46	10.27	10.36		
1991	10.29	10.11	10.08	9.80	
1992	10.03	9.83	9.71	9.39	8.98

§5.17 —Standard and Poor's High-Grade Municipal Bonds

Municipal bonds are debt instruments issued by governmental or quasi-governmental agencies. These agencies are not associated with the federal governments.[11] The unique thing about municipal bonds is that they are free of federal income tax. Table 5-17 shows the returns to municipal bonds over the period 1952 to 1992 inclusive. As the table indicates, the return on municipal bonds averaged 5.68 per cent.

The problem with using the municipal bond yield is that one must know the individual's marginal tax rate. For example, suppose an individual paid no federal income tax. Then there would be no reason for the individual to purchase bonds free of federal taxation. Thus, corporate bonds would be the best investment. As the individual's tax rate increases, the tax-free bonds become more and more attractive.

After-tax returns on taxable corporate bonds must be compared to returns on tax-free municipal bonds. The following equation shows how to calculate the before-tax equivalent yield for municipal bonds:

[Before-Tax Yield - Tax Free Yield] / [1 - Marginal Tax Rate]

If a municipal bond was paying 8 per cent tax free and the individual has a marginal tax rate of 30 per cent, then the taxable equivalent yield would be:

Before tax yield = .08/(1-.30)
Before tax yield = .08/(.70)
Before tax yield = 11.42%

The desirability of holding a municipal bond is dependent on the individual's tax position. Thus, there is no way to determine the before-tax equivalent for a municipal bond since it is different for each individual. However, as Table 5-17 indicates, the average annual yield on high-grade municipal bonds has averaged 5.68 per cent for the period 1952 through 1992.

---

[11] R. Ibbotson & R. Sinquefield, Stocks, Bonds, Bills and Inflation: The Past and the Future 7 (Fin Analyst Research Foundation, Univ of Va 1987); Harris, *Selecting Income Growth and Discount Rates in Wrongful Death and Injury Cases: Comment*, 44, No 1 J Risk & Ins 117 (Mar 1977).

Table 5-17   Yield on High-Grade Municipal Bonds

Year	Yield	Year	Yield
1952	2.19	1973	5.18
1953	2.72	1974	6.09
1954	2.37	1975	6.89
1955	2.53	1976	6.49
1956	2.93	1977	5.56
1957	3.60	1978	5.90
1958	3.56	1979	6.39
1959	3.95	1980	8.51
1960	3.73	1981	11.23
1961	3.46	1982	11.57
1962	3.18	1983	9.47
1963	3.23	1984	10.15
1964	3.22	1985	9.18
1965	3.27	1986	7.38
1966	3.82	1987	7.73
1967	3.98	1988	7.76
1968	4.51	1989	7.24
1969	5.81	1990	7.25
1970	6.51	1991	6.89
1971	5.70	1992	6.41
1972	5.27	Average Yield	5.68

Table 5-18 Yield on High-Grade Municipal Bonds

Table 5-18A

Year	1952	1953	1954	1955	1956	1957	1958	1959	1960
1952	2.19								
1953	2.46	2.72							
1954	2.43	2.55	2.37						
1955	2.45	2.54	2.45	2.53					
1956	2.55	2.64	2.61	2.73	2.93				
1957	2.72	2.83	2.86	3.02	3.27	3.60			
1958	2.84	2.95	3.00	3.16	3.36	3.58	3.56		
1959	2.98	3.09	3.16	3.31	3.51	3.70	3.76	3.95	
1960	3.06	3.17	3.24	3.38	3.55	3.71	3.75	3.84	3.73
1961	3.10	3.21	3.27	3.39	3.54	3.66	3.68	3.71	3.60
1962	3.11	3.20	3.26	3.37	3.49	3.58	3.58	3.58	3.46
1963	3.12	3.21	3.25	3.35	3.46	3.53	3.52	3.51	3.40
1964	3.13	3.21	3.25	3.34	3.43	3.49	3.48	3.46	3.36
1965	3.14	3.21	3.25	3.33	3.41	3.47	3.45	3.43	3.35
1966	3.18	3.26	3.30	3.37	3.45	3.50	3.49	3.48	3.42
1967	3.23	3.30	3.35	3.42	3.49	3.55	3.54	3.54	3.49
1968	3.31	3.38	3.42	3.50	3.57	3.63	3.63	3.64	3.60
1969	3.45	3.52	3.57	3.65	3.73	3.79	3.81	3.83	3.82
1970	3.61	3.69	3.74	3.83	3.92	3.99	4.02	4.06	4.07
1971	3.71	3.79	3.85	3.94	4.03	4.10	4.14	4.18	4.20
1972	3.79	3.87	3.93	4.01	4.10	4.18	4.21	4.26	4.28
1973	3.85	3.93	3.99	4.08	4.16	4.23	4.27	4.32	4.35
1974	3.95	4.03	4.09	4.18	4.26	4.34	4.38	4.43	4.46
1975	4.07	4.15	4.22	4.31	4.39	4.47	4.52	4.58	4.62
1976	4.17	4.25	4.32	4.41	4.49	4.57	4.62	4.68	4.73
1977	4.22	4.30	4.37	4.46	4.54	4.62	4.67	4.73	4.77
1978	4.28	4.36	4.43	4.52	4.60	4.68	4.73	4.79	4.83
1979	4.36	4.44	4.51	4.59	4.68	4.75	4.80	4.86	4.91
1980	4.50	4.58	4.65	4.74	4.83	4.91	4.97	5.03	5.08
1981	4.73	4.81	4.89	4.98	5.08	5.16	5.23	5.30	5.36
1982	4.95	5.04	5.12	5.22	5.32	5.41	5.48	5.56	5.63
1983	5.09	5.18	5.26	5.36	5.46	5.56	5.63	5.72	5.79
1984	5.24	5.34	5.42	5.52	5.63	5.72	5.80	5.89	5.96
1985	5.36	5.45	5.54	5.64	5.74	5.84	5.92	6.01	6.09
1986	5.42	5.51	5.59	5.70	5.80	5.89	5.97	6.06	6.14
1987	5.48	5.57	5.66	5.76	5.86	5.95	6.03	6.12	6.19
1988	5.54	5.63	5.72 .	5.82	5.92	6.01	6.09	6.17	6.25
1989	5.59	5.68	5.76	5.86	5.95	6.05	6.12	6.21	6.28
1990	5.63	5.72	5.80	5.90	5.99	6.08	6.16	6.24	6.31
1991	5.66	5.75	5.83	5.92	6.02	6.10	6.18	6.26	6.33
1992	5.68	5.77	5.84	5.94	6.03	6.11	6.18	6.26	6.33

Table 5-18B

Year	1961	1962	1963	1964	1965	1966	1967	1968	1969
1961	3.46								
1962	3.32	3.18							
1963	3.29	3.21	3.23						
1964	3.27	3.21	3.23	3.22					
1965	3.27	3.23	3.24	3.25	3.27				
1966	3.36	3.34	3.39	3.44	3.55	3.82			
1967	3.45	3.45	3.50	3.57	3.69	3.90	3.98		
1968	3.58	3.60	3.67	3.76	3.90	4.10	4.25	4.51	
1969	3.83	3.88	3.98	4.10	4.28	4.53	4.77	5.16	5.81
1970	4.10	4.17	4.29	4.45	4.65	4.93	5.20	5.61	6.16
1971	4.24	4.32	4.45	4.60	4.80	5.06	5.30	5.63	6.01
1972	4.33	4.41	4.53	4.68	4.86	5.09	5.30	5.56	5.82
1973	4.40	4.47	4.59	4.73	4.89	5.10	5.28	5.50	5.69
1974	4.52	4.60	4.72	4.85	5.01	5.21	5.38	5.58	5.76
1975	4.67	4.76	4.88	5.02	5.18	5.38	5.55	5.75	5.92
1976	4.79	4.88	5.00	5.13	5.29	5.48	5.64	5.83	5.99
1977	4.83	4.92	5.04	5.16	5.31	5.48	5.64	5.80	5.94
1978	4.89	4.98	5.09	5.21	5.36	5.52	5.66	5.81	5.94
1979	4.97	5.06	5.17	5.29	5.42	5.58	5.71	5.86	5.98
1980	5.15	5.24	5.35	5.48	5.62	5.77	5.91	6.06	6.19
1981	5.44	5.54	5.66	5.80	5.95	6.12	6.27	6.43	6.58
1982	5.72	5.82	5.96	6.10	6.26	6.44	6.60	6.77	6.94
1983	5.88	5.99	6.12	6.27	6.43	6.60	6.77	6.94	7.10
1984	6.06	6.17	6.31	6.45	6.62	6.79	6.96	7.13	7.30
1985	6.18	6.30	6.43	6.58	6.74	6.91	7.07	7.25	7.41
1986	6.23	6.34	6.47	6.61	6.77	6.93	7.09	7.25	7.40
1987	6.28	6.39	6.52	6.66	6.81	6.97	7.12	7.28	7.42
1988	6.34	6.44	6.57	6.70	6.85	7.00	7.15	7.30	7.44
1989	6.37	6.47	6.59	6.72	6.86	7.01	7.15	7.30	7.43
1990	6.40	6.50	6.62	6.74	6.88	7.02	7.16	7.29	7.42
1991	6.41	6.51	6.63	6.75	6.88	7.02	7.15	7.28	7.40
1992	6.41	6.51	6.62	6.74	6.86	7.00	7.12	7.24	7.36

Table 5-18C

Year	1970	1971	1972	1973	1974	1975	1976	1977	1978
1970	6.51								
1971	6.11	5.70							
1972	5.83	5.49	5.27						
1973	5.67	5.38	5.23	5.18					
1974	5.75	5.56	5.51	5.64	6.09				
1975	5.94	5.83	5.86	6.05	6.49	6.89			
1976	6.02	5.94	5.98	6.16	6.49	6.69	6.49		
1977	5.96	5.88	5.91	6.04	6.26	6.31	6.03	5.56	
1978	5.95	5.89	5.91	6.02	6.19	6.21	5.98	5.73	5.90
1979	6.00	5.94	5.97	6.07	6.22	6.25	6.09	5.95	6.15
1980	6.23	6.20	6.25	6.38	6.55	6.62	6.57	6.59	6.93
1981	6.64	6.66	6.75	6.92	7.13	7.28	7.35	7.52	8.01
1982	7.02	7.07	7.19	7.38	7.63	7.82	7.95	8.19	8.72
1983	7.20	7.25	7.38	7.57	7.81	8.00	8.14	8.38	8.85
1984	7.39	7.46	7.59	7.79	8.02	8.22	8.36	8.60	9.03
1985	7.51	7.57	7.71	7.89	8.12	8.30	8.45	8.66	9.05
1986	7.50	7.56	7.68	7.86	8.06	8.23	8.35	8.53	8.86
1987	7.51	7.57	7.69	7.85	8.04	8.19	8.30	8.46	8.75
1988	7.52	7.58	7.69	7.84	8.02	8.16	8.26	8.40	8.66
1989	7.51	7.56	7.67	7.81	7.97	8.10	8.18	8.31	8.54
1990	7.50	7.55	7.64	7.78	7.93	8.04	8.12	8.24	8.44
1991	7.47	7.52	7.61	7.73	7.87	7.98	8.04	8.15	8.33
1992	7.42	7.47	7.55	7.66	7.79	7.89	7.95	8.04	8.20

Table 5-18D

Year	1979	1980	1981	1982	1983	1984	1985	1986	1987
1979	6.39								
1980	7.45	8.51							
1981	8.71	9.87	11.23						
1982	9.43	10.44	11.40	11.57					
1983	9.43	10.20	10.76	10.52	9.47				
1984	9.55	10.19	10.61	10.40	9.81	10.15			
1985	9.50	10.02	10.32	10.09	9.60	9.18	9.18		
1986	9.24	9.64	9.83	9.55	9.05	8.90	8.28	7.38	
1987	9.07	9.40	9.53	9.25	8.78	8.61	8.10	7.56	7.73
1988	8.94	9.22	9.31	9.03	8.61	8.44	8.01	7.62	7.75
1989	8.78	9.02	9.08	8.81	8.42	8.24	7.86	7.53	7.58
1990	8.66	8.86	8.90	8.64	8.27	8.10	7.76	7.47	7.50
1991	8.52	8.70	8.71	8.46	8.12	7.95	7.63	7.38	7.37
1992	8.37	8.52	8.52	8.28	7.95	7.78	7.48	7.24	7.21

Table 5-18E

Year	1988	1989	1990	1991	1992
1988	7.76				
1989	7.50	7.24			
1990	7.42	7.25	7.25		
1991	7.29	7.13	7.07	6.89	
1992	7.11	6.95	6.85	6.65	6.41

§5.18 —Common Stock

Common stock represents fractional ownership in a corporation. The corporation may be large or small. For the common stock of a company to be traded on the New York Stock Exchange, certain conditions must have been met by the company. Of importance is that the corporate stock is widely held and there is a ready market for the stock. This means that if the individual wishes to buy or sell a security on the exchange it can be done almost immediately.

Returns on common stock may be in two forms. The return may be in the form of dividends or in the form of capital gains or both. Capital gains occur when the investment is sold for more than the original purchase price.

Table 5-19 shows the return on common stock. The common stock total return index is based upon the Standard and Poor's Composite Index. The return was calculated by adding the dividends received to the change in price and dividing this sum by the beginning price.

Table 5-19 Returns on Common Stock

Year	% Return
1952	18.40
1953	-1.00
1954	52.60
1955	31.60
1956	6.60
1957	-10.80
1958	43.40
1959	12.00
1960	0.50
1961	26.90
1962	-8.70
1963	22.80
1964	16.50
1965	12.50
1966	-10.10
1967	24.00
1968	11.10

Year	% Return
1969	-8.50
1970	4.00
1971	14.30
1972	19.00
1973	-14.70
1974	-26.50
1975	37.20
1976	23.80
1977	-7.20
1978	6.60
1979	18.40
1980	32.40
1981	-4.90
1982	21.41
1983	22.51
1984	6.27
1985	32.16
1986	18.47
1987	5.23
1988	16.81
1989	31.49
1990	-3.17
1991	30.55
1992	7.67
Average	12.97

Source: Ibbotson Assocs, Stock, Bonds, Bills and Inflation: 1993 Yearbook Market Results, 1926-1992 (Chicago 1993).

§5.19 —Combinations of Investments

Some economists argue that present value should be discounted at a combination of various returns. For example, an economist may argue that the appropriate investment would be one-third of the money invested in one-year Treasury Bills and the balance in long-term government bonds. Using the average historic returns on long-term government bonds, 6.84 per cent, and the average historic return on Treasury Bills, 6.05 per cent, the weighted average of these returns can be calculated. The weighted average would be 6.57 per cent and this would be the discount rate used to calculate present value.

Table 5-20   Weighted Return to a Portfolio

Investment	Return	Weight	Weighted Average Return
Treasury Bill	6.05%	33.3%	2.01%
LT Government	6.84%	66.7%	4.56%
		Portfolio Return	6.57%

§5.20   Evaluating Returns

The above tables show the historical returns that have been achieved through alternative investments. The lowest 1952 to 1992 average return was from the three-month Treasury Bills which averaged 5.51 per cent annually. The largest return was from investments in common stocks, which averaged 12.97% for the same period of time.

What is of importance is that as the return on the investment increases so does the risk associated with earning the return. That is to say, the return on common stock is more risky than the return on three-month Treasury Bills.

Table 5-21 shows the present value of a future income stream using the various discount rates established by various investment vehicles. The present value is based on an annual income of $20,000 starting today and being paid each year for an additional 29 years. It is assumed that the annual growth rate of the future income is zero, and only the discount rate changes.

Table 5-21   Present Value of the Future Income Stream Using Different Discount Rates

Investment	Yield (%)	Present Value of Salary in 29 Yrs	Present Value of Total Future Wages
3-Month Treasury Bill	5.51	$4,222	$306,873
6-Month Treasury Bill	6.38	3,327	281,328
1-Year Treasury Bill	6.05	3,641	290,397
Long-Term Government	6.84	2,936	269,475
Moody's Aaa Bond	7.31	2,585	258,235
Moody's Baa Bond	8.28	1,991	237,497
S&P Municipal	5.68	4,029	301,173
Weighted Portfolio	6.57	3,159	276,324

The present value of the salary paid in the twenty-ninth year ranges from a low of $1,991 to a high of $4,222. Likewise, the present value of the future income stream varies from a low of $237,497 to a high of $306,873. The only variable which can account for this difference is the discount rate or the rate earned on invested funds.

§5.21 Summary

The investment chosen by the economist as the appropriate one will have a significant impact on the size of the present value estimate. The higher the return, the lower will be the present value estimate.

The range of investment returns can be determined from Table 5-21. The range of investment returns is from the low of 5.51 per cent earned on the three-month Treasury Bill to a high of 8.28 per cent earned on the Baa corporate bond.

6 Combining Growth and Discount

$$\text{Present Value of Future Income} = \sum_{t=0}^{n} \$ * M * (1+g)^t / (1+d)^t * P_L * P_S * P_F * C * HS * Tx$$

§6.01 Introduction

The calculation of the present value of an income stream requires establishing values for four variables. The variables are the dollars to be used as the beginning value, "$" in the formula, the growth rate of the dollars, the discount rate, and the number of years into the future the estimate is made. Chapter 3, "Base Dollars," showed various sources on which the current dollar value could be based. Chapter

4, "The Growth Rate," examined various methods to calculate growth rates of earnings or expenses and presented sources from which growth rates could be estimated. Chapter 5, "Discount Rates: The Present Value Calculation," showed how discounting to the present value is accomplished and presented source material for establishing the appropriate discount rate.

It is the purpose of this chapter to demonstrate how the present value is determined when a growth rate and a discount rate are used simultaneously. This method of calculating the present value is known as the *simultaneous method*, or simultaneous growth and discount. The relationship between the growth rate and the discount rate establishes a "spread." This relationship will be examined.

Finally, a worksheet will be developed so anyone can calculate the present value of a future stream of dollars using the simultaneous method. Note that the simultaneous method is the appropriate method to use when calculating the present value of an income stream. The calculation requires deciding what values to use for dollars, "$"; growth, "g"; discount, "d"; and time, "t."

§6.02 Reviewing the Growth Factor

The growth formula has been used to calculate the future value of one dollar. The formula for growth is:

$$\text{Future Value} = (1+g)^t$$

Where:

"g" is the rate of growth per year
"t" is the number of years growth will occur

The growth factor can be determined by using a calculator or by looking up the growth factor in Appendix A. A portion of Appendix A appears in Table 6-1.

Table 6-1   Growth Table

Growth Rate in Per Cent

Year	0.00	0.02	0.04	0.06	0.08	0.10
0	1.000	1.000	1.000	1.000	1.000	1.000
1	1.000	1.020	1.040	1.060	1.080	1.100
2	1.000	1.040	1.082	1.124	1.166	1.210
3	1.000	1.061	1.125	1.191	1.260	1.331
4	1.000	1.082	1.170	1.262	1.360	1.464
5	1.000	1.104	1.217	1.338	1.469	1.611
6	1.000	1.126	1.265	1.419	1.587	1.772
7	1.000	1.149	1.316	1.504	1.714	1.949
8	1.000	1.172	1.369	1.594	1.851	2.144
9	1.000	1.195	1.423	1.689	1.999	2.358
10	1.000	1.219	1.480	1.791	2.159	2.594

Year

	0.00	0.02	0.04	0.06	0.08	0.10
11	1.000	1.243	1.539	1.898	2.332	2.853
12	1.000	1.268	1.601	2.012	2.518	3.138
13	1.000	1.294	1.665	2.133	2.720	3.452
14	1.000	1.319	1.732	2.261	2.937	3.797
15	1.000	1.346	1.801	2.397	3.172	4.177
16	1.000	1.373	1.873	2.540	3.426	4.595
17	1.000	1.400	1.948	2.693	3.700	5.054
18	1.000	1.428	2.026	2.854	3.996	5.560
19	1.000	1.457	2.107	3.026	4.316	6.116
20	1.000	1.486	2.191	3.207	4.661	6.727
21	1.000	1.516	2.279	3.400	5.034	7.400
22	1.000	1.546	2.370	3.604	5.437	8.140
23	1.000	1.577	2.465	3.820	5.871	8.954
24	1.000	1.608	2.563	4.049	6.341	9.850
25	1.000	1.641	2.666	4.292	6.848	10.835

If $1,000 were to be received in 12 years and the investment were growing at 4 per cent annually, the future value would be $1,601. This is the present value of $1,000 times the future value factor of 1.601.

§6.03   Reviewing the Discount Factor

The discount formula is used to calculate the present value of a dollar to be received in the future. The present value formula is:

$$\text{Present Value} = 1/(1+i)^t$$

Where:

"i" is the interest or discount

"t" is the number of years until money is to be received

The discount factor can be determined by using a calculator or by looking up the present value factor in Appendix B. A portion of Appendix B is presented in Table 6-2.

Table 6-2   Discount Table

Discount Rate

Year

	0.00	0.02	0.04	0.06	0.08	0.10
0	1.000	1.000	1.000	1.000	1.000	1.000
1	1.000	0.980	0.962	0.943	0.926	0.909
2	1.000	0.961	0.925	0.890	0.857	0.826

Year

	0.00	0.02	0.04	0.06	0.08	0.10
3	1.000	0.942	0.889	0.840	0.794	0.751
4	1.000	0.924	0.855	0.792	0.735	0.683
5	1.000	0.906	0.822	0.747	0.681	0.621
6	1.000	0.888	0.790	0.705	0.630	0.564
7	1.000	0.871	0.760	0.665	0.583	0.513
8	1.000	0.853	0.731	0.627	0.540	0.467
9	1.000	0.837	0.703	0.592	0.500	0.424
10	1.000	0.820	0.676	0.558	0.463	0.386
11	1.000	0.804	0.650	0.527	0.429	0.350
12	1.000	0.788	0.625	0.497	0.397	0.319
13	1.000	0.773	0.601	0.469	0.368	0.290
14	1.000	0.758	0.577	0.442	0.340	0.263
15	1.000	0.743	0.555	0.417	0.315	0.239
16	1.000	0.728	0.534	0.394	0.292	0.218
17	1.000	0.714	0.513	0.371	0.270	0.198
18	1.000	0.700	0.494	0.350	0.250	0.180
19	1.000	0.686	0.475	0.331	0.232	0.164
20	1.000	0.673	0.456	0.312	0.215	0.149
21	1.000	0.660	0.439	0.294	0.199	0.135
22	1.000	0.647	0.422	0.278	0.184	0.123
23	1.000	0.634	0.406	0.262	0.170	0.112
24	1.000	0.622	0.390	0.247	0.158	0.102
25	1.000	0.610	0.375	0.233	0.146	0.092

To determine the present value of $1,000 to be received in 15 years when the money is invested at 8 per cent, the future value, $1,000, is multiplied by the present value factor from Table 6-2. The present value factor is .315. The present value of the $1,000 is $315.

§6.04 Combining Growth and Discount

When the present value of a future stream of money is being estimated, the calculation for growth and the calculation for discount must be made. When both calculations are being made, the equation can be written as follows:

$$\text{Present Value} = (1+g)^t / (1+d)^t$$

Where:

"g" is the annual rate of growth

"d" is the annual rate of discount

"t" is the number of years being considered

This formula gives the present value factor of $1. There is a factor for each year and for each growth and discount rate combination. Table 6-3 shows the present value factors for various growth and discount combinations when "t" equals 25 years. A more complete table appears in Appendix C.

Table 6-3   Present Value Year 25

Discount Rate	Growth Rate					
	0.00	.02	.04	.06	.08	.10
.00	25.00	32.67	43.31	58.16	78.95	108.18
.02	19.52	25.00	32.50	42.82	57.14	77.06
.04	15.62	19.61	25.00	32.33	42.36	56.18
.06	12.78	15.75	19.70	25.00	32.17	41.92
.08	10.67	12.93	15.88	19.79	25.00	32.01
.10	9.08	10.82	13.07	16.00	19.87	25.00
.12	7.84	9.22	10.96	13.21	16.12	19.95
.14	6.87	7.97	9.35	11.10	13.34	16.24
.16	6.10	6.99	8.10	9.49	11.24	13.47
.18	5.47	6.21	7.11	8.23	9.62	11.37

Table 6-3 can be used to determine the present value of a stream of money to be received or expended for the next 26 years. The first payment would occur today, followed by 25 additional payments.

Suppose an individual will receive 26 annual payments. The first payment is today for $2,000 and will be followed by 25 more annual payments each growing at 4 per cent annually. This can be viewed as an annuity growing at 4 per cent annually. The present value of such an annuity depends on the current interest rate. If the current interest is 8 per cent, then the present value factor would be found where the row headed ".08" intersects the column headed ".04." The present value factor is 15.88. Multiplying the present value factor by the annual income of $2,000 gives the present value of $31,760. To this amount the first payment of $2,000 must be added. The present value totals $33,760.

Likewise, if an individual were to receive $1,000 per year starting immediately and continuing for an additional 25 years, with a growth rate of 2 per cent and a discount rate of 10 per cent, the present value factor would be 10.82. The present value of the stream on future payments would be $10,820. The total present value would be $12,820.

§6.05   Constructing a Worksheet to Calculate the Present Value of Future Income

When a stream of income is to start immediately, the following worksheet can be used to determine the present value of that stream.

Worksheet # 1
Present Value of Annual Income

1. The monthly payment of _____
    times 12 equals an annual payment of _____ .
    The annual payments will be made
    this year plus _____ more years.
    (Year number from Appendix C.)

    The annual payments will grow
    at _____ per year. (Column Number)

    The interest rate, or discount
    rate, is _____. (Row Number)

2. The present value factor is on
    year number column _____
    _____ of Appendix C where
    column _____ and row _____
    Intersect. The factor is _____ .

3. Multiply the annual payment which
    is _____ by the factor of _____ .
    The present value of the future payments is _____ .

4. The present value of the future
    income plus the income paid in year 1 is
    (the sum of line 1 and line 3) _____ .

Example 1. Suppose the income stream to be evaluated is $1,000 per month for 26 years with the monthly payment growing at 2 per cent annually. The appropriate interest rate is 8 per cent. The first payment is made immediately, and there are 25 years of future payments. Worksheet #2 is used to calculate the present value of the stream. The worksheet converts the monthly payments to annual payments for the purpose of calculating present value.

Worksheet #1
Present Value of Annual Income
2% Annual Growth of Wages
8% Annual Interest Rate

1. The monthly payment of $1,000
    times 12 equals an annual payment of $12,000.

    The annual payments will be made
    this year plus 25 more years.
    (Year #25 from Appendix C.)

    The annual payments will grow
    at 2% per year. (Column headed 2%)

        The interest rate, or discount
rate, is 8%. (Row for 8%)

2.   The present value factor is on
year number 25 of Appendix C where
column 2% and row 8%
intersect. The factor is 12.93.

3.   Multiply the annual payment which
is $12,000 by the factor of 12.93.
The present value of the future payments is $155,160.

4.   The present value of the future income
plus the income paid in year 1 is
(the sum of line 1 and line 3) $167,160.

Example 2. Suppose a 35-year-old plaintiff was earning $800 per month at the time of the injury. The economist has forecast an annual salary increase of 4 per cent and assumed an interest rate, or discount rate, of 6 per cent annually. The plaintiff is expected to have worked to age 65, or for 30 more years. Worksheet #1 can be used to determine the present value of the income stream.

Worksheet # 1
Present Value of Annual Income

1.   The monthly payment of $800
times 12 equals an annual payment of $ 9,600.

        The annual payments will be made
for this year plus 29 more years.
(Year number from Appendix C.)

        The annual payments will grow
at 4% per year. (Column Number)

        The interest rate, or discount
rate, is 6%. (Row Number)

2.   The present value factor is on
year number 29 of Appendix C where
column 4% and row 6%
intersect. The factor is   22.07.

3.   Multiply the annual payment which
is $9,600 by the factor of 22.07.

        The present value of the future payments is $211,872.

4.   The present value of the future income
plus the income paid in year 1 is
(the sum of line 1 and line 3) $221,472.

§6.06 Using the Worksheet to Cross-Examine the Economist about Growth Rates

On cross-examination the defense attorney may wish to question the size of the growth rate of wages assumed by plaintiff's economist. The lower the growth rate the lower will be the present value. The defense attorney will want the economist to assume that the plaintiff's income would experience no growth at all. Then the present value would be lower. Worksheet # 1 can be used to recalculate the present value of the income stream in Example 1. Change the assumed growth rate to zero per cent, let the discount rate remain at 8 per cent annually, and the monthly income remains $1,000.

Worksheet # 1
Present Value of Annual Income
0% Annual Growth of Wages
8% Annual Interest Rate

1. The monthly payment of $ 1,000
   times 12 equals an annual payment of $ 12,000.

   The annual payments will be made
   for this year plus 25 more years.
   (Year number from Appendix C.)

   The annual payments will grow
   at 0% per year. (Column Number)

   The interest rate, or discount
   rate, is 8%. (Row Number)

2. The present value factor is on
   year number 25 of Appendix C where
   column 0% and row 8%
   intersect. The factor is   10.675.

3. Multiply the annual payment which
   is $12,000 by the factor of 10.675.
   The present value of the future income is $128,100.

4. The present value of the future income
   plus the income paid in year 1 is
   (the sum of line 1 and line 3) $140,100.

The reduction on the present value from $167,160 to $140,100 is due to the decrease in the growth rate of wages. An additional reduction on the present value can be achieved if the interest rate is assumed to be larger than the economist's stated rate of 8 per cent annually.

The tables from Chapter 4 concerning growth can be used to provide different growth rates. For example, if the growth rate employed is CPI for 1952 to 1992, the growth rate is 4.30 per cent. This can be "plugged" into the worksheet.

§6.07   Using the Worksheet to Cross-Examine the Economist about Discount Rates

On cross-examination the defense attorney may wish to question the size of the interest rate assumption made by plaintiff's economist. The higher the discount rate, the lower will be the present value. Using the same example as in §6.06, the defense attorney may wish to pursue the present value question using a different discount rate. Assume the fact situation is the same except the discount rate, at the defense attorney's suggestion, is now 10 per cent.

Worksheet # 1
Present Value of Annual Income
0% Annual Growth of Wages
10% Annual Interest Rate

1. The monthly payment of $1,000
    times 12 equals an annual payment of $12,000.

    The annual payments will be made
    for this year plus 25 more years.
    (Year number from Appendix C.)

    The annual payments will grow
    at 0% per year. (Column Number)

    The interest rate, or discount
    rate, is 10%. (Row Number)

2. The present value factor is on
    year number 25 of Appendix C
    where column 0% and row 10%
    intersect. The factor is   9.077.

3. Multiply the annual payment which
    is $12,000 by the factor of 9.077.
    The present value of the future income is $108.924.

4. The present value of the future income
    plus the income paid in year 1 is
    (the sum of line 1 and line 3) $120,924.

The present value of the future income stream was $167,160 when the economist used the growth rate of 2 per cent annually and a discount rate of 8 per cent. When the growth rate was permitted to be 0 per cent and the discount rate was increased to 10 per cent annually, the present value of the future income stream declined to $120,924. The decline in present value of $46,236 is because of the decline in the annual growth rate and the increase in the annual discount rate.

Chapter 5 allows for the choice of various discount rates from different time periods and different investment vehicles.

§6.08 The Concept of *Spread* and How It is Used

An economist has been asked to establish the present value of $20,000 per year for 20 years. The growth rate and discount rate used in the analysis are 4 per cent and 6 per cent respectively. As Table 6-4 indicates, the present value of the stream of money is $335,805.

Table 6-4 Present Value

$20,000 Per Year for 20 Years
4% Annual Growth
6% Annual Discount

Period	Present Value	Sum
0	$20,000	$ 20,000
1	19,623	39,623
2	19,252	58,875
3	18,889	77,764
4	18,533	96,297
5	18,183	114,480
6	17,840	132,320
7	17,503	149,823
8	17,173	166,997
9	16,849	183,846
10	16,531	200,377
11	16,219	216,596
12	15,913	232,509
13	15,613	248,123
14	15,318	263,441
15	15,029	278,470
16	14,746	293,216
17	14,468	307,684
18	14,195	321,878
19	13,927	335,805

If the relationship between the growth and discount rate does not change, the present value of the future income stream will not change. The economist will testify that it is not the growth rate and discount rate that are being testified to, but rather the relationship between the two values—that is, the *spread* will remain constant over time.

The *spread* between the two values is computed by dividing the interest rate by the growth rate. The following formula establishes the spread:

Spread = (1 + Discount Rate)/ (1 + Growth Rate)

In the example with a 4 per cent growth rate and a 6 per cent discount rate the spread would be:

Spread = (1 + Discount Rate)/ (1 + Growth Rate)
Spread = (1 + .06)/ (1 + .04)
Spread = 1.0192307692

As long as the discount rate is 1.0192307692 times larger than the growth rate the present value of the future stream of money will remain the same. The idea presented here is that the growth and discount rates do not have to remain the same for long periods of time, only the relationship between the two must remain the same.

Suppose the spread remains constant but the growth rate increases to 10 per cent. If the spread remains at 1.0192307692 then the interest rate would be 12.115385 per cent, which is 1.0192307692 times 10 per cent. Table 6-5 presents the present values using the higher growth and discount rates.

Table 6-5   Present Value

$20,000 Per Year for 20 Years
10% Annual Growth
12.115385% Annual Discount

Period	Present Value	Sum
0	$20,000	$ 20,000
1	19,623	39,623
2	19,252	58,875
3	18,889	77,764
4	18,533	96,297
5	18,183	114,480
6	17,840	132,320
7	17,503	149,823
8	17,173	166,997
9	16,849	183,846
10	16,531	200,377
11	16,219	216,596
12	15,913	232,509
13	15,613	248,123
14	15,318	263,441
15	15,029	278,470
16	14,746	293,216
17	14,468	307,684
18	14,195	321,878
19	13,927	335,805

It is the concept of spread that allows the economist to avoid the need to forecast all the future growth and discount rates. What needs to be examined now are the historic relationships between the growth rate and the discount rate. That is, did the time frame used by the economist to establish the spread seem appropriate? How would different time frames alter the spread?

§6.09 Examining Different Time Frames to Determine the Spread Between the Growth and Discount Rates

We will examine the relationship between a growth rate and a discount rate in order to determine the impact of the decision regarding the appropriate time frame. The growth rate will be based on the rate of change in the Consumer Price Index. The interest rate will be the average rate of return on one-year Treasury Bills. Table 6-6 presents the average rate of change in the Consumer Price Index and the average rate of return on the one-year Treasury Bill from 1952 through 1992.

Table 6-6   Real Returns

Year	T-Bill Yield	Consumer Price Index	Percentage Change	Spread
1952		26.50		
1953	2.11	26.70	.75	1.36
1954	0.93	26.90	.75	0.18
1955	1.93	26.80	-.37	2.30
1956	2.91	27.20	1.49	1.42
1957	3.66	28.10	3.31	0.35
1958	2.13	28.90	2.85	-0.72
1959	4.29	29.10	.69	3.60
1960	3.66	29.60	1.72	1.94
1961	2.89	29.90	1.01	1.88
1962	3.10	30.20	1.00	2.10
1963	3.41	30.60	1.32	2.09
1964	3.89	31.00	1.31	2.58
1965	4.23	31.50	1.61	2.62
1966	5.34	32.40	2.86	2.48
1967	4.94	33.40	3.09	1.85
1968	5.76	34.80	4.19	1.57
1969	7.28	36.70	5.46	1.82
1970	6.94	38.80	5.72	1.22
1971	4.90	40.50	4.38	0.52
1972	5.01	41.80	3.21	1.80

Year	T-Bill Yield	Consumer Price Index	Percentage Change	Spread
1973	7.54	44.40	6.22	1.32
1974	8.35	49.30	11.04	-2.69
1975	6.72	53.80	9.13	-2.41
1976	5.84	56.90	5.76	0.08
1977	6.06	60.60	6.50	-0.44
1978	8.39	65.20	7.59	0.80
1979	10.80	72.60	11.35	-0.55
1980	12.22	82.40	13.50	-1.28
1981	15.13	90.90	10.32	4.81
1982	12.45	96.50	6.16	6.29
1983	9.65	99.60	3.21	6.44
1984	11.01	103.90	4.32	6.69
1985	8.47	107.60	3.56	4.91
1986	6.07	109.60	1.86	4.21
1987	6.33	113.60	3.65	2.68
1988	7.17	118.30	4.14	3.03
1989	7.91	124.00	4.82	3.09
1990	7.36	130.70	5.40	1.96
1991	5.54	136.20	4.21	1.33
1992	3.75	140.30	3.01	.74
Average Change				1.85

From Table 6-6 the relationship between the return on one-year Treasury Bills and the rate of inflation can be seen. The real returns have ranged from a low of negative 2.69 per cent in 1974 to a high of 6.69 per cent in 1984. Note that these returns are one-year spreads and not indicative of a period of time. The average real return for the period 1953 through 1992 is 1.85 per cent. Any growth and discount rate that maintains the spread of 1.85% will have the same present value.

The average return on one-year Treasury Bills from 1952 through 1992 is 6.05% and the average rate of inflation for the same time period is 4.30%. The relationship between these two variables is 1.01678.

§6.10   Present Value Using Different Growth and Discount Rates

In Chapters 4 and 5 different growth and discount rates were established. Table 6-7 presents the present value of $20,000 per year for 30 years. The first payment is today and there are 29 future payments. The various present values result from using the various growth and discount rates in different combinations.

Table 6-7 Present Values

Discount Rates

		Treasury Bills		Moody's
		3 Mo	1 year	AAA
		5.51%	6.05%	7.31%
Growth Rates				
Employer Records	7.42%	$787,684	$727,207	$609,004
Tot. Private Nonag	4.99	559,031	520,633	444,895
SIC 3841	6.93	733,231	678,111	570,186
CPI	4.30	510,127	476,281	409,336

The range in present value runs from a low of $409,336 to a high of $787,684. The difference in the present values is due strictly to the selection of the growth and discount rates.

§6.11 Summary

The present value of a future stream of income can be calculated when the base wage, the annual growth rate, the annual interest rate, and the number of years the payments are to be made are known. The worksheet developed calculates the present value when the monthly or annual payments start immediately. There is an error introduced into the analysis when the monthly payments are converted to annual payments.

The use of this worksheet permits the attorney to estimate the present value of the future income stream, given various assumptions regarding the growth rate and the discount rate of the stream of money. The same worksheet can be used if the calculation is for the present value of future medical expenses.

7

Wages, Salaries, and Fringes

$$\text{Present Value of Future Income} = \sum_{t=0}^{n} \underline{\$} * M * (1+g)^t / (1+d)^t * P_L * P_S * P_F * C * HS * T_X$$

§7.01   Introduction

The base dollar amount in the present value equation is "$" and represents the current dollar amount of what is being forecast. When estimating a present value figure, the economist will be forecasting the present value of a future cash inflow, like income, or the present value of a future cash outflow, such as medical expenses, or both.

This chapter explains where the economist may obtain the data used as the basis for the economic forecast and how the economist uses the data. The critical point is that base dollars are the current dollars. The base dollars may be historic data which has been obtained and moved to current dollars. *Moving to current dollars* means taking a historic value and increasing or projecting it to the current value, i.e., today's value. The higher the base dollars used in the present value equation, the greater will be the present value of the cash inflow or outflow.

§7.02   What Economists Estimate

Economists attempt to estimate two different types of dollar flows. The first type is the income flow. The second type is the expense flow. In the cash inflow analysis, the economist estimates the present value of a future stream of dollars that the plaintiff will not receive as a result of an action, for example, an injury or wrongful discharge from employment. In the cash outflow analysis, the economist estimates the present value of future expenses the party will incur. The analysis of medical expenses are addressed in Chapter 10, "Life Care Plans."

§7.03   Types of Income Losses

Income losses experienced by the plaintiff may be cash losses or in-kind losses. Cash losses are the result of reduced earning capacity and are reflected in loss of wages and salaries or a lowering of wages or salaries. Since fringe benefits are usually a percentage of wages or salaries, lower wages and salaries will result in lower fringe benefits. Other cash losses the plaintiff may experience include reduced rental income, reduced interest income, reduced dividend income, reduced capital gains, and reduced business or farm income.

In addition to the loss of cash income, the economist may calculate the in-kind loss. An in-kind income is a nonmonetary income. The most common example of in-kind income is the value to a family of household services. If an accident leaves a family member unable to perform housework, then the rest of the family experiences a loss of in-kind services.

§7.04   Sources for Determining the Base Dollar Amount of Wages and Salaries When Calculating the Present Value of Future Wages

The base dollar amount used to calculate the present value of the plaintiff's future income stream may be obtained from different sources. The particular source utilized by the economist will depend on what information can be made available to the economist.

Sources of information which can be utilized by the economist to establish the base dollar income include the plaintiff's spouse, federal income tax form, W-2 form, employer records, the Standard Industrial Classification Tables, the Statistical Abstracts of the United States, Bureau of Census data published for each state, and various professional publications that establish income levels. Which source is used depends on what is available.

§7.05   —The Plaintiff or Spouse

While information provided by the plaintiff or spouse may be very helpful, it must be considered suspect. Usually, the plaintiff or spouse can provide accurate information regarding income from employment, and this information can be further verified. But often in a death case the value of the deceased increases in the eyes of the survivors.

Consider the letter written by a widowed plaintiff. The plaintiff, separated from her husband, lived in Florida, while he lived in Arizona. He was killed while riding in his girlfriend's car in Arizona. The plaintiff anticipated that she and her husband would reconcile and wrote:

> He maintained various capabilities, and skills such as tuning and maintenance on his own vehicles, electrical, plumbing, repair work on the home, yard work, and also the painting of the exterior of the home. He could fix just about everything in the home such as the furnace and maintenance on appliances around the home. He was a jack-of-all-trades. He would baby-sit for his children, fix their bicycles and put together toys for them. It seemed that anything that needed to be done, he was capable of doing.

The attorney and the economist must take care to not put too much weight on some of a spouse's statements.

§7.06   —Plaintiff's Income Tax Return

The plaintiff's 1040 federal income tax return may be used as a basis for determining his or her level of income. The tax return contains information concerning income from wages, salaries, tips, interest, dividends, and capital gains. Business, partnership, and farm incomes are included on the tax returns, as well as income from rents, royalties, trusts, and estates.

When the 1040 tax form is used to determine the level of plaintiff's income, care must be used to distinguish between income that would be affected as a result of an injury and income that would not be affected. For example, wages may cease as a result of an injury, but dividend income may continue. Therefore, it would not be proper to include the dividend income as part of the lost income.

Wages, Salaries, and Tips

Wages, salaries, and tips generally constitute the largest portion of income for most working families. The line item on the 1040 form represents the sum of the wages, salaries, and tips of both the husband and wife when a joint tax return is being filed. The distribution of income between husband and wife must be determined by examining the employees' copies of the W-2 forms attached to the tax return.

The W-2 form will state the name of the employee, the name of the employer, the tax year, the employee's social security number, the name of the state to which state income tax was sent, the total number of dollars paid to the employee, and the total amount of the taxes withheld by the employer.

The W-2 form does not indicate the hourly rate of compensation or the number of hours worked per year. Suppose a plaintiff's W-2 form indicated an annual income of $18,000. There are several questions that would need to be answered before an economic analysis could proceed. How many hours did the plaintiff work during the year? Was part of the $18,000 overtime pay? If so, what is the rate of overtime pay, and how many overtime hours did the plaintiff work? Would overtime hours have continued in the future? If so, how many hours per year and for how many years into the future?

Interest and Dividend Income

Interest is the payment for the use of capital. Dividends are payments to the owners of a corporation from the earnings of the corporation. Interest is paid to debt holders; dividends are paid to owners, or equity holders.

The return on debt and equity is not usually affected by the actions of an owner of the securities unless it is a closely held corporation. The level of interest and dividend income would not be affected as a result of an injury to the owner and, therefore, should not be included in the base dollar amount used to estimate the present value of the future income stream.

The level of interest and dividend income to a family may be reduced as the result of an injury to an individual if the injured party is the manager of the funds. In this case, the loss of income would not be total; what needs to be estimated is the difference in income, if any, before and after the injury. Interest and dividend income may stop, or decline, if the injured party owns a business in which he or she is a major factor in its success. Suppose the president of a small construction company had loaned the corporation money. Interest would be paid to the debt holder (president) periodically. If the president were injured, and the company's success was dependent on the president, then the interest income may cease. The interest income would properly be an amount that should be included in the present value calculation. The same line of reasoning could also be applied to dividends.

Income from Capital Gains

Capital gains occur when an asset is sold for more than the purchase price. The capital gains typically reported on the individual 1040 form are from the purchase and sale of bonds and common stocks, although gains from the sale of other types of assets, such as art, may be reported here.

The loss a family could experience is the loss of management expertise provided by the injured or deceased party. However, the principal would not be lost.

For example, an insurance company's portfolio manager borrowed $25,000 in 1985 to make personal investments. At the time of his death in 1991, the portfolio had grown to $395,000. In addition to the portfolio, he had repaid the $25,000 loan and retired a $77,000 mortgage on his home. Of the total portfolio, $50,000 was divided among his three minor children. The children ranged in age from 2 to 14. Following his death a wrongful death suit was filed. The family recognized that the principal of the portfolio would remain in tact, but argued that the loss of expertise in portfolio management was the loss to the family. His personal records, and the records at the brokerage houses where he did business, indicated that his portfolio appreciated more than 50 per cent per year for the 6 years he managed the funds.

The loss of capital gains is a loss the economist can estimate. The economist estimates the increase in principal rather than a level of income.

Income from Businesses, Partnerships, and Farms

The income reported from a business, partnership, or farm which appears on the 1040 form is an accounting figure properly designed to minimize an individual's personal tax liability. To determine the economic value of the business to an individual, or his or her family, requires the examination of more detailed records.

In the most basic evaluation, the economist estimates the cash flow from the business rather than the reported income from the business. The cash flow is the earnings from the business plus the noncash expenses. The most common type of noncash expenses is depreciation. Thus, the cash flow would equal earnings after taxes plus depreciation. The cash flow would be used as the base dollar amount in the calculation of the present value of the future income stream.

A more detailed analysis may reveal that the benefits of the business or partnership far exceed the level indicated by the tax return. The business may provide an automobile and its maintenance, travel funds, life and health insurance policies, and retirement plans. In the case of a farm, maintenance to the home may be written off as a business expense. Personal vehicles may also use "farm gas." All these considerations would fall into the category of business valuation.

The examination of a medical doctor's income statements may reveal that a certain amount of travel required to keep current in the profession is combined with vacations. The economist could estimate the portion of the travel which is business and the portion which is pleasure. Appropriate adjustments would be made to the base dollar estimate.

Some businesses have buy-out agreements. These agreements establish how the ownership of the business will be transferred at the time of an owner's withdrawal. The amount of money may be stipulated in the buy-out agreement, or a formula may be stated. In either case, the plaintiff, or the plaintiff's heirs, may suffer a loss of income and may also suffer a loss of principal. The loss of income is used as a base dollar amount in the calculation of the present value of the future income. The loss of principal is a one-time loss.

Income from Rents, Royalties, Trusts, and Estates

Income from rent may be much like income from stocks and bonds. The income may continue regardless of the health of the owner of the property. If injury has caused the owner of the property to hire maintenance or management, then the economist may use these added expenses as the base dollar amount used to calculate the present value of the future expenses. The increase in expenses represents a decrease in income from the rental properties.

Royalty is an income from a copyright, patent, or other such property. Royalty income may or may not continue, depending on the source of the income. If the royalty is from ownership of a song or book or something that does not have to be updated, then the royalty will continue regardless of the health of the owner. In this case the income would not be included as a base dollar loss.

What might be included as a base dollar loss is royalty from a book which needs to be updated to be marketable. For example, a college text book on income tax needs to be updated as the tax laws change. If injury prevents the author from being able to update the book, then it would become outdated resulting in a loss of income.

Income from estates and trusts is not usually dependent on the health of the recipient. There is, however, the potential loss where the proceeds from an estate or trust would go to a different family member after the death of an individual. Likewise, if the full value of the estate had not been received, there could be a loss to heirs. In these cases survivors may experience a loss that should be included in the economic anaylsis.

§7.07   —Employer Records

Employer records can be the basis for estimating the present value of a future income stream. The records will usually state the name of the employee, the date of initial employment, the hourly rate of compensation or salary paid at the time of the initial hiring, and any subsequent increases in compensation. All this information is valuable to the economist.

Consider the situation where the deceased had gone to work for a firm producing medical instruments and supplies. His initial employment date was January 2, 1971. The employer records indicate that the deceased received wage increases on the anniversary of his employment (*see* Table 7-1). Employment was terminated January 2, 1991, the date of the employee's death.

Table 7-1   Employer Records

January 1 of Each Year	Hourly Wage Rate
1977	$3.46
1978	3.75
1979	3.96
1980	4.27
1981	4.55
1982	4.80
1983	5.05
1984	5.38
1985	6.05
1986	6.70
1987	7.23
1988	7.75
1989	8.35
1990	8.99

Employment Terminated January 2, 1991

1991	9.65
1992	10.10

The wages that appear in Table 7-1 after employment was terminated are hourly wages the deceased never actually earned. The wages represent what the employer states the deceased would have earned had employment continued. The base dollar amount that the economist will employ is the $10.10 per hour. The annual dollar loss appearing in the formula will be $21,008, which is 2,080 hours per year times the hourly wage of $10.10.

However, the defense attorney will, on cross-examination, point out that the deceased never did earn $10.10 per hour. The most he ever earned was $8.99 per hour. Thus, the annual salary that should have been used was $18,699 (2,080 hours times $8.99 per hour).

The economist should be able to tie the $8.99 per hour, appearing on the employer's records, to the W-2 form filed with the employee's 1990 federal tax return. If the income shown on the W-2 form is in excess of $18,699, it would be reasonable to assume overtime.

The question of overtime compensation should be resolved by the economist before the economic analysis proceeds. Suppose the W-2 form indicates an income in 1990 of $18,699. This would appear to be straight-time of $8.99 per hour for 2,080 hours. But it is also possible that the deceased worked 26 weeks for 60 hours per week at double-time for hours in excess of 40 hours per week. This raises the question for the defense of how long the overtime would have continued. What happens if no overtime was assumed and employment was just half of the year? Clearly, the annual income would be $9,350.

§7.08   —Total Private Nonagricultural Sector Wages

In some cases there is no earnings history available, and the economist must turn to other sources to establish a base dollar amount. One such source is the government publication showing the average hourly wages paid in the private nonagricultural sector of the economy (*see* Table 7-2).

Table 7-2   Total Private Nonagricultural Hourly Wages

Year	Hourly Wage Rate
1980	$6.66
1981	7.25
1982	7.68
1983	8.02
1984	8.33
1985	8.58
1986	8.76
1987	8.98
1988	9.28
1989	9.66
1990	10.01
1991	10.33
1992	10.59

Source: Economic Report of the President 396, Table B-42 (1993).

The 1992 wage rate of $10.59 is the most recent data available. The annual income would be $22,027 (2,080 hours per year times $10.59 per hour). This would be the base dollar amount used in the formula to make the present value analysis.

§7.09   —The Standard Industrial Classification Tables

The Standard Industrial Classification (SIC)[1] system was developed by the United States government to facilitate collection and analysis of economic data on economic establishments. The goal is to make sure the data is comparable. An *establishment* is defined as an economic unit generally at a single physical location where business is conducted or where services or industrial operations are performed. All establishments are assigned a three- or four-digit code based on broad economic divisions. The code may be obtained from the SIC Manual or from

---

[1] US Govt Printing Office, Standard Indus Classification Tables Manual (Washington, DC).

other business handbooks or directories. The directories include Standard and Poor's *Register of Corporations* or the *Million Dollar Directory*.[2] The economic categories are as follows:

01-09 Agricultural, Forestry, Fishing, Hunting, and Trapping
10-14 Mining
15-17 Construction
20-39 Manufacturing
40-49 Transportation, Communications, Electric, Gas, and Sanitary Services
50-51 Wholesale Trade
52-59 Retail Trade
60-67 Finance, Insurance, Real Estate
70-89 Services
91-97 Public Administration
99   Nonclassifiable Establishments

The SIC tables state the average number of hours worked per week by the production workers, the average weekly overtime hours, and the average hourly rate of pay. A specific SIC table may be used to estimate the base dollar amount used in the present value equation.

Example: SIC Code #384 is Medical Instruments and Supplies. This category is further broken down into SIC 3841, Surgical and Medical Instruments, and SIC 3842, Surgical Appliances and Supplies. Table 7-3 shows the average hourly wage paid for the years 1972 to 1989.

Table 7-3   Hourly Wages SIC Code 3841 and 3842

Year	Hourly Wage Rate	
	SIC 3841	SIC 3842
1972	3.04	3.25
1973	3.23	3.45
1974	3.54	3.73
1975	3.93	4.06
1976	4.11	4.40
1977	4.36	4.72
1978	4.70	5.12
1979	5.03	5.54
1980	5.57	6.00
1981	6.32	6.54
1982	7.05	6.98
1983	7.41	7.38
1984	7.84	7.69

[2] R. Vukas, Description of SIC Codes (Washburn Univ 1987) (unpublished manuscript); Standard & Poor's Register of Corporations (McGraw-Hill, Inc 1987); Duns Mktg Serv, Million Dollar Directory (1987).

Year	Hourly Wage Rate	
	SIC 3841	SIC 3842
1985	8.28	8.05
1986	8.62	8.33
1987	8.76	8.53
1988	9.18	8.68
1989	9.43	9.15

Source: United States Employment, Hours and Earnings 1909-90, vol 1 Bulletin 2370, at 375 (1991).

This information can be used to calculate the base dollar amount in the present value equation. If the category SIC 3841 is used, the average hourly rate of compensation of $9.43 per hour and multiplied by 2,080 hours per year yields the base dollar amount of $19,614.40. Since the most recent data is 1989, the economist would move the hourly rate forward to reflect a more current rate of compensation. The current rate of compensation would be used as the basis for calculating the present value.

§7.10   —Median Income as Reported in the Statistical Abstracts of the United States

Another source of information available to the economist, when there is no history of earnings available, is the Statistical Abstracts of the United States which provide income data based on the sex and educational attainment of the individual. Table 7-4 presents median income data.

Table 7-4   Mean Money Earnings of Persons by Educational Attainment and Sex

	Male		Female	
	1987	1990	1987	1990
Elementary				
Less than 8 yrs	16,863	NA	10,163	NA
8 years	18,946	19,188	12,655	13,222
Secondary				
1-3 years	21,327	22,564	13,136	15,381
4 years	24,745	28,043	16,223	18,954
College				
1-3 years	29,253	34,188	19,336	22,654
4 years	38,117	44,554	23,506	28,911
5+ years	47,903	55,831	30,255	35,827

Source: Statistical Abstracts of the United States Table 713 (1992) and Table 737 (1990).

The most recent data, 1990, is used as the basis for the income calculation. The dollar amount is then inflated to reflect current dollars. The current dollars are the base dollar amount used to make the present value calculation.

§7.11   —State Data Published by the Bureau of Census

The United States Department of Commerce, Bureau of Census, publishes income data. The income data is based on sex, age, education attainment, and race. Table 7-5 shows census data on income levels for men.

Table 7-5   Educational Attainment-Median Income of Persons 25 Years Old and Over by Sex

MALE

Year	8th Grade	High School Graduate	College Graduate
1988	na	21,186	32,328
1987	na	20,262	31,406
1986	11,804	19,772	31,602
1985	10,818	18,997	29,698
1984	10,325	18,825	28,206
1983	10,419	17,616	26,253
1982	9,501	17,055	24,630
1981	9,270	16,989	23,640
1980	8,732	16,211	21,838
1979	8,032	15,466	20,125
1978	7,604	14,341	18,774
1977	7,155	13,207	17,391
1976	6,959	12,393	16,466
1975	6,642	11,834	15,659
1974	6,511	11,338	14,401
1973	6,371	10,832	13,939
1972	5,786	9,915	13,520
1971	5,469	9,088	12,573
1970	5,410	8,772	12,144
1969	5,345	8,434	11,893
1968	5,096	7,731	10,866
1967	4,778	7,244	10,090

Source: US Department of Commerce, Bureau of the Census, Trends in Income by Selected Characteristics: 1947 to 1988, at 41 (1989).

If the injured party was a 40-year-old male with a high school education, then the mean annual earnings in 1988 were $21,186. This figure would be used as the base for calculating a current level of income. The current level of income would be used as the base dollar amount in the present value calculation.

The economist must be careful to use *earnings* rather than *income*, since *income* is a broader term than *earnings*. *Earnings* refers to wages, while *income* includes wages, interest, dividends, and other sources of money.

§7.12   —State Data Published by the State

Some states also have statistical abstracts. Kansas, for example, has a Statistical Abstract that presents income data by county. The Kansas 1990-91 Statistical Abstract reports that the average annual pay in the construction industry in 1988 was $21,989. This figure increased to $22,539 by 1990. These figures can be compared to the average income for the United States. For the two years 1988 and 1990, the national average pay in the construction industry was $24,433 and $26,150, respectively.

In addition to the industry data, the Kansas Statistical Abstract presents income data for metropolitan areas, and by county. For example, if the plaintiff resided in Chase County, Kansas, the average wage per job in that county in 1989 was $11,093.

§7.13   —The Federal Minimum Wage

In the absence of an earnings history, the minimum wage can serve as the base dollar amount. The federal minimum wage as of April 1, 1992 was $4.25 per hour. Full-time employment would result in an annual income of $8,840. The $8,840 would be the base dollar amount used to calculate the present value of a future income stream.

§7.14   —Professional Publications

There are professional organizations that publish income data. One such organization is the American Assembly of Collegiate Schools of Business (AACSB).[3]

---

[3] The American Assembly of Collegiate Schools of Business (AACSB) is a nonprofit corporation comprised of member organizations and institutions devoted to the promotion and improvement of higher education for business administration and management. The AACSB publishes a variety of literature, including the *AACSB Membership Directory*, its *Articles of Incorporation* and *Bylaws*, the *Accreditation Council Policies and Procedures*, a brochure describing the full range of programs and activities undertaken in addition to accreditation, and the AACSB *Salary Survey* compiled by the AACSB Statistical Service.

Table 7-6 presents the 1992-1993 median salaries of finance faculty for participating AACSB member schools. The salary data can be broken down into private and nonprivate and accredited and nonaccredited schools.

Table 7-6   Median Salaries, School of Business, Finance Faculty

Rank	1992-1993 Mean
Professor	$61,900
Associate Professor	52,300
Assistant Professor	49,000
Instructor	33,100

These earnings figures can be used by the economist as the base dollar amount used to calculate the present value of the future income stream. In addition to mean salaries, the report also states the number of salaries used to calculate the median, the range of salaries, and the 90th, 75th, 25th, and 10th percentiles. In addition to the current data, previous years' salary data may also be available.

Similar income data can be obtained for attorneys, accountants, nurses, and many other professional occupations. Starting salaries for most occupations requiring a college education can be obtained from the placement offices of most colleges and universities.

§7.15   Determining the Base Dollar Amount When Calculating the Present Value of Fringe Benefits

Fringe benefits can cover a vast array of items. The benefits can range from parking privileges to child care. Many times the benefits are taken for granted and not considered as a form of compensation. This is particularly true of an employer-subsidized cafeteria. It is the responsibility of the economist to assist in identifying the fringe benefits and the value of the fringe benefits.

As a starting point, fringe benefits, and the cost of fringe benefits to employers, are identified in the Statistical Abstracts of the United States. The total benefit package is broken down into paid leave, supplemental pay, pension and savings, legally required, and other benefits. Table 7-7 presents the employer costs for employee compensation per hour worked.

Table 7-7   Employer Cost for Employee Compensation per Hour Worked, 1989 - 1991

	1988	1989	1990	1991
Total Compensation	13.79	14.28	14.96	15.40
Wage & Salaries	10.02	10.38	10.84	11.14
Total Benefits	3.77	3.90	4.13	4.27
Paid Leave	0.97	1.00	1.03	1.05
Vacation	0.48	0.50	0.51	0.52
Holiday	0.33	0.34	0.34	0.35
Sick	0.12	0.12	0.13	0.13
Other	0.04	0.04	0.04	0.05
Supplemental Pay	0.33	0.34	0.37	0.36
Premium Pay	0.17	0.17	0.17	0.17
NonProduction Bonus	0.12	0.12	0.16	0.13
Shift Pay	0.04	0.05	0.05	0.05
Insurance	0.78	0.85	0.92	1.01
Pension & Savings	0.45	0.42	0.45	0.11
Pension	0.38	0.34	0.36	0.35
Savings & Thrift	0.07	0.08	0.09	0.10
Legally Required	1.22	1.27	1.35	1.40
Social Security	0.81	0.84	0.89	0.92
Fed Unemployment	0.03	0.03	0.03	0.03
State Unemployment	0.12	0.11	0.09	0.09
Workers Compensation	0.24	0.27	0.31	0.33
Other Benefits	0.02	0.02	Rounds to Zero	

Source: Statistical Abstracts of the United States Table 684 (1991), and Table 660 (1992).

These figures can be used to form the basis for the calculation of the fringe benefit package. In 1991 the average hourly rate of pay was $11.14 while the fringe benefits cost $4.27. Caution should be taken not to view the fringe benefit to the employee as being an additional 38.33% of the wage. It is true that the cost of $4.27 is 38.33% of the $11.14 per hour wage; however, some of the fringe benefits are already included in the analysis.

Consider the full-time employee earning $11.14 per hour. This would translate to an annual income of $23,171. Included in the 2,080 hours per year of work is 80 hours of vacation time. This portion of the fringe benefit has already been included in the compensation figure. The cost of the vacation pay would be deducted from the total fringe benefit package being paid the employee. The hourly cost of 52¢ per hour would be deducted from the cost of fringe benefits. The benefit cost becomes $3.75 which is 33.66% of the hourly rate. In a similar fashion holiday pay and sick pay can be deducted.

The area of supplemental pay can usually be identified. That is, there are usually records indicating whether or not the employee received any of the supplemental pay categories. If any of these are received it is usually clearer to separate out each of the supplemental pay areas for analysis.

One approach is to say that the individual was earning $10.00 in 1991 and was eligible for premium pay. If the actual premium pay is not known an estimate could be made. It would be estimated that the premium pay is 1.53% of the hourly wage. This is 17¢, the premium pay in 1991, divided by the hourly rate paid in 1991 of $11.14.

The same approach is made in all the fringe categories. However, one of the major problem areas is health insurance. While the cost to the employer can be calculated, the benefit to the employee cannot be calculated. Often the individual cannot replace the health insurance provided by an employer with the same benefits at the same cost. In addition, for the health insurance to have any value one must have a need for the insurance. To estimate the need one must estimate the nature of an illness, its severity, and when it will occur.

Not all firms provide the same level of fringe benefits. Some firms may not have pension plans or savings plans. The minimum fringe benefit can be estimated by use of the legally required fringe benefits. However, this too can create a problem. For the four years of information presented in Table 7-7 the legally required fringe benefits have steadily increased from 12.18% of the hourly wage in 1988 to 12.57% of the hourly wage in 1991.

The typical method used to forecast the value of fringe benefits is based on what percentage the cost of the fringe is compared to the hourly wage.

§7.16 Determining the Base Dollar Amount When Calculating the Present Value of Retirement Benefits

Most retirement benefits are a defined benefit plan, a money purchase plan, or a profit-sharing plan. A *defined benefit plan* is one in which the benefit an employee receives upon retirement can be determined from a formula defined in the plan. Annual contributions to the plan are in the amount needed to provide for the benefit.

A *money purchase plan* provides for a stipulated annual contribution by the employee. No specific benefit is formulated in advance. Each employee will receive whatever benefit the total contributions made during employment will purchase at the time of the employee's retirement. Suppose an employee contributes 4% of his or her income to a money purchase plan and the employer contributes one-half of what the employee contributes. The contribution which would be a fringe benefit would be 2% of whatever the present value of the income would be. The employee's contribution is already included in the wage calculation.

A *profit-sharing plan* has a defined annual contribution by the employer. The contribution is usually from the employer's current or accumulated profits. At retirement the employee's benefit is a portion of the contributions the employer has made.

Under the defined benefit plan the economist will calculate the present value of the retirement benefit by using the specified formula. Usually the formula will specify benefits as a percentage of the last five years' earnings times a factor. The factor may represent the number of months or years the employee has been with the firm. The plaintiff's last five years of earnings have been calculated by the economist when the present value analysis was done. Under the money purchase plan the economist will have to make judgments about how much money will be available to purchase the retirement benefits, and what the money will be able to purchase. If this occurrence is very far in the future, the economist will be reluctant to make a very definite statement about what retirement benefits can be purchased.

§7.17   Cross-Examining the Economist

The primary purpose of cross-examination about the base dollar amount is to show that the figure does not represent what the plaintiff earned and, therefore, that the present value of the loss has been overstated. For example, if a person were injured two years ago, and at the time of trial, the economist used a base dollar amount which represented an increased wage from the time of the injury to what the individual would have earned today had the injury not occurred, counsel should attempt to point out that the plaintiff never earned the amount of money the economist has used as the base dollar amount in the present value calculation. It can also be argued that the use of the increased base dollar amount also resulted in a higher fringe benefit being lost. Had the economist used the actual earnings that the plaintiff received, the present value of the loss would have been less.

§7.18   Summary

The economist is retained to calculate the present value of a cash inflow and/or outflow. The cash inflows represents lost wages, fringe benefits, dividend income, rental income, in-kind income, and other income that will be diminished or interrupted as a result of the plaintiff's injury. The base dollar amount used will depend on what information is made available to the economist. If the employee's records or employer's records are available, they will serve as the basis for the economic analysis. In the absence of this type of information, the economist will turn to other published sources as a basis for calculating the current dollar amount of the loss or expense.

8

Modifications and the Vocational Expert

$$\text{Present Value of Future Income} = \sum_{t=0}^{n} \$ * \underline{M} * (1+g)^t / (1+d)^t * P_L * P_S * P_F * C * HS * T_X$$

§8.01   Introduction

Chapter 3 established the base dollar amount used to calculate the present value of the future income stream. The basis for the dollar amount was that the plaintiff would be unable to return to work. The modifications to base dollar amounts represent adjustments for disability, since the future income may not be totally eliminated when the plaintiff is injured. The nature of the injury may render the plaintiff only partially disabled, reducing the earning capacity of the plaintiff but not totally eliminating the plaintiffs ability to earn. This chapter distinguishes between total disability and partial disability.

Degrees of disability are usually in medical terms and must be translated to economic terms. The chapter explores the methods for translating degrees of medical disability to degrees of economic disability.

§8.02 The Degrees of Disability

Disability may be either total or partial, temporary or permanent. If the injury has left the plaintiff totally disabled, then the plaintiff will be unable to obtain any type of gainful employment. In an economic sense the analysis can proceed as if the case were a wrongful death case. In other words, the "M" appearing in the formula is 100 per cent. The loss of future income is total. If the disability is temporary, then the analysis continues until the time the disability will cease. If the disability is not total, it is necessary to establish the degree to which the earning capacity has been reduced. This is difficult to do and is beyond the expertise of most economists. One expert who evaluates the earning capacity of the disabled is the vocational rehabilitation specialist. The data provided by the vocational rehabilitation specialist becomes the input data for the economist.

§8.03 Is There a Loss?

It is possible that an injury does not alter the capacity of the individual to earn an income. For instance, after injury, the plaintiff may be forced to retrain and, as a result, the income after retaining increases. In this case there would be no economic loss. Consider another situation where the plaintiff, a 22-year-old high school graduate, is paralyzed from the waist down as the result of an accident. The disability is judged to be permanent, and the plaintiff is unable to return to work in the construction industry. As a result, the injured party returns to college and graduates with a degree in accounting. It is very possible there is no loss in the present value of future income resulting from the injury.

There may be ongoing medical expenses, pain and suffering, and reduced income while the plaintiff attends school, but the present value of the lost income may be negative. Negative present value of lost income means the present value of the future income stream after the injury, and after retraining as an accountant, is higher than the present value of the future income stream as a construction worker.

§8.04 Using a Clinical Psychologist or Vocational Rehabilitation Specialist

A clinical psychologist or vocational rehabilitation specialist may be used to determine the reduced work capacity of the plaintiff. This is done by determining the occupational skill levels of the plaintiff before the injury and comparing them to the occupational skill levels after the injury. The result may be expressed in terms of the number of Standard Industrial Classification occupations that the party could handle before the injury as compared to the number that can be handled after the injury.

Using the information provided by the specialist, the economist then determines the wage levels that existed for the types of jobs the plaintiff could hold before the injury and compares them to the wage levels that existed for the types of jobs the plaintiff can hold after the injury. The difference in the wage rates represents the loss to the plaintiff and is the basis for the economist's forecast. Many times the vocational rehabilitation specialist has already done the analysis concerning the loss of job opportunities and provided the economist with the loss of earnings potential. The nature of the jobs and the income level that can be held by the plaintiff is determined by the specialist.

§8.05   Translating Injury to a Part of the Body to the Body as a Whole

When an injury occurs to one part of an individual's body, the medical profession may translate the injury to the body as a whole. For example, if a person loses the right arm, the translation may be that this is a 25 per cent disability to the body as a whole. Two publications that assist physicians in making the translation are *Guides to the Evaluation of Permanent Impairment*, published by the American Medical Association, and the *Manual for Orthopedic Surgeons*, published by the American Academy of Orthopedic Surgeons.

These publications are of no value in making the economic evaluation of the lost income. Consider the example of an individual who loses the little finger on the left hand. This may translate to a 10 per cent disability to the body as a whole. To the college professor, accountant, or lawyer, there may be no reduction of income. Thus, no economic loss exists. However, to the concert pianist the economic loss is 100 per cent, since the result is an inability to perform.

§8.06   Using Minimum Wage as the Alternative Income

After an injury occurs, the economist may use the minimum wage as the alternative source of income. The present value of the future loss can be handled one of two ways: as a reduction of earning capacity of a stated percentage, or as the difference between the two income figures.

For example, a plaintiff earned $8 an hour as a construction worker before a back injury. The testimony indicates the injury is permanent and such that the plaintiff should not return to the construction field. The injury will not permit heavy work, but the plaintiff is permitted to return to work. The economist, in the absence of alternative information, may assume an alternative income at the minimum wage of $4.25 per hour. The calculation of the present value of future income may be done in one of two ways. First, the $4.25 per hour represents

58.125 per cent of earnings before the injury. The loss of income is 46.875 per cent of the preinjury level (100% minus 53.125%). The present value calculation would enter $8 per hour as the income level and enter 46.875 per cent as the value "M" for modification, or reduction in income. The resulting present value represents the loss to the plaintiff.

The second method is to enter the dollar loss as $3.75 per hour. This is the $8 per hour earned before the accident less the $4.25 earned after the accident. In this case, there would be no entry for modifications to income for disability since the modification is reflected in the dollar amount used to calculate the loss of income. Both methods of evaluation would result in the same present value of future loss.

§8.07   Using Time and Motion Studies to Estimate Loss

In order to establish the degree of disability sustained by an individual, a time and motion specialist may be called. The specialist would take movies of the plaintiff performing certain types of jobs. The time to complete a job after the injury would be compared to the time required to perform the same task by a person who is not injured. The additional time reflects the degree of disability.

An example would be to film and evaluate the time it takes an injured person to get out a box of cereal, pour the cereal in a bowl, add milk and sugar, eat, and clean up. This amount of time would be compared to the time required for an uninjured person. The difference represents the degree of disability. The degree of disability established by the time and motion specialist can be translated to an economic value by the specialist. The economist then incorporates the economic value into the analysis of the lost income.

§8.08   Incorporating Government Statistics into the Economic Analysis

In the absence of specific information regarding the economic loss due to disability, the economist may turn to government publications in order to establish the loss. The reduction in income due to disability is categorized by race and by sex.[1] Tables 8-1 through 8-4 present the effect of disability on earnings.

Table 8-1   Effect of Disability on Earnings

Percentage decline in earnings by degree of disability and amount of work undertaken by those who worked as compared to a nondisabled individual working full-time (50-52 weeks)

---

[1] The data appears in the Health and Human Services, Social Security Administration, Disability Survey 72 (Apr 1981).

White Men	Severely Disabled	Occupationally Disabled	Secondary Disability
Full-Time			
(50-52 Weeks)	15.59%	20.30%	16.22%
(26-49 Weeks)	46.66%	42.34%	34.89%
Part-Time			
(26 Weeks +)	77.48%	71.98%	67.20%
Intermittent	78.60%	54.96%	48.15%
AVERAGE	52.42%	32.37%	26.95%
Percentage Who Worked	41.90%	91.60%	91.40%

Severely disabled means unable to work or unable to work regularly.

Occupationally disabled means able to work regularly, but unable to do the same work as before the onset of disability, or unable to work full-time.

Secondary disability means able to work full-time, regularly, doing the same work as before onset, but with some limitation to the kind or amount of work.

Table 8-2   Effect of Disability on Earnings

Percentage decline in earnings by degree of disability and amount of work undertaken by those who worked as compared to a nondisabled individual working full-time (50-52 weeks)

Black Men	Severely Disabled	Occupationally Disabled	Secondary Disability
Full-Time			
(50-52 Weeks)	*	23.56%	2.47%
(26-49 Weeks)	*	59.40%	
Part-Time			
(26 weeks +)	*	*	*
Intermittent	86.12%	*	86.01%
AVERAGE	72.26%	50.36%	28.75%
Percentage Who Worked	60.10%	29.70%	79.80%

*Means the number in the cell was less than 50,000 people.

Table 8-3   Effect of Disability on Earnings

Percentage decline in earnings by degree of disability and amount of work undertaken by those who worked as compared to a nondisabled individual working full-time (50-52 weeks)

White Women	Severely Disabled	Occupationally Disabled	Secondary Disability
Full-Time			
(50-52 Weeks)	19.78%	16.04%	5.84%
(26-49 Weeks)	43.60%	39.50%	36.89%
Part-Time			
(26 weeks)	71.89%	72.01%	63.17%
Intermittent	78.62%	86.58%	70.56%
AVERAGE	63.84%	55.15%	29.72%
Percentage Who Worked	8.00%	53.40%	54.40%

Table 8-4   Effect of Disability on Earnings

Percentage decline in earnings by degree of disability and amount of work undertaken by those who worked as compared to a nondisabled individual working full-time (50-52 weeks)

Black Women	Severely Disabled	Occupationally Disabled	Secondary Disability
Full-Time			
(50-52 Weeks)	*	*	34.85%
(26-49 Weeks)	*	*	17.10%
Part-Time			
(26 weeks +)	83.58%		*
Intermittent	93.78%	85.01%	*
AVERAGE	84.13%	79.03%	37.81%
Percentage Who Worked	25.10%	71.70%	79.90%

*Means the number in the cell was less than 50,000 people.

The economist uses the percentage decline in earnings as "M" in the present value formula. The economist will want someone else to determine the degree of disability. That is, the economist will say: "If the plaintiff is occupationally disabled, then the loss of income is _____ ." The economist will not want to say: "In my opinion the plaintiff is occupationally disabled."

§8.09   The Report from the Vocational Rehabilitation Specialist

The following report is typical of a report provided by a vocational rehabilitation specialist. This report was provided by Mr. Michael Dreiling, Director of the Menninger Foundation's Return to Work Center in Prairie Village, Kansas.

REFERRAL:

Your client was referred to the Center in Kansas City for the purpose of participating in a vocational evaluation and assessment in order to determine what impact injuries from a May 20, 1991 automobile accident may have on her vocational opportunities. As part of the vocational work-up, your client was interviewed on December 4, 1992 and also participated in two days of vocational testing at the Center.

LIST OF AVAILABLE RECORDS:

Reports Which Identify Functional Limitations

EDUCATION BACKGROUND:

She is a high school graduate graduating from (name of high school) in 1960. She indicated making mostly Bs and Cs and enjoyed math, music, and physical education classes. She attended the (name of university) for one semester in 1961 and took primarily preparatory classes.

In 1973 she took the emergency medical technician training course at (name of institution) and received three credit hours.

Other than the one semester at (name of university) and one class at (name of institution), she has not participated in any other formal academic or schooling programs.

SOCIAL BACKGROUND:

The client is presently divorced and has no dependent children. Her present income is derived from her employment.

PRIOR MEDICAL INFORMATION:

She reported that in 1991 she was involved in an on-the-job injury where she sustained a sprain and strain to the back area and received a three to five per cent permanent rating. She indicated she did not receive any permanent medical restrictions and did not have any problems with performing work in the open labor market.

MILITARY HISTORY:

She has not participated in the military in this country.

WORK BACKGROUND:

During her junior and senior year in high school she worked for the (name of firm) during the evenings and weekends. Her job required her to do counter work which included cashiering and working with the customers. Her job required her to be able to stand constantly and to lift trays of pastries weighing up to 20 pounds. She also reported having to push large containers containing the ingredients for the pastries. The work history continues.

After high school she went to work for the summer for (_____). This job required her to be able to stand constantly and to stoop, bend, and lift up to 50 to 75 pounds.

She then went to work at (name of institution) in 1962 through 1964 in the (_____) department. She was responsible for the timekeeping activities and helped prepare the payroll information. This job required her to be able to sit in order to work the calculator and also to do a considerable amount of walking in order to retrieve the time cards from the various departments.

In the late 1960s she worked approximately three-and-one-half years as an owner/operator of a restaurant in (name of city). Her job included doing cooking, ordering supplies, waiting on customers, cleaning, and supervising employees including five part-time and five full-time. This job required her to lift supplies weighing anywhere from several pounds up to and including 110 pounds of meat packages. This job required her to stand constantly except when she did do her daily bookkeeping and she did report that she had an accountant that took care of the more detailed financial matters. She reported making approximately $ _____ per year but eventually sold the restaurant for personal reasons.

In the late 1960s and early 1970s she worked at (name of institution) as the head of the housekeeping department. She was responsible for supervising 50 or more housekeepers and described herself as a working supervisor. This job physically would require her to be able to walk and stand constantly in order to inspect the work of the other housekeepers as well as to perform the cleaning activities in the hallways in the front of the hotel. She reported receiving a straight salary and believes she made approximately $ _____ yearly.

From approximately 1972 to 1973 (name) owned a western store in (name of city). She was responsible for ordering, stocking, and selling to the customers. Additionally, she was responsible for cleaning the store and supervising three employees. In addition to the western store (name) had a horse arena right next door where she would have horse shows on the weekends. She was responsible for putting on the horse shows which included picking up the trophies, keeping the grounds maintained and performing announcing activities during the show. All of these activities were very physically demanding and required her to be able to stand, walk, and lift on a regular basis.

During this same time period she also was a volunteer firefighter and emergency medical technician where she was on call 24 hours per day. Her responsibilities included fighting fires as well as responding to various types of automobile accidents and other emergency situations. This was a very physically demanding job in terms of being able to lift victims as well as to carry and work with 40 to 50 pounds of firefighting equipment. (Name) reported doing this work for approximately five years between 1972 and 1978.

During this same time period she also indicated that she was chairman of the (name of city) zoning board and also served on the (name) Planning Commission.

In 1978 she reported expanding her store to include a store in (name of city) where she took on additional partners. She continued to operate both of these stores up until 1981 at which time she developed (an illness) and had to let her store go.

From 1980 to 1984 she moved to (name) and worked for (name) where she was a working manager at a truck stop. This truck stop was a 24-hour location and she was involved in all activities including ordering, cashiering, book work, scheduling, and stocking activities. This was a very physically demanding job and required her to be quite active in fact, even responsible for changing the advertising signs which were some 60 feet in the air. She indicated she would work anywhere between 50 to 80 hours per week and would receive a salary including bonuses between $28,000.00 to $29,000.00 yearly. She also described this as a working manager position where she would have to fill in for any workers who did not show up for their shift.

She moved back to (name of city) and in 1984 and 1985 continued to work for (name) doing a similar job here in the (name of city) area. She described the job as being very consistent with the one in (name) with the only exception is that she received less money for her work.

She then went to work for (name of company) in (city) for approximately six months where she was a manager of a small truck stop and again performed very similar tasks as a manager for (name of firm).

From 1985 to 1988 she was a manager for a convenience store for (name) located at (address). She was again responsible for all the same type of activities as she had done in the past and reported earning approximately $26,000.00 to $27,000.00 yearly which included a base salary and bonuses.

During this same time period she also was an owner/operator of a small (type of business) in the (name of city) area. She would work primarily in the evenings and on weekends. Later she went into business with a cousin.

She next went to work for (name of company) which was the in (name of city) where she again was the manager of the truck stop. She reported that (company name) eventually bought the corporation and she was relieved of her duties which she reported was the first time this had happened to her in her work career.

In April 1991 she went to work for (name of company) out of (city) where she was responsible for managing a convenience store and truck stop. She continues to work at this location but has had a modified job setting since her automobile accident. The job has required her to be able to do bookwork, stocking, ordering, waiting on customers, maintaining the premises including minor plumbing, replacing lights and climbing ladders. Additionally, she is responsible for cleaning the grounds around the store. She reports that her salary is $1,600.00 per month gross and additionally, is provided health and dental insurance as well as sick leave, paid holidays, and two weeks vacation. While at the same time performing this work she was continuing her own business on a part time basis and was doing this on weekends. Since the automobile accident she has not been able to continue the part time work and has had to sell off the assets of the company.

A review of her work history would indicate that she primarily has been either an owner/operator or a working manager of retail sales activities. She is an individual who has put in numerous hours over the years in order to build up a business or manage a business and has been physically involved with the hands-on work of the businesses. She has learned bookkeeping skills by actually performing these during her jobs but the majority of her work has been more of a hands-on ordering, selling, and waiting on customers. Additionally, she has been quite involved with managing and supervising other employees.

CLIENT'S PERSPECTIVE OF INJURY: One page follows.

VOCATIONAL TESTING RESULTS:

ASSESSMENT INSTRUMENTS ADMINISTERED:

Your client was administered the following assessment instruments:

The Gates-MacGinitie Reading Tests
The Wide Range Achievement Test-Revised 2 (WRAT-R2)
The General Aptitude Test Battery (GATB)
The Revised BETA-Second Edition
The Personnel Tests for Industry-Oral Directions Test (PTI-ODT)
The Computer Operator Aptitude Battery (COAB)
The Wonderlic Personnel Test
The Short Employment Test (SET)
Three components of the Valpar Component Work Sample System
(Valpars 04, 05, and 08)

GENERAL IMPRESSIONS, BEHAVIORAL OBSERVATIONS:

Your client arrived early to begin her evaluation each day. She was dressed casually, but appropriately for the evaluation setting. She was observed to wear glasses throughout the evaluation, although she commented that she felt she needs new glasses as her eyes blur. Your client was friendly and cooperative during the evaluation and appeared to be motivated to try her best on all administered tasks. She was observed for approximately eleven and one half hours during the two days of testing.

During the orientation to testing, your client stated that she needed to walk around because she had been sitting too long (during the intake interview). She was then given a scheduled 10-minute break before starting testing. She reported after the break that her back pain was at 3 on a scale of 1 to 10 (1 being minimal pain and 10 being maximum pain). She further stated that the pain started at the base of her neck and ran all the way down to her hips, but was worst in the neck and low-back areas.

After sitting for nearly 40 minutes, your client stood to stretch and move about. She reported that her "muscles were tightening all the way around her waist to her low-back and up her spine." She rated her back pain at 4 and stated she also had a headache and pain radiating down her right arm. This occurred while sitting at a flat table in a regular chair. She was then moved to a drafting table with an elevated and tilted surface to see if this accommodation would be of benefit.

The 21-page report goes on to explain each of the tests administered and the results of the tests. Based on the tests and the intrepretation of the test results a conclusion is presented.

CONCLUSION:

It is my opinion that she has and will experience a change and loss in her vocational capacity. As previously indicated in this report, your client was quite an active individual who had a work history reflective of an individual who would work much more than 40 hours per week, and at times, would work several jobs during the same time period.

A review of her income tax records would indicate that her most productive years recently in terms of earning capacity were in (year) where she earned $ _____ and in (year) where she earned $ _____ . In (year) her actual wages went down as she became involved with her self employment in her personal business. In (year), the year she was involved in the automobile accident, she had returned to work in the (business) setting as well as continuing to work in (personal business) operation on the side. She presently reports that her current monthly salary is $ _____ which is an annual salary of $ _____ . Her current salary is reflective of a $10,000.00 yearly reduction from her earlier years earnings.

It is obvious after having reviewed the various medical records, reviewing her vocational testing results, and interviewing your client, that she continues to work at the (industry) even though she continues to experience considerable discomfort and difficulties in performing her job tasks. Since the accident, she has not been able to put in as many hours as she had in the past and when she does come home from work she finds herself completely exhausted. It would appear that unless she shows considerable improvement in her medical and emotional condition, she is an individual who is in jeopardy of not being able to continue in her modified work activities.

The results of the vocational testing and neuropsychological evaluation would indicate that she has lost the capacity to perform many of her previous job tasks. In the past, she was physically capable of doing a wide variety of physically oriented tasks in her jobs and the ability to put in more than 40 hours per week. She was also financially compensated for these activities. Now as a result of the medical restrictions identified by Dr. (Name) she will experience a loss of her access to the open labor market of at least 50%. Vocationally speaking, this means that she had a wide range of physically oriented type jobs that she would have had the capacity to perform prior to her automobile injury. Now as a result of the medical restrictions due to the automobile accident, she no longer has the physical capacity to exercise her choice to perform these jobs. Her choices of work have been reduced and if she finds herself competing for work in the open labor market, she will experience a significant reduction in her opportunities to perform various types of jobs.

It is my opinion that the current salary which she is earning at her current employment would represent her optimum earning capacity presently, and if she finds she is unable to physically and emotionally keep up with this employment and ends up losing this job, she would then experience additional ramifications on her earning capacity. Based upon her current vocational profile and functioning, it is my opinion that if she were to attempt to re-enter the open labor market in another job, that she currently possesses the capacity to perform work which would typically pay in the $5.00 to $6.00 per hour category. When considering the $6.00 per hour earning capacity over a full year, it would indicate earnings of $12,480.00. Comparing this to her present income this would indicate a loss of $6,720.00 yearly. When comparing the $6.00 hourly figure to her earning capacity in (year) of $ _____ , it would indicate a loss in earning capacity of $17,509.00 yearly. At the time of her accident, she was 49 years old and assuming a normal retirement age of 65, would indicate that she has 16 years of work where she will experience a loss of earning capacity.

In summary, it is my opinion that this individual's vocational capacity has been impacted as a result of the medical problems she is now experiencing from the (date) automobile accident. Her general labor market has been reduced due to the fact that she can no longer perform a full range of physically oriented type work as she had done in the past. Her capacity to improve through additional vocational rehabilitation training is not very good due to the ongoing emotional and pain behaviors which she continues to experience. Her earning capacity has been impacted evidenced by the annual salary she received in (year) and (year) when compared to what she is capable of earning since the accident.

Finally, this individual appeared to be a very active person in terms of the various types of vocational activities she participated in during her lifetime. Now as a result of the medical problems, she has had a significant impact on not only her vocational capacity but also her avocational activities. Unless her medical condition would improve significantly, I would not anticipate this individual's vocational earning capacity to improve.

If you have any questions regarding any of the information contained within this report, please direct them to me.

Sincerely,

_____

§8.10 —The Economist's Use of the Vocational Report

The only portion of the report used by the economist is found in the conclusion. The report states that loss of earnings potential is $17,509 annually. This is the dollar amount used as the base figure for the calculation of the present value of the future wages. This report does address the difference in income levels.

While not intended to be within the scope of the vocational specialist's expertise, the report does not address the areas of fringe benefits the employee is likely to receive. Additionally, the report does not address the areas of pain and suffering.

§8.11 A Caution Concerning Earnings Capacity

The typical report made by a vocational specialist will address earnings capacity. Capacity implies that the earnings are as high as the injured party could earn. In order to properly establish the size of the loss one needs to establish whether the injured party was working, earning, at capacity before the accident.

§8.12 Summary

If a vocational rehabilitation specialist is not involved in the estimate of earning capacity the economist typically estimates the loss of the present value in the future income stream resulting from disability as though the disability were total and permanent. The degree of disability will be left to someone else. If the rehabilitation specialist is involved the economist need only use the estimated loss in earning capacity established by the specialist.

9

Household Services

$$\text{Present Value of Future Income} = \sum_{t=0}^{n} \$ * M * (1+g)^t / (1+d)^t * P_L * P_S * P_F * C * \underline{HS} * T_X$$

§9.01   Introduction

Household services refer to the economic value provided to the household by either spouse or by minor children. These services are provided on a noncash basis.

149

Historically the most common analysis concerned the value of household services provided by a mother/housewife not employed outside the home. Today the value of household services is a part of most analysis addressing economic loss. This chapter will review some of the sources that can be used to estimate the value of household services and how the estimates of the value of household services are made.

§9.02   Sylvia Porter Study

The Sylvia Porter Study[1] estimates the value of a housewife's services. Table 9-1 shows the types of jobs a housewife performs, the number of hours spent on each job, and the economic value of the jobs.[2] As the table indicates, the housewife spends 99.6 hours per week in domestic work. The 1979 dollar estimate of household services is $18,862.48.[3] This is the economic value, or base value, of the housewife not employed outside the home. The value would be the dollars in the present value equation.

The problem with the study's household service figure is that it does not identify the size of the family and the number or age of the children. Consequently, the housewife is expected to contribute equally each year regardless of family size or age of the family members.

Table 9-1   Hours Spent by a Housewife in Domestic Work

	Hours per week
Nursemaid	44.5
Housekeeper	17.5
Cook	13.1
Dishwasher	6.2
Laundress	5.9
Food Buyer	3.3
Chauffeur	2.0
Gardener	2.3
Maintenance	1.7
Seamstress	1.3
Dietitian	1.2
Practical Nurse	.6
Total	99.6

---

[1] S. Porter, New Money Book For The 80's 621 (1980); Stewart & Greenhalgh, *Work History Patterns and the Occupational Attainment of Women*, 94 Econ J 498 (Sept 1984).

[2] Porter, *supra* note 1.

[3] *Id.*

§9.03   Gauger-Walker Study

The Gauger-Walker study[4] estimates the economic value of household services of the husband, wife, and teenage children. Based on whether or not the wife is employed outside the home, the economic values of the husband, wife, and teenage children are estimated. The economic values are a function of the number of children in the family, the age of the youngest child in the family, and the age of the head of household. The economic values are presented in Table 9-2.

Table 9-2   Dollar Value of Household Services
Gauger-Walker Study 1979 Dollars

# Of Children	Age of Wife	Employed Wife Households			Nonemp Wife Households		
		Wife	Husband	Teen	Wife	Husband	
0	Under 25	4,700	1,800		7,000	1,100	
	25-39	5,000	1,900		8,000	1,600	
	40-54	5,900	1,100		8,400	2,100	
	55 plus	6,000	1,500		7,400	2,700	
	Youngest Child	Wife	Husband		Wife	Husband	Teen
1	12-17	6,700	2,400	1,400	9,600	2,700	1,200
	6-11	8,000	1,500		9,400	2,000	+
	2-5	6,200	2,000		9,100	2,400	+
	1	3,000	600		9,900	2,300	+
	Under 1				10,900	2,100	+
2	12-17	6,300	2,100	1,000	10,000	2,200	1,100
	6-11	7,200	2,000	1,100	9,900	2,100	1,100
	2-5	8,300	2,400	1,500	11,100	2,200	900
	1	8,400	5,000		11,700	2,200	*
	Under 1	10,200	2,100		12,600	2,000	*
3	12-17	5,000	2,100	1,100	9,000	1,400	1,000
	6-11	8,600	2,000	1,700	9,900	2,200	1,600
	2-5	10,200	2,800		10,700	1,900	1,000
	1	11,500	3,200		11,600	2,200	1,400
	Under 1	8,700	2,800		13,300	2,000	*
4	12-17	8,700	1,900	1,700	8,400	1,400	1,000
	6-11	7,200	1,400	1,100	10,700	1,900	1,100
	2-5	*	*	*	12,000	2,000	1,100
	1	*	*	*	11,800	2,600	800
	Under 1	*	*	*	13,700	2,600	*
5-6	12-17	*	*	*	+	+	+

[4] Gauger & Walker, *The Dollar Value of Household Work*, 60 Info Bull 11 (New York State College of Human Ecology 1980).

# of Children	Youngest Child	Wife	Husband	Teen	Wife	Husband	Teen
	6-11	*	*	*	11,500	2,000	1,700
	2-5	*	*	*	12,200	2,100	900
	1	*	*	*	9,900	700	
	Under 1	*	*	*	13,600	2,600	1,000
7-9	12-17	*	*	*			
	6-11	+	+	+	*	*	*
	2-5	*	*	*	11,900	2,900	1,400
	1	+	+	+	*	*	*
	Under 1	+	+	+	15,200	2600	*

* Average not calculated
+ no cases

Gauger & Walker, *The Dollar Value of Household Services*, 60 Information Bulletin 11 (New York State College of Human Ecology 1980)

As the family structure changes, the economic contributions of each member of the household changes. In order to calculate the present value of household services, the economist must know the birth date of the husband, wife, and each of the children.

In addition to establishing the economic value of the household members the study also identifies the number of hours worked by each of the members of the household. Table 9-3 shows the number of hours each member of the household works per day.

Table 9-3   Average Number of Hours Worked per Day

# of Children	Age of Wife	Employed Wife			Non employed Wife		
		Wife	Husband	Teen	Wife	Husband	Teen
0	Under 25	4.0	1.5		5.0	1.0	0
	25-39	4.0	1.5		6.0	1.0	
	40-54	4.0	1.0		6.0	1.5	
	55+	4.0	1.0		5.0	2.0	
1	Youngest Child						
	12-17	5.0	2.0	1.0	7.0	2.0	1.0
	6-11	6.0	1.0		7.0	1.5	.5
	2-5	5.0	1.5		5.0	1.5	
	1	6.0	.5		8.0	1.5	
	Under 1	*	.*		8.0	1.5	
2	12-17	5.0	1.5	1.0	7.0	1.5	1.0
	6-11	5.0	1.5	1.0	7.0	1.5	1.0
	2-5	6.0	1.5	1.0	8.0	1.5	1.0
	1	6.0	3.0		9.0	1.5	
	Under 1	8.0	1.5		10.0	1.5	

# of Children	Youngest Child	Employed Wife			Non employed Wife		
		Wife	Husband	Teen	Wife	Husband	Teen
3	12-17	4.0	1.5	1.0	7.0	1.0	1.0
	6-11	6.0	1.5	1.5	7.0	1.5	1.0
	2-5	8.0	2.0	1.5	8.0	1.5	1.0
	1	8.0	2.0		9.0	1.5	
	Under 1	7.0	2.0		10.0	1.5	
4	12-17	6.0	1.0	1.5	6.0	1.0	1.0
	6-11	5.0	1.0		8.0	1.5	1.0
	2-5				9.0	1.5	1.0
	1				9.0	1.5	
	Under 1				11.0	1.5	
5-6							
	6-11				9.0	2.0	1.5
	2-5				9.0	1.5	1.0
	1				8.0	1.5	1.0
	Under 1				10.0	2.0	1.0
7-9							
	2-5				9.0	2.0	1.0
	1						
	Under 1				12.0	2.0	1.0

The value of household activities in the Gauger-Walker study was based on the hourly rate of compensation paid in occupational areas presented in Table 9-4. The hourly rates were obtained from agencies in central New York and the US Bureau of Labor Statistics' "Job Banks for May 1979."[5]

Table 9-4 Household Activities and Hourly Compensation

Activity	Hourly Rate
Cooks	$4.48
Kitchen Helpers	3.02
Cleaning Persons	4.75
Yard Workers	3.21
Laundry Workers	3.20
Dressmakers	4.48
Child Care Workers	3.50
Housekeepers	3.18
Homemaker Aides	3.58
Average Hourly Rate	$3.77

In order to establish a value of household services the amount of time spent in various categories was multiplied by the hourly rate. The economic activities reported included marketing, management and record keeping, food preparation, after meal cleanup, house care and maintenance, yard and car care, washing, ironing and special care of clothing, and physical care of family members.

[5] *Id.*

§9.04   The Douglass, Kenney, and Miller Study

An article, "Which Estimates of Household Production are Best?"[6] is an excellent review of the current research being done questioning the value of household services. The article presents the results of several studies addressing the number of hours spent in household activity. The number of hours spent in household production for women ranges from 35.6 hours per week to 51.4 hours. The range of hours for men is from 10.8 hours to 12.7 hours.[7]

In addition to the number of hours spent in household production the article also estimates the dollar value of household production. The estimate, presented in 1987 dollars, is by age group and employment status. The information is presented in Table 9-5.

Table 9-5   Mean Annual Values of Household Production for 1987

	Women				Men		
	Employed		Not Employed		Employed		Not Employed
Age	Rice & Hodgson Gauger & Walker	DK&M Using Peskin	Rice & Hodgson Gauger & Walker	DK&M Using Peskin	Rice & Hodgson Gauger & Walker	DK&M Using Peskin	DK&M Using Peskin
15-19	7,295	4,626	10,793	9,837	2,471	1,910	4,682
20-24	8,285	5,359	13,569	10,570	2,667	2,893	5,665
25-29	10,431	7,083	16,430	12,294	3,134	3,347	6,118
30-34	11,559	8,275	16,279	13,486	3,303	3,737	6,509
35-39	11,104	8,619	15,591	13,829	3,236	3,976	6,748
40-44	10,400	8,323	14,639	13,534	3,239	4,094	6,866
45-49	9,589	7,725	13,772	12,935	3,037	4,111	6,883
50-54	9,151	7,725	13,091	12,935	3,037	4,111	6,883
55-59	8,886	7,717	11,391	12,928	3,752	4,216	6,988
60-64	7,225	7,717	9,262	12,928	3,703	4,216	6,988
65-69	5,526	7,524	7,083	12,605	2,333	4,216	6,988
70-74	3,934	5,357	5,044	8,975	1,662	3,002	4,975
75-79	2,677	3,643	3,432	6,103	1,131	2,041	3,383
80-84	1,557	2,117	1,995	3,546	657	1,186	1,966
85+	881	1,198	1,129	2,007	372	671	1,113

§9.05   The Bryant, Zick, and Kim Study

The work of Bryant, Zick, and Kim reported in their study *Household Work: What's it Worth and Why?*[8] is a study published in 1992. The study addresses the value of household work. *Household work* is defined as the sum of the time the

---

[6] Douglass, Kenney & Miller, *Which Estimates of Household Production are Best?*, IV, No 1 J Forensic Econ (Winter 1990).

[7] *Id* Table 3.

[8] Bryant, Zick & Kim, *Household Work: What's It Worth and Why?*, Info Bull 322 IB228 (Cornell Univ 1992).

individual spends preparing food, cleaning up after cooking and meals, cleaning both indoor and out, doing laundry, doing indoor and outdoor repairs on houses, cars, furniture and appliances, gardening, looking after pets, caring for family members, chauffeuring, shopping, running errands, and managing family finances.[9]

The study addresses the economic value of household services provided by husband and wife of intact families. The study presents values for the number of hours worked by black and nonblack parents.

Table 9-6   Median Hours Per Week Spent in Household Work by Married Men and Women

Sex	Black	Nonblack	Black as % of Nonblack
Males	9.94	12.75	77.96
Females	30.3	34.85	86.94

The study finds the two major variables in determining the value of household services are the age of the youngest child and the number of hours the parent is employed outside the home. Table 9-7 presents the 1988 value of household services for nonblack families.

Table 9-7   1988 Value of Household Services

1988 Values Age of Youngest Child	Nonblack Females			
	Not Emp	0-34 hrs	35-40 hrs	40+ hrs
1	14,833	16,997	11,295	11,489
2-5	15,920	11,551	10,349	11,489
6-14	13,739	11,383	8,418	7,809
15-17	12,283	9,726	6,344	7,809
18+	12,924	9,097	6,948	5,802

1988 Values Age of Youngest Child	Nonblack Males			
	Not Emp	0-34 hrs	35-40 hrs	40+ hrs
1			7,871	7,808
2-5			9,291	5,958
6-14			9,409	7,903
15-17			6,586	6,341
18+	11,155	9,650	6,724	6,284

---

[9] *Id* 2.

By using the proportions presented in Table 9-6 and applying them to the dollar value presented in Table 9-7 the value of household services can be established for the black wife and black husband. Those figures are presented in Table 9-8.

Table 9-8   Value of Household Services: Black Wife and Husband

1988 Values		Black Females		
Age of Youngest Child	Not Emp	0-34 hrs	35-40 hrs	40+ hrs
1	12,896	14,778	9,820	9,989
2-5	13,841	10,043	8,998	9,989
6-14	11,945	9,897	7,319	6,789
15-17	10,679	8,456	5,516	6,789
18+	11,237	7,909	6,041	5,044

1988 Values		Black Males		
Age of Youngest Child	Not Emp	0-34 hrs	35-40 hrs	40+ hrs
1			6,136	6,087
2-5			7,243	4,645
6-14			7,335	6,161
15-17			5,134	4,943
18+	8,697	9,650	5,242	4,899

§9.06   Fact Situation

A Caucasian couple, both celebrating their thirty-eighth birthday today, have two children. The children, ages ten and eight, are also celebrating their birthdays today. The reason for assuming the birthdays are all the same is to avoid having to deal with fractions of years. The wife is not employed outside the home. The present value of household services of the wife is calculated in §§9.07 through 9.10.

The present value of household services of the wife will be calculated in §9.07 and §9.08 using the information presented in the Gauger-Walker study. Section 9.09 calculates the present value of the wife using the dollar information presented in the Douglass, Kenney, and Miller study while §9.10 uses the information in the Bryant, Zick, and Kim study.

§9.07 Calculating the Present Value of the Household Services of the Wife Using the Gauger-Walker Value Estimate

The analysis begins by examining the family structure and the age of the family members and the value of the wife's household services. From Table 9-2 the annual value of the wife's household services is determined to be $9,900. This is the 1979 value of household services of a wife not employed outside the home. She has two children ages 10 and 8. Table 9-9 shows the dollar value of household services as the children get older.

Table 9-9 Dollar Value of Household Services for a Mother with Two Children and Not Employed Outside the Home

Age of Mother	Age of Father	Age of Oldest Child	Age of Youngest Child	1979 Value of Mother's Work
38	38	10	8	$ 9,900
39	39	11	9	9,900
40	40	12	10	10,000
41	41	13	11	10,000
42	42	14	12	10,000
43	43	15	13	10,000
44	44	16	14	10,000
45	45	17	15	10,000
46	46	18	16	9,600
47	47	19	17	9,600
48	48	20	18	8,400
49	49	21	19	8,400
50	50	22	20	8,400
51	51		21	8,400
52	52		22	8,400
53	53			8,400
54	54			8,400
55	55			7,400
56	56			7,400
57	57			7,400
58	58			7,400
59	59			7,400
60	60			7,400
61	61			7,400

Age of Mother	Age of Father	Age of Oldest Child	Age of Youngest Child	1979 Value of Mother's Work
62	62			7,400
63	63			7,400
64	64			7,400
65	65			7,400
66	66			7,400
67	67			7,400
68	68			7,400

Table 9-9 indicates that the value of a mother's household services changes as the age and composition of the family changes. After the youngest child reaches age 18 the value of the household services decreases to $8,400 per year. This is the value attributed to a two member household with no children at home.

The last column in Table 9-9 is the 1979 dollar value of the household services. These numbers are inflated to 1991 dollar values by using the Consumer Price Index. The index value of the Consumer Price Index in 1992 is 140.3 and it was 72.6 in 1979. The increase in the price index for the twelve years was 93.25%. This increase is applied to all the 1979 values appearing in Table 9-9. These values are presented in Table 9-10.

Table 9-10   Value of Household Services in 1979 and 1991

Age of Mother	Father	Age of Children		Value of Household Services 1979 Dollars	1991 Dollars
38	38	10	8	9,900	19,131
39	39	11	9	9,900	19,131
40	40	12	10	10,000	19,325
41	41	13	11	10,000	19,325
42	42	14	12	10,000	19,325
43	43	15	13	10,000	19,325
44	44	16	14	10,000	19,325
45	45	17	15	10,000	19,325
46	46	18	16	9,600	18,552
47	47	19	17	9,600	18,552
48	48	20	18	8,400	16,232
49	49	21	19	8,400	16,232
50	50	22	20	8,400	16,232
51	51		21	8,400	16,232
52	52		22	8,400	16,232
53	53			8,400	16,232
54	54			8,400	16,232

Age of Mother	Father	Age of Children	Value of Household Services 1979 Dollars	1991 Dollars
55	55		7,400	14,300
56	56		7,400	14,300
57	57		7,400	14,300
58	58		7,400	14,300
59	59		7,400	14,300
60	60		7,400	14,300
61	61		7,400	14,300
62	62		7,400	14,300
63	63		7,400	14,300
64	64		7,400	14,300
65	65		7,400	14,300
66	66		7,400	14,300
67	67		7,400	14,300
68	68		7,400	14,300

To the 1992 value of household services the growth rate and the discount rate are applied. The last column in Table 9-10 is the current value and is the base value that is used to compute the present value of future services.

Assume that a growth rate of 4 per cent and a discount rate of 6 per cent are assumed by the economist to be the appropriate values. Table 9-11 presents the present value of the household services of the wife.

The calculation of the present value and the sum are completed by using the present value formula. Recall the formula was:

$$\text{Present Value of Future Income} = \$ \sum_{t=0}^{n} (1+g)^t / (1+d)^t$$

Where "$" represents the 1991 dollar value of services, "t" is the number of years in the future, "g" is the growth rate, and "d" is the interest or discount rate. Inserting the variables in the formula yields:

Present Value of = $19,131 $(1+04)^0 / (1+.06)^0$ = $19,131
Present Value of = 19,131 $(1+.04)^1 / (1+.06)^1$ = 18,770
Present Value of = 19,325 $(1+.04)^2 / (1+.06)^2$ = 18,603
Present Value of = 19,325 $(1+.04)^3 / (1+.06)^3$ = 18,252

The column titled "sum" is the running total. That is, the first year's loss is $19,131, the second year's loss is the "sum" of the first two years, $37,902 and so on.

Table 9-11   Present Value of Household Services

Age of Mother	Children		Years in Future	1991 Value	Present Value	Sum
38	10	8	0	19,131	19,131	19,131
39	11	9	1	19,131	18,770	37,901
40	12	10	2	19,325	18,603	56,504
41	13	11	3	19,325	18,252	74,755
42	14	12	4	19,325	17,907	92,663
43	15	13	5	19,325	17,569	110,232
44	16	14	6	19,325	17,238	127,470
45	17	15	7	19,325	16,913	144,383
46	18	16	8	18,552	15,930	160,312
47	19	17	9	18,552	15,629	175,942
48	20	18	10	16,232	13,417	189,358
49	21	19	11	16,232	13,164	202,522
50	22	20	12	16,232	12,915	215,437
51		21	13	16,232	12,672	228,109
52		22	14	16,232	12,432	240,541
53			15	16,232	12,198	252,739
54			16	16,232	11,968	264,707
55			17	14,300	10,344	275,051
56			18	14,300	10,149	285,200
57			19	14,300	9,958	295,158
58			20	14,300	9,770	304,928
59			21	14,300	9,585	314,513
60			22	14,300	9,405	323,918
61			23	14,300	9,227	333,145
62			24	14,300	9,053	342,198
63			25	14,300	8,882	351,080
64			26	14,300	8,715	359,795
65			27	14,300	8,550	368,345

The present value of the household services is calculated through each of the ages. The present value of household services until the oldest child reaches age 18 is $160,312, while the present value until the youngest child reaches age 18 is $189,358. The present value of household services to age 65 is also computed.

To properly evaluate the value of household services it is necessary to mortality adjust the values. That is, each of the future values needs to be adjusted for the probability of living each successive year. Table 9-12 makes the mortality adjustment for a Caucasian female.

Table 9-12   The Mortality Adjusted Value of Household Services

Mother's Age	Period	1991 Value	Present Value	Probability of: Dying	Probability of: Living	Adjusted PV	Adjusted Sum
38	0	19,131	19,131	0.99	.9990	19,112	19,112
39	1	19,131	18,770	1.09	.9979	18,731	37,843
40	2	19,325	18,603	1.20	.9967	18,542	56,385
41	3	19,325	18,252	1.33	.9954	18,168	74,552
42	4	19,325	17,907	1.46	.9939	17,799	92,351
43	5	19,325	17,569	1.59	.9924	17,435	109,786
44	6	19,325	17,238	1.73	.9906	17,077	126,863
45	7	19,325	16,913	1.89	.9888	16,723	143,586
46	8	18,552	15,930	2.07	.9867	15,718	159,304
47	9	18,552	15,629	2.29	.9845	15,387	174,691
48	10	16,232	13,417	2.54	.9820	13,175	187,866
49	11	16,232	13,164	2.84	.9792	12,890	200,755
50	12	16,232	12,915	3.16	.9761	12,606	213,362
51	13	16,232	12,672	3.51	.9727	12,325	225,687
52	14	16,232	12,432	3.90	.9689	12,045	237,732
53	15	16,232	12,198	4.31	.9647	11,767	249,499
54	16	16,232	11,968	4.76	.9601	11,490	260,989
55	17	14,300	10,344	5.24	.9551	9,880	270,869
56	18	14,300	10,149	5.77	.9496	9,637	280,506
57	19	14,300	9,958	6.34	.9435	9,395	289,902
58	20	14,300	9,770	6.97	.9370	9,154	299,055
59	21	14,300	9,585	7.64	.9298	8,913	307,968
60	22	14,300	9,405	8.39	.9220	8,671	316,639
61	23	14,300	9,227	9.18	.9135	8,429	325,068
62	24	14,300	9,053	10.02	.9044	8,187	333,256
63	25	14,300	8,882	10.91	.8945	7,945	341,201
64	26	14,300	8,715	11.84	.8839	7,703	348,904
65	27	14,300	8,550	12.85	.8726	7,461	356,365
66	28	14,300	8,389	14.04	.8603	7,217	363,582
67	29	14,300	8,231	15.35	.8471	6,972	370,554
68	30	14,300	8,075	16.77	.8329	6,726	377,280
69	31	14,300	7,923	18.33	.8176	6,478	383,758
70	32	14,300	7,773	20.03	.8013	6,229	389,987
71	33	14,300	7,627	21.94	.7837	5,977	395,964
72	34	14,300	7,483	24.04	.7648	5,723	401,687
73	35	14,300	7,342	26.34	.7447	5,467	407,154
74	36	14,300	7,203	28.85	.7232	5,209	412,364
75	37	14,300	7,067	31.61	.7003	4,950	417,313
76	38	14,300	6,934	34.87	.6759	4,687	422,000
77	39	14,300	6,803	38.46	.6499	4,422	426,422
78	40	14,300	6,675	42.42	.6224	4,154	430,576
79	41	14,300	6,549	46.80	.5932	3,885	434,461
80	42	14,300	6,425	51.62	.5626	3,615	438,076
81	43	14,300	6,304	59.87	.5289	3,334	441,410
82	44	14,300	6,185	69.43	.4922	3,044	444,454
83	45	14,300	6,068	80.52	.4526	2,746	447,201
84	46	14,300	5,954	93.38	.4103	2,443	449,644
85	47	14,300	5,842	108.30	.3659	2,137	451,781
86	48	14,300	5,731	125.60	.3199	1,834	453,615
87	49	14,300	5,623	145.66	.2733	1,537	455,152

Mother's Age	Period	1991 Value	Present Value	Probability of: Dying	Probability of: Living	Adjusted PV	Adjusted Sum
88	50	14,300	5,517	168.92	.2272	1,253	456,405
89	51	14,300	5,413	195.91	.1827	989	457,393
90	52	14,300	5,311	227.20	.1412	750	458,143
91	53	14,300	5,211	263.49	.1040	542	458,685
92	54	14,300	5,112	305.58	.0722	369	459,054
93	55	14,300	5,016	354.39	.0466	234	459,288
94	56	14,300	4,921	411.00	.0275	135	459,423
95	57	14,300	4,828	476.66	.0144	69	459,492
96	58	14,300	4,737	552.79	.0064	30	459,523
97	59	14,300	4,648	641.10	.0023	11	459,533
98	60	14,300	4,560	743.50	.0006	3	459,536
99	61	14,300	4,474	862.27	.0001	0	459,536

The mortality adjusted present value of the household services continues to age 99 and is $459,536. One thing that the analysis does not consider is the reduced ability of the individual to perform the household services.

§9.08 Calculating the Present Value of the Household Services of the Wife Using the Gauger-Walker Hour Estimate

In addition to the dollar value of household services presented in the Gauger-Walker study, the number of hours worked per day was presented. These figures were presented in Table 9-3. The Table indicates that a mother of two children, the youngest between ages 6 and 11, works 7 hours per day. Table 9-13 presents the number of hours the mother works per day and per year. The information in Table 9-13 is based on the information in Table 9-3.

Table 9-13   Hours Worked Per Day and Per Year

Age of Mother	Age of Oldest Child	Age of Youngest Child	Hours per Day	Hours per Year
38	10	8	7	2,555
39	11	9	7	2,555
40	12	10	7	2,555
41	13	11	7	2,555
42	14	12	7	2,555
43	15	13	7	2,555
44	16	14	7	2,555
45	17	15	7	2,555
46	18	16	7	2,555
47	19	17	7	2,555
48	20	18	6	2,190
49	21	19	6	2,190

Age of Mother	Age of Oldest Child	Age of Youngest Child	Hours per Day	Hours per Year
50	22	20	6	2,190
51		21	6	2,190
52		22	6	2,190
53			6	2,190
54			6	2,190
55			5	1,825
56			5	1,825
57			5	1,825
58			5	1,825
59			5	1,825
60			5	1,825
61			5	1,825
62			5	1,825
63			5	1,825
64			5	1,825
65			5	1,825
66			5	1,825
67			5	1,825
68			5	1,825
69			5	1,825
70			5	1,825
71			5	1,825
72			5	1,825
73			5	1,825
74			5	1,825
75			5	1,825
76			5	1,825
77			5	1,825
78			5	1,825
79			5	1,825
80			5	1,825
81			5	1,825
82			5	1,825
83			5	1,825
84			5	1,825
85			5	1,825
86			5	1,825
87			5	1,825
88			5	1,825
89			5	1,825

Age of Mother	Age of Oldest Child	Age of Youngest Child	Hours per Day	Hours per Year
90			5	1,825
91			5	1,825
92			5	1,825
93			5	1,825
94			5	1,825
95			5	1,825
96			5	1,825
97			5	1,825
98			5	1,825
99			5	1,825

In order to determine the dollar value of the household services the economist must estimate how the housewife spends her time and what the prevailing wage rate for those services is in the area where the family lives.

Many states provide information concerning wage rates in the area. For example, in 1990-91, the Department of Human Resources of the State of Kansas published the Kansas Wage Survey. According to the survey the following median range of wages were paid for the following job categories:

Occupation	High Hourly Rate	Low Hourly Rate
Financial Manager	18.21	20.94
Purchasing Agent	11.96	13.75
Dietitian	10.39	11.95
Housekeeper	5.13	5.90
Baker	5.13	5.90
Cook	5.91	6.80
Dishwasher	4.45	5.12
Maid	5.13	5.90
Child Care Worker	4.45	5.12
Average	7.86	9.04

Considering the hours suggested in the Walker-Gauger study, the 1990 value of household services would range from $20,082 ($7.86 * 2,555) to $23,097 ($9.04 * 2,555). Had the number of hours of work reported by Sylvia Porter been used then the annual value of household services would range from $40,708 ($7.86 * 99.6 hours per week * 52 weeks per year) to $46,820.

It is these values that would be used to compute the present value of the household services. When this approach is taken the time spent in each category is weighted equally. If the time spent in child care was proportionately more than the time spent in financial planning then the average wage would be less and the annual value would be less.

Table 9-14   Present Value of Household Services Using Local Wage Rates

Period	Hours Year	Value	Value	Sum	Probability Living	Adjusted: PV	Sum
38	2,555	20,082	20,082	20,082	0.9990	20,062	20,062
39	2,555	20,082	19,703	39,786	0.9979	19,662	39,724
40	2,555	20,082	19,332	59,117	0.9967	19,268	58,992
41	2,555	20,082	18,967	78,084	0.9954	18,880	77,872
42	2,555	20,082	18,609	96,693	0.9939	18,495	96,367
43	2,555	20,082	18,258	114,951	0.9924	18,119	114,486
44	2,555	20,082	17,913	132,865	0.9906	17,745	132,231
45	2,555	20,082	17,575	150,440	0.9888	17,379	149,610
46	2,555	20,082	17,244	167,684	0.9867	17,014	166,624
47	2,555	20,082	16,918	184,602	0.9845	16,656	183,281
48	2,190	17,213	14,228	198,830	0.9820	13,972	197,252
49	2,190	17,213	13,959	212,790	0.9792	13,669	210,922
50	2,190	17,213	13,696	226,486	0.9761	13,369	224,290
51	2,190	17,213	13,438	239,923	0.9727	13,071	237,361
52	2,190	17,213	13,184	253,107	0.9689	12,774	250,135
53	2,190	17,213	12,935	266,043	0.9647	12,479	262,614
54	2,190	17,213	12,691	278,734	0.9601	12,185	274,799
55	1,825	14,345	10,377	289,111	0.9551	9,911	284,710
56	1,825	14,345	10,181	299,291	0.9496	9,668	294,377
57	1,825	14,345	9,989	309,280	0.9435	9,424	303,801
58	1,825	14,345	9,800	319,080	0.9370	9,183	312,984
59	1,825	14,345	9,615	328,696	0.9298	8,940	321,925
60	1,825	14,345	9,434	338,129	0.9220	8,698	330,623
61	1,825	14,345	9,256	347,385	0.9135	8,455	339,078
62	1,825	14,345	9,081	356,467	0.9044	8,213	347,291
63	1,825	14,345	8,910	365,376	0.8945	7,970	355,261
64	1,825	14,345	8,742	374,118	0.8839	7,727	362,988
65	1,825	14,345	8,577	382,695	0.8726	7,484	370,472
66	1,825	14,345	8,415	391,110	0.8603	7,239	377,711
67	1,825	14,345	8,256	399,366	0.8471	6,994	384,705
68	1,825	14,345	8,100	407,467	0.8329	6,747	391,452
69	1,825	14,345	7,948	415,414	0.8176	6,498	397,950
70	1,825	14,345	7,798	423,212	0.8013	6,248	404,198
71	1,825	14,345	7,651	430,863	0.7837	5,996	410,194
72	1,825	14,345	7,506	438,369	0.7648	5,741	415,935
73	1,825	14,345	7,365	445,733	0.7447	5,484	421,419
74	1,825	14,345	7,226	452,959	0.7232	5,226	426,645
75	1,825	14,345	7,089	460,048	0.7003	4,965	431,609
76	1,825	14,345	6,956	467,004	0.6759	4,701	436,310
77	1,825	14,345	6,824	473,828	0.6499	4,435	440,746
78	1,825	14,345	6,696	480,524	0.6224	4,167	444,913
79	1,825	14,345	6,569	487,093	0.5932	3,897	448,810
80	1,825	14,345	6,445	493,538	0.5626	3,626	452,436
81	1,825	14,345	6,324	499,862	0.5289	3,345	455,780
82	1,825	14,345	6,204	506,066	0.4922	3,054	458,834
83	1,825	14,345	6,087	512,153	0.4526	2,755	461,589
84	1,825	14,345	5,972	518,126	0.4103	2,450	464,040
85	1,825	14,345	5,860	523,985	0.3659	2,144	466,184
86	1,825	14,345	5,749	529,734	0.3199	1,839	468,023
87	1,825	14,345	5,641	535,375	0.2733	1,542	469,565

Period	Hours Year	Value	Value	Sum	Probability Living	Adjusted: PV	Sum
88	1,825	14,345	5,534	540,909	0.2272	1,257	470,822
89	1,825	14,345	5,430	546,339	0.1827	992	471,814
90	1,825	14,345	5,327	551,667	0.1412	752	472,566
91	1,825	14,345	5,227	556,894	0.1040	544	473,110
92	1,825	14,345	5,128	562,022	0.0722	370	473,480
93	1,825	14,345	5,031	567,053	0.0466	234	473,714
94	1,825	14,345	4,937	571,990	0.0275	136	473,850
95	1,825	14,345	4,843	576,833	0.0144	70	473,920
96	1,825	14,345	4,752	581,585	0.0064	30	473,950
97	1,825	14,345	4,662	586,248	0.0023	11	473,961
98	1,825	14,345	4,574	590,822	0.0006	3	473,964
99	1,825	14,345	4,488	595,310	0.0001	0	473,964

The mortality adjusted present value of the household services is $473,964. This uses the hours presented in Gauger-Walker study and an hourly rate of $7.86. Had the hourly rate of $9.04 been used the mortality adjusted present value would increase to $545,119.

Another consideration ignored by this analysis is the fact that the Mother/ Housewife is "on call" 24 hours a day. If one were to value this by saying that a Mother is available additional hours per day then the value of the household services would be even greater.

§9.09   Calculating the Present Value of Household Services Using the Douglass, Kenney, and Miller Study

Table 9-4 presents the economic value of household services as estimated by Douglass, Kenney, and Miller (DKM). The values are calculated for men and for women. Using the current fact situation of a 38-year-old housewife not employed outside the home the DKM estimate of value is $13,829 in 1987 dollars. Table 9-15 presents the present value calculation using the DKM statistics.

In order to "move" the 1987 values to 1992 figures the Consumer Price Index was used. The 1992 Consumer Price Index was 140.3 while the 1987 value was 113.6. The 1987 values were increased by 1.235 (140.3/113.6) in order to obtain the 1992 values. The 1992 values were permitted to grow at 4 per cent annually and then were discounted at 6 per cent annually. The values were then mortality adjusted by multiplying by the probability of living. The mortality adjusted present value of household services is $412,612.

Table 9-15   Present Value of Household Services Using the DKM Values

Age	Period	1987 Value	1992 Value	Present Value	Sum	Probability Living	Adjusted: PV	Sum
38	0	13,829	17,079	17,079	0.99	.9990	17,062	17,062
39	1	13,829	17,079	16,757	1.09	.9979	16,722	33,785
40	2	13,534	16,715	16,090	1.2	.9967	16,037	49,822
41	3	13,534	16,715	15,787	1.33	.9954	15,714	65,536

Age	Period	1987 Value	1992 Value	Present Value	Sum	Probability Living	Adjusted: PV	Sum
42	4	13,534	16,715	15,489	1.46	.9939	15,395	80,931
43	5	13,534	16,715	15,196	1.59	.9924	15,080	96,011
44	6	13,534	16,715	14,910	1.73	.9906	14,770	110,782
45	7	12,935	15,975	13,981	1.89	.9888	13,824	124,606
46	8	12,935	15,975	13,717	2.07	.9867	13,535	138,141
47	9	12,935	15,975	13,458	2.29	.9845	13,249	151,390
48	10	12,935	15,975	13,204	2.54	.9820	12,966	164,357
49	11	12,935	15,975	12,955	2.84	.9792	12,686	177,042
50	12	12,935	15,975	12,711	3.16	.9761	12,407	189,449
51	13	12,935	15,975	12,471	3.51	.9727	12,130	201,579
52	14	12,935	15,975	12,236	3.90	.9689	11,855	213,434
53	15	12,935	15,975	12,005	4.31	.9647	11,581	225,015
54	16	12,935	15,975	11,778	4.76	.9601	11,308	236,323
55	17	12,928	15,967	11,550	5.24	.9551	11,031	247,354
56	18	12,928	15,967	11,332	5.77	.9496	10,760	258,115
57	19	12,928	15,967	11,118	6.34	.9435	10,490	268,605
58	20	12,928	15,967	10,908	6.97	.9370	10,221	278,826
59	21	12,928	15,967	10,703	7.64	.9298	9,951	288,777
60	22	12,928	15,967	10,501	8.39	.9220	9,682	298,459
61	23	12,928	15,967	10,302	9.18	.9135	9,412	307,870
62	24	12,928	15,967	10,108	10.02	.9044	9,142	317,012
63	25	12,928	15,967	9,917	10.91	.8945	8,871	325,883
64	26	12,928	15,967	9,730	11.84	.8839	8,601	334,484
65	27	12,605	15,568	9,308	12.85	.8726	8,122	342,606
66	28	12,605	15,568	9,133	14.04	.8603	7,857	350,463
67	29	12,605	15,568	8,960	15.35	.8471	7,590	358,053
68	30	12,605	15,568	8,791	16.77	.8329	7,322	365,375
69	31	12,605	15,568	8,625	18.33	.8176	7,052	372,428
70	32	8,975	11,084	6,025	20.03	.8013	4,828	377,256
71	33	8,975	11,084	5,912	21.94	.7837	4,633	381,889
72	34	8,975	11,084	5,800	24.04	.7648	4,436	386,325
73	35	8,975	11,084	5,691	26.34	.7447	4,238	390,563
74	36	8,975	11,084	5,583	28.85	.7232	4,038	394,601
75	37	6,103	7,537	3,725	31.61	.7003	2,609	397,210
76	38	6,103	7,537	3,655	34.87	.6759	2,470	399,680
77	39	6,103	7,537	3,586	38.46	.6499	2,331	402,011
78	40	6,103	7,537	3,518	42.42	.6224	2,190	404,200
79	41	6,103	7,537	3,452	46.80	.5932	2,048	406,248
80	42	3,546	4,379	1,968	51.62	.5626	1,107	407,355
81	43	3,546	4,379	1,931	59.87	.5289	1,021	408,376
82	44	3,546	4,379	1,894	69.43	.4922	932	409,308
83	45	3,546	4,379	1,858	80.52	.4526	841	410,150
84	46	3,546	4,379	1,823	93.38	.4103	748	410,898
85	47	2,007	2,479	1,013	108.30	.3659	370	411,268
86	48	2,007	2,479	993	125.60	.3199	318	411,586
87	49	2,007	2,479	975	145.66	.2733	266	411,852
88	50	2,007	2,479	956	168.92	.2272	217	412,070
89	51	2,007	2,479	938	195.91	.1827	171	412,241
90	52	2,007	2,479	921	227.20	.1412	130	412,371
91	53	2,007	2,479	903	263.49	.1040	94	412,465
92	54	2,007	2,479	886	305.58	.0722	64	412,529
93	55	2,007	2,479	869	354.39	.0466	41	412,569
94	56	2,007	2,479	853	411.00	.0275	23	412,593
95	57	2,007	2,479	837	476.66	.0144	12	412,605

Age	Period	1987 Value	1992 Value	Present Value	Sum	Probability Living	Adjusted: PV	Sum
96	58	2,007	2,479	821	552.79	.0064	5	412,610
97	59	2,007	2,479	806	641.10	.0023	2	412,612
98	60	2,007	2,479	790	743.50	.0006	0	412,612
99	61	2,007	2,479	776	862.27	.0001	0	412,612

§9.10   Calculating the Present Value of Household Services Using the Bryant, Zick, and Kim Study

In order to estimate the 1993 values of household services the values established in this study are "moved" to 1992 values using the Consumer Price Index. Table 9-16 presents the 1988 value of a wife's household services and the 1992 values of services.

Table 9-16   1992 Mortality Adjusted Value of Household Services Using the Bryant, Zick, and Kim Study

Age	Period	1988 Value	1992 Value	Present Value	Sum	Probability Living	Adjusted: PV	Sum
38	0	13,739	16,294	16,294	0.99	.9990	16,278	16,278
39	1	13,739	16,294	15,987	1.09	.9979	15,953	32,231
40	2	13,739	16,294	15,685	1.2	.9967	15,634	47,865
41	3	13,739	16,294	15,389	1.33	.9954	15,318	63,183
42	4	13,739	16,294	15,099	1.46	.9939	15,007	78,190
43	5	13,739	16,294	14,814	1.59	.9924	14,701	92,891
44	6	13,739	16,294	14,534	1.73	.9906	14,398	107,289
45	7	12,283	14,567	12,749	1.89	.9888	12,606	119,895
46	8	12,283	14,567	12,508	2.07	.9867	12,342	132,237
47	9	12,283	14,567	12,272	2.29	.9845	12,082	144,319
48	10	12,924	15,327	12,669	2.54	.9820	12,441	156,759
49	11	12,924	15,327	12,430	2.84	.9792	12,171	168,931
50	12	12,924	15,327	12,195	3.16	.9761	11,904	180,834
51	13	12,924	15,327	11,965	3.51	.9727	11,638	192,473
52	14	12,924	15,327	11,740	3.90	.9689	11,374	203,847
53	15	12,924	15,327	11,518	4.31	.9647	11,111	214,958
54	16	12,924	15,327	11,301	4.76	.9601	10,850	225,808
55	17	12,924	15,327	11,088	5.24	.9551	10,589	236,398
56	18	12,924	15,327	10,878	5.77	.9496	10,330	246,727
57	19	12,924	15,327	10,673	6.34	.9435	10,070	256,798
58	20	12,924	15,327	10,472	6.97	.9370	9,812	266,609
59	21	12,924	15,327	10,274	7.64	.9298	9,553	276,162
60	22	12,924	15,327	10,080	8.39	.9220	9,294	285,456
61	23	12,924	15,327	9,890	9.18	.9135	9,035	294,491
62	24	12,924	15,327	9,704	10.02	.9044	8,776	303,267
63	25	12,924	15,327	9,520	10.91	.8945	8,516	311,783
64	26	12,924	15,327	9,341	11.84	.8839	8,257	320,040
65	27	12,924	15,327	9,165	12.85	.8726	7,997	328,036
66	28	12,924	15,327	8,992	14.04	.8603	7,736	335,772
67	29	12,924	15,327	8,822	15.35	.8471	7,473	343,245
68	30	12,924	15,327	8,656	16.77	.8329	7,209	350,454
69	31	12,924	15,327	8,492	18.33	.8176	6,944	357,398
70	32	12,924	15,327	8,332	20.03	.8013	6,676	364,074

Age	Period	1988 Value	1992 Value	Present Value	Sum	Probability Living	Adjusted: PV	Sum
71	33	12,924	15,327	8,175	21.94	.7837	6,406	370,481
72	34	12,924	15,327	8,021	24.04	.7648	6,134	376,615
73	35	12,924	15,327	7,869	26.34	.7447	5,860	382,475
74	36	12,924	15,327	7,721	28.85	.7232	5,584	388,059
75	37	12,924	15,327	7,575	31.61	.7003	5,305	393,364
76	38	12,924	15,327	7,432	34.87	.6759	5,024	398,388
77	39	12,924	15,327	7,292	38.46	.6499	4,739	403,127
78	40	12,924	15,327	7,154	42.42	.6224	4,453	407,579
79	41	12,924	15,327	7,019	46.80	.5932	4,164	411,743
80	42	12,924	15,327	6,887	51.62	.5626	3,875	415,618
81	43	12,924	15,327	6,757	59.87	.5289	3,574	419,192
82	44	12,924	15,327	6,629	69.43	.4922	3,263	422,455
83	45	12,924	15,327	6,504	80.52	.4526	2,944	425,399
84	46	12,924	15,327	6,382	93.38	.4103	2,618	428,017
85	47	12,924	15,327	6,261	108.30	.3659	2,291	430,308
86	48	12,924	15,327	6,143	125.60	.3199	1,965	432,273
87	49	12,924	15,327	6,027	145.66	.2733	1,647	433,921
88	50	12,924	15,327	5,913	168.92	.2272	1,343	435,264
89	51	12,924	15,327	5,802	195.91	.1827	1,060	436,324
90	52	12,924	15,327	5,692	227.20	.1412	804	437,127
91	53	12,924	15,327	5,585	263.49	.1040	581	437,708
92	54	12,924	15,327	5,480	305.58	.0722	396	438,104
93	55	12,924	15,327	5,376	354.39	.0466	251	438,354
94	56	12,924	15,327	5,275	411.00	.0275	145	438,499
95	57	12,924	15,327	5,175	476.66	.0144	74	438,573
96	58	12,924	15,327	5,078	552.79	.0064	33	438,606
97	59	12,924	15,327	4,982	641.10	.0023	11	438,617
98	60	12,924	15,327	4,888	743.50	.0006	3	438,620
99	61	12,924	15,327	4,796	862.27	.0001	0	438,621

§9.11 Calculating the Present Value of the Household Services of the Husband

The analysis of the economic value of the husband would be computed in exactly the same manner. In the fact situation of a 38-year-old father/husband the economic value would be computed using any of the above approaches. The following example will use the Douglass, Kenney, and Miller approach. The values of the father/husband services are presented in Table 9-2.

Table 9-17 The Household Value of the Father/Husband

Age	Period	1987 Value	1992 Value	Present Value	Sum	Probability Living	Adjusted: PV	Sum
38	0	3,967	4,899	4,899	4,899	.9975	4,887	4,887
39	1	3,967	4,899	4,807	9,706	.9949	4,782	9,669
40	2	4,094	5,056	4,867	14,574	.9921	4,829	14,498
41	3	4,094	5,056	4,775	19,349	.9892	4,724	19,222
42	4	4,094	5,056	4,685	24,034	.9861	4,620	23,842
43	5	4,094	5,056	4,597	28,631	.9828	4,518	28,360
44	6	4,094	5,056	4,510	33,141	.9792	4,416	32,776
45	7	4,111	5,077	4,443	37,585	.9753	4,334	37,110

Age	Period	1987 Value	1992 Value	Present Value	Sum	Probability Living	Adjusted: PV	Sum
46	8	4,111	5,077	4,360	41,944	.9711	4,233	41,343
47	9	4,111	5,077	4,277	46,222	.9665	4,134	45,477
48	10	4,111	5,077	4,197	50,418	.9615	4,035	49,512
49	11	4,111	5,077	4,117	54,536	.9562	3,937	53,449
50	12	4,111	5,077	4,040	58,576	.9503	3,839	57,288
51	13	4,111	5,077	3,964	62,539	.9439	3,741	61,030
52	14	4,111	5,077	3,889	66,428	.9369	3,643	64,673
53	15	4,111	5,077	3,815	70,243	.9290	3,545	68,218
54	16	4,111	5,077	3,743	73,987	.9204	3,445	71,663
55	17	4,216	5,207	3,767	77,753	.9109	3,431	75,094
56	18	4,216	5,207	3,696	81,449	.9006	3,328	78,423
57	19	4,216	5,207	3,626	85,075	.8893	3,224	81,647
58	20	4,216	5,207	3,557	88,632	.8770	3,120	84,767
59	21	4,216	5,207	3,490	92,122	.8637	3,015	87,781
60	22	4,216	5,207	3,424	95,547	.8493	2,908	90,690
61	23	4,216	5,207	3,360	98,906	.8339	2,802	93,492
62	24	4,216	5,207	3,296	102,203	.8176	2,695	96,187
63	25	4,216	5,207	3,234	105,437	.8003	2,588	98,775
64	26	4,216	5,207	3,173	108,610	.7820	2,481	101,256
65	27	4,216	5,207	3,113	111,723	.7626	2,374	103,631
66	28	4,216	5,207	3,055	114,778	.7420	2,267	105,897
67	29	4,216	5,207	2,997	117,775	.7202	2,159	108,056
68	30	4,216	5,207	2,940	120,715	.6972	2,050	110,106
69	31	4,216	5,207	2,885	123,600	.6730	1,941	112,047
70	32	3,002	3,708	2,015	125,616	.6475	1,305	113,352
71	33	2,041	2,521	1,344	126,960	.6207	834	114,187
72	34	2,041	2,521	1,319	128,279	.5927	782	114,968
73	35	2,041	2,521	1,294	129,573	.5635	729	115,698
74	36	2,041	2,521	1,270	130,843	.5333	677	116,375
75	37	2,041	2,521	1,246	132,089	.5021	625	117,000
76	38	2,041	2,521	1,222	133,311	.4700	574	117,575
77	39	2,041	2,521	1,199	134,510	.4373	524	118,099
78	40	2,041	2,521	1,177	135,687	.4041	475	118,575
79	41	2,041	2,521	1,154	136,841	.3706	428	119,002
80	42	1,186	1,465	658	137,499	.3358	221	119,223
81	43	1,186	1,465	646	138,145	.3001	194	119,417
82	44	1,186	1,465	634	138,779	.2640	167	119,584
83	45	1,186	1,465	622	139,400	.2280	142	119,726
84	46	1,186	1,465	610	140,010	.1928	118	119,844
85	47	671	829	339	140,349	.1591	54	119,898
86	48	671	829	332	140,681	.1276	42	119,940
87	49	671	829	326	141,007	.0990	32	119,972
88	50	671	829	320	141,326	.0738	24	119,996
89	51	671	829	314	141,640	.0526	16	120,012
90	52	671	829	308	141,948	.0354	11	120,023
91	53	671	829	302	142,250	.0223	7	120,030
92	54	671	829	296	142,546	.0130	4	120,034
93	55	671	829	291	142,837	.0068	2	120,036
94	56	671	829	285	143,122	.0032	1	120,037
95	57	671	829	280	143,402	.0012	0	120,037
96	58	671	829	275	143,676	.0004	0	120,037
97	59	671	829	269	143,946	.0001	0	120,037
98	60	671	829	264	144,210	.0000	0	120,037
99	61	671	829	259	144,469	.0000	0	120,037

As with the calculation of the household services of the wife, the 1987 dollar values were inflated to 1992 using the rate of change reported in the Consumer Price Index. These values were permitted to grow and be discounted at 4 and 6 per cent respectively. The economic values were then adjusted by the probability of living using the 1989 mortality table for white males. The mortality adjusted present value of a 38-year-old caucasian male's household services is $120,037.

§9.12   Taxes and Household Services

Household services are noncash services. To replace the services requires purchasing the services in the open market. This requires replacing services with after-tax dollars. To estimate the present value of household services in before-tax dollars, the present value is divided by one minus the marginal tax rate. If the family is in the 28 per cent tax bracket, then to replace $100 of household services requires the family to have $139 ($139 less 28 per cent for taxes leaves the $100 necessary to purchase the household services in the open market). The proper calculation of the present value of the household services requires valuing the household services at the before-tax equivalent.

The value of the housewife's household service was valued in a range from $280,237 to $482,559, while the husband's value of household services was $120,037. If the family is in the 28 per cent marginal tax rate then these range of values increase.

	Without Tax	With Tax
Housewife	$473,964	$658,283
	412,612	573,072
Husband	$120,037	166,718

Taxes increase the economic loss associated with the inability to perform household services. This analysis also ignores the requirement of Social Security payments if the individual is employed in the home for a period exceeding three months. Inclusion of the Social Security taxes would further increase the size of the loss.

§9.13   Summary

Household services are provided by husbands and wives. When household services are valued, the economist must decide what time frame the analysis will cover and what methodology will be employed. Should the analysis cover the time period until the person providing the services reaches age 65, or should the analysis run, with certainty, until the person providing the services reaches life expectancy, or until the person receiving the service reaches life expectancy? Should the analysis run, mortality-adjusted, to age 100? If so, should the mortality adjustment be made according to the person receiving or providing the service, or both?

The impact of mortality on the present value of the analysis can be affected by the selection of the mortality table. Government mortality tables do not contain the same bias that insurance company tables do. This means that using the government mortality tables would result in a lower present value than would using a life insurance mortality table.

Regardless of how the analysis is performed, the household services are an after-tax service. The value should be recalculated on a before-tax basis since the services are paid for after taxes are paid.

10 Life Care Plans

§10.01 Introduction

When people are disabled it may be necessary for them to alter their life style. Occasionally the injuries are such that the individual is unable to provide part or all of the care necessary for normal living. When the individual is unable to care for himself or herself a life care plan is constructed. This chapter will present a life care plan and explain how an economist uses the life care plan to compute the cost of the plan.

§10.02 What Is a Life Care Plan?

Life care plans are constructed by health care professionals, often a nurse. The plan is designed to outline what an individual will need throughout his or her lifetime in order to maintain the goal established in the life care plan, for example, independent living. It is the economist's responsibility to take the information in the life care plan and estimate the cost of funding the plan.

§10.03   An Example of a Life Care Plan[1]

Life Care Plan for: Name of the Client

Date of Birth: 6 years ago

Race: Caucasian

Sex: Female

Present Age: 6 years old

Diagnosis: Cerebral Palsy

Date of Disabling Condition: From Birth

SS#:

As a result of client's disabling condition some of the deficits client has are as follows:

1. Impaired physical mobility, physical stamina, and physical stability
2. Impaired activities of daily living, i.e., self-bathing/hygiene, self-dressing/grooming, self-feeding, self-toileting, etc.
3. Impaired visual motor skills
4. Impaired ability to communicate with oral language

To attain the goal of independent living (without supervision or assistance) at age 25 for client, the following are probably necessary:

1. Appropriate mobility equipment, augmentative communication aids, physical aids, home environment modification, and educational and vocational technological aids/equipment
2. On-going physical, occupational and speech/language therapies, educational technology consultations and psychometric testing
3. On-going medical evaluations, i.e., pediatric, neurology, orthopedic, etc. laboratory, radiology or diagnostic studies at discretion of medical specialists and orthopedic surgical procedure, and
4. Academic programs and vocational services to achieve maximum educational and vocational potential

Items listed for Life Care Plan are representative of needs although not all inclusive.

---

[1] This plan was developed by Marjorie Wright, R.N., C.R.R.N. while at the Menninger Return to Work Center in Topeka, Kansas. Ms. Wright is currently affiliated with Bud Langston and Associates also of Topeka. Permission to use the Life Care Plan was granted by Michael Drieling of the Menninger Return to Work Center.

Item or Service	Duration	Frequency	Purpose	Estimated Cost
PHYSICAL AIDS				
1. Manual pediatric	To full growth	5-7 years	Mobility aid	1,757
2. W/C Modifications	To full growth	As needed	Cross braces	170
			Seat upholstery	55
			Back upholstery	66
			Back post	35 each
			Rear side frame	150 each
			Foot rest hangers	60
			Front side frame	60 each
OR				
1. Amigo Mini	To full growth	5-7 years	Mobility aid	2,010
2. Basket platform	Lifetime	1		49
3. Basket tote bag	Lifetime	3-4 years		35
4. Life-all Trunk lift	Lifetime	1	Vehicle storage	795
5. 12v, Gel-cel Battery	To full growth	6-12 months		85
6. Front Wheel (1)	To full growth	4-5 years		80
7. Rear Wheels (2)	To full growth	4-5 years		96 each
8. Fiberglas seat	To full growth	4-5 years		75
9. Maintenance Hot Line		As needed	Toll Free Number	
OR				
Quickie Wheelchair with Lifetime Warranty				
1. Pediatric PowerW/C	To full growth	5-7 years	Mobility aid	5,795
2. Seat/back upholstery		1.5-2.5 yrs	Accommodate Growth	300
3. Power battery	To full growth	1-2 years		180
4. Airless rear tires	To full growth	2-3 years	Replacements	45 pair
5. Front tires (2)	To full growth	2-3 years	Replacements	35 each
6. Bearings front/rear	To full growth	2-5 years	Replacements	15-30 each
7. Power maintenance	To full growth	2 weeks	N/C	
8. Bearings & General Maintenance	To full growth	Every year		45
AND				
1. Ultralite Manual	At full growth	5-7 years	Mobility aid	1,694
2. Rear Tires	Lifetime	2-3 years	Replacement	45 each
3. Front Tires	Lifetime	2-3 years	Replacements	35 each
4. Bearings Front/Rear	Lifetime	2-5 years	Replacements	15-35
PHYSICAL AIDS				
1. Adjustable tap turner	Lifetime	1-2 years	Stove and Water faucets	30
2. Door knob opener	Lifetime	1-2 years		12

Item or Service	Duration	Frequency	Purpose	Estimated Cost
3. Key holder	Lifetime	1-2 years		5.25
4. Button loop	Lifetime	1-2 years	Button aid	12
5. Scoop bowl	Lifetime	1-2 years	Eating aid	4.50
6. Scoop plate	Lifetime	1-2 years	Eating aid	4.50
7. Curved spoon	Lifetime	1-2 years	Eating aid	6.50
8. Curved fork	Lifetime	1-2 years	Eating aid	6.50
9. Non-skid pads	Lifetime	1-2 years	Non-skid surface	10.50-17.65
10. Adjustable chair	To full growth	Each year	Posture stability	375-425

MEDICATIONS

Item or Service	Duration	Frequency	Purpose	Estimated Cost
1. Phenobarbital 60 mg	Lifetime	As needed	Anticonvulsant	$3.87/60

COMMUNICATION AIDS

Item or Service	Duration	Frequency	Purpose	Estimated Cost
1. Communication board/notebook Alphabet & Numbers	@Elementary school age	As needed	Supplement verbal skills Alphabet & Numbers	26-49 12.5-39
2. Augmentative communication	Lifetime	Unit update As needed	Augment impaired verbal skills	3,595
3. Accessories	Lifetime	Every year	Plastic screwdriver Battery charger Wire keyguard	1.35 30 100
4. Service contract	Lifetime	Every year	Covers electronics	175/yr
5. Software kit	Lifetime	As needed		125

MEDICAL/PSYCHOLOGICAL

Item or Service	Duration	Frequency	Purpose	Estimated Cost
1. General Medicine	To age 21	3-4/yr	Checkups	20-30
OR				
2. Pediatrician	To age 21	3-4/yr	Checkups	35 initial exam 27 each std visit
3. Lab tests	As long as anticonvulsant medication used	2-4/yr	Monitor Status	28 each
4. General Medicine	After 21	1-2/yr	Monitor	20-30/visit
5. Neurologist	Lifetime	Every 1-2 years	Manage seizure disorders	35-102
6. Radiology Proc	As needed	Every	Monitor	CAT Tech 155-315
CAT scan & MRI		1-2 yrs		CAT Prof 85-315 MRI Tech 600 MRI Prof 190

Item or Service	Duration	Frequency	Purpose	Estimated Cost
7. Diag Procedure	As needed	Every 1-2 years	Monitor	120
8. Orthopedist	Lifetime	2/yr	Monitor	25-55
9. Radiology	Lifetime	1-2/yr	Monitor	Both hips 35-55 Feet 45 Back 40
10. Orthopedic Surgery	1 time		As determined by Orthopedist	1,020
11. Hospital I-patient	1 time	3-5 days	For surgery	30+310/day 8.57/min op room 3.12/min recovery
12. Anesthesia	1 time	3-4 hours	For surgery	250/1 hr
13. Psychological	As needed	Intermittent		32-47/hr
14. Support group	Lifetime	1/mo		N/C

HOME ENVIRONMENT MODIFICATIONS

Item or Service	Duration	Frequency	Purpose	Estimated Cost
1. Grab bar/bathtub	Lifetime	1 time	Safety	24-25
2. Bathtub rail	Lifetime	1 time	Safety	27-36
3. Padded tub bench	Lifetime	1/7 yrs	Safety	133-166
4. Shower hose	Lifetime	1/7-10 yrs		24-48
5. Diverter valve	Lifetime	1		14-28
6. Toilet safety frame	Lifetime	1/7-10 yrs		48-50
7. Railings	Lifetime	1		320

PHYSICAL, OCCUPATIONAL,
SPEECH-LANGUAGE THERAPIES/EDUCATION TECHNOLOGY

Item or Service	Duration	Frequency	Purpose	Estimated Cost
1. Physical Therapy	To age 21	30-45 min 3x/wk 9 min		By School system
2. Physical Therapy	To age 21	30-45 min 3X/wk		$30/30 min
3. Occupational Ther	To age 21	30 min 2/wk 9 months		By School system
4. Occupational Ther	To age 21	30 min 2/wk		$20/30 min
5. Speech Language	To age 21	30 min 2/wk 9 months		By School system
6. Speech Language	To age 21	30 min 2/wk 3 months		$20/30 min
	Age 21-25	1-2 hr/yr	Monitor status	$20/30 min
7. Comprehensive Eval	To age 21	1/yr		500
8. Consultation	To age 21	2-3 hrs/2 yrs	Evaluate Program	$30/hr

Item or Service	Duration	Frequency	Purpose	Estimated Cost
EDUCATIONAL/VOCATIONAL				
1. Public Education	To age 21		Provided by Public School System	
2. Academic Tutoring	To age 21			
3. Vocational Eval	@ age 16			575
4. Vocational Counsel	@ age 16	2-3/mo		
	For 1 year	for 6 mo		55/hr
		1/mo next 6 mo	55/hr	
	Next 3 years	2/yr		55/hr
TECHNOLOGY AIDS/EQUIPMENT				
1. Apple II GS	Lifetime	4-5 yrs		2,500
2. Glare screen	Lifetime	As needed		39.92
3. Surge protector	Lifetime			19.95-29.95
4. Desk or table	Lifetime	1		150-160
5. Keyguard	Lifetime	4-5 yrs		97
6. Software	Lifetime	As needed		50
7. Maintenance	Lifetime	As needed		
8. Software	Lifetime	As needed		
9. Portable typewriter	To age 21	4-5 yrs		219
	To age 21	As needed	Ribbons	3.50 each
	To age 21	As needed	Batteries	27 for 5
	To age 21	As needed	Charger	18
10. Keyguard	To age 21	4-5 yrs		30-50
11. Lap top	After 21	4-5 yrs		698
12. Tape recorder	Lifetime	4-5 yrs	Education Aid	29.95-49.95
TRANSPORTATION ACCOMMODATIONS				
1. Driver's education	Provided by school			
2. Hand controls	Lifetime	5-7 yrs		350-450
ADDITIONAL EVALUATION/TRAINING FOR LICENSED DRIVER				
3. Initial evaluation	1 time	3-4 hours		96/hr
4. Behind wheel training	1 time	Five 1/2 hr sessions	48/1/2 hr	
5. Driving eval	1 time	1 time		96/hr
TRANSPORTATION				
1. Basic Ford conversion package	Lifetime	5-7 years		26,090-27,340
2. CB radio	Lifetime	7-10 years		39.95-179.95
3. Antenna	Lifetime	7-10 years		19.95-60

The economist must take each item in the life care plan and, when possible, estimate the present value of each item in order to estimate the cost of implementing the plan.

§10.04   Factors the Economist Must Consider

The calculation of the present value of the expenses requires the use of the present value formula. There are five variables that must be established for the present value to be calculated.

$$\text{Present Value of Future Income} = \$ \sum_{t=0}^{n} [(1+g)^t / (1+d)^t] * M_a$$

The five variables are:

"$" represents today's cost of the good or service being provided by the life care plan. The current dollar amount is provided by the life care plan.

"t" represents time. This indicates the length of time and the frequency the goods or services are needed. This too is provided by the life care plan.

"M_a" is the mortality adjustment. The appropriate mortality adjustment is determined by the race and sex of the individual for whom the life care plan is constructed.

"d" represents the interest or discount rate used in the analysis to reduce the future costs to present value.

"g" represents the growth rate in the costs and services required in the life care plan. There are several alternatives available to the economist.

Many of the items required in the life care plan are medically related. Accordingly, the economist may elect to use the Medical Price Index as the basis for estimating future costs. However, here are also several subcategorizes in the Medical Price Index that may be more appropriate.

Table 10-1 presents the various medical related price indices that may be used to estimate the annual rate of growth in costs. Also presented in the table is the length of time the index number covers and the average rate of change in the index.

Table 10-1   Medical Price Indices

Medical Care	1952-1992	6.31
Medical Care Commodities	1952-1992	3.94
Prescription Drugs	1952-1990	3.94
Non-Pres Drug & Supplies*	1988-1990	5.36

Medical Care Services	1952-1992	6.73
Professional Med Services*	1970-1990	7.46
Physician Services*	1970-1990	8.00
Dental Services*	1970-1990	7.14
Eye Services*	1987-1990	4.26
Hosp & Related Services	1952-1990	9.45
Consumer Price Index	1952-1992	4.30

*Rate of change is computed using the exponential growth rate.

The economist will have to determine which of the growth rates applies to the various components of the life care plan. For example, if prescription drugs are part of the life care plan then the appropriate growth in drug prices is 3.78%. If transportation costs are considered then the appropriate rate of increase in the cost of the van may be best reflected by the historic rate of change in the Consumer Price Index.

§10.05   Applying Growth Rates to the Life Care Plan

The appropriate growth rate of each component of the life care plan is established. Once this is done the present value factor and the present value of each component is computed.

The first item on the life care plan is a manual pediatric wheelchair. It is needed now and will be needed until the age of full growth. The age of full growth is usually 14. The wheelchair will have to be replaced every 5 to 7 years and has a current cost of $1,757.

The fact that there is uncertainty about when the wheelchair must be replaced means there will be a high and low value to the life care plan. The low value means the wheelchair will be replaced in 7 years and the high value will require replacing the chair in 5 years.

In a similar fashion high and low values are established when there is a range of costs and a range of occurrences. For example, the category under Medical/Psychological has "general medicine." The patient needs to visit 3 to 4 times per year with a cost of $20 to $30 per visit. The low cost is $60 per year, three visits at $20 per visit while the high cost is $120, four visits at $30 per visit.

The calculation of life care expenses is established for each item. Table 10-2 presents the calculation of the low present value of the cost of the van with the conversion package. The van needs to be replaced every 5 to 7 years. The low cost of the van is $26,090 and price increases are expected to parallel the Consumer Price Index.

Table 10-2   Present Value of a Conversion Van

Growth Rate	4.30%
Interest Rate	6.05%
Price of the Van	$27,340

Age	Period	Present Value	Sum	Probability of Living	Adjusted PV	Sum
6	0	27,340	27,340	.9998	27,334	27,334
7	1		27,340	.9996	0	27,334
8	2		27,340	.9994	0	27,334
9	3		27,340	.9993	0	27,334
10	4		27,340	.9992	0	27,334
11	5	25,157	52,497	.9990	25,133	52,467
12	6		52,497	.9989	0	52,467
13	7		52,497	.9986	0	52,467
14	8		52,497	.9983	0	52,467
15	9		52,497	.9980	0	52,467
16	10	23,149	75,647	.9975	23,091	75,558
17	11		75,647	.9969	0	75,558
18	12		75,647	.9964	0	75,558
19	13		75,647	.9959	0	75,558
20	14		75,647	.9954	0	75,558
21	15	21,301	96,948	.9949	21,192	96,750
22	16		96,948	.9944	0	96,750
23	17		96,948	.9940	0	96,750
24	18		96,948	.9935	0	96,750
25	19		96,948	.9930	0	96,750
26	20	19,601	116,548	.9925	19,453	116,203
27	21		116,548	.9919	0	116,203
28	22		116,548	.9914	0	116,203
29	23		116,548	.9908	0	116,203
30	24		116,548	.9902	0	116,203
31	25	18,036	134,584	.9895	17,847	134,050
32	26		134,584	.9888	0	134,050
33	27		134,584	.9881	0	134,050
34	28		134,584	.9873	0	134,050
35	29		134,584	.9866	0	134,050
36	30	16,596	151,181	.9857	16,359	150,409
37	31		151,181	.9848	0	150,409
38	32		151,181	.9838	0	150,409

Age	Period	Present Value	Sum	Probability of Living	Adjusted PV	Sum
39	33		151,181	.9828	0	150,409
40	34		151,181	.9816	0	150,409
41	35	15,271	166,452	.9803	14,970	165,379
42	36		166,452	.9789	0	165,379
43	37		166,452	.9773	0	165,379
44	38		166,452	.9756	0	165,379
45	39		166,452	.9738	0	165,379
46	40	14,052	180,504	.9718	13,655	179,034
47	41		180,504	.9695	0	179,034
48	42		180,504	.9671	0	179,034
49	43		180,504	.9643	0	179,034
50	44		180,504	.9613	0	179,034
51	45	12,930	193,434	.9579	12,386	191,420
52	46		193,434	.9542	0	191,420
53	47		193,434	.9500	0	191,420
54	48		193,434	.9455	0	191,420
55	49		193,434	.9406	0	191,420
56	50	11,898	205,333	.9351	11,127	202,547
57	51		205,333	.9292	0	202,547
58	52		205,333	.9227	0	202,547
59	53		205,333	.9157	0	202,547
60	54		205,333	.9080	0	202,547
61	55	10,948	216,281	.8997	9,850	212,397
62	56		216,281	.8907	0	212,397
63	57		216,281	.8809	0	212,397
64	58		216,281	.8705	0	212,397
65	59		216,281	.8593	0	212,397
66	60	10,074	226,355	.8473	8,536	220,932
67	61		226,355	.8343	0	220,932
68	62		226,355	.8203	0	220,932
69	63		226,355	.8052	0	220,932
70	64		226,355	.7891	0	220,932
71	65	9,270	235,625	.7718	7,155	228,087
72	66		235,625	.7532	0	228,087
73	67		235,625	.7334	0	228,087
74	68		235,625	.7122	0	228,087
75	69		235,625	.6897	0	228,087
76	70	8,530	244,155	.6657	5,678	233,765
77	71		244,155	.6401	0	233,765
78	72		244,155	.6129	0	233,765
79	73		244,155	.5842	0	233,765

Age	Period	Present Value	Sum	Probability of Living	Adjusted PV	Sum
80	74		244,155	.5541	0	233,765
81	75	7,849	252,005	.5209	4,089	237,854
82	76		252,005	.4847	0	237,854
83	77		252,005	.4457	0	237,854
84	78		252,005	.4041	0	237,854
85	79		252,005	.3603	0	237,854
86	80	7,223	259,227	.3151	2,276	240,129
87	81		259,227	.2692	0	240,129
88	82		259,227	.2237	0	240,129
89	83		259,227	.1799	0	240,129
90	84		259,227	.1390	0	240,129
91	85	6,646	265,873	.1024	680	240,810
92	86		265,873	.0711	0	240,810
93	87		265,873	.0459	0	240,810
94	88		265,873	.0270	0	240,810
95	89		265,873	.0141	0	240,810
96	90	6,115	271,989	.0063	39	240,848
97	91		271,989	.0023	0	240,848
98	92		271,989	.0006	0	240,848
99	93		271,989	.0001	0	240,848

Today's cost of the van is $27,340. The van needs to be replaced in five years. The present value of replacing the van in five years is $25,157. The table presents the present value of replacing the van every five years. The column headed adjusted present value is the mortality adjusted cost of the van. The mortality adjustment is the probability of living each successive year. The mortality adjusted present value of the cost of the van is $240,848. It is this value that will appear as the high cost of replacing the van.

In a similar fashion the cost of the van can be computed if the van is replaced every seventh year. The mortality adjusted present value of replacing the van is $168,020.

§10.06 The Cost of the Life Care Plan

The cost of the life care plan is presented in Table 10-3.

Table 10-3   The Cost of the Life Care Plan

Item or Service	Frequency	Cost	Rate	High	Low
PHYSICAL AIDS					
1. Manual pediatric	5-7 years*	1,757	5.36	6,522	3,315
	As needed	170			
	As needed	55			
	As needed	66			
	As needed	35 each			
	As needed	150 each			
	As needed	60			
	As needed	60 each			

*to age of full growth (age 14)

OR

1. Amigo Mini*	5-7 years	2,010	5.36	3,966	3,927
2. Basket platform	1	49		49	49
3. Basket tote bag	3-4 years	35	5.36	103	69
4. Life-all trunk lift	1	795		795	795
5. 12v, Gel-cel battery	6-12 months	85	5.36	1,328	664
6. Front wheel (1)	4-5 years	80	5.36	158	157
7. Rear wheels (2)	4-5 years	96 each	5.36	379	378
8. Fiberglas seat	4-5 years	75	5.36	148	147
9. Maintenance hot line as needed toll free number				6,926	6,186

*to age of full growth (age 14)

OR

Quickie Wheelchair with Lifetime Warranty

1. Pediatric powerW.C*	5-7 years	5,795	5.36	11,398	11,323
2. Seat/back upholstery	1-2 yrs	300	5.36	2,344	1,176
3. Power battery	1-2 years	180	5.36	1,406	705
4. Airless rear tires	2-3 years	45 pair	5.36	353	265
5. Front tires (2)	2-3 years	35 each	5.36	274	206
6. Bearings front rear	2-5 years	15-30 each	5.36	236	59
7. Power maintenance	2 weeks	N/C			
8. Bearings & general maintenance	Every year	45	4.30	.339	339

*to age of full growth (age 14)

				16,350	14,073

AND

1. Ultralite manual*	5-7 years	1,694	5.36	17,540	12,761
2. Rear tires	2-3 years	45 each	5.36	2,265	1,525
3. Front tires	2-3 years	35 each	5.36	1,762	1,186

Item or Service	Frequency	Cost	Rate	High	Low
4. Bearings front/rear	2-5 years	15-35	5.36	3,524	621
*Beginning at the age of full growth (age 14)				25,091	16,093

PHYSICAL AIDS

Item or Service	Frequency	Cost	Rate	High	Low
1. Adjustable tap	1-2 years	30	5.36	1,730	872
2. Door knob opener	1-2 years	12	5.36	692	349
3. Key holder	1-2 years	5.25	5.36	303	152
4. Button loop	1-2 years	12	5.36	692	349
5. Scoop bowl	1-2 years	4.50	5.36	260	131
6. Scoop plate	1-2 years	4.50	5.36	260	131
7. Curved spoon	1-2 years	6.50	5.36	375	189
8. Curved fork	1-2 years	6.50	5.36	375	189
9. Non-skid pads	1-2 years	10.50-17.65	5.36	1,018	305
10. Adjustable chair	Each year	375-425	5.36	24,513	21,629
				30,218	24,296

MEDICATIONS

Item or Service	Frequency	Cost	Rate	High	Low
1. Phenobarbital 60 mg	As needed	$3.87/60			

COMMUNICATION AIDS

Item or Service	Frequency	Cost	Rate	High	Low
1. Communication	Supplement	26-49	4.30		
board/notebook	As needed	verbal skills			
Alphabet & Numbers		12.5-39	4.30		
2. Augmentative		3,595	4.30		
communication	As needed				
3. Accessories	1 time	1.35	4.30	1	1
		30	4.30	30	30
		100	4.30	100	100
4. Service contract	Every year	175/yr	4.30	7,352	7,352
5. Software kit	As needed	125	4.30		
				7,483	3,483

MEDICAL/PSYCHOLOGICAL

Item or Service	Frequency	Cost	Rate	High	Low
1. General medicine	3-4/yr	20-30	8.00	1,563	784
OR					
2. Pediatrician	3-4/yr	35 initial exam	8.00	35	35
		27 each std visit	8.00	1,407	1,058
				1,442	1,093

AND

Item or Service	Frequency	Cost	Rate	High	Low
3. Lab tests	2-4/yr	28 each	7.46	1,735	878
4. General medicine	1-2/yr	20-30/visit	8.00	4,659	1,558
5. Neurologist	1-2 yrs	35-102	8.00	15,841	2,727
6. Radiology proc	1-2 yrs	155-315	7.46	39,041	9,603

Item or Service	Frequency	Cost	Rate	High	Low
CAT scan & MRI		85-165	7.46	24,450	5,266
		600	7.46	74,363	74,363
		190	7.46	23,548	23,548
7. Diag procedure	1-2 years	120	7.46	14,873	7,434
8. Orthopedist	2/yr	25-55	8.00	17,084	7,765
9. Radiology	1-2/yr	Both hips 35-50	7.46	6,147	2,168
		Feet 45	7.46	5,577	2,788
		Back 40	7.46	4,958	2,478
10. Orthopedic surgery	1 time	1,020			
11. Hospital I-patient	1 time	304-310/day			
		8.57/min op room			
		3.12/min recovery			
12. Anesthesia	3-4 hours	250/1 hr			
13. Psychological	Intermittent	32-47/hr	8.00		
14. Support group	1/mo	N/C			
				232,276	140,576

HOME ENVIRONMENT MODIFICATIONS

1. Grab bar/bathtub	1 time	24-25		25	24
2. Bathtub rail	1 time	27-36		36	27
3. Padded tub bench	1/7 yrs	133-166	4.30	1,069	620
4. Shower hose	1/7-10 yrs	24-48	4.30	309	112
5. Diverter valve	1	14-28		28	28
6. Toilet safety frame	1/7-10 yrs	48-50	4.30	322	234
7. Railings	1	320		320	320
				2,110	1,365

PHYSICAL, OCCUPATIONAL,
SPEECH-LANGUAGE THERAPIES/EDUCATION TECHNOLOGY*

1. Physical Therapy	30-45 min				
	By School system				
2. Physical Therapy	30-45 min	$30/30 min	7.46	19,263	19,263
3. Occupational Ther3	0 min 2/wk				
	By School system				
4. Occupational Ther	30 min 2/wk	$20/30 min	7.46	8,561	8,561
5. Speech Language	30 min 2/wk				
	By School system				
6. Speech Language	30 min 2/wk	$20/30 min	7.46	8,561	8,561
	1-2 hr/yr	$20/30 min	7.46	988	329
7. Comprehensive Eval	1/yr	1,000	7.46	16,461	16,461
8. Consultation	2-3 hrs/2 yrs	$30/hr	7.46	1,482	988
*To age 21				55,636	54,163

EDUCATIONAL/VOCATIONAL

1. Public Education   Provided by Public School System
2. Academic Tutoring   To age 21

Item or Service	Frequency	Cost	Rate	High	Low
3. Vocational Eval	@ age 16	575	4.30	486	486
4. Vocational Counsel	2-3/mo				
	for 6 mo	55/hr	4.30	139	93
	1/mo next 6 mo	55/hr	4.30	279	279
	2/yr for 3 yrs	55/hr	4.30	269	269
				1,183	1,137

TECHNOLOGY AIDS/EQUIPMENT

1. Apple II GS	4-5 yrs	2,500	4.30	27,210	24,323
2. Glare screen	As needed	39.95		40	40
3. Surge protector		19.95-29.95			
4. Desk or table	1 time	150-160		160	150
5. Keyguard	4-5 yrs	97	4.30	1,052	944
6. Software	As needed	50		50	50
7. Maintenance	As needed				
8. Software	As needed				
9. Portable typewriter	4-5 yrs	219	4.30	2,384	2,130
	As needed	3.50 each			
	As needed	27 for 5			
	As needed	18			
10. Keyguard	4-5 yrs	30-50	4.30	544	292
11. Lap top	4-5 yrs	698	4.30	7,597	6,791
12. Tape recorder	4-5 yrs	29.95-49.95	4.30	544	291
				39,581	34,981

TRANSPORTATION ACCOMMODATIONS

1. Driver's education	Provided by school				
2. Hand controls	5-7 years	350-450	4.30	4,354	3,405

ADDITIONAL EVALUATION/TRAINING FOR LICENSED DRIVER

3. Initial evaluation	3-4 hours	96/hr	4.30	324	243
4. Behind wheel training	5 1/2 hr sess	48/session	4.30	696	696
5. Driving eval	1 time	96/hr	4.30	81	81
				1,101	1,020

TRANSPORTATION

1. Basic Ford conversion
   package   5-7 years   26,090-27,340   4.30   265,991   168,020
2. CB radio   7-10 years   39.95-179.95   4.30   1,159   187
3. Antenna   7-10 years   19.95-60   4.30   386   93
                                                             _____   _____
                                                              242,393   169,320

The total cost of the life care plan is summarized in Table 10-4.

Table 10-4   Cost of Life Care Plan

Category		High Cost	Low Cost
PHYSICAL AIDS			
	Manual wheelchair	6,522	3,315
or	Amigo Mini	6,926	6,186
or	Quickie Wheelchair	16,350	14,073
AND			
	Ultralite @ age 14	25,091	16,093
PHYSICAL AIDS		30,218	24,296
MEDICATIONS			
COMMUNICATION AIDS		7,483	3,483
MEDICAL/PSYCHOLOGICAL			
	General Medicine	1,563	784
or	Pediatrician	1,442	1,093
AND		232,276	140,576
HOME ENVIRONMENT MODIFICATIONS		2,110	1,365
PHYSICAL, OCCUPATIONAL,		55,636	54,163
EDUCATIONAL/VOCATIONAL		1,183	1,137
TECHNOLOGY AIDS/EQUIPMENT		39,581	34,981
TRANSPORTATION ACCOMMODATIONS		4,354	3,405
TRAINING FOR LICENSED DRIVER		1,101	1,020
TRANSPORTATION		242,393	169,320

The cost of the life care plan ranges from a low of $453,938 to a high of $659,339. What the actual cost will be depends on the type of wheelchair, the type of medical care, and the type of transportation. In addition to the costs outlined in the life care plan the following costs were not included: any item listed "as needed," any surgery and hospital care, anesthesia, and psychological care, any mileage costs associated with care, and any additional insurance costs resulting from the injury. The other factor that makes many life care plans so costly but was not included in this plan is the cost of care. For example, if the cost of care were required at $100 per day, the cost of care of this person's life would be an additional $1,521,261. But depending on the nature of the care facility it may be possible to deduct the transportation costs, the medical costs, and the therapy costs.

In addition to the costs the analysis has not addressed any reduction in earnings resulting from the injury. Additionally no consideration was given for a diminished ability to enjoy life.

§10.07 Summary

When the present value of a life care plan is computed, the present value of each component is computed independently. Both the high and the low values are computed using a mortality adjustment. Care must be taken to avoid double counting. For example, in the category "durable medical equipment" there is an option between purchasing the manual pediatric wheelchair or the Amigo mini wheelchair.

It is to be noted that there are two parties involved in the construction of the life care plan. The economist's work and testimony, is based on the work of the person who constructs the life care plan. Typically the cost of each of the broad categories, those presented in Table 10-4, are presented to the jury. It may be necessary to present how one of the totals is reached. In this manner the jury is presented with each of the components of the plan and is not so overwhelmed with one very large present value figure.

11

Hedonics

§11.01 Introduction

The term *hedonics* is defined as "pertaining to or marked by pleasure; the study of pleasant and unpleasant sensations." In personal injury and death cases hedonics has come to be understood as the economic value attributed to the joy of living. In personal injury and death cases, hedonics refers to the losses associated with the pleasure of life. Loss can result from pain but can also result from the cessation of pleasure.

A great deal has been written in the area of hedonic losses. One of the best sources of information is the Journal of Forensic Economics Volume III, Number 3. The entire edition is devoted to the question of hedonics. Another excellent source of information is *Economic/Hedonic Damages* by Brookshire and Smith.[1]

---

[1] Michael L. Brookshire & Stan V. Smith, Economic/Hedonic Damages: The Practice Book for Plaintiff and Defense Attorneys (1990).

§11.02   Why Consider Hedonics?

Life is worth living, and from this life we receive pleasure. The pleasure may be in watching our children grow, achieve, and eventually leave home or from listening to music, watching television, or visiting friends.

If someone is deprived of the ability to enjoy any of the pleasures of life, that person has suffered a loss. One can also be deprived of the joys of life if the ability to experience pain is removed. While appearing circuitous, the loss of the ability to enjoy pain is loss to the enjoyment of life. With the death of a friend, we feel a loss. Recognizing the loss and feeling the pain is one of the joys of life.

Life has both pleasure and pain and when the ability to experience either is removed, a loss is suffered. That a loss exists is not argued. What is argued is whether or not the loss is measurable. If measurable, can the loss be translated to dollars, how may dollars?

A good case can be made that a loss can not be measured. For example, the loss of sight is immeasurable as is the loss of hearing, walking, talking, smelling. However, if the loss is immeasurable, does it follow that some attempt to compensate the injured party should not be made? Obviously not. If the ability to earn a living is impaired, a person may attempt redress if such a disability is the result of an other's act, but should an attempt to compensate the injured party be limited to the impact such an injury has on the ability to earn a living or should the compensation extend to the pleasure of life outside the workplace?

Many people receive satisfaction from being able to work. This satisfaction goes beyond the monetary compensation received from employment. An injury may reduce or eliminate the ability to earn from employment and may eliminate the added satisfaction from the intrinsic joys of job fulfillment.

The inclusion of hedonics in determining monetary damages has significant implications in other areas of the economy. Hedonics could greatly increase monetary recovery to a plaintiff. Thus, while a plaintiff may stand to benefit, so would the plaintiff's attorney. On the defense side, the defense attorney might argue that hedonic losses should not be considered in an award, however, the defense attorney also benefits from the time spent preparing to argue against the inclusion of hedonics.

As a consideration for liability carriers, the inclusion of hedonic losses would increase the exposure to the carriers. As the exposure increases, the premiums would also increase. How much the exposure increases and how much the losses might increase is not known. But the uncertainty associated with increased exposure and possible increased losses are not the reasons to include or exclude hedonic considerations from the courtroom.

§11.03   Pleasures of Life versus Value of Life

The question of hedonics also leads to the problem of trying to distinguish between the value of life and the deprivation of the pleasure of life. Some might argue there is no difference between the value of life and the pleasure of life. Others would argue the two are not at all alike. If a person loses a life, there is also a termination of the pleasure of living. If a person is injured, the pleasure of living has been altered but life has not been terminated.

Can the removal of the pleasure of living be so great that it is preferable not to be alive at all? These are the questions concerning euthanasia and the right to die. If euthanasia is the action of inducing a painless death of a person for reasons assumed to be merciful, the act of placing a person in a position where euthanasia is contemplated is the act of depriving a person of the pleasures of life.

The attempt to value life is based on different approaches, willingness to pay, wage risk, contingent valuation, consumer market studies and earnings at the time of the accident. These approaches do not attempt to measure the pleasure of living but rather attempt to place a value on life itself. And that is the critical point in the discussion of hedonics. Is the evaluation based on an estimate of the value of life or on the joy associated with living?

§11.04   Hedonic Loss, Lost Income, Pain, and Suffering

Economists are identifying different types of losses associated with the injured person: (1) loss of economic compensation associated with earnings and fringe benefits; (2) loss of in-kind compensation such as household services, gardening, etc.; (3) loss of the ability to enjoy the pleasures of living; (4) loss associated with pain and suffering as distinct from the cessation of pleasure; and (5) the increase in expenses that result from the injury.

There is an ongoing debate as to whether loss resulting from pain and suffering is different from loss of the pleasure of life. The two are entwined at times and separate at others. For example, a person is disfigured in an accident. The accident imposes physical pain on the individual. At the same time, family members are uncomfortable viewing the injured person and do not visit. Consequently, the injured party suffers the pain associated with the accident and the additional pain of being deprived of the pleasure of seeing family members. Are these two losses separate and distinct?

It should be noted that in addition to the losses that result from an injury, there may be increased expenses. These expenses may range from increased use of nonprescription drugs to round-the-clock nursing care. This is not treated as a loss of economic benefits, but as an increase in costs.

§11.05   The Three Parts for Estimating Hedonic Loss

There are three components in the hedonic value estimate. The first component establishing the statistical value of life. There are studies that become the basis for the statistical value of life model. The second component is the degree of suffering imposed on the injured party. This component is usually evaluated by a psychologist. The second component establishes the degree of the loss. The third component is the economist's work and is the combining of the first two in order to establish a value. Note that the economist providing the report has removed himself or herself from the responsibility of information contained in the first two components.

§11.06 —Valuing Life: Component Number One

Economist's try to estimate the value of life through several different approaches. These include "willingness to pay" studies which are broken down into the following categories: (1) wage risk studies; (2) contingent valuation studies, and (3) consumer market studies.[2] A second approach to estimating hedonic values utilizes the earnings at the time of the accident.

The consumer market approach to hedonic value attempts to determine how much a cross-section of people will pay for a reduction in the probability of death. For example, if there is a group of 1 million people and each member of the group is willing to pay $10 in order to reduce probability of dying by 10 deaths per one million people then the value of one life is $1,000,000. Each of the one million people spending $10 each puts $10 million in the fund. Since ten fewer deaths occur, each life is valued at $1,000,000.

Wage risk studies estimate the wage premium paid for performing jobs that have a greater risk of death associated with the job. If two jobs are identical except that one job has a greater degree of risk of death than the other a wage premium is usually paid. Suppose the premium paid is $200 per year to each of 5,000 workers. If the risk of death is increased by 1 in 1,000, then the statistical value of the life is $1,000,000. Since no two jobs are identical in every way, regression analysis is used with the wage data to explain other factors. In other words, the risk of death factor can be isolated and identified.[3]

Contingent valuation studies and consumer market studies are also employed to give estimates to the value of life. An explanation of these concepts can be found in the Fisher, Chestnut, and Violette study. Their study indicated the value of life ranged from $1.6 million to $8.5 million in 1986 dollars.

Ted R. Miller estimates the statistical value of life to range from $1.5 million to $2.8 million. This is in 1988 dollars and is for a 38-year-old person with a 39-year life expectancy.[4] Miller goes on to state that "The value of pain, suffering, and lost enjoyment of life, which some courts have labeled hedonic damages, can be separated from this value."[5] Miller goes on to suggest that from this value, the hedonic damages, one should subtract the after-tax earnings, the value of household production, and the value of financial security.[6]

---

[2] Ann Fisher, Lauraine G. Chestnut & Daniel M. Violette, *The Value of Reducing Risks of Death: A Note on New Evidence*, 8, No 1 J Poly Analysis & Mgmt 88-100 (Winter 1989).

[3] *Id.*

[4] Ted R. Miller, *The Plausible Range for the Value of Life - Red Herrings Among the Mackerel*, III, No 3 J Forensic Econs 17-39 (Fall 1990).

[5] *Id.*

[6] *Id.*

There is some disagreement about the validity of subtracting anything from the statistical value of life. If one were to subtract the wages of a very highly paid individual it is possible the difference would be zero or negative. It seems more appropriate to establish the statistical value of life, and in the context of the lifetime the other components add value, i.e., income and household services. It should also be noted that the joy of living is not what is being addressed, rather the statistical value of life is being addressed.

Perhaps an analogy can be drawn from the parable of the talents from the Book of Matthew. We can view each person as having a statistical value of life. The value may be increased or decreased by other factors. Thus, the value associated with life consists of "a statistical value of life," and this is independent of the economic activity of life and also independent of the joy associated with living that life.

As an example consider two people having the same quantity and quality of paint. Both paint a picture. The value of the painting is independent of the amount of paint used, and the joy of painting the picture is in addition to the other values. This can be true of life also. The life has a certain statistical value, but what one does with the life is independent of life itself, and the joy of living the life is yet another consideration.

Now the economist must decide how to allocate the statistical value of life over the life of an individual. The Miller study indicated a value of $2.2 million for a person with a life expectancy of 39 years. If the value were equally divided by the life expectancy then each year would have a value of $56,410. This amount becomes the base amount of dollars used in the analysis. This is the base dollar amount and is used in the present value formula. Recall that the present value formula is:

$$\text{Present Value of Future Income} = \$ \sum_{t=0}^{n} * M * (1+g)^t / (1+d)^t]$$

The dollar value in the formula is the $56,410. As with any present value analysis the question of growth rate, discount rate, and time must be considered. In the following Table, 11-1, is the present statistical value of the life using various growth and discount rates. The time frame is the 39-year life expectancy.

Table 11-1 Present Value of $54,610 for 39 Years At Various Growth and Discount Rates

Year	Growth = 0% Discount = 0%		Growth = 2% Discount = 4%		Growth = 4% Discount = 6%	
	Present Value	Sum	Present Value	Sum	Present Value	Sum
0	56,410	56,410	56,410	56,410	56,410	56,410
1	56,410	112,820	55,325	111,735	55,346	111,756
2	56,410	169,230	54,261	165,996	54,301	166,057

Year	Present Value	Sum	Present Value	Sum	Present Value	Sum
3	56,410	225,640	53,218	219,214	53,277	219,334
4	56,410	282,050	52,194	271,409	52,272	271,606
5	56,410	338,460	51,191	322,599	51,285	322,891
6	56,410	394,870	50,206	372,805	50,318	373,209
7	56,410	451,280	49,241	422,046	49,368	422,577
8	56,410	507,690	48,294	470,340	48,437	471,014
9	56,410	564,100	47,365	517,705	47,523	518,537
10	56,410	620,510	46,454	564,159	46,626	565,163
11	56,410	676,920	45,561	609,720	45,747	610,910
12	56,410	733,330	44,685	654,404	44,883	655,793
13	56,410	789,740	43,825	698,230	44,037	699,830
14	56,410	846,150	42,983	741,212	43,206	743,035
15	56,410	902,560	42,156	783,368	42,390	785,426
16	56,410	958,970	41,345	824,713	41,591	827,016
17	56,410	1,015,380	40,550	865,263	40,806	867,822
18	56,410	1,071,790	39,770	905,034	40,036	907,858
19	56,410	1,128,200	39,006	944,039	39,281	947,139
20	56,410	1,184,610	38,255	982,295	38,539	985,678
21	56,410	1,241,020	37,520	1,019,814	37,812	1,023,491
22	56,410	1,297,430	36,798	1,056,612	37,099	1,060,589
23	56,410	1,353,840	36,091	1,092,703	36,399	1,096,988
24	56,410	1,410,250	35,396	1,128,100	35,712	1,132,700
25	56,410	1,466,660	34,716	1,162,815	35,038	1,167,739
26	56,410	1,523,070	34,048	1,196,863	34,377	1,202,116
27	56,410	1,579,480	33,393	1,230,257	33,729	1,235,844
28	56,410	1,635,890	32,751	1,263,008	33,092	1,268,937
29	56,410	1,692,300	32,121	1,295,129	32,468	1,301,404
30	56,410	1,748,710	31,504	1,326,633	31,855	1,333,260
31	56,410	1,805,120	30,898	1,357,531	31,254	1,364,514
32	56,410	1,861,530	30,304	1,387,835	30,664	1,395,178
33	56,410	1,917,940	29,721	1,417,555	30,086	1,425,264
34	56,410	1,974,350	29,149	1,446,705	29,518	1,454,782
35	56,410	2,030,760	28,589	1,475,294	28,961	1,483,744
36	56,410	2,087,170	28,039	1,503,332	28,415	1,512,158
37	56,410	2,143,580	27,500	1,530,832	27,879	1,540,037
38	56,410	2,199,990	26,971	1,557,803	27,353	1,567,390

The table indicates that the present value of a statistical life over the next 39 years, this year and 38 future years, is $2,199,990 if the growth rate and discount rate are both zero. The present value decreases as the growth and discount rate increase.

If a person has a shorter life expectancy then the present value would be higher. Conversely, if the life expectancy is shorter then the statistical value of the life would be lower. Using this approach, the present value of the statistical value of life for each age can be computed. The base dollar amount is $56,410. The younger the person is the higher will be the statistical value of the life while the older the person is, the lower will be the statistical value of the life.

The underlying assumptions are that a 38-year-old has a life expectancy of 39 years and those 39 years have a statistical value of $2.2 million, or $56,410 per year. Tables 11-2 and 11-3 present the present value of the statistical life for white males, white females, black males, and black females using growth and discount rates of zero.

Table 11-2 The Present Value of the Statistical Life for White Males and Females Ages 0 to 65 In 1988 Dollars

Age	White Male Life Expectancy	White Male Present Value	White Female Life Expectancy	White Female Present Value
0	72.7	$4,101,007	79.2	4,467,672
1	72.3	4,078,443	78.8	4,445,108
2	71.4	4,027,674	77.8	4,388,698
3	70.4	3,971,264	76.9	4,337,929
4	69.5	3,920,495	75.9	4,281,519
5	68.5	3,864,085	74.9	4,225,109
6	67.5	3,807,675	73.9	4,168,699
7	66.5	3,751,265	73	4,117,930
8	65.5	3,694,855	72	4,061,520
9	64.5	3,638,445	71	4,005,110
10	63.6	3,587,676	70	3,948,700
11	62.6	3,531,266	69	3,892,290
12	61.6	3,474,856	68	3,835,880
13	60.6	3,418,446	67	3,779,470
14	59.6	3,362,036	66	3,723,060
15	58.6	3,305,626	65.1	3,672,291
16	57.7	3,254,857	64.1	3,615,881
17	56.8	3,204,088	63.1	3,559,471
18	55.8	3,147,678	62.1	3,503,061
19	54.9	3,096,909	61.2	3,452,292
20	54	3,046,140	60.2	3,395,882
21	53	2,989,730	59.2	3,339,472
22	52.1	2,938,961	58.3	3,288,703
23	51.2	2,888,192	57.3	3,232,293

| | White Male | | White Female | |
| | Life | Present | Life | Present |
Age	Expectancy	Value	Expectancy	Value
24	50.3	2,837,423	56.3	3,175,883
25	49.4	2,786,654	55.3	3,119,473
26	48.4	2,730,244	54.4	3,068,704
27	47.5	2,679,475	53.4	3,012,294
28	46.6	2,628,706	52.4	2,955,884
29	45.7	2,577,937	51.5	2,905,115
30	44.7	2,521,527	50.5	2,848,705
31	43.8	2,470,758	49.5	2,792,295
32	42.9	2,419,989	48.6	2,741,526
33	42	2,369,220	47.6	2,685,116
34	41	2,312,810	46.6	2,628,706
35	40.1	2,262,041	45.7	2,577,937
36	39.2	2,211,272	44.7	2,521,527
37	38.3	2,160,503	43.7	2,465,117
38	37.4	2,109,734	42.8	2,414,348
39	36.5	2,058,965	41.8	2,357,938
40	35.6	2,008,196	40.9	2,307,169
41	34.7	1,957,427	39.9	2,250,759
42	33.8	1,906,658	39	2,199,990
43	32.9	1,855,889	38	2,143,580
44	32	1,805,120	37.1	2,092,811
45	31.1	1,754,351	36.1	2,036,401
46	30.2	1,703,582	35.2	1,985,632
47	29.3	1,652,813	34.3	1,934,863
48	28.4	1,602,044	33.4	1,884,094
49	27.5	1,551,275	32.4	1,827,684
50	26.7	1,506,147	31.5	1,776,915
51	25.8	1,455,378	30.6	1,726,146
52	25	1,410,250	29.7	1,675,377
53	24.2	1,365,122	28.8	1,624,608
54	23.3	1,314,353	28	1,579,480
55	22.5	1,269,225	27.1	1,528,711
56	21.7	1,224,097	26.2	1,477,942
57	21	1,184,610	25.4	1,432,814
58	20.2	1,139,482	24.6	1,387,686
59	19.4	1,094,354	23.7	1,336,917
60	18.7	1,054,867	22.9	1,291,789
61	18	1,015,380	22.1	1,246,661

	White Male		White Female	
Age	Life Expectancy	Present Value	Life Expectancy	Present Value
62	17.3	975,893	20.5	1,156,405
63	16.6	936,406	21.3	1,201,533
64	15.9	896,919	19.7	1,111,277
65	15.2	857,432	19	1,071,790

Table 11-3   The Present Value of the Statistical Life for Black Males and Black Females Ages 0 to 65 In 1988 Dollars

	Black Male		Black Female	
Age	Life Expectancy	Present Value	Life Expectancy	Present Value
0	64.8	3,655,368	73.5	4,146,135
1	65.2	3,677,932	73.8	4,163,058
2	64.2	3,621,522	72.9	4,112,289
3	63.3	3,570,753	71.9	4,055,879
4	62.3	3,514,343	71.0	4,005,110
5	61.4	3,463,574	70.0	3,948,700
6	60.4	3,407,164	69.0	3,892,290
7	59.4	3,350,754	68.0	3,835,880
8	58.5	3,299,985	67.1	3,785,111
9	57.5	3,243,575	66.1	3,728,701
10	56.5	3,187,165	65.1	3,672,291
11	55.5	3,130,755	64.1	3,615,881
12	54.5	3,074,345	63.1	3,559,471
13	53.5	3,017,935	62.1	3,503,061
14	52.6	2,967,166	61.2	3,452,292
15	51.6	2,910,756	60.2	3,395,882
16	50.7	2,859,987	59.2	3,339,472
17	49.8	2,809,218	58.2	3,283,062
18	48.8	2,752,808	57.3	3,232,293
19	47.9	2,702,039	56.3	3,175,883
20	47.1	2,656,911	55.3	3,119,473
21	46.2	2,606,142	54.4	3,068,704
22	45.3	2,555,373	53.4	3,012,294
23	44.4	2,504,604	52.4	2,955,884
24	43.6	2,459,476	51.5	2,905,115

| | Black Male | | Black Female | |
| | Life | Present | Life | Present |
Age	Expectancy	Value	Expectancy	Value
25	42.7	2,408,707	50.6	2,854,346
26	41.9	2,363,579	49.6	2,797,936
27	41.0	2,312,810	48.7	2,747,167
28	40.2	2,267,682	47.7	2,690,757
29	39.3	2,216,913	46.8	2,639,988
30	38.5	2,171,785	45.9	2,589,219
31	37.6	2,121,016	44.9	2,532,809
32	36.8	2,075,888	44.0	2,482,040
33	36.0	2,030,760	43.1	2,431,271
34	35.1	1,979,991	42.2	2,380,502
35	34.3	1,934,863	41.3	2,329,733
36	33.5	1,889,735	40.4	2,278,964
37	32.7	1,844,607	39.5	2,228,195
38	32.0	1,805,120	38.6	2,177,426
39	31.2	1,759,992	37.7	2,126,657
40	30.4	1,714,864	36.8	2,075,888
41	29.7	1,675,377	35.9	2,025,119
42	28.9	1,630,249	35.0	1,974,350
43	28.1	1,585,121	34.1	1,923,581
44	27.4	1,545,634	33.3	1,878,453
45	26.6	1,500,506	32.4	1,827,684
46	25.9	1,461,019	31.5	1,776,915
47	25.1	1,415,891	30.7	1,731,787
48	24.4	1,376,404	29.8	1,681,018
49	23.7	1,336,917	29.0	1,635,890
50	23.0	1,297,430	28.2	1,590,762
51	22.3	1,257,943	27.3	1,539,993
52	21.6	1,218,456	26.5	1,494,865
53	20.9	1,178,969	25.7	1,449,737
54	20.3	1,145,123	24.9	1,404,609
55	19.6	1,105,636	24.1	1,359,481
56	18.9	1,066,149	23.4	1,319,994
57	18.3	1,032,303	22.6	1,274,866
58	17.7	998,457	21.8	1,229,738
59	17.1	964,611	21.1	1,190,251
60	16.4	925,124	20.4	1,150,764
61	15.9	896,919	19.7	1,111,277
62	15.3	863,073	19.0	1,071,790

| | Black Male | | Black Female | |
Age	Life Expectancy	Present Value	Life Expectancy	Present Value
63	14.7	829,227	18.3	1,032,303
64	14.1	795,381	17.7	998,457
65	13.6	767,176	17.0	958,970

The value of the statistical life is presented in Tables 11-2 and 11-3. If a person were killed it is these values that would be used as the value of life.

§11.07   —The Psychologist's Report: Component Number Two

If a person is disabled then it is necessary to determine the degree to which the person has been disabled. This responsibility falls to the psychologist. The psychologist, through testing, etc., is able to qualify the degree to which an injured party is able to function. An example of a psychologist's scale is presented in Table 11-4.[7]

Table 11-4   Degree of Loss

Minimal	1 - 17%
Mild	17 - 33%
Moderate	33 - 50%
Severe	50 - 67%
Extreme	67 - 83%
Catastrophic	83 - 100%

The ranges are determined by dividing 100% disability by 6, the number of categories. Each category has a 16.66% spread. Each category is described by the degree of disability. For example, Burla, Brookshire, and Smith describe the minimal loss by example. Minimal loss is when a person is injured, misses some work, and has personal and family relationships disrupted for a short period, but then returns to the preinjury level of function. At the other extreme is catastrophic loss. This would require round the clock care, and the person being unable to work.[8]

These degrees of disability are established by the psychologist and are incorporated into the economic analysis by the economist. The psychologist may rate the degree of disability as different for various periods of time. The

---

[7] Edward P. Burla, Michael L. Brookshire, & Stan V. Smith, *Hedonic Damages and Personal Injury: A Conceptual Approach*, III, No 1 J Forensic Econs 1-8 (Dec 1989).

[8] *Id.*

psychologist might testify the injuries to the injured party are extreme for the next five years, followed by ten years of severe disability and moderate disability thereafter.

§11.08 —The Economist's Report: Component Number Three

Consider a 50-year-old Caucasian male injured in an automobile accident one year ago. From Table 11-2 the present value of a statistical life of a 50-year-old is $1,506,147, or $56,410 per year of life expectancy ($1,506,147 ÷ 26.7 years). This information was provided by the studies that identify the statistical value of life. The life expectancy is 26.7 years; this information is from the National Center of Health Statistics.

The dollar information would be used by the economist to estimate the impact on the statistical life value. The degree of loss is used to determine the proportion of the loss experienced by the injured party. Table 11-5 presents the present value of the loss throughout the life expectancy of the 50-year-old. The present value of the loss is $815,914.

Table 11-5 Present Value of the Lost Value of Statistical Life Growth and Discount Rate are 0%

Age	Period	Present Value	Sum	Degree of Loss	Adjusted PV	Sum
50	0	56,410	56,410	0.75	42,308	42,308
51	1	56,410	112,820	0.75	42,308	84,615
52	2	56,410	169,230	0.75	42,308	126,923
53	3	56,410	225,640	0.75	42,308	169,230
54	4	56,410	282,050	0.75	42,308	211,538
55	5	56,410	338,460	0.58	32,718	244,255
56	6	56,410	394,870	0.58	32,718	276,973
57	7	56,410	451,280	0.58	32,718	309,691
58	8	56,410	507,690	0.58	32,718	342,409
59	9	56,410	564,100	0.58	32,718	375,127
60	10	56,410	620,510	0.58	32,718	407,844
61	11	56,410	676,920	0.58	32,718	440,562
62	12	56,410	733,330	0.58	32,718	473,280
63	13	56,410	789,740	0.58	32,718	505,998
64	14	56,410	846,150	0.58	32,718	538,716
65	15	56,410	902,560	0.42	23,692	562,408
66	16	56,410	958,970	0.42	23,692	586,100
67	17	56,410	1,015,380	0.42	23,692	609,792
68	18	56,410	1,071,790	0.42	23,692	633,484
69	19	56,410	1,128,200	0.42	23,692	657,177
70	20	56,410	1,184,610	0.42	23,692	680,869

Age	Period	Present Value	Sum	Degree of Loss	Adjusted PV	Sum
71	21	56,410	1,241,020	0.42	23,692	704,561
72	22	56,410	1,297,430	0.42	23,692	728,253
73	23	56,410	1,353,840	0.42	23,692	751,945
74	24	56,410	1,410,250	0.42	23,692	775,637
75	25	56,410	1,466,660	0.42	23,692	799,330
70% of	yr	39,487	1,506,147	0.42	16,585	815,914

§11.09 Conclusion

The size of the loss of the statistical value of life in §11.08 has been estimated to be $815,914. If the economist had elected to permit the "value," the $56,410, to grow and be discounted, then the present value of the loss would have been even less, assuming the growth rate was less than the discount rate.

The critical point to note in this analysis is that the economist uses two sources of information for which he claims no responsibility. That is, the statistical value of life is determined by economists other than the one testifying and the degree of disability is determined by the psychologist. The economist is responsible for the calculation of the present value of the estimated values.

12

Mortality Adjustment

$$\text{Present Value of Future Income} = \$ \sum_{t=0}^{n} * M * (1+g)^t / (1+d)^t * \underline{P_L} * P_S * P_F * C * HS * Tx$$

§12.01   Introduction

Mortality expectations are sometimes introduced with the expectation that the present value of the future income stream can be reduced. This may or may not be the case. However, when the calculation of the present value of future medical expenses is made, the use of mortality expectation to determine present value is essential.

This chapter will look at what a mortality table is, what types of mortality tables there are, how mortality tables are constructed, and how mortality tables may be used in the present value calculation.

§12.02   Mortality Tables

Mortality tables reflect the number of persons per thousand for age 0 to age 100 expected to die during a particular year.[1] Mortality tables do not reflect *which* persons will die, however, but rather *how many* persons will die. In addition to the probability of dying, most mortality tables will also state the life expectancy. Mortality tables can be constructed for the entire population or for a part of the population. Mortality tables are constructed for the different sexes and for the different races.

Table 12-1 is a mortality table for the entire population of the United States.[2] The first column shows the age of the individual. The third column shows the life expectancy of an individual of that age. The second column states the probability a person of that age will die. For example, a four-year-old has a life expectancy of 72.1 years, and the probability of death occurring during the age of four is .33 per cent, about one-third of a per cent. The mortality table shows the life expectancy at each age and the probability of dying at each of the ages.

[1] G. Reynolds, The Mortality Merchants 46 (1978).

[2] US Dept of Commerce, Economics and Statistics Administration, Bureau of the Census, Statistical Abstracts of the United States, Table 105 (112th ed 1992).

Table 12-1 Mortality Table and Life Expectancy for the Total Population

Age	Deaths Per 1000	Life Exp	Age	Deaths Per 1000	Life Exp	Age	Deaths Per 1000	Life Exp
birth	9.86	75.3	25	1.18	51.9	50	4.85	28.9
1	0.69	75.0	26	1.20	50.9	51	5.31	28.1
2	0.52	74.1	27	1.23	50.0	52	5.84	27.2
3	0.40	73.1	28	1.27	49.1	53	6.43	26.4
4	0.33	72.1	29	1.32	48.1	54	7.08	25.6
5	0.29	71.1	30	1.38	47.2	55	7.79	24.7
6	0.26	70.2	31	1.45	46.2	56	8.55	23.9
7	0.24	69.2	32	1.51	45.3	57	9.37	23.1
8	0.21	68.2	33	1.59	44.4	58	10.27	22.3
9	0.18	67.2	34	1.66	43.5	59	11.23	21.6
10	0.16	66.2	35	1.75	42.5	60	12.27	20.8
11	0.17	65.2	36	1.85	41.6	61	13.37	20.1
12	0.22	64.3	37	1.94	40.7	62	14.52	19.3
13	0.32	63.3	38	2.04	39.8	63	15.69	18.6
14	0.47	62.3	39	2.14	38.8	64	16.91	17.9
15	0.63	61.3	40	2.25	37.9	65	18.20	17.2
16	0.79	60.4	41	2.38	37.0	70	27.31	14.5
17	0.91	59.4	42	2.53	36.1	75	41.31	11.4
18	0.99	58.5	43	2.71	35.2	80	63.71	8.8
19	1.03	57.5	44	2.92	34.3	85	126.81	4.7
20	1.06	56.6	45	3.15	33.4			
21	1.10	55.6	46	3.41	32.5			
22	1.13	54.7	47	3.71	31.6			
23	1.15	53.8	48	4.05	30.7			
24	1.17	52.8	49	4.43	29.8			

There are different mortality tables constructed for each race and for each sex. Thus, there are four tables which are subsets of the mortality table of the total population. The four tables are white-male, white-female, black-male, and black-female. These tables appear in the Table 12-2 and Appendix F.

Table 12-2

	1989 Expectation of Life in Years				1989 Expected Deaths per Thousand			
	White		Black		White		Black	
Age	Male	Female	Male	Female	Male	Female	Male	Female
0	72.7	79.2	64.8	73.5	9.08	7.15	20.04	17.17
1	72.3	78.8	65.2	73.8	0.69	0.53	1.18	0.91
2	71.4	77.8	64.2	72.9	0.50	0.41	0.91	0.75

| | 1989 Expectation of Life in Years | | | | 1989 Expected Deaths per Thousand | | | |
| | White | | Black | | White | | Black | |
Age	Male	Female	Male	Female	Male	Female	Male	Female
3	70.4	76.9	63.3	71.9	0.38	0.32	0.72	0.61
4	69.5	75.9	62.3	71.0	0.32	0.27	0.59	0.49
5	68.5	74.9	61.4	70.0	0.29	0.23	0.51	0.40
6	67.5	73.9	60.4	69.0	0.27	0.21	0.45	0.32
7	66.5	73.0	59.4	68.0	0.26	0.19	0.40	0.27
8	65.5	72.0	58.5	67.1	0.23	0.17	0.34	0.23
9	64.5	71.0	57.5	66.1	0.20	0.15	0.28	0.22
10	63.6	70.0	56.5	65.1	0.17	0.13	0.24	0.23
11	62.6	69.0	55.5	64.1	0.17	0.13	0.24	0.25
12	61.6	68.0	54.5	63.1	0.24	0.16	0.34	0.27
13	60.6	67.0	53.5	62.1	0.39	0.22	0.55	0.30
14	59.6	66.0	52.6	61.2	0.59	0.30	0.83	0.33
15	58.6	65.1	51.6	60.2	0.82	0.39	1.16	0.37
16	57.7	64.1	50.7	59.2	1.03	0.48	1.47	0.42
17	56.8	63.1	49.8	58.2	1.21	0.53	1.78	0.48
18	55.8	62.1	48.8	57.3	1.31	0.55	2.07	0.54
19	54.9	61.2	47.9	56.3	1.37	0.53	2.33	0.62
20	54.0	60.2	47.1	55.3	1.42	0.50	2.61	0.70
21	53.0	59.2	46.2	54.4	1.47	0.48	2.89	0.79
22	52.1	58.3	45.3	53.4	1.51	0.47	3.10	0.88
23	51.2	57.3	44.4	52.4	1.53	0.47	3.23	0.95
24	50.3	56.3	43.6	51.5	1.55	0.49	3.28	1.03
25	49.4	55.3	42.7	50.6	1.55	0.50	3.32	1.10
26	48.4	54.4	41.9	49.6	1.56	0.52	3.38	1.18
27	47.5	53.4	41.0	48.7	1.58	0.54	3.50	1.28
28	46.6	52.4	40.2	47.7	1.62	0.56	3.69	1.39
29	45.7	51.5	39.3	46.8	1.67	0.59	3.94	1.51
30	44.7	50.5	38.5	45.9	1.73	0.62	4.20	1.65
31	43.8	49.5	37.6	44.9	1.79	0.66	4.47	1.78
32	42.9	48.6	36.8	44.0	1.86	0.70	4.78	1.91
33	42.0	47.6	36.0	43.1	1.93	0.73	5.14	2.02
34	41.0	46.6	35.1	42.2	2.02	0.76	5.53	2.13
35	40.1	45.7	34.3	41.3	2.11	0.80	5.96	2.25
36	39.2	44.7	33.5	40.4	2.22	0.85	6.39	2.37
37	38.3	43.7	32.7	39.5	2.32	0.91	6.79	2.53
38	37.4	42.8	32.0	38.6	2.42	0.99	7.11	2.71
39	36.5	41.8	31.2	37.7	2.52	1.09	7.40	2.92
40	35.6	40.9	30.4	36.8	2.63	1.20	7.69	3.16
41	34.7	39.9	29.7	35.9	2.76	1.33	8.02	3.40
42	33.8	39.0	28.9	35.0	2.93	1.46	8.38	3.65
43	32.9	38.0	28.1	34.1	3.13	1.59	8.78	3.90
44	32.0	37.1	27.4	33.3	3.38	1.73	9.23	4.15

| | 1989 Expectation of Life in Years | | | | 1989 Expected Deaths per Thousand | | | |
| | White | | Black | | White | | Black | |
Age	Male	Female	Male	Female	Male	Female	Male	Female
45	31.1	36.1	26.6	32.4	3.66	1.89	9.69	4.43
46	30.2	35.2	25.9	31.5	3.98	2.07	10.19	4.74
47	29.3	34.3	25.1	30.7	4.33	2.29	10.80	5.07
48	28.4	33.4	24.4	29.8	4.71	2.54	11.53	5.43
49	27.5	32.4	23.7	29.0	5.12	2.84	12.37	5.83
50	26.7	31.5	23	28.2	5.58	3.16	13.30	6.27
51	25.8	30.6	22.3	27.3	6.10	3.51	14.25	6.75
52	25.0	29.7	21.6	26.5	6.73	3.90	15.21	7.30
53	24.2	28.8	20.9	25.7	7.49	4.31	16.14	7.91
54	23.3	28.0	20.3	24.9	8.35	4.76	17.07	8.59
55	22.5	27.1	19.6	24.1	9.29	5.24	18.04	9.31
56	21.7	26.2	18.9	23.4	10.29	5.77	19.09	10.09
57	21.0	25.4	18.3	22.6	11.37	6.34	20.27	11.01
58	20.2	24.6	17.7	21.8	12.55	6.97	21.61	12.12
59	19.4	23.7	17.1	21.1	13.81	7.64	23.10	13.38
60	18.7	22.9	16.4	20.4	15.18	8.39	24.68	14.76
61	18.0	22.1	15.9	19.7	16.63	9.18	26.36	16.17
62	17.3	20.5	15.3	19.0	18.12	10.02	28.15	17.51
63	16.6	21.3	14.7	18.3	19.62	10.91	30.07	18.72
64	15.9	19.7	14.1	17.7	21.18	11.84	32.12	19.85
65	15.2	19.0	13.6	17.0	22.80	12.85	34.31	21.00
70	12.1	15.3	11.0	13.9	34.70	20.03	47.63	29.38
75	9.4	11.9	8.8	11.0	53.66	31.61	65.79	42.53
80	7.1	8.9	6.9	8.5	82.84	51.62	94.32	65.05
85+	5.3	6.5	5.6	6.7	1000.	1000.	1000.	1000.

Source: US Dept of Labor, Bureau of Labor Statistics, Statistical Abstracts of the United States, Expectation of Life and Expected Deaths By Race, Sex and Age: 1989, Table 105 (1992).

As Table 12-2 indicates, females have a greater life expectancy than males, and whites have a greater life expectancy than blacks.

§12.03   Types of Mortality Tables

Mortality tables may be select tables, ultimate tables, or aggregate tables. *Select mortality tables* are based on the mortality experience of persons recently insured. *Ultimate mortality tables* exclude those insured in the early years of the insurance contract. *Aggregate mortality tables* include all insured.[3]

---

[3] K. Black, Jr & H. Skipper, Jr, Insurance 317 (11th ed 1987).

Select mortality tables reflect the life expectancy based on the experience of the persons insured in the most recent years. This group has a low mortality expectation relative to others in the same age group, since to become insured they must be in good health. This select period may run from five years to as long as fifteen years.[4]

The ultimate table is the mortality table covering the period after the select period. This means the benefits of "healthy selection" have worn off.[5]

The aggregate table includes the mortality data of both tables.[6]

The mortality tables used by an insurance company have a healthy bias. The insurance company requires the insured to pass a medical examination prior to being insured; thus, the unhealthy are not insured. In addition to this bias, the insurance company makes two other adjustments. The first is gradation, and the second is margin.[7]

Gradation is used to modify mortality results that do not appear to be supported by the population. The objective of gradation is to provide for smooth changes in life expectancy and in the probability of dying. If, for some unexplained reason, there were no deaths among all the 38-year-old persons insured, gradation would be used to smooth the results.

Margin is used to provide a cushion. The death rates are increased over what was actually experienced in order to provide a cushion of safety.

Mortality tables are calculated by assuming that no person lives beyond age 100. If a person reaches age 100, the insurance company will pay the face value of the life insurance policy as if the person had died. When this occurs, the person is said "to have outlived the mortality table."

§12.04 Annuities

An *annuity* is a series of payments made at various designated times in the future.[8] The payments may be weekly, monthly, semiannually, or whatever is agreed. The annuity may start immediately or it may be deferred. If the annuity is deferred, then the date on which the first payment will be made by the insurance company is stated in the contract.

Annuities may be *ordinary annuities* or *annuities due*. An ordinary annuity is paid at the beginning of the payment period. An annuity due is paid at the end of the payment period.

For example, consider an annual annuity for $10,000. The annuity is to start in one year. If the annuity is an ordinary annuity, the first payment will be made one year from today. If the annuity is an annuity due, then the first payment will be made in two years.

---

[4] *Id* 55.

[5] *Id.*

[6] *Id.*

[7] *Id* 318.

[8] J. Viscione & G. Roberts, Contemporary Financial Management 65 (1987).

§12.05   Annuity Mortality Tables

Mortality tables used for life insurance purposes are different from the mortality tables used for annuity purposes. Persons who purchase annuities are usually in better health than the general population. In order for the insurance company to charge a proper annuity premium, the mortality expectation for the annuity table is lower than the life insurance mortality table.

To be more explicit, the life insurance contract pays off when the insured dies. In order to assure enough money to pay all the claims, the mortality table and will be "padded." That is, the probability of dying will be increased, causing the premium to be higher. Likewise, for the annuity contract the "padding" is done by reducing the probability of dying. The annuity contract pays if the individual is alive. To lower the probability of dying increases the premiums for the annuity.

§12.06   Calculating the Probability of Living

The probability of living can be calculated from the mortality tables appearing in Table 12-2. To calculate the probability of living, the probability of dying must be known for each age.

It is critical to recognize that there is one mortality table for each and every age. There is a mortality table for a one-year-old, a different mortality table for a ten-year-old, and so on for each age. For the person age 1 there is the probability of living to age 2, and to age 3, and to age 98, and to age 99. The probability of a person living from age 1 to age 99 is different from the probability of a person age 2 living to age 99. The person age 2 has already survived to age 2; the person age 1 has not.

The construction of the probability of living requires knowing the individual's race and age. Suppose the probability of living is being constructed for a 40-year-old black male. The probability of living can be constructed from the data presented in Table 12-2. The table states the life expectancy of a 40-year-old black male is 30.4 years and the probability of dying is 7.69 per thousand. The probability of a 40-year-old black male living to age 41 is 99.391 per cent. The formula for this calculation is:

Probability of Living $= 1-[7.69/1000]$

The 40-year-old individual has a 99.231 per cent chance of living to age 41. The 41-year-old black male has a life expectancy of 29.7 years, and the probability of dying is 8.02 per thousand. As expected, as the individual ages the life expectancy decreases and the probability of death increases. The probability of a 41-year-old black male living to age 42 is 99.198% $= (1-(8.02/1,000))$. The question, though, is what is the probability that a 40-year-old black male will live to age 42. The probability of living from age 40 to age 41 is 99.231 per cent. The probability of living from age 41 to age 42 is 99.198 per cent. The probability of living from age 40 to age 42 is the multiplication of the two values, or 98.435 per cent.

Table 12-3 presents several probabilities. The second column is the probability of dying during that year. Out of 1,000 40-year-old black males, 6.09 will die. This does not mean that a fraction of a person will die, but rather that 609 men out of 100,000 will die. The third column is the probability of living. It is 1 minus the probability of dying. The fourth column is the probability of living from age 40 to any successive age through age 70. It is the fourth column that is used when the present value of a future income stream or medical payment stream is calculated, and for the payment to be made the individual must be alive.[9]

Table 12-3   Probability of Living, 40-Year-Old Black Male

Age	Deaths per Thousand	Prob of Living	Prob of Being Alive at Age
40	7.69	0.99231	0.99231
41	8.02	0.99198	0.98435
42	8.38	0.99162	0.97610
43	8.78	0.99122	0.96753
44	9.23	0.99077	0.95860
45	9.69	0.99031	0.94931
46	10.19	0.98981	0.93964
47	10.80	0.98920	0.92949
48	11.53	0.98847	0.91877
49	12.37	0.98763	0.90741
50	13.30	0.98670	0.89534
51	14.25	0.98575	0.88258
52	15.21	0.98479	0.86916
53	16.14	0.98386	0.85513
54	17.07	0.98293	0.84053
55	18.04	0.98196	0.82537
56	19.09	0.98091	0.80961
57	20.27	0.97973	0.79320
58	21.61	0.97839	0.77606
59	23.10	0.97690	0.75813
60	24.68	0.97532	0.73942
61	26.36	0.97364	0.71993
62	28.15	0.97185	0.69967
63	30.07	0.96993	0.67863
64	32.12	0.96788	0.65683
65	34.31	0.96569	0.63429
66	36.64	0.96336	0.61106

[9] The probability of dying is presented in the Statistical Abstracts. Those probabilities not presented are exponential interpolations.

Age	Deaths per Thousand	Prob of Living	Prob of Being Alive at Age
67	39.12	0.96088	0.58715
68	41.77	0.95823	0.56262
69	44.61	0.95539	0.53753
70	47.63	0.95237	0.51193

§12.07   Two Approaches to Mortality-Adjusted Medical Payments

The purpose of adjusting a stream of medical payments for mortality is to recognize the probability that a person may die any year. Even economists recognize that individuals may die before age 100. The mortality adjustment to future payments is done using one of two methods: (1) by calculating the present value to life expectancy, or (2) by making the annual adjustment for the probability of living each year to age 100.

Consider a situation where a 40-year-old black male is injured. The annual medical expense is $20,000. The appropriate growth rate is 4 per cent annually, and the appropriate discount rate is 6 per cent annually. Table 12-4 shows the present value calculations with annual mortality adjustments.

Table 12-4   Present Value

Age	Period	Present Value	Sum	Deaths/ Thousand	Prob of Living	Adjusted PV	Adjusted Sum
40	0	20,000	20,000	7.69	.9923	19,846	19,846
41	1	19,623	39,623	8.02	.9844	19,316	39,162
42	2	19,252	58,875	8.38	.9761	18,792	57,954
43	3	18,889	77,764	8.78	.9675	18,276	76,230
44	4	18,533	96,297	9.23	.9586	17,766	93,996
45	5	18,183	114,480	9.69	.9493	17,261	111,257
46	6	17,840	132,320	10.19	.9396	16,763	128,020
47	7	17,503	149,823	10.80	.9295	16,269	144,289
48	8	17,173	166,997	11.53	.9188	15,778	160,068
49	9	16,849	183,846	12.37	.9074	15,289	175,357
50	10	16,531	200,377	13.30	.8953	14,801	190,158
51	11	16,219	216,596	14.25	.8826	14,315	204,473
52	12	15,913	232,509	15.21	.8692	13,831	218,304
53	13	15,613	248,123	16.14	.8551	13,351	231,655
54	14	15,318	263,441	17.07	.8405	12,876	244,531
55	15	15,029	278,470	18.04	.8254	12,405	256,935
56	16	14,746	293,216	19.09	.8096	11,938	268,874
57	17	14,468	307,684	20.27	.7932	11,476	280,350
58	18	14,195	321,878	21.61	.7761	11,016	291,366

Age	Period	Present Value	Sum	Deaths/ Thousand	Prob of Living	Adjusted PV	Adjusted Sum
59	19	13,927	335,805	23.10	.7581	10,558	301,924
60	20	13,664	349,469	24.68	.7394	10,104	312,027
61	21	13,406	362,876	26.36	.7199	9,652	321,679
62	22	13,153	376,029	28.15	.6997	9,203	330,882
63	23	12,905	388,934	30.07	.6786	8,758	339,640
64	24	12,662	401,596	32.12	.6568	8,317	347,956
65	25	12,423	414,018	34.31	.6343	7,880	355,836
66	26	12,188	426,207	36.64	.6111	7,448	363,284
67	27	11,958	438,165	39.12	.5872	7,021	370,305
68	28	11,733	449,898	41.77	.5626	6,601	376,906
69	29	11,511	461,409	44.61	.5375	6,188	383,094
70	30	11,294	472,703	47.63	.5119	5,782	388,876
71	31	11,081	483,784	50.81	.4859	5,384	394,260
72	32	10,872	494,656	54.20	.4596	4,997	399,257
73	33	10,667	505,323	57.82	.4330	4,619	403,875
74	34	10,466	515,789	61.67	.4063	4,252	408,128
75	35	10,268	526,057	65.79	.3796	3,897	412,025
76	36	10,074	536,131	70.70	.3527	3,554	415,579
77	37	9,884	546,016	75.99	.3259	3,222	418,800
78	38	9,698	555,713	81.66	.2993	2,903	421,703
79	39	9,515	565,228	87.76	.2730	2,598	424,301
80	40	9,335	574,564	94.32	.2473	2,309	426,610
81	41	9,159	583,723	106.14	.2210	2,025	428,634
82	42	8,986	592,709	119.44	.1946	1,749	430,383
83	43	8,817	601,526	134.40	.1685	1,485	431,869
84	44	8,650	610,176	151.25	.1430	1,237	433,106
85	45	8,487	618,664	170.20	.1187	1,007	434,113
86	46	8,327	626,991	191.52	.0959	799	434,912
87	47	8,170	635,161	215.52	.0753	615	435,527
88	48	8,016	643,177	242.53	.0570	457	435,984
89	49	7,865	651,041	272.92	.0414	326	436,310
90	50	7,716	658,757	307.12	.0287	222	436,531
91	51	7,571	666,328	345.60	.0188	142	436,673
92	52	7,428	673,756	388.90	.0115	85	436,759
93	53	7,288	681,043	437.63	.0065	47	436,806
94	54	7,150	688,194	492.47	.0033	23	436,829
95	55	7,015	695,209	554.18	.0015	10	436,840
96	56	6,883	702,092	623.62	.0006	4	436,843
97	57	6,753	708,845	701.76	.0002	1	436,844
98	58	6,626	715,470	789.70	.0000	0	436,845
99	59	6,501	721,971	888.65	.0000	0	436,845

The life expectancy of a 40-year-old black male is 30.4 years, rounded to 30 years. From the fourth column the present value of the $20,000 per year of medical expenses to life expectancy of age 70 is found to be $472,703. If the entire life to age 100 is considered, the present value of the future medical expenses, mortality adjusted, is $436,845.

§12.08 Comparing Mortality Results

Consider again the fact situation outlined in §12.07. The present value of $20,000 per year for 25 years, growing at 4 per cent annually and being discounted at 6 per cent annually, was calculated to be $401,596. Recall, the first payment is today and there are 24 future payments. When mortality adjustments are made, the present value of the expense stream changes.

Table 12-5 presents the present value of an expense stream of $20,000 per year beginning at age 40, growing at 4 per cent and discounted at 6 per cent: (1) life expectancy and (2) mortality adjusted to age 99. The different values in the table indicate the difference in the life expectancy based on sex and race. The difference in the mortality adjusted present value to age 99 is because of the different probabilities of living.

The life expectancy of a 40-year-old white male is 35.6 years and 30.4 years for a black male. Women typically live longer than men. The life expectancy of a 40-year-old white woman is 40.9 years, while for a black woman it is 36.8 years.

The present values of the $20,000 per year expense stream, growing at 4 per cent and discounted at 6 per cent, are presented in table 12-5. The difference in the present values is strictly due to the life expectancy and the probability of living. With no mortality adjustment the present value of the $20,000 to age 65 is $401,596.

Table 12-5 Present Value with Mortality Adjustment to Life Expectancy and to Age 99

	Life Expectancy	PV to Life Expectancy	PV to Age 99
White Male	35.6	546,016	488,400
Black Male	30.4	472,703	436,845
White Female	40.9	583,793	548,593
Black Female	36.7	546,016	504,375

§12.09 Conclusion

The mortality adjustment is needed when the present value of future medical expenses is being calculated. Economists either calculate the present value annually, adjusting for mortality, or calculate the present value with certainty to life expectancy.

The choice of mortality tables will have an effect on the size of the present value figure. Government life expectancy tables are based on the total population, while insurance company mortality tables are based on only that part of the population which is healthy enough to be insured. Additionally, insurance company mortality tables are "padded" in order to provide for a margin of error.

13

The Probability of Seeking and the Probability of Finding Employment

$$\text{Present Value of Future Income} = \$ \sum_{t=0}^{n} * M * (1+g)^{t} / (1+d)^{t} * P_L * P_S * P_F * C * HS * Tx$$

§13.01 Introduction

When the uncertainties of life are introduced into the computation of the present value of a future income stream, then the probability of a person seeking a job and the probability of finding a job enter the calculation. This chapter will present data on the probability of seeking employment, present data on the probability of finding employment, explain what the data mean, and demonstrate one way to use the data in the present value calculation.

§13.02   The Probability of Seeking Employment

The probability that an individual will seek employment is referred to by government statistics as *participation rates*. A person may seek employment but not find employment; he or she is, however, participating in the labor force. To participate in the labor force one must have a job or be looking for a job.

Participation rates represent the proportion of the population in the labor force.[1] The labor force participation rate is the ratio of the labor force to the noninstitutional population.[2] The labor force includes all resident armed forces. The civilian labor force ratio excludes the armed forces and is defined as the ratio of the civilian labor force to the civilian noninstitutional population. The participation rates are calculated based on race and sex of the individual. Tables 13-1 through 13-6 present the participation rates for white males, white females, black males, black females, Hispanic males, and Hispanic females respectively. The most recent data ends in 1988. Data for blacks only goes back to 1972 and for Hispanics to 1980.

Table 13-1   Participation Rates, White Males 1954-1988

Year				Age				
	16-17	18-19	20-24	25-34	35-44	45-54	55-64	65+
1954	47.1	70.5	86.3	97.5	98.2	96.8	89.1	40.4
1955	48.1	71.7	86.5	97.8	98.2	96.7	88.4	39.6
1956	51.3	71.8	87.6	97.4	98.1	96.8	88.9	40.0
1957	49.6	71.5	86.6	97.2	98.0	96.7	88.0	37.7
1958	46.8	69.4	86.7	97.2	98.0	96.6	88.2	35.7
1959	45.4	70.3	87.3	97.5	98.0	96.3	87.9	34.3
1960	46.0	69.0	87.8	97.7	97.9	96.1	87.2	33.3
1961	44.3	66.2	87.6	97.7	97.9	95.9	87.8	31.9
1962	42.9	66.4	86.5	97.4	97.9	96.0	86.7	30.6
1963	42.4	67.8	85.8	97.4	97.8	96.2	86.6	28.4
1964	43.5	66.6	85.7	97.5	97.6	96.1	86.1	27.9
1965	44.6	65.8	85.3	97.4	97.7	95.9	85.2	27.9
1966	47.1	65.4	84.4	97.5	97.6	95.8	84.9	27.2
1967	47.9	66.1	84.0	97.5	97.7	95.6	84.9	27.1
1968	47.7	65.7	82.4	97.2	97.6	95.4	84.7	27.4
1969	48.8	66.3	82.6	97.0	97.4	95.1	83.9	27.3
1970	48.9	67.4	83.3	96.7	97.3	94.9	83.3	26.7
1971	49.3	67.8	83.2	96.3	97.0	94.7	82.6	25.6
1972	50.2	71.1	84.3	96.0	97.0	94.0	81.1	24.4
1973	52.7	72.3	85.8	96.2	96.8	93.5	78.9	22.7
1974	53.3	73.6	86.6	96.3	96.7	93.0	78.0	22.4

---

[1] US Dept of Labor Technical Notes, Current Population Survey (Household Survey), Handbook of Labor Statistics, Bulletin 2217, at 1-3 (June 1985).

[2] *Id* 2.

Year	Age							
	16-17	18-19	20-24	25-34	35-44	45-54	55-64	65+
1954	51.8	72.8	85.5	95.8	96.4	92.9	76.4	21.7
1976	51.8	73.5	86.3	95.9	96.0	92.5	75.2	20.2
1977	53.8	74.9	86.8	96.0	96.2	92.1	74.6	20.0
1978	55.3	75.3	87.3	95.9	96.3	92.1	73.7	20.3
1979	55.3	74.5	87.6	96.0	96.4	92.2	73.4	20.0
1980	53.6	74.1	87.2	95.9	96.2	92.1	73.1	19.1
1981	51.5	73.5	87.0	95.8	96.1	92.4	71.5	18.5
1982	49.3	70.5	86.3	95.6	96.0	92.2	71.0	17.9
1983	46.9	71.3	86.1	95.2	96.0	91.9	70.0	17.7
1984	47.0	70.8	86.5	95.4	96.1	92.0	69.5	16.4
1985	48.5	71.2	86.4	95.7	95.7	92.0	68.8	15.9
1986	48.7	70.5	87.3	95.5	95.4	91.8	68.0	16.3
1987	48.8	70.0	86.9	95.5	95.4	91.6	68.1	16.5
1988	49.3	71.0	86.6	95.2	95.4	91.8	67.9	16.7
Ave:	48.8	70.2	86.0	96.6	97.0	94.2	79.8	25.6

Table 13-2 Participation Rates, White Females 1954-1988

Year	Age							
	16-17	18-19	20-24	25-34	35-44	45-54	55-64	65+
1954	29.3	52.1	44.4	32.5	39.3	39.8	29.1	9.1
1955	29.9	52.0	45.8	32.6	40.0	42.7	31.8	10.5
1956	33.5	53.0	46.5	33.2	41.5	44.4	34.0	10.6
1957	32.1	52.6	45.8	33.6	41.5	45.4	33.7	10.2
1958	28.8	52.3	46.0	33.6	41.4	46.5	34.5	10.1
1959	29.9	50.8	44.5	33.4	41.4	47.8	35.7	10.0
1960	30.0	51.9	45.7	34.1	41.5	48.6	36.2	10.6
1961	29.4	51.9	46.9	34.3	41.8	48.9	37.2	10.5
1962	27.9	51.6	47.1	34.1	42.2	48.9	38.0	9.8
1963	27.8	51.3	47.3	34.8	43.1	49.5	38.9	9.4
1964	28.4	49.6	48.8	35.0	43.3	50.2	39.4	9.9
1965	28.7	50.6	49.2	36.3	44.4	49.9	40.3	9.7
1966	31.8	53.1	51.0	37.7	45.0	50.6	41.1	9.4
1967	32.3	52.7	53.1	39.7	46.4	50.9	41.9	9.3
1968	33.0	53.3	54.0	40.6	47.5	51.5	42.0	9.4
1969	35.2	54.6	56.4	41.7	48.6	53.0	42.6	9.7
1970	36.6	55.0	57.7	43.2	49.9	53.7	42.6	9.5
1971	36.3	55.0	58.0	43.7	50.2	53.6	42.5	9.3
1972	39.3	57.4	59.4	46.0	50.7	53.4	42.0	9.0
1973	41.7	58.8	61.7	48.7	52.2	53.4	40.7	8.7
1974	43.3	60.4	63.9	51.3	53.6	54.3	40.4	8.0
1975	42.7	60.4	65.5	53.6	54.9	54.3	40.6	8.0
1976	43.8	61.7	66.3	56.0	57.1	54.7	40.7	7.9
1977	45.8	63.3	67.8	58.5	58.9	55.3	40.7	7.9
1978	48.8	64.6	69.3	61.2	60.7	56.7	41.1	8.1

Year	Age							
	16-17	18-19	20-24	25-34	35-44	45-54	55-64	65+
1979	49.0	65.7	70.5	63.3	63.0	58.1	41.5	8.1
1980	47.2	65.1	70.6	64.8	65.0	59.6	40.9	7.9
1981	46.1	64.2	71.5	66.4	66.4	60.9	40.9	7.9
1982	44.6	64.6	71.8	67.8	67.5	61.4	41.5	7.8
1983	43.9	64.1	72.1	68.7	68.2	61.9	41.1	7.8
1984	44.8	65.2	72.5	69.8	69.6	62.7	41.2	7.5
1985	45.2	64.8	73.8	70.9	71.4	64.2	41.5	7.0
1986	47.2	65.3	74.1	71.8	72.9	65.8	42.1	7.3
1987	48.2	64.9	74.8	72.5	74.2	67.2	42.4	7.2
1988	47.7	66.3	74.9	73.0	74.9	69.2	43.6	7.7
Ave:	38.0	57.7	59.1	49.1	53.4	54.0	39.6	8.9

Table 13-3   Participation Rate, Black Males 1972-1988

Year	Age							
	16-17	18-19	20-24	25-34	35-44	45-54	55-64	65+
1972	34.3	60.2	82.7	92.7	91.1	85.4	72.5	24.2
1973	32.3	61.2	83.7	91.8	91.0	87.4	69.5	22.3
1974	34.0	61.9	83.6	92.8	90.4	84.0	68.9	21.6
1975	29.8	57.2	78.7	91.6	89.4	83.5	67.7	20.7
1976	29.0	55.0	79.0	90.9	89.9	82.4	65.1	19.8
1977	30.2	58.0	79.2	90.7	91.0	82.0	65.5	20.0
1978	31.9	59.7	78.8	90.9	90.5	83.2	67.9	21.1
1979	30.7	58.1	80.7	90.8	90.4	84.5	64.8	19.5
1980	30.9	56.6	79.9	90.9	89.1	83.0	61.9	16.9
1981	29.2	55.0	79.2	88.9	89.3	82.7	62.1	16.0
1982	24.6	55.3	78.7	89.2	89.8	82.2	61.9	15.9
1983	24.7	55.0	79.4	89.0	89.7	84.5	62.6	14.0
1984	26.9	56.2	79.1	88.9	90.0	83.7	58.9	13.7
1985	29.8	60.0	79.0	88.8	89.8	83.0	58.9	13.9
1986	30.0	58.5	80.1	89.6	89.6	84.1	59.1	12.6
1987	31.7	57.0	77.8	89.4	88.6	83.7	62.1	13.7
1988	32.7	56.0	79.3	89.3	88.2	83.5	59.4	14.3
Ave:	30.0	57.7	79.9	90.4	89.9	83.7	64.3	17.7

Table 13-4   Participation Rate, Black Females 1972-1988

Year	Age							
	16-17	18-19	20-24	25-34	35-44	45-54	55-64	65+
1972	21.0	44.3	57.0	60.8	61.4	57.2	44.0	12.6
1973	23.9	45.1	58.0	62.7	61.7	56.1	44.7	11.4
1974	22.7	44.3	58.8	62.4	62.2	56.4	42.8	10.4
1975	25.0	43.5	55.9	62.8	62.0	56.6	43.1	10.7
1976	23.2	42.6	56.9	66.7	63.0	56.8	43.7	11.3
1977	21.5	44.3	59.3	68.5	64.1	57.9	43.7	10.5

Year	Age							
	16-17	18-19	20-24	25-34	35-44	45-54	55-64	65+
1978	26.4	48.3	62.7	70.6	67.2	59.4	43.8	11.1
1979	27.5	45.6	61.5	70.1	68.0	59.6	44.0	10.9
1980	24.6	45.0	60.2	70.5	68.1	61.4	44.8	10.2
1981	23.9	44.0	61.1	70.0	69.8	62.0	45.4	9.3
1982	23.3	43.3	60.1	70.2	71.7	62.4	44.8	8.5
1983	20.8	44.4	59.1	72.3	72.6	62.3	44.8	8.2
1984	23.9	45.3	60.7	71.5	73.7	64.5	46.1	8.0
1985	27.6	47.9	62.5	72.4	74.8	65.7	45.3	9.4
1986	29.0	49.2	64.6	72.4	75.8	66.5	43.6	7.8
1987	28.2	51.4	64.4	73.5	77.8	67.5	44.4	8.6
1988	28.1	48.2	63.2	73.7	78.1	68.3	43.4	9.6
Ave:	25.2	45.7	60.4	68.9	68.9	61.2	44.3	9.9

Table 13-5 Participation Rate, Hispanic Males 1980-1988

Year	Age							
	16-17	18-19	20-24	25-34	35-44	45-54	55-64	65+
1980	45.2	74.8	88.0	93.3	93.8	91.7	73.6	20.7
1981	39.8	68.2	88.8	93.8	92.6	90.6	70.9	19.4
1982	34.4	65.1	86.1	93.9	93.5	88.8	70.0	17.9
1983	34.0	70.3	86.0	93.5	93.0	89.4	71.3	17.4
1984	35.4	68.8	87.0	93.4	93.6	89.0	71.2	14.9
1985	36.0	65.7	87.3	93.1	92.4	89.5	69.6	14.9
1986	34.5	68.3	88.3	93.4	93.3	89.9	69.3	15.2
1987	33.3	69.6	87.8	93.6	93.0	88.0	70.2	14.4
1988	38.6	70.1	89.4	93.4	93.8	88.5	68.8	17.4
Ave:	36.6	69.0	87.6	93.5	93.2	89.5	70.5	16.9

Table 13-6 Participation Rate, Hispanic Females 1980-1988

Year	Age							
	16-17	18-19	20-24	25-34	35-44	45-54	55-64	65+
1980	29.9	50.4	57.0	54.0	55.3	54.5	34.7	5.7
1981	27.0	49.2	59.8	55.5	55.9	54.8	34.5	6.4
1982	25.7	52.2	58.4	56.4	55.2	53.6	33.2	6.4
1983	25.5	49.1	56.5	54.8	54.7	55.4	37.5	6.4
1984	30.6	53.5	56.2	56.9	58.6	55.2	38.5	7.2
1985	26.5	49.2	57.7	57.1	59.1	55.1	36.4	5.9
1986	27.1	46.1	58.9	59.0	60.6	57.4	33.9	5.5
1987	29.7	49.6	60.4	60.9	62.2	57.8	36.8	5.3
1988	32.4	55.5	62.3	60.9	62.1	57.9	41.5	6.5
Ave:	27.5	50.5	58.6	57.3	58.2	55.7	36.3	6.1

The average participation rate is calculated for each of the age groups. As the tables indicate, there is a chance that men and women will be participating in the labor force at age 16. Likewise, there is a chance each will be participating in the labor force after age 65. Since the age category 65+ is open-ended, there is a statistical chance of participating in the labor force each year after an individual reaches age 65.

Note the significant change in the participation rate of women in the labor force. In 1954, white women between the ages of 25 and 54 had a probability of participating in the labor force ranging between 32 per cent and 40 per cent. By 1980 the probability of participating in the labor force had increased to a range of 60 to 65 per cent and by 1988 the participation rate was between 70 and 75 per cent.

§13.03   Interpreting the Participation Rate

The participation rates are cross-sectional data. This means the figures are determined for each age independently of the other age groups. If one-third of persons age 38 are not participating in the labor force it does not follow that a 37-year-old has a 33% chance of exiting the labor force when they turn 38. The participation rate tells what portion of that age group, for one reason or another, is not participating in the labor force.

Assume there are two people age 46. One is working and one, by choice, is not working. Does this mean that a 45-year-old, turning 46, has a 50% chance of not participating in the labor force. No. What may be the case is the person not participating in the labor force may be retired military with 20 years of active duty.

Another situation which can be misleading is the choice of a spouse to remain outside the labor force. Assume a situation with three women all are 30 years old. Two are participating in the labor force and one has elected to remain in the home. It does not follow that a 29-year-old working woman has a 33.3% chance of not participating in the labor force when she turns 30 years old.

§13.04   The Probability of Finding Employment

The probability of holding a job, that is, having employment, is the *employment rate*. It is one (1) minus the unemployment rate. To determine the employment rate, the labor force must be estimated.

The civilian labor force is the total of all employed and unemployed persons. The labor force, as distinguished from the civilian labor force, includes the members of the armed forces serving in the United States.[3] The full-time labor force includes all civilians working full-time schedules. This definition would include persons with full-time schedules but temporarily employed part-time due to economic reasons. Also included in the definition of full-time labor force are unemployed persons seeking full-time work.[4] The employment rate is one (1)

---

[3] US Dept of Labor Technical Notes, Current Population Survey (Household Survey), Handbook of Labor Statistics, Bulletin 2217, at 2 (June 1985).

[4] *Id.*

minus the ratio of the number of workers unemployed to the labor force. For an individual to be employed or unemployed he or she must be a participant in the labor force.

Table 13-7 Employment Rates, White Males 1954-1988

Year	Age							
	16-17	18-19	20-24	25-34	35-44	45-54	55-64	65+
1954	14.0	13.0	9.8	4.2	3.6	3.8	4.3	4.2
1955	12.2	10.4	7.0	2.7	2.6	2.9	3.9	3.8
1956	11.2	9.7	6.1	2.8	2.2	2.8	3.1	3.4
1957	11.9	11.1	7.0	2.7	2.5	3.0	3.4	3.2
1958	14.9	16.5	11.7	5.6	4.4	4.8	5.2	5.0
1959	15.0	13.0	7.5	3.8	3.2	3.7	4.2	4.5
1960	14.6	13.5	8.3	4.1	3.3	3.6	4.1	4.0
1961	16.5	15.2	10.1	4.9	4.0	4.4	5.3	5.2
1962	15.2	12.7	8.1	3.8	3.1	3.5	4.1	4.0
1963	17.8	14.2	7.8	3.9	2.9	3.3	4.0	4.1
1964	16.1	13.3	7.4	3.0	2.5	2.9	3.5	3.6
1965	14.7	11.3	5.9	2.6	2.3	2.3	3.1	3.4
1966	12.5	8.9	4.1	2.1	1.7	1.7	2.5	3.0
1967	12.7	9.0	4.2	1.9	1.6	1.8	2.2	2.7
1968	12.6	8.3	4.6	1.7	1.4	1.5	1.7	2.8
1969	12.5	7.9	4.6	1.7	1.4	1.4	1.7	2.2
1970	15.7	12.0	7.8	3.1	2.3	2.3	2.7	3.2
1971	17.1	13.5	9.4	4.0	2.9	2.9	3.2	3.4
1972	16.4	12.4	8.5	3.4	2.5	2.5	3.0	3.3
1973	15.2	10.0	6.6	3.0	1.8	2.0	2.4	2.9
1974	16.2	11.5	7.8	3.6	2.4	2.2	2.5	3.0
1975	19.7	17.2	13.1	6.3	4.5	4.4	4.1	5.0
1976	19.7	15.5	10.9	5.6	3.7	3.7	4.0	4.7
1977	17.6	13.0	9.3	5.0	3.1	3.0	3.3	4.9
1978	16.9	10.8	7.7	3.8	2.5	2.5	2.6	3.9
1979	16.1	12.2	7.5	3.7	2.5	2.5	2.5	3.2
1980	18.5	14.5	11.1	5.9	3.6	3.3	3.1	2.5
1981	19.9	16.4	11.6	6.1	4.0	3.6	3.4	2.4
1982	24.2	20.0	14.3	8.9	6.2	5.3	5.1	3.2
1983	22.6	18.7	13.8	9.0	6.4	5.7	5.6	3.2
1984	19.7	15.0	9.8	6.2	4.6	4.2	4.7	2.6
1985	19.2	14.7	9.7	5.7	4.3	4.1	4.0	2.7
1986	18.4	14.7	9.2	5.8	4.4	4.0	4.0	3.0
1987	17.9	13.7	8.4	5.2	3.9	3.9	3.4	2.5
1988	16.1	12.4	7.4	4.6	3.4	3.2	3.3	2.2
Ave:	16.3	13.0	8.5	4.3	3.2	3.2	3.5	3.5

Table 13-8   Employment Rates, White Females 1954-1988

Year				Age				
	16-17	18-19	20-24	25-34	35-44	45-54	55-64	65+
1954	12.0	9.4	6.4	5.7	4.9	4.4	4.5	2.8
1955	11.6	7.7	5.1	4.3	3.8	3.4	3.6	2.2
1956	12.1	8.3	5.1	4.0	3.5	3.3	3.5	2.3
1957	11.9	7.8	5.1	4.7	3.7	3.0	2.6	3.4
1958	15.6	11.0	7.3	6.6	5.6	4.9	4.3	3.5
1959	13.3	11.1	7.0	5.2	4.7	3.9	4.0	2.9
1960	14.5	11.5	7.2	5.7	4.2	4.0	3.3	2.8
1961	17.0	13.6	8.4	6.6	5.6	4.8	4.3	3.8
1962	15.6	11.3	7.7	5.4	4.5	3.7	3.5	4.0
1963	18.1	13.2	7.4	5.8	4.6	3.9	3.5	3.3
1964	17.1	13.2	7.1	5.2	4.5	3.6	3.5	3.4
1965	15.0	13.4	6.3	4.9	4.1	3.0	2.7	2.7
1966	14.5	10.7	5.3	3.7	3.3	2.7	2.2	2.7
1967	12.9	10.6	6.0	4.7	3.7	2.9	2.3	2.6
1968	13.9	11.0	5.9	3.9	3.1	2.3	2.1	2.8
1969	13.7	10.0	5.5	4.2	3.2	2.4	2.1	2.4
1970	15.3	11.9	6.9	5.3	4.3	3.4	2.6	3.3
1971	16.7	14.1	8.5	6.3	4.9	3.9	3.3	3.6
1972	17.0	12.3	8.2	5.5	4.4	3.5	3.3	3.7
1973	15.8	10.9	7.1	5.1	3.7	3.2	2.7	2.8
1974	16.4	13.0	8.2	5.8	4.4	3.6	3.2	3.9
1975	19.2	16.1	11.2	8.4	6.5	5.8	5.0	5.3
1976	18.2	15.1	10.4	7.6	5.8	5.0	4.8	5.3
1977	18.2	14.2	9.3	6.7	5.3	5.0	4.4	4.9
1978	17.1	12.4	8.3	5.8	4.5	3.8	3.0	3.7
1979	15.9	12.5	7.8	5.6	4.2	3.7	3.0	3.1
1980	17.3	13.1	8.5	6.3	4.9	4.3	3.1	3.0
1981	18.4	15.3	9.1	6.6	5.1	4.2	3.7	3.4
1982	21.2	17.6	10.9	8.0	6.4	5.5	5.0	3.1
1983	21.4	16.4	10.3	7.6	6.2	5.5	4.7	3.1
1984	17.8	13.6	8.8	6.1	5.0	4.8	4.0	3.7
1985	17.2	13.1	8.5	6.2	4.9	4.5	4.1	3.1
1986	16.7	13.6	8.1	6.1	4.5	4.3	3.7	2.6
1987	15.5	11.7	7.4	5.0	4.1	3.3	2.7	2.4
1988	14.4	10.8	6.7	4.5	3.7	3.1	2.5	2.6
Ave:	16.0	12.3	7.6	5.7	4.6	3.9	3.5	3.3

Table 13-9 Employment Rates, Black Males 1972-1988

Year	Age							
	16-17	18-19	20-24	25-34	35-44	45-54	55-64	65+
1972	36.7	28.4	14.9	7.2	4.8	3.8	4.4	5.4
1973	35.7	23.0	13.2	6.2	3.9	3.2	3.2	3.3
1974	39.9	28.3	16.2	8.1	4.3	4.2	3.6	5.3
1975	41.9	35.9	24.7	12.7	8.7	9.3	6.3	8.7
1976	40.8	36.0	22.6	12.0	7.5	7.3	6.3	8.7
1977	41.0	38.2	23.0	11.8	6.2	4.9	6.0	7.8
1978	43.0	32.9	21.0	9.8	5.1	4.9	4.4	6.6
1979	37.9	32.2	18.7	9.6	6.3	5.2	5.1	6.4
1980	39.7	36.2	23.7	13.4	8.2	7.2	6.2	8.7
1981	43.2	39.2	26.4	14.4	9.3	7.8	6.1	7.5
1982	52.7	47.1	31.5	20.1	13.4	9.0	10.3	9.3
1983	52.2	47.3	31.4	19.4	13.5	11.4	11.0	11.8
1984	44.0	42.2	26.6	15.0	10.4	7.9	8.9	7.9
1985	42.9	40.0	23.5	13.8	9.6	9.7	7.9	8.9
1986	41.4	38.2	23.5	13.5	10.9	7.8	8.0	4.3
1987	39.0	31.6	20.3	12.2	8.7	6.7	6.6	4.3
1988	34.4	31.7	19.4	11.0	7.6	6.2	5.2	5.6
Ave:	42.0	35.8	22.4	12.4	8.1	6.9	6.4	7.1

Table 13-10 Employment Rates, Black Females 1972-1988

Year	Age							
	16-17	18-19	20-24	25-34	35-44	45-54	55-64	65+
1972	42.0	40.1	17.9	10.5	7.6	4.6	3.7	2.6
1973	38.6	34.2	18.4	10.3	5.6	3.9	3.3	3.7
1974	40.2	36.0	19.0	9.0	6.6	4.4	3.6	1.9
1975	41.2	40.6	24.3	13.4	9.0	7.0	5.3	3.6
1976	48.4	37.6	22.5	13.6	8.2	5.9	5.4	2.4
1977	49.5	40.4	25.5	13.6	8.7	5.8	4.8	3.4
1978	45.0	38.7	22.7	11.9	7.8	5.6	5.2	4.7
1979	42.7	36.9	22.6	12.1	7.2	5.2	4.7	3.9
1980	42.9	38.2	23.5	13.2	8.2	6.4	4.5	4.9
1981	46.5	39.8	26.4	14.9	9.8	6.9	4.7	6.0
1982	44.2	48.6	29.6	17.8	10.7	8.5	6.1	4.5
1983	48.6	48.0	31.8	18.6	11.4	9.9	7.3	6.3
1984	47.5	40.2	25.6	15.4	9.4	8.6	5.9	4.9
1985	44.3	36.4	25.6	15.1	9.3	6.8	6.0	5.2
1986	44.6	36.1	24.7	14.6	8.5	6.4	5.0	4.9
1987	40.5	31.7	23.3	13.5	8.1	6.7	4.5	3.4
1988	35.9	29.6	19.8	12.7	7.4	5.6	4.3	5.4
Ave:	44.2	38.4	23.7	13.5	8.4	6.4	5.0	4.2

Table 13-11   Employment Rates, Hispanic Males 1980-1988

Year	Age							
	16-17	18-19	20-24	25-34	35-44	45-54	55-64	65+
1980	26.2	19.3	12.2	8.3	7.1	6.0	5.9	7.6
1981	30.9	20.3	14.1	8.9	6.5	5.9	6.7	6.7
1982	40.2	26.8	18.2	12.4	9.9	7.5	10.0	7.4
1983	34.7	25.9	17.0	11.6	10.8	10.3	11.7	6.8
1984	31.5	22.2	12.5	9.2	7.6	7.2	10.4	8.2
1985	29.1	22.4	13.0	9.6	7.2	6.8	7.0	9.4
1986	28.5	22.4	13.0	9.5	8.5	7.0	8.0	9.6
1987	28.2	19.3	10.2	7.6	6.9	7.1	6.7	7.9
1988	29.5	19.5	9.2	7.0	5.9	6.1	6.7	6.9
Ave:	31.2	22.0	13.3	9.3	7.8	7.1	8.1	7.8

Table 13-12   Employment Rates, Hispanic Females 1980-1988

Year	Age							
	16-17	18-19	20-24	25-34	35-44	45-54	55-64	65+
1980	29.7	19.8	12.0	10.6	8.6	5.3	5.8	1.1
1981	23.5	23.4	13.5	8.7	8.9	7.2	8.4	2.5
1982	35.1	25.0	16.8	12.2	11.9	9.9	10.4	4.8
1983	32.5	25.7	16.2	12.5	12.2	9.7	9.6	3.5
1984	26.1	21.0	12.2	10.3	9.1	7.9	8.8	3.4
1985	26.2	22.6	12.1	10.6	8.5	8.1	9.2	5.5
1986	27.6	23.6	12.9	9.8	5.2	8.9	6.2	11.2
1987	27.1	19.9	11.4	7.8	6.5	6.7	5.0	3.7
1988	24.5	18.9	10.7	7.2	6.2	5.9	4.6	3.0
Ave:	28.5	22.2	13.1	10.0	8.6	7.7	7.6	4.3

§13.05   Incorporating the Probability of Seeking Employment and the Probability of Finding Employment into the Present Value Analysis

Since the probability of seeking employment and the probability of finding employment are measures of uncertainty, it seems reasonable to include these probabilities in the present value calculation when mortality adjustments are made. Stated differently, if the uncertainty of living is included in the calculation of the present value of wages and salary, then the uncertainty of seeking employment and the uncertainty of finding employment should also be included in the analysis.

This not the case since for a loss of wages to have occurred the individual must already be participating in the labor force. Including the probability of seeking employment (participation) will lead to an understatement of the present value of the income stream experienced by the individual.

The government statistics indicate that there is a probability of seeking employment after age 65. Likewise, there is a probability of finding employment after age 65.

The seeking and finding employment figures are incorporated into the analysis by using the averages. That is, each of the Tables 13-1 through 13-12 presents the average probability of seeking and finding employment. These averages are employed in the present value analysis.

§13.06 An Example of Using the Probability of Seeking Employment, the Probability of Finding Employment, and the Mortality Adjustment in the Present Value Analysis

Consider the fact situation where the present value of a 40-year-old white male is being calculated. The earnings are $25,000 annually. The present value calculation employs a growth rate of wages of 2 per cent and a discount, or interest rate, of 4 per cent. Table 13-13 shows the present value of the future income if the individual were to work uninterrupted to age 65.

Table 13-13 Present Value of An Income Stream to Age 65

Age	Period	Future Value	Present Value	Sum
40	0	25,000	25,000	25,000
41	1	25,500	24,519	49,519
42	2	26,010	24,048	73,567
43	3	26,530	23,585	97,152
44	4	27,061	23,132	120,284
45	5	27,602	22,687	142,971
46	6	28,154	22,251	165,221
47	7	28,717	21,823	187,044
48	8	29,291	21,403	208,447
49	9	29,877	20,991	229,438
50	10	30,475	20,588	250,026
51	11	31,084	20,192	270,218
52	12	31,706	19,804	290,021
53	13	32,340	19,423	309,444
54	14	32,987	19,049	328,493
55	15	33,647	18,683	347,176
56	16	34,320	18,324	365,500
57	17	35,006	17,971	383,471
58	18	35,706	17,626	401,096
59	19	36,420	17,287	418,383

Age	Period	Future Value	Present Value	Sum
60	20	37,149	16,954	435,337
61	21	37,892	16,628	451,965
62	22	38,649	16,308	468,274
63	23	39,422	15,995	484,268
64	24	40,211	15,687	499,955
65	25	41,015	15,385	515,341
66	26	41,835	15,090	530,431
67	27	42,672	14,799	545,230
68	28	43,526	14,515	559,745
69	29	44,396	14,236	573,980
70	30	45,284	13,962	587,942
71	31	46,190	13,693	601,636
72	32	47,114	13,430	615,066
73	33	48,056	13,172	628,238
74	34	49,017	12,919	641,156
75	35	49,997	12,670	653,826
76	36	50,997	12,426	666,253
77	37	52,017	12,187	678,440
78	38	53,057	11,953	690,393
79	39	54,119	11,723	702,116
80	40	55,201	11,498	713,614
81	41	56,305	11,277	724,891
82	42	57,431	11,060	735,951
83	43	58,580	10,847	746,798
84	44	59,751	10,639	757,436
85	45	60,946	10,434	767,870
86	46	62,165	10,233	778,103
87	47	63,409	10,036	788,140
88	48	64,677	9,843	797,983
89	49	65,970	9,654	807,637
90	50	67,290	9,469	817,106
91	51	68,635	9,286	826,392
92	52	70,008	9,108	835,500
93	53	71,408	8,933	844,433
94	54	72,837	8,761	853,194
95	55	74,293	8,592	861,786
96	56	75,779	8,427	870,213
97	57	77,295	8,265	878,479
98	58	78,841	8,106	886,585
99	59	80,417	7,950	894,535

Table 13-13 shows the present value of working uninterrupted to each age through age 99. But the present value of the income stream reported by the economist is $499,995. This is the present value of the income stream working uninterrupted to age 65. If the probability of living and the probabilities of seeking and finding employment are included in the analysis, then the present value figure should be calculated through age 99. This calculation is presented in Table 13-14.

Table 13-14   Present Value of Future Income. The Probability of Living and the Probabilities of Seeking and Finding Employment Are Included

White Male

Age	Period	Present Value	Sum	Prob of Living	Emp Rate	Part Rate	Adjusted PV	Adjusted Sum
40	0	25,000	25,000	.9972	.938	.970	22,684	22,684
41	1	24,519	49,519	.9943	.938	.970	22,182	44,866
42	2	24,048	73,567	.9912	.938	.970	21,688	66,554
43	3	23,585	97,152	.9879	.938	.970	21,199	87,752
44	4	23,132	120,284	.9842	.938	.970	20,715	108,467
45	5	22,687	142,971	.9803	.912	.942	19,107	127,574
46	6	22,251	165,221	.9761	.912	.942	18,658	146,232
47	7	21,823	187,044	.9715	.912	.942	18,213	164,446
48	8	21,403	208,447	.9665	.912	.942	17,772	182,217
49	9	20,991	229,438	.9611	.912	.942	17,333	199,550
50	10	20,588	250,026	.9553	.912	.942	16,896	216,445
51	11	20,192	270,218	.9488	.912	.942	16,459	232,904
52	12	19,804	290,021	.9417	.912	.942	16,022	248,926
53	13	19,423	309,444	.9339	.912	.942	15,582	264,508
54	14	19,049	328,493	.9252	.912	.942	15,141	279,649
55	15	18,683	347,176	.9157	.770	.798	10,512	290,161
56	16	18,324	365,500	.9052	.770	.798	10,192	300,353
57	17	17,971	383,471	.8939	.770	.798	9,871	310,224
58	18	17,626	401,096	.8815	.770	.798	9,547	319,771
59	19	17,287	418,383	.8682	.770	.798	9,222	328,992
60	20	16,954	435,337	.8537	.770	.798	8,894	337,886
61	21	16,628	451,965	.8383	.770	.798	8,565	346,451
62	22	16,308	468,274	.8218	.770	.798	8,235	354,686
63	23	15,995	484,268	.8044	.770	.798	7,906	362,592
64	24	15,687	499,955	.7861	.770	.798	7,577	370,169
65	25	15,385	515,341	.7666	.235	.256	710	370,878
66	26	15,090	530,431	.7459	.235	.256	677	371,555
67	27	14,799	545,230	.7240	.235	.256	645	372,200
68	28	14,515	559,745	.7008	.235	.256	612	372,812
69	29	14,236	573,980	.6765	.235	.256	579	373,391
70	30	13,962	587,942	.6508	.235	.256	547	373,938

Age	Period	Present Value	Sum	Prob of Living	Emp Rate	Part Rate	Adjusted PV	Adjusted Sum
71	31	13,693	601,636	.6239	.235	.256	514	374,452
72	32	13,430	615,066	.5957	.235	.256	481	374,933
73	33	13,172	628,238	.5664	.235	.256	449	375,382
74	34	12,919	641,156	.5360	.235	.256	417	375,798
75	35	12,670	653,826	.5047	.235	.256	385	376,183
76	36	12,426	666,253	.4724	.235	.256	353	376,536
77	37	12,187	678,440	.4396	.235	.256	322	376,859
78	38	11,953	690,393	.4062	.235	.256	292	377,151
79	39	11,723	702,116	.3725	.235	.256	263	377,413
80	40	11,498	713,614	.3376	.235	.256	233	377,647
81	41	11,277	724,891	.3017	.235	.256	205	377,852
82	42	11,060	735,951	.2654	.235	.256	177	378,028
83	43	10,847	746,798	.2292	.235	.256	150	378,178
84	44	10,639	757,436	.1938	.235	.256	124	378,302
85	45	10,434	767,870	.1599	.235	.256	100	378,402
86	46	10,233	778,103	.1282	.235	.256	79	378,481
87	47	10,036	788,140	.0995	.235	.256	60	378,541
88	48	9,843	797,983	.0742	.235	.256	44	378,585
89	49	9,654	807,637	.0528	.235	.256	31	378,616
90	50	9,469	817,106	.0356	.235	.256	20	378,636
91	51	9,286	826,392	.0225	.235	.256	13	378,649
92	52	9,108	835,500	.0131	.235	.256	7	378,656
93	53	8,933	844,433	.0069	.235	.256	4	378,659
94	54	8,761	853,194	.0032	.235	.256	2	378,661
95	55	8,592	861,786	.0013	.235	.256	1	378,662
96	56	8,427	870,213	.0004	.235	.256	0	378,662
97	57	8,265	878,479	.0001	.235	.256	0	378,662
98	58	8,106	886,585	.0000	.235	.256	0	378,662
99	59	7,950	894,535	.0000	.235	.256	0	378,662

The probabilities of living and seeking and finding employment reduce the present value of the future income from $499,995 to age 65 to $378,662. It should again be noted that the inclusion of the participation rates understates the present value of the income stream.

The impact of including the probabilities of living and seeking and finding employment vary with race and sex. The actual calculations are not present here, but Table 13-15 shows the present value of an income stream using the current fact situation but altering the race and sex. Note that, if the person works uninterrupted to age 65, the present value of the future income stream will be $499,995 since the race and sex of the individual will have no impact on the present value.

Table 13-15 Present Value by Race and Sex

	Male	Female
White	$378,662	$114,215
Black	$343,493	$262,126

The present value of a future income stream adjusted for the probabilities of seeking and finding employment for women are biased downward. The present value calculation uses the average seeking employment rate and the average finding employment rate. This means that the early years keep the average much lower than would be indicated by the more recent patterns.

§13.07 An Example of Using the Probability of Finding Employment and the Mortality Adjustment in the Present Value Analysis

Since the inclusion of participating in the labor force understates the present value of the future income the analysis can proceed with just the inclusion of the probability of employment and the probability of living. If the analysis only has these two variables then the present value of the income stream to age 99 would be $440,158. This is very close to the present value of the income stream to age 65, which is $499,955.

Table 13-16 Present Value of a $25,000 Per Year Stream Adjusted for Unemployment Rate and Mortality Rate

Growth 2%
Discount 4%
White Male

Age	Period	Present Value	Sum	Probability of Living	Emp	Adjusted PV	Sum
40	0	25,000	25,000	0.9972	0.938	23,384	23,384
41	1	24,519	49,519	0.9943	0.938	22,868	46,252
42	2	24,048	73,567	0.9912	0.938	22,359	68,611
43	3	23,585	97,152	0.9879	0.938	21,855	90,466
44	4	23,132	120,284	0.9842	0.938	21,355	111,821
45	5	22,687	142,971	0.9803	0.912	20,283	132,104
46	6	22,251	165,221	0.9761	0.912	19,808	151,911
47	7	21,823	187,044	0.9715	0.912	19,335	171,247
48	8	21,403	208,447	0.9665	0.912	18,866	190,112
49	9	20,991	229,438	0.9611	0.912	18,399	208,512
50	10	20,588	250,026	0.9553	0.912	17,937	226,449
51	11	20,192	270,218	0.9488	0.912	17,472	243,921
52	12	19,804	290,021	0.9417	0.912	17,008	260,929

Age	Period	Present Value	Sum	Probability of Living	Emp	Adjusted PV	Sum
53	13	19,423	309,444	0.9339	0.912	16,543	277,472
54	14	19,049	328,493	0.9252	0.912	16,073	293,545
55	15	18,683	347,176	0.9157	0.77	13,173	306,718
56	16	18,324	365,500	0.9052	0.77	12,772	319,490
57	17	17,971	383,471	0.8939	0.77	12,369	331,860
58	18	17,626	401,096	0.8815	0.77	11,964	343,823
59	19	17,287	418,383	0.8682	0.77	11,557	355,380
60	20	16,954	435,337	0.8537	0.77	11,145	366,525
61	21	16,628	451,965	0.8383	0.77	10,733	377,258
62	22	16,308	468,274	0.8218	0.77	10,319	387,577
63	23	15,995	484,268	0.8044	0.77	9,907	397,485
64	24	15,687	499,955	0.7861	0.77	9,495	406,980
65	25	15,385	515,341	0.7666	0.235	2,772	409,751
66	26	15,090	530,431	0.7459	0.235	2,645	412,397
67	27	14,799	545,230	0.724	0.235	2,518	414,914
68	28	14,515	559,745	0.7008	0.235	2,390	417,305
69	29	14,236	573,980	0.6765	0.235	2,263	419,568
70	30	13,962	587,942	0.6508	0.235	2,135	421,703
71	31	13,693	601,636	0.6239	0.235	2,008	423,711
72	32	13,430	615,066	0.5957	0.235	1,880	425,591
73	33	13,172	628,238	0.5664	0.235	1,753	427,344
74	34	12,919	641,156	0.536	0.235	1,627	428,972
75	35	12,670	653,826	0.5047	0.235	1,503	430,474
76	36	12,426	666,253	0.4724	0.235	1,379	431,854
77	37	12,187	678,440	0.4396	0.235	1,259	433,113
78	38	11,953	690,393	0.4062	0.235	1,141	434,254
79	39	11,723	702,116	0.3725	0.235	1,026	435,280
80	40	11,498	713,614	0.3376	0.235	912	436,192
81	41	11,277	724,891	0.3017	0.235	800	436,992
82	42	11,060	735,951	0.2654	0.235	690	437,682
83	43	10,847	746,798	0.2292	0.235	584	438,266
84	44	10,639	757,436	0.1938	0.235	485	438,750
85	45	10,434	767,870	0.1599	0.235	392	439,142
86	46	10,233	778,103	0.1282	0.235	308	439,451
87	47	10,036	788,140	0.0995	0.235	235	439,685
88	48	9,843	797,983	0.0742	0.235	172	439,857
89	49	9,654	807,637	0.0528	0.235	120	439,977
90	50	9,469	817,106	0.0356	0.235	79	440,056
91	51	9,286	826,392	0.0225	0.235	49	440,105
92	52	9,108	835,500	0.0131	0.235	28	440,133
93	53	8,933	844,433	0.0069	0.235	14	440,148
94	54	8,761	853,194	0.0032	0.235	7	440,154
95	55	8,592	861,786	0.0013	0.235	3	440,157
96	56	8,427	870,213	0.0004	0.235	1	440,158

Age	Period	Present Value	Sum	Probability of Living	Emp	Adjusted PV	Sum
97	57	8,265	878,479	0.0001	0.235	0	440,158
98	58	8,106	886,585	0	0.235	0	440,158
99	59	7,950	894,535	0	0.235	0	440,158

§13.08 Summary

The adjustment to present value of future income for the probabilities of seeking and finding employment reduce the dollar loss. If the person was a member of the labor force, employed or unemployed, then the analysis should be computed with the probability of employment and the probability of living. If the person is not a member of the labor force then the probability of participating in the labor forces would also be included.

14

Consumption

$$\text{Present Value of Future Income} = \sum_{t=0}^{n} \$ * M * (1+g)^t / (1+d)^t * P_L * P_S * P_F * \underline{C} * HS * T_X$$

§14.01 Introduction

The purpose of this chapter is to define *consumption* and discuss the impact consumption has on the present value of a future income stream. To this end, different sources addressing the question of individual consumption are examined. Finally, the short-coming of the consumption data is examined.

§14.02   Definitions

An economist defines *consumption* as the total demand for all consumer goods and services.[1] However, this is not the appropriate definition for the forensic economist. The forensic economist is concerned with what portion of income goes solely to the support of an individual. For example: suppose a house payment is $700 per month. If it is a two-member household, it may be viewed that half of that house payment is for each of the individuals. However, if one of the individuals is deceased, the house payment does not decrease by half. Consequently, in a wrongful death case, what is being examined is not what portion of the house payment would be attributed to the deceased, but what sorts of expenditures on the deceased will in fact cease with his or her death. Examples of expenditures which cease at death would be a clothing expenditure, a portion of the food budget, life insurance and disability insurance premiums. Examples of expenditures which would not cease would be home-owner's insurance, house payments, lawn care, subscriptions, and utilities.

§14.03   When Consumption Matters

The economist is employed to estimate the present value of an income stream. The methodology for calculating the present value of the income stream is the same whether the plaintiff was injured or killed. However, how consumption alters the present value of the income stream depends on whether the plaintiff was disabled or killed.[2] If the plaintiff was disabled, there may be no reason to reduce the present value of the future income stream. In some cases consumption may increase as a result of the disability. The injury may result in increased needs for medication, home or transportation modification, and other medical expenses. These factors affecting the present value should be treated individually rather than simply indicating that consumption increases. That is, rather than saying consumption will be higher, an estimate should be made for the present value of future medication or the present value of future home or transportation modifications which are a result of the disability.

When the present value analysis is addressing the income stream of a deceased person it may then be appropriate to reduce the present value by an amount to reflect the deceased's consumption.

§14.04   Sources of Consumption Information

Traditionally the major sources of consumption information used by economists have been *Injury and Recovery in the Course of Employment* by Earl F. Cheit,[3] and

---

[1] W. Boumol & A. Binder, Economics 114 (3d ed 1985).

[2] Franz, *Should Income Taxes Be Included When Calculating Lost Earnings*, Trial, Oct 1982, at 53-57.

[3] E. Cheit, Injury and Recovery in the Course of Employment (1961).

the Revised Equivalency Scale published by the United States Department of Labor.[4] More recently there have been several other studies addressing the question of consumption. These studies have also incorporated more recent government statistic into the analysis. Three of these studies are *Estimating Personal Consumption of a Deceased Family Member*, by Roy Gilbert,[5] *Estimating Personal Consumption Costs in Wrongful Death Cases*, by Robert Patton and David Nelson,[6] and *Estimating Personal Expenditure Deduction in Multi-Income Families in Cases of Wrongful Death* by Melvin Harju and Clarence Adams.[7]

§14.05   Consumption Using the 1961 Cheit Report

Cheit reports that consumption of head of household ranges from 18 per cent of income when there are two adults and four minor children, to 30 per cent of income when there are two adults and no minor children. The consumption of the head of household is dependent on the number of minor children present. Table 14-1 presents the relationship between consumption of head of household and number of minor children at home.

Table 14-1   Consumption by Head of Household with Dependent Children

Number of Dependent Children	Per Cent of Income Consumed by Head of Household
0	30%
1	26%
2	22%
3	20%
4	18%

Table 14-1 indicates that, if the household consists of two adults and two minor dependent children, the head of household consumes 22 per cent of the family income. As the children grow and eventually leave home, the head of the household consumes more of the family income. With only one minor dependent child at

---

[4] US Dept of Labor, Revised Equivalency Scale for Urban Families of Different Size, Age and Composition, Derived from the Bureau of Labor Statistics of Consumer Expenditures (1960-61).

[5] Gilbert, *Estimating Personal Consumption of a Deceased Family Member*, 4, No 2 Forensic Econs 175 (1991).

[6] Patton & Nelson, *Estimating Personal Consumption Costs in Wrongful Death Cases*, 4, No 2 Forensic Econs 233 (1991).

[7] Harju & Adams, *Estimating Personal Expenditure Deductions in Multi-Income Families in Cases of Wrongful Death*, 4, No 2 Forensic Econs 65 (1990).

home the head of the household consumes 26 per cent of the income. With no dependent children the consumption increases to 30 per cent of the family income.

Assume the present value of the income of a 40-year-old person earning $20,000 per year is being calculated. The growth rate and discount rate are both 4%. The present value of the income to age 65 is $500,000, see Table 14-2. If the family is a two person household then the reduction of 30% in the total income could be made for the self consumption. The lost income to the surviving spouse would be $350,000.

If there are children present, then the age of the children must be known. Assume the couple have two children, ages 12 and 15 at the time of the death of the parent. The Cheit report indicates that one adult would consume 22% of the income until the oldest child leaves home, assume age 18, and 26% until the second child leaves home. After the second child leaves home, then self consumption would increase to 30% of the income. The consumption reduces the loss of future income to $357,200.

Table 14-2   Reducing the Present Value of Income for Consumption

Age	Period	Present Value	Sum	Age of Child #2	#1	Per Cent Consumed	Present Value Less Consumption Annual	Sum
40	0	20,000	20,000	12	15	22	15,600	15,600
41	1	20,000	40,000	13	16	22	15,600	31,200
42	2	20,000	60,000	14	17	22	15,600	46,800
43	3	20,000	80,000	15		26	14,800	61,600
44	4	20,000	100,000	16		26	14,800	76,400
45	5	20,000	120,000	17		26	14,800	91,200
46	6	20,000	140,000			30	14,000	105,200
47	7	20,000	160,000			30	14,000	119,200
48	8	20,000	180,000			30	14,000	133,200
49	9	20,000	200,000			30	14,000	147,200
50	10	20,000	220,000			30	14,000	161,200
51	11	20,000	240,000			30	14,000	175,200
52	12	20,000	260,000			30	14,000	189,200
53	13	20,000	280,000			30	14,000	203,200
54	14	20,000	300,000			30	14,000	217,200
55	15	20,000	320,000			30	14,000	231,200
56	16	20,000	340,000			30	14,000	245,200
57	17	20,000	360,000			30	14,000	259,200
58	18	20,000	380,000			30	14,000	273,200
59	19	20,000	400,000			30	14,000	287,200

Age	Period	Present Value	Sum	Age of Child #2	#1	Per Cent Consumed	Present Value Less Consumption Annual	Sum
60	20	20,000	420,000			30	14,000	301,200
61	21	20,000	440,000			30	14,000	315,200
62	22	20,000	460,000			30	14,000	329,200
63	23	20,000	480,000			30	14,000	343,200
64	24	20,000	500,000			30	14,000	357,200

§14.06   Consumption Using the Revised Equivalency Scale

Table 14-3 presents the consumption for the head of household based on the age of head of household and the number of family members. The proportion of income the head of household consumes is a function of his/her age and the age of the oldest child.

The Revised Equivalency Scale, from which Table 14-3 is derived, is an index. The "typical" family had two parents present and two minor children. The oldest child is between ages 6 and 15, and the head of the household is between ages 35 and 54. The Revised Equivalency Scale sets the consumption of the family at 100 per cent. That is, to maintain a stated standard of living takes 100 per cent of their income. All other family structure are relative to this family and this standard of living.

If the family structure is the same as the "typical" family, except there is only one child present and the child is between the ages 6 and 15, then the index number in Table 14-3 is 82. This means the family of three, husband, wife and one child, needs 82 per cent of what the family of four needs in order to maintain the same standard of living.

If the family consists of two parents and four children, with the oldest child between the ages 6 and 15 and the head of the household between the ages 35 and 54, then the index number is 132. This means the family of six needs 132 per cent of the income the "typical" family of four needs in order to maintain the same standard of living.

By comparing positions on the table, the head of household's consumption can be estimated. Suppose the head of the household of the "typical" family is killed. The family structure changes from two adults, head of household between the ages 35 and 54, with two children, oldest between the ages 6 and 15, to a family of one adult, two children. The index value is 76. This means the family of three needs 76 per cent of what the family of four needed to maintain the same standard of living. The head of the household consumed 24 per cent of the family income.

As with the Cheit analysis this consumption pattern would be traced through the aging of the children in order to determine the reduction in the present value of the future income stream.

Table 14-3   Revised Equivalency Scale for Urban Families of Different Sizes, Ages, and Composition

A 4-person family, husband, age 35 to 54; wife; 2 children, older child 6 to 15 years of age, equals 100%.

Size and Type of Family	Age of Head			
	Under 35	35-54	55-64	65+
One person	35	36	32	28
Two persons: average	47	59	59	52
Husband, wife	49	60	59	51
Husband, wife (child under 6)	40	57	60	58
One parent, one child	62	81	86	77
Three persons: average				
Husband, wife, one child (child under 6)	62	69	—	—
Husband, wife, one child (child 6-15)	62	82	88	81
Husband, wife, one child (child 16-17)	—	91	88	77
Husband, wife, one child (child over 18)	—	82	85	77
One parent, 2 children	67	76	82	75
Four persons: average	74	99	109	91
Husband, wife, two children under 6	72	80	—	—
Husband, wife, two children (oldest child 6-15)	77	100	105	95
Husband, wife, two children (oldest child 16-17)	—	113	125	—
Husband, wife, two children (oldest child over 18)	—	96	110	89
One parent, 3 children	94	118	124	—
Five persons: average	94	118	124	—
Husband, wife, children under 6	87	97	—	—
Husband, wife, three children (oldest 6-15)	96	116	120	—
Husband, wife, three children (oldest 16-17)	—	128	138	—
Husband, wife, three children (oldest over 18)	—	119	124	—
One parent, 4 children	108	117	—	—
Six persons: average	111	138	143	—
Husband, wife, children under 6	101	—	—	—
Husband, wife, four children (oldest 6-15)	110	132	140	—
Husband, wife, four children (oldest 16-17)	—	146	—	—
Husband, wife, four children (oldest over 18)	—	149	—	—
One parent, 5 children	125	137	—	—

§14.07   Consumption of Husband and Wife

The Patton and Nelson study addresses the portion of family income spent by the husband and wife members of the family based on the number of members in the family and the family income. Table 14-4 presents the percentage of income that is consumed by an adult male or adult female family member. The proportion of the income spent of personal consumption by each spouse depends on the income level of the household. As one might expect, as the income increases, or the number of family members increases, the proportion of income consumed by the adult family member decreases. The Patton and Nelson approach differs from Revised Equivalency Scale in that no adjustments are made for the age of the children.

The interpretation of the table is straightforward. Suppose a family of four, two adults and two children, has an income of $45,000 per year. The adult male consumes 15.4% of the income and the adult female consumes 16% of the income. In estimating the reduction for consumption to the present value of an income stream it would be necessary to know the ages of the children.

Table 14-4 Percent of Income Consumed by Adult Family Members

MALE

Income Level	One Person Low	One Person High	Two	Three	Four	Five	Six
0 - 5,000	138.7	149.1	68.6	45.0	49.2	45.4	31.5
5 - 10,000	102.2	113.3	47.4	33.7	34.1	31.3	24.2
10 - 15,000	85.5	96.5	38.2	28.5	27.5	25.2	20.7
15 - 20,000	75.4	86.1	32.7	25.3	23.7	21.6	18.5
20 - 25,000	68.3	78.8	29.1	23.0	21.0	19.2	17.0
25 - 30,000	63.0	73.3	26.4	21.3	19.1	17.4	15.9
30 - 35,000	58.9	69.0	24.3	20.0	17.6	16.0	15.0
35 - 40,000	55.6	65.4	22.6	18.9	16.4	14.9	14.2
40 - 45,000	52.8	62.4	21.2	18.0	15.4	14.0	13.6
45 - 50,000	50.4	59.9	20.1	17.2	14.6	13.2	13.1
50 - 55,000	48.3	57.7	19.1	16.6	13.9	12.6	12.6
55 - 60,000	46.5	55.7	18.2	16.0	13.2	12.0	12.2
60 - 65,000	44.9	54.0	17.4	15.4	12.7	11.5	11.8
65 - 70,000	43.4	52.4	16.8	15.0	12.2	11.0	11.5
70 - 75,000	42.1	51.0	16.2	14.6	11.8	10.6	11.2
75 - 80,000	41.0	49.7	15.6	14.2	11.4	10.3	10.9

FEMALE

Family Size

Income Level	One Person Low	One Person High	Two	Three	Four	Five	Six
0 - 5,000	138.7	149.1	70.2	50.0	50.0	48.3	37
5 - 10,000	102.2	113.3	48.8	36.5	34.9	33.0	27.3
10 - 15,000	85.5	96.5	39.4	30.5	28.3	26.4	22.8
15 - 20,000	75.4	86.1	33.9	26.8	24.3	22.6	20.1
20 - 25,000	68.3	78.8	30.1	24.2	21.7	19.6	18.2
25 - 30,000	63.0	73.3	27.4	22.3	19.7	18.0	16.8
30 - 35,000	58.9	69.0	25.3	20.9	18.2	16.6	15.7
35 - 40,000	55.6	65.4	23.6	19.6	17.0	15.4	14.8
40 - 45,000	52.8	62.4	22.1	18.6	16.0	14.4	14.0
45 - 50,000	50.4	59.9	20.9	17.8	15.1	13.6	13.4
50 - 55,000	48.3	57.7	19.9	17.0	14.4	12.9	12.8
55 - 60,000	46.5	55.7	19.0	16.4	13.8	12.3	12.3
60 - 65,000	44.9	54.0	18.3	15.8	13.2	11.8	11.9
65 - 70,000	43.4	52.4	17.6	15.3	12.7	11.3	11.5
70 - 75,000	42.1	51.0	16.9	14.8	12.3	10.9	11.2
75 - 80,000	41.0	49.7	16.4	14.4	11.9	10.5	10.9

§14.08 Using the Patton and Nelson Consumption Figures

The question we are addressing is, "What portion of the family income is consumed by the husband?" Let us assume the income is $45,000 per year, growing at 2% and discounted at 4%. The family has two children, ages 12 and 15. Table 14-5 presents the present value of the income stream to age 65 and a reduction in the income stream for the husband's personal consumption.

Table 14-5

Age	Period	Future Income	Present Value	Sum	Child #2	#1	Cons	Adjusted PV	Sum
40	0	45,000	45,000	45,000	12	15	15.4	38,070	38,070
41	1	45,900	44,135	89,135	13	16	15.4	37,338	75,408
42	2	46,818	43,286	132,420	14	17	15.4	36,620	112,028
43	3	47,754	42,453	174,874	15		18	34,812	146,840
44	4	48,709	41,637	216,511	16		18	34,142	180,982
45	5	49,684	40,836	257,347	17		18	33,486	214,468
46	6	50,677	40,051	297,398			21.2	31,560	246,028
47	7	51,691	39,281	336,679			21.2	30,953	276,981
48	8	52,725	38,525	375,205			21.2	30,358	307,339
49	9	53,779	37,785	412,989			21.2	29,774	337,113
50	10	54,855	37,058	450,047			21.2	29,202	366,315
51	11	55,952	36,345	486,392			21.2	28,640	394,955
52	12	57,071	35,646	522,039			21.2	28,089	423,044
53	13	58,212	34,961	556,999			21.2	27,549	450,594
54	14	59,377	34,288	591,288			21.2	27,019	477,613
55	15	60,564	33,629	624,917			21.2	26,500	504,113
56	16	61,775	32,982	657,899			21.2	25,990	530,103
57	17	63,011	32,348	690,247			21.2	25,490	555,593
58	18	64,271	31,726	721,973			21.2	25,000	580,593
59	19	65,557	31,116	753,089			21.2	24,519	605,112
60	20	66,868	30,518	783,607			21.2	24,048	629,160
61	21	68,205	29,931	813,537			21.2	23,585	652,746
62	22	69,569	29,355	842,892			21.2	23,132	675,877
63	23	70,960	28,791	871,683			21.2	22,687	698,564
64	24	72,380	28,237	899,920			21.2	22,251	720,815

Table 14-5 indicates that the present value of the future income through age 64 is $899,920. When consumption is taken into account the present value of the income stream after deducting for consumption is $720,815.

Column 3 in Table 14-5 is the future value of the income level. If the rate of inflation is forecast to be 2% per year for the next 25 years then there is no change in the purchasing power of the income level.

When using the Patton and Nelson figures to determine the proportion of income consumed by a member of the household it is important to recognize that the analysis is taking place in 1986-87 dollars. If it is judged that the *real* income is changing, then appropriate adjustments must be made to the consumption figures.

Allow the fact situation outlined above to be modified to permit an increase in real income of 1.5%. Where the growth rate was 2%, allowing for no increase in purchasing power, the growth rate is now increased to 3.5% allowing for a 1.5% increase in purchasing power each year. Table 14-6 shows the increase in real income. Column 3 represents future income with no increase in purchasing power. Column 4 represents future income with a 1.5% annual increase in purchasing power. By comparing the income level in Column 4, the real income in future years, to the income levels in Table 14-4 we can determine when the level of consumption changes.

Table 14-6 indicates that the real income reaches $50,000 when the husband would reach age 48. From Table 14-5 we can determine that both children are over 18. The household now consists of two adults. From Table 14-4 the husband's consumption is 19.1% of the income. Table 14-6 indicates that the real income would rise above $60,000 at age 60 and accordingly consumption would decrease to 18.2%. These changes in real income can be traced through the future income stream.

Table 14-6

| | | Future Income | |
Age	Period	No Growth	1.5% Growth
40	0	45,000	45,000
41	1	45,000	45,675
42	2	45,000	46,360
43	3	45,000	47,056
44	4	45,000	47,761
45	5	45,000	48,478
46	6	45,000	49,205
47	7	45,000	49,943
48	8	45,000	50,692
49	9	45,000	51,453
50	10	45,000	52,224
51	11	45,000	53,008
52	12	45,000	53,803
53	13	45,000	54,610
54	14	45,000	55,429
55	15	45,000	56,260
56	16	45,000	57,104
57	17	45,000	57,961
58	18	45,000	58,830

| | | Future Income | |
Age	Period	No Growth	1.5% Growth
59	19	45,000	59,713
60	20	45,000	60,608
61	21	45,000	61,518
62	22	45,000	62,440
63	23	45,000	63,377
64	24	45,000	64,328

§14.09   Consumption for One Family Member

The Gilbert study presents findings in a different format. The results of the Gilbert study present consumption for one person as a function of income level and family size. Table 14-7 present the results of the Gilbert study. The income levels are in 1987-1988 dollars.

Table 14-7   Consumption as a Percentage of Income and Family Size

Income Range		Family Size			
		Two	Three	Four	Five+
10,000	15,000	32.5	21.8	16.5	11.6
15,000	20,000	34.0	22.6	16.7	11.8
20,000	30,000	34.5	22.8	16.9	11.7
30,000	40,000	34.9	23.0	17.2	12.4
40,000	Plus	34.2	22.8	17.1	12.4

§14.10   Consumption Based on Dual Incomes

The study by Harju and Adams adds another variable to the consumption equation. Their conclusions address the proportion of income that would have been consumed by the deceased had both parties been working. The proportion of net income consumed by the deceased is a function of the gross income level of the survivor and the gross income of the deceased. Table 14-8 presents the results of the Harju and Adams study. The study points out that fringe benefits and child care expense should be considered separately.

Table 14-8

Survivor's Gr Income	Decedent's Gr Income				
	10,000	20,000	30,000	40,000	50,000
0	17.6%	17.6%	17.6%	17.6%	17.6%
$10,000	38.5	29.2	26.0	24.9	24.0
20,000	53.9	37.7	33.5	30.8	29.0
30,000	72.8	50.7	42.2	37.5	34.4
40,000	95.8	61.7	49.5	43.0	39.5
50,000	111.1	68.9	54.1	47.3	42.9
50,000	126.9	76.4	60.5	52.0	46.6

§14.11 Problems Interpreting the Consumption Table

There are certain relationships presented on the Revised Equivalency Table that imply that a head of household has negative consumption. If the family were husband, wife, and three children under six years of age, and the head of the household is under 35, then the family would need 87 per cent of what the typical family of four would need to maintain a lifestyle. If the husband died, then the family of four, with one parent, would need 88 per cent of what the typical family needed in order to maintain that lifestyle. This implies that the husband had negative consumption.

Another problem is with interpretation of the numbers on the table. Consider a family of two adults with the head of household between ages 55 and 64. The two adults need 59 per cent of the income of the family of four. If the head of household dies, then the single adult needs 32 per cent of what the family of four would need. This implies that the head of household consumed 27 per cent of the income.

There is an improper way to interpret the table. Some argue that 32 per cent of the income needed to support one adult is 54 per cent of the 59 per cent needed to support both adults (54% = 32% / 59%). Thus, the consumption of the head of household is 46 per cent of the total income (100% - 54% = 46%).

The major problems with the studies by Patton and Nelson and Harju and Adams are the difficulty in applying the data. In the Patton and Nelson study the increase in real income must be taken into consideration in order to make a correct reduction for consumption. In the Harju and Adams study the same criticism can be made, except that in their approach forecasts must be made of the income levels of both earners.

§14.12 Cross-Examining the Economist

During the pretrial discovery, defense counsel will have had the opportunity to determine what information the economist obtained regarding personal consumption of the decedent. More likely than not, the economist did not obtain such information for the simple reason that the actual figures on an individual's personal consumption are extremely difficult to determine. During cross-examination defense counsel will want to obtain an admission from the economist that the individual's personal consumption figures were not taken into account. An argument might be made that the opinion of the economist is not supported by factual information regarding the decedent.[8]

§14.13   Summary

When an economist is making an extended analysis of the present value of the future income it is possible to make the reduction for personal consumption. However, it would be inappropriate to reduce the present value of future income for consumption without attempting to account for the other variables such as fringe benefits, taxes, and household services.

---

[8] Higgins v Kinebrew Motors, Inc, 547 F2d 1223, 1225-36 (5th Cir 1977).

15 Federal Income Taxes

$$\text{Present Value of Future Income} = \sum_{t=0}^{n} \$ * M * (1+g)^t / (1+d)^t * P_L * P_S * P_F * C * HS * \underline{Tx}$$

§15.01 Introduction

Initially it would appear that taxes would reduce the size of the present value award. This chapter will address that question and review the major problems arising from including taxes in the present value calculation.[1]

---

[1] In Norfolk & Western Ry v Liepelt, 444 US 490, *rehg denied*, 445 US 972 (1980), the Supreme Court of the United States addressed the issue of whether a state court could prohibit admission of evidence concerning the effect of income taxation on future earnings in the context of an action under the Federal Employer's Liability Act (FELA), 45 USC §51 *et seq.* The Court

§15.02   The Federal Income Tax

Since taxes are a fact of life today, any discussion of loss and compensation for that loss is incomplete without discussion of the effect of taxes on the present value of future income. Taxes may be paid at the point of a sale, i.e., sales tax, or taxes may be withheld by an employer, i.e., state and federal income tax and social security tax. Taxes are paid on investment income, although they may not be withheld. Regardless of how the taxes are paid, they represent a reduction in the discretionary income available to the plaintiff or the plaintiff's survivors. This chapter will limit the discussion to federal income taxes.

The 1992 Individual Federal Income Tax rates are presented in Tables 15-1, 15-2, and 15-3. As the tables indicate, there are three categories of taxpayers: single, married, and head of household. There are two categories of married taxpayers, married filing jointly and married filing separately.

Table 15-1   1992 Federal Income Tax Rate

Filing Status	Taxable Income	But not Over	Tax owed is this amount Plus	of the amount over
Single				
	0	21,450	15%	
	21,450	51,900	3,127.50 + 28%	21,450
	51,900		11,743.50 + 31%	51,900
Married filing Jointly				
	0	35,800	15%	
	35,800	86,500	5,370.00 + 28%	35,800
	86,500		19,566.00 + 31%	86,500
Married filing Separately				
	0	17,900	15%	
	17,900	43,250	2,685.00 + 28%	17,900
	43,250		9,783.00 + 31%	43,250

---

held that the recovery of damages in FELA actions was a matter of federal law, rejecting the argument that the effect of future income taxes was too speculative. However, a majority of jurisdictions still hold that the jury should not be instructed regarding the effects of income taxation on the amount of any damages received in a wrongful death action. *See generally* Annotation, *Propriety of Taking Income Tax into Consideration in Fixing Damages in Personal Injury or Death Action*, 16 ALR4th 589 (1983); Annotation, *Propriety of Considering Future Income Taxes in Awarding Damages Under Federal Tort Claims Act*, 47 ALR Fed 735 (1980).

Filing Status	Taxable Income	But not Over	Tax owed is this amount Plus	of the amount over
Head of Household				
	0	28,750	15%	
	28,750	74,150	4,312.50 + 28%	28,750
	74,150		17,024.50 + 31%	74,150

Tax rates are described two ways: the *average* tax rate and the *marginal* tax rate. The average tax rate is the tax liability divided by the taxable income. The marginal tax rate is the proportion of the last dollar of income that is paid in taxes. The marginal tax rates are 15, 28, and 31 per cent.

Which marginal tax rate is in effect depends on the income level of the taxpayer. Table 15-1 states that for the single taxpayer having a taxable income of less than $21,450 the tax due is 15 per cent. If the taxable income is above $21,450 and below $51,900, then the tax liability is $3,217.50 plus 28 per cent of the income above $21,450. In a like fashion, if the taxable income is over $51,900 the tax due is $11,743.50 plus 31 per cent of the earnings above $51,900.

Consider a taxable income of $25,000. If the taxpayer is single, the tax liability is $4,211.50 ($3,217.50 + 15% * $3,550). For this taxpayer the average tax rate is 16.85 per cent, and the marginal tax rate is 28 per cent. If the taxpayer's filing status is head of household, the tax liability is $4,312.50. The average tax rate is 15 per cent, and the marginal tax rate is 15 per cent.

For the married taxpayer filing separately the tax liability is $4,673. The average tax rate is 18.69 per cent and the marginal tax rate is 28 per cent.

§15.03   Reducing Future Income for Federal Income Taxes

Based on the data in Table 15-1, the present value of a future income stream, reduced for federal income taxes, will decline by an amount ranging from 15 to 31 per cent depending on the taxable income. The present value will be reduced by 15 per cent when the future income to be earned never exceeds $21,450 for a single person, $35,800 for married filing jointly, $17,900 for married filing separately, and $28,750 for head of household. If the income always exceeds these amounts, then the reduction in present value will require knowing what the taxable income is each future year and applying the appropriate reduction. If the current income level is $25,000 and is being forecast for the next 20 years, with an annual growth of wages of 4 per cent and an annual discount rate of 6 per cent, then the present value of the future income stream is $501,995. To reduce future income for taxes, the forecast of income for each future year must be made. The forecast value for each future year is presented in Table 15-2. The columns without taxes have a current income of $25,000 and the columns with taxes have a current income of $20,789.

Table 15-2   Present Value of Future Income Streams

| | | Without Taxes | | With Taxes | |
| | | Present | | Present | |
Age	Period	Value	Sum	Value	Sum
40	0	25,000	25,000	20,789	20,789
41	1	24,528	49,528	20,396	41,185
42	2	24,066	73,594	20,011	61,196
43	3	23,611	97,205	19,634	80,830
44	4	23,166	120,371	19,263	100,093
45	5	22,729	143,100	18,900	118,993
46	6	22,300	165,400	18,543	137,537
47	7	21,879	187,279	18,193	155,730
48	8	21,466	208,746	17,850	173,580
49	9	21,061	229,807	17,513	191,094
50	10	20,664	250,471	17,183	208,277
51	11	20,274	270,745	16,859	225,136
52	12	19,892	290,637	16,541	241,676
53	13	19,516	310,153	16,229	257,905
54	14	19,148	329,301	15,922	273,827
55	15	18,787	348,088	15,622	289,449
56	16	18,432	366,520	15,327	304,776
57	17	18,085	384,605	15,038	319,814
58	18	17,743	402,348	14,754	334,569
59	19	17,409	419,757	14,476	349,044
60	20	17,080	436,837	14,203	363,247
61	21	16,758	453,594	13,935	377,182
62	22	16,442	470,036	13,672	390,854
63	23	16,131	486,167	13,414	404,268
64	24	15,827	501,995	13,161	417,429

How much of an income reduction occurs for taxes depends on the filing status of the taxpayers. Table 15-2 also presents the after-tax dollars available each year to the single taxpayer. The table also shows the present value of the after-tax income. In order to make the after-tax calculation, the economist assumes that the filing status of the taxpayer will not change and that the tax structure will not change. The reduction for taxes causes the present value of the future income stream to decrease from $501,995 to $417,429.

Table 15-3 makes exactly the same calculations but for someone with a filing statue of married filing separately. If income taxes are ignored, the present value of the future income stream remains $501,995, while inclusion of income taxes reduces the present value of the income stream to $408,162. Note the difference in the filing status makes a difference in the present value of $9,267.

Table 15-3   Present Value after Taxes for Married Filing Separately

Age	Period	Without Taxes		With Taxes	
		Present Value	Sum	Present Value	Sum
40	0	25,000	25,000	20,327	20,327
41	1	24,528	49,528	19,943	40,270
42	2	24,066	73,594	19,567	59,838
43	3	23,611	97,205	19,198	79,036
44	4	23,166	120,371	18,836	97,871
45	5	22,729	143,100	18,480	116,352
46	6	22,300	165,400	18,132	134,483
47	7	21,879	187,279	17,790	152,273
48	8	21,466	208,746	17,454	169,727
49	9	21,061	229,807	17,125	186,852
50	10	20,664	250,471	16,801	203,653
51	11	20,274	270,745	16,484	220,138
52	12	19,892	290,637	16,173	236,311
53	13	19,516	310,153	15,868	252,179
54	14	19,148	329,301	15,569	267,748
55	15	18,787	348,088	15,275	283,023
56	16	18,432	366,520	14,987	298,010
57	17	18,085	384,605	14,704	312,714
58	18	17,743	402,348	14,427	327,141
59	19	17,409	419,757	14,155	341,296
60	20	17,080	436,837	13,887	355,183
61	21	16,758	453,594	13,625	368,809
62	22	16,442	470,036	13,368	382,177
63	23	16,131	486,167	13,116	395,293
64	24	15,827	501,995	12,869	408,162

§15.04   Evaluating the Reduction for Taxes

If the present value analysis is done properly there will be no remaining principal when the plaintiff reaches age 65. The economists estimated the present value of the future income stream, without consideration of taxes, to be $501,995.

Assume that an award of this amount is made. The recipient would take $25,000 for the first year's consumption and invest the remaining $476,995 at 6% interest. At the beginning of the second year the balance in the account would be

$505,615, having earned $28,620 in interest during the year. From the fund the second year's income would be withdrawn. The second year's income is $26,000, reflecting the 4% annual growth in income.

If this sequence is followed there will be a zero balance in the fund after 25 years. This is shown in Table 15-4.

Table 15-4   Impact of Taxes on the Award

Age	Beginning Balance	Annual Income	Principal @ Interest	Interest Income	Ending Bal
40	501,995	25,000	476,995	28,620	505,615
41	505,615	26,000	479,615	28,777	508,392
42	508,392	27,040	481,352	28,881	510,233
43	510,233	28,122	482,111	28,927	511,038
44	511,038	29,246	481,791	28,907	510,699
45	510,699	30,416	480,282	28,817	509,099
46	509,099	31,633	477,466	28,648	506,114
47	506,114	32,898	473,216	28,393	501,609
48	501,609	34,214	467,395	28,044	495,439
49	495,439	35,583	459,856	27,591	487,447
50	487,447	37,006	450,441	27,026	477,467
51	477,467	38,486	438,981	26,339	465,320
52	465,320	40,026	425,294	25,518	450,812
53	450,812	41,627	409,185	24,551	433,736
54	433,736	43,292	390,444	23,427	413,871
55	413,871	45,024	368,847	22,131	390,978
56	390,978	46,825	344,153	20,649	364,803
57	364,803	48,698	316,105	18,966	335,071
58	335,071	50,645	284,426	17,066	301,492
59	301,492	52,671	248,820	14,929	263,750
60	263,750	54,778	208,972	12,538	221,510
61	221,510	56,969	164,541	9,872	174,413
62	174,413	59,248	115,165	6,910	122,075
63	122,075	61,618	60,457	3,627	64,085
64	64,085	64,085	0	0	5

Table 15-5 shows that with the tax rate applicable to the married filing jointly taxpayer, when the award is reduced for taxes there will be insufficient funds and the principal will be exhausted at age 62. In fact the fund will be about $150,000 short of meeting the goal.

Table 15-5 Impact of Federal Income Tax

Age	Beg Balance	Annual Income	Prin @ Interest	Int Income	After Tax Income	Ending Bal
40	417,429	20,789	396,640	23,798	20,229	416,869
41	416,869	21,621	395,248	23,715	20,158	415,406
42	415,406	22,485	392,920	23,575	20,039	412,959
43	412,959	23,385	389,574	23,374	19,868	409,443
44	409,443	24,320	385,123	23,107	19,641	404,764
45	404,764	25,293	379,471	22,768	19,353	398,824
46	398,824	26,305	372,519	22,351	18,998	391,518
47	391,518	27,357	364,161	21,850	18,572	382,733
48	382,733	28,451	354,282	21,257	18,068	372,350
49	372,350	29,589	342,761	20,566	17,481	360,242
50	360,242	30,773	329,469	19,768	16,803	346,272
51	346,272	32,004	314,268	18,856	16,028	330,296
52	330,296	33,284	297,012	17,821	15,148	312,160
53	312,160	34,615	277,544	16,653	14,155	291,699
54	291,699	36,000	255,699	15,342	13,041	268,740
55	268,740	37,440	231,300	13,878	11,796	243,096
56	243,096	38,937	204,159	12,250	10,412	214,571
57	214,571	40,495	174,076	10,445	8,878	182,954
58	182,954	42,115	140,839	8,450	7,183	148,022
59	148,022	43,799	104,223	6,253	5,315	109,538
60	109,538	45,551	63,987	3,839	3,263	67,250
61	67,250	47,373	19,877	1,193	1,014	20,891
62	20,891	49,268	-28,377	-1,703	-1,447	-29,825
63	-29,825	51,239	-81,064	-4,864	-4,134	-85,198
64	-85,198	53,289	-138,487	-8,309	-7,063	-145,549

The reason for the shortfall is two-fold. The award to plaintiff is not a taxable income but the interest income is taxable. The present value of the award is computed using after-tax dollars, but the after-tax dollars earn taxable income. Second, the status of the taxpayer is changed from married filing jointly to single.

§15.05 Problems Associated with Reducing the Present Value of a Future Income Stream for Taxes

In order to reduce the future income stream for income taxes, the economist must make accurate forecasts concerning the future income, family structure, expenditures by type and size, and the level of household services. Sections 15.06 through 15.10 briefly address the difficulty of forecasting each of these items.

§15.06   —Income Forecasting

Income is received from wages and salaries, investment income, rents, royalties, and farm income. In order to reduce future income levels for income tax, the exact dollar amount of income must be known and the source of the income must be known.

For example, an individual has income from investments, dividends, and capital gains totaling $20,000 annually, plus a taxable salary of $20,000. Total taxable income for the individual is $40,000. The tax liability for a married couple filing jointly would be $6,546. If the couple had no investment income, the tax liability would be only $3,000. Is the difference of $3,546 in the tax liability due to the salary or to the investment income?

If the present value of the future income stream is calculated ignoring income tax, the present value is $403,292. Reduced for income tax, the award would be $671,749. The award would be insufficient, and the principal would be exhausted when plaintiff reaches age 62. Had the award been reduced at the higher tax rate, the principal would be exhausted sooner.

This same problem exists when there are two incomes in the family. Suppose each party earned $20,000 each. Is the injured party's income to be reduced for income tax at the higher or lower of the two rates? In either case the reduction for taxes will cause the principal to be exhausted before fully compensating the plaintiff.

§15.07   —Family Structure

When income streams are being reduced for income taxes, the age of each of the dependents must be known since the personal exemptions reduce the taxable income. Since the family can claim each child as a dependent under certain conditions through college, a decision must be made regarding the likelihood that the child will attend college. In a similar manner the mortality of each of the family members must be considered since, if premature death occurs, the number of dependents will change. As the number of dependents changes, the taxable income changes. Since alimony is a deductible expense when calculating taxable income, the analysis must consider the likelihood of the marriage surviving.

§15.08   —Expenditure Forecasting

Just as the family structure must be forecast, so must the level of expenditures be forecast. Income taxes are based on taxable income. Taxable income is total income less certain expenses. Deductible expenses include medical expenses after a deductible is met, state and local taxes, interest on the home mortgage.

To properly forecast the level of taxes, the medical expenses must be forecast by year. What illnesses will each family member have? Will the illnesses require medical care, and if so will the expenses be covered by the health insurance policy? If the policy does not cover the illnesses, will the expense be large enough to qualify for a deduction of medical expenses? How many years will the illnesses continue?

This type of analysis of medical expenses requires the economist to forecast the exact nature of illness and the coverage provided by the health insurance carrier and to perform the analysis on an annual basis. The same problems arise with interest deductions. To properly estimate the tax liability, the annual mortgage interest must be known. This requires knowing the amortization schedule for the mortgage and determining if the home will ever be refinanced or paid off at an accelerated rate. If refinancing or acceleration occurs, the economist must determine at what rate these occur.

§15.09   —Tax Schedules

To reduce the income stream for taxes, the economist must forecast the tax schedule for each year the analysis is being performed. Typically, the economist would assume the current tax structure would remain unchanged throughout the period the analysis occurs. To do otherwise would require the economist to predict how the Congress will alter the tax structure. This analysis would also have to be done year by year.

If there are state and local income taxes to be considered, the same forecast would have to be made. The economist must determine, by year, how the state and local governments will act. Since state and local taxes are deductible when calculating federal income tax liability, the economist, to be accurate in the analysis, must also calculate, by year, all local levies, school taxes, and other assessments.

§15.10   —Household Services

If taxes are to be included in the present value analysis, the household services must be calculated on a before-tax basis. To do this requires forecasting the annual value of the household services and the tax rate that will be applicable in each of those years.

Let the value of household services be estimated at $8,000 per year. If the family income is less than $35,800 married filing jointly the marginal tax rate is 15 per cent. The replacement value of the household services is $9,412. This is $8,000 divided by one minus the marginal tax rate, or $8,000/(1−.15). Since the value of household services is expected to increase annually, the marginal tax rate may change. Table 15-6 shows the after-tax and before-tax value of household services calculated for a 25-year period. The marginal tax rate is based on the assumption that no additional family income is being earned. Household services are assumed to grow in value at 4 per cent annually.

Table 15-6   Value of Household Services

Period	Future Value	Before Tax	Present Value After Tax
0	8,000	9,412	9,412
1	8,320	9,788	9,234
2	8,653	10,180	9,060
3	8,999	10,587	8,889
4	9,359	11,010	8,721
5	9,733	11,451	8,557
6	10,123	11,909	8,395
7	10,527	12,385	8,237
8	10,949	12,881	8,081
9	11,386	13,396	7,929
10	11,842	13,932	7,779
11	12,316	14,489	7,633
12	12,808	15,069	7,489
13	13,321	15,671	7,347
14	13,853	16,298	7,209
15	14,408	16,950	7,073
16	14,984	17,628	6,939
17	15,583	18,333	6,808
18	16,207	19,067	6,680
19	16,855	19,829	6,554
20	17,529	20,622	6,430
21	18,230	21,447	6,309
22	18,959	22,305	6,190
23	19,718	23,197	6,073
24	20,506	24,125	5,958
Total Present Value			$188,986

Had taxes not been considered the present value of the household services for the 25-year period is $160,638. The inclusion of taxes in the value of household services will cause the present value of the service to increase by $28,348, from $160,638 to $188,986. This value would be much higher if the analysis also included lost income and the family is in a higher tax bracket. The other factor causing the value to be low is that the interest income from the award is taxable.

§15.11   Summary

The inclusion of taxes considerably complicates the present value calculation. The economist is required to make annual forecasts of income, types of income, expenditures, tax rates, and value of household services. It is evident that the inclusion of income taxes in the present value analysis will cause the present value of the award to be increased.

16

Worklife Expectancy

§16.01 What Is Worklife?

The purpose of this chapter is to explain what the worklife expectancy is, and how worklife expectancy is employed in the calculation of the present value of the future income stream.

Worklife refers to how long an individual is in the labor force.[1] Table 16-1 presents the working life for white men and black men using 1979-1980 data. Table 16-2 presents the same data for women.

The estimation of the worklife indicates the probability that an individual will be classified in one of three states: economically active; economically inactive; or deceased. *Economically active* means the individual is in the labor force, while *economically inactive* means the individual is out of the labor force.[2]

Table 16-1 indicates that a 40-year-old white male has a 34-year life expectancy and that 20.5 of those years will be spent in the labor force. The same table indicates that a 40-year-old black male has a 30.5-year life expectancy and that 16.8 of those years will be spent in the labor force.

---

[1] US Dept of Labor, Bureau of Labor Statistics, Worklife Estimates: Effects of Race and Education, Bulletin 2254 (Feb 1986).

[2] *Id* 31.

Table 16-1   Working Life Tables for Men 1979-1980

Age	White Life Expectancy	White Active Years in Labor Force	Black Life Expectancy	Black Active Years in Labor Force
16	56.1	39.9	51.4	33.6
17	55.2	39.4	50.4	33.2
18	54.3	38.8	49.5	32.8
19	53.3	38.2	48.6	32.4
20	52.4	37.5	47.6	31.9
21	51.5	36.9	46.6	31.3
22	50.6	36.1	45.9	30.7
23	49.7	35.4	45.0	30.0
24	48.8	34.6	44.1	29.3
25	47.9	33.8	43.3	28.6
26	47.0	32.9	42.4	27.9
27	46.1	32.1	41.5	27.1
28	45.2	31.2	40.7	26.4
29	44.2	30.3	39.8	25.6
30	43.3	29.5	39.0	24.8
31	42.4	28.6	38.1	24.0
32	41.4	27.7	37.2	23.2
33	40.5	26.8	36.4	22.3
34	39.6	25.9	35.5	21.5
35	38.6	25.0	34.7	20.7
36	37.7	24.1	33.8	19.9
37	36.8	23.2	33.0	19.1
38	35.9	22.3	32.2	18.4
39	34.9	21.4	31.3	17.6
40	34.0	20.5	30.5	16.8
41	33.1	19.6	29.7	16.0
42	32.2	18.7	28.9	15.3
43	31.3	17.8	28.8	14.5
44	30.4	16.9	27.3	13.8
45	29.5	16.1	26.5	13.1
46	28.6	15.2	25.8	12.4
47	27.8	14.4	25.0	11.6
48	26.9	13.5	24.3	10.9
49	26.1	12.7	23.5	10.2
50	25.2	11.9	22.8	9.5
51	24.4	11.1	22.1	8.8
52	23.6	10.3	21.5	8.1

Age	White		Black	
	Life Expectancy	Active Years in Labor Force	Life Expectancy	Active Years in Labor Force
53	22.8	9.5	20.8	7.4
54	22.0	8.7	20.2	6.8
55	21.3	8.0	19.5	6.1
56	20.5	7.2	18.9	5.5
57	19.7	6.5	18.3	4.9
58	19.0	5.8	17.7	4.3
59	18.3	5.2	17.1	3.7
60	17.6	4.5	16.5	3.3
61	16.9	4.0	15.9	2.9
62	16.2	3.5	15.4	2.5
63	15.6	3.1	14.9	2.2
64	14.9	2.7	14.3	2.0
65	14.3	2.3	13.8	1.8
66	13.7	2.1	13.3	1.6
67	13.1	1.8	12.8	1.4
68	12.5	1.6	12.3	1.3
69	11.9	1.4	11.8	1.2
70	11.4	1.2	11.4	1.0
71	10.9	1.1	10.9	0.9
72	10.4	0.9	10.5	0.7
73	9.9	0.8	10.0	0.6
74	9.4	0.7	9.6	0.5
75	8.9	0.6	9.2	3.0

Source: US Dept of Labor, Bureau of Labor Statistics, Worklife Estimates: Effects of Race and Education, Bulletin 2254 (Feb 1986).

Table 16-2 Working Life Tables for Women 1979-1980

Age	White		Black	
	Life Expectancy	Active Years in Labor Force	Life Expectancy	Active Years in Labor Force
16	63.4	29.6	59.7	27.8
17	62.5	29.1	58.7	27.5
18	61.5	28.5	57.7	27.1
19	60.5	27.9	56.8	26.7
20	59.6	27.3	55.8	26.3
21	58.6	26.7	54.8	25.8
22	57.6	26.0	53.9	25.3

| Age | White | | Black | |
---	Life Expectancy	Active Years in Labor Force	Life Expectancy	Active Years in Labor Force
23	56.7	25.4	52.9	24.7
24	55.7	24.7	52.0	24.2
25	54.7	24.1	51.0	23.5
26	53.8	23.4	50.1	22.9
27	52.8	22.8	49.2	22.3
28	51.8	22.1	48.2	21.6
29	50.9	21.5	47.3	21.0
30	49.9	20.8	46.3	20.3
31	48.9	20.2	45.4	19.7
32	48.0	19.6	44.5	19.0
33	47.0	19.0	43.5	18.3
34	46.0	18.3	42.6	17.7
35	45.1	17.7	41.7	17.0
36	44.1	17.0	40.7	16.3
37	43.1	16.4	39.8	15.7
38	42.2	15.8	38.9	15.0
39	41.2	15.1	38.0	14.4
40	40.3	14.4	37.1	13.8
41	39.3	13.8	36.2	13.1
42	38.4	13.1	35.3	12.5
43	37.5	12.4	34.5	11.9
44	36.5	11.8	33.6	11.3
45	35.6	11.1	32.7	10.8
46	34.7	10.5	31.9	10.2
47	33.8	9.9	31.1	9.6
48	32.9	9.2	30.2	9.0
49	32.0	8.6	29.4	8.5
50	31.1	8.0	28.6	7.9
51	30.2	7.4	27.8	7.4
52	29.3	6.9	27.0	6.8
53	28.4	6.3	26.2	6.3
54	27.6	5.8	25.5	5.7
55	26.7	5.3	24.7	5.2
56	25.9	4.7	23.9	4.7
57	25.0	4.3	23.2	4.2
58	24.2	3.8	22.4	3.8
59	23.4	3.4	21.7	3.4
60	22.6	3.0	21.0	3.0
61	21.8	2.6	20.3	2.6

| Age | White | | Black | |
---	Life Expectancy	Active Years in Labor Force	Life Expectancy	Active Years in Labor Force
62	21.0	2.3	19.6	2.3
63	20.2	2.0	19.0	2.0
64	19.4	1.8	18.3	1.7
65	18.7	1.5	17.7	1.5
66	17.9	1.4	17.0	1.3
67	17.2	1.2	16.4	1.1
68	16.4	1.0	15.7	0.9
69	15.7	0.9	15.1	8.0
70	15.0	0.8	14.5	0.7
71	14.3	0.7	13.9	0.6
72	13.6	0.6	13.4	0.5
73	13.0	0.5	12.9	0.5
74	12.3	0.4	12.3	0.4
75	11.7	0.3	11.8	0.4

Source: US Dept of Labor, Bureau of Labor Statistics, Worklife Estimates: Effects of Race and Education, Bulletin 2254 (Feb 1986).

§16.02 How Worklife Expectancy Is Used in the Present Value Calculation: Cross-Examination

Table 16-3 presents the present value of a future income stream. The analysis starts with a 25-year-old male who was earning $20,000 at the time of the injury. The growth rate employed is 4 per cent, and the discount rate employed is 6 per cent. As the table shows, the present value of the future income stream, assuming the individual worked uninterrupted to age 65, is $565,228.

Table 16-3 Present Value of Future Income

Age	Period	Present Value of Future Income	Total Income
25	0	20,000	20,000
26	1	19,623	39,623
27	2	19,252	58,875
28	3	18,889	77,764
29	4	18,533	96,297
30	5	18,183	114,480

Age	Period	Present Value of Future Income	Total Income
31	6	17,840	132,320
32	7	17,503	149,823
33	8	17,173	166,997
34	9	16,849	183,846
35	10	16,531	200,377
36	11	16,219	216,596
37	12	15,913	232,509
38	13	15,613	248,123
39	14	15,318	263,441
40	15	15,029	278,470
41	16	14,746	293,216
42	17	14,468	307,684
43	18	14,195	321,878
44	19	13,927	335,805
45	20	13,664	349,469
46	21	13,406	362,876
47	22	13,153	376,029
48	23	12,905	388,934
49	24	12,662	401,596
50	25	12,423	414,018
51	26	12,188	426,207
52	27	11,958	438,165
53	28	11,733	449,898
54	29	11,511	461,409
55	30	11,294	472,703
56	31	11,081	483,784
57	32	10,872	494,656
58	33	10,667	505,323
59	34	10,466	515,789
60	35	10,268	526,057
61	36	10,074	536,131
62	37	9,884	546,016
63	38	9,698	555,713
64	39	9,515	565,228

The defense attorney will want to ask the plaintiff's economist whether the figure of $565,228 takes into account the worklife expectancy calculation. It does not.

The economist will be asked to examine the worklife expectancy table (Table 16-1). The table shows that a 25-year-old white male has a work life expectancy of 33.8 years. This means the individual would exit the labor force at age 58.8

years. From Table 16-3, the present value of the income stream to age 58.8 is $513,696. This figure is arrived at by taking 80 per cent times $10,466 (the difference between $515,789 and $505,323) plus $505,323 ($8,373 + $505,323 = $513,696).

Using the worklife expectancy table has decreased the present value of the future income stream from $565,228 to $513,696. This is a decline in the present value of the future income stream of $51,532.

Had the plaintiff been a 25-year-old black male, the worklife would be 28.6 years. This would reduce the present value of future income to $456,805. This is a reduction of $108,423.

In a similar fashion, the worklife expectancy of women can be employed to reduce the present value of the future income stream. For example, the worklife expectancy for a 25-year-old white female is 24.1 years, and for a 25-year-old black female the worklife expectancy is 23.5 years. The reduction in the present value of the future income stream for a 25-year-old white female is from $565,228 to $402,835, and for the black female the present value of the future income is reduced to $395,265.

§16.03   Reconsidering the Worklife Table

Care must be taken not to put too much meaning on the worklife tables. The worklife tables state how many years will be spent in the labor force, not which years will be spent in the labor force.

The worklife expectancy table indicates that a 25-year-old white female will spend 24.1 years in the labor force. As illustrated in §16.02, this caused the present value of the future income to decrease from $565,228 to $402,835. But the illustration assumes the woman was in the labor force for the next 24.1 years. Suppose the woman exited the labor force at age 25 to have a family and returned to the labor force at age 40. If the woman worked uninterrupted to age 65, she would have "fulfilled" the worklife expectancy of 24.1 years.

Under the latter approach the present value of the future income stream would be $301,787. This is the present value of the income stream if the woman works uninterrupted from age 25 to age 65 less the present value of the income stream from age 25 to age 40. The worklife is 25 years, and is between ages 40 and 65, after the childbearing years.

This example points out the problem with the worklife expectancy table. The table indicates how many years the individual is expected to be an active participant in the labor force but not which years the participation in the labor force will occur. The timing of the participation will affect the present value of the income stream.

Another problem with the worklife table is that the likelihood of seeking employment is biased by personal decisions. A 47-year-old retired military person who does not have other employment would reduce the worklife expectancy. It does not, however, reflect that the individual may have adequate income to meet living expenses. In a similar fashion the spouse not employed outside the home would reduce the worklife expectancy.

The worklife table measures movement into and out of the labor force. It does not mean the person is employed, only that he or she is actively seeking employment.[3] This means that worklife years can include a person who is unemployed but seeking employment.

During the course of discovery, the defense counsel should have determined the method by which the economist calculated the plaintiff's worklife expectancy. It is generally agreed that the United States Department of Labor publishes the most authoritative study on worklife.[4] Often the economist has decided that the individual would have exited the labor force at 65. The argument for this age is that it is when the individual is eligible for full retirement benefits.

§16.04   Summary

The worklife tables show how many years an individual is expected to be active in the labor force. The tables do not distinguish between employment and unemployment, nor do they indicate which years an individual will be economically active. The work life tables do not address reasons for exiting the labor force.

---

[3] US Dept of Labor, Bureau of Labor Statistics, Worklife Estimates: Effects of Race and Education, Bulletin 2254, at 33 (Feb 1986).

[4] US Dept of Labor, Bureau of Labor Statistics, Special Labor Force Report, Length of Working Life for Men and Women 187 (rev ed 1976).

17

Age Earnings Profile

§17.01   Introduction

The *age earnings profile* is used by some economists when estimating the present value of a future income stream. This chapter will explain what the age earnings profile is, how it is constructed, how it is interpreted, and how it is combined with the present value formula to make the calculation of the present value of future wages. The last part of the chapter will be devoted to demonstrating what the age earnings profile does not show and why the age earnings profile is inappropriate and should not be used when making the present value calculations.

§17.02   The Age Earnings Profile

"At any given point in time, earnings of individuals in virtually all careers are a mathematical function of the age of the individual worker."[1] The age earnings profile is constructed from cross-sectional data and shows the income of different individuals at different ages for a given year. Cross-sectional data means that the data is gathered at a specific point or moment in time. For example, an age earnings profile could be constructed for earnings on a given day, or for average earnings during a given month, or, as is more common, average earnings during a given year. Since the age earnings profile is constructed at a point in time, the earnings at each age represent earnings of different individuals.

§17.03   Calculating Median Income

The following example is used to show how the age earnings profile is constructed. In the table below there are 24 different workers identified as worker A through worker X. Each worker is referred to as an *observation*. Each of these workers, or observations, is between the ages of 25 and 64 inclusively. Finally, the income level of each observation is given.

Table 17-1   Raw Data

Worker	Age	Income
A	42	$ 8,942
B	37	14,311
C	28	8,943
D	63	9,071
E	51	10,261
F	52	9,882
G	48	9,980
H	54	8,146
I	32	5,000
J	29	9,126
K	46	9,871
L	48	9,871
M	39	10,546
N	36	9,954
O	40	10,258
P	61	9,001
Q	54	9,990
R	53	14,333
S	58	10,100

[1] L. Bassett, The Use of Economists in Personal Injury Actions (No 2 1984).

Worker	Age	Income
T	32	11,346
U	26	12,469
V	59	100,000
W	64	9,070
X	57	9,071

In order to make the data more understandable, the data could be reclassified in various statistical ways. One way is to construct a frequency distribution that would indicate the median income by age groups. Permit the age groupings to be by 10 year intervals, starting with age 25. In this case the class interval is 10 years. One would construct four class intervals, each with a 10-year spread or interval. Within each class interval the median income can be calculated.[2]

In the age group 25-34 there are five observations, or workers. They are workers C, I, J, T, and U. When ranked from the lowest to the highest salary, the ranking appears as follows:

Table 17-2 Median Income Age Group 25-34

Worker	Age	Income
I	32	$ 5,000
C	28	8,943
J	29	9,126
T	32	11,346
U	26	12,469

By definition, the median number of a group is the number that divides the group into two equal parts. In this case the median income would be $9,126. There are two observations with incomes less than $9,126, and two observations with incomes greater than $9,126. Again, the median income for the age group 25-34 is $9,126.

In the age group 35-44 there are five observations. They are workers A, B, M, N, and O. When ranked by salary the order appears as follows:

Table 17-3 Median Income Age group 35-44

Worker	Age	Income
A	42	$ 8,942
N	36	9,954
O	40	10,258
M	39	10,546
B	37	14,311

---

[2] T. Yamane, Statistics, An Introductory Analysis 368 (1964).

The 40 year-old worker O, with an income of $10,258, represents the median income. There are two workers with an income less than $10,258 and two workers with incomes above $10,258.

The age group 45-54 is a little different from the previous two groups. The previous group had an odd number of observations. This meant the middle observation was the median income. In the age group 45-54 there is an even number of observations. The eight workers are ranked by salary:

Table 17-4   Median Income Age Group 45-54

Worker	Age	Income
H	54	$ 8,146
K	46	9,871
L	48	9,871
F	52	9,882
G	48	9,980
Q	54	9,990
E	51	10,261
R	53	14,333

Since there is an even number of observations, the median income will be found between the fourth and fifth observations in the class interval. The income for worker F is $9,882 and the income for worker G is $9,980. The median income for this age group would be half-way between these two observations. In this case the median income for the age group 45-54 is $9,931 = (($9,882 + $9,980)/2).

Finally, the median income for the age group 55-64 is calculated in exactly the same manner. That is, the six observations in this category are ranked by salary as follows:

Table 17-5   Median Income Age Group 55-64

Worker	Age	Income
P	61	$ 9,001
W	64	9,070
D	63	9,071
X	57	9,071
S	58	10,100
V	59	100,000

Since there is an even number of observations in the class interval 55-64, the average of the middle two observations is used to determine the class median. However, in this case the third and fourth observations, when ranked by salary have the same value; thus, the median income would be this value, or $9,071. The thing to note in this class interval is the $100,000 income does not affect the median income of the class interval. The median income of the age categories is used to estimate the age earnings profile.

§17.04 The Source of the Data

The following table presents the 1980, 1985, and 1990 median money income for year-round full-time male workers with income.[3] This is an age earnings profile. This type of data may be found in the Statistical Abstracts of the United States and the "Monthly Labor Review."

Table 17-6 Age Earnings Profile

Age	1980 Wages	1985 Wages	1990 Wages
14 - 19			
25 - 34	17,724	22,321	25,502
35 - 44	21,777	28,966	32,611
45 - 54	22,323	29,880	35,731
55 - 64	21,053	28,387	33,180
65 +			

There are several things to notice concerning the table. First, and this is of great significance, the data are cross-sectional in nature. This means that in 1980, 1985, and 1990 each full-time, year-round male worker was categorized by age. Once the workers were categorized by age, the median income for each age group was calculated. Thus, the age earnings profile is for a specific moment in time.

Second, the class intervals are of different sizes, i.e., the age categories do not contain the same number of years. The age group 14-19 inclusive includes six years, while the age group 20-24 contains only five years. Each of the categories 25-34, 35-44, 45-54, and 55-64 contain 10 years while the last category, 65 plus, is open-ended.

A third thing to note is that earnings peak prior to the "normal" retirement age of 65. The data for all three periods show that wages peaked somewhere between the ages of 45 and 54. The data presented by these age earnings profiles suggest that earnings peak but do not show at what age, only what age category.

§17.05 The Equation for Calculating the Age Earnings Profile

The age categories and median incomes are restated in the following table:

---

[3] US Dept of Commerce, Bureau of the Census, Statistical Abstracts of the United States Table 710 (1992).

Table 17-7   Age Earnings Profile

Age	1980 Wages	1985 Wages	1990 Wages
25 - 34	17,724	22,321	25,502
35 - 44	21,777	28,966	32,611
45 - 54	22,323	29,880	35,731
55 - 64	21,053	28,387	33,180

The equation used to construct the age earnings profile is called a second degree polynomial.[4] The equation is:

$$\text{Income} = C(0) + C(2)*A + C(2)*A$$

Where:

"A" represents the age of the individual.
"C" represents the coefficient.

It is beyond our scope to demonstrate how the coefficients in the above equations are determined from the age earnings profile. Let it be sufficient to say the coefficients are as follows:

Table 17-8   Age Earnings Coefficients

	1980	1985	1990
C(0)	-8656.67128	-18861.3966	-24686.8022
C(1)	1289.69736	2001.82479	2410.88928
C(2)	-13.3074985	-20.3449978	-24.1499921

Using the above equation and inserting the 1990 coefficients into the equation, the income for a 25-year-old is calculated to be:

$$\text{Income} = -24686.8022 + 2410.88928 * (25)$$
$$+ -24.1499921 * (25)^2$$
$$= \$20,492$$

At age 63 the equation yields an income of $19,868:

$$\text{Income} = -24686.8022 + 2410.88928 * (63)$$
$$+ -24.1499921 * (63)^2$$
$$= \$31,348$$

---

[4] Harry Nagy, Ph.D., Professor of Physics and Astronomy Dept of Washburn Univ, wrote the program used to calculate the coefficients in the equations in this chapter.

§17.06 Using the Equation to Construct the Age Earnings Profile

By letting age be the variable (A) and using the coefficients estimated in §17.05, the following age earnings profiles are determined for the years 1980, 1985, and 1990:

Table 17-9 Age Earnings Profile

Age	Age Earnings Profile for Year		
	1980	1985	1990
22	13,367	15,332	16,664
23	14,058	16,418	17,988
24	14,722	17,464	19,264
25	15,360	18,469	20,492
26	15,971	19,433	21,671
27	16,555	20,356	22,802
28	17,113	21,239	23,885
29	17,644	22,081	24,919
30	18,149	22,883	25,905
31	18,626	23,644	26,843
32	19,078	24,364	27,732
33	19,502	25,043	28,573
34	19,901	25,682	29,366
35	20,272	26,280	30,111
36	20,617	26,837	30,807
37	20,935	27,354	31,455
38	21,227	27,830	32,054
39	21,492	28,265	32,606
40	21,730	28,660	33,109
41	21,942	29,013	33,564
42	22,127	29,327	33,970
43	22,286	29,599	34,328
44	22,418	29,831	34,638
45	22,523	30,022	34,899
46	22,602	30,173	35,113
47	22,654	30,282	35,278
48	22,679	30,351	35,394
49	22,678	30,380	35,463
50	22,650	30,367	35,483
51	22,596	30,314	35,454
52	22,515	30,221	35,378
53	22,408	30,086	35,253

| Age | Age Earnings Profile for Year | | |
	1980	1985	1990
54	22,273	29,911	35,080
55	22,113	29,695	34,858
56	21,925	29,439	34,589
57	21,711	29,142	34,271
58	21,470	28,804	33,904
59	21,203	28,425	33,490
60	20,909	28,006	33,027
61	20,589	27,546	32,515
62	20,242	27,046	31,956
63	19,868	26,504	31,348
64	19,467	25,922	30,692

Note that the median income of the age groups does not appear in the above table. This is true because the median income corresponds to the midpoints of the class intervals. The midpoint of the first class, 25-34, is 29.5 years of age. The corresponding income would be the median income in 1980 of $17,808.55. Similarly, the midpoints of the other class intervals would be 39.5, 49.5, and 59.5, respectively.

All three profiles show that individual's wages peak. Using the 1980 data, wages peak at age 48 at $22,679, while the 1985 data suggest that wages peak at age 49 with earnings of $30,380. In 1990 wages peaked at age 50 when earnings were $35,483. The increasing and decreasing of the wages at various ages is known as the *age earnings effect*. This is sometimes stated as the effect that age has on the individual earnings.

§17.07   The Age Earnings Effect

The *age earnings effect* is calculated by dividing each successive earnings by the previous year's (age) earnings. Thus, in 1990 the age earnings effect for a 23-year-old is that the earnings are 7.95 per cent higher than those of a 22-year-old. A 24-year-old's income is 7.09 per cent higher than a 23-year-old's. It is the percentage changes that are important when the economist uses the age earnings profile in the calculation of economic loss. The following table shows how, in 1990, each successive year's income is related to the previous year's income:

Table 17-10   Age Earnings Effect (1990)

Age	1990 Age Earnings Profile	Age Earnings Effect (Percentage)
22	$16,664	
23	17,988	7.95
24	19,264	7.09
25	20,492	6.37
26	21,671	5.75
27	22,802	5.22
28	23,885	4.75
29	24,919	4.33
30	25,905	3.96
31	26,843	3.62
32	27,732	3.31
33	28,573	3.03
34	29,366	2.77
35	30,111	2.54
36	30,807	2.31
37	31,455	2.10
38	32,054	1.91
39	32,606	1.72
40	33,109	1.54
41	33,564	1.37
42	33,970	1.21
43	34,328	1.05
44	34,638	0.90
45	34,899	0.76
46	35,113	0.61
47	35,278	0.47
48	35,394	0.33
49	35,463	0.19
50	35,483	0.06
51	35,454	-0.08
52	35,378	-0.22
53	35,253	-0.35
54	35,080	-0.49
55	34,858	-0.63
56	34,589	-0.77
57	34,271	-0.92
58	33,904	-1.07

Age	1990 Age Earnings Profile	Age Earnings Effect (Percentage)
59	33,490	-1.22
60	33,027	-1.38
61	32,515	-1.55
62	31,956	-1.72
63	31,348	-1.90
64	30,692	-2.09

§17.08   Making the Data Current

Since the most recent data presented is the 1990 age earnings profile, it is necessary to *move* the data to 1992 data. This is done by applying a growth rate which would represent the growth rate of wages from 1990 to 1993. Let us assume that wages have grown at the rate of 3 per cent per year for the two-year period. This would mean that each wage would grow by 6.09 per cent. This is calculated by using the growth formula $((1+g)^2)$. The value of the expression equals 1.0609 when "g" equals 3 per cent and means that the 1992 wages are 1.0609 per cent higher than the 1990 wages. In this manner the economist has moved the 1990 wages to a 1992 wage level. It is the 1992 earnings that are used to estimate the future earnings if the individual has no earnings history. The following are the 1992 wage levels:

Table 17-11   Current Income

Age	1990 Age Earnings Profile	1992 Age Earnings Profile
22	16,664	17,679
23	17,988	19,084
24	19,264	20,437
25	20,492	21,740
26	21,671	22,991
27	22,802	24,190
28	23,885	25,339
29	24,919	26,436
30	25,905	27,482
31	26,843	28,477
32	27,732	29,421
33	28,573	30,313
34	29,366	31,154

Age	1990 Age Earnings Profile	1992 Age Earnings Profile
36	30,807	32,683
35	30,111	31,944
37	31,455	33,370
38	32,054	34,007
39	32,606	34,591
40	33,109	35,125
41	33,564	35,608
42	33,970	36,039
43	34,328	36,419
44	34,638	36,747
45	34,899	37,025
46	35,113	37,251
47	35,278	37,426
48	35,394	37,550
49	35,463	37,622
50	35,483	37,644
51	35,454	37,614
52	35,378	37,532
53	35,253	37,400
54	35,080	37,216
55	34,858	36,981
56	34,589	36,695
57	34,271	36,358
58	33,904	35,969
59	33,490	35,529
60	33,027	35,038
61	32,515	34,496
62	31,956	33,902
63	31,348	33,257
64	30,692	32,561

As expected, the 1990 data and the current 1992 data show the same trend. That is, both income levels peak at age 50. It is 1992 data that is used in making the economic forecast of present value. The economist uses the appropriate growth and discount rates to establish the present value of the income stream.

§17.09 Two Ways to Go

When the economist is estimating present value of future income, the plaintiff either will have an earnings history or will not have an earnings history. Section

17.10 demonstrates how the present value of the future income is determined if the individual has no earnings history. Section **17.11** demonstrates how the present value of the future income is determined if the individual has an earnings history.

§17.10 —Calculating the Present Value of Future Income When the Individual Has No Earnings History

In the absence of an earnings history, the current data, as calculated in §17.08, are used as the basis for making the economic forecast. If the plaintiff is a 39-year-old high school graduate with no earnings history, then the economist would state that the age earnings profile indicates that the salary, or base wage, would be $34,591, as shown on the previous table.

Using the age earnings effect, an age earnings profile for the plaintiff is constructed. The age earnings effect indicates that a 40-year-old high school graduate will earn 1.11 per cent more than a 39-year-old worker. Accordingly, the $34,591 is increased by 1.11 per cent to become earnings of $34,975 at age 40. In like manner, the earnings of a 41-year-old worker are 1.37 per cent larger than a 40-year-old worker. The earnings of $34,975 are increased by 1.37 per cent to become earnings of $35,454 for the 41-year-old worker. It is the last column in Table 17-12 below, Age Earnings Profile for a 39-year-old, that is considered the 1992 earnings of the individual. The numbers in this column are used in calculating the present value of the future income.

Table 17-12   Earnings Profile No Previous Earnings History

Age	1986 Base Earnings	Age Earnings Effect (Per Cent)	Age Earnings Profile for a 39-Year-Old
39	34,591		34,591
40		1.54	35,125
41		1.37	35,608
42		1.21	36,039
43		1.05	36,419
44		0.90	36,747
45		0.76	37,025
46		0.61	37,251
47		0.47	37,426
48		0.33	37,550
49		0.19	37,622
50		0.06	37,644

Age	1986 Base Earnings	Age Earnings Effect (Per Cent)	Age Earnings Profile for a 39-Year-Old
51	.	-0.08	37,614
52		-0.22	37,532
53		-0.35	37,400
54		-0.49	37,216
55		-0.63	36,981
56		-0.77	36,695
57		-0.92	36,358
58		-1.07	35,969
59		-1.22	35,529
60		-1.38	35,038
61		-1.55	34,496
62		-1.72	33,902
63		-1.90	33,257
64		-2.09	32,561

The formula used to calculate the present value is:

$$\text{Present Value} = \$ \sum_{t=0}^{n} [(1+g)^t /[1+d]^t]$$

Where $ is the annual wage.
g is the growth rate of wages.
d is the interest or discount rate.
t is the number of years to be calculated.
n is the last year.

Assume the annual growth rate of wages is 3 per cent (g), and the annual discount rate is 4 per cent (d). The annual salary ($) is the salary shown in Table 17-12 in the column Age Earnings Profile for a 39-Year-Old. For the first year the present value of the future wage would be $34,258. The calculations are as follows:

Year	Present Value
1 =	$34,591 $[1+.03]^1/[1+.04]^1$ = $34,258
2 =	35,125 $[1+.03]^2/[1+.04]^2$ = 34,453
3 =	35,608 $[1+.03]^3/[1+.04]^3$ = 34,591

The calculations would continue until the plaintiff reaches age 64. There would be one calculation for each year being estimated. The sum of the calculations for each year is the present value of the future income stream. The following table shows the age of the plaintiff, the year, the period, the base wage calculated from the age earnings profile, the future wage after the growth rate has been applied, the present value of each year's wage, and, finally, the sum of the present value. The sum of the present value of each of the future wages, $930,559, represents the loss estimated by the economist.

Table 17-13   Present Value of Future Income No Previous Earnings History

Age	1990 Age Earnings Profile	1992 Age Earnings Profile	PV with 3% Growth & 4% Discount
39	32,606	34,591	34,259
40	33,109	35,125	34,787
41	33,564	35,608	35,265
42	33,970	36,039	35,692
43	34,328	36,419	36,069
44	34,638	36,747	36,394
45	34,899	37,025	36,669
46	35,113	37,251	36,893
47	35,278	37,426	37,066
48	35,394	37,550	37,189
49	35,463	37,622	37,261
50	35,483	37,644	37,282
51	35,454	37,614	37,252
52	35,378	37,532	37,171
53	35,253	37,400	37,040
54	35,080	37,216	36,858
55	34,858	36,981	36,626
56	34,589	36,695	36,342
57	34,271	36,358	36,008
58	33,904	35,969	35,623
59	33,490	35,529	35,187
60	33,027	35,038	34,701
61	32,515	34,496	34,164
62	31,956	33,902	33,576
63	31,348	33,257	32,937
64	30,692	32,561	32,248
			$930,559

§17.11 —Calculating the Present Value of Future Income When the Individual Has an Earnings History

When the analysis is for a person with an earnings history, the current wages are substituted in the age earnings profile at the individual's current age. The current wage becomes the base wage in the earnings profile. The percentage changes calculated in the profile are used to increase or decrease the future income based on the starting wage. Consider the 39-year-old high school graduate earning $30,000 at the time of the accident. The following age earnings profile would be established.

Table 17-14   Earnings Profile Previous Earnings History

Age	1990 Base Earnings	Age Earnings Effect %	Age Earnings Earnings Profile for 39-Yr-Old
39	30,000	1.72	
40		1.54	30,463
41		1.37	30,881
42		1.21	31,255
43		1.05	31,585
44		0.90	31,870
45		0.76	32,110
46		0.61	32,307
47		0.47	32,458
48		0.33	32,566
49		0.19	32,629
50		0.06	32,647
51		-0.08	32,621
52		-0.22	32,551
53		-0.35	32,436
54		-0.49	32,276
55		-0.63	32,073
56		-0.77	31,824
57		-0.92	31,532
58		-1.07	31,195
59		-1.22	30,813
60		-1.38	30,387
61		-1.55	29,917
62		-1.72	29,402
63		-1.90	28,843
64		-2.09	28,239

As before, the age earnings profile is used to calculate the present value of the future wage. The following table shows the age of the plaintiff the year, the base wage calculated from the age earnings profile, the future wage after the growth rate has been applied, the present value of each year's wage, and, finally, the sum of the present value. The sum of the present value of each of the future wages, $724,894, represents the loss estimated by the economist.

Table 17-15   Present Value of Future-Income Previous Earnings History

Period	Age	Beginning Wage	Age Earnings Profile	Present Value 3% Growth 4% Discount
0	39	30,000		30,000
1	40		30,463	30,170
2	41		30,881	30,290
3	42		31,255	30,362
4	43		31,585	30,387
5	44		31,870	30,367
6	45		32,110	30,302
7	46		32,307	30,194
8	47		32,458	30,044
9	48		32,566	29,854
10	49		32,629	29,624
11	50		32,647	29,355
12	51		32,621	29,050
13	52		32,551	28,708
14	53		32,436	28,332
15	54		32,276	27,922
16	55		32,073	27,479
17	56		31,824	27,004
18	57		31,532	26,498
19	58		31,195	25,963
20	59		30,813	25,399
21	60		30,387	24,807
22	61		29,917	24,188
23	62		29,402	23,543
24	63		28,843	22,873
25	64		28,239	22,179
				724,894

§17.12   Shortcomings of Using the Age Earnings Profile

Recall that the age earnings profile is constructed from cross-sectional data. The profiles presented in the table below show that, in 1980, wages peaked when the worker was 48 years of age and earning $22,679. In 1985, wages peaked at age 49 when earnings were $30,380 and, in 1990, wages peaked at age 50 when earnings reached $35,483.

Some economists will argue that all three age earnings profiles indicate that the income of the worker will decline after the peak age, 48 to 50 years of age. This is wrong. What the three profiles do indicate is that a worker over age 50 will earn less than a younger worker. The profile does not say that earnings will decline.

Intuitively one can see that claiming that an individual's income will decline after age 50 does not make sense. We, as members of the labor force, do not expect a decrease in salary because we get older. By the same token, it is not unreasonable to say that a person age 55 will earn less than a person age 50, and this is what the profile is demonstrating.

Approaching the age earnings profile in a different fashion, we could examine the earnings in 1980 of any worker in the labor force. For example the 42-year-old worker's earnings were $21,730 in 1980. According to the economist using the profile, earnings should decline after age 48. However, in 1985, when the worker is 47 years of age, the earnings have grown to $30,282, and by 1990, when the worker is 52 years of age, earnings have grown to $35,378. The table does not suggest that earnings fall as a person gets older, but rather suggests that earnings of younger workers may exceed earnings of older workers.

Table 17-16   Age Earnings Profiles

	Age Earnings Profile for Year		
Age	1980	1985	1990
22	13,367	15,332	16,664
23	14,058	16,418	17,988
24	14,722	17,464	19,264
25	15,360	18,469	20,492
26	15,971	19,433	21,671
27	16,555	20,356	22,802
28	17,113	21,239	23,885
29	17,644	22,081	24,919
30	18,149	22,883	25,905
31	18,626	23,644	26,843
32	19,078	24,364	27,732
33	19,502	25,043	28,573
34	19,901	25,682	29,366

	Age Earnings Profile for Year		
Age	1980	1985	1990
35	20,272	26,280	30,111
36	20,617	26,837	30,807
37	20,935	27,354	31,455
38	21,227	27,830	32,054
39	21,492	28,265	32,606
40	21,730	28,660	33,109
41	21,942	29,013	33,564
42	22,127	29,327	33,970
43	22,286	29,599	34,328
44	22,418	29,831	34,638
45	22,523	30,022	34,899
46	22,602	30,173	35,113
47	22,654	30,282	35,278
48	22,679	30,351	35,394
49	22,678	30,380	35,463
50	22,650	30,367	35,483
51	22,596	30,314	35,454
52	22,515	30,221	35,378
53	22,408	30,086	35,253
54	22,273	29,911	35,080
55	22,113	29,695	34,858
56	21,925	29,439	34,589
57	21,711	29,142	34,271
58	21,470	28,804	33,904
59	21,203	28,425	33,490
60	20,909	28,006	33,027
61	20,589	27,546	32,515
62	20,242	27,046	31,956
63	19,868	26,504	31,348
64	19,467	25,922	30,692

If the profiles were graphed, each year would peak, but the 1985 profile would indicate higher earnings at each age level than would the 1980 profile. In the same fashion, the 1990 profile would peak, but earnings at each age would be higher than that indicated by the 1985 profile.

Chart 17.1   Age Earnings Profiles

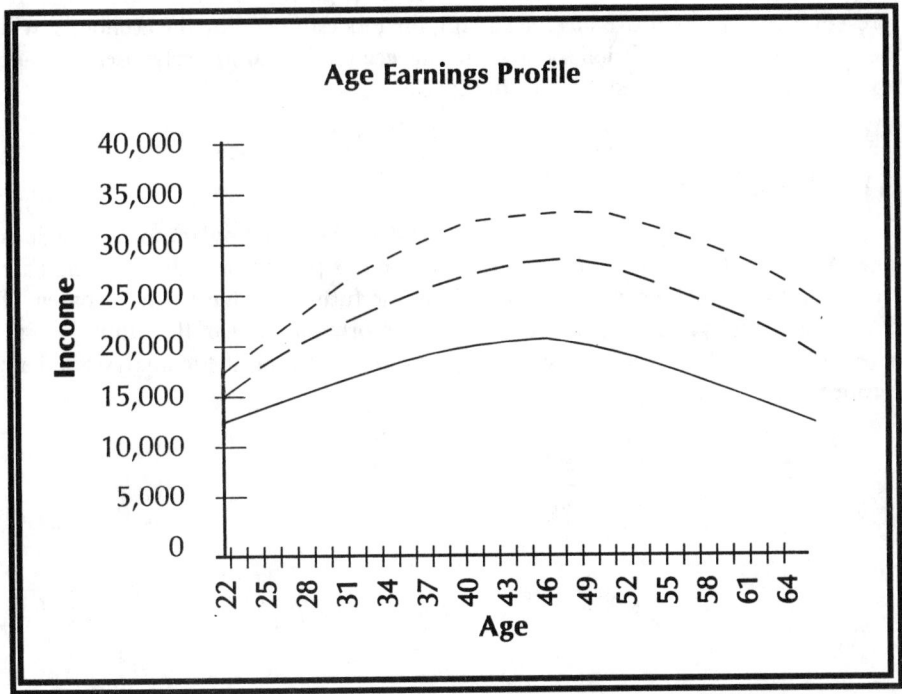

When estimating the present value of a future income stream, the economist is dealing in time series analysis. Time series analysis refers to analyzing data, or making estimates, from different points in time, or for different points in time. The error the economist has made when using the age earnings profile is using cross-sectional data to estimate a time series phenomenon.

§17.13   Proper Use of the Age Earnings Profile

If the economist plans to use the age earnings profile as the basis for making the economic forecast, the economist would be analyzing a case where the plaintiff has no earnings history. The economist would be concerned only with the wage indicated by the age earnings profile as a median income for that age person. For example, suppose the plaintiff were a 24-year-old male military veteran recently separated from the service but not yet in the labor force. The economist might suggest that the 1992 age earnings profile, see Table 17-11, for a 24-year-old full-time male worker indicates earnings of $20,437 per year. This would become the base wage which would be permitted to grow and be discounted to present value.

§17.14   An Interesting Observation

If the economist properly uses the age earnings profile in the calculation of the present value of the future income stream, the loss estimated by the economist will be a larger amount of dollars than if the economist improperly uses the age earnings profile in the estimate of the loss.

§17.15   Conclusion

The age earnings profile is cross-sectional data showing how incomes at various ages are related. If used properly, the age earnings profile provides only the base year's income on which the present value of the future income stream is based. If the age earnings profile is used improperly, the present value of the future income stream will result in a lower estimated economic loss than if the analysis is done properly.

18

A Quick Method for Estimating the Present Value of Future Income

$$\text{Present Value of Future Income} = \$ \sum_{t=0}^{n} * M * \underline{[(1+g)^t/(1+d)^t]} * P_L * P_S * \\ P_F * C * HS * Tx$$

§18.01 Introduction

When the economist is estimating the present value of a future income stream, it is necessary to estimate the growth rate of wages and the discount rate, or interest rate, that should be used to obtain the present value. If all variables are constant except the growth rate, the larger the growth rate employed by the economist the larger the present value of the future income stream. Likewise, if all variables are constant except the discount rate, the larger the discount rate employed by the economist the smaller the present value of the future income stream.

A debate between economists, and one that spills over into the courtroom, is over the appropriate growth and discount rates. Some states have attempted to resolve this issue by requiring the growth and discount rates to be equal. Two states which have done this are Alaska and Pennsylvania.[1]

§18.02   The Alaska Plan: A Quick Estimate of the Present Value of the Future Income Stream

The Alaska plan states that the growth rate and the discount rate employed by the economist must be equal. When this occurs, the formula for present value reduces to a multiplication of the dollar loss times the number of years the loss is to be experienced. The present value formula is:[2]

Present Value = $ * N

The "$" amount is the base dollar amount and "N" is the number of years the loss occurs.

The term *Alaska plan* has come to mean that the growth and discount rates are equal. The Alaska plan does provide a quick method for estimating the present value of a future income stream. While not technically accurate, the equating of the growth and discount rates, thus making the present value calculation a quick multiplication, does provide the attorney with a good "ball park" figure which should not be far off what the economist will conclude.

However, the Alaska plan has two problems. First, the plan is not based on economic fact. This means that either the growth rate or discount rate employed by the economist will be too high or too low. Second, if the income stream does not have a growth rate, then the use of different growth and discount rates can lead to different figures. This can best be seen when calculating the present value of a retirement program.

§18.03   An Example of Estimating the Present Value of Lost Income Using the Alaska Plan

Mr. Smith was injured and is unable to pursue gainful employment. At the time he was injured he was earning $20,000 per year. Today is Mr. Smith's thirty-fifth birthday. The present value of the future income until Mr. Smith retires at age 65, using the Alaska plan, is $600,000.

Present Value - $ * N
Present Value = $20,000 * 30
Present Value = $600,000

---

[1] Baulieu v Elliott, 434 P2d 665 (Ala 1967); Kuczkowski v Boluhasz, 491 Pa 561, 421 A2d 1027 (1980).

[2] Franz, *Simplified Calculation of Future Lost Earnings*, Trial, Aug 1977, at 34-37.

Suppose the economist is estimating the present value of the future income using a 6 per cent growth rate and a 6 per cent discount rate. Table 18-1 shows the present value calculation by year. The last column, Total Loss, represents the present value of the future income stream and indicates the present value of the total loss of income to age 65 is $600,000.

Table 18-1 Present Value of Future Income With 6 Per Cent Growth and Discount Rates

Age	Annual Wage	Growth Rate	Discount Rate	Annual Wage	Total Loss
35	20,000	(1+.06)/	(1+.06)	20,000	20,000
36	20,000	(1+.06)/	(1+.06)	20,000	40,000
37	20,000	(1+.06)/	(1+.06)	20,000	60,000
38	20,000	(1+.06)/	(1+.06)	20,000	80,000
39	20,000	(1+.06)/	(1+.06)	20,000	100,000
40	20,000	(1+.06)/	(1+.06)	20,000	120,000
41	20,000	(1+.06)/	(1+.06)	20,000	140,000
42	20,000	(1+.06)/	(1+.06)	20,000	160,000
43	20,000	(1+.06)/	(1+.06)	20,000	180,000
44	20,000	(1+.06)/	(1+.06)	20,000	200,000
45	20,000	(1+.06)/	(1+.06)	20,000	220,000
46	20,000	(1+.06)/	(1+.06)	20,000	240,000
47	20,000	(1+.06)/	(1+.06)	20,000	260,000
48	20,000	(1+.06)/	(1+.06)	20,000	280,000
49	20,000	(1+.06)/	(1+.06)	20,000	300,000
50	20,000	(1+.06)/	(1+.06)	20,000	320,000
51	20,000	(1+.06)/	(1+.06)	20,000	340,000
52	20,000	(1+.06)/	(1+.06)	20,000	360,000
53	20,000	(1+.06)/	(1+.06)	20,000	380,000
54	20,000	(1+.06)/	(1+.06)	20,000	400,000
55	20,000	(1+.06)/	(1+.06)	20,000	420,000
56	20,000	(1+.06)/	(1+.06)	20,000	440,000
57	20,000	(1+.06)/	(1+.06)	20,000	460,000
58	20,000	(1+.06)/	(1+.06)	20,000	480,000
59	20,000	(1+.06)/	(1+.06)	20,000	500,000
60	20,000	(1+.06)/	(1+.06)	20,000	520,000
61	20,000	(1+.06)/	(1+.06)	20,000	540,000
62	20,000	(1+.06)/	(1+.06)	20,000	560,000
63	20,000	(1+.06)/	(1+.06)	20,000	580,000
64	20,000	(1+.06)/	(1+.06)	20,000	600,000

Table 18-2 shows exactly the same calculations, but the growth and discount rates have been increased to 10 per cent annually. The present value of the future income stream does not change; it remains $600,000.

Table 18-2   Present Value of Future Income With 10 Per Cent Growth and Discount Rates

Age	Annual Wage	Growth Rate	Discount Rate	Annual Wage	Total Loss
35	20,000	(1+.10)/	(1+.10)	20,000	20,000
36	20,000	(1+.10)/	(1+.10)	20,000	40,000
37	20,000	(1+.10)/	(1+.10)	20,000	60,000
38	20,000	(1+.10)/	(1+.10)	20,000	80,000
39	20,000	(1+.10)/	(1+.10)	20,000	100,000
40	20,000	(1+.10)/	(1+.10)	20,000	120,000
41	20,000	(1+.10)/	(1+.10)	20,000	140,000
42	20,000	(1+.10)/	(1+.10)	20,000	160,000
43	20,000	(1+.10)/	(1+.10)	20,000	180,000
44	20,000	(1+.10)/	(1+.10)	20,000	200,000
45	20,000	(1+.10)/	(1+.10)	20,000	220,000
46	20,000	(1+.10)/	(1+.10)	20,000	240,000
47	20,000	(1+.10)/	(1+.10)	20,000	260,000
48	20,000	(1+.10)/	(1+.10)	20,000	280,000
49	20,000	(1+.10)/	(1+.10)	20,000	300,000
50	20,000	(1+.10)/	(1+.10)	20,000	320,000
51	20,000	(1+.10)/	(1+.10)	20,000	340,000
52	20,000	(1+.10)/	(1+.10)	20,000	360,000
53	20,000	(1+.10)/	(1+.10)	20,000	380,000
54	20,000	(1+.10)/	(1+.10)	20,000	400,000
55	20,000	(1+.10)/	(1+.10)	20,000	420,000
56	20,000	(1+.10)/	(1+.10)	20,000	440,000
57	20,000	(1+.10)/	(1+.10)	20,000	460,000
58	20,000	(1+.10)/	(1+.10)	20,000	480,000
59	20,000	(1+.10)/	(1+.10)	20,000	500,000
60	20,000	(1+.10)/	(1+.10)	20,000	520,000
61	20,000	(1+.10)/	(1+.10)	20,000	540,000
62	20,000	(1+.10)/	(1+.10)	20,000	560,000
63	20,000	(1+.10)/	(1+.10)	20,000	580,000
64	20,000	(1+.10)/	(1+.10)	20,000	600,000

No matter what growth or discount rates are used, as long as the two values are equal, the calculation reduces to the multiplication of the current income level times the number of years being forecast.

This can further be seen by looking at each page in Appendix C. Appendix C combines the growth and discount rates and presents the present value factor by year. Table 18-3 presents the present value factors of one dollar received each year for 30 years.

Table 18-3   Present Value Factors 30-Year Discount

Discount Rate	Growth Rates					
	0%	2%	4%	6%	8%	10%
0%	30.000	41.379	58.328	83.802	122.346	180.943
2%	22.396	30.000	41.110	57.527	81.995	118.708
4%	17.292	22.518	30.000	40.854	56.768	80.300
6%	13.765	17.458	22.635	30.000	40.609	56.048
8%	11.258	13.940	17.620	22.749	30.000	40.374
10%	9.427	11.426	14.112	17.777	22.859	30.000
12%	8.055	9.583	11.593	14.280	17.931	22.967
14%	7.003	8.198	9.738	11.756	14.445	18.082
16%	6.177	7.132	8.339	9.891	11.918	14.607
18%	5.517	6.294	7.261	8.479	10.042	12.077

Note that on the diagonal, where the growth rate and discount rates are the same, the present value factor is 30.00. Again this demonstrates that, when the growth rate and the discount rate are the same, the present value factor is equal to the number of years for which the loss is being calculated.

The use of the Alaska plan does provide a good indicator of the present value of an income stream that is expected to grow. However, when calculating the present value of a retirement benefit that is not expected to grow, the growth and discount rates assumed prior to retirement do matter. Section 18.04 examines the present value of a defined contribution plan, and §18.05 examines the present value of a defined benefit plan.

§18.04   An Example of Estimating the Present Value of Retirement Benefits Using a Defined Contribution Plan

A defined contribution plan specifies, or defines, the moneys contributed by the employee and employer to the retirement plan. For example, the plan may specify that 8 per cent of the employee's salary will be contributed to the retirement plan. The size of the retirement annuity is determined when the individual retires. The retirement annuity purchased depends on the amount of money available.

Table 18-4 shows the income earned each year with differing growth assumptions. In each case the current, or beginning salary is $20,000. The annual growth of income ranges from 2 to 10 per cent. The defined contribution is 8 per cent of the annual income. In each case the present value of the future income stream is $600,000 if the discount rate used is the same as the growth rate.

Table 18-4   Future Value of $20,000 Annual Income Growing at Different Rates

Age	Years in the Future	Annual Growth Rate				
		0.02	0.04	0.06	0.08	0.10
35	0	20,000	20,000	20,000	20,000	20,000
36	1	20,400	20,800	21,200	21,600	22,000
37	2	20,808	21,632	22,472	23,328	24,200
38	3	21,224	22,497	23,820	25,194	26,620
39	4	21,649	23,397	25,250	27,210	29,282
40	5	22,082	24,333	26,765	29,387	32,210
41	6	22,523	25,306	28,370	31,737	35,431
42	7	22,974	26,319	30,073	34,276	38,974
43	8	23,433	27,371	31,877	37,019	42,872
44	9	23,902	28,466	33,790	39,980	47,159
45	10	24,380	29,605	35,817	43,178	51,875
46	11	24,867	30,789	37,966	46,633	57,062
47	12	25,365	32,021	40,244	50,363	62,769
48	13	25,872	33,301	42,659	54,392	69,045
49	14	26,390	34,634	45,218	58,744	75,950
50	15	26,917	36,019	47,931	63,443	83,545
51	16	27,456	37,460	50,807	68,519	91,899
52	17	28,005	38,958	53,855	74,000	101,089
53	18	28,565	40,516	57,087	79,920	111,198
54	19	29,136	42,137	60,512	86,314	122,318
55	20	29,719	43,822	64,143	93,219	134,550
56	21	30,313	45,575	67,991	100,677	148,005
57	22	30,920	47,398	72,071	108,731	162,805
58	23	31,538	49,294	76,395	117,429	179,086
59	24	32,169	51,266	80,979	126,824	196,995
60	25	32,812	53,317	85,837	136,970	216,694
61	26	33,468	55,449	90,988	147,927	238,364
62	27	34,138	57,667	96,447	159,761	262,200
63	28	34,820	59,974	102,234	172,542	288,420
64	29	35,517	62,373	108,368	186,345	317,262
Average of last 5 years		34,151	57,756	96,775	160,709	264,588

Table 18-5 represents 8 per cent of the employee's annual income. This would represent the amount of money contributed to the retirement program. The contributions are different since the annual growth rate of wages ranges from 2 to 10 per cent.

Table 18-5   The Contribution of the Employer Plus the Employee Assuming 3 Per Cent by Both

Age	Years in Future	Annual Growth Rate				
		0.02	0.04	0.06	0.08	0.10
35	0	1,200	1,200	1,200	1,200	1,200
36	1	1,224	1,248	1,272	1,296	1,320
37	2	1,248	1,298	1,348	1,400	1,452
38	3	1,273	1,350	1,429	1,512	1,597
39	4	1,299	1,404	1,515	1,633	1,757
40	5	1,325	1,460	1,606	1,763	1,933
41	6	1,351	1,518	1,702	1,904	2,126
42	7	1,378	1,579	1,804	2,057	2,338
43	8	1,406	1,642	1,913	2,221	2,572
44	9	1,434	1,708	2,027	2,399	2,830
45	10	1,463	1,776	2,149	2,591	3,112
46	11	1,492	1,847	2,278	2,798	3,424
47	12	1,522	1,921	2,415	3,022	3,766
48	13	1,552	1,998	2,560	3,264	4,143
49	14	1,583	2,078	2,713	3,525	4,557
50	15	1,615	2,161	2,876	3,807	5,013
51	16	1,647	2,248	3,048	4,111	5,514
52	17	1,680	2,337	3,231	4,440	6,065
53	18	1,714	2,431	3,425	4,795	6,672
54	19	1,748	2,528	3,631	5,179	7,339
55	20	1,783	2,629	3,849	5,593	8,073
56	21	1,819	2,735	4,079	6,041	8,880
57	22	1,855	2,844	4,324	6,524	9,768
58	23	1,892	2,958	4,584	7,046	10,745
59	24	1,930	3,076	4,859	7,609	11,820
60	25	1,969	3,199	5,150	8,218	13,002
61	26	2,008	3,327	5,459	8,876	14,302
62	27	2,048	3,460	5,787	9,586	15,732
63	28	2,089	3,598	6,134	10,353	17,305
64	29	2,131	3,742	6,502	11,181	19,036
"Σ of Contribution		48,682	67,302	94,870	135,940	197,393
Present Value		26,876	20,750	16,518	13,509	11,312

Table 18-5 also shows the total contributions made by the employee and employer to the retirement fund. When the wages are assumed to grow at 2 per cent annually, the total contribution made by both the employee and employer is $48,682. When the growth rate of wages increases to 10 per cent annually, the total contribution increases to $197,393. In both cases contributions to the retirement program are 6 per cent of wages.

It is this amount of money, ranging from $48,682 to $197,393, which is used to purchase the retirement annuity. These figures represent the future value of the pension plan. The size of the annuity will depend on the market conditions which prevail and the terms included in the annuity.

The question facing the economist is: "What is the present value of the defined contribution plan?" The appropriate discount factor to employ under the Alaska plan is the same as the growth factor. Therefore, the present value of the $48,682 must be discounted for 30 years in order to determine the present value.

Table 18-5 shows the present value of the defined contribution plan of 6 per cent of the wage using a discount rate equal to the assumed growth rate. The present value of the defined contribution plan, using a 2 per cent growth and discount rate is $26,876. If the annual growth and discount rate is 10 per cent, then the present value of the defined contribution plan is $11,312.

§18.05   An Example of Estimating the Present Value of Retirement Benefits Using a Defined Benefit Plan

A defined benefit plan states a formula which will be used to calculate the employee's retirement benefit. For example, a defined retirement benefit might be 10 per cent of the average annual income earned the last five years of employment. The growth assumption will change the amount of income earned the last years, thus changing the annual retirement income.

If the present value of the retirement benefit is to be estimated, the economist will use 10 per cent of the average income earned the last five years as the annual retirement income. Using the example in Table 18-5, the annual retirement would range from $3,415, when the growth rate and discount rate were assumed to be 2 per cent, to $26,459, when the growth and discount rates were assumed to be 10 per cent. Recall that Table 18-1 and Table 18-2 show the present value of the future income to be $600,000 regardless of the growth and interest assumptions. The difference is the retirement benefit and the cost of the retirement benefit.

Table 18-6 shows the annual retirement income for the 16-year period from age 65 to age 80. The economist must discount the income to present value. In other words, the economist will state the dollars needed today in order to fund a 16-year annuity starting in 30 years when Mr. Smith reaches age 65. What is different about this annuity is that it does not grow, i.e., the annual retirement benefit is level.

Table 18-6   Annual Retirement Benefits Defined Benefit Plan

Age	Annual Growth Rate				
	2%	4%	6%	8%	10%
65	3,415	5,776	9,677	16,071	26,459
66	3,415	5,776	9,677	16,071	26,459
67	3,415	5,776	9,677	16,071	26,459
68	3,415	5,776	9,677	16,071	26,459
69	3,415	5,776	9,677	16,071	26,459
70	3,415	5,776	9,677	16,071	26,459
71	3,415	5,776	9,677	16,071	26,459
72	3,415	5,776	9,677	16,071	26,459
73	3,415	5,776	9,677	16,071	26,459
74	3,415	5,776	9,677	16,071	26,459
75	3,415	5,776	9,677	16,071	26,459
76	3,415	5,776	9,677	16,071	26,459
77	3,415	5,776	9,677	16,071	26,459
78	3,415	5,776	9,677	16,071	26,459
79	3,415	5,776	9,677	16,071	26,459
80	3,415	5,776	9,677	16,071	26,459

Determining the present value of the retirement benefit is a two-step process. First, the cost of the 16-year annuity, which starts at age 65, must be determined; and second, the present value of a 16-year annuity which starts paying in 30 years must be determined.

Table 18-7 shows the cost of the retirement annuity which is to be purchased when Mr. Smith reaches age 65. The price of a 16-year annuity, paying $3,415 annually and earning interest at 2 per cent per year is $47,295. The price of an annuity paying $26,459 annually and earning 10 per cent a year is $227,706. However, these annuities do not start for another 30 years, when Mr. Smith reaches age 65. Therefore, the present value calculation requires discounting the cost of the annuity another 30 years. This last step is determining the present value of the cost of the annuity which is to begin in 30 years. Stated differently, how much money does it take today to provide $47,295 in 30 years? The $47,295 would be used to purchase a 16-year annuity paying $3,415 annually.

For the larger annuity the same question would be asked, that is, how much money does it take today to provide $227,706 in 30 years? The $227,706 would be used to purchase a 16-year annuity paying $26,459 annually.

What is the appropriate interest rate to use when discounting the money needed in 30 years? The answer is provided in the Alaska plan. The discount rate is the same rate as the growth rate. If the growth and discount rate of wages were 2 per cent when the present value of the future income was calculated, the appropriate discount rate is 2 per cent. If the growth and discount rate used was 10 per cent, then the appropriate discount rate is 10 per cent.

Table 18-7   Retirement Benefits at Age 65 Discount Rate

Age	Yrs in Future	Discount Rate				
		0.02	0.04	0.06	0.08	0.10
65	0	3,415	5,776	9,677	16,071	26,459
66	1	3,348	5,554	9,129	14,881	24,054
67	2	3,282	5,340	8,612	13,778	21,867
68	3	3,218	5,135	8,125	12,758	19,879
69	4	3,155	4,937	7,665	11,813	18,072
70	5	3,093	4,747	7,231	10,938	16,429
71	6	3,032	4,565	6,822	10,127	14,935
72	7	2,973	4,389	6,436	9,377	13,578
73	8	2,915	4,220	6,071	8,683	12,343
74	9	2,858	4,058	5,728	8,040	11,221
75	10	2,801	3,902	5,404	7,444	10,201
76	11	2,747	3,752	5,098	6,893	9,274
77	12	2,693	3,608	4,809	6,382	8,431
78	13	2,640	3,469	4,537	5,909	7,664
79	14	2,588	3,335	4,280	5,472	6,967
80	15	2,537	3,207	4,038	5,066	6,334
Cost at age 65		47,295	69,996	103,662	153,630	227,708
Pr Value @ 35		26,111	21,580	18,050	15,267	13,050

The present value of $47,295 to be received in 30 years, and discounted at 2 per cent per year, is $26,111. Had the rate of growth of the wage been 6 per cent annually, the discount rate would have to be 6 per cent. In this case the annual retirement income, starting at age 65, would be $9,677. The present value of the retirement annuity would be $18,050. Likewise, the present value of the retirement benefit with a 10 per cent annual growth and discount rate would be $13,050.

The Alaska plan requires that the growth and discount rates be equal. This results in the present value of the future stream of income being the same regardless of the growth and discount assumption. When the present value of the retirement benefit is being estimated, the higher the assumed growth and discount rate, the lower the present value of the benefit.

§18.06   An Example of Estimating the Present Value of Medical Expenses

Suppose an injured party is 30 years old and expected to need medical attention every fifth year. Further assume that the cost of such attention costs $10,000 today. The economist is attempting to forecast the present value of the medical expenses, with certainty, to age 65. The first medical attention will be required five years from today. Table 18-8 shows the age of the individual when the medical attention is required and the cost in today's dollars, i.e., $10,000.

Table 18-8 Medical Expense Every Five Years

Age	Cost in Current Dollars
30	$10,000
35	10,000
40	10,000
45	10,000
50	10,000
55	10,000
60	10,000
65	10,000

It is the goal of the economist to forecast the present value of the future medical expenses. The sum of the total expenses is $80,000. Since medical expenses are expected to grow annually, the economist's job is to forecast an appropriate growth and discount rate. Under the Alaska plan the growth and discount rate must be the same. Table 18-9 shows the present value of each future medical expense given different growth and discount assumptions.

Table 18-9 Present Value of Future Medical Expenses

Age	Years in Future	Growth and Discount Rate				
		2%	4%	6%	8%	10%
30	0	10,000	10,000	10,000	10,000	10,000
35	5	10,000	10,000	10,000	10,000	10,000
40	10	10,000	10,000	10,000	10,000	10,000
45	15	10,000	10,000	10,000	10,000	10,000
50	20	10,000	10,000	10,000	10,000	10,000
55	25	10,000	10,000	10,000	10,000	10,000
60	30	10,000	10,000	10,000	10,000	10,000
65	35	10,000	10,000	10,000	10,000	10,000
Present Value		80,000	80,000	80,000	80,000	80,000

Regardless of the growth and discount rate assumptions, the present value of the future medical expenses does not change. The implied assumption made under the Alaska plan is that the rate of growth of wages is the same as the rate of growth of medical expenses and both are equal to the discount rate.

§18.07 Summary

When calculating the present value of a future stream of money using the Alaska plan, the growth rate used in the calculation must equal the discount rate.

This permits the quick calculation of the present value of the future stream of money. The present value of the future stream is the current dollar amount times the number of years the money is to be received.

When the present value of periodic payments is to be estimated, the same assumption of growth rate equal to discount rate is made. Again, the present value is equal to the current payment times the number of future payments to be made.

A shortcoming of the method is the assumption that all growth rates are the same and equal to all discount rates. There is justification for the assumption of a constant discount. Regardless of what the future expenses are, the same investment can be made, therefore the same discount rate. But the assumption that the growth rate of wages and the growth rate of medical expenses will be the same over time does not have economic justification.

Finally, when the present value of a retirement plan is being calculated, the assumption of the growth rate does have an impact on the present value of the benefit. This is true because the retirement benefit does not grow.

The larger the growth rate used under the Alaska plan, the larger will be the income used to calculate the retirement benefit. The larger the growth rate and discount rate assumed, the larger the retirement benefit and the smaller the present value of the benefit.

19 Judging the Economist's Estimate of Present Value

$$\text{Present Value of Future Income} = \sum_{t=0}^{n} \$ * M * (1+g)^t / (1+d)^t * \text{PL} * \text{PS} * \text{PF} * C * \text{HS} * \text{Tx}$$

§19.01   Introduction

After the economist has rendered a report, it is necessary to determine the accuracy of the work. The purpose is to see whether the economist's assumptions give the result intended by the economist.

Using the basic formula, shown above, the economist must determine a value for each of the four variables, "$," "t," "g," and "d." The variables are the current dollar amount, the number of years over which the estimate is being made, the annual growth rate of dollars, and the discount rate.

§19.02   Fact Situation

The plaintiff is the widow of a 45-year-old white male killed one year ago today. At the time of the accident the deceased was earning $25,000 per year. The economist has assumed the deceased would have worked uninterrupted to age 65. The growth and discount rates assumed by the economist are 5 and 6 per cent, respectively.

§19.03   Present Value Calculation

Table 19-1 shows the present value calculation of future income using the formula stated above and the assumptions stated in §19.02.

Table 19-1   Present Value of Future Income

Growth Rate = 5%
Discount Rate - 6%

Age	Period	Future Income	Present Value	Sum
45	0	25,000	25,000	25,000
46	1	26,250	24,764	49,764
47	2	27,563	24,531	74,295
48	3	28,941	24,299	98,594
49	4	30,388	24,070	122,664
50	5	31,907	23,843	146,506
51	6	33,502	23,618	170,124
52	7	35,178	23,395	193,519
53	8	36,936	23,174	216,694
54	9	38,783	22,956	239,649
55	10	40,722	22,739	262,389
56	11	42,758	22,525	284,913
57	12	44,896	22,312	307,225
58	13	47,141	22,102	329,327
59	14	49,498	21,893	351,220
60	15	51,973	21,687	372,907
61	16	54,572	21,482	394,389
62	17	57,300	21,279	415,668
63	18	60,165	21,079	436,747
64	19	63,174	20,880	457,626

The economist's testimony is that the present value of the future income is $457,626. This assumes that the first payment of future income is $25,000 and occurs today. Future income grows at 5 per cent annually, while interest is 6 per cent annually. If the calculations are done properly and the economist's assumptions are followed, then when the final payment is made 19 years from today, there should be no money left in the fund.

§19.04 How to Test the Economist's Estimate

Table 19-2 shows how to test the economist's estimate. The economist has determined that $457,626 is the present value of the future income stream. At the beginning of the first year the economist deducts $25,000 from the principal to make the first year's salary payment. The remaining principal of $432,626 is invested at 6 per cent. The annual interest income of $25,958 is added to the principal, resulting in the ending principal of $458,584.

At the beginning of the second year the annual salary of $25,000 has grown at 5 per cent annually and became $26,250. This is in accordance with the assumption of an annual 5 per cent growth in wages. The salary for the second year is deducted from the balance of $458,584, leaving a balance of $432,334 to earn annual interest of 6 per cent. Table 19-2 shows the annual interest income and salary paid.

If the economist's analysis has been done properly, there should be no money left in the fund when the person would have reached age 65. This is the case shown in Table 19-2.

Table 19-2 Judging the Present Value of Loss

Age	Beginning Principal	Annual Income	Principal Interest	Annual Income	Ending Principal
45	457,625	25,000	432,625	25,958	458,583
46	458,583	26,250	432,333	25,940	458,272
47	458,272	27,563	430,710	25,843	456,553
48	456,553	28,941	427,612	25,657	453,269
49	453,269	30,388	422,881	25,373	448,254
50	448,254	31,907	416,347	24,981	441,328
51	441,328	33,502	407,825	24,470	432,295
52	432,295	35,178	397,117	23,827	420,944
53	420,944	36,936	384,008	23,040	407,048
54	407,048	38,783	368,265	22,096	390,361
55	390,361	40,722	349,639	20,978	370,617
56	370,617	42,758	327,859	19,672	347,530
57	347,530	44,896	302,634	18,158	320,792
58	320,792	47,141	273,650	16,419	290,069
59	290,069	49,498	240,571	14,434	255,005
60	255,005	51,973	203,032	12,182	215,214
61	215,214	54,572	160,642	9,639	170,281
62	170,281	57,300	112,980	6,779	119,759
63	119,759	60,165	59,594	3,576	63,169
64	63,169	63,174*			

*due to rounding

When the economist testifies that a growth rate and the discount rate are not equal but to simplify the calculation the two have been set equal, the economist is making improper economic judgments. The economist usually argues that the assumption of growth being equal to the discount rate will simplify the present value calculation but have no significant impact on the dollar amount estimated to be the present value of the future stream of income.

When the economist sets the growth and discount rates equal, one of two possible conditions exists. The growth rate is less than the discount rate but the two are set equal to each other.

Section **19.05** shows the present value calculation when the growth and discount rates are equal. If the two are equal and that has justification, then there would be no money left in the fund at the end of the annuity period. Section **19.07** shows the present value calculation when the growth rate of wages exceeds the discount rate but they are assumed to be equal.

§19.05   Calculating the Present Value When the Growth Rate Equals the Discount Rate

The economist has testified that the growth rate for wages has an historical average which is equal to the historical average for the discount rate. Tables 19-3 and 19-4 shows the present value of the two possible assumptions. That is, Table 19-3 shows the present value of the income stream if the annual growth and discount rates are equal at 4.5 per cent.

Table 19-3   Present Value of Future Income

Growth Rate = 4.5%
Discount Rate = 4.5%

Age	Period	Future Income	Present Value	Sum
45	0	25,000	25,000	25,000
46	1	26,125	25,000	50,000
47	2	27,301	25,000	75,000
48	3	28,529	25,000	100,000
49	4	29,813	25,000	125,000
50	5	31,155	25,000	150,000
51	6	32,557	25,000	175,000
52	7	34,022	25,000	200,000
53	8	35,553	25,000	225,000
54	9	37,152	25,000	250,000
55	10	38,824	25,000	275,000
56	11	40,571	25,000	300,000
57	12	42,397	25,000	325,000
58	13	44,305	25,000	350,000
59	14	46,299	25,000	375,000

Age	Period	Future Income	Present Value	Sum
60	15	48,382	25,000	400,000
61	16	50,559	25,000	425,000
62	17	52,834	25,000	450,000
63	18	55,212	25,000	475,000
64	19	57,697	25,000	500,000

Table 19-4 shows exactly the same present value even though the growth and discount rates have increased to 6 per cent annually. Whenever the growth and discount rates are assumed to be the same, the present value will be the same, regardless of what rate is used.

Table 19-4   Present Value of Future Income

Growth Rate = 6%
Discount Rate = 6%

Age	Period	Future Income	Present Value	Sum
45	0	25,000	25,000	25,000
46	1	26,125	25,000	50,000
47	2	27,301	25,000	75,000
48	3	28,529	25,000	100,000
49	4	29,813	25,000	125,000
50	5	31,155	25,000	150,000
51	6	32,557	25,000	175,000
52	7	34,022	25,000	200,000
53	8	35,553	25,000	225,000
54	9	37,152	25,000	250,000
55	10	38,824	25,000	275,000
56	11	40,571	25,000	300,000
57	12	42,397	25,000	325,000
58	13	44,305	25,000	350,000
59	14	46,299	25,000	375,000
60	15	48,382	25,000	400,000
61	16	50,559	25,000	425,000
62	17	52,834	25,000	450,000
63	18	55,212	25,000	475,000
64	19	57,697	25,000	500,000

Tables 19-5 and 19-6 show how the 20-year annuity will be paid out under the different growth and interest assumptions. As indicated on both tables, there would be no money left in the fund at the end of the 20-year period.

Table 19-5   Judging the Present Value of Future Income

Growth Rate = 4.5%
Discount Rate = 4.5%

Age	Principal	Income	Principal Interest	Annual Int Income	Ending Principal
45	500,000	25,000	475,000	21,375	496,375
46	496,375	26,125	470,250	21,161	491,411
47	491,411	27,301	464,111	20,885	484,996
48	484,996	28,529	456,466	20,541	477,007
49	477,007	29,813	447,194	20,124	467,318
50	467,318	31,155	436,164	19,627	455,791
51	455,791	32,557	423,235	19,046	442,280
52	442,280	34,022	408,259	18,372	426,630
53	426,630	35,553	391,078	17,598	408,676
54	408,676	37,152	371,524	16,719	388,242
55	388,242	38,824	349,418	15,724	365,142
56	365,142	40,571	324,571	14,606	339,176
57	339,176	42,397	296,779	13,355	310,134
58	310,134	44,305	265,829	11,962	277,792
59	277,792	46,299	231,493	10,417	241,910
60	241,910	48,382	193,528	8,709	202,237
61	202,237	50,559	151,678	6,825	158,503
62	158,503	52,834	105,669	4,755	110,424
63	110,424	55,212	55,212	2,485	57,697
64	57,697	57,697	0	0	

Table 19-6   Judging the Present Value of Future Income
Year Age

Growth Rate = 6%
Discount Rate = 6%

Age	Beginning Principal	Annual Income	Principal Interest	Annual Int Income	Ending Principal
45	500,000	25,000	475,000	28,500	503,500
46	503,500	26,500	477,000	28,620	505,620
47	505,620	28,090	477,530	28,652	506,182
48	506,182	29,775	476,406	28,584	504,991
49	504,991	31,562	473,429	28,406	501,835
50	501,835	33,456	468,379	28,103	496,482
51	496,482	35,463	461,019	27,661	488,680

Age	Beginning Principal	Annual Income	Principal Interest	Annual Int Income	Ending Principal
52	488,680	37,591	451,089	27,065	478,154
53	478,154	39,846	438,308	26,298	464,607
54	464,607	42,237	422,370	25,342	447,712
55	447,712	44,771	402,941	24,176	427,117
56	427,117	47,457	379,660	22,780	402,439
57	402,439	50,305	352,134	21,128	373,262
58	373,262	53,323	319,939	19,196	339,136
59	339,136	56,523	282,613	16,957	299,570
60	299,570	59,914	239,656	14,379	254,035
61	254,035	63,509	190,526	11,432	201,958
62	201,958	67,319	134,639	8,078	142,717
63	142,717	71,358	71,358	4,282	75,640
64	75,640	75,640			

§19.06 Testing the Assumption of Equivalence: The Growth Rate is Less Than the Discount Rate

The economist may testify that the appropriate growth rate to use in the analysis is 4.5 per cent and the appropriate discount rate is 6 per cent. But in order to simplify the analysis the growth and discount rate have been set equal to each other. Since the two are equal, the present value is the multiplication of the current income level, $25,000, times the number of years being forecast, 20 years. The present value is $500,000.

In reality the growth rate was less than the discount rate. Thus the assumption that the growth and discount rates should be equal does not have a basis in economic fact. Table 19-7 shows what happens to the principal of $500,000 when a growth rate of 4.5 per cent and a discount rate of 6 per cent are used.

Table 19-7 Judging the Present Value of Future Income

Growth Rate = 4.5%
Discount Rate = 6%

Age	Beginning Principal	Annual Income	Principal Interest	Annual Int Income	Ending Principal
45	500,000	25,000	475,000	28,500	503,500
46	503,500	26,125	477,375	28,643	506,018
47	506,018	27,301	478,717	28,723	507,440
48	507,440	28,529	478,911	28,735	507,645
49	507,645	29,813	477,832	28,670	506,502
50	506,502	31,155	475,348	28,521	503,869

Age	Beginning Principal	Annual Income	Principal Interest	Annual Int Income	Ending Principal
51	503,869	32,557	471,312	28,279	499,591
52	499,591	34,022	465,569	27,934	493,504
53	493,504	35,553	457,951	27,477	485,428
54	485,428	37,152	448,276	26,897	475,172
55	475,172	38,824	436,348	26,181	462,529
56	462,529	40,571	421,958	25,317	447,275
57	447,275	42,397	404,878	24,293	429,171
58	429,171	44,305	384,866	23,092	407,958
59	407,958	46,299	361,659	21,700	383,359
60	383,359	48,382	334,977	20,099	355,075
61	355,075	50,559	304,516	18,271	322,787
62	322,787	52,834	269,952	16,197	286,150
63	286,150	55,212	230,938	13,856	244,794
64	244,794	57,697	187,097	11,226	198,323

Table 19-7 shows that, when the individual reaches age 64, the money has not been used up. In fact, when a growth rate of 4.5 per cent and a discount rate of 6 per cent are employed, as the economist testified and were the true rates, there is an excess of $198,323. In fact, the larger the spread, i.e., the more the discount rate exceeds the growth rate, the greater will be the excess in the fund.

§19.07   Testing the Assumption of Equivalence: The Growth Rate Exceeds the Discount Rate

If the growth rate is larger than the discount rate, the fund will have an insufficient amount of money to properly compensate the plaintiff. The economist may testify that the appropriate growth rate to use in the analysis is 7 per cent and the appropriate discount rate is 6 per cent. In order to simplify the analysis, the economist has set the growth and discount rates equal to each other at 6 per cent. The present value of the income stream would be $500,000.

Table 19-8   Judging the Present Value of Future Income

Growth Rate = 7%
Discount Rate = 6%

Age	Beginning Principal	Annual Income	Principal Interest	Annual Int Income	Ending Principal
45	500,000	25,000	475,000	28,500	503,500
46	503,500	26,750	476,750	28,605	505,355
47	505,355	28,623	476,733	28,604	505,336

Age	Beginning Principal	Annual Income	Principal Interest	Annual Int Income	Ending Principal
48	505,336	30,626	474,710	28,483	503,193
49	503,193	32,770	470,423	28,225	498,648
50	498,648	35,064	463,585	27,815	491,400
51	491,400	37,518	453,882	27,233	481,114
52	481,114	40,145	440,970	26,458	467,428
53	467,428	42,955	424,473	25,468	449,942
54	449,942	45,961	403,980	24,239	428,219
55	428,219	49,179	379,040	22,742	401,783
56	401,783	52,621	349,161	20,950	370,111
57	370,111	56,305	313,806	18,828	332,635
58	332,635	60,246	272,389	16,343	288,732
59	288,732	64,463	224,269	13,456	237,725
60	237,725	68,976	168,749	10,125	178,874
61	178,874	73,804	105,070	6,304	111,374
62	111,374	78,970	32,404	1,944	34,348
63	34,348	84,498	-50,151	-3,009	-53,160
64	-53,160	90,413	-143,573	-8,614	-152,187

Table 19-8 shows that there is insufficient money in the fund to allow for the expected 7 per cent growth of wages. The fund is exhausted when the individual would have reached age 63.

The more the growth rate exceeds the discount rate the greater will be the inadequacy of the fund. Stated differently, the more the growth rate exceeds the discount rate, the sooner the fund will be exhausted.

§19.08 Summary

When an economist calculates the present value of a future income stream, it is necessary to state the growth rate and the discount rate. If the economist arbitrarily alters the growth or discount rate, the present value will be improperly altered.

If the "true" growth rate is less than the "true" discount rate but the economist sets the two values equal, the present value will be overstated. This would over-compensate the plaintiff. If the "true" growth rate is greater than the "true" discount rate but the economist sets the two values equal, the present value will be understated. This would under-compensate the plaintiff.

20

Selecting an Economist

§20.01 The Plaintiff's Economist
§20.02 The Defense Economist

§20.01 The Plaintiff's Economist

It is not necessary to search far and wide for an expert economist. They can be found at local junior colleges, colleges, and universities. The academic affiliation will usually give credibility to an economist's testimony.

The plaintiff's economist should have all the characteristics of "a good witness"—one head, neatly dressed, articulate, confident but not argumentative. Often what the economist says is not as important as how well he or she says it.

Experience as an expert witness is helpful, but every economist has to have a first case. If the individual understands present value and comes across as a sincere and caring person, in all likelihood the jury will listen to what he or she has to say.

Whatever has not been included in the analysis—probability of seeking employment, probability of being employed, the worklife expectancy table, the higher returns on long-term government bonds—will not bother the jury if the economist appears sincere and confident. The points of contention on cross-examination will provide a learning experience for the novice economist-witness, but will not generally harm the credibility.

§20.02 The Defense Economist

The number of heads the defense economist has is not important since he or she is only needed to help prepare for the cross-examination of the plaintiff's economist. Competent economists can be found in all types of businesses, banks, brokerage firms, insurance companies, federal and state government, and the local junior colleges and universities. Since the defense economist's job is to help prepare the defense attorney for the cross-examination of the plaintiff's economist, there is no such thing as "proper credentials." The economist needs only to understand the present value concept and be aware of areas of disagreement. The defense economist is truly the case of an economist who is heard but not seen. The defense economist does not usually testify since his or her testimony would permit the plaintiff's attorney to establish a floor for the economic loss.

21 Case Studies

§21.01 Introduction

Economists submit reports to attorneys all the time. In order to evaluate the economist's report properly, the attorney, or the attorney's economists, should try to review several different reports prepared by the same economist. When examining different reports, the goal is to find where the economist is consistent from report to report and where he or she is inconsistent.

If any of the variables in the analysis change, the defense attorney should attempt to determine whether the economist has sufficient reason for the changes. In some cases the variables will change. For example, in two cases involving a wrongful death, there is no expectation that both descendants would have exactly the same income. However, both might be the same age. If the analysis by plaintiff's economist took place in the same year, the growth rate for wages may be the same. If this is not the case, why not? There may be a perfectly good explanation.

This chapter presents different reports submitted by the same economist in different cases. There are different types of losses. From reading the reports of the economists, the nature of the loss estimated should be evident. If the report is not clear, then it is necessary to get additional information, either through interrogatories or deposition.[1]

Sections **21.02** and **21.04** present the fact situations addressed by the economist. Sections **21.03** and **21.05** present the economist's reports in their entirety. There is some duplication in the reports presented. The purpose is to compare and contrast the reports.

§21.02   Wrongful Death of a Housewife and Mother Not Employed Outside the Home

Mrs. Smith was a white female, 27 years old at the time of her death. She was born September 18, 1963 and died March 18, 1991. She was married and was the mother of two small children. Section **21.03** is the economist's report.

§21.03   Economist's Report on the Economic Loss of a Housewife Not Employed Outside the Home

Consultant

Washburn University
School of Business
Topeka, Kansas 66621
913-231-1010 ext. 1586

Post Office Box 4431
Topeka, Kansas 66604-0431
Telephone and Fax
913-232-4499

May 5, 1993

Elizabeth and Craig
ATTN: Ms. Anne Elizabeth
P.O. Box 4431
Topeka, Kansas 66604

RE: Mrs. Smith

Dear Ms. Elizabeth,

I have evaluated the economic loss resulting from the death of Mrs. Smith and estimate the present value of the loss to be $570,293. This amount is the sum of

---

[1] Fed R Civ P 26(b)(4)(A)i.

the historic loss plus the present value of the future loss. This figure is exclusive of any value for the pleasure of living, any pain and suffering, and exclusive of the moral teaching, training, guidance, etc., that a mother provides for a child.

This evaluation is based on information received from your office as detailed in Part I of this report. If there is an error in the information please contact me immediately so I may correct the error and provide you with a revised evaluation.

The methodology and other sources of information employed in preparing this report appear in the subsequent Parts of the report. If I may be of further assistance please do not hesitate to contact me.

Sincerely,

Economist, Ph. D.

Economic Loss
to Mrs. Smith

The economic loss suffered as a result of the death of Mrs. Smith is $570,293. The dollar amount consists of a historic loss and the present value of the future loss.

The historic loss represents the value of household services from the date of the accident, March 18, 1991, to September 18, 1993. This loss is $46,843.

The present value of future loss begins September 18, 1993. The loss is $523,450.

HISTORIC LOSS:

From March 18, 1991 to September 18, 1993

Household Services $46,843

PRESENT VALUE OF FUTURE LOSS:

Beginning September 18, 1993

Household Services $523,450

TOTAL LOSS $570,293

ECONOMIC ANALYSIS
Mrs. Smith

PART I. BACKGROUND STATISTICS:

Date of Birth:	September 18, 1963
Current Age:	29
Race:	Caucasian
Sex:	Female
Date of Accident:	March 18, 1991
Accident resulted in:	Death
Life Expectancy:	53.4 years
Education:	College Graduate
Earnings History:	Not employed outside the home
Marital Status:	Married
Dependents:	Two minor children
	Frank, DOB: May 9, 1987
	Craig, DOB: April 7, 1989
Date of Analysis:	May 3, 1993
Date of Present Value:	September 18, 1993

PART II. CALCULATION OF HISTORIC ECONOMIC LOSS

The historic loss begins on the date of Mrs. Smith's death, March 18, 1991, and continues until the present value date of September 18, 1993. The economic loss is based on the value of household services provided by a mother of two children, the youngest being four years old.

The economic values are based on the study *Household Work: What's It Worth and Why?* by W. Keith, Cathleen D. Zick, and Hyoshin Kim, Cornell University Bulletin 322 IB228 (1992). The values reported in the study are 1988 values according to the Consumer Price Index, and are presented in the following table.

Table 1

	1988	1989	1990	1991	1992
CPI	118.3	124.00	130.70	136.20	140.30
Change in CPI		4.82	5.40	4.21	3.01

Age of Youngest Child	1988	1989	1990	1991	1992
1	$17,591	18,439	19,434	20,253	20,862
2 thru 5	15,920	16,687	17,589	18,329	18,881
6 thru 14	13,739	14,401	15,179	15,818	16,294
15 thru 17	12,283	12,875	13,570	14,142	14,567
over 18	12,924	13,547	14,279	14,880	15,327

The historic loss is based on two considerations: First, Mrs. Smith did not work outside the home, and second, the youngest child is age four. The calculation of the historic loss is presented in the next table.

Table 2

Year	Value of Services	Per Cent of Year	Loss
1991	$18,329	78.9	$14,462
1992	18,881	100.0	18,881
1993	18,881	71.5	13,500
			$46,843

PART III.   CALCULATION OF FUTURE ECONOMIC LOSS

The present value of the loss is calculated by using the following formula:

$$\text{Present Value of Future Income} = \$ \sum_{t=0}^{n} [(1+g)^t / (1+d)^t] * M_a$$

The five variables in this formula are:

$\$, t, g, d$ and M_a

$\$$ = Represents the basis for calculating the economic loss resulting from the death of Mrs. Smith. The 1992 values of the household services are presented in Table 1. It is these values that are used as "$\$$" in the present value formula. Enclosed please find a printout showing the present value computation.

t = Represents time and starts on the present value date and runs throughout the life of Mrs. Smith.

g = Represents the growth rate. The growth rate is 4.30% and is the 1952-1992 historic rate of change in the Consumer Price Index.

d = Represents the discount rate or rate at which dollars received will earn interest. The discount rate is 6.05% and is the 1952-1992 historic yield on one-year treasury bills. There are many types of investments which can be made today, ranging from passbook savings to speculating in future markets. While there is no such thing as a risk-free investment, the United States one-year Treasury Bill is used as a surrogate.

For example, if we are receiving $1,000 one year from today we might be willing to receive some amount less than $1,000 today. This is true because we could invest the money for one year and earn interest. The rate of earnings is the interest rate or discount rate.

The actual calculation of the present value of the future income stream assumes that the relationship between the growth and discount rate will remain unchanged. That is, the discount rate will be 1.0168 times the growth rate. This relationship is established by dividing 1.0605, the interest rate, by 1.0430, the growth rate.

The analysis does *not* assume that the growth rate of wages and the interest rate will always be the same. The analysis *does* assume that the interest rate is 1.0168 times the growth rate.

M_a = Represents the mortality adjustment. In the calculation of the present value of the future household services each value is multiplied by the probability that Mrs. Smith will be alive. This is the mortality adjustment.

PART IV. BIBLIOGRAPHY

PROBABILITY OF LIVING:

US National Center for Health Statistics, *Life Expectancy Tables*, Vital Statistics of US 1989, *cited in Statistical Abstracts of U.S. 1992*, Table 105 (1992).

CONSUMER PRICE INDEX:

Economic Report of the President Table B-56 (1993). Federal Reserve Bulletin (Apr 1993).

INTEREST RATES:

Various Federal Reserve Bulletins

VALUE OF HOUSEHOLD SERVICES:

W. Keith Bryant, Cathleen D. Zick & Hyoshin Kim,
Household Work: What's It Worth and Why?,
Cornell University Bulletin 322 IB228 (1992).

Annual Value of
Household Services

Mrs. Smith

Date of Birth: September 18, 1963
Date of Death: March 18, 1991
Date of Present Value: September 18, 1993

	1988	1989	1990	1991	1992
CPI	118.3	124.00	130.70	136.20	140.30
Change in CPI		4.82	5.40	4.21	3.01

Age of Youngest Child	1988	1989	1990	1991	1992
1	$17,591	18,439	19,434	20,253	20,862
2 thru 5	15,920	16,687	17,589	18,329	18,881
6 thru 14	13,739	14,401	15,179	15,818	16,294
15 thru 17	12,283	12,875	13,570	14,142	14,567
over 18	12,924	13,547	14,279	14,880	15,327

Present Value of
Future Economic Loss

Mother's Age	Period	Child's Age	Present Value	Sum	Probability of Living	Adjusted PV	Adjusted Sum
30	0	4	18,881	18,881	.9994	18,869	18,869
31	1	5	18,569	37,450	.9987	18,545	37,414
32	2	6	15,761	53,210	.9980	15,730	53,144
33	3	7	15,501	68,711	.9973	15,459	68,602
34	4	8	15,245	83,956	.9965	15,192	83,794
35	5	9	14,993	98,949	.9957	14,929	98,724
36	6	10	14,746	113,695	.9949	14,671	113,394
37	7	11	14,503	128,197	.9940	14,415	127,810
38	8	12	14,263	142,461	.9930	14,163	141,973
39	9	13	14,028	156,488	.9919	13,914	155,887
40	10	14	13,796	170,285	.9907	13,668	169,556
41	11	15	12,131	182,416	.9894	12,002	181,558
42	12	16	11,931	194,346	.9880	11,787	193,345
43	13	17	11,734	206,080	.9864	11,574	204,919
44	14	18	12,142	218,222	.9847	11,956	216,876
45	15	19	11,942	230,164	.9828	11,737	228,612
46	16	20	11,745	241,909	.9808	11,519	240,132
47	17	21	11,551	253,460	.9785	11,303	251,435
48	18	22	11,360	264,820	.9761	11,089	262,524
49	19	23	11,173	275,993	.9733	10,875	273,398
50	20	24	10,989	286,982	.9702	10,661	284,059
51	21		10,807	297,789	.9668	10,449	294,508
52	22		10,629	308,418	.9630	10,236	304,744
53	23		10,454	318,872	.9589	10,024	314,768

Mother's Age	Period	Child's Age	Present Value	Sum	Probability of Living	Adjusted PV	Adjusted Sum
54	24		10,281	329,153	.9543	9,811	324,579
55	25		10,111	339,264	.9493	9,599	334,178
56	26		9,945	349,209	.9438	9,386	343,564
57	27		9,780	358,989	.9379	9,173	352,737
58	28		9,619	368,608	.9313	8,958	361,696
59	29		9,460	378,069	.9242	8,743	370,439
60	30		9,304	387,373	.9165	8,527	378,966
61	31		9,151	396,523	.9080	8,309	387,275
62	32		9,000	405,523	.8989	8,090	395,365
63	33		8,851	414,374	.8891	7,870	403,235
64	34		8,705	423,079	.8786	7,648	410,883
65	35		8,561	431,641	.8673	7,426	418,309
66	36		8,420	440,061	.8551	7,200	425,509
67	37		8,281	448,342	.8420	6,973	432,482
68	38		8,145	456,487	.8279	6,743	439,225
69	39		8,010	464,497	.8127	6,510	445,735
70	40		7,878	472,375	.7964	6,274	452,009
71	41		7,748	480,123	.7790	6,035	458,045
72	42		7,620	487,743	.7602	5,793	463,838
73	43		7,494	495,237	.7402	5,547	469,385
74	44		7,371	502,608	.7189	5,298	474,684
75	45		7,249	509,857	.6961	5,046	479,730
76	46		7,129	516,987	.6719	4,790	484,520
77	47		7,012	523,998	.6460	4,530	489,050
78	48		6,896	530,895	.6186	4,266	493,316
79	49		6,782	537,677	.5897	3,999	497,315
80	50		6,670	544,347	.5592	3,730	501,046
81	51		6,560	550,908	.5257	3,449	504,495
82	52		6,452	557,360	.4892	3,157	507,651
83	53		6,346	563,705	.4499	2,855	510,506
84	54		6,241	569,946	.4078	2,545	513,051
85	55		6,138	576,084	.3637	2,232	515,283
86	56		6,037	582,121	.3180	1,920	517,203
87	57		5,937	588,058	.2717	1,613	518,816
88	58		5,839	593,897	.2258	1,318	520,134
89	59		5,743	599,639	.1816	1,043	521,177
90	60		5,648	605,287	.1403	792	521,969
91	61		5,555	610,842	.1033	574	522,543
92	62		5,463	616,305	.0718	392	522,935
93	63		5,373	621,678	.0463	249	523,184
94	64		5,284	626,962	.0273	144	523,329
95	65		5,197	632,159	.0143	74	523,403
96	66		5,111	637,271	.0064	33	523,435
97	67		5,027	642,297	.0023	12	523,447
98	68		4,944	647,241	.0006	3	523,450
99	69		4,862	652,104	.0001	0	523,450

§21.04   Fact Situation for a Disabled Worker

A woman was injured in an automobile accident. It is not clear if she will be able to continue in her employment. In order to access her employment opportunities a vocational rehabilitation expert has been consulted. The report provides one of the bases for the economist's estimate of the economic loss. *See* §21.05.

§21.05   Economist's Report on the Economic Loss Suffered by a Disabled Worker

Consultant

Washburn University
School of Business
Topeka, Kansas 66621
913-231-1010 ext. 1586

Post Office Box 4431
Topeka, Kansas 66604-0431
Telephone and Fax
913-232-4499

February 17, 1993

Firm's Name
Attn:
Address
Address

RE: (Client's Name)

Dear Attorney:

I have made a preliminary estimate of the economic loss to (client's name) resulting from the May 20, 1991 automobile accident. The loss ranges from a low of $154,197 to a high of $489,568. The lower figure assumes (client's name) is able to retain her current job earning $18,000 per year and retire at age 65 while the higher figure assumes she is unable to obtain employment and would retire at age 70. The differences are more clearly spelled out later in the report. The dollar amounts include the historic loss plus the present value of the future loss.

The estimate of economic loss is exclusive of any consideration of a loss of fringe benefits and any loss of ability to perform household services. The loss also excludes any consideration of pain and suffering.

This evaluation is based on information received from your office as detailed in Part I of this report. If there is an error in the information please contact me immediately so I may correct the error and provide you with a revised evaluation.

The methodology and other sources of information employed in preparing this report appear in the subsequent Parts of the report. If I may be of further assistance please do not hesitate to contact me.

Sincerely,

Economist, Ph. D.

Economic Loss to
(Client's Name)

HISTORIC LOSS:

From May 5, 1991 to February 27, 1993

Wages	$11,145
Catering	9,920
Historic Loss	$21,065

PRESENT VALUE OF FUTURE LOSS:

Beginning February 27, 1993

No Employment after February 27, 1993

Wages	$283,989	$370,181
Catering	75,429	98,322
Present Value	$359,418	$468,503
Historic Loss	21,065	21,065
Total Loss	$380,483	$489,568

Current Employment at $18,000 per year

	To Age 65	To Age 70
Wages	$57,703	$75,216
Catering	75,429	98,322
Present Value	$133,132	$173,538
Historic Loss	21,065	21,065
Total Loss	$154,197	$194,603

Alternative Employment at $12,480 per year ($6.00 per hour)

	To Age 65	To Age 70
Wages	$127,097	$165,672
Catering	75,429	98,322
Present Value	$192,526	$263,994
Historic Loss	21,065	21,065
Total Loss	$213,591	$285,059

ECONOMIC ANALYSIS
(Client's Name)

PART I. BACKGROUND STATISTICS:

Date of Birth:	February 27, 1942
Current Age:	50
Race:	Caucasian
Sex:	Female
Date of Accident:	May 20, 1991
Accident resulted in:	Disability
Life Expectancy:	30.6
Education:	High School Graduate

Earnings History:

1984	$16,038
1985	21,628
1986	22,709
1987	29,546
1988	28,686
1989	14,464
1990	20,435
1991	18,541
1992	18,063

Age at Retirement:	65 or 70
Marital Status:	Divorced
Date of Analysis:	February 15, 1993
Date of Present Value:	February 27, 1993

PART II. CALCULATION OF HISTORIC ECONOMIC LOSS

The historic loss includes both wages from employment and income from the catering business. The income estimated to be earned, absent the accident, is the average income from 1984 through 1990. The average was $21,930. The 1991 and 1992 loss are calculated as follows:

1991

Average Income	$21,930
Actual Income	18,541
Loss	3,389
Plus Bonus	
@$500/Mo.5 Mo.	2,500
Total Loss	$5,889

The 1992 loss of income is calculated by letting the 1991 income increase by 3.01%, the increase in the Consumer Price Index for the year 1992. The 1992 income would be $22,590. From this the actual income of $18,063 is subtracted leaving a loss of $4,527. To this figure the loss of cash flow of $6,000 from the catering business is added. The total loss is $10,527.

The 1993 loss is calculated in the same way. From the base income of $22,590 the current income of $18,000 is subtracted leaving $4,590 in lost income. The portion of the year to February 27th is 15.9% or $729. The same calculation is done for the catering business. The loss from catering is $954. The total loss for 1993 is $1,683.

In addition to the wages, the cash flow associated with the catering business was estimated. The estimate of cash flow assumes that the gross profit (sales less cost of goods sold) reported on the 1991 tax return is applicable to any sales. It is also assumed that the operating expenses, depreciation, interest, taxes, etc., are fully reported on the tax return and are independent of sales. Consequently the 1991 cash flow, absent the accident, is estimated as follows:

	To May 20, 1991	Annualized
Sales	$3,775	$9,815
Cost of Goods Sold	1,222	3,177
Gross Profit	2,553	6,638
Operating Expenses	5,672	5,672
Earnings	<3,119>	966
Depreciation	2,000	2,000
Cash Flow	<$1,119>	$2,966

The benefits from operating the catering business are grossly understated since the analysis is based on only the beginning of the year. The auction "season" really runs from April or May through October to November. Accordingly, the benefits of operating the business is estimated to be $6,000 annually beginning in 1992.

PART III. CALCULATION OF FUTURE ECONOMIC LOSS

The present value of the loss is calculated by using the following formula:

$$\text{Present Value of Future Income} = \$ \sum_{t=0}^{n} [(1+g)^t / (1+d)^t]$$

The four variables in this formula are:

$, t, g, and d

$ =   Represents the basis for calculating the economic loss resulting from the accident. The wage calculation is based on different earnings levels. The highest level of earnings is $22,590. This analysis assumes (client's name) would be unable to work after February 27, 1993. The reason alternative employment may not be possible is that employers will not hire her because of her preexisting condition. There is some concern for this scenario since her employer has been bought out.

The second alternative is to assume (client's name) continues at her current rate of compensation, $18,000 per year. Her annual loss under this scenario would be $22,590 less $18,000 or $4,590 per year.

The third alternative assumes (client's name) would be unable to continue her current employment but would find alternative employment at $6.00 per hour, $12,480 annually. The annual loss of income would be $22,590 less $12,480 or $10,110. This information is based on the report from the Return to Work Center.

The analysis is exclusive of any consideration of any type of fringe benefits other than the paid holidays (client's name) currently receives. No consideration was given for the cost of replacing health insurance if she is forced to seek alternative employment.

The analysis also excludes any consideration of future medical expenses, pain and suffering, inability to perform household services, or the reduced capacity to enjoy life.

t =   Represents time and starts on the present value date and runs until period "n." The analyses concluded with retirement at either 65 or 70. The analysis assumes uninterrupted work until retirement.

g =   Represents the growth rate. The growth rate is 4.34% and is the 1952-1991 historic rate of change in the Consumer Price Index. The growth rate is applied to increases in wages, regardless of where employed, and to the cash flows resulting from operating the catering business.

d =   Represents the discount rate or rate at which dollars received will earn interest. The discount rate is 6.10% and is the 1952-1991 historic yield on one-year treasury bills. There are many types of investments which can be made today, ranging from passbook savings to speculating in future markets. While there is no such thing as a risk free investment, the U.S. one-year Treasury Bill is used as a surrogate.

For example, if we are receiving $1,000 one year from today we might be willing to receive some amount less than $1,000 today. This is true because we could invest the money for one year and earn interest. The rate of earnings is the interest rate or discount rate.

The actual calculation of the present value of the future income stream assumes the relationship between the growth and discount rate will remain unchanged. That is, the discount rate will be 1.0169 times the growth rate. This relationship is established by dividing 1.0610, the interest rate, by 1.0434, the growth rate.

The analysis does *not* assume that the growth rate of wages and the interest rate will always be the same. The analysis *does* assume that the interest rate is 1.0169 times the growth rate.

PART IV.   BIBLIOGRAPHY

PROBABILITY OF LIVING:

US National Center for Health Statistics, *Life Expectancy Tables*, Vital Statistics of U.S. 1992, *cited in Statistical Abstracts of U.S. 1992*, Table 105 (1992).

JOB PARTICIPATION RATE:

Bureau of Labor Statistics, Handbook of Labor Statistics, Civilian Labor Participation Rate By Sex, Race and Age, Bulletin 2070, at 14-15 (Dec 1980).

CONSUMER PRICE INDEX:

Economic Report of the President Table B-59 (1992).

INTEREST RATES:

Various Federal Reserve Bulletins

ALTERNATIVE EMPLOYMENT:

Menninger Return to Work Center
Topeka, Kansas

Client's Name

DOB: February 27, 1942
DOA: May 20, 1991
Date of Present Value:
February 27, 1993

GROWTH 0.0434
DISCOUNT 0.0612
INCOME 4,590 $21,590 less 18,000

Age	Per	Present Value	Sum	Prob of Living	Emp	Adjusted Pres Val	Sum
51	0	4,590	4,590	.9965	.961	4,396	4,396
52	1	4,513	9,103	.9926	.961	4,305	8,700
53	2	4,437	13,540	.9883	.961	4,214	12,915
54	3	4,363	17,903	.9836	.961	4,124	17,039
55	4	4,290	22,193	.9785	.965	4,050	21,089
56	5	4,218	26,411	.9728	.965	3,960	25,049
57	6	4,147	30,558	.9667	.965	3,868	28,917
58	7	4,077	34,635	.9599	.965	3,777	32,694
59	8	4,009	38,644	.9526	.965	3,685	36,380
60	9	3,942	42,586	.9446	.965	3,593	39,973

Age	Per	Present Value	Sum	Prob of Living	Emp	Adjusted Pres Val	Sum
61	10	3,876	46,462	.9359	.965	3,500	43,473
62	11	3,811	50,272	.9265	.965	3,407	46,880
63	12	3,747	54,019	.9164	.965	3,313	50,194
64	13	3,684	57,703	.9056	.965	3,219	53,413
65	14	3,622	61,325	.8939	.967	279	53,692
66	15	3,561	64,886	.8814	.967	270	53,962
67	16	3,502	68,388	.8679	.967	262	54,223
68	17	3,443	71,831	.8533	.967	253	54,476
69	18	3,385	75,216	.8377	.967	244	54,720
70	19	3,328	78,545	.8209	.967	235	54,955
71	20	3,273	81,817	.8029	.967	226	55,182
72	21	3,218	85,035	.7836	.967	217	55,399
73	22	3,164	88,198	.7629	.967	208	55,606
74	23	3,111	91,309	.7409	.967	198	55,805
75	24	3,058	94,367	.7175	.967	189	55,993
76	25	3,007	97,375	.6925	.967	179	56,173
77	26	2,957	100,331	.6659	.967	169	56,342
78	27	2,907	103,238	.6376	.967	160	56,502
79	28	2,858	106,097	.6078	.967	150	56,651
80	29	2,810	108,907	.5764	.967	139	56,791
81	30	2,763	111,670	.5419	.967	129	56,919
82	31	2,717	114,387	.5043	.967	118	57,037
83	32	2,671	117,059	.4637	.967	107	57,144
84	33	2,627	119,685	.4204	.967	95	57,239
85	34	2,582	122,268	.3748	.967	83	57,322
86	35	2,539	124,807	.3278	.967	72	57,394
87	36	2,497	127,303	.2800	.967	60	57,454
88	37	2,455	129,758	.2327	.967	49	57,503
89	38	2,414	132,171	.1871	.967	39	57,542
90	39	2,373	134,544	.1446	.967	30	57,572
91	40	2,333	136,878	.1065	.967	21	57,593
92	41	2,294	139,172	.0740	.967	15	57,608
93	42	2,256	141,427	.0477	.967	9	57,617
94	43	2,218	143,645	.0281	.967	5	57,622
95	44	2,181	145,826	.0147	.967	3	57,625
96	45	2,144	147,970	.0066	.967	1	57,626
97	46	2,108	150,078	.0024	.967	0	57,627
98	47	2,073	152,150	.0006	.967	0	57,627
99	48	2,038	154,188	.0001	.967	0	57,627

22 Evaluating Structured Settlements

§22.01 Introduction

This chapter will define structured settlements and the terms used in discussing structured settlements. In addition, it will explain interest assumptions, growth assumptions, and mortality assumptions used in evaluating and designing structured settlements. The latter part of the chapter focuses on evaluating structured settlements and designing structured settlements.

§22.02 Defining the Terms—Structured Settlement

A *structured settlement* occurs whenever the plaintiff will receive a payment at some date in the future. A structured settlement might be one in which the plaintiff will receive $100,000 in 29 years. Or it may be in the form of an annuity; that is, the plaintiff will receive $1,000 per month for life. The fact that payments occur at dates other than at the time of settlement makes the settlement a structured settlement.

§22.03 —Present Value

The *present value* of a structured settlement refers to the cost of providing the future payments. The present value will depend on the number of dollars being paid, when the dollars are being paid, the growth rate, the current rate of interest, and whether the payments are certain.

§22.04 —Payout

The *payout* of a structured settlement is the number of dollars the plaintiff will receive over the life of the structured settlement. It has nothing to do with the cost or present value of providing the settlement.

For example, suppose a five-year-old female is bitten by a dog, and a settlement is to provide the girl with $1 million. The payout is $1 million. The cost, or present value, of the settlement will depend on when the $1 million is to be received. If the money is to be received today, then the present value is $1 million. The longer the time until the money is to be received, the smaller the present value.

§22.05 —Dollars Received

There are different types of payments which can be made to a plaintiff. Payments will be lump sums or in the form of annuities. A *lump sum payment* is a one-time payment. An *annuity* is a series of payments.

§22.06   —Dollars Received as Lump Sums

A *lump sum* is a one-time payment. For instance, $10,000 received in 10 years is a lump sum payment, as is $50,000 received at age 65. There may be more than one lump sum payment in a settlement. For example, the settlement may be in the following form:

Table 22-1   Structured Lump Sum Payments

$20,000 to be received in 5 years
$20,000 to be received in 10 years
$20,000 to be received in 15 years
$20,000 to be received in 20 years
$20,000 to be received in 25 years
$20,000 to be received in 30 years
$20,000 to be received in 35 years
$20,000 to be received in 40 years

This is a settlement containing eight lump sum payments. Rather than specify that a payment will occur in five, or ten years, the settlement may specify that the money will be paid when the recipient reaches a certain age. Table 22-2 specifies when the money is to be paid based on age.

Table 22-2   Structured Lump Sum Payments

$20,000 to be received at age 30
$20,000 to be received at age 35
$20,000 to be received at age 40
$20,000 to be received at age 45
$20,000 to be received at age 50
$20,000 to be received at age 55
$20,000 to be received at age 60
$20,000 to be received at age 65

The examples in lump sum payouts in Tables 22-1 and 22-2 have the same number of payments, eight. Both have the same payout, $160,000 (eight times $20,000). The lump sum payments do not have to be the same amount. Table 22-3 presents a different lump sum package.

Table 22-3   Structured Lump Sum Payments

$20,000 to be received at age 30
$25,000 to be received at age 35
$30,000 to be received at age 40
$35,000 to be received at age 45
$40,000 to be received at age 50
$45,000 to be received at age 55
$50,000 to be received at age 60
$55,000 to be received at age 65

§22.07   —Dollars Received as Annuities

An *annuity* was defined in §22.05 as a series of payments. Annuity payments may be made annually or monthly. An annuity payment may be $1,000 per month for life, or $10,000 per year for life.

Suppose a college fund is to be established for a minor. The money to be received is $10,000 per year at ages 18, 19, 20, and 21. This could be a series of four lump sum payments or a four-year annuity of $10,000 per year.

§22.08   —Certain or Uncertain Payments; The Mortality Adjustment

Payments are said to be *certain* or *uncertain* depending on whether the recipient is living when the payment is to be made. Payments which are *certain* are made to the plaintiff or the plaintiff's estate. If the payments are *uncertain* the payments are made only if the recipient is alive.

Using the example in Table 22-1, the settlement offer is modified to *uncertain* as follows:

Table 22-4   Structured Lump Sum Payments

$20,000 to be received in 5 years if living
$20,000 to be received in 10 years if living
$20,000 to be received in 15 years if living
$20,000 to be received in 20 years if living
$20,000 to be received in 25 years if living
$20,000 to be received in 30 years if living
$20,000 to be received in 35 years if living
$20,000 to be received in 40 years if living

Certain and uncertain lump sum payments may be combined into the same offer. For example, the following offer might be made:

Table 22-5   Structured Lump Sum Payments

$20,000 to be received in 5 years
$20,000 to be received in 10 years
$20,000 to be received in 15 years
$20,000 to be received in 20 years
$20,000 to be received in 25 years if living
$20,000 to be received in 30 years if living
$20,000 to be received in 35 years if living
$20,000 to be received in 40 years if living

In this case the first five payments are certain. The payments are made to the individual or the individual's estate. The last four payments are made to the individual only if he or she is living.

In a like fashion, annuities may be certain or uncertain. For example, an annuity of $ 1,000 per month for life is an uncertain annuity; the money will be paid to the recipient only if living.

Payment may be made where part of the payments are certain and part of the payments are uncertain. For example, an annuity may read as follows: "$1,000 per month, starting immediately, continuing for life, payments guaranteed to age 65." In this case $1,000 will be paid each month to the recipient for as long as he or she is alive. If the individual dies before age 65, then the $1,000 per month is paid to his or her estate. The payments to the estate continue until the individual would have reached age 65.

The calculation of the present value of uncertain payment requires estimating the probability of an individual being alive in the future years. This requires knowing the sex, race, and current age of the individual who is to receive the lump sum payments.

Many times the term *guaranteed* is used in the structured settlement discussion. *Guaranteed* usually means the same as *certain*.

Lump sum payments and annuities may be combined in a structured settlement. For example, the following structured settlement offer contains both:

Table 22-6 Structured Lump Sum Payments

Lump Sum Payments
$20,000 to be received in 5 years
$20,000 to be received in 10 years
$20,000 to be received in 15 years
$20,000 to be received in 20 years
$20,000 to be received in 25 years if living
$20,000 to be received in 30 years if living
$20,000 to be received in 35 years if living
$20,000 to be received in 40 years if living

Annuities
$1,000 per month for life guaranteed to age 65

The structured settlement presented in Table 22-6 might be written as follows: "$20,000 every five years for 40 years, with the first four payments guaranteed, plus a life annuity of $1,000 per month guaranteed to age 65."

§22.09 —Deferred Annuities

Annuities do not have to start immediately. An annuity which does not start immediately is a deferred annuity. Suppose the plaintiff is a 10-year-old child. The annuity offered might read: "$1,000 per month for life, starting at age 20, guaranteed to age 65."

§22.10 —Growth Rate

When a structured settlement contains a *growth rate*, it usually refers to the annuity portion of the settlement. The growth rate is usually an annual growth rate. The growth rate can be whatever is agreed upon, but typically runs between 2 and 6 per cent annually.

If the annuity is $1,000 per month starting immediately and growing at 4 per cent annually, then during the first year the party will receive $1,000 per month. During the second year the annuity would grow at 4 per cent and be $1,040 per month. During the third year the third annuity again would be 4 per cent larger, or $1,084. The annual growth is compounded.

If the annuity is a deferred annuity, the growth of the annuity does not take effect until the annuity begins. If the annuity is $2,000 per month starting in 20 years and growing at 3 per cent per year, then the monthly annuity will grow to $2,060 in 21 years.

§22.11 —Interest Rate

The *interest rate*, or *discount rate*, is used to determine the cost, or present value, of a structured settlement. It is the fact that money can earn interest that makes the present value and the payout of a structured settlement different. The higher the interest rate in effect, the lower the cost of purchasing a given structured settlement package. The *cost* of a structured settlement and the *present value* of a structured settlement mean the same thing. An appropriate interest rate may be determined by examining a financial publication such as *The Wall Street Journal*.

The interest earned on an individual's investment is taxable income. If an individual purchases an annuity, the interest earned on the investment is not taxable. This point is of major importance to an individual considering settling a case. Suppose $100,000 has been offered to settle a case. The individual may take the $100,000 now or receive $100,000 in the form of a structured settlement. Once the individual takes the $100,000 and invests it, for example, at 10 per cent annually, the interest income becomes taxable income. In this case the individual would pay tax on the interest income of $10,000. If a structured settlement is accepted, the interest income is not taxable.[1] The structure allows the principal left with the annuity company to compound at a higher rate.

§22.12 Overview of Evaluating Structured Settlements

To evaluate a structured settlement offer means to calculate the cost, or present value, of the offer. To determine the present value requires knowledge of: (1) the

---

[1] IRC (a)(2) provides that gross income does not include the amount of any damages received whether by suit or agreement and whether by lump sums or as periodic payments on account of personal injuries or sickness.

date of birth of the recipient; (2) the race and sex of the recipient; (3) when the payments will occur; (4) the size of the payments; (5) how long the payments are to continue; (6) whether the payments are certain or uncertain; (7) the growth of annuities; and (8) the current rate of interest.

§22.13   Worksheet for Calculating Present Value of Certain Lump Sum Payments

The following structured settlement offer has been made:

$10,000 to be paid in 5 years
$20,000 to be paid in 10 years
$40,000 to be paid in 15 years
$80,000 to be paid in 20 years

In order to evaluate the present value of the offer, the current rate of interest must be known. Having determined that the appropriate rate of interest to employ is 6 per cent, the present value can be calculated. Appendix B contains the present value factors for single payments. A portion of Appendix B appears below.

Table 22-7   Present Value of $1 Received in "t" years

| | | | Interest Rate | | |
Period	2%	4%	6%	8%	10%
0	1.0000	1.0000	1.0000	1.0000	1.0000
1	0.9804	0.9615	0.9434	0.9259	0.9091
2	0.9612	0.9246	0.8900	0.8573	0.8264
3	0.9423	0.8890	0.8396	0.7938	0.7513
4	0.9238	0.8548	0.7921	0.7350	0.6830
5	0.9057	0.8219	0.7473	0.6806	0.6209
6	0.8880	0.7903	0.7050	0.6302	0.5645
7	0.8706	0.7599	0.6651	0.5835	0.5132
8	0.8535	0.7307	0.6274	0.5403	0.4665
9	0.8368	0.7026	0.5919	0.5002	0.4241
10	0.8203	0.6756	0.5584	0.4632	0.3855
11	0.8043	0.6496	0.5268	0.4289	0.3505
12	0.7885	0.6246	0.4970	0.3971	0.3186
13	0.7730	0.6006	0.4688	0.3677	0.2897
14	0.7579	0.5775	0.4423	0.3405	0.2633
15	0.7430	0.5553	0.4173	0.3152	0.2394
16	0.7284	0.5339	0.3936	0.2919	0.2176
17	0.7142	0.5134	0.3714	0.2703	0.1978
18	0.7002	0.4936	0.3503	0.2502	0.1799

	Interest Rate				
Period	2%	4%	6%	8%	10%
19	0.6864	0.4746	0.3305	0.2317	0.1635
20	0.6730	0.4564	0.3118	0.2145	0.1486

Table 20-7 shows the present value factor of $1 received in five years to be .7473. The present value of $10,000 received in five years would be $7,473.

The present value of the lump sum payments can be estimated using the following form. The spaces filled in show the information that must be determined before the present value can be calculated.

Worksheet 22-1

Worksheet for Calculating the

Present Value of Lump Sum Payments

All Payments Certain

6% Interest Rate

Dollars	In "t" Years	Present Value Factor	Present Value
$10,000	5	_____	_____
$20,000	10	_____	_____
$40,000	15	_____	_____
$80,000	20	_____	_____
$150,000 is the Payout		Present Value	_____

The blank spaces have to be filled in. The present value factors are from Appendix B. The present value factors are where the column headed with the appropriate interest rate and the row representing when the payment is to be received intersect. Worksheet 22-2 shows the present value factors filled in.

Worksheet 22-2

Worksheet for Calculating the

Present Value of Lump Sum Payments

All Payments Certain

6% Interest Rate

Dollars	In "t" Years	Present Value Factor	Present Value
$10,000	5	.7473	_____
$20,000	10	.5584	_____
$40,000	15	.4173	_____
$80,000	20	.3118	_____
$150,000 is the Payout		Present Value	_____

The calculation of the present value of the lump sum payments is the multiplication of the payment times the present value factor. The present value of $10,000 received in five years is $7,473. Worksheet 22-3 completes the present value calculations. The present value of the four lump sum payments is $60,277. The structure has a payout of $150,000, but with a 6 per cent annual interest has a cost of $60,277.

Worksheet 22-3

Worksheet for Calculating the

Present Value of Lump Sum Payments

All Payments Certain

6% Interest Rate

Dollars	In "t" Years	Present Value Factor	Present Value
$10,000	5	.7473	$ 7,473
$20,000	10	.5584	11,168
$40,000	15	.4173	16,692
$80,000	20	.3118	24,944
$150,000 is the Payout		Present Value	$60,277

The interest rate assumption is of critical importance in the cost of providing lump sum payments. If the appropriate interest rate increases, then the cost of providing the future payments decreases. Worksheet 22-4 presents the calculation of the present value of the same settlement offer but the interest assumption is 10 per cent.

Worksheet 22-4

Worksheet for Calculating the

Present Value of Lump Sum Payments

All Payments Certain

10% Interest Rate

Dollars	In "t" Years	Present Value Factor	Present Value
$10,000	5	.6209	$ 6,209
$20,000	10	.3855	17,710
$40,000	15	.2394	19,576
$80,000	20	.1486	11,888
$150,000 is the Payout		Present Value	$35,383

The payout of the structure is $150,000 regardless of the interest assumption. The cost of providing the settlement decreases from $60,277 to $35,383 because of the increase in the interest rate used to calculate the present value.

§22.14   Worksheet for Calculating Present Value of Uncertain Lump Sum Payments

When the payments are *uncertain*, the payments are made only if the recipient is alive. The payout and the present value are both adjusted for probability of the recipient being alive when the payment is to occur.

When payments are uncertain, the race, sex, and current age of the recipient must be known. Worksheet 22-5 is the same lump sum payment schedule as in 22-1, but the payments are uncertain. The worksheet has been modified to reflect the necessary adjustments to the present value and payout calculation.

The modification is to determine the probability of the individual living the number of years necessary to receive the payments. Assume the individual is a 20-year-old white male. The probability of living to age 25 is found in Appendix F. The probability of a 20-year-old white male living to age 25 is 99.241 per cent. This value is entered in the column headed "Probability of Living." Likewise, from Appendix F, the probability of a 20-year-old white male living to age 30 is 98.258 per cent. The column is completed in this manner.

Worksheet 22-5

Worksheet for Calculating the

Present Value of Lump Sum Payments

for a 20-Year-Old White Male

All Payments Uncertain

6% Interest Rate

Dollars	Received at Age	Present Value Factor	Probability of Living	Present Value
$10,000	25	.7473	.99428	$ 7,430
$20,000	30	.5584	.98434	10,993
$40,000	35	.4173	.97482	16,272
$80,000	40	.3118	.96307	24,023
$143,198 is the Payout			Present Value	$58,718

The payout is also adjusted to reflect the uncertainty of the payments. As seen on Worksheet 22-5, the payout decreased from $150,000, when all payments were guaranteed, to $145,982 when payments are uncertain. The older the recipient is, the lower the cost of providing the settlement. This is because of the decreasing chance of survival as one gets older. Worksheets 22-6 and 22-7 show calculation of the present value of uncertain payments to 40- and 60-year-old white males, respectively.

Worksheet 22-6
Worksheet for Calculating the
Present Value of Lump Sum Payments
for a 40-Year-Old White Male
All Payments Uncertain
6% Interest Rate

Dollars	Received at Age	Present Value Factor	Probability of Living	Present Value
$10,000	45	.7473	.98424	$ 7,355
$20,000	50	.5584	.96111	10,734
$40,000	55	.4173	.92518	15,443
$80,000	60	.3118	.86816	21,655
$135,525 is the Payout			Present Value	$55,187

Worksheet 22-7
Worksheet for Calculating the
Present Value of Lump Sum Payments
for a 60-Year-Old White Male
All Payments Uncertain
6% Interest Rate

Dollars	Received at Age	Present Value Factor	Probability of Living	Present Value
$10,000	65	.7473	.90543	$ 6,766
$20,000	70	.5584	.77918	8,702
$40,000	75	.4173	.61744	10,306
$80,000	80	.3118	.42909	10,703
$83,663 is the Payout			Present Value	$36,478

When the payments are certain, there are two things that influence the present value of the payments. They are the interest rate and the length of time until the payments made. The higher the interest rate, the smaller the present value. The farther away the payments are, the lower the present value.

§22.15 Worksheet for Calculating Present Value of Certain Annuities with No Growth Rate

A no-growth certain annuity pays a stated amount of money each month or each year. The payment is made for a specified number of years. The recipient may change since the annuity is certain.

To calculate the present value of a certain annuity, the annual payment, current rate of interest, and the number of years the payments will occur must be known. Assume the annuity will pay $1,000 per month for 20 years, and the current interest rate is 8 per cent. Worksheet 22-8 presents the steps necessary to calculate the present value of the annuity. With the blanks which must be known filled in the present value is determined.

Worksheet 22-8

Worksheet for Calculating the

Present Value of a No-Growth Annuity

All Payments Certain

8% Interest Rate

1. The monthly annuity of . _____ . times 12 = $. _____ .
    The annuity payments will be made for . _____ .
    years in the future (Year Number from Appendix
    C.) The annuity will grow at . _____ . per year
    (Column Number). The interest rate is . _____ .
    (Row Number).

2. The present value factor is found in Year . _____ .
    of Appendix C where column . _____ . and row . _____ .
    intersect. The factor is . _____ .

3. Multiply the annual payment of . _____ . by the
    factor of . _____ . The present value of the future
    payments is   . _____ .

4. The present value of the future income is the
    sum of lines 1 and 3. $. _____ .

Worksheet 22-9

Worksheet for Calculating the

Present Value of a No-Growth Annuity

All Payments Certain

8% Interest Rate

1. The monthly annuity of .$1,000. times 12 = $.12,000.
    The annuity payments will be made for .19.
    years in the future (Year Number from Appendix
    C.) The annuity will grow at .0%. per year
    (Column Number). The interest rate is .8%.
    (Row Number).

2. The present value factor is found in Year .19.
    of Appendix C where column .0%. and row .8%.
    intersect. The factor is .9.60.

3. Multiply the annual payment of .12,000. by the
    factor of .9.60. The present value of the future
    payments is $.115,200.

4. The present value of the future income is the
    sum of lines 1 and 3. $.127,200.

§22.16   Worksheet for Calculating Present Value of Certain Annuities with a Growth Rate

The calculation of the present value of annuities which have a growth rate is
done in exactly the same manner as the no-growth annuity, except the column in
which the present value factor in Appendix C appears is different. If the annuity
had a 2 per cent annual growth rate, the present value factor would increase to
11.26.

The changes made on the worksheet should reflect that there is a growth rate
in the annuity; thus the present value factor changes. With a 2 per cent growth rate
the present value of the annuity becomes $151,440 (*see* Worksheet 22-10).

Worksheet 22-10

Worksheet for Calculating the

Present Value of an Annuity Growing at 2% Annually

All Payments Certain

8% Interest Rate

1. The monthly annuity of .$1,000. times 12 = $. 12,000.
    The annuity payments will be made for .19.
    years in the future (Year Number from Appendix
    C.) The annuity will grow at .2%. per year
    (Column Number). The interest rate is .8%.
    (Row Number).

2. The present value factor is found in Year .19.
    of Appendix C where column .0%. and row .8%.
    intersect. The factor is .11.62.

3. Multiply the annual payment of .12,000. by the
    factor of .11.62. The present value of the
    future payments is $.139,440.

4. The present value of the future income is the
    sum of lines 1 and 3. $.151,440.

§22.17   Worksheet for Calculating Present Value of Uncertain Annuities with No Growth Rate

When the annuity to be paid is paid only if the recipient is living, the present value of the annuity is adjusted to reflect the probability that the individual will be alive to receive payment. To calculate the present value of a no-growth uncertain annuity, the age, sex, and race of the recipient must be known. Worksheets 22-11A and 22-11B show the calculation of an annuity paying $1,000 per month for the next 20 years. Worksheet 22-11A is the present value of payments made for 20 years while 22-11B is the present value of payments if living. The recipient is a 25-year-old black male. The probabilities for living each year are obtained from Appendix F. As the worksheet indicates, the present value of the annuity, when interest rates are 8 per cent, is $122,721.

Worksheet 22-11A

Worksheet for Calculating the

Present Value of a No-Growth Annuity

All Payments Certain

Black Male

8% Interest

Age	Per	Income in Current $	Growth Factor	Future Value	Discount Factor	Present Value
25	0	12,000	1.00	12,000	1.000	12,000
26	1	12,000	1.00	11,111	0.926	11,111
27	2	12,000	1.00	10,288	0.857	10,288
28	3	12,000	1.00	9,526	0.794	9,526
29	4	12,000	1.00	8,820	0.735	8,820
30	5	12,000	1.00	8,167	0.681	8,167
31	6	12,000	1.00	7,562	0.630	7,562
32	7	12,000	1.00	7,002	0.583	7,002
33	8	12,000	1.00	6,483	0.540	6,483
34	9	12,000	1.00	6,003	0.500	6,003
35	10	12,000	1.00	5,558	0.463	5,558
36	11	12,000	1.00	5,147	0.429	5,147
37	12	12,000	1.00	4,765	0.397	4,765
38	13	12,000	1.00	4,412	0.368	4,412
39	14	12,000	1.00	4,086	0.340	4,086
40.	15	12,000	1.00	3,783	0.315	3,783
41	16	12,000	1.00	3,503	0.292	3,503
42	17	12,000	1.00	3,243	0.270	3,243
43	18	12,000	1.00	3,003	0.250	3,003
44	19	12,000	1.00	2,781	0.232	2,781

Worksheet 22-11B
Worksheet for Calculating the
Present Value of a No-Growth Annuity
All Payments Uncertain
Black Male
8% Interest

Age	Per	Present Value	Prob of Living	Adjusted Pres Value	Adjusted Sum
25	0	12,000	.9967	11,960	11,960
26	1	11,111	.9933	11,037	22,997
27	2	10,288	.9898	10,183	33,180
28	3	9,526	.9862	9,394	42,575
29	4	8,820	.9823	8,664	51,239
30	5	8,167	.9782	7,989	59,228
31	6	7,562	.9738	7,364	66,592
32	7	7,002	.9691	6,786	73,377
33	8	6,483	.9642	6,251	79,628
34	9	6,003	.9588	5,756	85,384
35	10	5,558	.9531	5,298	90,682
36	11	5,147	.9470	4,874	95,556
37	12	4,765	.9406	4,482	100,038
38	13	4,412	.9339	4,121	104,159
39	14	4,086	.9270	3,787	107,946
40	15	3,783	.9199	3,480	111,426
41	16	3,503	.9125	3,196	114,622
42	17	3,243	.9048	2,935	117,557
43	18	3,003	.8969	2,693	120,250
44	19	2,781	.8886	2,471	122,721

§22.18   Worksheet for Calculating Present Value of Uncertain Annuities with a Growth Rate

If the annuity is growing at 2 per cent annually, the present value increases to $141,428 (*see* Worksheet 22-12). As the worksheet shows, the annuity will grow to an annual payment of $17,482.

Worksheet 22-12A

Worksheet for Calculating the

Present Value of an Annuity

2% Annual Growth

All Payments Certain

Black Male

8% Interest

Age	Per	Income in Current $	Growth Factor	Future Value	Discount Factor	Present Value
25	0	12,000	1.00	12,000	1.000	12,000
26	1	12,000	1.02	12,240	0.926	11,333
27	2	12,000	1.04	12,485	0.857	10,704
28	3	12,000	1.06	12,734	0.794	10,109
29	4	12,000	1.08	12,989	0.735	9,547
30	5	12,000	1.10	13,249	0.681	9,017
31	6	12,000	1.13	13,514	0.630	8,516
32	7	12,000	1.15	13,784	0.583	8,043
33	8	12,000	1.17	14,060	0.540	7,596
34	9	12,000	1.20	14,341	0.500	7,174
35	10	12,000	1.22	14,628	0.463	6,776
36	11	12,000	1.24	14,920	0.429	6,399
37	12	12,000	1.27	15,219	0.397	6,044
38	13	12,000	1.29	15,523	0.368	5,708
39	14	12,000	1.32	15,834	0.340	5,391
40	15	12,000	1.35	16,150	0.315	5,091
41	16	12,000	1.37	16,473	0.292	4,808
42	17	12,000	1.40	16,803	0.270	4,541
43	18	12,000	1.43	17,139	0.250	4,289
44	19	12,000	1.46	17,482	0.232	4,051

Worksheet 22-12B
Worksheet for Calculating the
Present Value of a 2% Annual Growth
All Payments Uncertain
Black Male
8% Interest

Age	Per	Present Value	Prob of Living	Adjusted Pres Value	Adjusted Sum
25	0	12,000	.9967	11,960	11,960
26	1	11,333	.9933	11,258	23,218
27	2	10,704	.9898	10,595	33,813
28	3	10,109	.9862	9,969	43,782
29	4	9,547	.9823	9,378	53,160
30	5	9,017	.9782	8,820	61,981
31	6	8,516	.9738	8,293	70,274
32	7	8,043	.9691	7,795	78,068
33	8	7,596	.9642	7,324	85,392
34	9	7,174	.9588	6,879	92,271
35	10	6,776	.9531	6,458	98,729
36	11	6,399	.9470	6,060	104,789
37	12	6,044	.9406	5,685	110,474
38	13	5,708	.9339	5,331	115,804
39	14	5,391	.9270	4,997	120,801
40	15	5,091	.9199	4,683	125,485
41	16	4,808	.9125	4,388	129,872
42	17	4,541	.9048	4,109	133,982
43	18	4,289	.8969	3,847	137,828
44	19	4,051	.8886	3,600	141,428

If the annuity is a life annuity the calculation can be quite long. Worksheet 22-13 shows the present value calculation year by year for a life annuity. The recipient is a 25-year-old black male. The present value of the annuity is $184,651.

Worksheet 22-13A
Present Value of a Life Annuity
2% Annual Growth, 8% Interest
All Payments Uncertain
Black Male

Age	Per	Current Income	Growth Factor	Future Value	Discount Factor	Present Value
25	0	12,000	1.000	12,000	1.000	12,000
26	1	12,000	1.020	12,240	0.926	11,333
27	2	12,000	1.040	12,485	0.857	10,704
28	3	12,000	1.061	12,734	0.794	10,109
29	4	12,000	1.082	12,989	0.735	9,547
30	5	12,000	1.104	13,249	0.681	9,017
31	6	12,000	1.126	13,514	0.630	8,516
32	7	12,000	1.149	13,784	0.583	8,043
33	8	12,000	1.172	14,060	0.540	7,596
34	9	12,000	1.195	14,341	0.500	7,174
35	10	12,000	1.219	14,628	0.463	6,776
36	11	12,000	1.243	14,920	0.429	6,399
37	12	12,000	1.268	15,219	0.397	6,044
38	13	12,000	1.294	15,523	0.368	5,708
39	14	12,000	1.319	15,834	0.340	5,391
40	15	12,000	1.346	16,150	0.315	5,091
41	16	12,000	1.373	16,473	0.292	4,808
42	17	12,000	1.400	16,803	0.270	4,541
43	18	12,000	1.428	17,139	0.250	4,289
44	19	12,000	1.457	17,482	0.232	4,051
45	20	12,000	1.486	17,831	0.215	3,826
46	21	12,000	1.516	18,188	0.199	3,613
47	22	12,000	1.546	18,552	0.184	3,412
48	23	12,000	1.577	18,923	0.170	3,223
49	24	12,000	1.608	19,301	0.158	3,044
50	25	12,000	1.641	19,687	0.146	2,875
51	26	12,000	1.673	20,081	0.135	2,715
52	27	12,000	1.707	20,483	0.125	2,564
53	28	12,000	1.741	20,892	0.116	2,422
54	29	12,000	1.776	21,310	0.107	2,287
55	30	12,000	1.811	21,736	0.099	2,160
56	31	12,000	1.848	22,171	0.092	2,040
57	32	12,000	1.885	22,614	0.085	1,927
58	33	12,000	1.922	23,067	0.079	1,820
59	34	12,000	1.961	23,528	0.073	1,719

Age	Per	Current Income	Growth Factor	Future Value	Discount Factor	Present Value
60	35	12,000	2.000	23,999	0.068	1,623
61	36	12,000	2.040	24,479	0.063	1,533
62	37	12,000	2.081	24,968	0.058	1,448
63	38	12,000	2.122	25,468	0.054	1,367
64	39	12,000	2.165	25,977	0.050	1,291
65	40	12,000	2.208	26,496	0.046	1,220
66	41	12,000	2.252	27,026	0.043	1,152
67	42	12,000	2.297	27,567	0.039	1,088
68	43	12,000	2.343	28,118	0.037	1,027
69	44	12,000	2.390	28,681	0.034	970
70	45	12,000	2.438	29,254	0.031	916
71	46	12,000	2.487	29,839	0.029	866
72	47	12,000	2.536	30,436	0.027	817
73	48	12,000	2.587	31,045	0.025	772
74	49	12,000	2.639	31,666	0.023	729
75	50	12,000	2.692	32,299	0.021	689
76	51	12,000	2.745	32,945	0.020	650
77	52	12,000	2.800	33,604	0.018	614
78	53	12,000	2.856	34,276	0.017	580
79	54	12,000	2.913	34,962	0.016	548
80	55	12,000	2.972	35,661	0.015	517
81	56	12,000	3.031	36,374	0.013	489
82	57	12,000	3.092	37,101	0.012	462
83	58	12,000	3.154	37,843	0.012	436
84	59	12,000	3.217	38,600	0.011	412
85	60	12,000	3.281	39,372	0.010	389
86	61	12,000	3.347	40,160	0.009	367
87	62	12,000	3.414	40,963	0.008	347
88	63	12,000	3.482	41,782	0.008	328
89	64	12,000	3.551	42,618	0.007	309
90	65	12,000	3.623	43,470	0.007	292
91	66	12,000	3.695	44,340	0.006	276
92	67	12,000	3.769	45,226	0.006	261
93	68	12,000	3.844	46,131	0.005	246
94	69	12,000	3.921	47,054	0.005	232
95	70	12,000	4.000	47,995	0.005	220
96	71	12,000	4.080	48,955	0.004	207
97	72	12,000	4.161	49,934	0.004	196
98	73	12,000	4.244	50,932	0.004	185
99	74	12,000	4.329	51,951	0.003	175

Worksheet 22-13B
Present Value of a Life Annuity
2% Annual Growth, 8% Interest
All Payments Uncertain
Black Male

Age	Per	Present Value	Prob of Living	Adjusted Pres Value	Adjusted Sum
25	0	12,000	.9967	11,960	11,960
26	1	11,333	.9933	11,258	23,218
27	2	10,704	.9898	10,595	33,813
28	3	10,109	.9862	9,969	43,782
29	4	9,547	.9823	9,378	53,160
30	5	9,017	.9782	8,820	61,981
31	6	8,516	.9738	8,293	70,274
32	7	8,043	.9691	7,795	78,068
33	8	7,596	.9642	7,324	85,392
34	9	7,174	.9588	6,879	92,271
35	10	6,776	.9531	6,458	98,729
36	11	6,399	.9470	6,060	104,789
37	12	6,044	.9406	5,685	110,474
38	13	5,708	.9339	5,331	115,804
39	14	5,391	.9270	4,997	120,801
40	15	5,091	.9199	4,683	125,485
41	16	4,808	.9125	4,388	129,872
42	17	4,541	.9048	4,109	133,982
43	18	4,289	.8969	3,847	137,828
44	19	4,051	.8886	3,600	141,428
45	20	3,826	.8800	3,367	144,795
46	21	3,613	.8710	3,147	147,942
47	22	3,412	.8616	2,940	150,882
48	23	3,223	.8517	2,745	153,627
49	24	3,044	.8412	2,560	156,187
50	25	2,875	.8300	2,386	158,573
51	26	2,715	.8182	2,221	160,795
52	27	2,564	.8057	2,066	162,861
53	28	2,422	.7927	1,920	164,780
54	29	2,287	.7792	1,782	166,562
55	30	2,160	.7651	1,653	168,215
56	31	2,040	.7505	1,531	169,746
57	32	1,927	.7353	1,417	171,163
58	33	1,820	.7194	1,309	172,472

Age	Per	Present Value	Prob of Living	Adjusted Pres Value	Adjusted Sum
59	34	1,719	.7028	1,208	173,680
60	35	1,623	.6854	1,113	174,792
61	36	1,533	.6674	1,023	175,815
62	37	1,448	.6486	939	176,754
63	38	1,367	.6291	860	177,615
64	39	1,291	.6089	786	178,401
65	40	1,220	.5880	717	179,118
66	41	1,152	.5664	652	179,771
67	42	1,088	.5443	592	180,363
68	43	1,027	.5216	536	180,899
69	44	970	.4983	484	181,382
70	45	916	.4746	435	181,817
71	46	866	.4504	390	182,207
72	47	817	.4260	348	182,555
73	48	772	.4014	310	182,865
74	49	729	.3766	275	183,140
75	50	689	.3519	242	183,382
76	51	650	.3270	213	183,595
77	52	614	.3021	186	183,780
78	53	580	.2775	161	183,941
79	54	548	.2531	139	184,080
80	55	517	.2292	119	184,199
81	56	489	.2049	100	184,299
82	57	462	.1804	83	184,382
83	58	436	.1562	68	184,450
84	59	412	.1326	55	184,505
85	60	389	.1100	43	184,547
86	61	367	.0889	33	184,580
87	62	347	.0698	24	184,604
88	63	328	.0528	17	184,622
89	64	309	.0384	12	184,633
90	65	292	.0266	8	184,641
91	66	276	.0174	5	184,646
92	67	261	.0106	3	184,649
93	68	246	.0060	1	184,650
94	69	232	.0030	1	184,651
95	70	220	.0014	0	184,651
96	71	207	.0005	0	184,651
97	72	196	.0002	0	184,651
98	73	185	.0000	0	184,651
99	74	175	.0000	0	184,651

§22.19 Short Cut to Estimating Present Value of Life Annuities

Rather than go through all the calculations necessary to determine the present value of the life annuity, the present value may be estimated by considering the annuity a little differently. The annuity shown in Worksheet 22-12 is a life annuity paying $1,000 per month, growing at 2 per cent per year. It is being discounted at 8 per cent.

Instead of considering the annuity a life annuity, evaluate the annuity as though it is an annuity certain to life expectancy. Appendix F indicates that the life expectancy for a 25-year-old black male is 42.7 years, or rounded off it is 43 years. Using Worksheet 22-14, which is the same as Worksheet 22-10, the present value of the annuity to life expectancy is $198,480. If the goal of the calculation is to *estimate* the present value, then treating the life annuity as an annuity certain to life expectancy is a much faster calculation.

Worksheet 22-14

Worksheet for Calculating the

Present Value of an Annuity Growing at 2% Annually

All Payments Certain

8% Interest Rate

1. The monthly annuity of .$1,000. times 12 = $.12,000.
    The annuity payments will be made for .42.
    years in the future (Year Number from Appendix
    C). The annuity will grow at .2%. per year
    (Column Number). The interest rate is .8%.
    (Row Number).

2. The present value factor is found in Year .42.
    of Appendix C where column .2%. and row .8%.
    intersect. The factor is .15.459.

3. Multiply the annual payment of .12,000. by the
    factor of .15.54. The present value of the
    future payments is $.186,480.

4. The present value of the future income is the
    sum of lines 1 and 3. $.198,480.

§22.20 Evaluating Deferred Annuities

On occasion the offer may be an annuity that does not start for a period of years. The present value can be determined by considering this as two annuities, one which is received and one which is not received.

Consider the offer of a 20-year annuity certain paying $1,000 per month growing at 4 per cent annually. The annuity does not start for 10 years. The appropriate interest rate is deemed to be 10 per cent annually.

The annuity the individual receives is an annuity paying $1,000 per month growing at 4 per cent annually for 30 years. The individual does not receive any annuity for the first 10 years. The difference between the two present values is the present value of the deferred annuity. The present value of the 30-year annuity is shown on Worksheet 22-15. Worksheet 22-16 shows the 10-year annuity with the same conditions. The way this annuity is stated, the annuity that will be paid beginning 10 years is $17,079.

Worksheet 22-15
Worksheet for Calculating the
Present Value of a 30-year Annuity
Growing at 4% Annually
All Payments Certain
10% Interest Rate

1. The monthly annuity of .$1,000. times 12 = $.12,000.
    The annuity payments will be made for .29.
    years in the future (Year Number from Appendix
    C). The annuity will grow at .4%. per year
    (Column Number). The interest rate is .10%.
    (Row Number).

2. The present value factor is found in Year .29.
    of Appendix C where column .4%. and row.
    .10%. intersect. The factor is .13.93.

3. Multiply the annual payment of .12,000. by the
    factor of .13.93. The present value of the
    future payments is $.167,160.

4. The present value of the future income is the
    sum of lines 1 and 3. $.179,160.

Worksheet 22-16
Worksheet for Calculating the
Present Value of a 30-year Annuity
Growing at 4% Annually
All Payments Certain
10% Interest Rate

1. The monthly annuity of .$1,000. times 12 = $.12,000.
    The annuity payments will be made for .9.
    years in the future (Year Number from Appendix
    C). The annuity will grow at .4%. per year
    (Column Number). The interest rate is .10%.
    (Row Number).

2. The present value factor is found in Year .9.
    of Appendix C where column .4%. and row.
    .10%. intersect. The factor is .6.87.

3. Multiply the annual payment of .12,000. by the
    factor of .6.87. The present value of the future
    payments is $.82,440.

4. The present value of the future income is the
    sum of lines 1 and 3. $.94,440.

§22.21   Evaluating Structured Settlement Offers: Example 1

An injured 30-year-old white male has been offered $100,000 plus one of three different structures to settle the claim. If one of the three offers is to be accepted which should be accepted? What is the present value of each offer?

1. $1,460 per month for life
2. $1,083.90 per month for life increasing at 2% annually
3. $962.09 per month for life increasing at 4% annually
4. $842.27 per month for life increasing at 6% annually

To determine the present value of each offer the economist, or person evaluating the offer, must know how long the annuity will be paid and what the appropriate discount rate is. Appendix F indicates the life expectancy of a 30-year-old white male is 44.7 years, rounded to 45 years. Assume the appropriate interest rate is 10 per cent.

For annuity 1 the present value factor is 10.50. Multiplying the factor by the annual income of $17,520 ($1,460 * 12) gives the present value of $184,028. Table 22-8 shows the present value of the four annuities. Worksheets 22-17 through 22-20 show the calculation of the present values.

Table 22-8   Present Value of the Life Annuities Discount Rate of 10%

Monthly Payment	Annual Payment	Growth Rate	Value Factor	Value of Annuity
$1,460.00	$17,520.00	0.0%	10.5	184,028
1,083.90	13,006.80	2.0	12.77	166,080
962.09	11,545.08	4.0	16.07	185,537
842.27	10,107.24	6.0	21.12	213,450

Annuity 4 has the highest present value. However, other considerations may enter into the decision of which annuity to accept. The second payout and the total payout of two of the annuities are presented in Tables 22-9 and 22-10.

Worksheet 22-17

Present Value of Life Annuity 1

1. The monthly annuity of .$1,460. times 12 = $.17,520.
    The annuity payments will be made for .45.
    years (Year Number from Appendix C). The
    annuity will grow at .0%. per year (Column
    Number). The interest rate is .10%. (Row
    Number).

2. The present value factor is found in Year .45.
    of Appendix C where column .0%. and row.
    .10%. intersect. The factor is .10.5.

3. Multiply the annual payment of .17,520. by the
    factor of .10.5. The present value of the future
    payments is $.184,028.

Worksheet 22-18

Present Value of Life Annuity 2

1. The monthly annuity of .$1,083.90. times 12 = $.13,008.80.
    The annuity payments will be made for .45.
    years (Year Number from Appendix C). The
    annuity will grow at .2%. per year (Column
    Number). The interest rate is .10%. (Row
    Number).

2. The present value factor is found in Year .45.
    of Appendix C where column .2%. and row.
    .10%. intersect. The factor is .12.77.

3. Multiply the annual payment of .13,006.80. by
    the factor of .12.77. The present value of the
    future payments is $.166,080.

Worksheet 22-19

Present Value of Life Annuity 3

1. The monthly annuity of .$962.09. times 12 = $.11,545.08.
    The annuity payments will be made for .45.
    years (Year Number from Appendix C). The
    annuity will grow at .4%. per year (Column
    Number). The interest rate is .10%. (Row
    Number).

2. The present value factor is found in Year .45.
    of Appendix C where column .4%. and row.
    .10%. intersect. The factor is .16.07.

3. Multiply the annual payment of .11,545.08. by
    the factor of .16.07. The present value of the
    future payments is $.166,080.

Worksheet 22-20
Present Value of Life Annuity 4

1. The monthly annuity of .$842.27. times 12 = $.10,107.24.
    The annuity payments will be made for .45.
    years (Year Number from Appendix C). The
    annuity will grow at .6%. per year (Column
    Number). The interest rate is .10%. (Row
    Number).

2. The present value factor is found in Year .45.
    of Appendix C where column .6%. and row.
    .10%. intersect. The factor is .21.12.

3. Multiply the annual payment of .10,107.24. by
    the factor of .21.12. The present value of the
    future payments is $.213,450.

Table 22-9   Annual Payout and Total Payout

Age	Period	Growth Rate 0%	Payout	Growth Rate 2%	Payout
30	0	17,520	17,520	13,007	13,007
31	1	17,520	35,040	13,267	26,274
32	2	17,520	52,560	13,532	39,807
33	3	17,520	70,080	13,803	53,610
34	4	17,520	87,600	14,079	67,689
35	5	17,520	105,120	14,361	82,050
36	6	17,520	122,640	14,648	96,698
37	7	17,520	140,160	14,941	111,639
38	8	17,520	157,680	15,240	126,878
39	9	17,520	175,200	15,545	142,423
40	10	17,520	192,720	15,855	158,278
41	11	17,520	210,240	16,173	174,451
42	12	17,520	227,760	16,496	190,947
43	13	17,520	245,280	16,826	207,773
44	14	17,520	262,800	17,162	224,935
45	15	17,520	280,320	17,506	242,441

Age	Period	Growth Rate 0%	Payout	Growth Rate 2%	Payout
46	16	17,520	297,840	17,856	260,297
47	17	17,520	315,360	18,213	278,510
48	18	17,520	332,880	18,577	297,087
49	19	17,520	350,400	18,949	316,036
50	20	17,520	367,920	19,328	335,364
51	21	17,520	385,440	19,714	355,078
52	22	17,520	402,960	20,109	375,186
53	23	17,520	420,480	20,511	395,697
54	24	17,520	438,000	20,921	416,618
55	25	17,520	455,520	21,339	437,957
56	26	17,520	473,040	21,766	459,724
57	27	17,520	490,560	22,201	481,925
58	28	17,520	508,080	22,646	504,571
59	29	17,520	525,600	23,098	527,669
60	30	17,520	543,120	23,560	551,229
61	31	17,520	560,640	24,032	575,261
62	32	17,520	578,160	24,512	599,773
63	33	17,520	595,680	25,002	624,776
64	34	17,520	613,200	25,503	650,278
65	35	17,520	630,720	26,013	676,291
66	36	17,520	648,240	26,533	702,824
67	37	17,520	665,760	27,063	729,887
68	38	17,520	683,280	27,605	757,492
69	39	17,520	700,800	28,157	785,649
70	40	17,520	718,320	28,720	814,369
71	41	17,520	735,840	29,294	843,663
72	42	17,520	753,360	29,880	873,543
73	43	17,520	770,880	30,478	904,021
74	44	17,520	788,400	31,087	935,108
75	45	17,520	805,920	31,709	966,818
76	46	17,520	823,440	32,343	999,161
77	47	17,520	840,960	32,990	1,032,151
78	48	17,520	858,480	33,650	1,065,801
79	49	17,520	876,000	34,323	1,100,124
80	50	17,520	893,520	35,009	1,135,134
81	51	17,520	911,040	35,710	1,170,843
82	52	17,520	928,560	36,424	1,207,267
83	53	17,520	946,080	37,152	1,244,420
84	54	17,520	963,600	37,895	1,282,315
85	55	17,520	981,120	38,653	1,320,968
86	56	17,520	998,640	39,426	1,360,395

Age	Period	Growth Rate 0%	Payout	Growth Rate 2%	Payout
87	57	17,520	1,016,160	40,215	1,400,610
88	58	17,520	1,033,680	41,019	1,441,629
89	59	17,520	1,051,200	41,840	1,483,468
90	60	17,520	1,068,720	42,676	1,526,145
91	61	17,520	1,086,240	43,530	1,569,675
92	62	17,520	1,103,760	44,400	1,614,075
93	63	17,520	1,121,280	45,289	1,659,364
94	64	17,520	1,138,800	46,194	1,705,558
95	65	17,520	1,156,320	47,118	1,752,676
96	66	17,520	1,173,840	48,061	1,800,737
97	67	17,520	1,191,360	49,022	1,849,758
98	68	17,520	1,208,880	50,002	1,899,760
99	69	17,520	1,226,400	51,002	1,950,763

Table 22-10   Annual Payout and Total Payout

Age	Period	4% Growth Rate	Payout	6% Growth Rate	Payout
30	0	11,545	11,545	10,107	10,107
31	1	12,007	23,552	10,713	20,820
32	2	12,487	36,039	11,356	32,177
33	3	12,987	49,025	12,038	44,214
34	4	13,506	62,531	12,760	56,974
35	5	14,046	76,578	13,525	70,500
36	6	14,608	91,186	14,337	84,837
37	7	15,192	106,378	15,197	100,034
38	8	15,800	122,178	16,109	116,143
39	9	16,432	138,611	17,076	133,218
40	10	17,089	155,700	18,100	151,318
41	11	17,773	173,473	19,186	170,504
42	12	18,484	191,957	20,337	190,842
43	13	19,223	211,180	21,558	212,399
44	14	19,992	231,172	22,851	235,250
45	15	20,792	251,964	24,222	259,472
46	16	21,624	273,588	25,675	285,148
47	17	22,489	296,076	27,216	312,363
48	18	23,388	319,464	28,849	341,212
49	19	24,324	343,788	30,580	371,792
50	20	25,297	369,084	32,415	404,206

Age	Period	4% Growth Rate	Payout	6% Growth Rate	Payout
51	21	26,308	395,393	34,359	438,566
52	22	27,361	422,754	36,421	474,987
53	23	28,455	451,209	38,606	513,593
54	24	29,593	480,802	40,923	554,516
55	25	30,777	511,579	43,378	597,894
56	26	32,008	543,587	45,981	643,874
57	27	33,288	576,876	48,739	692,614
58	28	34,620	611,496	51,664	744,277
59	29	36,005	647,501	54,764	799,041
60	30	37,445	684,946	58,049	857,091
61	31	38,943	723,888	61,532	918,623
62	32	40,501	764,389	65,224	983,847
63	33	42,121	806,510	69,138	1,052,985
64	34	43,805	850,315	73,286	1,126,271
65	35	45,558	895,873	77,683	1,203,955
66	36	47,380	943,252	82,344	1,286,299
67	37	49,275	992,528	87,285	1,373,584
68	38	51,246	1,043,774	92,522	1,466,106
69	39	53,296	1,097,070	98,073	1,564,179
70	40	55,428	1,152,497	103,958	1,668,137
71	41	57,645	1,210,142	110,195	1,778,332
72	42	59,951	1,270,093	116,807	1,895,139
73	43	62,349	1,332,442	123,815	2,018,954
74	44	64,843	1,397,284	131,244	2,150,199
75	45	67,436	1,464,721	139,119	2,289,318
76	46	70,134	1,534,855	147,466	2,436,784
77	47	72,939	1,607,794	156,314	2,593,098
78	48	75,857	1,683,650	165,693	2,758,791
79	49	78,891	1,762,541	175,634	2,934,425
80	50	82,047	1,844,588	186,172	3,120,597
81	51	85,329	1,929,917	197,343	3,317,940
82	52	88,742	2,018,658	209,183	3,527,124
83	53	92,291	2,110,950	221,734	3,748,858
84	54	95,983	2,206,933	235,038	3,983,897
85	55	99,822	2,306,755	249,141	4,233,037
86	56	103,815	2,410,570	264,089	4,497,127
87	57	107,968	2,518,538	279,935	4,777,061
88	58	112,287	2,630,824	296,731	5,073,792
89	59	116,778	2,747,602	314,535	5,388,327
90	60	121,449	2,869,052	333,407	5,721,733

Age	Period	4% Growth Rate	Payout	6% Growth Rate	Payout
91	61	126,307	2,995,359	353,411	6,075,144
92	62	131,359	3,126,718	374,616	6,449,760
93	63	136,614	3,263,332	397,093	6,846,852
94	64	142,078	3,405,410	420,918	7,267,770
95	65	147,761	3,553,171	446,173	7,713,944
96	66	153,672	3,706,843	472,944	8,186,887
97	67	159,819	3,866,662	501,320	8,688,208
98	68	166,211	4,032,873	531,399	9,219,607
99	69	172,860	4,205,733	563,283	9,782,890

Tables 22-9 and 22-10 show that, while the annual payment under Annuity 1 is the highest annual payment until the payments in the tenth year under Annuity 4, the total money received by the recipient is highest under Annuity 1 until the eighteenth year when the total dollars paid out under Annuity 4 exceed the money paid out under Annuity 1.

The point is that present value may not always be in the best interest of the recipient. This is particularly true if the recipient has a short life expectancy.

§22.22   Evaluating Structured Settlement Offers: Example 2

The plaintiff is a 40-year-old white male. He has been offered $150,000 when the case is settled, plus the following payments: $25,000 in 5 years, $50,000 in 10 years, and $100,000 in 25 years. All payments are guaranteed. In addition he will receive a life annuity of $1,200 per month starting immediately and growing at 2 per cent annually with payments guaranteed to age 65.

To calculate the present value of the offer, the life expectancy must be known. From Appendix F, the life expectancy is determined to be 35 years. This figure is of concern only in the estimation of the annuity payments since the lump sum payments are guaranteed. The appropriate rate of interest is 8 per cent.

The present value of the offer is $427,553: $150,000 paid at the time of settlement plus the present value of the deferred payments, which totaled $277,553. Worksheets 22-21 and 22-22 present the calculations of the present value of the lump sum payments and the annuity, respectively. The present value factors for the lump sum value come from Appendix B and the present value factor for the annuity comes from Appendix C.

Worksheet 22-21
Present Value of the Lump Sum Payments
All Payments Certain
8% Interest

Dollars	In "t" Years	PV Factor	Present Value
$ 25,000	5	.6807	$17,018
50,000	10	.3971	19,855
100,000	25	.1460	14,600
$175,000 Payout			Total $51,473

Worksheet 22-22
Worksheet for Calculating the
Present Value of a Life Annuity
Growing at 2% Annually
All Payments Certain
8% Interest Rate

1. The monthly annuity of .$1,200. times 12 = $.14,400.
   The annuity payments will be made for .35.
   years in the future (Year Number from Appendix
   C). The annuity will grow at .2%. per year
   (Column Number). The interest rate is .8%.
   (Row Number).

2. The present value factor is found in Year .935.
   of Appendix C where column .2%. and row .8%.
   intersect. The factor is .14.70.

3. Multiply the annual payment of .14,400. by the
   factor of .14.70. The present value of the
   future payments is $.211,680.

4. The present value of the future income is the
   sum of lines 1 and 3. $.226,080.

§22.23   Overview of Designing a Structured Settlement

If a structured settlement is desired, it can be designed by the attorney. What needs to be determined at the outset is the goal of the structured settlement. Is the structured settlement to replace a monthly income? Is the structured settlement to provide lump sums of money at some future date to provide a fund for education or training? Is the structured settlement to provide retirement benefits? Is the structured settlement to provide for future medical expenses? The purpose of the settlement will help determine how it should be designed.

The present value of the settlement is known. The present value is how much the settlement costs today. Suppose there is a $300,000 policy limit that is expected to be paid to plaintiff. Of the $300,000, one-third, or $100,000, is attorneys' fees. This leaves $200,000 to structure for the plaintiff. The $200,000 is the present value of the structured settlement.

There are an infinite number of ways in which the $200,000 can be structured. One way to structure the settlement is to pay the entire amount, $200,000, to the plaintiff at the time of settlement. In this case the present value and the payout would be the same thing, since the payment of $200,000 is being made at the time of settlement.

The money could be paid in lump sums of so-many dollars every five years or the money could be paid in the form of an annuity, or a combination of the two.

Suppose the plaintiff is a 22-year-old male. If the plaintiff wants a life annuity then Appendix C can be used to estimate the dollar amount that can be received each year. From Appendix F a 22-year-old white male has a life expectancy of 52.1 years, rounded to 52 years.

Using Appendix C, the present value factors of $1 received each year for 52 years can be found. Remember that the money available for the structure is $200,000.

The size of the annuity will depend on the growth rate of the annuity and the market rate of interest when the annuity is purchased. The annual growth rate may be determined by the plaintiff, but the interest rate is determined by conditions in the financial markets. Assume that the appropriate interest rate is 8 per cent.

If the growth rate desired is 0 per cent, then the present value factor is 12.27. This factor may be interpreted to mean that in order to receive $1 per year for 52 years, the annuity starting in one year requires an investment of $12.27.

Since the plaintiff desires the annuity to start immediately, the value "1" must be added to the present value factor, making the present value factor 13.27. If $200,000 is available to buy the annual annuity, and each $1 of annual income costs 13.27, an annual annuity of $15,072 ($200,000/13.27) can be purchased. Dividing the $15,072 by 12 (months) gives a monthly annuity of approximately, $1,256.

Had the plaintiff wanted a 2 per cent annual growth rate in the annuity, then the present value factor would have been 16.13. To this is added "1" for the annuity to start immediately. The present value factor is 17.13. The $200,000 divided by 17.13 equals $11,675 per year or $973 per month. But the $973 will be 2 per cent more next year and each year thereafter.

Suppose the plaintiff wants some money at the time of the settlement and the rest of the money in the form of a life annuity. If $50,000 is paid to the client at settlement, then $150,000 is available for the life annuity. If the growth rate of the annuity is 0 per cent then the annual annuity would equal $11,304, or $942 per month. If the annuity included a 2 per cent annual growth rate then the annual annuity would be $8,757 and the monthly payment would be $730.

When the plaintiff is receiving $50,000 at settlement, it means the total cash paid at settlement to the plaintiff is $150,000 less $100,000 attorney fees. The remaining $150,000 is used to purchase the life annuity.

Had the plaintiff preferred to have lump sum payments the amount of each payment can be calculated. Since these are one-time payments the present value factor can be found in Appendix B.

Consider the situation where the plaintiff has $150,000 available at settlement. One-third is attorney fees, leaving $100,000 to structure. Plaintiff would like six payments starting in five years, with each payment five years apart. Thus plaintiff will receive a payment in 5 years, 10, 15, 20, 25, and 30 years. The present value factor for each of the one-time payments is in Appendix B. Table 22-11 shows the present value factors for the six future payments.

Table 22-11   Calculating the Present Value of Future Lump Sum Payments

In "t" Years	Present Value Factor
5	.6806
10	.4632
15	.3152
20	.2145
25	.1460
30	.0994
	Total 1.9189

By adding up all the present value factors, the total cost of providing $1 in each of the six years can be determined. In this case the cost of providing $1 in each year is 1.9189. Since there is $100,000 available to provide the future payments, $52,113.19 can be provided at each future period ($100,000/1.989). Table 22-12 presents the present value of the six payments.

Table 22-12   Present Value of Future Lump Sum Payments

In "t" years	Payment	Present Value Factor	Present Value
5	$52,113.19	.6806	$35,468.23
10	$52,113.19	.4632	24,138,83
15	$52,113.19	.3152	16,426.08
20	$52,113.19	.2145	11,178.28
25	$52,113.19	.1460	7,608.53
30	$52,113.19	.0994	5,180.05
Payout $312,679.14			Present Value $100,000

On the other hand, the client may prefer to specify how many dollars to receive at various points in the future. This is acceptable but one of the future payments is treated as a residual. That is, one of the payments will be determined by how much money is left in the fund after the five desired payments are determined.

Suppose the plaintiff would like payments of $20,000 in 5 years, $40,000 in 10 years, $60,000 in 15 years, $80,000 in 20 years, and $100,000 in 25 years. Is there any money available for a payment in 30 years, and if so, how large will the payment be? Table 22-13 shows the present value of the five future payments. The appropriate discount rate is 8 per cent.

Table 22-13   Calculating the Present Value of Future Lump Sum Payments

In "t" years	Payment	Present Value Factor	Present Value
5	$ 20,000	.6806	$13,612
10	40,000	.4632	18,528
15	60,000	.3152	18,912
20	80,000	.2145	17,160
25	100,000	.1460	14,600
Payout $312,679.14		Present Value $82,812	

Since the present value of the first five payments is $82,812, the entire present value of $100,000 has not been used. In fact, $17,188 remains to purchase a payment in 30 years. Recall that the present value factor of $1 to be received in 30 years was .0994 when interest rates were 8 per cent. Therefore, $17,188 will purchase a lump sum payment of $172,918 to be received in 30 years. Table 22-14 presents the present value and the payout of the structured settlement. If the size of the payments or the timing of the payments are not acceptable to the plaintiff, he or she may wish to restructure the future payments.

Table 22-14   Calculating the Present Value of Future Lump Sum Payments

In "t" years	Payment	Present Value Factor	Present Value
5	$ 20,000	.6806	$13,612
10	40,000	.4632	18,528
15	60,000	.3152	18,912
20	80,000	.2145	17,160
25	100,000	.1460	14,600
30	172,918	.0994	17,188
Payout $472,918		Present Value $100,000	

§22.24 Concluding Structured Settlements

The designing of a structured settlement is left to the imagination, but many things should be considered when designing the settlement. What is the life expectancy of the plaintiff, what are the expected medical needs, what are the educational goals of the individual or the individual's dependents. Will a structured settlement relieve the plaintiff of the responsibility of handling large sums of money, meaning is a structure in the best interest of the individual.

§22.25 Summary

Structured settlements permit the money from a settlement to be paid over a period of time. Management responsibility of the funds not dispersed falls to the company from which the annuity was purchased. The interest earned on an annuity is free of federal income tax. If a lump sum is paid to the plaintiff and plaintiff invests the money, interest earned on the investments is subject to federal income tax.

The purchasing of an annuity permits the reinvestment of funds at a tax-free, or on a tax-deferred, basis. This permits a higher monthly annuity than the individual can probably provide through the management of his or her own funds.

The cost of an annuity is greatly affected by the current interest rates. The higher the interest rates, the lower the cost of the annuity. This also means the higher the interest rates, the larger the annuity or lump sum payments a given amount of money will purchase. Likewise, the lower the interest rates, the higher the cost of the annuity.

23

Sample Testimony

§23.01   Introduction

This chapter presents a sample report of an economist and scripts of a direct examination, a cross-examination, and a redirect examination. The premise for the direct examination is two-fold. First, the quality of the expert's testimony is directly related to the quality of the direct examination, and second, all things related to the economic evidence should be previously offered as foundation in previous testimony.

Section **23.02** is the economist's report to the plaintiff's attorney. The fact situation and all relevant variables should be presented in the report. The direct examination begins in **§23.03** and the cross-examination begins in **§23.21**. The concluding section presents the redirect examination.

§23.02   The Economist's Report

Economist's Name
CONSULTANT

Washburn University
School of Business
Topeka, Kansas
Post Office Box
Telephone and Fax

May 9, 1993

ADDRESS
ADDRESS
ADDRESS
ADDRESS

RE: Mr. John Doe

Dear Mr. Attorney:

I have evaluated the above cited case and estimate the present value of the loss to be $671,234. This amount is the sum of the historic loss plus the present value of the future loss.

The loss is the economic loss sustained by Mr. Doe's family and does not include loss of services, attention, marital care, or advice. The analysis is also exclusive of any consideration of any reduction in the ability to enjoy life.

This evaluation is based on information received from your office as detailed in Part I of this report. If there is an error in the information please contact me immediately so I may correct the error and provide you with a revised evaluation.

The methodology and other sources of information employed in preparing this report appear in the subsequent Parts of the report. If I may be of further assistance please do not hesitate to contact me.

Sincerely,

Gary Baker, Ph. D.

Economic Loss To John Doe

The total economic loss suffered as a result of the accident to Mr. Doe is $671,234. The dollar amount consists of a historic loss and the present value of the future loss.

The historic loss represents the lost income, fringe benefits, and household services from the date of the accident, September 1, 1991, to July 4, 1993. This loss is $48,859.

The present value of future loss begins July 4, 1993. The loss is $622,375.

HISTORIC LOSS:

From September 1, 1991 to July 4, 1993

Wages	$29,387
Fringe Benefits	5,839
Household Services	13,633
Total	$48,859

PRESENT VALUE OF FUTURE LOSS:

Beginning July 4, 1993

Wages	$320,619
Fringe Benefits	63,675
Household Services	238,081
Total	$622,375
TOTAL LOSS:	$671,234

ECONOMIC ANALYSIS
John Doe

PART I.   BACKGROUND STATISTICS:

Date of Birth:	July 4, 1952
Current Age:	41
Race:	Caucasian
Sex:	Male
Date of Accident:	September 1, 1991
Accident resulted in:	Permanent Disability
Life Expectancy:	
Education:	High School Graduate
Earnings History:	1991 $7.50 per hour
	1990 7.14 per hour
	1989 6.74 per hour
	1988 6.39 per hour
Age at Retirement:	65
Marital Status:	Married
Dependents:	No Children
Date of Analysis:	May 9, 1993
Date of Present Value:	July 4, 1993

PART II.   CALCULATION OF HISTORIC ECONOMIC LOSS

The historic loss consists of wages, fringe benefits, and household services. The loss begins the day of the accident, September 1, 1991, and continues until the present value date of July 4, 1993.

At the time of the accident, Mr. Doe was earning $7.50 per hour. The fringe benefit package consisted of two weeks paid vacation, holidays, sick days, health insurance, and a pension fund. The value of these benefits are estimated at 19.86% of the base wage (Statistical Abstracts of the United States, Table 684 (1991) and Table 660 (1992)). The calculation of the historic loss is presented in the following table.

Historic Wage Loss:

Year	Income	% of Year	Loss
1991	15,600	33.2%	$ 5,172
1992	16,070	100.0	16,070
1993	16,070	50.7	8,145
		Total Loss	29,387

The fringe benefits are calculated as 19.86% of the wages. The loss of fringe benefits totals $5,836.

The value of household services are computed in the same manner as were historic wages. The value of household services is computed in the following table:

Value of Household Services:

Year	Income	% of Year	Loss
1991	$ 7,235	33.2%	$ 2,402
1992	7,453	100.0	7,453
1993	7,453	50.7	3,779
		Total Loss	13,633

PART III.   CALCULATION OF FUTURE ECONOMIC LOSS

The present value of the loss is calculated by using the following formula:

$$\text{Present Value of Future Income} = \$ \sum_{t=0}^{n} [(1+g)^t / (1+d)^t]$$

The four variables in this formula are:

$, t, g, and, d

$ = Represents the basis for calculating the economic loss resulting from the accident. The wage calculation is based on annual earnings.

t = Represents time and starts on the present value date. When the present value of wages is being computed the analysis continues each year until Mr. Doe reaches age 65. The analysis assumes uninterrupted work until retirement on the 65th birthday. The 1993 salary is $16,070. The fringe benefits package is computed as 19.86% of the earnings.

When the present value of household services is being computed the beginning value is $7,453. This assumes Mr. Doe would work in excess of 40 hours each week outside the home. In other words, Mr. Doe is employed full time. The analysis further assumes that upon Mr. Doe's retirement he would spend more time working around the home. Accordingly, the value of household services is increased to $13,229. When the value of household services is being computed the analysis mortality adjusts the value of the services. That is, the present value of household services is adjusted to reflect the probability that Mr. Doe is alive each year.

g = Represents the growth rate. The growth rate is 4.30% and is the 1952-1992 historic rate of change in the Consumer Price Index.

d = Represents the discount rate or rate at which dollars received will earn interest. The discount rate is 6.05% and is the 1952-1992 historic yield on one-year treasury bills. There are many types of investments which can be made today, ranging from passbook savings to speculating in future markets. While there is no such thing as a risk-free investment, the U.S. one-year Treasury Bill is used as a surrogate.

For example, if we are receiving $1,000 one year from today we might be willing to receive some amount less than $1,000 today. This is true because we could invest the money for one year and earn interest. The rate of earnings is the interest rate or discount rate.

The actual calculation of the present value of the future income stream assumes that the relationship between the growth and discount rate will remain unchanged. That is, the discount rate will be 1.0168 times the growth rate. This relationship is established by dividing 1.0605, the interest rate, by 1.0430, the growth rate.

The analysis does *not* assume that the growth rate of wages and the interest rate will always be the same. The analysis *does* assume the interest rate is 1.0168 times the growth rate.

PART IV.   BIBLIOGRAPHY

PROBABILITY OF LIVING:

US National Center for Health Statistics, Life Expectancy Tables, Vital Statistics of U.S. (1989) *cited in* Statistical Abstracts of the United States Table 105 (1992).

JOB PARTICIPATION RATE

Bureau of Labor Statistics, Civilian Labor Force Participation Rate By Sex, Race, and Age, Handbook of Labor Statistics, Bulletin 2340, at 25-30 (Aug 1989).

PROBABILITY OF EMPLOYMENT:

US Department of Labor, Bureau of Labor Statistics, Unemployment Rates by Sex, Race, and Age, Handbook of Labor Statistics, Bulletin 2340, at 136-41 (Aug 1989).

VALUE OF HOUSEHOLD SERVICES:

Source: W. Keith Bryant, Cathleen D. Zick & Hyoshin Kim, *Household Work: What's It Worth and Why?*, Cornell University Bulletin 322 IB228 (1992).

ENCLOSURES

Enclosure #1

John Doe

Date of Birth: July 4, 1952
Date of Accident: September 1, 1991
Present Value Date: July 4, 1993

Growth   .0430
Discount 0.0605
Income   16,070

Age	Per	Present Value	Sum	Prob of Living	Emp Rate	Adjusted PV	Adjusted Sum
41	0	16,070	16,070	.9971	.968	15,510	15,510
42	1	15,804	31,874	.9939	.968	15,206	30,716
43	2	15,544	47,418	.9906	.968	14,905	45,620
44	3	15,287	62,705	.9870	.968	14,605	60,225
45	4	15,035	77,739	.9830	.968	14,307	74,532
46	5	14,787	92,526	.9788	.968	14,010	88,542
47	6	14,543	107,069	.9742	.968	13,714	102,256
48	7	14,303	121,372	.9692	.968	13,418	115,674
49	8	14,067	135,438	.9638	.968	13,123	128,797
50	9	13,835	149,273	.9579	.968	12,828	141,626
51	10	13,606	162,879	.9514	.968	12,531	154,157
52	11	13,382	176,261	.9443	.968	12,232	166,389
53	12	13,161	189,422	.9364	.968	11,930	178,319
54	13	12,944	202,366	.9277	.968	11,624	189,943
55	14	12,730	215,096	.9182	.965	11,280	201,223
56	15	12,520	227,616	.9078	.965	10,967	212,190
57	16	12,314	239,930	.8964	.965	10,651	222,841
58	17	12,110	252,040	.8840	.965	10,331	233,172
59	18	11,910	263,950	.8706	.965	10,006	243,178
60	19	11,714	275,664	.8561	.965	9,677	252,855
61	20	11,521	287,185	.8406	.965	9,345	262,200
62	21	11,331	298,516	.8241	.965	9,010	271,211
63	22	11,144	309,659	.8066	.965	8,674	279,885
64	23	10,960	320,619	.7882	.965	8,336	288,221
65	24	10,779	331,398	.7687	.956	7,921	296,142
66	25	10,601	341,999	.7479	.956	7,580	303,722
67	26	10,426	352,425	.7260	.956	7,236	310,958
68	27	10,254	362,679	.7028	.956	6,889	317,847
69	28	10,085	372,763	.6783	.956	6,540	324,387
70	29	9,918	382,682	.6526	.956	6,188	330,575
71	30	9,755	392,436	.6256	.956	5,834	336,409
72	31	9,594	402,030	.5974	.956	5,479	341,888
73	32	9,435	411,465	.5680	.956	5,124	347,011
74	33	9,280	420,745	.5375	.956	4,769	351,780
75	34	9,127	429,872	.5061	.956	4,415	356,195
76	35	8,976	438,848	.4738	.956	4,065	360,261
77	36	8,828	447,676	.4408	.956	3,720	363,980
78	37	8,682	456,358	.4073	.956	3,381	367,361
79	38	8,539	464,897	.3736	.956	3,049	370,410
80	39	8,398	473,295	.3385	.956	2,718	373,128
81	40	8,259	481,554	.3025	.956	2,389	375,517

Age	Per	Present Value	Sum	Prob of Living	Emp Rate	Adjusted PV	Adjusted Sum
82	41	8,123	489,677	.2661	.956	2,067	377,583
83	42	7,989	497,666	.2298	.956	1,755	379,339
84	43	7,857	.505,524	.1943	.956	1,460	380,799
85	44	7,728	513,251	.1604	.956	1,185	381,983
86	45	7,600	520,851	.1286	.956	934	382,918
87	46	7,475	528,326	.0997	.956	713	383,630
88	47	7,351	535,677	.0744	.956	523	384,153
89	48	7,230	542,907	.0530	.956	366	384,519
90	49	7,111	550,018	.0357	.956	243	384,762
91	50	6,993	557,011	.0225	.956	151	384,913
92	51	6,878	563,889	.0131	.956	86	384,999
93	52	6,764	570,654	.0069	.956	45	385,044
94	53	6,653	577,306	.0032	.956	20	385,064
95	54	6,543	583,849	.0013	.956	8	385,072
96	55	6,435	590,285	.0004	.956	2	385,074
97	56	6,329	596,613	.0001	.956	1	385,075
98 ·	57	6,224	602,838	.0000	.956	0	385,075
99	58	6,122	608,960	.0000	.956	0	385,075

Enclosure #2

John Doe
PV WM 89
Growth .0430
Discount 0.0605
Income 6,070

Date of Birth: July 4, 1952
Date of Accident: September 1, 1991
Present Value Date: July 4, 1993

	Value of HHS	Chg in CPI
1988	6,284	
1989	6,587	4.82%
1990	6,943	5.40
1991	7,235	4.21
1992	7,453	3.01
	$13,229	

Age	Per	PV	Sum	Prob of Living	Adjusted PV	Adjusted Sum
41	0	7,453	7,453	.9971	7,431	7,431
42	1	7,330	14,782	.9939	7,285	14,716
43	2	7,209	21,991	.9906	7,141	21,857
44	3	7,090	29,081	.9870	6,997	28,854
45	4	6,973	36,053	.9830	6,854	35,709
46	5	6,858	42,911	.9788	6,712	42,421
47	6	6,745	49,656	.9742	6,570	48,991
48	7	6,633	56,289	.9692	6,429	55,420

Age	Per	PV	Sum	Prob of Living	Adjusted PV	Adjusted Sum
49	8	6,524	62,813	.9638	6,287	61,707
50	9	6,416	69,229	.9579	6,146	67,853
51	10	6,310	75,539	.9514	6,004	73,857
52	11	6,206	81,745	.9443	5,861	79,718
53	12	6,104	87,849	.9364	5,716	85,434
54	13	6,003	93,852	.9277	5,569	91,003
55	14	5,904	99,756	.9182	5,421	96,424
56	15	5,806	105,562	.9078	5,271	101,695
57	16	5,711	111,273	.8964	5,119	106,813
58	17	5,616	116,889	.8840	4,965	111,778
59	18	5,524	122,413	.8706	4,809	116,587
60	19	5,433	127,846	.8561	4,651	121,238
61	20	5,343	133,189	.8406	4,491	125,729
62	21	5,255	138,444	.8241	4,330	130,059
63	22	5,168	143,612	.8066	4,169	134,228
64	23	5,083	148,694	.7882	4,006	138,234
65	24	8,873	157,568	.7687	6,821	145,055
66	25	10,601	168,169	.7479	7,929	152,984
67	26	10,426	178,595	.7260	7,569	160,553
68	27	10,254	188,849	.7028	7,206	167,759
69	28	10,085	198,934	.6783	6,841	174,600
70	29	9,918	208,852	.6526	6,473	181,073
71	30	9,755	218,607	.6256	6,103	187,175
72	31	9,594	228,200	.5974	5,731	192,907
73	32	9,435	237,636	.5680	5,359	198,266
74	33	9,280	246,915	.5375	4,988	203,254
75	34	9,127	256,042	.5061	4,619	207,873
76	35	8,976	265,018	.4738	4,252	212,125
77	36	8,828	273,846	.4408	3,891	216,016
78	37	8,682	282,528	.4073	3,536	219,552
79	38	8,539	291,067	.3736	3,190	222,742
80	39	8,398	299,465	.3385	2,843	225,585
81	40	8,259	307,724	.3025	2,499	228,083
82	41	8,123	315,847	.2661	2,162	230,245
83	42	7,989	323,837	.2298	1,836	232,081
84	43	7,857	331,694	.1943	1,527	233,608
85	44	7,728	339,421	.1604	1,239	234,848
86	45	7,600	347,021	.1286	977	235,825
87	46	7,475	354,496	.0997	746	236,570
88	47	7,351	361,847	.0744	547	237,117
89	48	7,230	369,077	.0530	383	237,500

Age	Per	PV	Sum	Prob of Living	Adjusted PV	Adjusted Sum
90	49	7,111	376,188	.0357	254	237,754
91	50	6,993	383,181	.0225	158	237,912
92	51	6,878	390,059	.0131	90	238,002
93	52	6,764	396,824	.0069	47	238,049
94	53	6,653	403,477	.0032	21	238,070
95	54	6,543	410,020	.0013	8	238,078
96	55	6,435	416,455	.0004	3	238,081
97	56	6,329	422,784	.0001	1	238,081
98	57	6,224	429,008	.0000	0	238,081
99	58	6,122	435,130	.0000	0	238,081

Enclosure #3

Employment Rates
White Males
Based on Table XX

Year	16 to 17 Years	18 to 19 Years	20 to 24 Years	25 to 34 Years	35 to 44 Years	45 to 54 Years	55 to 64 Years	65 plus Years
1954	86.0	87.0	90.2	95.8	96.4	96.2	95.7	95.8
1955	87.8	89.6	93.0	97.3	97.4	97.1	96.1	96.2
1956	88.8	90.3	93.9	97.2	97.8	97.2	96.9	96.6
1957	88.1	88.9	93.0	97.3	97.5	97.0	96.6	96.8
1958	85.1	83.5	88.3	94.4	95.6	95.2	94.8	95.0
1959	85.0	87.0	92.5	96.2	96.8	96.3	95.8	95.5
1960	85.4	86.5	91.7	95.9	96.7	96.4	95.9	96.0
1961	83.5	84.8	89.9	95.1	96.0	95.6	94.7	94.8
1962	84.8	87.3	91.9	96.2	96.9	96.5	95.9	96.0
1963	82.2	85.8	92.2	96.1	97.1	96.7	96.0	95.9
1964	83.9	86.7	92.6	97.0	97.5	97.1	96.5	96.4
1965	85.3	88.7	94.1	97.4	97.7	97.7	96.9	96.6
1966	87.5	91.1	95.9	97.9	98.3	98.3	97.5	97.0
1967	87.3	91.0	95.8	98.1	98.4	98.2	97.8	97.3
1968	87.4	91.7	95.4	98.3	98.6	98.5	98.3	97.2
1969	87.5	92.1	95.4	98.3	98.6	98.6	98.3	97.8
1970	84.3	88.0	92.2	96.9	97.7	97.7	97.3	96.8
1971	82.9	86.5	90.6	96.0	97.1	97.1	96.8	96.6
1972	83.6	87.6	91.5	96.6	97.5	97.5	97.0	96.7
1973	84.8	90.0	93.4	97.0	98.2	98.0	97.6	97.1
1974	83.8	88.5	92.2	96.4	97.6	97.8	97.5	97.0
1975	80.3	82.8	86.9	93.7	95.5	95.6	95.9	95.0
1976	80.3	84.5	89.1	94.4	96.3	96.3	96.0	95.3
1977	82.4	87.0	90.7	95.0	96.9	97.0	96.7	95.1
1978	83.1	89.2	92.3	96.2	97.5	97.5	97.4	96.1
1979	83.9	87.8	92.5	96.3	97.5	97.5	97.5	96.8
1980	81.5	85.5	88.9	94.1	96.4	96.7	96.9	97.5
1981	80.1	83.6	88.4	93.9	96.0	96.4	96.6	97.6
1982	75.8	80.0	85.7	91.1	93.8	94.7	94.9	96.8
1983	77.4	81.3	86.2	91.0	93.6	94.3	94.4	96.8

Year	16 to 17 Years	18 to 19 Years	20 to 24 Years	25 to 34 Years	35 to 44 Years	45 to 54 Years	55 to 64 Years	65 plus Years
1984	80.3	85.0	90.2	93.8	95.4	95.8	95.3	97.4
1985	80.8	85.3	90.3	94.3	95.7	95.9	96.0	97.3
1986	81.6	85.3	90.8	94.2	95.6	96.0	96.0	97.0
1987	82.1	86.3	91.6	94.8	96.1	96.1	96.6	97.5
1988	83.9	87.6	92.6	95.4	96.6	96.8	96.7	97.8
Average:	83.7	87.0	91.5	95.7	96.8	96.8	96.5	96.5

Enclosure #4

1988 Value of Household Services for Nonblack Males

Age of Youngest Child	Not Emp	0-34 hrs	35-40 hrs	40+ hrs
1			7,871	7,808
2-5			9,291	5,958
6-14			9,409	7,903
15-17			6,586	6,341
18+	11,155	9,650	6,724	6,284

1988 CPI =	118.3
1992 CPI =	140.3
Growth Factor	1.1860

1992 Values	Nonblack Males			
Age of Youngest Child	Not Emp	0-34 hrs	35-40 hrs	40+ hrs
1			9,335	9,260
2-5			11,019	7,066
6-14			11,159	9,373
15-17			7,811	7,520
18+	13,229	11,445	7,974	7,453

Source: W. Keith Bryant, Cathleen D. Zick & Hyoshin Kim, *Household Work: What's It Worth and Why?*, Cornell University Bulletin 322 IB228 (19 __).

Enclosure #5

Average Rate of Change in the Consumer Price Index

1952-1992

Year	1952	1953	1954	1955	1956	1957	1958	1959	1960
1952									
1953	0.75								
1954	0.75	0.75							

1952-1992

Year	1952	1953	1954	1955	1956	1957	1958	1959	1960
1955	0.38	0.19	-0.37						
1956	0.66	0.62	0.56	1.49					
1957	1.19	1.29	1.48	2.40	3.31				
1958	1.46	1.61	1.82	2.55	3.08	2.85			
1959	1.35	1.45	1.59	2.09	2.28	1.77	0.69		
1960	1.40	1.49	1.61	2.01	2.14	1.75	1.21	1.72	
1961	1.36	1.43	1.53	1.85	1.92	1.57	1.14	1.37	1.01
1962	1.32	1.38	1.46	1.73	1.76	1.45	1.11	1.25	1.01
1963	1.32	1.38	1.45	1.67	1.70	1.43	1.15	1.26	1.11
1964	1.32	1.37	1.43	1.63	1.65	1.42	1.18	1.27	1.16
1965	1.34	1.39	1.45	1.63	1.65	1.44	1.24	1.33	1.25
1966	1.45	1.50	1.57	1.74	1.77	1.60	1.44	1.55	1.52
1967	1.56	1.62	1.68	1.86	1.89	1.75	1.62	1.74	1.74
1968	1.72	1.79	1.86	2.04	2.08	1.97	1.88	2.01	2.05
1969	1.94	2.02	2.10	2.28	2.34	2.26	2.21	2.36	2.43
1970	2.15	2.24	2.33	2.51	2.58	2.53	2.50	2.66	2.76
1971	2.27	2.36	2.45	2.63	2.70	2.66	2.64	2.81	2.91
1972	2.32	2.40	2.49	2.66	2.73	2.70	2.68	2.84	2.93
1973	2.50	2.59	2.69	2.86	2.94	2.92	2.92	3.08	3.18
1974	2.89	2.99	3.11	3.29	3.39	3.39	3.43	3.61	3.74
1975	3.16	3.27	3.39	3.58	3.69	3.71	3.76	3.95	4.10
1976	3.27	3.38	3.50	3.68	3.79	3.82	3.87	4.06	4.21
1977	3.40	3.51	3.63	3.81	3.92	3.95	4.01	4.20	4.34
1978	3.56	3.67	3.80	3.98	4.09	4.13	4.19	4.38	4.52
1979	3.85	3.97	4.10	4.28	4.41	4.46	4.53	4.72	4.88
1980	4.19	4.32	4.46	4.65	4.78	4.85	4.94	5.14	5.31
1981	4.41	4.54	4.68	4.87	5.01	5.08	5.17	5.38	5.55
1982	4.46	4.59	4.73	4.92	5.05	5.12	5.21	5.41	5.58
1983	4.42	4.55	4.68	4.86	4.98	5.05	5.13	5.32	5.48
1984	4.42	4.54	4.67	4.84	4.96	5.02	5.10	5.28	5.43
1985	4.39	4.51	4.63	4.80	4.91	4.97	5.05	5.21	5.35
1986	4.32	4.43	4.54	4.70	4.81	4.86	4.93	5.09	5.22
1987	4.30	4.40	4.52	4.67	4.77	4.82	4.89	5.04	5.16
1988	4.30	4.40	4.50	4.65	4.75	4.80	4.86	5.01	5.12
1989	4.31	4.41	4.51	4.66	4.75	4.80	4.86	5.00	5.11
1990	4.34	4.44	4.54	4.68	4.77	4.82	4.88	5.01	5.12
1991	4.34	4.43	4.53	4.67	4.76	4.80	4.86	4.99	5.09
1992	4.30	4.39	4.49	4.62	4.71	4.75	4.80	4.93	5.03

Average Rate of Change in the Consumer Price Index

1952-1992   Continued

Year	1961	1962	1963	1964	1965	1966	1967	1968	1969
1961									
1962	1.00								
1963	1.16	1.32							
1964	1.21	1.32	1.31						
1965	1.31	1.41	1.46	1.61					
1966	1.62	1.78	1.93	2.24	2.86				
1967	1.87	2.04	2.22	2.52	2.97	3.09			
1968	2.20	2.40	2.61	2.94	3.38	3.64	4.19		
1969	2.61	2.83	3.09	3.44	3.90	4.25	4.83	5.46	
1970	2.95	3.20	3.46	3.82	4.26	4.61	5.12	5.59	5.72
1971	3.09	3.33	3.58	3.90	4.28	4.57	4.94	5.19	5.05
1972	3.11	3.32	3.54	3.82	4.13	4.34	4.59	4.69	4.44
1973	3.36	3.58	3.80	4.08	4.39	4.61	4.86	5.00	4.88
1974	3.95	4.20	4.46	4.78	5.13	5.41	5.75	6.00	6.11
1975	4.32	4.58	4.85	5.17	5.53	5.83	6.17	6.45	6.62
1976	4.42	4.66	4.92	5.22	5.55	5.82	6.12	6.36	6.49
1977	4.55	4.79	5.03	5.32	5.63	5.88	6.16	6.38	6.50
1978	4.73	4.96	5.20	5.48	5.78	6.02	6.29	6.50	6.62
1979	5.10	5.34	5.59	5.87	6.18	6.43	6.71	6.94	7.09
1980	5.54	5.79	6.05	6.35	6.67	6.94	7.23	7.49	7.67
1981	5.78	6.03	6.29	6.58	6.89	7.16	7.45	7.71	7.89
1982	5.80	6.04	6.28	6.56	6.85	7.10	7.37	7.60	7.76
1983	5.68	5.90	6.13	6.38	6.65	6.87	7.11	7.30	7.43
1984	5.62	5.83	6.04	6.28	6.53	6.73	6.94	7.12	7.23
1985	5.53	5.73	5.93	6.15	6.38	6.56	6.76	6.91	7.00
1986	5.39	5.57	5.75	5.96	6.16	6.33	6.50	6.63	6.70
1987	5.32	5.49	5.67	5.86	6.05	6.20	6.36	6.47	6.53
1988	5.28	5.44	5.61	5.78	5.97	6.11	6.25	6.35	6.40
1989	5.26	5.42	5.57	5.75	5.92	6.05	6.19	6.28	6.32
1990	5.26	5.42	5.57	5.73	5.90	6.02	6.15	6.24	6.28
1991	5.23	5.38	5.52	5.68	5.83	5.95	6.07	6.15	6.18
1992	5.16	5.30	5.43	5.58	5.73	5.84	5.95	6.02	6.05

Average Rate of Change in the Consumer Price Index

1952-1992 Continued

Year	1970	1971	1972	1973	1974	1975	1976	1977	1978
1970									
1971	4.38								
1972	3.80	3.21							
1973	4.60	4.71	6.22						
1974	6.21	6.82	8.63	11.04					
1975	6.80	7.40	8.79	10.08	9.13				
1976	6.62	7.07	8.04	8.64	7.44	5.76			
1977	6.61	6.98	7.73	8.11	7.13	6.13	6.50		
1978	6.73	7.06	7.71	8.00	7.25	6.62	7.05	7.59	
1979	7.24	7.60	8.23	8.56	8.07	7.80	8.48	9.47	11.35
1980	7.87	8.26	8.89	9.27	8.97	8.94	9.74	10.81	12.42
1981	8.09	8.46	9.04	9.40	9.16	9.17	9.85	10.69	11.72
1982	7.93	8.25	8.76	9.04	8.79	8.74	9.24	9.78	10.33
1983	7.57	7.83	8.25	8.46	8.17	8.05	8.38	8.69	8.91
1984	7.33	7.56	7.92	8.08	7.78	7.63	7.87	8.06	8.14
1985	7.08	7.28	7.59	7.70	7.40	7.23	7.39	7.50	7.49
1986	6.76	6.91	7.18	7.25	6.94	6.74	6.84	6.87	6.78
1987	6.57	6.71	6.94	7.00	6.69	6.48	6.55	6.55	6.44
1988	6.44	6.56	6.77	6.81	6.50	6.30	6.35	6.33	6.21
1989	6.35	6.46	6.65	6.68	6.39	6.20	6.23	6.21	6.08
1990	6.31	6.41	6.58	6.61	6.33	6.14	6.17	6.14	6.02
1991	6.21	6.30	6.46	6.47	6.20	6.02	6.04	6.01	5.88
1992	6.06	6.14	6.29	6.29	6.03	5.84	5.85	5.81	5.68

Average Rate of Change in the Consumer Price Index

1952-1992 Continued

Year	1979	1980	1981	1982	1983	1984	1985	1986	1987
1979									
1980	13.50								
1981	11.91	10.32							
1982	9.99	8.24	6.16						
1983	8.30	6.56	4.69	3.21					
1984	7.50	6.00	4.56	3.76	4.32				
1985	6.84	5.51	4.31	3.70	3.94	3.56			
1986	6.13	4.90	3.82	3.24	3.25	2.71	1.86		
1987	5.82	4.73	3.79	3.32	3.35	3.02	2.75	3.65	
1988	5.63	4.65	3.84	3.46	3.50	3.30	3.22	3.89	4.14
1989	5.55	4.67	3.96	3.65	3.72	3.61	3.62	4.20	4.48
1990	5.54	4.74	4.12	3.87	3.96	3.90	3.97	4.50	4.79
1991	5.43	4.69	4.13	3.91	3.99	3.95	4.01	4.44	4.64
1992	5.24	4.55	4.03	3.82	3.88	3.83	3.87	4.20	4.32

Average Rate of Change in the Consumer Price Index

1952-1992   Continued

Year	1988	1989	1990	1991
1988				
1989	4.82			
1990	5.11	5.40		
1991	4.81	4.81	4.2	
1992	4.36	4.21	3.61	3.01

Enclosure #6

Year	1952	1953	1954	1955	1956	1957	1958	1959	1960
1952	1.84								
1953	1.98	2.11							
1954	1.63	1.52	0.93						
1955	1.70	1.66	1.43	1.93					
1956	1.94	1.97	1.92	2.42	2.91				
1957	2.23	2.31	2.36	2.83	3.29	3.66			
1958	2.22	2.28	2.31	2.66	2.90	2.90	2.13		
1959	2.48	2.57	2.64	2.98	3.25	3.36	3.21	4.29	
1960	2.61	2.70	2.79	3.10	3.33	3.44	3.36	3.98	3.66
1961	2.64	2.72	2.80	3.07	3.26	3.33	3.24	3.61	3.28
1962	2.68	2.76	2.83	3.07	3.23	3.29	3.21	3.49	3.22
1963	2.74	2.82	2.89	3.11	3.26	3.31	3.25	3.47	3.27
1964	2.83	2.91	2.98	3.19	3.33	3.38	3.34	3.54	3.39
1965	2.93	3.01	3.09	3.28	3.42	3.47	3.45	3.64	3.53
1966	3.09	3.18	3.26	3.45	3.59	3.66	3.66	3.85	3.79
1967	3.20	3.29	3.38	3.57	3.70	3.78	3.79	3.97	3.93
1968	3.35	3.45	3.54	3.72	3.86	3.94	3.97	4.15	4.14
1969	3.57	3.67	3.77	3.96	4.11	4.20	4.24	4.44	4.45
1970	3.75	3.86	3.96	4.15	4.30	4.39	4.45	4.64	4.68
1971	3.81	3.91	4.01	4.19	4.33	4.43	4.48	4.66	4.70
1972	3.86	3.97	4.06	4.24	4.37	4.46	4.52	4.69	4.72
1973	4.03	4.14	4.24	4.41	4.55	4.65	4.71	4.88	4.92
1974	4.22	4.33	4.43	4.61	4.75	4.85	4.92	5.10	5.15
1975	4.32	4.43	4.54	4.71	4.85	4.95	5.02	5.19	5.25
1976	4.38	4.49	4.59	4.76	4.89	4.99	5.06	5.23	5.28
1977	4.45	4.55	4.65	4.82	4.95	5.04	5.11	5.27	5.33
1978	4.59	4.70	4.80	4.97	5.10	5.20	5.27	5.43	5.49
1979	4.82	4.93	5.03	5.20	5.34	5.44	5.52	5.68	5.75
1980	5.07	5.19	5.30	5.47	5.61	5.72	5.81	5.98	6.06
1981	5.41	5.53	5.65	5.83	5.98	6.10	6.20	6.38	6.47
1982	5.63	5.76	5.89	6.06	6.22	6.34	6.45	6.63	6.73
1983	5.76	5.89	6.01	6.19	6.34	6.47	6.57	6.75	6.85
1984	5.92	6.05	6.17	6.35	6.50	6.63	6.74	6.92	7.02

Year	1952	1953	1954	1955	1956	1957	1958	1959	1960
1985	5.99	6.12	6.24	6.42	6.57	6.69	6.80	6.97	7.08
1986	6.00	6.12	6.24	6.41	6.55	6.67	6.77	6.94	7.04
1987	6.01	6.12	6.24	6.40	6.54	6.66	6.76	6.92	7.01
1988	6.04	6.15	6.27	6.43	6.56	6.68	6.77	6.93	7.02
1989	6.09	6.20	6.31	6.47	6.60	6.71	6.81	6.96	7.05
1990	6.12	6.23	6.34	6.49	6.62	6.73	6.83	6.97	7.06
1991	6.10	6.21	6.32	6.47	6.59	6.70	6.79	6.93	7.01
1992	6.05	6.15	6.26	6.40	6.52	6.62	6.70	6.84	6.91

Yield on 1-Year Treasury Bills

1952-1992   Continued

Year	1961	1962	1963	1964	1965	1966	1967	1968	1969
1961	2.89								
1962	3.00	3.10							
1963	3.13	3.26	3.41						
1964	3.32	3.47	3.65	3.89					
1965	3.50	3.66	3.84	4.06	4.23				
1966	3.81	3.99	4.22	4.49	4.79	5.34			
1967	3.97	4.15	4.36	4.60	4.84	5.14	4.94		
1968	4.20	4.38	4.60	4.83	5.07	5.35	5.35	5.76	
1969	4.54	4.74	4.98	5.24	5.51	5.83	5.99	6.52	7.28
1970	4.78	4.99	5.22	5.48	5.75	6.05	6.23	6.66	7.11
1971	4.79	4.98	5.19	5.41	5.63	5.86	5.96	6.22	6.37
1972	4.81	4.98	5.17	5.37	5.55	5.74	5.81	5.98	6.03
1973	5.02	5.20	5.39	5.58	5.77	5.96	6.05	6.24	6.33
1974	5.26	5.44	5.63	5.83	6.03	6.23	6.34	6.54	6.67
1975	5.35	5.53	5.72	5.91	6.09	6.28	6.38	6.56	6.68
1976	5.38	5.55	5.73	5.90	6.07	6.24	6.33	6.48	6.57
1977	5.42	5.58	5.75	5.91	6.07	6.22	6.30	6.44	6.52
1978	5.59	5.75	5.91	6.08	6.24	6.39	6.48	6.62	6.70
1979	5.86	6.03	6.20	6.37	6.54	6.71	6.81	6.97	7.08
1980	6.18	6.35	6.53	6.72	6.90	7.07	7.20	7.37	7.50
1981	6.61	6.79	6.99	7.19	7.38	7.58	7.73	7.92	8.09
1982	6.87	7.06	7.26	7.46	7.66	7.86	8.02	8.23	8.40
1983	6.99	7.18	7.37	7.57	7.77	7.96	8.12	8.32	8.49
1984	7.16	7.35	7.54	7.74	7.93	8.12	8.28	8.47	8.64
1985	7.21	7.39	7.58	7.77	7.95	8.14	8.29	8.47	8.63
1986	7.17	7.34	7.52	7.70	7.87	8.04	8.18	8.35	8.49
1987	7.14	7.30	7.47	7.64	7.80	7.96	8.09	8.25	8.38
1988	7.14	7.30	7.46	7.62	7.78	7.93	8.05	8.19	8.32
1989	7.17	7.32	7.47	7.63	7.78	7.93	8.04	8.18	8.30
1990	7.17	7.32	7.47	7.62	7.76	7.91	8.01	8.15	8.25
1991	7.12	7.26	7.40	7.55	7.68	7.81	7.91	8.04	8.14
1992	7.01	7.15	7.28	7.42	7.54	7.66	7.75	7.87	7.95

Yield on 1-Year Treasury Bills

1952-1992 Continued

Year	1970	1971	1972	1973	1974	1975	1976	1977	1978
1970	6.94								
1971	5.92	4.90							
1972	5.62	4.96	5.01						
1973	6.10	5.82	6.28	7.54					
1974	6.55	6.45	6.97	7.95	8.35				
1975	6.58	6.50	6.91	7.54	7.54	6.72			
1976	6.47	6.39	6.69	7.11	6.97	6.28	5.84		
1977	6.42	6.35	6.59	6.90	6.74	6.21	5.95	6.06	
1978	6.64	6.60	6.84	7.15	7.07	6.75	6.76	7.23	8.39
1979	7.06	7.07	7.34	7.67	7.69	7.56	7.77	8.42	9.60
1980	7.52	7.58	7.88	8.24	8.34	8.34	8.66	9.37	10.47
1981	8.16	8.27	8.61	9.01	9.19	9.31	9.74	10.52	11.64
1982	8.49	8.62	8.96	9.35	9.55	9.70	10.13	10.84	11.80
1983	8.57	8.70	9.01	9.38	9.56	9.70	10.07	10.67	11.44
1984	8.73	8.86	9.17	9.51	9.69	9.83	10.17	10.71	11.38
1985	8.72	8.84	9.12	9.43	9.59	9.70	10.00	10.46	11.02
1986	8.56	8.66	8.91	9.19	9.32	9.40	9.64	10.03	10.47
1987	8.44	8.53	8.75	9.00	9.11	9.16	9.37	9.69	10.05
1988	8.37	8.45	8.66	8.89	8.98	9.02	9.20	9.48	9.79
1989	8.35	8.42	8.62	8.83	8.91	8.95	9.11	9.36	9.63
1990	8.30	8.37	8.55	8.75	8.82	8.85	8.99	9.22	9.46
1991	8.18	8.23	8.40	8.58	8.64	8.65	8.78	8.97	9.18
1992	7.98	8.03	8.18	8.34	8.38	8.38	8.48	8.64	8.82

Yield on 1-Year Treasury Bills

1952-1992 Continued

Year	1979	1980	1981	1982	1983	1984	1985	1986	1987
1979	10.80								
1980	11.51	12.22							
1981	12.72	13.68	15.13						
1982	12.65	13.27	13.79	12.45					
1983	12.05	12.36	12.41	11.05	9.65				
1984	11.88	12.09	12.06	11.04	10.33	11.01			
1985	11.39	11.49	11.34	10.40	9.71	8.47	8.47		
1986	10.73	10.71	10.46	9.53	8.80	8.52	7.27	6.07	
1987	10.24	10.17	9.87	9.00	8.31	7.97	6.96	6.20	6.33
1988	9.93	9.83	9.54	8.74	8.12	7.81	7.01	6.52	6.75
1989	9.75	9.64	9.35	8.63	8.09	7.83	7.19	6.87	7.14
1990	9.55	9.43	9.16	8.49	8.00	7.76	7.22	6.97	7.19
1991	9.24	9.11	8.83	8.20	7.72	7.48	6.98	6.73	6.86
1992	8.85	8.70	8.40	7.79	7.33	7.07	6.58	6.30	6.34

Yield on 1-Year Treasury Bills

1952-1992 Continued

Year	1988	1989	1990	1991	1992
1988	7.17				
1989	7.54	7.91			
1990	7.48	7.64	7.36		
1991	7.00	6.94	6.45	5.54	
1992	6.35	6.14	5.55	4.65	3.75

Enclosure #7

Employer Cost for Employee Compensation per Hour Worked, 1989-1991

	1988	1989	1990	1991
Total Compensation	13.79	14.28	14.96	15.40
Wage & Salaries	10.02	10.38	10.84	11.14
Total Benefits	3.77	3.90	4.13	4.27
Paid Leave	0.97	1.00	1.03	1.05
Vacation	0.48	0.50	0.51	0.52
Holiday	0.33	0.34	0.34	0.35
Sick	0.12	0.12	0.13	0.13
Other	0.04	0.04	0.04	0.05
Supplemental Pay	0.33	0.34	0.37	0.36
Premium Pay	0.17	0.17	0.17	0.17
NonProduction Bonus	0.12	0.12	0.16	0.13
Shift Pay	0.04	0.05	0.05	0.05
Insurance	0.78	0.85	0.92	1.01
Pension & Savings	0.45	0.42	0.45	0.11
Pension	0.38	0.34	0.36	0.35
Savings & Thrift	0.07	0.08	0.09	0.10
Legally Required	1.22	1.27	1.35	1.40
Social Security	0.81	0.84	0.89	0.92
Fed Unemployment	0.03	0.03	0.03	0.03
Sate Unemployment	0.12	0.11	0.09	0.09
Workers Compensation	0.24	0.27	0.31	0.33
Other Benefits	0.02	0.02	Rounds to Zero	

Source: Statistical Abstracts of the United States Table 684 (1991) and Table 660 (1992).

§23.03   Direct Examination: Identify the Expert

Examination by plaintiff's attorney:

Q. Please state your name for the court.

A. My name is "The Economist".

Q. Where are you employed?

A. I am employed at the University.

Q. In what capacity are you employed?

A. I am Professor of Economics.

Q. How long have you been employed in that capacity?

A. I have been employed at the University for the last 12 years.

Q. What courses do you currently teach?

Q. Have you taught other courses over the last five years?

Q. Do you have other duties, responsibilities, or expectations as an employee of the University?

A. Yes.

Q. Would you please explain these other responsibilities.

A. The University expects performance in three areas. These areas are teaching, research, and community service.

Q. Please explain how you discharge the responsibilities in the area of research and community service.

A. In the area of research I present and publish papers in the area of forensic economics. In the area of community service I conduct training seminars on what forensic economists do. These seminars are presented through the University and are available for continuing legal education credit.

Q. Is the list of papers, articles, and seminars listed in your resume?

A. Yes.

§23.04   Direct Examination: Why the Expert is Here

Examination by plaintiff's attorney:

Q. Just what is it that forensic economists attempt to determine?

A. The purpose of the analysis is to estimate the economic loss sustained by an individual, or family, as a result of death or injury.

Q. What types of losses might an individual sustain as a result of an injury?

A. The losses to an individual and family can include the loss of wages, fringe benefits, the ability to perform household services, and the ability to enjoy life, hedonics.

Q. Do all parties disabled by an injury suffer the same degree of economic loss?

A. No. A person may be only partially disabled, or temporarily disabled.

Q. Did I retain you to do an economic calculation concerning the economic loss suffered by Mr. Doe as a result of an automobile accident he had on September 1, 1991?

A. Yes.

Q. Do you do this type of work as community service?

A. No, this is consulting.

Q. Are you paid to do this type of work?

A. Yes.

Q. Who pays you to do this type of analysis?

A. In this case, you did.

Q. Have you ever done this type of analysis before?

A. Yes.

Q. How long have you been involved in this type of analysis?

A. Approximately 15 years.

Q. How many cases have you handled in that time?

A. I would estimate over 500.

Q. Of those cases what proportion are for plaintiffs and what proportion are for defense?

A. I would judge 25% are for defense.

Q. Have you ever testified by deposition or in person before?

A. Yes.

Q. How often?

A. Probably 150 times.

Q. Do you ever testify for the defense?

A. No.

Q. Why not?

A. My analysis for the plaintiff is to determine the economic loss sustained by the plaintiff. My work for the defense is to assist in the cross-examination of the plaintiff's economist. As a defense economist I am required to estimate the loss to the plaintiff. This establishes a floor for the economic loss. The defense does not wish to have a high figure from the plaintiff's economist and a low figure from the defendant's economist, since this provides the jury with a high and a low figure for a verdict if the defendant is found at fault.

Q. So, I have asked you to compute the economic loss sustained by Mr. Doe and his family as a result of the accident he sustained on September 1, 1991, and for this you are being compensated. Is that correct?

A. Yes.

§23.05 Direct Examination: The Facts

Examination by plaintiff's attorney:

Q. How does an economic analysis like this begin?

A. First it is necessary to establish certain facts.

Q. What facts do you need?

A. I need to know the client's name, date of birth, race, sex, the date of the accident, and the result of the accident. That is, was the accident fatal or disabling. The analysis also requires knowing the earnings history, educational attainment, marital status, and dates of birth of dependents. If the accident necessitates on-going medical care, it is necessary to know the current cost of the care and when the care will be required in the future.

Q. Were these facts provided to you?

A. Yes.

Q. Who provided the facts?

A. Your office.

Q. And what are the facts in this case?

A. Mr. Doe is a 41-year-old Caucasian male born July 4, 1952. He was permanently disabled in an accident September 1, 1991. He is a high school graduate, married to his first wife and they have no children. His earnings increased from $6.39 per hour in 1988 to $7.50 in 1991, at the time of the accident.

§23.06 Direct Examination: The Time Frame

Examination by plaintiff's attorney:

Q. Using the information provided by my office, you were then able to make an economic forecast concerning the economic loss sustained by Mr. Doe?[1]

A. Yes.

Q. Please explain how the analysis proceeds.

A. In an analysis such as this there are two parts of the economic loss: the historic loss and the future loss. The historic loss is from the date of the accident until today, the date of the trial. The future loss is from today on into the future and in the case of wages would be at Mr. Doe's retirement date.

Q. What do you mean until Mr. Doe retires?

A. When calculating the future loss it is necessary to determine when a loss stops. When the loss stops depends on what type of loss is being estimated. If the loss

---

[1] Rule 703 of the Federal Rules of Evidence permits the expert to base an opinion on facts or data perceived by or made known to him at or before the hearing. Thus, the expert need not testify in response to a hypothetical question given by the attorney given in open court.

of wages is being estimated, then the future loss will terminate at retirement. If the loss being estimated is retirement benefits then the beginning point is the time of retirement. If the loss being calculated is household services then loss will continue through out Mr. Doe's life. The same is true of ongoing medical expenses.

Q. So, the historic loss begins on the date of the accident and continues until today, and the future loss starts today and continues until some date in the future.

A. Yes.

§23.07   Direct Examination: The Historic Loss

Examination by plaintiff's attorney:

Q. When calculating the historic loss, what sort of losses are considered by the economist?

A. The losses which can be calculated by an economist include the loss of wages, the loss of supervisory differential, the loss of the fringe benefits received, the loss resulting from the inability of the injured party to perform household services, and the medical expenses.

Q. In this case what losses were you asked to calculate?

A. I was asked to calculate the economic loss resulting from the lost wages, the lost fringe benefits, and the loss in value of household services.

Q. How do you calculate the historic loss?

A. The calculation of the historic loss begins by establishing the date of the accident, September 1, 1991. After determining the annual income for 1991, I multiply the annual income by the proportion of the year remaining after the accident. For the years 1992 I increased the 1991 earnings by the amount of inflation experienced that year in order to arrive at the 1992 loss. I use the 1992 income lever as the 1993 income and determine what fraction of the year is covered. The 1993 income level is also used to compute the future income level. The fringe benefits are 19.86 per cent of the wages.

The household services are computed the same way using the study published by _____ University.

Q. What is the historic loss of wages?

A. $29,387.

Q. What is the historic loss of fringe benefits?

A. $5,839.

Q. What is the historic loss of household services?

A. $13,633.

Q. The total historic loss is what?

A. $48,859.

Q. Does this loss include medical expenses?

A. No.

Q. Does this loss include pain and suffering or the ability to enjoy life?

A. No.

Q. You said earlier that there were two losses, a historic loss and the present value of the future loss. Is that correct?

A. Yes.

§23.08   Direct Examination: Present Value

Examination by plaintiff's attorney:

Q. Just exactly what is meant by the concept of *present value*?

A. Let me use an example to explain the concept of present value. Suppose the individual is to receive $1,000 one year from today. That individual might be willing to accept something less than $1,000 today. How much less depends on the interest rates and other factors. But the point is $1,000 to be received one year from today has a present value which is less than $1,000. What is attempting to be calculated in a case such as this is how many dollars Mr. Doe needs today in order to provide a stream of income over the remaining time that he would have been in the labor force.

Q. Then if I understand you correctly, the economist is attempting to determine the size of a fund, and this fund would be sufficient to provide an income for Mr. Doe each year until he reaches age 65.

A. Correct.

Q. Is this concept of present value used only in the calculation of the income stream?

A. No. We use the concept of present value to value bonds, stocks, businesses; the value of any stream of money can be estimated in this manner.

Q. Is there a formula which an economist would use to calculate the present value?

A. Yes.

Q. What is that formula?

A. The formula is:
$$\text{Present Value of Future Income} = \$ \sum_{t=0}^{n} [(1+g)^t / (1+d)^t]$$

Q. What are the variables in the formula?

A. There are four variables, dollars represented by the symbol "$"; the growth rate, "g"; the discount rate, "d"; and the time period, "t".

Q. What do each of the symbols represent? (See the following sections.)

§23.09   Direct Examination: The Dollar Amount

Examination by plaintiff's attorney:

A.   The dollar sign represents the current income, current medical expense, or the current value of household services. It is today's value of what we are attempting to estimate.

Q.   When you calculated a dollar loss for Mr. Doe, what was the dollar amount used in the analysis?

A.   There were two different values used in the analysis. When the income was being calculated the dollar amount was $16,070, the current annual income. The other value was $7,453, the current value of household services.

§23.10   Direct Examination: The Time Factor

Examination by plaintiff's attorney:

Q.   What does the letter "t" stand for?

A.   "T" represents time in the analysis.

Q.   What is the time frame?

A.   As the formula indicates, "t" is equal to zero and runs to value "n". "T" increases by increments of 1. Another way to explain it is to say that period "0" is today, period "1" is one year from today, period "2" is two years from today and so on. The wage analysis would run until "n" = 24, when Mr. Doe would be 65 years old.

Q.   So the wage analysis stops at age 65 because you assumed Mr. Doe would retire at age 65. Is that correct?

A.   Yes.

Q.   How large is "t" when the household services are computed?

A.   The value of household services are computed throughout the life of Mr. Doe. The value for "t" would be 58. This would mean the value of Mr. Doe's household services are computed to age 100. However, I must caution that each of these values is mortality adjusted to reflect the probability Mr. Doe will live each successive year.

§23.11   Direct Examination: The Growth Rate

Examination by plaintiff's attorney:

Q.   You have used the symbol "g" in the analysis. What does this represent?

A.   "G" represents the growth rate of wages which Mr. Doe may expect. The growth rate occurs annually.

Q.   On what is the growth rate based?

A.   The growth rate is based on the historic rate of change in the Consumer Price Index (or whatever the economist used).

Q.   In this case what was the growth rate?

A.   The growth rate was 4.30 per cent.

Q.   Per Year?

A.   Yes.

Q.   How does the growth rate affect the present value of the future income?

A.   The larger the growth rate assumed in the analysis, the larger the present value of the future income.

§23.12   Direct Examination: The Discount Rate

Examination by plaintiff's attorney:

Q.   What is the significance of the discount rate?

A.   First, let's explain that the dollar amount, when multiplied by the expression, 1+g, gives a future value. For example, the $16,070 would grow at 4.30 per cent and become $16,761 in one year. It is the discount rate which reduces that future value to present value. The larger the discount rate the smaller the present value.

Q.   What discount rate did you use?

A.   6.05% annually.

Q.   What is the basis for selecting that rate?

A.   This is the average return paid on One-Year Treasury Bills from 1952 through 1992.

Q.   How does the present value change when the interest rate changes?

A.   The larger the interest rate, the smaller the present value.

§23.13   Direct Examination: Growth and Discount Together

Examination by plaintiff's attorney:

Q.   You stated that you have used a growth rate of 4.30 per cent and a discount rate of 6.05 per cent. Is it your belief that the growth rate and interest rate will remain the same each year into the future?

A.   No. What I believe to be correct is that the relationship between the growth rate and interest rate will be maintained. That is, historically we have seen about a 2 per cent difference, spread if you will, between the growth rate and interest rate. I believe the relationship will be maintained.

Q.   How do the growth rate and discount rate interact?

A. The point is, as long as the growth rate and interest rate maintain the same spread, the present value will always be the same. If the growth rate was 8 per cent and the discount rate was 9.8 per cent, the present value will be the same as with a growth rate of 4.30 and a discount of 6.05. It is the spread that is important, the relationship between the two variables.

§23.14 Direct Examination: Present Value of Future Income—Basic Analysis

Examination by plaintiff's attorney:

Q. When I first contacted you to calculate the present value of the loss for Mr. Doe, what did I ask you to calculate?

A. You asked me to calculate the present value of the future wages, fringes, and household services.

Q. What is the present value of each of those?

A. They are: Wages, $320,619; Fringe benefits $63,675; and Household services, $238,081.

Q. What is the total of the present value of the future losses?

A. $622,375.

Q. How was the loss of wages computed?

A. The wages use the basic present value formula. The dollar amount is $16,070, the growth rate is 4.30 per cent, and the discount rate is 6.05 per cent. The time frame is until Mr. Doe reaches age 65. The analysis assumes no uninterrupted work.

Q. How was the value of household services computed?

A. This is what might be referred to as an extended analysis.

§23.15 Direct Examination: Present Value of Future Income—Extended Analysis

Examination by plaintiff's attorney:

A. The extended analysis would expand the number of variables considered in the analysis.

Q. What other factors would be included in the analysis?

A. When computing the present value future income the variables would include the probability of living and the probability of being unemployed, consumption, and taxes.

Q. How would these variables be added to the analysis?

A.   The formula would be:

$$\text{Present Value of Future Income} = \$ \sum_{t=0}^{n} [(1+g)^t/(1+d^t)] * M_a * PE * C * Tx$$

Q.   What are the variables?

A.   The M_a stands for the mortality adjustment, the probability of living, and PE is the probability of being employed.

Q.   How do these variables enter into the analysis?

A.   If the probability of living and employment are included in the analysis of wages, I believe the analysis should extend beyond the traditional retirement age of 65. After all, there is probability of working beyond age 65. In this case if the adjustments are included in the analysis then the present value of future income would increase from $320,619 to $385,075. The one factor that is not included in this analysis is the probability of seeking employment after age 65. It is my opinion that this probability may be included after the individual reaches age 65. In that case the present value would equal $313,024.

Q.   Under the extended analysis how long would Mr. Doe be working?

A.   He would have a statistical probability of working to age 100. While this may sound silly, please realize that the present value of future wages for working from age 65 to 100, with all the adjustments, is $22,767. Also, the present value of future wages for working from age 70 to 100, with all the adjustments, is $12,952.

§23.16   Direct Examination: Probability of Living

Examination by plaintiff's attorney:

Q.   When do you include the probability of living?

A.   The probability of living is used for medical expenses, household services, anything that will continue after the normal retirement age.

Q.   Where do you get the information for the probability of living?

A.   The probability of living is obtained from data published by the U.S. National Center for Health Statistics. The data is published in Statisical Abstracts of the United States.

Q.   How do you use the information?

A.   The information permits the construction of a mortality table for any individual of any given age, sex, and race. The probability of surviving to each future age is computed. The extended analysis takes into consideration the probability of reaching each future age.

§23.17   Direct Examination: Probability of Employment

Examination by plaintiff's attorney:

Q. How do the probabilities of looking for work, seeking employment, and finding work, being employed enter into the analysis?

A. For each age there is a probability that one will look for work, called seeking employment. Another statistic is the probability of being employed. In this case Mr. Doe was employed. Therefore the only relevant statistic is the probability of employment.

Q. Do you ever use the probability of seeking employment?

A. Yes. I think the statistic may be relevant after age 65.

§23.18   Direct Examination: Consumption

Examination by plaintiff's attorney:

Q. In this analysis you also said that consumption could be effective. Has consumption entered into the analysis?

A. It has not.

Q. When does consumption enter into the analysis?

A. If a person is killed then the future income level may be reduced by the amount the individual would have consumed.

Q. Are there times when consumption will be altered when a person is disabled?

A. Yes. A disability may require vehicle modifications, drugs, or therapy.

§23.19   Direct Examination: Household Services

Examination by plaintiff's attorney:

Q. Under the analysis you considered household services. What is the basis for computing the value of household services?

A. The basis in this analysis is the study published by _____ University. The figures presented are 1988 values. I increased them to current values. The study indicates that the value of household services is a function of the age of the youngest child and the number of hours worked outside the home.

Q. What did you use in you analysis?

A. I assumed that Mr. Doe would work full time until age 65 and then retire. I also assume the value of household services for a man with no children is the same as for those whose children are grown.

§23.20   Direct Examination: Taxes

Examination by plaintiff's attorney:

Q. Does the extended analysis allow for the reduction of the present value because of taxes?

A. No.

Q. Why not?

A. The inclusion of taxes actually causes the present value of the losses to increase. The money would have to be invested. The interest would be taxable income. In order to provide the appropriate number of dollars today the present value would have to be increased.

Q. Have you tried to estimate the impact of taxes?

A. No.

Q. Why not?

A. In order to do that it would be necessary to forecast the tax rates of every future year and when the rates change. This would require knowing the feelings of the House and Ways Committee of the House of Representatives. In addition to knowing how the House might act it would be necessary to know what the Doe family plans to do. Will they have a child, children? If so, when? What is the standard deduction going to be? Will they buy a bigger home? How many years will they plan to finance the house? What interest rate, will the interest rate be deductible?

Q. Would you again state the historic loss, the present value of the future loss, and the total loss experienced by the Doe family?

A. The historic loss was $48,859; the future loss is $320,619; and the total loss is $639,478.

Q. No further questions.

§23.21   Cross-Examination: An Overview

The purpose of cross-examining a witness is to discredit the witness. When the witness is an economist there are three areas in which the economist can be attacked; the first area is personal integrity, the second area is the methodology employed by the economist, and the third are is the fact provided to the economist.

If the integrity is to be attacked it must be demonstrated that the economist has a bias favoring the plaintiff, or favoring the size of the award. Is the economist related to the plaintiff? Is his or her fee contingent upon the award?

If the methodology employed is to be attacked, then the methodology must be conceptually incorrect or the method used changes when the type of loss being evaluated changes.

If the defense wishes to attack the methodology, then a defense economist may be necessary. If the method employed has changed over time perhaps the attorney can demonstrate different results using the various methods employed by the economist.

Often defense attorneys retain their own economist in order to assist in what questions to ask during the cross-examination. The most headway can be made when the dollar values are altered. In other words, the "$" amount can be in question. The dollar amount is usually information provided the economist. The values for growth, discount, mortality, etc., are within the economist's "area" and little headway is likely to be made.

§23.22 Cross-Examination: The Introduction

Q. Thank You Mr. Economist. Would you be more comfortable if I called you Mr. or Doctor.?

A. It really doesn't matter.

Q. Well Mr. Economist, I have only a few brief questions.

(The defense attorney will now refer to the witness as "Mr." This is an attempt to reduce the creditability of the witness.)

Q. Have you ever met Mr. Doe?

A. No.

Q. Have you ever met any member of his family?

A. No.

The point being established by the defense attorney is that the economist does not know the individual or any of his family. This means the economist knows nothing of the plaintiff's personal habits unless the information was provided by the plaintiff's attorney. This will permit defense to ask a series of questions about which the economist has no knowledge. It underscores the "statistical package" presented by the economist.

§23.23 Cross-Examination: The Dollar Amount

Q. When you calculated the historic loss did you consider the overtime pay?

A. No.

Q. Do you know if Mr. Doe earned overtime pay?

A. I assumed he was paid for overtime.

Q. I asked, "Do you know if Mr. Doe earned overtime pay?"

A. No.

Q. Where did you get the hourly rate of $7.50 per hour?

A. That was provided by the attorney's office.

Q. Did you know Mr. Doe was injured the second day on the job?

A. No.

Q. Would that affect your analysis? I know it would mine. If Mr. Doe returns to work at the same job, at the same rate and at the same rate of benefits, there would be no loss, would there?

A. No.

Q. If Mr. Doe is able to get any job, the loss would be reduced, wouldn't it?

A. Yes.

Q. You did not consider that possiblity at all did you?

A. No.

Q. Did you consider the possibility that Mr. Doe could be retrained?

A. No.

Q. Had you considered retraining, isn't it possible Mr. Doe could have returned to the labor force with some employment?

Q. In fact with retraining isn't it possible that Mr. Doe would earn more that he earned prior to the accident?

A. Yes.

Q. Assume with me that Mr. Doe is retrained and earns $5.00 per hour. Then the loss would be how much?

A. The loss would be $5,670 per year.

Q. How did you arrive at the $5,670 per year?

A. That is $16,070 per year less the income of $5.00 per hour times 2,080 hours per year. The loss is $5,670.

Q. When did Mr. Doe earn $16,070?

A. He would have earned the money in 1993.

Q. The question was, "When did Mr. Doe earn $16,070?"

A. He did not earn $16,070.

Q. According to your report the most Mr. Doe ever earned in a full year would have been $14,851. And that is $7.14 per hour in 1990 times the 2,080 per hour. Is my math correct, Sir, 2,080 hours times $7.14 is $14,851?

A. Yes.

Q. If Mr. Doe earned $5.00 per hour, or 10,400 per year, then the loss would be $4,451 per year. Right?

A. No. The loss would be . . . .

Q. My question is if you subtract $10,400 from the earnings of Mr. Doe the last year he worked, $14,851, don't you get $4,451?

A. Yes, but . . . .

Q. If you use $4,451 as the basis of the loss, what would happen to the present value of the loss?

A. The loss would be reduced.

Q. How much?

A. $4,451 divided by $16,070 is 27.7 per cent. The present value of $16,070 is $320,619. The present value of $4,451 would be 27.7% of this amount or $88,811.

Q. The loss is $88,811. As I recall you estimated the fringe benefits to be 19.86% of the wage. What would the fringe benefits total?

A. Well, you can't . . . .

Q. Sir, I asked what 19.86% of $88,811 equals.

A. $17,638.

§23.24 Cross-Examination: Household Services

Q. Sir, I would like now to turn to household services. The study you cite, was it done in this city?

A. I believe it was done to reflect the national average.

Q. Is Mr. Doe a national average in your judgment?

A. Well . . . .

Q. What sort of household services does Mr. Doe perform?

A. The services include preparing food, cleaning up after cooking and meals, cleaning both indoors and out, doing laundry, doing indoor and outdoor repairs to home, yard, car, etc.

Q. How many hours a day did Mr. Doe work on household services?

A. I do not know.

Q. What was the hourly rate at which household services were computed?

A. The average hourly rate of pay for household services was $8.33.

Q. Is that a local wage rate?

A. Local to where the study was done, yes.

Q. Does that mean if you paint your house then the value of the painting is based on what a painter would earn?

A. I believe so.

Q. Would you expect Mr. Doe to have all the expertise a professional painter would have?

A. I do not know.

Q. But your analysis assumes that Mr. Doe has the expertise of whatever person is hired. Is this valid? Frankly, doesn't this overstate the value of the services?

A. I don't think so.

Q. Surely you jest.

§23.25 Cross-Examination: The Time Factor

Q. I believe you used a period of 24 years in your analysis.

A. Correct.

Q. That would be starting employment today and continuing uninterrupted until retirement at age 65. Correct?

A. Yes.

Q. There is no place in your report that refers to the nature of Mr. Doe's employment. Were you aware that he worked only seasonally?

A. I was aware that he worked for a contracting firm.

Q. Were you aware of the seasonal nature of Mr. Doe's employment?

A. No.

Q. Did you factor into your analysis the fact that Mr. Doe spent a good portion of the year unemployed?

A. No.

Q. If you considered that Mr. Doe only worked a fraction of the year, would the loss you estimated be increased or decreased?

A. It's hard to say.

Q. But if Mr. Doe only worked, say 80% of the year, then you have overstated the loss by assuming he worked 52 weeks per year. Correct?

A. Yes, but . . . .

Q. Let's consider some other factors. Did you know Mr. Doe smoked?

A. No.

Q. What impact would smoking have on your report?

A. None.

Q. Wouldn't smoking have an effect on life expectancy?

A. Yes, but it would not shorten the life to less than 65 years of age.

Q. But it could, couldn't it? And you did not consider this, did you?

A. No.

Q. Did you know Mr. Doe had heart problems?

Q. Did you know Mr. Doe's family had an unusually short life expectancy?

Q. Did you know Mr. Doe was diabetic?

The questioning is designed to show how little the economist knows about the individual. All the factors mentioned can be used to show a reduced life expectancy.

Q. Are you aware of Mr. Doe's hobbies?

A. No.

Q. Do you think riding a motorcycle is risky?

Q. Do you think skydiving is dangerous?

§23.26 Cross-Examination: The Growth Rate

The goal of the cross-examination is to show that the lower the growth rate the lower the present value will be. The attorney will present alternative growth rates in order to show lower present values.

Q. You used a growth rate of 4.30 per cent in your analysis, didn't you?

A. Yes.

Q. What was the growth rate of wages Mr. Doe had experienced over the last 10 years?

A. I do not know.

Q. Did you know that Mr. Doe had averaged a 3.2 per cent annual increase in wages over the last 10 years?

A. No.

Q. Would that have reduced the size of the loss you estimated if you had used 3.2 per cent?

A. Yes.

Q. How much?

A. It would have reduced the loss to $289,989.

Q. What was the annual loss you used to arrive at $289,989?

A. $16,070.

Q. If you used the amount we agreed on earlier, the $4,451, what would the present value be?

A. The loss would have been $79,489.

Q. Suppose the wages did not grow. What would the present value be?

A. If the growth rate were zero, then the present value would be $212,901.

Q. What is the wage rate used in this analysis?

A. $16,070.

Q. If the wage loss was the $4,451 we agreed on, what would the present value be?

A. $58,969.

§23.27   Cross-Examination: The Discount Factor

The higher the discount rate the lower the present value of the future income stream. The attorney will merely suggest alternative investment vehicles.

Q. You estimated the loss to be $369,478, using a discount rate of 6.05%, correct?

A. Yes.

Q. If the investment had been in a Moody's Aaa bond would the return have been higher or lower than the return you used?

A. Higher.

Q. What would the return have been?

A. For the same time period the return would have been 7.31%.

Q. What would the present value of $4,451 be if the discount rate of 7.31% is used with a growth rate of zero?

A. The present value would be $53,281.

Q. If we could invest in a certificate of deposit yielding 8% what would the present value be?

A. You can not invest in a CD yielding . . . .

Q. What would the present value be if the discount rate or interest rate is 8%?

A. The present value would be $50,613.

A different approach to the investment can be made.

Q. If an award of approximately $770,000 is made, as you indicate in your report is appropriate, and the money is invested at 6.05%, what will be earned annually?

A. $46,585.

Q. This is more than Mr. Doe earned in any previous year. In fact it is nearly 3 times more than Mr. Doe ever earned in one year. Correct?

A. Yes, but . . . .

Q. And the principle would never have to be touched. In other words, when Mr. Doe retires he will have the $770,000 intact.

§23.28 Redirect

Q. In your judgment what was the total economic loss sustained by the Doe family?

A. $369,478. $48,859 historic loss and $320,619 future loss.

Q. Thank you, no further questions.

Appendix A
Growth Factors

Growth Factors

Year	Growth Rates						
	0.00	0.02	0.04	0.06	0.08	0.10	0.12
1	1.000	1.020	1.040	1.060	1.080	1.100	1.120
2	1.000	1.040	1.082	1.124	1.166	1.210	1.254
3	1.000	1.061	1.125	1.191	1.260	1.331	1.405
4	1.000	1.082	1.170	1.262	1.360	1.464	1.574
5	1.000	1.104	1.217	1.338	1.469	1.611	1.762
6	1.000	1.126	1.265	1.419	1.587	1.772	1.974
7	1.000	1.149	1.316	1.504	1.714	1.949	2.211
8	1.000	1.172	1.369	1.594	1.851	2.144	2.476
9	1.000	1.195	1.423	1.689	1.999	2.358	2.773
10	1.000	1.219	1.480	1.791	2.159	2.594	3.106
11	1.000	1.243	1.539	1.898	2.332	2.853	3.479
12	1.000	1.268	1.601	2.012	2.518	3.138	3.896
13	1.000	1.294	1.665	2.133	2.720	3.452	4.363
14	1.000	1.319	1.732	2.261	2.937	3.797	4.887
15	1.000	1.346	1.801	2.397	3.172	4.177	5.474
16	1.000	1.373	1.873	2.540	3.426	4.595	6.130
17	1.000	1.400	1.948	2.693	3.700	5.054	6.866
18	1.000	1.428	2.026	2.854	3.996	5.560	7.690
19	1.000	1.457	2.107	3.026	4.316	6.116	8.613
20	1.000	1.486	2.191	3.207	4.661	6.727	9.646
21	1.000	1.516	2.279	3.400	5.034	7.400	10.804
22	1.000	1.546	2.370	3.604	5.437	8.140	12.100
23	1.000	1.577	2.465	3.820	5.871	8.954	13.552
24	1.000	1.608	2.563	4.049	6.341	9.850	15.179
25	1.000	1.641	2.666	4.292	6.848	10.835	17.000
26	1.000	1.673	2.772	4.549	7.396	11.918	19.040
27	1.000	1.707	2.883	4.822	7.988	13.110	21.325
28	1.000	1.741	2.999	5.112	8.627	14.421	23.884
29	1.000	1.776	3.119	5.418	9.317	15.863	26.750
30	1.000	1.811	3.243	5.743	10.063	17.449	29.960
31	1.000	1.848	3.373	6.088	10.868	19.194	33.555

Growth Factors

				Growth Rates			
Year	0.00	0.02	0.04	0.06	0.08	0.10	0.12
32	1.000	1.885	3.508	6.453	11.737	21.114	37.582
33	1.000	1.922	3.648	6.841	12.676	23.225	42.092
34	1.000	1.961	3.794	7.251	13.690	25.548	47.143
35	1.000	2.000	3.946	7.686	14.785	28.102	52.800
36	1.000	2.040	4.104	8.147	15.968	30.913	59.136
37	1.000	2.081	4.268	8.636	17.246	34.004	66.232
38	1.000	2.122	4.439	9.154	18.625	37.404	74.180
39	1.000	2.165	4.616	9.704	20.115	41.145	83.081
40	1.000	2.208	4.801	10.286	21.725	45.259	93.051
41	1.000	2.252	4.993	10.903	23.462	49.785	104.217
42	1.000	2.297	5.193	11.557	25.339	54.764	116.723
43	1.000	2.343	5.400	12.250	27.367	60.240	130.730
44	1.000	2.390	5.617	12.985	29.556	66.264	146.418
45	1.000	2.438	5.841	13.765	31.920	72.890	163.988
46	1.000	2.487	6.075	14.590	34.474	80.180	183.666
47	1.000	2.536	6.318	15.466	37.232	88.197	205.706
48	1.000	2.587	6.571	16.394	40.211	97.017	230.391
49	1.000	2.639	6.833	17.378	43.427	106.719	258.038
50	1.000	2.692	7.107	18.420	46.902	117.391	289.002
51	1.000	2.745	7.391	19.525	50.654	129.130	323.682
52	1.000	2.800	7.687	20.697	54.706	142.043	362.524
53	1.000	2.856	7.994	21.939	59.083	156.247	406.027
54	1.000	2.913	8.314	23.255	63.809	171.872	454.751
55	1.000	2.972	8.646	24.650	68.914	189.059	509.321
56	1.000	3.031	8.992	26.129	74.427	207.965	570.439
57	1.000	3.092	9.352	27.697	80.381	228.762	638.892
58	1.000	3.154	9.726	29.359	86.812	251.638	715.559
59	1.000	3.217	10.115	31.120	93.757	276.801	801.426
60	1.000	3.281	10.520	32.988	101.257	304.482	897.597
61	1.000	3.347	10.940	34.967	109.358	334.930	1005.309
62	1.000	3.414	11.378	37.065	118.106	368.423	1125.946
63	1.000	3.482	11.833	39.289	127.555	405.265	1261.059
64	1.000	3.551	12.306	41.646	137.759	445.792	1412.386
65	1.000	3.623	12.799	44.145	148.780	490.371	1581.872
66	1.000	3.695	13.311	46.794	160.682	539.408	1771.697
67	1.000	3.769	13.843	49.601	173.537	593.349	1984.301
68	1.000	3.844	14.397	52.577	187.420	652.683	2222.417
69	1.000	3.921	14.973	55.732	202.413	717.952	2489.107
70	1.000	4.000	15.572	59.076	218.606	789.747	2787.800
71	1.000	4.080	16.194	62.620	236.095	868.722	3122.336
72	1.000	4.161	16.842	66.378	254.983	955.594	3497.016
73	1.000	4.244	17.516	70.360	275.381	1051.153	3916.658
74	1.000	4.329	18.217	74.582	297.412	1156.269	4386.657
75	1.000	4.416	18.945	79.057	321.205	1271.895	4913.056
76	1.000	4.504	19.703	83.800	346.901	1399.085	5502.623
77	1.000	4.594	20.491	88.828	374.653	1538.993	6162.937
78	1.000	4.686	21.311	94.158	404.625	1692.893	6902.490
79	1.000	4.780	22.163	99.808	436.995	1862.182	7730.788
80	1.000	4.875	23.050	105.796	471.955	2048.400	8658.483
81	1.000	4.973	23.972	112.144	509.711	2253.240	9697.501
82	1.000	5.072	24.931	118.872	550.488	2478.564	10861.201
83	1.000	5.174	25.928	126.005	594.527	2726.421	12164.545

Growth Factors

Year	0.00	0.02	Growth Rates 0.04	0.06	0.08	0.10	0.12
84	1.000	5.277	26.965	133.565	642.089	2999.063	13624.291
85	1.000	5.383	28.044	141.579	693.456	3298.969	15259.206
86	1.000	5.491	29.165	150.074	748.933	3628.866	17090.310
87	1.000	5.600	30.332	159.078	808.848	3991.753	19141.148
88	1.000	5.712	31.545	168.623	873.555	4390.928	21438.085
89	1.000	5.827	32.807	178.740	943.440	4830.021	24010.656
90	1.000	5.943	34.119	189.465	1018.915	5313.023	26891.934
91	1.000	6.062	35.484	200.832	1100.428	5844.325	30118.966
92	1.000	6.183	36.903	212.882	1188.463	6428.757	33733.242
93	1.000	6.307	38.380	225.655	1283.540	7071.633	37781.231
94	1.000	6.433	39.915	239.195	1386.223	7778.796	42314.979
95	1.000	6.562	41.511	253.546	1497.121	8556.676	47392.777
96	1.000	6.693	43.172	268.759	1616.890	9412.344	53079.910
97	1.000	6.827	44.899	284.885	1746.241	10353.578	59449.499
98	1.000	6.963	46.695	301.978	1885.941	11388.936	66583.439
99	1.000	7.103	48.562	320.096	2036.816	12527.829	74573.452

Appendix B
Discount Factors

Discount Factors

	Interest Rates						
Year	0.00	0.02	0.04	0.06	0.08	0.10	0.12
1	1.000	0.980	0.962	0.943	0.926	0.909	0.893
2	1.000	0.961	0.925	0.890	0.857	0.826	0.797
3	1.000	0.942	0.889	0.840	0.794	0.751	0.712
4	1.000	0.924	0.855	0.792	0.735	0.683	0.636
5	1.000	0.906	0.822	0.747	0.681	0.621	0.567
6	1.000	0.888	0.790	0.705	0.630	0.564	0.507
7	1.000	0.871	0.760	0.665	0.583	0.513	0.452
8	1.000	0.853	0.731	0.627	0.540	0.467	0.404
9	1.000	0.837	0.703	0.592	0.500	0.424	0.361
10	1.000	0.820	0.676	0.558	0.463	0.386	0.322
11	1.000	0.804	0.650	0.527	0.429	0.350	0.287
12	1.000	0.788	0.625	0.497	0.397	0.319	0.257
13	1.000	0.773	0.601	0.469	0.368	0.290	0.229
14	1.000	0.758	0.577	0.442	0.340	0.263	0.205
15	1.000	0.743	0.555	0.417	0.315	0.239	0.183
16	1.000	0.728	0.534	0.394	0.292	0.218	0.163
17	1.000	0.714	0.513	0.371	0.270	0.198	0.146
18	1.000	0.700	0.494	0.350	0.250	0.180	0.130
19	1.000	0.686	0.475	0.331	0.232	0.164	0.116
20	1.000	0.673	0.456	0.312	0.215	0.149	0.104
21	1.000	0.660	0.439	0.294	0.199	0.135	0.093
22	1.000	0.647	0.422	0.278	0.184	0.123	0.083
23	1.000	0.634	0.406	0.262	0.170	0.112	0.074
24	1.000	0.622	0.390	0.247	0.158	0.102	0.066
25	1.000	0.610	0.375	0.233	0.146	0.092	0.059
26	1.000	0.598	0.361	0.220	0.135	0.084	0.053
27	1.000	0.586	0.347	0.207	0.125	0.076	0.047
28	1.000	0.574	0.333	0.196	0.116	0.069	0.042
29	1.000	0.563	0.321	0.185	0.107	0.063	0.037
30	1.000	0.552	0.308	0.174	0.099	0.057	0.033
31	1.000	0.541	0.296	0.164	0.092	0.052	0.030
32	1.000	0.531	0.285	0.155	0.085	0.047	0.027

Discount Factors

			Interest Rates			
Year	0.00	0.02	0.04	0.06	0.08	0.10	0.12
33	1.000	0.520	0.274	0.146	0.079	0.043	0.024
34	1.000	0.510	0.264	0.138	0.073	0.039	0.021
35	1.000	0.500	0.253	0.130	0.068	0.036	0.019
36	1.000	0.490	0.244	0.123	0.063	0.032	0.017
37	1.000	0.481	0.234	0.116	0.058	0.029	0.015
38	1.000	0.471	0.225	0.109	0.054	0.027	0.013
39	1.000	0.462	0.217	0.103	0.050	0.024	0.012
40	1.000	0.453	0.208	0.097	0.046	0.022	0.011
41	1.000	0.444	0.200	0.092	0.043	0.020	0.010
42	1.000	0.435	0.193	0.087	0.039	0.018	0.009
43	1.000	0.427	0.185	0.082	0.037	0.017	0.008
44	1.000	0.418	0.178	0.077	0.034	0.015	0.007
45	1.000	0.410	0.171	0.073	0.031	0.014	0.006
46	1.000	0.402	0.165	0.069	0.029	0.012	0.005
47	1.000	0.394	0.158	0.065	0.027	0.011	0.005
48	1.000	0.387	0.152	0.061	0.025	0.010	0.004
49	1.000	0.379	0.146	0.058	0.023	0.009	0.004
50	1.000	0.372	0.141	0.054	0.021	0.009	0.003
51	1.000	0.364	0.135	0.051	0.020	0.008	0.003
52	1.000	0.357	0.130	0.048	0.018	0.007	0.003
53	1.000	0.350	0.125	0.046	0.017	0.006	0.002
54	1.000	0.343	0.120	0.043	0.016	0.006	0.002
55	1.000	0.337	0.116	0.041	0.015	0.005	0.002
56	1.000	0.330	0.111	0.038	0.013	0.005	0.002
57	1.000	0.323	0.107	0.036	0.012	0.004	0.002
58	1.000	0.317	0.103	0.034	0.012	0.004	0.001
59	1.000	0.311	0.099	0.032	0.011	0.004	0.001
60	1.000	0.305	0.095	0.030	0.010	0.003	0.001
61	1.000	0.299	0.091	0.029	0.009	0.003	0.001
62	1.000	0.293	0.088	0.027	0.008	0.003	0.001
63	1.000	0.287	0.085	0.025	0.008	0.002	0.001
64	1.000	0.282	0.081	0.024	0.007	0.002	0.001
65	1.000	0.276	0.078	0.023	0.007	0.002	0.001
66	1.000	0.271	0.075	0.021	0.006	0.002	0.001
67	1.000	0.265	0.072	0.020	0.006	0.002	0.001
68	1.000	0.260	0.069	0.019	0.005	0.002	0.000
69	1.000	0.255	0.067	0.018	0.005	0.001	0.000
70	1.000	0.250	0.064	0.017	0.005	0.001	0.000
71	1.000	0.245	0.062	0.016	0.004	0.001	0.000
72	1.000	0.240	0.059	0.015	0.004	0.001	0.000
73	1.000	0.236	0.057	0.014	0.004	0.001	0.000
74	1.000	0.231	0.055	0.013	0.003	0.001	0.000
75	1.000	0.226	0.053	0.013	0.003	0.001	0.000
76	1.000	0.222	0.051	0.012	0.003	0.001	0.000
77	1.000	0.218	0.049	0.011	0.003	0.001	0.000
78	1.000	0.213	0.047	0.011	0.002	0.001	0.000
79	1.000	0.209	0.045	0.010	0.002	0.001	0.000
80	1.000	0.205	0.043	0.009	0.002	0.000	0.000
81	1.000	0.201	0.042	0.009	0.002	0.000	0.000
82	1.000	0.197	0.040	0.008	0.002	0.000	0.000
83	1.000	0.193	0.039	0.008	0.002	0.000	0.000
84	1.000	0.189	0.037	0.007	0.002	0.000	0.000

Discount Factors

			Interest Rates				
Year	0.00	0.02	0.04	0.06	0.08	0.10	0.12
85	1.000	0.186	0.036	0.007	0.001	0.000	0.000
86	1.000	0.182	0.034	0.007	0.001	0.000	0.000
87	1.000	0.179	0.033	0.006	0.001	0.000	0.000
88	1.000	0.175	0.032	0.006	0.001	0.000	0.000
89	1.000	0.172	0.030	0.006	0.001	0.000	0.000
90	1.000	0.168	0.029	0.005	0.001	0.000	0.000
91	1.000	0.165	0.028	0.005	0.001	0.000	0.000
92	1.000	0.162	0.027	0.005	0.001	0.000	0.000
93	1.000	0.159	0.026	0.004	0.001	0.000	0.000
94	1.000	0.155	0.025	0.004	0.001	0.000	0.000
95	1.000	0.152	0.024	0.004	0.001	0.000	0.000
96	1.000	0.149	0.023	0.004	0.001	0.000	0.000
97	1.000	0.146	0.022	0.004	0.001	0.000	0.000
98	1.000	0.144	0.021	0.003	0.001	0.000	0.000
99	1.000	0.141	0.021	0.003	0.000	0.000	0.000

Appendix C
Ordinary Annuity

Year 1
Annual Payments
Ordinary Annuity
(Payments at the end of the Year)

Growth Rates
Per Cent

Discount Rate	0%	2%	4%	6%	8%	10%
0%	1.000	1.020	1.040	1.060	1.080	1.100
2%	.980	1.000	1.020	1.039	1.059	1.078
4%	.962	.981	1.000	1.019	1.038	1.058
6%	.943	.962	.981	1.000	1.019	1.038
8%	.926	.944	.963	.981	1.000	1.019
10%	.909	.927	.945	.964	.982	1.000
12%	.893	.911	.929	.946	.964	.982
14%	.877	.895	.912	.930	.947	.965
16%	.862	.879	.897	.914	.931	.948
18%	.847	.864	.881	.898	.915	.932

Year 2
Annual Payments
Ordinary Annuity
(Payments at the end of the Year)

Growth Rates
Per Cent

Discount Rate	0%	2%	4%	6%	8%	10%
0%	2.000	2.060	2.122	2.184	2.246	2.310
2%	1.942	2.000	2.059	2.119	2.180	2.241
4%	1.886	1.943	2.000	2.058	2.117	2.176
6%	1.833	1.888	1.944	2.000	2.057	2.115
8%	1.783	1.836	1.890	1.945	2.000	2.056
10%	1.736	1.787	1.839	1.892	1.946	2.000
12%	1.690	1.740	1.791	1.842	1.894	1.947
14%	1.647	1.695	1.745	1.794	1.845	1.896
16%	1.605	1.652	1.700	1.749	1.798	1.848
18%	1.566	1.612	1.658	1.705	1.753	1.801

Year 3
Annual Payments
Ordinary Annuity
(Payments at the end of the Year)

Growth Rates
Per Cent

Discount Rate	0%	2%	4%	6%	8%	10%
0%	3.000	3.122	3.246	3.375	3.506	3.641
2%	2.884	3.000	3.119	3.242	3.367	3.496
4%	2.775	2.886	3.000	3.117	3.237	3.360
6%	2.673	2.779	2.888	3.000	3.115	3.232
8%	2.577	2.679	2.783	2.890	3.000	3.112
10%	2.487	2.584	2.684	2.787	2.892	3.000
12%	2.402	2.495	2.591	2.690	2.791	2.894
14%	2.322	2.412	2.504	2.598	2.695	2.794
16%	2.246	2.332	2.421	2.512	2.605	2.700
18%	2.174	2.257	2.343	2.430	2.520	2.611

Year 4
Annual Payments
Ordinary Annuity
(Payments at the end of the Year)

Growth Rates
Per Cent

Discount Rate	0%	2%	4%	6%	8%	10%
0%	4.000	4.204	4.416	4.637	4.867	5.105
2%	3.808	4.000	4.200	4.408	4.624	4.848
4%	3.630	3.811	4.000	4.196	4.400	4.611
6%	3.465	3.637	3.815	4.000	4.192	4.392
8%	3.312	3.474	3.643	3.818	4.000	4.189
10%	3.170	3.324	3.483	3.649	3.821	4.000
12%	3.037	3.183	3.335	3.492	3.655	3.825
14%	2.914	3.052	3.196	3.346	3.501	3.661
16%	2.798	2.930	3.067	3.209	3.356	3.509
18%	2.690	2.816	2.946	3.081	3.221	3.366

Year 5
Annual Payments
Ordinary Annuity
(Payments at the end of the Year)

Growth Rates
Per Cent

Discount Rate	0%	2%	4%	6%	8%	10%
0%	5.000	5.308	5.633	5.975	6.336	6.716
2%	4.713	5.000	5.302	5.620	5.955	6.307
4%	4.452	4.719	5.000	5.296	5.607	5.935
6%	4.212	4.462	4.724	5.000	5.290	5.595
8%	3.993	4.226	4.471	4.729	5.000	5.285
10%	3.791	4.009	4.239	4.480	4.734	5.000
12%	3.605	3.810	4.025	4.252	4.489	4.738
14%	3.433	3.626	3.828	4.041	4.264	4.498
16%	3.274	3.456	3.646	3.846	4.056	4.276
18%	3.127	3.298	3.478	3.666	3.864	4.070

Year 6
Annual Payments
Ordinary Annuity
(Payments at the end of the Year)

Growth Rates
Per Cent

Discount Rate	0%	2%	4%	6%	8%	10%
0%	6.000	6.434	6.898	7.394	7.923	8.487
2%	5.601	6.000	6.425	6.880	7.364	7.880
4%	5.242	5.609	6.000	6.417	6.862	7.335
6%	4.917	5.256	5.616	6.000	6.409	6.844
8%	4.623	4.936	5.268	5.623	6.000	6.401
10%	4.355	4.645	4.953	5.281	5.630	6.000
12%	4.111	4.380	4.666	4.970	5.293	5.636
14%	3.889	4.139	4.405	4.687	4.987	5.305
16%	3.685	3.918	4.166	4.428	4.707	5.003
18%	3.498	3.716	3.947	4.192	4.451	4.727

Year 7
Annual Payments
Ordinary Annuity
(Payments at the end of the Year)

Growth Rates
Per Cent

Discount Rate	0%	2%	4%	6%	8%	10%
0%	7.000	7.583	8.214	8.897	9.637	10.436
2%	6.472	7.000	7.571	8.189	8.856	9.577
4%	6.002	6.4,8200001	7.000	7.560	8.164	8.816
6%	5.582	6.019	6.491	7.000	7.549	8.140
8%	5.206	5.606	6.036	6.500	7.000	7.538
10%	4.868	5.234	5.628	6.053	6.509	7.000
12%	4.564	4.900	5.262	5.650	6.068	6.5,1700001
14%	4.288	4.598	4.931	5.288	5.672	6.084
16%	4.039	4.325	4.631	4.960	5.314	5.692
18%	3.812	4.076	4.360	4.664	4.989	5.338

Year 8
Annual Payments
Ordinary Annuity
(Payments at the end of the Year)

**Growth Rates
Per Cent**

Discount Rate	0%	2%	4%	6%	8%	10%
0%	8.000	8.755	9.583	10.491	11.488	12.579
2%	7.325	8.000	8.739	9.549	10.436	11.406
4%	6.733	7.338	8.000	8.724	9.516	10.382
6%	6.210	6.755	7.350	8.000	8.710	9.485
8%	5.747	6.239	6.776	7.361	8.000	8.696
10%	5.335	5.781	6.267	6.796	7.372	8.000
12%	4.968	5.373	5.814	6.294	6.816	7.383
14%	4.639	5.009	5.410	5.847	6.321	6.835
16%	4.344	4.682	5.049	5.447	5.878	6.346
18%	4.078	4.388	4.724	5.088	5.482	5.909

Year 9
Annual Payments
Ordinary Annuity
(Payments at the end of the Year)

**Growth Rates
Per Cent**

Discount Rate	0%	2%	4%	6%	8%	10%
0%	9.000	9.950	11.006	12.181	13.487	14.937
2%	8.162	9.000	9.930	10.963	12.108	13.379
4%	7.435	8.178	9.000	9.911	10.921	12.039
6%	6.802	7.462	8.192	9.000	9.893	10.881
8%	6.247	6.837	7.488	8.207	9.000	9.876
10%	5.759	6.288	6.871	7.513	8.220	9.000
12%	5.328	5.804	6.328	6.903	7.537	8.234
14%	4.946	5.376	5.848	6.366	6.935	7.560
16%	4.607	4.996	5.423	5.891	6.404	6.966
18%	4.303	4.657	5.045	5.469	5.933	6.440

Year 10
Annual Payments
Ordinary Annuity

(Payments at the end of the Year)

Growth Rates
Per Cent

Discount Rate	0%	2%	4%	6%	8%	10%
0%	10.000	11.169	12.486	13.972	15.645	17.531
2%	8.983	10.000	11.144	12.432	13.879	15.507
4%	8.111	9.001	10.000	11.121	12.379	13.791
6%	7.360	8.143	9.019	10.000	11.099	12.329
8%	6.710	7.401	8.173	9.036	10.000	11.077
10%	6.145	6.758	7.441	8.203	9.053	10.000
12%	5.650	6.197	6.804	7.480	8.232	9.069
14%	5.216	5.705	6.247	6.849	7.518	8.260
16%	4.833	5.272	5.759	6.297	6.893	7.554
18%	4.494	4.890	5.328	5.811	6.345	6.936

Year 11
Annual Payments
Ordinary Annuity
(Payments at the end of the Year)

Growth Rates
Per Cent

Discount Rate	0%	2%	4%	6%	8%	10%
0%	11.000	12.412	14.026	15.870	17.977	20.384
2%	9.787	11.000	12.383	13.958	15.755	17.802
4%	8.760	9.809	11.000	12.354	13.894	15.644
6%	7.887	8.798	9.830	11.000	12.327	13.832
8%	7.139	7.935	8.834	9.850	11.000	12.301
10%	6.495	7.194	7.981	8.868	9.870	11.000
12%	5.938	6.554	7.247	8.026	8.902	9.889
14%	5.453	5.999	6.612	7.298	8.069	8.935
16%	5.029	5.515	6.059	6.668	7.349	8.112
18%	4.656	5.092	5.577	6.118	6.723	7.398

Year 12
Annual Payments
Ordinary Annuity
(Payments at the end of the Year)

**Growth Rates
Per Cent**

Discount Rate	0%	2%	4%	6%	8%	10%
0%	12.000	13.680	15.627	17.882	20.495	23.523
2%	10.575	12.000	13.645	15.545	17.740	20.276
4%	9.385	10.601	12.000	13.611	15.467	17.605
6%	8.384	9.428	10.625	12.000	13.578	15.392
8%	7.536	8.438	9.469	10.649	12.000	13.547
10%	6.814	7.598	8.491	9.510	10.672	12.000
12%	6.194	6.880	7.658	8.542	9.549	10.694
14%	5.660	6.263	6.944	7.716	8.592	9.586
16%	5.197	5.729	6.329	7.007	7.773	8.640
18%	4.793	5.266	5.797	6.394	7.068	7.829

Year 13
Annual Payments
Ordinary Annuity
(Payments at the end of the Year)

**Growth Rates
Per Cent**

Discount Rate	0%	2%	4%	6%	8%	10%
0%	13.000	14.974	17.292	20.015	23.215	26.975
2%	11.348	13.000	14.932	17.194	19.842	22.945
4%	9.986	11.378	13.000	14.892	17.100	19.678
6%	8.853	10.034	11.406	13.000	14.854	17.010
8%	7.904	8.914	10.082	11.434	13.000	14.817
10%	7.103	7.972	8.973	10.127	11.460	13.000
12%	6.424	7.176	8.039	9.031	10.172	11.486
14%	5.842	6.498	7.247	8.104	9.087	10.215
16%	5.342	5.917	6.571	7.317	8.168	9.142
18%	4.910	5.416	5.990	6.642	7.384	8.230

Year 14
Annual Payments
Ordinary Annuity
(Payments at the end of the Year)

Growth Rates
Per Cent

Discount Rate	0%	2%	4%	6%	8%	10%
0%	14.000	16.293	19.024	22.276	26.152	30.772
2%	12.106	14.000	16.245	18.907	22.068	25.823
4%	10.563	12.140	14.000	16.198	18.796	21.871
6%	9.295	10.618	12.172	14.000	16.153	18.690
8%	8.244	9.363	10.671	12.203	14.000	16.110
10%	7.367	8.320	9.429	10.723	12.233	14.000
12%	6.628	7.446	8.394	9.494	10.773	12.263
14%	6.002	6.709	7.524	8.466	9.556	10.821
16%	5.468	6.082	6.788	7.600	8.536	9.617
18%	5.008	5.546	6.161	6.865	7.674	8.604

Year 15
Annual Payments
Ordinary Annuity
(Payments at the end of the Year)

Growth Rates
Per Cent

Discount Rate	0%	2%	4%	6%	8%	10%
0%	15.000	17.639	20.825	24.673	29.324	34.950
2%	12.849	15.000	17.583	20.688	24.425	28.927
4%	11.118	12.887	15.000	17.528	20.558	24.190
6%	9.712	11.180	12.924	15.000	17.476	20.433
8%	8.559	9.787	11.239	12.959	15.000	17.426
10%	7.606	8.642	9.860	11.297	12.993	15.000
12%	6.811	7.692	8.723	9.931	11.352	13.026
14%	6.142	6.897	7.776	8.801	10.001	11.407
16%	5.575	6.227	6.982	7.858	8.878	10.068
18%	5.092	5.658	6.311	7.065	7.939	8.953

Year 16
Annual Payments
Ordinary Annuity
(Payments at the end of the Year)

Growth Rates
Per Cent

Discount Rate	0%	2%	4%	6%	8%	10%
0%	16.000	19.012	22.698	27.213	32.750	39.545
2%	13.578	16.000	18.947	22.538	26.921	32.274
4%	11.652	13.620	16.000	18.885	22.387	26.644
6%	10.106	11.720	13.661	16.000	18.825	22.242
8%	8.851	10.188	11.786	13.700	16.000	18.768
10%	7.824	8.941	10.268	11.849	13.738	16.000
12%	6.974	7.916	9.028	10.346	11.911	13.775
14%	6.265	7.066	8.006	9.114	10.422	11.971
16%	5.668	6.355	7.156	8.095	9.197	10.495
18%	5.162	5.756	6.444	7.245	8.181	9.278

Year 17
Annual Payments
Ordinary Annuity
(Payments at the end of the Year)

Growth Rates
Per Cent

Discount Rate	0%	2%	4%	6%	8%	10%
0%	17.000	20.412	24.645	29.906	36.450	44.599
2%	14.292	17.000	20.338	24.462	29.563	35.884
4%	12.166	14.339	17.000	20.267	24.286	29.239
6%	10.477	12.240	14.384	17.000	20.199	24.119
8%	9.122	10.566	12.312	14.428	17.000	20.134
10%	8.022	9.218	10.653	12.382	14.470	17.000
12%	7.120	8.120	9.312	10.738	12.450	14.511
14%	6.373	7.217	8.216	9.404	10.821	12.516
16%	5.749	6.467	7.313	8.311	9.494	10.901
18%	5.222	5.840	6.561	7.407	8.403	9.581

Year 18
Annual Payments
Ordinary Annuity
(Payments at the end of the Year)

**Growth Rates
Per Cent**

Discount Rate	0%	2%	4%	6%	8%	10%
0%	18.000	21.841	26.671	32.760	40.446	50.159
2%	14.992	18.000	21.757	26.460	32.361	39.776
4%	12.659	15.044	18.000	21.676	26.259	31.983
6%	10.828	12.740	15.094	18.000	21.599	26.067
8%	9.372	10.924	12.819	15.142	18.000	21.525
10%	8.201	9.475	11.018	12.895	15.189	18.000
12%	7.250	8.306	9.575	11.109	12.970	15.234
14%	6.467	7.352	8.408	9.674	11.198	13.042
16%	5.818	6.566	7.453	8.508	9.770	11.285
18%	5.273	5.912	6.664	7.552	8.606	9.864

Year 19
Annual Payments
Ordinary Annuity
(Payments at the end of the Year)

**Growth Rates
Per Cent**

Discount Rate	0%	2%	4%	6%	8%	10%
0%	19.000	23.297	28.778	35.786	44.762	56.275
2%	15.678	19.000	23.203	28.537	35.324	43.975
4%	13.134	15.735	19.000	23.112	28.307	34.886
6%	11.158	13.222	15.790	19.000	23.025	28.088
8%	9.604	11.261	13.307	15.843	19.000	22.942
10%	8.365	9.713	11.362	13.390	15.895	19.000
12%	7.366	8.475	9.820	11.460	13.471	15.945
14%	6.550	7.473	8.582	9.925	11.556	13.549
16%	5.877	6.653	7.578	8.688	10.027	11.650
18%	5.316	5.975	6.754	7.682	8.792	10.128

Year 20
Annual Payments
Ordinary Annuity
(Payments at the end of the Year)

Growth Rates
Per Cent

Discount Rate	0%	2%	4%	6%	8%	10%
0%	20.000	24.783	30.969	38.993	49.423	63.002
2%	16.351	20.000	24.677	30.695	38.460	48.502
4%	13.590	16.413	20.000	24.576	30.434	37.956
6%	11.470	13.685	16.473	20.000	24.479	30.186
8%	9.818	11.580	13.777	16.531	20.000	24.386
10%	8.514	9.934	11.688	13.867	16.588	20.000
12%	7.469	8.629	10.047	11.793	13.954	16.642
14%	6.623	7.581	8.742	10.158	11.895	14.039
16%	5.929	6.729	7.691	8.853	10.267	11.996
18%	5.353	6.029	6.834	7.799	8.962	10.373

Year 21
Annual Payments
Ordinary Annuity
(Payments at the end of the Year)

Growth Rates
Per Cent

Discount Rate	0%	2%	4%	6%	8%	10%
0%	21.000	26.299	33.248	42.392	54.457	70.403
2%	17.011	21.000	26.181	32.938	41.782	53.384
4%	14.029	17.079	21.000	26.068	32.643	41.204
6%	11.764	14.131	17.144	21.000	25.959	32.363
8%	10.017	11.881	14.230	17.207	21.000	25.856
10%	8.649	10.139	11.996	14.326	17.268	21.000
12%	7.562	8.769	10.258	12.108	14.420	17.327
14%	6.687	7.678	8.887	10.375	12.217	14.511
16%	5.973	6.797	7.792	9.004	10.490	12.323
18%	5.384	6.076	6.905	7.904	9.118	10.602

Year 22
Annual Payments
Ordinary Annuity
(Payments at the end of the Year)

Growth Rates
Per Cent

Discount Rate	0%	2%	4%	6%	8%	10%
0%	22.000	27.845	35.618	45.996	59.893	78.543
2%	17.658	22.000	27.714	35.269	45.298	58.650
4%	14.451	17.731	22.000	27.588	34.937	44.639
6%	12.042	14.560	17.801	22.000	27.468	34.622
8%	10.201	12.166	14.666	17.870	22.000	27.353
10%	8.772	10.329	12.287	14.769	17.936	22.000
12%	7.645	8.897	10.454	12.405	14.869	18.000
14%	6.743	7.764	9.020	10.577	12.521	14.967
16%	6.011	6.856	7.882	9.141	10.697	12.634
18%	5.410	6.117	6.967	7.999	9.261	10.815

Year 23
Annual Payments
Ordinary Annuity
(Payments at the end of the Year)

Growth Rates
Per Cent

Discount Rate	0%	2%	4%	6%	8%	10%
0%	23.000	29.422	38.083	49.816	65.765	87.497
2%	18.292	23.000	29.277	37.691	49.022	64.328
4%	14.857	18.371	23.000	29.138	37.320	48.272
6%	12.303	14.973	18.447	23.000	29.005	36.966
8%	10.371	12.434	15.086	18.520	23.000	28.878
10%	8.883	10.505	12.562	15.196	18.591	23.000
12%	7.718	9.013	10.636	12.687	15.302	18.660
14%	6.792	7.842	9.141	10.764	12.810	15.406
16%	6.044	6.907	7.963	9.267	10.891	12.929
18%	5.432	6.152	7.022	8.084	9.391	11.014

Year 24
Annual Payments
Ordinary Annuity
(Payments at the end of the Year)

Growth Rates
Per Cent

Discount Rate	0%	2%	4%	6%	8%	10%
0%	24.000	31.030	40.646	53.865	72.106	97.347
2%	18.914	24.000	30.870	40.209	52.964	70.452
4%	15.247	18.998	24.000	30.718	39.793	52.114
6%	12.550	15.370	19.080	24.000	30.571	39.398
8%	10.529	12.688	15.490	19.159	24.000	30.431
10%	8.985	10.668	12.822	15.607	19.235	24.000
12%	7.784	9.119	10.805	12.954	15.720	19.309
14%	6.835	7.911	9.252	10.939	13.083	15.831
16%	6.073	6.953	8.036	9.382	11.071	13.209
18%	5.451	6.182	7.070	8.160	9.510	11.200

Year 25
Annual Payments
Ordinary Annuity
(Payments at the end of the Year)

Growth Rates
Per Cent

Discount Rate	0%	2%	4%	6%	8%	10%
0%	25.000	32.671	43.312	58.156	78.954	108.182
2%	19.523	25.000	32.495	42.825	57.138	77.056
4%	15.622	19.614	25.000	32.327	42.362	56.178
6%	12.783	15.752	19.701	25.000	32.167	41.923
8%	10.675	12.928	15.879	19.785	25.000	32.013
10%	9.077	10.819	13.069	16.003	19.867	25.000
12%	7.843	9.216	10.961	13.207	16.123	19.947
14%	6.873	7.973	9.352	11.101	13.342	16.240
16%	6.097	6.993	8.101	9.487	11.238	13.474
18%	5.467	6.208	7.113	8.228	9.620	11.373

Year 26
Annual Payments
Ordinary Annuity
(Payments at the end of the Year)

Growth Rates
Per Cent

Discount Rate	0%	2%	4%	6%	8%	10%
0%	26.000	34.344	46.084	62.706	86.351	120.100
2%	20.121	26.000	34.152	45.543	61.558	84.178
4%	15.983	20.217	26.000	33.968	45.030	60.477
6%	13.003	16.120	20.310	26.000	33.793	44.543
8%	10.810	13.154	16.254	20.401	26.000	33.625
10%	9.161	10.960	13.301	16.384	20.488	26.000
12%	7.896	9.304	11.107	13.445	16.512	20.573
14%	6.906	8.028	9.444	11.252	13.587	16.635
16%	6.118	7.029	8.160	9.583	11.394	13.725
18%	5.480	6.231	7.150	8.290	9.720	11.534

Year 27
Annual Payments
Ordinary Annuity
(Payments at the end of the Year)

Growth Rates
Per Cent

Discount Rate	0%	2%	4%	6%	8%	10%
0%	27.000	36.051	48.968	67.528	94.339	133.210
2%	20.707	27.000	35.841	48.369	66.238	91.859
4%	16.330	20.809	27.000	35.641	47.801	65.024
6%	13.211	16.474	20.908	27.000	35.449	47.261
8%	10.935	13.367	16.615	21.004	27.000	35.266
10%	9.237	11.090	13.521	16.752	21.097	27.000
12%	7.943	9.384	11.242	13.672	16.886	21.187
14%	6.935	8.078	9.528	11.392	13.819	17.017
16%	6.136	7.060	8.212	9.671	11.539	13.963
18%	5.492	6.250	7.183	8.345	9.811	11.684

Year 28
Annual Payments
Ordinary Annuity
(Payments at the end of the Year)

Growth Rates
Per Cent

Discount Rate	0%	2%	4%	6%	8%	10%
0%	28.000	37.792	51.966	72.640	102.966	147.631
2%	21.281	28.000	37.564	51.305	71.193	100.142
4%	16.663	21.390	28.000	37.346	50.678	69.833
6%	13.406	16.815	21.495	28.000	37.137	50.082
8%	11.051	13.569	16.963	21.597	28.000	36.938
10%	9.307	11.211	13.729	17.107	21.695	28.000
12%	7.984	9.456	11.368	13.886	17.247	21.791
14%	6.961	8.123	9.605	11.522	14.039	17.384
16%	6.152	7.087	8.259	9.751	11.675	14.189
18%	5.502	6.267	7.212	8.395	9.895	11.824

Year 29
Annual Payments
Ordinary Annuity
(Payments at the end of the Year)

Growth Rates
Per Cent

Discount Rate	0%	2%	4%	6%	8%	10%
0%	29.000	39.568	55.085	78.058	112.283	163.494
2%	21.844	29.000	39.320	54.356	76.440	109.075
4%	16.984	21.959	29.000	39.083	53.665	74.920
6%	13.591	17.143	22.070	29.000	38.857	53.010
8%	11.158	13.760	17.297	22.178	29.000	38.640
10%	9.370	11.323	13.926	17.448	22.283	29.000
12%	8.022	9.523	11.484	14.088	17.596	22.384
14%	6.983	8.162	9.674	11.644	14.247	17.739
16%	6.166	7.111	8.301	9.824	11.800	14.404
18%	5.510	6.282	7.238	8.439	9.972	11.955

Year 30
Annual Payments
Ordinary Annuity
(Payments at the end of the Year)

**Growth Rates
Per Cent**

Discount Rate	0%	2%	4%	6%	8%	10%
0%	30.000	41.379	58.328	83.802	122.346	180.943
2%	22.396	30.000	41.110	57.527	81.995	118.708
4%	17.292	22.518	30.000	40.854	56.768	80.300
6%	13.765	17.458	22.635	30.000	40.609	56.048
8%	11.258	13.940	17.620	22.749	30.000	40.374
10%	9.427	11.426	14.112	17.777	22.859	30.000
12%	8.055	9.583	11.593	14.280	17.931	22.967
14%	7.003	8.198	9.738	11.756	14.445	18.082
16%	6.177	7.132	8.339	9.891	11.918	14.607
18%	5.517	6.294	7.261	8.479	10.042	12.077

Year 31
Annual Payments
Ordinary Annuity
(Payments at the end of the Year)

**Growth Rates
Per Cent**

Discount Rate	0%	2%	4%	6%	8%	10%
0%	31.000	43.227	61.701	89.890	133.214	200.138
2%	22.938	31.000	42.936	60.822	87.877	129.097
4%	17.588	23.065	31.000	42.659	59.989	85.990
6%	13.929	17.761	23.189	31.000	42.394	59.201
8%	11.350	14.110	17.930	23.309	31.000	42.140
10%	9.479	11.523	14.287	18.095	23.426	31.000
12%	8.085	9.638	11.693	14.461	18.255	23.539
14%	7.020	8.230	9.796	11.861	14.632	18.412
16%	6.187	7.151	8.373	9.952	12.027	14.800
18%	5.523	6.305	7.280	8.515	10.106	12.190

Year 32
Annual Payments
Ordinary Annuity
(Payments at the end of the Year)

Growth Rates
Per Cent

Discount Rate	0%	2%	4%	6%	8%	10%
0%	32.000	45.112	65.210	96.343	144.951	221.252
2%	23.468	32.000	44.798	64.246	94.106	140.301
4%	17.874	23.603	32.000	44.498	63.335	92.009
6%	14.084	18.053	23.733	32.000	44.212	62.473
8%	11.435	14.270	18.229	23.859	32.000	43.939
10%	9.526	11.612	14.453	18.400	23.982	32.000
12%	8.112	9.689	11.787	14.633	18.568	24.100
14%	7.035	8.258	9.849	11.959	14.809	18.731
16%	6.196	7.167	8.403	10.008	12.128	14.983
18%	5.528	6.315	7.298	8.548	10.165	12.296

Year 33
Annual Payments
Ordinary Annuity
(Payments at the end of the Year)

Growth Rates
Per Cent

Discount Rate	0%	2%	4%	6%	8%	10%
0%	33.000	47.034	68.858	103.184	157.627	244.477
2%	23.989	33.000	46.696	67.805	100.700	152.383
4%	18.148	24.130	33.000	46.373	66.810	98.374
6%	14.230	18.334	24.266	33.000	46.065	65.868
8%	11.514	14.422	18.517	24.399	33.000	45.771
10%	9.569	11.695	14.610	18.695	24.527	33.000
12%	8.135	9.734	11.873	14.796	18.869	24.652
14%	7.048	8.284	9.897	12.049	14.977	19.039
16%	6.203	7.181	8.431	10.059	12.223	15.156
18%	5.532	6.323	7.314	8.577	10.219	12.394

Year 34
Annual Payments
Ordinary Annuity
(Payments at the end of the Year)

Growth Rates
Per Cent

Discount Rate	0%	2%	4%	6%	8%	10%
0%	34.000	48.994	72.652	110.435	171.317	270.024
2%	24.499	34.000	48.631	71.503	107.682	165.413
4%	18.411	24.646	34.000	48.284	70.418	105.108
6%	14.368	18.605	24.789	34.000	47.953	69.391
8%	11.587	14.565	18.794	24.928	34.000	47.638
10%	9.609	11.771	14.759	18.979	25.063	34.000
12%	8.157	9.776	11.954	14.949	19.159	25.194
14%	7.060	8.306	9.941	12.134	15.136	19.336
16%	6.210	7.194	8.455	10.106	12.311	15.320
18%	5.536	6.330	7.327	8.603	10.268	12.486

Year 35
Annual Payments
Ordinary Annuity
(Payments at the end of the Year)

Growth Rates
Per Cent

Discount Rates	0%	2%	4%	6%	8%	10%
0%	35.000	50.994	76.598	118.121	186.102	298.127
2%	24.999	35.000	50.604	75.346	115.075	179.465
4%	18.665	25.153	35.000	50.232	74.165	112.229
6%	14.498	18.865	25.303	35.000	49.877	73.048
8%	11.655	14.701	19.061	25.448	35.000	49.538
10%	9.644	11.843	14.899	19.252	25.589	35.000
12%	8.176	9.814	12.028	15.095	19.439	25.726
14%	7.070	8.327	9.982	12.212	15.287	19.622
16%	6.215	7.205	8.477	10.148	12.393	15.476
18%	5.539	6.336	7.339	8.626	10.313	12.572

Year 36
Annual Payments
Ordinary Annuity
(Payments at the end of the Year)

Growth Rates
Per Cent

Discount Rate	0%	2%	4%	6%	8%	10%
0%	36.000	53.034	80.702	126.268	202.070	329.039
2%	25.489	36.000	52.616	79.340	122.903	194.619
4%	18.908	25.650	36.000	52.217	78.055	119.762
6%	14.621	19.115	25.807	36.000	51.837	76.842
8%	11.717	14.828	19.318	25.958	36.000	51.474
10%	9.677	11.909	15.032	19.516	26.106	36.000
12%	8.192	9.848	12.098	15.233	19.709	26.249
14%	7.079	8.345	10.018	12.285	15.430	19.899
16%	6.220	7.215	8.497	10.187	12.469	15.624
18%	5.541	6.341	7.350	8.647	10.354	12.652

Year 37
Annual Payments
Ordinary Annuity
(Payments at the end of the Year)

Growth Rates
Per Cent

Discount Rate	0%	2%	4%	6%	8%	10%
0%	37.000	55.115	84.970	134.904	219.316	363.043
2%	25.969	37.000	54.667	83.491	131.192	210.962
4%	19.143	26.138	37.000	54.241	82.096	127.729
6%	14.737	19.356	26.301	37.000	53.834	80.779
8%	11.775	14.949	19.565	26.459	37.000	53.446
10%	9.706	11.970	15.158	19.770	26.613	37.000
12%	8.208	9.880	12.162	15.363	19.970	26.763
14%	7.087	8.361	10.052	12.352	15.565	20.165
16%	6.224	7.223	8.514	10.223	12.540	15.764
18%	5.543	6.346	7.359	8.666	10.392	12.726

Year 38
Annual Payments
Ordinary Annuity
(Payments at the end of the Year)

Growth Rates
Per Cent

Discount Rate	0%	2%	4%	6%	8%	10%
0%	38.000	57.237	89.409	144.058	237.941	400.448
2%	26.441	38.000	56.759	87.804	139.968	228.586
4%	19.368	26.616	38.000	56.303	86.292	136.155
6%	14.846	19.588	26.786	38.000	55.869	84.865
8%	11.829	15.063	19.804	26.951	38.000	55.454
10%	9.733	12.027	15.276	20.014	27.111	38.000
12%	8.221	9.908	12.222	15.486	20.221	27.267
14%	7.094	8.376	10.082	12.415	15.693	20.423
16%	6.228	7.231	8.530	10.255	12.607	15.897
18%	5.545	6.350	7.367	8.683	10.427	12.796

Year 39
Annual Payments
Ordinary Annuity
(Payments at the end of the Year)

Growth Rates
Per Cent

Discount Rate	0%	2%	4%	6%	8%	10%
0%	39.000	59.402	94.026	153.762	258.057	441.593
2%	26.903	39.000	58.891	92.287	149.260	247.593
4%	19.584	27.085	39.000	58.405	90.649	145.068
6%	14.949	19.811	27.261	39.000	57.942	89.105
8%	11.879	15.171	20.033	27.433	39.000	57.500
10%	9.757	12.079	15.389	20.250	27.600	39.000
12%	8.233	9.934	12.278	15.603	20.463	27.762
14%	7.100	8.389	10.110	12.474	15.815	20.671
16%	6.231	7.237	8.544	10.285	12.668	16.023
18%	5.547	6.353	7.375	8.699	10.458	12.860

Year 40
Annual Payments
Ordinary Annuity
(Payments at the end of the Year)

Growth Rates
Per Cent

Discount Rate	0%	2%	4%	6%	8%	10%
0%	40.000	61.610	98.827	164.048	279.781	486.852
2%	27.355	40.000	61.065	96.945	159.099	268.090
4%	19.793	27.545	40.000	60.547	95.174	154.495
6%	15.046	20.026	27.728	40.000	60.054	93.506
8%	11.925	15.272	20.254	27.907	40.000	59.583
10%	9.779	12.128	15.495	20.478	28.080	40.000
12%	8.244	9.958	12.329	15.714	20.696	28.248
14%	7.105	8.401	10.136	12.528	15.930	20.911
16%	6.233	7.243	8.557	10.312	12.726	16.142
18%	5.548	6.356	7.381	8.712	10.487	12.921

Year 41
Annual Payments
Ordinary Annuity
(Payments at the end of the Year)

Growth Rates
Per Cent

Discount Rate	0%	2%	4%	6%	8%	10%
0%	41.000	63.862	103.820	174.951	303.244	536.637
2%	27.799	41.000	63.282	101.786	169.516	290.196
4%	19.993	27.996	41.000	62.731	99.873	164.466
6%	15.138	20.232	28.186	41.000	62.206	98.072
8%	11.967	15.368	20.467	28.371	41.000	61.705
10%	9.799	12.173	15.595	20.697	28.551	41.000
12%	8.253	9.980	12.377	15.818	20.921	28.726
14%	7.110	8.411	10.159	12.579	16.039	21.142
16%	6.236	7.248	8.568	10.337	12.779	16.256
18%	5.549	6.359	7.387	8.725	10.514	12.977

Year 42
Annual Payments
Ordinary Annuity
(Payments at the end of the Year)

Growth Rates
Per Cent

Discount Rate	0%	2%	4%	6%	8%	10%
0%	42.000	66.159	109.012	186.508	328.583	591.401
2%	28.235	42.000	65.543	106.817	180.547	314.034
4%	20.186	28.438	42.000	64.957	104.753	175.012
6%	15.225	20.431	28.635	42.000	64.398	102.810
8%	12.007	15.459	20.672	28.827	42.000	63.866
10%	9.817	12.215	15.690	20.908	29.014	42.000
12%	8.262	9.999	12.422	15.917	21.139	29.195
14%	7.114	8.420	10.180	12.626	16.142	21.365
16%	6.238	7.253	8.578	10.360	12.829	16.363
18%	5.550	6.361	7.392	8.736	10.538	13.029

Year 43
Annual Payments
Ordinary Annuity
(Payments at the end of the Year)

Growth Rates
Per Cent

Discount Rate	0%	2%	4%	6%	8%	10%
0%	43.000	68.503	114.413	198.758	355.950	651.641
2%	28.662	43.000	67.848	112.045	192.226	339.743
4%	20.371	28.872	43.000	67.225	109.821	186.167
6%	15.306	20.623	29.076	43.000	66.632	107.728
8%	12.043	15.544	20.869	29.275	43.000	66.067
10%	9.834	12.254	15.779	21.111	29.468	43.000
12%	8.270	10.017	12.463	16.011	21.348	29.656
14%	7.117	8.429	10.199	12.670	16.240	21.580
16%	6.239	7.257	8.587	10.380	12.875	16.465
18%	5.551	6.363	7.396	8.746	10.560	13.078

Year 44
Annual Payments
Ordinary Annuity
(Payments at the end of the Year)

Growth Rates
Per Cent

Discount Rate	0%	2%	4%	6%	8%	10%
0%	44.000	70.893	120.029	211.744	385.506	717.905
2%	29.080	44.000	70.198	117.478	204.592	367.468
4%	20.549	29.297	44.000	69.537	115.083	197.965
6%	15.383	20.807	29.509	44.000	68.908	112.831
8%	12.077	15.625	21.059	29.714	44.000	68.309
10%	9.849	12.290	15.864	21.307	29.914	44.000
12%	8.276	10.033	12.501	16.100	21.550	30.109
14%	7.120	8.436	10.217	12.711	16.332	21.788
16%	6.241	7.260	8.596	10.399	12.918	16.562
18%	5.552	6.365	7.400	8.754	10.581	13.124

Year 45
Annual Payments
Ordinary Annuity
(Payments at the end of the Year)

Growth Rates
Per Cent

Discount Rate	0%	2%	4%	6%	8%	10%
0%	45.000	73.331	125.871	225.508	417.426	790.795
2%	29.490	45.000	72.594	123.124	217.686	397.367
4%	20.720	29.715	45.000	71.893	120.548	210.443
6%	15.456	20.984	29.933	45.000	71.227	118.126
8%	12.108	15.702	21.242	30.146	45.000	70.593
10%	9.863	12.324	15.944	21.496	30.352	45.000
12%	8.283	10.048	12.537	16.184	21.744	30.553
14%	7.123	8.443	10.233	12.749	16.420	21.988
16%	6.242	7.263	8.603	10.417	12.958	16.653
18%	5.552	6.366	7.403	8.763	10.599	13.166

Year 46
Annual Payments
Ordinary Annuity
(Payments at the end of the Year)

**Growth Rates
Per Cent**

Discount Rate	0%	2%	4%	6%	8%	10%
0%	46.000	75.817	131.945	240.099	451.900	870.975
2%	29.892	46.000	75.037	128.992	231.550	429.612
4%	20.885	30.124	46.000	74.295	126.223	223.642
6%	15.524	21.154	30.350	46.000	73.590	123.622
8%	12.137	15.774	21.418	30.569	46.000	72.919
10%	9.875	12.355	16.020	21.678	30.782	46.000
12%	8.288	10.062	12.570	16.263	21.932	30.990
14%	7.126	8.449	10.248	12.784	16.503	22.182
16%	6.243	7.266	8.610	10.432	12.996	16.740
18%	5.553	6.367	7.406	8.770	10.616	13.206

Year 47
Annual Payments
Ordinary Annuity
(Payments at the end of the Year)

**Growth Rates
Per Cent**

Discount Rate	0%	2%	4%	6%	8%	10%
0%	47.000	78.354	138.263	255.565	489.132	959.172
2%	30.287	47.000	77.528	135.090	246.229	464.385
4%	21.043	30.526	47.000	76.743	132.116	237.602
6%	15.589	21.318	30.758	47.000	75.997	129.324
8%	12.164	15.842	21.588	30.984	47.000	75.287
10%	9.887	12.383	16.092	21.853	31.204	47.000
12%	8.293	10.074	12.601	16.338	22.113	31.418
14%	7.128	8.454	10.261	12.816	16.582	22.368
16%	6.244	7.268	8.616	10.447	13.030	16.823
18%	5.553	6.368	7.409	8.776	10.632	13.243

Year 48
Annual Payments
Ordinary Annuity
(Payments at the end of the Year)

Growth Rates
Per Cent

Discount Rate	0%	2%	4%	6%	8%	10%
0%	48.000	80.941	144.834	271.958	529.343	1,056.190
2%	30.673	48.000	80.067	141.426	261.772	501.886
4%	21.195	30.919	48.000	79.238	138.236	252.368
6%	15.650	21.476	31.159	48.000	78.450	135.242
8%	12.189	15.906	21.752	31.392	48.000	77.700
10%	9.897	12.410	16.159	22.022	31.619	48.000
12%	8.297	10.085	12.629	16.410	22.288	31.840
14%	7.130	8.459	10.273	12.847	16.657	22.548
16%	6.245	7.271	8.621	10.460	13.063	16.901
18%	5.554	6.369	7.411	8.782	10.646	13.277

Year 49
Annual Payments
Ordinary Annuity
(Payments at the end of the Year)

Growth Rates
Per Cent

Discount Rate	0%	2%	4%	6%	8%	10%
0%	49.000	83.579	151.667	289.336	572.770	1,162.909
2%	31.052	49.000	82.657	148.012	278.229	542.328
4%	21.341	31.306	49.000	81.781	144.591	267.985
6%	15.708	21.628	31.552	49.000	80.949	141.383
8%	12.212	15.967	21.909	31.792	49.000	80.158
10%	9.906	12.435	16.223	22.185	32.026	49.000
12%	8.301	10.096	12.656	16.477	22.456	32.253
14%	7.131	8.463	10.284	12.875	16.727	22.722
16%	6.246	7.272	8.626	10.472	13.093	16.975
18%	5.554	6.370	7.413	8.787	10.659	13.309

Year 50
Annual Payments
Ordinary Annuity
(Payments at the end of the Year)

Growth Rates
Per Cent

Discount Rate	0%	2%	4%	6%	8%	10%
0%	50.000	86.271	158.774	307.756	619.672	1,280.299
2%	31.424	50.000	85.297	154.855	295.655	585.942
4%	21.482	31.684	50.000	84.373	151.191	284.504
6%	15.762	21.774	31.938	50.000	83.495	147.756
8%	12.233	16.024	22.060	32.185	50.000	82.660
10%	9.915	12.458	16.284	22.342	32.425	50.000
12%	8.304	10.105	12.680	16.541	22.618	32.659
14%	7.133	8.467	10.294	12.901	16.794	22.890
16%	6.246	7.274	8.630	10.483	13.121	17.045
18%	5.554	6.371	7.415	8.792	10.671	13.339

Year 51
Annual Payments
Ordinary Annuity
(Payments at the end of the Year)

Growth Rates
Per Cent

Discount Rate	0%	2%	4%	6%	8%	10%
0%	51.000	89.016	166.165	327.281	670.326	1,409.429
2%	31.788	51.000	87.989	161.967	314.105	632.977
4%	21.617	32.056	51.000	87.015	158.044	301.975
6%	15.813	21.914	32.316	51.000	86.090	154.370
8%	12.253	16.079	22.206	32.570	51.000	85.210
10%	9.923	12.479	16.341	22.493	32.817	51.000
12%	8.308	10.113	12.703	16.601	22.775	33.058
14%	7.134	8.471	10.304	12.926	16.858	23.052
16%	6.247	7.275	8.634	10.493	13.147	17.112
18%	5.554	6.371	7.417	8.796	10.682	13.367

Year 52
Annual Payments
Ordinary Annuity
(Payments at the end of the Year)

Growth Rates
Per Cent

Discount Rate	0%	2%	4%	6%	8%	10%
0%	52.000	91.817	173.851	347.978	725.032	1,551.472
2%	32.145	52.000	90.734	169.358	333.640	683.701
4%	21.748	32.420	52.000	89.708	165.161	320.454
6%	15.861	22.050	32.688	52.000	88.733	161.233
8%	12.272	16.130	22.347	32.949	52.000	87.806
10%	9.930	12.499	16.395	22.639	33.203	52.000
12%	8.310	10.121	12.724	16.658	22.926	33.450
14%	7.135	8.474	10.312	12.949	16.918	23.208
16%	6.247	7.277	8.637	10.502	13.171	17.175
18%	5.555	6.372	7.418	8.800	10.692	13.393

Year 53
Annual Payments
Ordinary Annuity
(Payments at the end of the Year)

Growth Rates
Per Cent

Discount Rate	0%	2%	4%	6%	8%	10%
0%	53.000	94.673	181.845	369.917	784.114	1,707.720
2%	32.495	53.000	93.533	177.039	354.325	738.403
4%	21.873	32.777	53.000	92.452	172.552	340.000
6%	15.907	22.180	33.052	53.000	91.426	168.355
8%	12.288	16.178	22.482	33.320	53.000	90.451
10%	9.936	12.517	16.447	22.779	33.581	53.000
12%	8.313	10.128	12.744	16.712	23.071	33.835
14%	7.136	8.477	10.320	12.970	16.975	23.358
16%	6.248	7.278	8.640	10.511	13.194	17.235
18%	5.555	6.372	7.419	8.803	10.701	13.417

Year 54
Annual Payments
Ordinary Annuity
(Payments at the end of the Year)

Growth Rates
Per Cent

Discount Rate	0%	2%	4%	6%	8%	10%
0%	54.000	97.587	190.159	393.172	847.923	1,879.591
2%	32.838	54.000	96.386	185.021	376.227	797.395
4%	21.993	33.128	54.000	95.249	180.227	360.673
6%	15.950	22.305	33.410	54.000	94.170	175.746
8%	12.304	16.224	22.612	33.684	54.000	93.144
10%	9.942	12.534	16.495	22.914	33.952	54.000
12%	8.315	10.135	12.762	16.763	23.211	34.213
14%	7.137	8.479	10.327	12.989	17.029	23.504
16%	6.248	7.279	8.643	10.519	13.215	17.292
18%	5.555	6.373	7.420	8.806	10.709	13.440

Year 55
Annual Payments
Ordinary Annuity
(Payments at the end of the Year)

Growth Rates
Per Cent

Discount Rate	0%	2%	4%	6%	8%	10%
0%	55.000	100.558	198.806	417.822	916.837	2,068.651
2%	33.175	55.000	99.296	193.316	399.416	861.014
4%	22.109	33.471	55.000	98.100	188.197	382.538
6%	15.991	22.426	33.760	55.000	96.966	183.415
8%	12.319	16.267	22.738	34.042	55.000	95.888
10%	9.947	12.550	16.541	23.045	34.316	55.000
12%	8.317	10.140	12.779	16.812	23.347	34.584
14%	7.138	8.481	10.333	13.008	17.080	23.644
16%	6.248	7.280	8.645	10.526	13.235	17.346
18%	5.555	6.373	7.421	8.809	10.717	13.461

Year 56
Annual Payments
Ordinary Annuity
(Payments at the end of the Year)

Growth Rates
Per Cent

Discount Rate	0%	2%	4%	6%	8%	10%
0%	56.000	103.589	207.798	443.952	991.264	2,276.616
2%	33.505	56.000	102.263	201.936	423.970	929.623
4%	22.220	33.809	56.000	101.006	196.474	405.666
6%	16.029	22.542	34.105	56.000	99.814	191.374
8%	12.332	16.308	22.859	34.393	56.000	98.682
10%	9.952	12.564	16.584	23.170	34.674	56.000
12%	8.319	10.146	12.795	16.857	23.477	34.949
14%	7.138	8.483	10.339	13.025	17.128	23.779
16%	6.248	7.280	8.648	10.532	13.253	17.397
18%	5.555	6.373	7.422	8.812	10.724	13.480

Year 57
Annual Payments
Ordinary Annuity
(Payments at the end of the Year)

Growth Rates
Per Cent

Discount Rate	0%	2%	4%	6%	8%	10%
0%	57.000	106.681	217.150	471.649	1,071.645	2,505.377
2%	33.828	57.000	105.287	210.894	449.969	1,003.613
4%	22.327	34.139	57.000	103.968	205.069	430.127
6%	16.065	22.653	34.442	57.000	102.716	199.634
8%	12.344	16.346	22.975	34.738	57.000	101.528
10%	9.956	12.578	16.625	23.292	35.026	57.000
12%	8.320	10.151	12.810	16.901	23.603	35.307
14%	7.139	8.485	10.344	13.041	17.174	23.910
16%	6.249	7.281	8.650	10.538	13.270	17.445
18%	5.555	6.373	7.423	8.814	10.731	13.499

Year 58
Annual Payments
Ordinary Annuity
(Payments at the end of the Year)

Growth Rates
Per Cent

Discount Rate	0%	2%	4%	6%	8%	10%
0%	58.000	109.835	226.876	501.008	1,158.457	2,757.015
2%	34.145	58.000	108.371	220.204	477.496	1,083.406
4%	22.430	34.463	58.000	106.986	213.995	456.000
6%	16.099	22.761	34.774	58.000	105.673	208.205
8%	12.356	16.382	23.087	35.076	58.000	104.427
10%	9.960	12.590	16.663	23.408	35.371	58.000
12%	8.322	10.155	12.823	16.942	23.724	35.658
14%	7.139	8.487	10.349	13.055	17.218	24.036
16%	6.249	7.282	8.651	10.543	13.286	17.491
18%	5.555	6.374	7.424	8.816	10.736	13.516

Year 59
Annual Payments
Ordinary Annuity
(Payments at the end of the Year)

Growth Rates
Per Cent

Discount Rate	0%	2%	4%	6%	8%	10%
0%	59.000	113.052	236.991	532.128	1,252.213	3,033.816
2%	34.456	59.000	111.516	229.879	506.643	1,169.458
4%	22.528	34.781	59.000	110.063	223.264	483.365
6%	16.131	22.864	35.099	59.000	108.686	217.099
8%	12.367	16.417	23.195	35.408	59.000	107.379
10%	9.964	12.602	16.700	23.521	35.709	59.000
12%	8.323	10.159	12.836	16.981	23.841	36.004
14%	7.140	8.488	10.354	13.069	17.259	24.157
16%	6.249	7.282	8.653	10.548	13.301	17.535
18%	5.555	6.374	7.424	8.818	10.742	13.532

Year 60
Annual Payments
Ordinary Annuity
(Payments at the end of the Year)

Growth Rates
Per Cent

Discount Rate	0%	2%	4%	6%	8%	10%
0%	60.000	116.333	247.510	565.116	1,353.470	3,338.298
2%	34.761	60.000	114.722	239.933	537.504	1,262.258
4%	22.623	35.093	60.000	113.199	232.890	512.309
6%	16.161	22.964	35.417	60.000	111.755	226.329
8%	12.377	16.449	23.299	35.734	60.000	110.386
10%	9.967	12.613	16.734	23.629	36.042	60.000
12%	8.324	10.163	12.848	17.017	23.954	36.343
14%	7.140	8.489	10.358	13.082	17.298	24.274
16%	6.249	7.282	8.654	10.553	13.315	17.576
18%	5.555	6.374	7.425	8.819	10.747	13.546

Year 61
Annual Payments
Ordinary Annuity
(Payments at the end of the Year)

Growth Rates
Per Cent

Discount Rate	0%	2%	4%	6%	8%	10%
0%	61.000	119.679	258.451	600.083	1,462.828	3,673.228
2%	35.060	61.000	117.991	250.381	570.181	1,362.337
4%	22.715	35.399	61.000	116.395	242.885	542.923
6%	16.190	23.059	35.730	61.000	114.883	235.908
8%	12.386	16.480	23.399	36.053	61.000	113.449
10%	9.970	12.623	16.767	23.733	36.369	61.000
12%	8.325	10.166	12.859	17.052	24.063	36.676
14%	7.140	8.490	10.362	13.093	17.335	24.388
16%	6.249	7.283	8.656	10.557	13.327	17.615
18%	5.555	6.374	7.425	8.821	10.751	13.560

Year 62
Annual Payments
Ordinary Annuity
(Payments at the end of the Year)

Growth Rates
Per Cent

Discount Rate	0%	2%	4%	6%	8%	10%
0%	62.000	123.093	269.829	637.148	1,580.934	4,041.651
2%	35.353	62.000	121.324	261.239	604.780	1,470.266
4%	22.803	35.699	62.000	119,652	253.265	575.304
6%	16.217	23.152	36.037	62.000	118.069	245.848
8%	12.394	16.509	23.495	36.367	62.000	116.568
10%	9.973	12.632	16.798	23.834	36.689	62.000
12%	8.326	10.169	12.869	17.085	24.168	37.003
14%	7.141	8.491	10.365	13.104	17.370	24.497
16%	6.249	7.283	8.657	10.560	13.339	17.652
18%	5.555	6.374	7.426	8.822	10.755	13.573

Year 63
Annual Payments
Ordinary Annuity
(Payments at the end of the Year)

Growth Rates
Per Cent

Discount Rate	0%	2%	4%	6%	8%	10%
0%	63.000	126.575	281.662	676.437	1,708.489	4,446.916
2%	35.640	63.000	124.723	272.523	641.414	1,586.659
4%	22.887	35.993	63.000	122.973	264.045	609.552
6%	16.242	23.240	36.338	63.000	121.316	256.163
8%	12.402	16.536	23.588	36.675	63.000	119.745
10%	9.975	12.640	16.827	23.931	37.004	63.000
12%	8.327	10.172	12.878	17.116	24.269	37.325
14%	7.141	8.492	10.368	13.115	17.403	24.602
16%	6.249	7.284	8.658	10.564	13.350	17.687
18%	5.555	6.374	7.426	8.823	10.759	13.585

Year 64
Annual Payments
Ordinary Annuity
(Payments at the end of the Year)

**Growth Rates
Per Cent**

Discount Rate	0%	2%	4%	6%	8%	10%
0%	64.000	130.126	293.968	718.083	1,846.248	4,892.707
2%	35.921	64.000	128.188	284.249	680.203	1,712.181
4%	22.969	36.282	64.000	126.357	275.239	645.776
6%	16.266	23.325	36.634	64.000	124.624	266.867
8%	12.409	16.562	23.677	36.977	64.000	122.981
10%	9.978	12.648	16.855	24.024	37.313	64.000
12%	8.327	10.174	12.887	17.146	24.367	37.640
14%	7.141	8.493	10.371	13.124	17.434	24.704
16%	6.250	7.284	8.659	10.567	13.361	17.721
18%	5.555	6.374	7.426	8.824	10.763	13.596

Year 65
Annual Payments
Ordinary Annuity
(Payments at the end of the Year)

**Growth Rates
Per Cent**

Discount Rate	0%	2%	4%	6%	8%	10%
0%	65.000	133.749	306.767	762.228	1,995.028	5,383.078
2%	36.197	65.000	131.721	296.436	721.274	1,847.549
4%	23.047	36.565	65.000	129.806	286.864	684.090
6%	16.289	23.407	36.924	65.000	127.994	277.975
8%	12.416	16.586	23.763	37.274	65.000	126.277
10%	9.980	12.656	16.881	24.114	37.616	65.000
12%	8.328	10.177	12.895	17.174	24.461	37.950
14%	7.141	8.494	10.373	13.133	17.464	24.802
16%	6.250	7.284	8.660	10.570	13.370	17.753
18%	5.555	6.375	7.427	8.825	10.766	13.607

Year 66
Annual Payments
Ordinary Annuity
(Payments at the end of the Year)

Growth Rates
Per Cent

Discount Rate	0%	2%	4%	6%	8%	10%
0%	66.000	137.444	320.078	809.022	2,155.710	5,922.486
2%	36.468	66.000	135.324	309.100	764.761	1,993.533
4%	23.122	36.843	66.000	133.321	298.935	724.614
6%	16.310	23.486	37.208	66.000	131.428	289.503
8%	12.422	16.609	23.846	37.565	66.000	129.634
10%	9.981	12.663	16.906	24.201	37.914	66.000
12%	8.329	10.179	12.902	17.200	24.551	38.255
14%	7.142	8.494	10.376	13.141	17.492	24.897
16%	6.250	7.284	8.660	10.572	13.379	17.783
18%	5.555	6.375	7.427	8.826	10.769	13.616

Year 67
Annual Payments
Ordinary Annuity
(Payments at the end of the Year)

Growth Rates
Per Cent

Discount Rate	0%	2%	4%	6%	8%	10%
0%	67.000	141.213	333.921	858.623	2,329.247	6,515.835
2%	36.733	67.000	138.997	322.261	810.805	2,150.967
4%	23.194	37.115	67.000	136.904	311.471	767.477
6%	16.331	23.562	37.487	67.000	134.926	301.465
8%	12.428	16.631	23.926	37.851	67.000	133.053
10%	9.983	12.669	16.929	24.285	38.207	67.000
12%	8.329	10.181	12.909	17.225	24.639	38.554
14%	7.142	8.495	10.378	13.149	17.519	24.988
16%	6.250	7.284	8.661	10.575	13.388	17.811
18%	5.555	6.375	7.427	8.827	10.771	13.625

Year 68
Annual Payments
Ordinary Annuity
(Payments at the end of the Year)

Growth Rates
Per Cent

Discount Rate	0%	2%	4%	6%	8%	10%
0%	68.000	145.057	348.318	911.200	2,516.667	7,168.518
2%	36.994	68.000	142.742	335.937	859.559	2,320.749
4%	23.264	37.382	68.000	140.556	324.489	812.812
6%	16.350	23.636	37.761	68.000	138.491	313.879
8%	12.433	16.651	24.003	38.132	68.000	136.536
10%	9.985	12.675	16.951	24.365	38.494	68.000
12%	8.330	10.182	12.916	17.249	24.723	38.848
14%	7.142	8.496	10.380	13.156	17.544	25.076
16%	6.250	7.285	8.662	10.577	13.395	17.838
18%	5.555	6.375	7.427	8.827	10.774	13.634

Year 69
Annual Payments
Ordinary Annuity
(Payments at the end of the Year)

Growth Rates
Per Cent

Discount Rate	0%	2%	4%	6%	8%	10%
0%	69.000	148.978	363.290	966.932	2,719.080	7,886.470
2%	37.249	69.000	146.560	350.151	911.180	2,503.846
4%	23.330	37.644	69.000	144.279	338.008	860.763
6%	16.368	23.706	38.030	69.000	142.123	326.761
8%	12.438	16.671	24.077	38.407	69.000	140.083
10%	9.986	12.680	16.972	24.443	38.776	69.000
12%	8.330	10.184	12.922	17.271	24.804	39.136
14%	7.142	8.496	10.382	13.163	17.568	25.161
16%	6.250	7.285	8.662	10.579	13.403	17.864
18%	5.555	6.375	7.427	8.828	10.776	13.642

Year 70
Annual Payments
Ordinary Annuity
(Payments at the end of the Year)

Growth Rates
Per Cent

Discount Rate	0%	2%	4%	6%	8%	10%
0%	70.000	152.977	378.862	1,026.008	2,937.687	8,676.217
2%	37.499	70.000	150.453	364.921	965.837	2,701.305
4%	23.395	37.901	70.000	148.073	352.047	911.480
6%	16.385	23.774	38.294	70.000	145.823	340.129
8%	12.443	16.689	24.148	38.677	70.000	143.695
10%	9.987	12.685	16.992	24.518	39.052	70.000
12%	8.330	10.185	12.927	17.292	24.883	39.419
14%	7.142	8.496	10.383	13.169	17.591	25.243
16%	6.250	7.285	8.663	10.581	13.409	17.888
18%	5.556	6.375	7.427	8.828	10.778	13.649

Year 71
Annual Payments
Ordinary Annuity
(Payments at the end of the Year)

Growth Rates
Per Cent

Discount Rate	0%	2%	4%	6%	8%	10%
0%	71.000	157.057	395.057	1,088.629	3,173.781	9,544.939
2%	37.744	71.000	154.423	380.271	1,023.710	2,914.251
4%	23.456	38.153	71.000	151.939	366.626	965.123
6%	16.401	23.839	38.552	71.000	149.594	354.002
8%	12.447	16.706	24.217	38.943	71.000	147.375
10%	9.988	12.690	17.010	24.590	39.324	71.000
12%	8.331	10.187	12.933	17.312	24.958	39.697
14%	7.142	8.497	10.385	13.174	17.613	25.322
16%	6.250	7.285	8.663	10.582	13.415	17.911
18%	5.556	6.375	7.428	8.829	10.780	13.656

Year 72
Annual Payments
Ordinary Annuity
(Payments at the end of the Year)

Growth Rates
Per Cent

Discount Rate	0%	2%	4%	6%	8%	10%
0%	72.000	161.218	411.899	1,155.006	3,428.764	10,500.532
2%	37.984	72.000	158.471	396.223	1,084.987	3,143.898
4%	23.516	38.400	72.000	155.880	381.765	1,021.861
6%	16.416	23.901	38.806	72.000	153.435	368.398
8%	12.451	16.723	24.283	39.203	72.000	151.123
10%	9.990	12.694	17.028	24.659	39.591	72.000
12%	8.331	10.188	12.937	17.331	25.031	39.971
14%	7.142	8.497	10.386	13.180	17.633	25.399
16%	6.250	7.285	8.663	10.584	13.421	17.933
18%	5.556	6.375	7.428	8.829	10.782	13.662

Year 73
Annual Payments
Ordinary Annuity
(Payments at the end of the Year)

Growth Rates
Per Cent

Discount Rate	0%	2%	4%	6%	8%	10%
0%	73.000	165.463	429.415	1,225.367	3,704.145	11,551.686
2%	38.220	73.000	162.597	412.800	1,149.869	3,391.556
4%	23.573	38.642	73.000	159.897	397.487	1,081.872
6%	16.430	23.962	39.055	73.000	157.349	383.338
8%	12.455	16.738	24.346	39.458	73.000	154.940
10%	9.990	12.699	17.044	24.726	39.853	73.000
12%	8.331	10.189	12.942	17.349	25.102	40.239
14%	7.142	8.497	10.387	13.185	17.652	25.473
16%	6.250	7.285	8.664	10.585	13.427	17.954
18%	5.556	6.375	7.428	8.830	10.783	13.668

Year 74
Annual Payments
Ordinary Annuity
(Payments at the end of the Year)

Growth Rates
Per Cent

Discount Rate	0%	2%	4%	6%	8%	10%
0%	74.000	169.792	447.631	1,299.949	4,001.557	12,707.954
2%	38.451	74.000	166.805	430.028	1,218.567	3,658.639
4%	23.628	38.880	74.000	163.992	413.813	1,145.345
6%	16.443	24.020	39.299	74.000	161.336	398.841
8%	12.458	16.753	24.407	39.709	74.000	158.827
10%	9.991	12.702	17.060	24.791	40.110	74.000
12%	8.331	10.190	12.946	17.366	25.169	40.503
14%	7.142	8.498	10.388	13.189	17.671	25.544
16%	6.250	7.285	8.664	10.587	13.432	17.973
18%	5.556	6.375	7.428	8.830	10.785	13.674

Year 75
Annual Payments
Ordinary Annuity
(Payments at the end of the Year)

Growth Rates
Per Cent

Discount Rate	0%	2%	4%	6%	8%	10%
0%	75.000	174.208	466.577	1,379.006	4,322.761	13,979.850
2%	38.677	75.000	171.096	447.931	1,291.306	3,946.670
4%	23.680	39.113	75.000	168.164	430.768	1,212.481
6%	16.456	24.076	39.539	75.000	165.399	414.930
8%	12.461	16.766	24.466	39.955	75.000	162.787
10%	9.992	12.706	17.075	24.853	40.363	75.000
12%	8.332	10.191	12.950	17.382	25.235	40.762
14%	7.142	8.498	10.389	13.193	17.688	25.612
16%	6.250	7.285	8.664	10.588	13.437	17.992
18%	5.556	6.375	7.428	8.830	10.786	13.679

Year 76
Annual Payments
Ordinary Annuity
(Payments at the end of the Year)

Growth Rates
Per Cent

Discount Rate	0%	2%	4%	6%	8%	10%
0%	76.000	178.712	486.280	1,462.806	4,669.662	15,378.935
2%	38.899	76.000	175.470	466.536	1,368.324	4,257.291
4%	23.731	39.341	76.000	172.418	448.374	1,283.489
6%	16.468	24.129	39.774	76.000	169.539	431.625
8%	12.464	16.779	24.523	40.197	76.000	166.820
10%	9.993	12.709	17.089	24.913	40.611	76.000
12%	8.332	10.192	12.953	17.398	25.298	41.016
14%	7.143	8.498	10.390	13.197	17.704	25.679
16%	6.250	7.285	8.665	10.589	13.441	18.010
18%	5.556	6.375	7.428	8.831	10.787	13.684

Year 77
Annual Payments
Ordinary Annuity
(Payments at the end of the Year)

Growth Rates
Per Cent

Discount Rate	0%	2%	4%	6%	8%	10%
0%	77.000	183.306	506.771	1,551.634	5,044.315	16,917.928
2%	39.117	77.000	179.930	485.871	1,449.873	4,592.274
4%	23.780	39.566	77.000	176.753	466.658	1,358.594
6%	16.479	24.181	40.004	77.000	173.757	448.951
8%	12.467	16.792	24.578	40.434	77.000	170.928
10%	9.994	12.712	17.103	24.970	40.854	77.000
12%	8.332	10.192	12.957	17.412	25.359	41.266
14%	7.143	8.498	10.391	13.201	17.720	25.742
16%	6.250	7.285	8.665	10.590	13.445	18.026
18%	5.556	6.375	7.428	8.831	10.788	13.688

Year 78
Annual Payments
Ordinary Annuity
(Payments at the end of the Year)

Growth Rates
Per Cent

Discount Rate	0%	2%	4%	6%	8%	10%
0%	78.000	187.992	528.082	1,645.792	5,448.940	18,610.821
2%	39.330	78.000	184.478	505.964	1,536.218	4,953.531
4%	23.827	39.785	78.000	181.171	485.644	1,438.032
6%	16.490	24.231	40.231	78.000	178.054	466.930
8%	12.469	16.803	24.631	40.667	78.000	175.112
10%	9.994	12.715	17.115	25.026	41.093	78.000
12%	8.332	10.193	12.960	17.426	25.417	41.511
14%	7.143	8.499	10.392	13.205	17.735	25.804
16%	6.250	7.285	8.665	10.591	13.449	18.042
18%	5.556	6.375	7.428	8.831	10.789	13.692

Year 79
Annual Payments
Ordinary Annuity
(Payments at the end of the Year)

Growth Rates
Per Cent

Discount Rate	0%	2%	4%	6%	8%	10%
0%	79.000	192.772	550.245	1,745.600	5,885.936	20,473.003
2%	39.539	79.000	189.115	526.845	1,627.643	5,343.122
4%	23.872	40.001	79.000	185.674	505.362	1,522.053
6%	16.500	24.279	40.453	79.000	182.432	485.588
8%	12.471	16.814	24.681	40.895	79.000	179.373
10%	9.995	12.717	17.127	25.080	41.328	79.000
12%	8.332	10.194	12.963	17.439	25.474	41.752
14%	7.143	8.499	10.393	13.208	17.749	25.864
16%	6.250	7.285	8.665	10.591	13.452	18.057
18%	5.556	6.375	7.428	8.831	10.790	13.696

Year 80
Annual Payments
Ordinary Annuity
(Payments at the end of the Year)

Growth Rates
Per Cent

Discount Rate	0%	2%	4%	6%	8%	10%
0%	80.000	197.647	573.295	1,851.396	6,357.890	22,521.403
2%	39.745	80.000	193.842	548.544	1,724.445	5,763.269
4%	23.915	40.213	80.000	190.264	525.837	1,610.922
6%	16.509	24.325	40.671	80.000	186.893	504.949
8%	12.474	16.824	24.730	41.119	80.000	183.714
10%	9.995	12.720	17.138	25.131	41.558	80.000
12%	8.332	10.194	12.965	17.451	25.528	41.988
14%	7.143	8.499	10.393	13.211	17.762	25.921
16%	6.250	7.285	8.665	10.592	13.456	18.072
18%	5.556	6.375	7.428	8.832	10.791	13.700

Year 81
Annual Payments
Ordinary Annuity
(Payments at the end of the Year)

Growth Rates
Per Cent

Discount Rate	0%	2%	4%	6%	8%	10%
0%	81.000	202.620	597.267	1,963.540	6,867.602	24,774.644
2%	39.946	81.000	198.663	571.095	1,826.942	6,216.368
4%	23.957	40.420	81.000	194.942	547.100	1,704.917
6%	16.518	24.369	40.885	81.000	191.439	525.042
8%	12.475	16.834	24.777	41.339	81.000	188.134
10%	9.996	12.722	17.149	25.181	41.785	81.000
12%	8.332	10.195	12.968	17.462	25.581	42.221
14%	7.143	8.499	10.394	13.213	17.774	25.976
16%	6.250	7.285	8.665	10.593	13.459	18.085
18%	5.556	6.375	7.428	8.832	10.792	13.703

Year 82
Annual Payments
Ordinary Annuity
(Payments at the end of the Year)

**Growth Rates
Per Cent**

Discount Rate	0%	2%	4%	6%	8%	10%
0%	82.000	207.693	622.197	2,082.412	7,418.090	27,253.208
2%	40.143	82.000	203.578	594.530	1,935.468	6,705.005
4%	23.997	40.624	82.000	199.710	569.181	1,804.336
6%	16.526	24.412	41.094	82.000	196.070	545.892
8%	12.477	16.843	24.823	41.555	82.000	192.637
10%	9.996	12.724	17.159	25.229	42.007	82.000
12%	8.333	10.195	12.970	17.473	25.632	42.449
14%	7.143	8.499	10.394	13.216	17.786	26.030
16%	6.250	7.286	8.666	10.593	13.461	18.098
18%	5.556	6.375	7.428	8.832	10.792	13.707

Year 83
Annual Payments
Ordinary Annuity
(Payments at the end of the Year)

**Growth Rates
Per Cent**

Discount Rate	0%	2%	4%	6%	8%	10%
0%	83.000	212.867	648.125	2,208.417	8,012.617	29,979.629
2%	40.336	83.000	208.589	618.884	2,050.378	7,231.966
4%	24.036	40.823	83.000	204.570	592.111	1,909.490
6%	16.534	24.453	41.300	83.000	200.788	567.530
8%	12.479	16.852	24.866	41.767	83.000	197.223
10%	9.996	12.726	17.168	25.275	42.225	83.000
12%	8.333	10.196	12.972	17.484	25.680	42.673
14%	7.143	8.499	10.395	13.218	17.798	26.082
16%	6.250	7.286	8.666	10.594	13.464	18.110
18%	5.556	6.375	7.428	8.832	10.793	13.709

Year 84
Annual Payments
Ordinary Annuity
(Payments at the end of the Year)

Growth Rates
Per Cent

Discount Rate	0%	2%	4%	6%	8%	10%
0%	84.000	218.144	675.090	2,341.982	8,654.706	32,978.692
2%	40.526	84.000	213.699	644.194	2,172.047	7,800.257
4%	24.073	41.019	84.000	209.523	615.923	2,020.710
6%	16.542	24.492	41.502	84.000	205.595	589.984
8%	12.481	16.860	24.908	41.975	84.000	201.893
10%	9.997	12.728	17.177	25.320	42.439	84.000
12%	8.333	10.196	12.974	17.493	25.728	42.893
14%	7.143	8.499	10.395	13.221	17.808	26.131
16%	6.250	7.286	8.666	10.595	13.467	18.122
18%	5.556	6.375	7.428	8.832	10.794	13.712

Year 85
Annual Payments
Ordinary Annuity
(Payments at the end of the Year)

Growth Rates
Per Cent

Discount Rate	0%	2%	4%	6%	8%	10%
0%	85.000	223.527	703.134	2,483.561	9,348.163	36,277.661
2%	40.711	85.000	218.908	670.495	2,300.874	8,413.121
4%	24.109	41.211	85.000	214.572	640.650	2,138.347
6%	16.549	24.530	41.700	85.000	210.493	613.285
8%	12.482	16.868	24.949	42.179	85.000	206.651
10%	9.997	12.729	17.186	25.363	42.649	85.000
12%	8.333	10.196	12.976	17.503	25.773	43.109
14%	7.143	8.499	10.396	13.223	17.818	26.179
16%	6.250	7.286	8.666	10.595	13.469	18.133
18%	5.556	6.375	7.428	8.832	10.794	13.715

Year 86
Annual Payments
Ordinary Annuity
(Payments at the end of the Year)

**Growth Rates
Per Cent**

Discount Rate	0%	2%	4%	6%	8%	10%
0%	86.000	229.017	732.299	2,633.634	10,097.096	39,906.527
2%	40.893	86.000	224.220	697.828	2,437.278	9,074.052
4%	24.143	41.399	86.000	219.718	666.329	2,262.771
6%	16.556	24.567	41.894	86.000	215.484	637.466
8%	12.483	16.875	24.987	42.380	86.000	211.496
10%	9.997	12.731	17.194	25.404	42.855	86.000
12%	8.333	10.197	12.978	17.512	25.817	43.322
14%	7.143	8.499	10.396	13.225	17.828	26.226
16%	6.250	7.286	8.666	10.595	13.471	18.143
18%	5.556	6.375	7.428	8.832	10.795	13.717

Year 87
Annual Payments
Ordinary Annuity
(Payments at the end of the Year)

**Growth Rates
Per Cent**

Discount Rate	0%	2%	4%	6%	8%	10%
0%	87.000	234.618	762.631	2,792.712	10,905.943	43,898.280
2%	41.072	87.000	229.636	726.233	2,581.706	9,786.821
4%	24.176	41.584	87.000	224.962	692.996	2,394.373
6%	16.562	24.602	42.085	87.000	220.568	662.559
8%	12.485	16.882	25.025	42.576	87.000	216.431
10%	9.997	12.732	17.202	25.444	43.058	87.000
12%	8.333	10.197	12.979	17.520	25.859	43.530
14%	7.143	8.499	10.396	13.226	17.837	26.270
16%	6.250	7.286	8.666	10.596	13.473	18.153
18%	5.556	6.375	7.428	8.833	10.795	13.719

Year 88
Annual Payments
Ordinary Annuity
(Payments at the end of the Year)

Growth Rates
Per Cent

Discount Rate	0%	2%	4%	6%	8%	10%
0%	88.000	240.330	794,.176001	2,961.335	11,779.499	48,289.208
2%	41.247	88.000	235.159	755.752	2,734.630	10,555.493
4%	24.207	41.765	88.000	230.308	720.688	2,533.568
6%	16.568	24.636	42.272	88.000	225.749	688.599
8%	12.486	16.889	25.061	42.769	88.000	221.458
10%	9.998	12.733	17.209	25.482	43.257	88.000
12%	8.333	10.197	12.981	17.528	25.900	43.735
14%	7.143	8.500	10.397	13.228	17.845	26.314
16%	6.250	7.286	8.666	10.596	13.475	18.162
18%	5.556	6.375	7.428	8.833	10.796	13.721

Year 89
Annual Payments
Ordinary Annuity
(Payments at the end of the Year)

Growth Rates
Per Cent

Discount Rate	0%	2%	4%	6%	8%	10%
0%	89.000	246.157	826.983	3,140.075	12,722.939	53,119.228
2%	41.419	89.000	240.789	786.429	2,896.550	11,384.453
4%	24.238	41.942	89.000	235.756	749.445	2,680.793
6%	16.573	24.669	42.456	89.000	231.027	715.621
8%	12.487	16.895	25.096	42.959	89.000	226.577
10%	9.998	12.735	17.216	25.519	43.452	89.000
12%	8.333	10.198	12.982	17.535	25.939	43.936
14%	7.143	8.500	10.397	13.230	17.854	26.355
16%	6.250	7.286	8.666	10.597	13.477	18.171
18%	5.556	6.375	7.428	8.833	10.796	13.723

Year 90
Annual Payments
Ordinary Annuity
(Payments at the end of the Year)
Growth Rates
Per Cent

Discount Rate	0%	2%	4%	6%	8%	10%
0%	90.000	252.100	861.103	3,329.540	13,741.854	58,432.251
2%	41.587	90.000	246.530	818.309	3,067.994	12,278.430
4%	24.267	42.116	90.000	241.309	779.308	2,836.512
6%	16.579	24.700	42.636	90.000	236.405	743.664
8%	12.488	16.901	25.129	43.145	90.000	231.792
10%	9.998	12.736	17.222	25.555	43.644	90.000
12%	8.333	10.198	12.984	17.542	25.977	44.134
14%	7.143	8.500	10.397	13.231	17.861	26.395
16%	6.250	7.286	8.666	10.597	13.478	18.179
18%	5.556	6.375	7.428	8.833	10.796	13.725

Year 91
Annual Payments
Ordinary Annuity
(Payments at the end of the Year)

Growth Rates
Per Cent

Discount Rate	0%	2%	4%	6%	8%	10%
0%	91.000	258.162	896.587	3,530.372	14,842.282	64,276.577
2%	41.752	91.000	252.384	851.438	3,249.523	13,242.522
4%	24.295	42.287	91.000	246.969	810.320	3,001.215
6%	16.584	24.730	42.812	91.000	241.884	772.764
8%	12.489	16.906	25.162	43.327	91.000	237.103
10%	9.998	12.737	17.228	25.589	43.832	91.000
12%	8.333	10.198	12.985	17.549	26.014	44.328
14%	7.143	8.500	10.398	13.232	17.869	26.434
16%	6.250	7.286	8.666	10.597	13.480	18.187
18%	5.556	6.375	7.428	8.833	10.797	13.727

Year 92
Annual Payments
Ordinary Annuity
(Payments at the end of the Year)

Growth Rates
Per Cent

Discount Rate	0%	2%	4%	6%	8%	10%
0%	92.000	264.345	933.490	3,743.255	16,030.745	70,705.334
2%	41.914	92.000	258.352	885.867	3,441.730	14,282.230
4%	24.323	42.455	92.000	252.737	842.525	3,175.419
6%	16.588	24.759	42.986	92.000	247.467	802.963
8%	12.489	16.912	25.193	43.506	92.000	242.512
10%	9.998	12.738	17.234	25.622	44.017	92.000
12%	8.333	10.198	12.986	17.555	26.049	44.518
14%	7.143	8.500	10.398	13.234	17.876	26.471
16%	6.250	7.286	8.666	10.597	13.481	18.195
18%	5.556	6.375	7.429	8.833	10.797	13.728

Year 93
Annual Payments
Ordinary Annuity
(Payments at the end of the Year)

Growth Rates
Per Cent

Discount Rate	0%	2%	4%	6%	8%	10%
0%	93.000	270.652	971.870	3,968.910	17,314.284	77,776.968
2%	42.072	93.000	264.437	921.646	3,645.243	15,403.483
4%	24.349	42.619	93.000	258.617	875.968	3,359.674
6%	16.593	24.787	43.156	93.000	253.155	834,301001
8%	12.490	16.916	25.223	43.682	93.000	248.021
10%	9.999	12.739	17.239	25.654	44.199	93.000
12%	8.333	10.198	12.987	17.561	26.083	44.705
14%	7.143	8.500	10.398	13.235	17.882	26.508
16%	6.250	7.286	8.666	10.598	13.482	18.202
18%	5.556	6.375	7.429	8.833	10.797	13.730

Year 94
Annual Payments
Ordinary Annuity
(Payments at the end of the Year)

**Growth Rates
Per Cent**

Discount Rate	0%	2%	4%	6%	8%	10%
0%	94.000	277.085	1,011.785	4,208.104	18,700.507	85,555.764
2%	42.228	94.000	270.642	958.829	3,860.728	16,612.678
4%	24.374	42.780	94.000	264.609	910.698	3,554.559
6%	16.597	24.814	43.323	94.000	258.950	866.822
8%	12.491	16.921	25.251	43.855	94.000	253.633
10%	9.999	12.739	17.244	25.685	44.377	94.000
12%	8.333	10.198	12.988	17.567	26.115	44.889
14%	7.143	8.500	10.398	13.236	17.888	26.542
16%	6.250	7.286	8.666	10.598	13.484	18.209
18%	5.556	6.375	7.429	8.833	10.797	13.731

Year 95
Annual Payments
Ordinary Annuity
(Payments at the end of the Year)

**Growth Rates
Per Cent**

Discount Rate	0%	2%	4%	6%	8%	10%
0%	95.000	283.647	1,053.296	4,461.651	20,197.628	94,112.441
2%	42.380	95.000	276.968	997.469	4,088.889	17,916.712
4%	24.398	42.938	95.000	270.717	946.763	3,760.688
6%	16.601	24.840	43.486	95.000	264.855	900.570
8%	12.492	16.925	25.279	44.024	95.000	259.348
10%	9.999	12.740	17.249	25.715	44.552	95.000
12%	8.333	10.199	12.989	17.572	26.147	45.070
14%	7.143	8.500	10.398	13.237	17.894	26.576
16%	6.250	7.286	8.666	10.598	13.485	18.215
18%	5.556	6.375	7.429	8.833	10.798	13.733

Year 96
Annual Payments
Ordinary Annuity
(Payments at the end of the Year)

Growth Rates
Per Cent

Discount Rate	0%	2%	4%	6%	8%	10%
0%	96.000	290.340	1,096.468	4,730.410	21,814.518	103,524.785
2%	42.529	96.000	283.419	1,037.625	4,330.471	19,323.022
4%	24.421	43.093	96.000	276.943	984.216	3,978.708
6%	16.605	24.865	43.647	96.000	270.871	935.591
8%	12.492	16.930	25.306	44.190	96.000	265.169
10%	9.999	12.741	17.254	25.743	44.724	96.000
12%	8.333	10.199	12.989	17.577	26.178	45.247
14%	7.143	8.500	10.398	13.238	17.900	26.608
16%	6.250	7.286	8.666	10.598	13.486	18.221
18%	5.556	6.375	7.429	8.833	10.798	13.734

Year 97
Annual Payments
Ordinary Annuity
(Payments at the end of the Year)

Growth Rates
Per Cent

Discount Rate	0%	2%	4%	6%	8%	10%
0%	97.000	297.166	1,141.367	5,015.294	23,560.760	113,878.364
2%	42.676	97.000	289.996	1,079.355	4,586.263	20,839.632
4%	24.443	43.246	97.000	283.288	1,023.108	4,209.307
6%	16.608	24.889	43.805	97.000	277.001	971.934
8%	12.493	16.934	25.331	44.353	97.000	271.099
10%	9.999	12.742	17.258	25.771	44.892	97.000
12%	8.333	10.199	12.990	17.582	26.207	45.421
14%	7.143	8.500	10.399	13.239	17.905	26.640
16%	6.250	7.286	8.666	10.598	13.487	18.227
18%	5.556	6.375	7.429	8.833	10.798	13.735

Year 98
Annual Payments
Ordinary Annuity
(Payments at the end of the Year)

Growth Rates
Per Cent

Discount Rate	0%	2%	4%	6%	8%	10%
0%	98.000	304.130	1,188.061	5,317.272	25,446.700	125,267.300
2%	42.820	98.000	296.701	1,122.722	4,857.102	22,475.191
4%	24.465	43.395	98.000	289.755	1,063.497	4,453.209
6%	16.611	24.912	43.959	98.000	283.246	1,009.649
8%	12.493	16.937	25.356	44.514	98.000	277.137
10%	9.999	12.742	17.262	25.797	45.058	98.000
12%	8.333	10.199	12.991	17.587	26.235	45.592
14%	7.143	8.500	10.399	13.239	17.910	26.670
16%	6.250	7.286	8.666	10.598	13.488	18.233
18%	5.556	6.375	7.429	8.833	10.798	13.736

Year 99
Annual Payments
Ordinary Annuity
(Payments at the end of the Year)

Growth Rates
Per Cent

Discount Rate	0%	2%	4%	6%	8%	10%
0%	99.000	311.232	1,236.624	5,637.368	27,483.516	137,795.130
2%	42.960	99.000	303.539	1,167.789	5,143.873	24,239.030
4%	24.485	43.541	99.000	296.346	1,105.439	4,711.183
6%	16.615	24.934	44.111	99.000	289.609	1,048.786
8%	12.494	16.941	25.380	44.671	99.000	283.288
10%	9.999	12.743	17.266	25.823	45.221	99.000
12%	8.333	10.199	12.992	17.591	26.263	45.760
14%	7.143	8.500	10.399	13.240	17.915	26.699
16%	6.250	7.286	8.666	10.599	13.489	18.238
18%	5.556	6.375	7.429	8.833	10.798	13.737

Appendix D
Participation Rates

Participation Rates White Males 1954 - 1988

Year	16-17	18-19	20-24	25-34	35-44	45-54	55-64	65+
1954	47.1	70.5	86.3	97.5	98.2	96.8	89.1	40.4
1955	48.1	71.7	86.5	97.8	98.2	96.7	88.4	39.6
1956	51.3	71.8	87.6	97.4	98.1	96.8	88.9	40.0
1957	49.6	71.5	86.6	97.2	98.0	96.7	88.0	37.7
1958	46.8	69.4	86.7	97.2	98.0	96.6	88.2	35.7
1959	45.4	70.3	87.3	97.5	98.0	96.3	87.9	34.3
1960	46.0	69.0	87.8	97.7	97.9	96.1	87.2	33.3
1961	44.3	66.2	87.6	97.7	97.9	95.9	87.8	31.9
1962	42.9	66.4	86.5	97.4	97.9	96.0	86.7	30.6
1963	42.4	67.8	85.8	97.4	97.8	96.2	86.6	28.4
1964	43.5	66.6	85.7	97.5	97.6	96.1	86.1	27.9
1965	44.6	65.8	85.3	97.4	97.7	95.9	85.2	27.9
1966	47.1	65.4	84.4	97.5	97.6	95.8	84.9	27.2
1967	47.9	66.1	84.0	97.5	97.7	95.6	84.9	27.1
1968	47.7	65.7	82.4	97.2	97.6	95.4	84.7	27.4
1969	48.8	66.3	82.6	97.0	97.4	95.1	83.9	27.3
1970	48.9	67.4	83.3	96.7	97.3	94.9	83.3	26.7
1971	49.3	67.8	83.2	96.3	97.0	94.7	82.6	25.6
1972	50.2	71.1	84.3	96.0	97.0	94.0	81.1	24.4
1973	52.7	72.3	85.8	96.2	96.8	93.5	78.9	22.7
1974	53.3	73.6	86.6	96.3	96.7	93.0	78.0	22.4
1975	51.8	72.8	85.5	95.8	96.4	92.9	76.4	21.7
1976	51.8	73.5	86.3	95.9	96.0	92.5	75.2	20.2
1977	53.8	74.9	86.8	96.0	96.2	92.1	74.6	20.0
1978	55.3	75.3	87.3	95.9	96.3	92.1	73.7	20.3
1979	55.3	74.5	87.6	96.0	96.4	92.2	73.4	20.0
1980	53.6	74.1	87.2	95.9	96.2	92.1	73.1	19.1
1981	51.5	73.5	87.0	95.8	96.1	92.4	71.5	18.5
1982	49.3	70.5	86.3	95.6	96.0	92.2	71.0	17.9
1983	46.9	71.3	86.1	95.2	96.0	91.9	70.0	17.7
1984	47.0	70.8	86.5	95.4	96.1	92.0	69.5	16.4

	Age							
Year	16-17	18-19	20-24	25-34	35-44	45-54	55-64	65+
1985	48.5	71.2	86.4	95.7	95.7	92.0	68.8	15.9
1986	48.7	70.5	87.3	95.5	95.4	91.8	68.0	16.3
1987	48.8	70.0	86.9	95.5	95.4	91.6	68.1	16.5
1988	49.3	71.0	86.6	95.2	95.4	91.8	67.9	16.7
Ave:	48.8	70.2	86.0	96.6	97.0	94.2	79.8	25.6

Participation Rates White Females 1954 - 1988

	Age							
Year	16-17	18-19	20-24	25-34	35-44	45-54	55-64	65+
1954	29.3	52.1	44.4	32.5	39.3	39.8	29.1	9.1
1955	29.9	52.0	45.8	32.6	40.0	42.7	31.8	10.5
1956	33.5	53.0	46.5	33.2	41.5	44.4	34.0	10.6
1957	32.1	52.6	45.8	33.6	41.5	45.4	33.7	10.2
1958	28.8	52.3	46.0	33.6	41.4	46.5	34.5	10.1
1959	29.9	50.8	44.5	33.4	41.4	47.8	35.7	10.0
1960	30.0	51.9	45.7	34.1	41.5	48.6	36.2	10.6
1961	29.4	51.9	46.9	34.3	41.8	48.9	37.2	10.5
1962	27.9	51.6	47.1	34.1	42.2	48.9	38.0	9.8
1963	27.8	51.3	47.3	34.8	43.1	49.5	38.9	9.4
1964	28.4	49.6	48.8	35.0	43.3	50.2	39.4	9.9
1965	28.7	50.6	49.2	36.3	44.4	49.9	40.3	9.7
1966	31.8	53.1	51.0	37.7	45.0	50.6	41.1	9.4
1967	32.3	52.7	53.1	39.7	46.4	50.9	41.9	9.3
1968	33.0	53.3	54.0	40.6	47.5	51.5	42.0	9.4
1969	35.2	54.6	56.4	41.7	48.6	53.0	42.6	9.7
1970	36.6	55.0	57.7	43.2	49.9	53.7	42.6	9.5
1971	36.3	55.0	58.0	43.7	50.2	53.6	42.5	9.3
1972	39.3	57.4	59.4	46.0	50.7	53.4	42.0	9.0
1973	41.7	58.8	61.7	48.7	52.2	53.4	40.7	8.7
1974	43.3	60.4	63.9	51.3	53.6	54.3	40.4	8.0
1975	42.7	60.4	65.5	53.6	54.9	54.3	40.6	8.0
1976	43.8	61.7	66.3	56.0	57.1	54.7	40.7	7.9
1977	45.8	63.3	67.8	58.5	58.9	55.3	40.7	7.9
1978	48.8	64.6	69.3	61.2	60.7	56.7	41.1	8.1
1979	49.0	65.7	70.5	63.3	63.0	58.1	41.5	8.1
1980	47.2	65.1	70.6	64.8	65.0	59.6	40.9	7.9
1981	46.1	64.2	71.5	66.4	66.4	60.9	40.9	7.9
1982	44.6	64.6	71.8	67.8	67.5	61.4	41.5	7.8
1983	43.9	64.1	72.1	68.7	68.2	61.9	41.1	7.8
1984	44.8	65.2	72.5	69.8	69.6	62.7	41.2	7.5
1985	45.2	64.8	73.8	70.9	71.4	64.2	41.5	7.0
1986	47.2	65.3	74.1	71.8	72.9	65.8	42.1	7.3
1987	48.2	64.9	74.8	72.5	74.2	67.2	42.4	7.2
1988	47.7	66.3	74.9	73.0	74.9	69.2	43.6	7.7
Ave:	38.0	57.7	59.1	49.1	53.4	54.0	39.6	8.9

Participation Rates Black Males 1972 - 1988

				Age				
Year	16-17	18-19	20-24	25-34	35-44	45-54	55-64	65+
1972	34.3	60.2	82.7	92.7	91.1	85.4	72.5	24.2
1973	32.3	61.2	83.7	91.8	91.0	87.4	69.5	22.3
1974	34.0	61.9	83.6	92.8	90.4	84.0	68.9	21.6
1975	29.8	57.2	78.7	91.6	89.4	83.5	67.7	20.7
1976	29.0	55.0	79.0	90.9	89.9	82.4	65.1	19.8
1977	30.2	58.0	79.2	90.7	91.0	82.0	65.5	20.0
1978	31.9	59.7	78.8	90.9	90.5	83.2	67.9	21.1
1979	30.7	58.1	80.7	90.8	90.4	84.5	64.8	19.5
1980	30.9	56.6	79.9	90.9	89.1	83.0	61.9	16.9
1981	29.2	55.0	79.2	88.9	89.3	82.7	62.1	16.0
1982	24.6	55.3	78.7	89.2	89.8	82.2	61.9	15.9
1983	24.7	55.0	79.4	89.0	89.7	84.5	62.6	14.0
1984	26.9	56.2	79.1	88.9	90.0	83.7	58.9	13.7
1985	29.8	60.0	79.0	88.8	89.8	83.0	58.9	13.9
1986	30.0	58.5	80.1	89.6	89.6	84.1	59.1	12.6
1987	31.7	57.0	77.8	89.4	88.6	83.7	62.1	13.7
1988	32.7	56.0	79.3	89.3	88.2	83.5	59.4	14.3
Ave:	30.0	57.7	79.9	90.4	89.9	83.7	64.3	17.7

Participation Rates Black Females 1972 - 1988

				Age				
Year	16-17	18-19	20-24	25-34	35-44	45-54	55-64	65+
1972	21.0	44.3	57.0	60.8	61.4	57.2	44.0	12.6
1973	23.9	45.1	58.0	62.7	61.7	56.1	44.7	11.4
1974	22.7	44.3	58.8	62.4	62.2	56.4	42.8	10.4
1975	25.0	43.5	55.9	62.8	62.0	56.6	43.1	10.7
1976	23.2	42.6	56.9	66.7	63.0	56.8	43.7	11.3
1977	21.5	44.3	59.3	68.5	64.1	57.9	43.7	10.5
1978	26.4	48.3	62.7	70.6	67.2	59.4	43.8	11.1
1979	27.5	45.6	61.5	70.1	68.0	59.6	44.0	10.9
1980	24.6	45.0	60.2	70.5	68.1	61.4	44.8	10.2
1981	23.9	44.0	61.1	70.0	69.8	62.0	45.4	9.3
1982	23.3	43.3	60.1	70.2	71.7	62.4	44.8	8.5
1983	20.8	44.4	59.1	72.3	72.6	62.3	44.8	8.2
1984	23.9	45.3	60.7	71.5	73.7	64.5	46.1	8.0
1985	27.6	47.9	62.5	72.4	74.8	65.7	45.3	9.4
1986	29.0	49.2	64.6	72.4	75.8	66.5	43.6	7.8
1987	28.2	51.4	64.4	73.5	77.8	67.5	44.4	8.6
1988	28.1	48.2	63.2	73.7	78.1	68.3	43.4	9.6
Ave:	25.2	45.7	60.4	68.9	68.9	61.2	44.3	9.9

Participation Rates Hispanic Males 1980 - 1988

				Age				
Year	16-17	18-19	20-24	25-34	35-44	45-54	55-64	64+
1980	45.2	74.8	88.0	93.3	93.8	91.7	73.6	20.7
1981	39.8	68.2	88.8	93.8	92.6	90.6	70.9	19.4
1982	34.4	65.1	86.1	93.9	93.5	88.8	70.0	17.9
1983	34.0	70.3	86.0	93.5	93.0	89.4	71.3	17.4
1984	35.4	68.8	87.0	93.4	93.6	89.0	71.2	14.9
1985	36.0	65.7	87.3	93.1	92.4	89.5	69.6	14.9
1986	34.5	68.3	88.3	93.4	93.3	89.9	69.3	15.2
1987	33.3	69.6	87.8	93.6	93.0	88.0	70.2	14.4
1988	38.6	70.1	89.4	93.4	93.8	88.5	68.8	17.4
Ave:	36.6	69.0	87.6	93.5	93.2	89.5	70.5	16.9

Participation Rates Hispanic Females 1980 - 1988

				Age				
Year	16-17	18-19	20-24	25-34	35-44	45-54	55-64	64+
1980	29.9	50.4	57.0	54.0	55.3	54.5	34.7	5.7
1981	27.0	49.2	59.8	55.5	55.9	54.8	34.5	6.4
1982	25.7	52.2	58.4	56.4	55.2	53.6	33.2	6.4
1983	25.5	49.1	56.5	54.8	54.7	55.4	37.5	6.4
1984	30.6	53.5	56.2	56.9	58.6	55.2	38.5	7.2
1985	26.5	49.2	57.7	57.1	59.1	55.1	36.4	5.9
1986	27.1	46.1	58.9	59.0	60.6	57.4	33.9	5.5
1987	29.7	49.6	60.4	60.9	62.2	57.8	36.8	5.3
1988	32.4	55.5	62.3	60.9	62.1	57.9	41.5	6.5
Ave:	27.5	50.5	58.6	57.3	58.2	55.7	36.3	6.1

Appendix E
Employment Rates

Employment Rates White Males 1954 - 1988

Year	16-17	18-19	20-24	25-34	35-44	45-54	55-64	65+
1954	14.0	13.0	9.8	4.2	3.6	3.8	4.3	4.2
1955	12.2	10.4	7.0	2.7	2.6	2.9	3.9	3.8
1956	11.2	9.7	6.1	2.8	2.2	2.8	3.1	3.4
1957	11.9	11.1	7.0	2.7	2.5	3.0	3.4	3.2
1958	14.9	16.5	11.7	5.6	4.4	4.8	5.2	5.0
1959	15.0	13.0	7.5	3.8	3.2	3.7	4.2	4.5
1960	14.6	13.5	8.3	4.1	3.3	3.6	4.1	4.0
1961	16.5	15.2	10.1	4.9	4.0	4.4	5.3	5.2
1962	15.2	12.7	8.1	3.8	3.1	3.5	4.1	4.0
1963	17.8	14.2	7.8	3.9	2.9	3.3	4.0	4.1
1964	16.1	13.3	7.4	3.0	2.5	2.9	3.5	3.6
1965	14.7	11.3	5.9	2.6	2.3	2.3	3.1	3.4
1966	12.5	8.9	4.1	2.1	1.7	1.7	2.5	3.0
1967	12.7	9.0	4.2	1.9	1.6	1.8	2.2	2.7
1968	12.6	8.3	4.6	1.7	1.4	1.5	1.7	2.8
1969	12.5	7.9	4.6	1.7	1.4	1.4	1.7	2.2
1970	15.7	12.0	7.8	3.1	2.3	2.3	2.7	3.2
1971	17.1	13.5	9.4	4.0	2.9	2.9	3.2	3.4
1972	16.4	12.4	8.5	3.4	2.5	2.5	3.0	3.3
1973	15.2	10.0	6.6	3.0	1.8	2.0	2.4	2.9
1974	16.2	11.5	7.8	3.6	2.4	2.2	2.5	3.0
1975	19.7	17.2	13.1	6.3	4.5	4.4	4.1	5.0
1976	19.7	15.5	10.9	5.6	3.7	3.7	4.0	4.7
1977	17.6	13.0	9.3	5.0	3.1	3.0	3.3	4.9
1978	16.9	10.8	7.7	3.8	2.5	2.5	2.6	3.9
1979	16.1	12.2	7.5	3.7	2.5	2.5	2.5	3.2
1980	18.5	14.5	11.1	5.9	3.6	3.3	3.1	2.5
1981	19.9	16.4	11.6	6.1	4.0	3.6	3.4	2.4
1982	24.2	20.0	14.3	8.9	6.2	5.3	5.1	3.2
1983	22.6	18.7	13.8	9.0	6.4	5.7	5.6	3.2
1984	19.7	15.0	9.8	6.2	4.6	4.2	4.7	2.6

Year	16-17	18-19	20-24	25-34	35-44	45-54	55-64	65+
				Age				
1985	19.2	14.7	9.7	5.7	4.3	4.1	4.0	2.7
1986	18.4	14.7	9.2	5.8	4.4	4.0	4.0	3.0
1987	17.9	13.7	8.4	5.2	3.9	3.9	3.4	2.5
1988	16.1	12.4	7.4	4.6	3.4	3.2	3.3	2.2
Ave:	16.3	13.0	8.5	4.3	3.2	3.2	3.5	3.5

Employment Rates White Females 1954 - 1988

Year	16-17	18-19	20-24	25-34	35-44	45-54	55-64	65+
				Age				
1954	12.0	9.4	6.4	5.7	4.9	4.4	4.5	2.8
1955	11.6	7.7	5.1	4.3	3.8	3.4	3.6	2.2
1956	12.1	8.3	5.1	4.0	3.5	3.3	3.5	2.3
1957	11.9	7.8	5.1	4.7	3.7	3.0	2.6	3.4
1958	15.6	11.0	7.3	6.6	5.6	4.9	4.3	3.5
1959	13.3	11.1	7.0	5.2	4.7	3.9	4.0	2.9
1960	14.5	11.5	7.2	5.7	4.2	4.0	3.3	2.8
1961	17.0	13.6	8.4	6.6	5.6	4.8	4.3	3.8
1962	15.6	11.3	7.7	5.4	4.5	3.7	3.5	4.0
1963	18.1	13.2	7.4	5.8	4.6	3.9	3.5	3.3
1964	17.1	13.2	7.1	5.2	4.5	3.6	3.5	3.4
1965	15.0	13.4	6.3	4.9	4.1	3.0	2.7	2.7
1966	14.5	10.7	5.3	3.7	3.3	2.7	2.2	2.7
1967	12.9	10.6	6.0	4.7	3.7	2.9	2.3	2.6
1968	13.9	11.0	5.9	3.9	3.1	2.3	2.1	2.8
1969	13.7	10.0	5.5	4.2	3.2	2.4	2.1	2.4
1970	15.3	11.9	6.9	5.3	4.3	3.4	2.6	3.3
1971	16.7	14.1	8.5	6.3	4.9	3.9	3.3	3.6
1972	17.0	12.3	8.2	5.5	4.4	3.5	3.3	3.7
1973	15.8	10.9	7.1	5.1	3.7	3.2	2.7	2.8
1974	16.4	13.0	8.2	5.8	4.4	3.6	3.2	3.9
1975	19.2	16.1	11.2	8.4	6.5	5.8	5.0	5.3
1976	18.2	15.1	10.4	7.6	5.8	5.0	4.8	5.3
1977	18.2	14.2	9.3	6.7	5.3	5.0	4.4	4.9
1978	17.1	12.4	8.3	5.8	4.5	3.8	3.0	3.7
1979	15.9	12.5	7.8	5.6	4.2	3.7	3.0	3.1
1980	17.3	13.1	8.5	6.3	4.9	4.3	3.1	3.0
1981	18.4	15.3	9.1	6.6	5.1	4.2	3.7	3.4
1982	21.2	17.6	10.9	8.0	6.4	5.5	5.0	3.1
1983	21.4	16.4	10.3	7.6	6.2	5.5	4.7	3.1
1984	17.8	13.6	8.8	6.1	5.0	4.8	4.0	3.7
1985	17.2	13.1	8.5	6.2	4.9	4.5	4.1	3.1
1986	16.7	13.6	8.1	6.1	4.5	4.3	3.7	2.6
1987	15.5	11.7	7.4	5.0	4.1	3.3	2.7	2.4
1988	14.4	10.8	6.7	4.5	3.7	3.1	2.5	2.6
Ave:	16.0	12.3	7.6	5.7	4.6	3.9	3.5	3.3

Employment Rates Black Males 1972 - 1988

Year	16-17	18-19	20-24	25-34	35-44	45-54	55-64	65+
				Age				
1972	36.7	28.4	14.9	7.2	4.8	3.8	4.4	5.4
1973	35.7	23.0	13.2	6.2	3.9	3.2	3.2	3.3
1974	39.9	28.3	16.2	8.1	4.3	4.2	3.6	5.3
1975	41.9	35.9	24.7	12.7	8.7	9.3	6.3	8.7
1976	40.8	36.0	22.6	12.0	7.5	7.3	6.3	8.7
1977	41.0	38.2	23.0	11.8	6.2	4.9	6.0	7.8
1978	43.0	32.9	21.0	9.8	5.1	4.9	4.4	6.6
1979	37.9	32.2	18.7	9.6	6.3	5.2	5.1	6.4
1980	39.7	36.2	23.7	13.4	8.2	7.2	6.2	8.7
1981	43.2	39.2	26.4	14.4	9.3	7.8	6.1	7.5
1982	52.7	47.1	31.5	20.1	13.4	9.0	10.3	9.3
1983	52.2	47.3	31.4	19.4	13.5	11.4	11.0	11.8
1984	44.0	42.2	26.6	15.0	10.4	7.9	8.9	7.9
1985	42.9	40.0	23.5	13.8	9.6	9.7	7.9	8.9
1986	41.4	38.2	23.5	13.5	10.9	7.8	8.0	4.3
1987	39.0	31.6	20.3	12.2	8.7	6.7	6.6	4.3
1988	34.4	31.7	19.4	11.0	7.6	6.2	5.2	5.6
Ave:	42.0	35.8	22.4	12.4	8.1	6.9	6.4	7.1

Employment Rates Black Females 1972 - 1988

Year	16-17	18-19	20-24	25-34	35-44	45-54	55-64	65+
				Age				
1972	42.0	40.1	17.9	10.5	7.6	4.6	3.7	2.6
1973	38.6	34.2	18.4	10.3	5.6	3.9	3.3	3.7
1974	40.2	36.0	19.0	9.0	6.6	4.4	3.6	1.9
1975	41.2	40.6	24.3	13.4	9.0	7.0	5.3	3.6
1976	48.4	37.6	22.5	13.6	8.2	5.9	5.4	2.4
1977	49.5	40.4	25.5	13.6	8.7	5.8	4.8	3.4
1978	45.0	38.7	22.7	11.9	7.8	5.6	5.2	4.7
1979	42.7	36.9	22.6	12.1	7.2	5.2	4.7	3.9
1980	42.9	38.2	23.5	13.2	8.2	6.4	4.5	4.9
1981	46.5	39.8	26.4	14.9	9.8	6.9	4.7	6.0
1982	44.2	48.6	29.6	17.8	10.7	8.5	6.1	4.5
1983	48.6	48.0	31.8	18.6	11.4	9.9	7.3	6.3
1984	47.5	40.2	25.6	15.4	9.4	8.6	5.9	4.9
1985	44.3	36.4	25.6	15.1	9.3	6.8	6.0	5.2
1986	44.6	36.1	24.7	14.6	8.5	6.4	5.0	4.9
1987	40.5	31.7	23.3	13.5	8.1	6.7	4.5	3.4
1988	35.9	29.6	19.8	12.7	7.4	5.6	4.3	5.4
Ave:	44.2	38.4	23.7	13.5	8.4	6.4	5.0	4.2

Employment Rates Hispanic Males 1980 - 1988

				Age				
Year	16-17	18-19	20-24	25-34	35-44	45-54	55-64	65+
1980	26.2	19.3	12.2	8.3	7.1	6.0	5.9	7.6
1981	30.9	20.3	14.1	8.9	6.5	5.9	6.7	6.7
1982	40.2	26.8	18.2	12.4	9.9	7.5	10.0	7.4
1983	34.7	25.9	17.0	11.6	10.8	10.3	11.7	6.8
1984	31.5	22.2	12.5	9.2	7.6	7.2	10.4	8.2
1985	29.1	22.4	13.0	9.6	7.2	6.8	7.0	9.4
1986	28.5	22.4	13.0	9.5	8.5	7.0	8.0	9.6
1987	28.2	19.3	10.2	7.6	6.9	7.1	6.7	7.9
1988	29.5	19.5	9.2	7.0	5.9	6.1	6.7	6.9
Ave:	31.2	22.0	13.3	9.3	7.8	7.1	8.1	7.8

Employment Rates Hispanic Females 1980 - 1988

				Age				
Year	16-17	18-19	20-24	25-34	35-44	45-54	55-64	65+
1980	29.7	19.8	12.0	10.6	8.6	5.3	5.8	1.1
1981	23.5	23.4	13.5	8.7	8.9	7.2	8.4	2.5
1982	35.1	25.0	16.8	12.2	11.9	9.9	10.4	4.8
1983	32.5	25.7	16.2	12.5	12.2	9.7	9.6	3.5
1984	26.1	21.0	12.2	10.3	9.1	7.9	8.8	3.4
1985	26.2	22.6	12.1	10.6	8.5	8.1	9.2	5.5
1986	27.6	23.6	12.9	9.8	5.2	8.9	6.2	11.2
1987	27.1	19.9	11.4	7.8	6.5	6.7	5.0	3.7
1988	24.5	18.9	10.7	7.2	6.2	5.9	4.6	3.0
Ave:	28.5	22.2	13.1	10.0	8.6	7.7	7.6	4.3

Appendix F
Probability of Living

PROBABILITY OF LIVING TO AGE 'X' STARTING FROM AGE 0

1989 U. S. POPULATION

	TOTAL POPULATION	WHITE MALE	WHITE FEMALE	BLACK MALE	BLACK FEMALE
LIFE EXPECTANCY TO AGE	75.30	72.70	79.20	64.80	73.50
1	99.931	99.931	99.947	99.882	99.909
2	99.879	99.881	99.906	99.791	99.834
3	99.839	99.843	99.874	99.719	99.773
4	99.806	99.811	99.847	99.660	99.724
5	99.777	99.782	99.824	99.610	99.684
6	99.751	99.755	99.803	99.565	99.652
7	99.727	99.729	99.784	99.525	99.626
8	99.706	99.706	99.767	99.491	99.603
9	99.688	99.686	99.752	99.463	99.581
10	99.672	99.669	99.739	99.439	99.558
11	99.656	99.653	99.726	99.416	99.533
12	99.634	99.629	99.710	99.382	99.506
13	99.602	99.590	99.688	99.327	99.476
14	99.555	99.531	99.659	99.145	99.443
15	99.492	99.449	99.620	99.030	99.407
16	99.414	99.347	99.572	98.885	99.365
17	99.323	99.227	99.519	98.709	99.317

1989 U. S. POPULATION

	TOTAL POPULATION	WHITE MALE	WHITE FEMALE	BLACK MALE	BLACK FEMALE
18	99.225	99.097	99.464	98.504	99.264
19	99.123	98.961	99.412	98.275	99.202
20	99.018	98.820	99.362	98.018	99.133
21	98.909	98.675	99.314	97.735	99.054
22	98.797	98.526	99.268	97.432	98.967
23	98.683	98.375	99.221	97.117	98.873
24	98.568	98.223	99.172	96.799	98.771
25	98.451	98.071	99.123	96.477	98.663
26	98.333	97.918	99.071	96.151	98.546
27	98.212	97.763	99.018	95.815	98.420
28	98.088	97.605	98.962	95.461	98.283
29	97.958	97.442	98.904	95.085	98.135
30	97.823	97.273	98.842	94.686	97.973
31	97.681	97.099	98.777	94.253	97.798
32	97.534	96.918	98.708	93.784	97.612
33	97.379	96.731	98.636	93.302	97.415
34	97.217	96.536	98.561	92.786	97.207
35	97.047	96.332	98.482	92.233	96.988
36	96.867	96.118	98.399	91.643	96.758
37	96.679	95.895	98.309	91.021	96.514
38	96.482	95.663	98.212	90.374	96.252
39	96.272	95.422	98.105	89.705	95.971
40	96.051	95.171	97.987	89.015	95.668
41	95.830	94.909	97.857	88.301	95.342
42	95.590	94.631	97.714	87.561	94.994
43	95.330	94.334	97.558	86.793	94.624
44	95.051	94.015	97.390	85.992	94.231
45	94.752	93.671	97.205	85.158	93.814
46	94.429	93.299	97.004	84.228	93.369
47	94.079	92.895	96.782	83.379	92.896
48	93.698	92.457	96.536	82.433	92.391
49	93.283	91.984	96.262	81.413	91.853
50	92.830	91.470	95.958	80.331	91.277
51	92.337	90.912	95.621	79.262	90.661
52	91.798	90.301	95.248	78.133	89.999
53	91.208	89.624	94.838	76.944	89.287
54	90.562	88.876	94.386	75.702	88.520
55	89.856	88.050	93.892	74.410	87.696
56	89.093	87.144	93.350	73.068	86.811

1989 U. S. POPULATION

	TOTAL POPULATION	WHITE MALE	WHITE FEMALE	BLACK MALE	BLACK FEMALE
57	88.264	86.153	92.758	71.673	85.855
58	87.364	85.072	92.112	70.220	84.815
59	86.385	83.897	91.408	68.703	83.680
60	85.331	82.624	90.641	67.116	82.445
61	84.197	81.250	89.809	65.459	81.112
62	82.976	79.777	88.909	63.734	79.691
63	81.681	78.212	87.939	61.940	78.200
64	80.301	76.556	86.898	60.077	76.647
65	78.839	74.810	85.781	58.147	75.038
66	77.286	72.954	84.752	56.152	73.352
67	75.632	70.985	83.489	54.095	71.590
68	73.878	68.900	82.203	51.976	69.751
69	72.023	66.698	80.822	49.805	67.835
70	70.057	64.379	79.343	47.581	65.842
71	67.983	61.938	77.756	45.313	63.759
72	65.794	59.376	76.053	43.007	61.587
73	63.492	56.698	74.228	40.676	59.328
74	61.079	53.908	72.276	38.321	56.984
75	58.556	51.015	70.194	35.958	54.561
76	55.921	48.030	67.976	33.593	52.035
77	53.176	44.963	65.604	31.215	49.411
78	50.331	41.833	63.078	28.844	46.700
79	47.391	38.655	60.404	26.488	43.909
80	44.372	35.453	57.577	24.163	41.053
81	41.129	32.127	54.606	21.884	37.992
82	37.678	28.712	51.335	19.556	34.744
83	34.054	25.256	47.772	17.220	31.339
84	30.291	21.813	43.927	14.912	27.817
85	26.450	18.445	39.824	12.656	24.234
86	22.601	15.219	35.511	10.502	20.656
87	18.827	12.204	31.051	8.491	17.159
88	15.220	9.466	26.527	6.661	13.829
89	11.873	7.061	22.046	5.045	10.752
90	8.876	5.028	17.727	3.668	8.010
91	6.306	3.389	13.700	2.542	5.668
92	4.210	2.138	10.090	1.663	3.768
93	2.604	1.244	7.006	1.016	2.320
94	1.464	.655	4.523	.572	1.298
95	.729	.303	2.664	.290	.643

| | 1989 U. S. POPULATION | | | | |
	TOTAL POPULATION	WHITE MALE	WHITE FEMALE	BLACK MALE	BLACK FEMALE
96	.309	.119	1.394	.129	.271
97	.104	.037	.623	.049	.091
98	.025	0.000	.224	.015	.022
99	0.000	0.000	.057	0.000	0.000

PROBABILITY OF LIVING TO AGE 'X' STARTING FROM AGE 1

1989 U. S. POPULATION

	TOTAL POPULATION	WHITE MALE	WHITE FEMALE	BLACK MALE	BLACK FEMALE
LIFE EXPECTANCY TO AGE	75.00	72.30	78.80	65.20	73.80
2	99.948	99.950	99.959	99.909	99.925
3	99.908	99.912	99.927	99.837	99.864
4	99.875	99.880	99.900	99.778	99.815
5	99.846	99.851	99.877	99.727	99.775
6	99.820	99.824	99.856	99.682	99.743
7	99.796	99.798	99.837	99.643	99.716
8	99.775	99.775	99.820	99.609	99.693
9	99.757	99.755	99.805	99.581	99.671
10	99.741	99.738	99.792	99.557	99.649
11	99.724	99.721	99.779	99.533	99.624
12	99.702	99.697	99.763	99.499	99.597
13	99.670	99.659	99.741	99.444	99.567
14	99.624	99.600	99.711	99.262	99.534
15	99.561	99.518	99.672	99.147	99.497
16	99.482	99.416	99.625	99.002	99.455
17	99.392	99.295	99.572	98.825	99.408
18	99.293	99.165	99.517	98.621	99.354
19	99.191	99.029	99.464	98.391	99.292
20	99.086	98.889	99.415	98.134	99.223
21	98.977	98.743	99.367	97.851	99.144
22	98.865	98.594	99.320	97.547	99.057
23	98.751	98.443	99.274	97.232	98.963
24	98.636	98.291	99.225	96.913	98.861
25	98.519	98.138	99.175	96.591	98.752
26	98.401	97.985	99.124	96.265	98.636
27	98.280	97.831	99.070	95.928	98.510
28	98.155	97.672	99.015	95.574	98.373
29	98.026	97.509	98.956	95.198	98.224
30	97.891	97.340	98.895	94.798	98.062
31	97.749	97.166	98.830	94.364	97.888
32	97.601	96.985	98.760	93.895	97.701
33	97.446	96.798	98.688	93.412	97.503
34	97.284	96.603	98.613	92.895	97.296

1989 U. S. POPULATION

	TOTAL POPULATION	WHITE MALE	WHITE FEMALE	BLACK MALE	BLACK FEMALE
35	97.114	96.399	98.534	92.342	97.077
36	96.934	96.185	98.451	91.752	96.847
37	96.746	95.962	98.361	91.129	96.602
38	96.549	95.729	98.264	90.481	96.340
39	96.338	95.488	98.157	89.811	96.058
40	96.118	95.237	98.039	89.120	95.755
41	95.897	94.974	97.908	88.406	95.429
42	95.656	94.696	97.766	87.665	95.081
43	95.396	94.399	97.610	86.895	94.710
44	95.117	94.080	97.441	86.093	94.317
45	94.817	93.736	97.257	85.259	93.899
46	94.494	93.363	97.056	84.328	93.454
47	94.144	92.959	96.833	83.478	92.980
48	93.762	92.521	96.587	82.530	92.476
49	93.347	92.047	96.313	81.509	91.936
50	92.894	91.534	96.009	80.425	91.360
51	92.401	90.975	95.672	79.356	90.743
52	91.861	90.363	95.299	78.225	90.081
53	91.271	89.686	94.888	77.035	89.368
54	90.624	88.937	94.436	75.792	88.601
55	89.918	88.111	93.941	74.498	87.776
56	89.154	87.204	93.399	73.154	86.890
57	88.325	86.213	92.807	71.758	85.933
58	87.424	85.131	92.160	70.303	84.892
59	86.445	83.955	91.456	68.784	83.756
60	85.390	82.681	90.689	67.195	82.520
61	84.255	81.306	89.856	65.537	81.186
62	83.033	79.833	88.956	63.809	79.764
63	81.738	78.266	87.986	62.013	78.271
64	80.356	76.609	86.944	60.148	76.717
65	78.894	74.862	85.827	58.216	75.106
66	77.340	73.005	84.797	56.219	73.419
67	75.685	71.034	83.533	54.159	71.656
68	73.929	68.948	82.247	52.037	69.815
69	72.073	66.744	80.865	49.864	67.897
70	70.105	64.424	79.385	47.637	65.902
71	68.030	61.981	77.798	45.367	63.817
72	65.840	59.417	76.094	43.058	61.643
73	63.535	56.737	74.268	40.724	59.382

1989 U. S. POPULATION

	TOTAL POPULATION	WHITE MALE	WHITE FEMALE	BLACK MALE	BLACK FEMALE
74	61.121	53.945	72.314	38.367	57.036
75	58.597	51.051	70.232	36.001	54.610
76	55.960	48.063	68.012	33.633	52.082
77	53.212	44.994	65.639	31.252	49.456
78	50.365	41.861	63.112	28.878	46.742
79	47.424	38.682	60.436	26.519	43.949
80	44.403	35.478	57.607	24.192	41.091
81	41.157	32.149	54.635	21.910	38.026
82	37.704	28.732	51.362	19.579	34.776
83	34.077	25.274	47.798	17.240	31.367
84	30.312	21.828	43.950	14.929	27.843
85	26.468	18.458	39.845	12.671	24.256
86	22.617	15.230	35.530	10.515	20.675
87	18.840	12.213	31.067	8.501	17.175
88	15.230	9.473	26.541	6.669	13.842
89	11.881	7.066	22.058	5.051	10.762
90	8.882	5.032	17.737	3.673	8.017
91	6.310	3.392	13.707	2.545	5.673
92	4.213	2.139	10.095	1.665	3.771
93	2.606	1.245	7.010	1.018	2.322
94	1.465	.655	4.526	.572	1.299
95	.729	.304	2.666	.290	.643
96	.309	.119	1.395	.129	.271
97	.104	.037	.624	.049	.091
98	.025	0.000	.224	.015	.022
99	0.000	0.000	.057	0.000	0.000

PROBABILITY OF LIVING TO AGE 'X' STARTING FROM AGE 2

1989 U. S. POPULATION

LIFE EXPECTANCY TO AGE	TOTAL POPULATION	WHITE MALE	WHITE FEMALE	BLACK MALE	BLACK FEMALE
	74.10	71.40	77.70	64.20	72.90
3	99.960	99.962	99.968	99.928	99.939
4	99.927	99.930	99.941	99.869	99.890
5	99.898	99.901	99.918	99.818	99.850
6	99.872	99.874	99.897	99.773	99.818
7	99.848	99.848	99.878	99.733	99.791
8	99.827	99.825	99.861	99.699	99.768
9	99.809	99.805	99.846	99.671	99.746
10	99.793	99.788	99.833	99.648	99.723
11	99.776	99.771	99.820	99.624	99.698
12	99.754	99.747	99.804	99.590	99.671
13	99.722	99.708	99.782	99.535	99.642
14	99.675	99.650	99.752	99.353	99.609
15	99.613	99.568	99.713	99.238	99.572
16	99.534	99.465	99.666	99.092	99.530
17	99.443	99.345	99.613	98.915	99.482
18	99.345	99.215	99.558	98.711	99.429
19	99.243	99.079	99.505	98.481	99.367
20	99.137	98.938	99.455	98.224	99.297
21	99.028	98.793	99.408	97.940	99.219
22	98.916	98.644	99.361	97.636	99.132
23	98.803	98.493	99.314	97.321	99.037
24	98.687	98.340	99.266	97.001	98.935
25	98.571	98.188	99.216	96.679	98.827
26	98.452	98.034	99.164	96.353	98.710
27	98.331	97.879	99.111	96.015	98.584
28	98.206	97.721	99.055	95.661	98.447
29	98.077	97.558	98.997	95.284	98.298
30	97.941	97.389	98.935	94.884	98.136
31	97.799	97.215	98.870	94.450	97.961
32	97.652	97.034	98.801	93.980	97.774
33	97.496	96.847	98.729	93.497	97.576
34	97.335	96.651	98.654	92.980	97.369
35	97.164	96.447	98.575	92.426	97.150

1989 U. S. POPULATION

	TOTAL POPULATION	WHITE MALE	WHITE FEMALE	BLACK MALE	BLACK FEMALE
36	96.985	96.233	98.491	91.835	96.919
37	96.796	96.010	98.401	91.212	96.674
38	96.599	95.777	98.304	90.563	96.412
39	96.388	95.536	98.197	89.893	96.131
40	96.168	95.285	98.079	89.202	95.827
41	95.946	95.022	97.949	88.486	95.501
42	95.706	94.743	97.806	87.745	95.152
43	95.445	94.447	97.650	86.974	94.781
44	95.167	94.127	97.481	86.172	94.388
45	94.867	93.783	97.297	85.337	93.970
46	94.543	93.410	97.096	84.405	93.524
47	94.193	93.005	96.873	83.554	93.050
48	93.811	92.567	96.627	82.606	92.545
49	93.396	92.093	96.353	81.584	92.005
50	92.943	91.579	96.048	80.499	91.429
51	92.449	91.021	95.711	79.428	90.811
52	91.909	90.408	95.338	78.296	90.148
53	91.318	89.731	94.927	77.105	89.435
54	90.672	88.982	94.475	75.861	88.667
55	89.965	88.155	93.980	74.566	87.842
56	89.201	87.248	93.438	73.221	86.955
57	88.371	86.256	92.845	71.823	85.998
58	87.470	85.173	92.198	70.367	84.956
59	86.490	83.997	91.494	68.846	83.819
60	85.435	82.722	90.726	67.256	82.582
61	84.298	81.346	89.893	65.596	81.246
62	83.076	79.872	88.993	63.867	79.824
63	81.780	78.305	88.022	62.069	78.330
64	80.398	76.647	86.980	60.203	76.775
65	78.935	74.899	85.862	58.269	75.162
66	77.380	73.041	84.831	56.270	73.474
67	75.724	71.070	83.567	54.208	71.709
68	73.967	68.982	82.281	52.085	69.867
69	72.111	66.778	80.898	49.909	67.948
70	70.142	64.456	79.418	47.680	65.952
71	68.066	62.012	77.829	45.408	63.865
72	65.874	59.447	76.125	43.098	61.689
73	63.568	56.765	74.298	40.761	59.426
74	61.153	53.972	72.344	38.402	57.079

1989 U. S. POPULATION

	TOTAL POPULATION	WHITE MALE	WHITE FEMALE	BLACK MALE	BLACK FEMALE
75	58.627	51.076	70.260	36.034	54.651
76	55.989	48.087	68.040	33.663	52.121
77	53.240	45.017	65.666	31.281	49.494
78	50.392	41.882	63.137	28.904	46.777
79	47.449	38.701	60.460	26.543	43.982
80	44.426	35.495	57.631	24.214	41.121
81	41.179	32.165	54.657	21.930	38.055
82	37.724	28.747	51.383	19.597	34.802
83	34.095	25.286	47.817	17.256	31.391
84	30.327	21.839	43.968	14.943	27.864
85	26.482	18.467	39.861	12.683	24.275
86	22.629	15.237	35.544	10.524	20.690
87	18.850	12.219	31.080	8.509	17.188
88	15.238	9.477	26.552	6.675	13.852
89	11.887	7.069	22.067	5.056	10.770
90	8.887	5.034	17.744	3.676	8.023
91	6.313	3.393	13.713	2.547	5.677
92	4.215	2.140	10.099	1.667	3.774
93	2.607	1.245	7.013	1.019	2.324
94	1.466	.655	4.528	.573	1.300
95	.730	.304	2.667	.291	.644
96	.309	.119	1.396	.130	.271
97	.105	.037	.624	.049	.091
98	.025	0.000	.224	.015	.022
99	0.000	0.000	.057	0.000	0.000

PROBABILITY OF LIVING TO AGE 'X' STARTING FROM AGE 3

1989 U. S. POPULATION

	TOTAL POPULATION	WHITE MALE	WHITE FEMALE	BLACK MALE	BLACK FEMALE
LIFE EXPECTANCY TO AGE	73.10	70.40	76.90	63.30	71.90
4	99.967	99.968	99.973	99.941	99.951
5	99.938	99.939	99.950	99.890	99.911
6	99.912	99.912	99.929	99.845	99.879
7	99.888	99.886	99.910	99.805	99.852
8	99.867	99.863	99.893	99.771	99.829
9	99.849	99.843	99.878	99.743	99.807
10	99.833	99.826	99.865	99.719	99.784
11	99.816	99.809	99.852	99.695	99.759
12	99.794	99.785	99.836	99.662	99.732
13	99.762	99.746	99.814	99.607	99.702
14	99.715	99.687	99.784	99.424	99.669
15	99.653	99.606	99.745	99.309	99.633
16	99.574	99.503	99.697	99.163	99.591
17	99.483	99.383	99.645	98.987	99.543
18	99.385	99.253	99.590	98.782	99.489
19	99.282	99.117	99.537	98.552	99.428
20	99.177	98.976	99.487	98.294	99.358
21	99.068	98.830	99.439	98.010	99.279
22	98.956	98.681	99.393	97.706	99.192
23	98.842	98.530	99.346	97.391	99.098
24	98.727	98.377	99.297	97.071	98.996
25	98.610	98.225	99.248	96.749	98.887
26	98.492	98.072	99.196	96.422	98.770
27	98.371	97.917	99.143	96.085	98.644
28	98.246	97.758	99.087	95.730	98.507
29	98.116	97.595	99.029	95.353	98.358
30	97.981	97.426	98.967	94.952	98.196
31	97.839	97.252	98.902	94.518	98.021
32	97.691	97.071	98.833	94.048	97.834
33	97.535	96.883	98.760	93.564	97.636
34	97.374	96.688	98.685	93.047	97.428
35	97.203	96.484	98.606	92.492	97.209
36	97.023	96.269	98.523	91.901	96.978

1989 U. S. POPULATION

	TOTAL POPULATION	WHITE MALE	WHITE FEMALE	BLACK MALE	BLACK FEMALE
37	96.835	96.046	98.433	91.277	96.733
38	96.638	95.814	98.336	90.628	96.471
39	96.427	95.572	98.228	89.958	96.189
40	96.206	95.321	98.110	89.266	95.885
41	95.985	95.058	97.980	88.550	95.559
42	95.744	94.779	97.837	87.808	95.210
43	95.483	94.483	97.681	87.037	94.839
44	95.205	94.163	97.512	86.234	94.446
45	94.905	93.819	97.328	85.398	94.027
46	94.581	93.445	97.127	84.466	93.581
47	94.230	93.041	96.904	83.614	93.107
48	93.849	92.602	96.658	82.665	92.601
49	93.433	92.128	96.384	81.643	92.062
50	92.980	91.614	96.079	80.557	91.484
51	92.486	91.055	95.742	79.485	90.867
52	91.946	90.443	95.368	78.353	90.204
53	91.355	89.765	94.957	77.161	89.490
54	90.708	89.016	94.505	75.915	88.721
55	90.001	88.189	94.010	74.620	87.895
56	89.236	87.281	93.468	73.273	87.008
57	88.406	86.289	92.875	71.875	86.050
58	87.505	85.206	92.228	70.418	85.008
59	86.525	84.029	91.523	68.896	83.870
60	85.469	82.754	90.755	67.305	82.632
61	84.332	81.377	89.922	65.643	81.296
62	83.109	79.903	89.021	63.913	79.873
63	81.813	78.335	88.050	62.114	78.377
64	80.430	76.676	87.007	60.246	76.822
65	78.966	74.928	85.889	58.311	75.208
66	77.411	73.069	84.859	56.310	73.519
67	75.754	71.097	83.594	54.247	71.753
68	73.997	69.009	82.307	52.122	69.910
69	72.139	66.803	80.924	49.945	67.989
70	70.170	64.480	79.443	47.715	65.992
71	68.093	62.035	77.854	45.441	63.904
72	65.900	59.469	76.149	43.129	61.727
73	63.594	56.787	74.322	40.790	59.463
74	61.177	53.993	72.367	38.429	57.114
75	58.651	51.096	70.283	36.060	54.685

1989 U. S. POPULATION

	TOTAL POPULATION	WHITE MALE	WHITE FEMALE	BLACK MALE	BLACK FEMALE
76	56.011	48.105	68.062	33.688	52.153
77	53.261	45.034	65.687	31.303	49.524
78	50.412	41.898	63.158	28.925	46.806
79	47.468	38.716	60.480	26.563	44.009
80	44.444	35.509	57.649	24.231	41.146
81	41.195	32.177	54.675	21.946	38.078
82	37.739	28.758	51.400	19.611	34.823
83	34.108	25.296	47.832	17.268	31.410
84	30.339	21.847	43.982	14.954	27.881
85	26.492	18.474	39.874	12.692	24.289
86	22.638	15.243	35.556	10.532	20.703
87	18.857	12.224	31.090	8.515	17.198
88	15.244	9.481	26.560	6.680	13.861
89	11.892	7.072	22.074	5.060	10.777
90	8.890	5.036	17.750	3.679	8.028
91	6.316	3.395	13.717	2.549	5.681
92	4.216	2.141	10.103	1.668	3.777
93	2.608	1.246	7.015	1.019	2.325
94	1.467	.656	4.529	.573	1.301
95	.730	.304	2.668	.291	.644
96	.309	.119	1.396	.130	.271
97	.105	.037	.624	.049	.091
98	.025	0.000	.224	.015	.022
99	0.000	0.000	.057	0.000	0.000

PROBABILITY OF LIVING TO AGE 'X' STARTING FROM AGE 4

1989 U. S. POPULATION

	TOTAL POPULATION	WHITE MALE	WHITE FEMALE	BLACK MALE	BLACK FEMALE
LIFE EXPECTANCY TO AGE	72.10	69.50	75.90	62.30	71.00
5	99.971	99.971	99.977	99.949	99.960
6	99.945	99.944	99.956	99.904	99.928
7	99.921	99.918	99.937	99.864	99.901
8	99.900	99.895	99.920	99.830	99.878
9	99.882	99.875	99.905	99.802	99.856
10	99.866	99.858	99.892	99.778	99.833
11	99.849	99.841	99.879	99.754	99.808
12	99.827	99.817	99.863	99.720	99.781
13	99.795	99.778	99.841	99.665	99.751
14	99.748	99.719	99.811	99.483	99.718
15	99.685	99.638	99.772	99.368	99.681
16	99.607	99.535	99.724	99.222	99.640
17	99.516	99.415	99.671	99.045	99.592
18	99.418	99.284	99.617	98.840	99.538
19	99.315	99.148	99.564	98.610	99.476
20	99.210	99.007	99.514	98.352	99.407
21	99.101	98.862	99.466	98.068	99.328
22	98.989	98.713	99.420	97.764	99.241
23	98.875	98.562	99.373	97.448	99.146
24	98.759	98.409	99.324	97.129	99.044
25	98.643	98.256	99.274	96.806	98.935
26	98.524	98.103	99.223	96.479	98.819
27	98.403	97.948	99.169	96.141	98.692
28	98.278	97.789	99.114	95.787	98.555
29	98.148	97.626	99.055	95.409	98.406
30	98.013	97.457	98.994	95.008	98.244
31	97.871	97.283	98.929	94.574	98.069
32	97.723	97.102	98.859	94.103	97.882
33	97.568	96.914	98.787	93.620	97.684
34	97.406	96.719	98.712	93.102	97.476
35	97.235	96.515	98.633	92.547	97.256
36	97.055	96.300	98.549	91.956	97.026
37	96.867	96.077	98.460	91.331	96.780

1989 U. S. POPULATION

	TOTAL POPULATION	WHITE MALE	WHITE FEMALE	BLACK MALE	BLACK FEMALE
38	96.669	95.844	98.362	90.682	96.518
39	96.459	95.603	98.255	90.011	96.236
40	96.238	95.351	98.137	89.319	95.932
41	96.017	95.088	98.006	88.602	95.606
42	95.776	94.810	97.863	87.860	95.257
43	95.515	94.513	97.708	87.088	94.886
44	95.236	94.193	97.539	86.285	94.492
45	94.936	93.849	97.354	85.448	94.073
46	94.612	93.475	97.153	84.515	93.627
47	94.261	93.070	96.930	83.663	93.153
48	93.880	92.632	96.684	82.714	92.647
49	93.464	92.158	96.410	81.691	92.107
50	93.010	91.643	96.105	80.604	91.529
51	92.517	91.084	95.768	79.532	90.911
52	91.976	90.471	95.394	78.399	90.248
53	91.385	89.794	94.983	77.206	89.534
54	90.738	89.044	94.531	75.960	88.765
55	90.031	88.217	94.035	74.664	87.938
56	89.266	87.309	93.493	73.317	87.051
57	88.436	86.316	92.900	71.917	86.093
58	87.534	85.233	92.253	70.459	85.049
59	86.553	84.056	91.548	68.937	83.911
60	85.497	82.780	90.780	67.344	82.673
61	84.360	81.403	89.946	65.682	81.336
62	83.137	79.928	89.045	63.951	79.912
63	81.840	78.360	88.074	62.151	78.416
64	80.457	76.701	87.031	60.282	76.859
65	78.993	74.952	85.912	58.346	75.245
66	77.436	73.092	84.882	56.344	73.555
67	75.779	71.119	83.617	54.279	71.788
68	74.021	69.031	82.329	52.153	69.944
69	72.163	66.824	80.946	49.975	68.023
70	70.193	64.501	79.465	47.743	66.024
71	68.115	62.055	77.875	45.467	63.935
72	65.922	59.488	76.170	43.154	61.757
73	63.615	56.805	74.342	40.814	59.492
74	61.197	54.010	72.387	38.452	57.142
75	58.670	51.112	70.302	36.081	54.712
76	56.030	48.120	68.080	33.708	52.178

1989 U. S. POPULATION

	TOTAL POPULATION	WHITE MALE	WHITE FEMALE	BLACK MALE	BLACK FEMALE
77	53.279	45.048	65.704	31.322	49.548
78	50.428	41.912	63.175	28.942	46.829
79	47.483	38.728	60.496	26.578	44.031
80	44.459	35.520	57.665	24.246	41.167
81	41.209	32.187	54.689	21.959	38.097
82	37.751	28.767	51.414	19.622	34.840
83	34.120	25.304	47.845	17.279	31.425
84	30.349	21.854	43.994	14.963	27.894
85	26.501	18.480	39.885	12.699	24.301
86	22.645	15.248	35.565	10.538	20.713
87	18.863	12.227	31.098	8.520	17.207
88	15.249	9.484	26.567	6.684	13.867
89	11.896	7.074	22.080	5.063	10.782
90	8.893	5.038	17.755	3.681	8.032
91	6.318	3.396	13.721	2.550	5.684
92	4.218	2.142	10.105	1.669	3.778
93	2.609	1.246	7.017	1.020	2.327
94	1.467	.656	4.530	.574	1.302
95	.730	.304	2.668	.291	.644
96	.309	.119	1.396	.130	.271
97	.105	.037	.624	.049	.091
98	.025	0.000	.224	.015	.022
99	0.000	0.000	.057	0.000	0.000

PROBABILITY OF LIVING TO AGE 'X' STARTING FROM AGE 5

1989 U. S. POPULATION

	TOTAL POPULATION	WHITE MALE	WHITE FEMALE	BLACK MALE	BLACK FEMALE
LIFE EXPECTANCY TO AGE	71.10	68.50	74.90	61.40	70.00
6	99.974	99.973	99.979	99.955	99.968
7	99.950	99.947	99.960	99.915	99.941
8	99.929	99.924	99.943	99.881	99.918
9	99.911	99.904	99.928	99.853	99.896
10	99.895	99.887	99.915	99.829	99.873
11	99.878	99.870	99.902	99.805	99.848
12	99.856	99.846	99.886	99.771	99.821
13	99.824	99.807	99.864	99.716	99.791
14	99.777	99.748	99.834	99.534	99.758
15	99.714	99.666	99.795	99.418	99.721
16	99.636	99.564	99.747	99.272	99.679
17	99.545	99.443	99.694	99.096	99.632
18	99.446	99.313	99.640	98.890	99.578
19	99.344	99.177	99.587	98.660	99.516
20	99.239	99.036	99.537	98.403	99.446
21	99.129	98.891	99.489	98.118	99.368
22	99.017	98.741	99.442	97.814	99.280
23	98.904	98.590	99.396	97.498	99.186
24	98.788	98.437	99.347	97.178	99.084
25	98.671	98.285	99.297	96.856	98.975
26	98.553	98.131	99.246	96.528	98.858
27	98.432	97.976	99.192	96.190	98.732
28	98.307	97.818	99.137	95.835	98.594
29	98.177	97.654	99.078	95.458	98.445
30	98.041	97.485	99.017	95.057	98.283
31	97.899	97.311	98.951	94.623	98.108
32	97.751	97.130	98.882	94.151	97.921
33	97.596	96.942	98.810	93.667	97.723
34	97.434	96.747	98.735	93.149	97.515
35	97.263	96.543	98.656	92.594	97.295
36	97.084	96.328	98.572	92.003	97.065
37	96.895	96.105	98.482	91.378	96.819
38	96.698	95.872	98.385	90.728	96.557

1989 U. S. POPULATION

	TOTAL POPULATION	WHITE MALE	WHITE FEMALE	BLACK MALE	BLACK FEMALE
39	96.487	95.631	98.277	90.057	96.275
40	96.266	95.379	98.160	89.364	95.971
41	96.044	95.116	98.029	88.648	95.644
42	95.803	94.837	97.886	87.905	95.295
43	95.543	94.540	97.730	87.133	94.924
44	95.264	94.221	97.561	86.329	94.530
45	94.964	93.876	97.377	85.492	94.111
46	94.640	93.502	97.175	84.559	93.665
47	94.289	93.097	96.953	83.706	93.190
48	93.907	92.659	96.706	82.756	92.684
49	93.491	92.184	96.432	81.732	92.144
50	93.037	91.670	96.127	80.645	91.566
51	92.543	91.111	95.790	79.573	90.948
52	92.003	90.498	95.416	78.439	90.284
53	91.411	89.820	95.005	77.246	89.570
54	90.764	89.070	94.553	75.999	88.800
55	90.057	88.242	94.057	74.702	87.974
56	89.292	87.334	93.514	73.354	87.086
57	88.461	86.341	92.922	71.954	86.127
58	87.559	85.258	92.274	70.495	85.083
59	86.578	84.080	91.569	68.972	83.945
60	85.522	82.804	90.801	67.379	82.706
61	84.385	81.427	89.967	65.716	81.368
62	83.161	79.952	89.066	63.983	79.944
63	81.864	78.383	88.094	62.182	78.447
64	80.480	76.723	87.051	60.313	76.890
65	79.015	74.974	85.932	58.375	75.275
66	77.459	73.113	84.901	56.372	73.585
67	75.801	71.140	83.636	54.307	71.817
68	74.043	69.051	82.348	52.180	69.972
69	72.184	66.844	80.965	50.000	68.050
70	70.214	64.520	79.483	47.767	66.051
71	68.135	62.073	77.893	45.491	63.961
72	65.941	59.506	76.187	43.176	61.782
73	63.633	56.821	74.359	40.835	59.516
74	61.215	54.026	72.403	38.471	57.165
75	58.687	51.127	70.318	36.099	54.733
76	56.046	48.134	68.096	33.725	52.199
77	53.294	45.061	65.719	31.338	49.568

1989 U. S. POPULATION

	TOTAL POPULATION	WHITE MALE	WHITE FEMALE	BLACK MALE	BLACK FEMALE
78	50.443	41.924	63.189	28.957	46.848
79	47.497	38.740	60.510	26.592	44.048
80	44.472	35.531	57.678	24.258	41.183
81	41.221	32.197	54.702	21.970	38.112
82	37.762	28.775	51.425	19.632	34.854
83	34.130	25.311	47.856	17.287	31.438
84	30.358	21.861	44.004	14.970	27.906
85	26.509	18.485	39.894	12.706	24.311
86	22.652	15.252	35.573	10.543	20.721
87	18.869	12.231	31.105	8.524	17.214
88	15.254	9.487	26.573	6.687	13.873
89	11.899	7.076	22.085	5.065	10.786
90	8.896	5.039	17.759	3.683	8.035
91	6.320	3.397	13.724	2.552	5.686
92	4.219	2.142	10.108	1.670	3.780
93	2.610	1.247	7.019	1.020	2.327
94	1.468	.656	4.531	.574	1.302
95	.730	.304	2.669	.291	.645
96	.309	.119	1.397	.130	.271
97	.105	.037	.625	.049	.091
98	.025	0.000	.224	.015	.022
99	0.000	0.000	.057	0.000	0.000

PROBABILITY OF LIVING TO AGE 'X' STARTING FROM AGE 6

1989 U. S. POPULATION

	TOTAL POPULATION	WHITE MALE	WHITE FEMALE	BLACK MALE	BLACK FEMALE
LIFE EXPECTANCY TO AGE	70.20	67.50	73.90	60.40	69.00
7	99.976	99.974	99.981	99.960	99.973
8	99.955	99.951	99.964	99.926	99.950
9	99.937	99.931	99.949	99.898	99.928
10	99.921	99.914	99.936	99.874	99.905
11	99.904	99.897	99.923	99.850	99.880
12	99.882	99.873	99.907	99.816	99.853
13	99.850	99.834	99.885	99.761	99.823
14	99.803	99.775	99.855	99.579	99.790
15	99.740	99.693	99.816	99.463	99.753
16	99.661	99.591	99.768	99.317	99.711
17	99.571	99.470	99.715	99.140	99.664
18	99.472	99.340	99.661	98.935	99.610
19	99.370	99.204	99.608	98.704	99.548
20	99.264	99.063	99.558	98.447	99.478
21	99.155	98.917	99.510	98.162	99.400
22	99.043	98.768	99.463	97.858	99.312
23	98.929	98.617	99.417	97.542	99.218
24	98.814	98.464	99.368	97.222	99.116
25	98.697	98.311	99.318	96.899	99.007
26	98.579	98.158	99.267	96.572	98.890
27	98.457	98.003	99.213	96.234	98.763
28	98.332	97.844	99.157	95.879	98.626
29	98.202	97.681	99.099	95.501	98.477
30	98.067	97.512	99.037	95.100	98.315
31	97.925	97.337	98.972	94.665	98.140
32	97.777	97.156	98.903	94.194	97.952
33	97.621	96.969	98.831	93.710	97.754
34	97.459	96.773	98.755	93.191	97.546
35	97.289	96.569	98.676	92.636	97.327
36	97.109	96.354	98.593	92.044	97.096
37	96.920	96.131	98.503	91.419	96.850
38	96.723	95.898	98.405	90.769	96.588
39	96.512	95.656	98.298	90.097	96.306

1989 U. S. POPULATION

	TOTAL POPULATION	WHITE MALE	WHITE FEMALE	BLACK MALE	BLACK FEMALE
40	96.291	95.405	98.180	89.404	96.001
41	96.069	95.141	98.050	88.687	95.675
42	95.828	94.863	97.906	87.944	95.326
43	95.568	94.566	97.751	87.172	94.954
44	95.289	94.246	97.582	86.367	94.560
45	94.988	93.901	97.397	85.531	94.141
46	94.664	93.527	97.196	84.597	93.695
47	94.313	93.123	96.973	83.744	93.220
48	93.931	92.684	96.727	82.793	92.714
49	93.515	92.209	96.452	81.769	92.173
50	93.062	91.695	96.147	80.682	91.595
51	92.567	91.135	95.810	79.609	90.977
52	92.027	90.522	95.436	78.474	90.313
53	91.435	89.844	95.025	77.281	89.598
54	90.788	89.094	94.572	76.033	88.829
55	90.081	88.266	94.077	74.735	88.002
56	89.315	87.358	93.534	73.387	87.114
57	88.484	86.365	92.941	71.986	86.155
58	87.582	85.281	92.293	70.527	85.110
59	86.601	84.103	91.588	69.003	83.972
60	85.544	82.826	90.820	67.409	82.732
61	84.406	81.449	89.986	65.745	81.394
62	83.183	79.973	89.084	64.012	79.969
63	81.885	78.404	88.112	62.210	78.472
64	80.501	76.744	87.069	60.340	76.915
65	79.036	74.994	85.950	58.402	75.299
66	77.479	73.133	84.919	56.398	73.608
67	75.821	71.159	83.654	54.331	71.840
68	74.062	69.069	82.365	52.203	69.995
69	72.203	66.862	80.982	50.023	68.072
70	70.232	64.537	79.500	47.789	66.072
71	68.153	62.090	77.910	45.511	63.981
72	65.958	59.522	76.203	43.195	61.801
73	63.650	56.837	74.375	40.853	59.535
74	61.231	54.040	72.419	38.489	57.183
75	58.702	51.141	70.333	36.116	54.751
76	56.061	48.147	68.110	33.740	52.216
77	53.308	45.074	65.733	31.352	49.584
78	50.456	41.935	63.203	28.970	46.863

1989 U. S. POPULATION

	TOTAL POPULATION	WHITE MALE	WHITE FEMALE	BLACK MALE	BLACK FEMALE
79	47.509	38.750	60.523	26.604	44.063
80	44.483	35.540	57.690	24.269	41.196
81	41.231	32.205	54.713	21.980	38.124
82	37.772	28.783	51.436	19.641	34.865
83	34.138	25.318	47.866	17.295	31.448
84	30.366	21.867	44.013	14.977	27.914
85	26.516	18.490	39.902	12.712	24.319
86	22.658	15.256	35.581	10.548	20.728
87	18.874	12.234	31.112	8.528	17.219
88	15.258	9.489	26.579	6.690	13.877
89	11.902	7.078	22.090	5.067	10.790
90	8.898	5.041	17.762	3.684	8.038
91	6.321	3.398	13.727	2.553	5.688
92	4.220	2.143	10.110	1.671	3.781
93	2.611	1.247	7.020	1.021	2.328
94	1.468	.656	4.532	.574	1.303
95	.730	.304	2.669	.291	.645
96	.309	.119	1.397	.130	.271
97	.105	.037	.625	.049	.091
98	.025	0.000	.224	.015	.022
99	0.000	0.000	.058	0.000	0.000

PROBABILITY OF LIVING TO AGE 'X' STARTING FROM AGE 7

1989 U. S. POPULATION

	TOTAL POPULATION	WHITE MALE	WHITE FEMALE	BLACK MALE	BLACK FEMALE
LIFE EXPECTANCY TO AGE	69.20	66.50	73.00	59.40	68.00
8	99.979	99.977	99.983	99.966	99.977
9	99.961	99.957	99.968	99.938	99.955
10	99.945	99.940	99.955	99.914	99.932
11	99.928	99.923	99.942	99.890	99.907
12	99.906	99.899	99.926	99.856	99.880
13	99.874	99.860	99.904	99.801	99.850
14	99.827	99.801	99.874	99.619	99.817
15	99.764	99.719	99.835	99.503	99.780
16	99.685	99.617	99.787	99.357	99.738
17	99.595	99.496	99.734	99.180	99.690
18	99.496	99.366	99.679	98.975	99.637
19	99.394	99.230	99.627	98.744	99.575
20	99.288	99.089	99.577	98.486	99.505
21	99.179	98.943	99.529	98.202	99.427
22	99.067	98.794	99.482	97.897	99.339
23	98.953	98.642	99.435	97.581	99.245
24	98.837	98.490	99.387	97.261	99.142
25	98.721	98.337	99.337	96.938	99.033
26	98.602	98.184	99.285	96.610	98.917
27	98.481	98.028	99.232	96.272	98.790
28	98.356	97.870	99.176	95.917	98.653
29	98.226	97.706	99.118	95.539	98.504
30	98.090	97.537	99.056	95.138	98.341
31	97.948	97.363	98.991	94.703	98.166
32	97.800	97.181	98.922	94.231	97.979
33	97.645	96.994	98.849	93.747	97.781
34	97.483	96.798	98.774	93.229	97.572
35	97.312	96.594	98.695	92.673	97.353
36	97.132	96.379	98.611	92.081	97.122
37	96.944	96.156	98.522	91.456	96.876
38	96.746	95.923	98.424	90.805	96.614
39	96.535	95.681	98.317	90.133	96.332
40	96.314	95.430	98.199	89.440	96.027

1989 U. S. POPULATION

	TOTAL POPULATION	WHITE MALE	WHITE FEMALE	BLACK MALE	BLACK FEMALE
41	96.092	95.166	98.068	88.723	95.701
42	95.851	94.887	97.925	87.979	95.352
43	95.591	94.590	97.769	87.207	94.980
44	95.311	94.271	97.600	86.402	94.585
45	95.011	93.926	97.416	85.565	94.166
46	94.687	93.552	97.214	84.630	93.720
47	94.336	93.147	96.991	83.777	93.245
48	93.954	92.708	96.745	82.826	92.739
49	93.538	92.233	96.470	81.802	92.198
50	93.084	91.719	96.165	80.714	91.620
51	92.590	91.159	95.828	79.640	91.001
52	92.049	90.546	95.454	78.506	90.337
53	91.457	89.868	95.043	77.312	89.623
54	90.810	89.117	94.590	76.064	88.853
55	90.102	88.289	94.095	74.765	88.025
56	89.336	87.381	93.552	73.417	87.137
57	88.505	86.387	92.959	72.015	86.178
58	87.603	85.303	92.311	70.555	85.133
59	86.622	84.125	91.606	69.031	83.994
60	85.565	82.848	90.837	67.436	82.755
61	84.427	81.470	90.003	65.772	81.416
62	83.203	79.994	89.101	64.038	79.991
63	81.905	78.425	88.129	62.235	78.493
64	80.520	76.763	87.086	60.364	76.935
65	79.055	75.013	85.967	58.425	75.320
66	77.498	73.152	84.935	56.420	73.628
67	75.839	71.178	83.670	54.353	71.859
68	74.080	69.087	82.381	52.224	70.013
69	72.220	66.879	80.997	50.043	68.090
70	70.249	64.554	79.515	47.808	66.090
71	68.169	62.106	77.924	45.529	63.999
72	65.974	59.537	76.218	43.213	61.818
73	63.665	56.852	74.389	40.870	59.551
74	61.246	54.054	72.432	38.504	57.198
75	58.716	51.154	70.346	36.130	54.766
76	56.074	48.160	68.123	33.753	52.230
77	53.321	45.085	65.746	31.364	49.597
78	50.468	41.946	63.215	28.981	46.875
79	47.521	38.760	60.534	26.614	44.074

1989 U. S. POPULATION

	TOTAL POPULATION	WHITE MALE	WHITE FEMALE	BLACK MALE	BLACK FEMALE
80	44.494	35.549	57.701	24.279	41.207
81	41.241	32.214	54.724	21.989	38.135
82	37.781	28.790	51.446	19.649	34.874
83	34.147	25.325	47.876	17.302	31.456
84	30.373	21.872	44.022	14.983	27.922
85	26.522	18.495	39.910	12.717	24.325
86	22.663	15.260	35.588	10.552	20.733
87	18.878	12.238	31.118	8.531	17.224
88	15.261	9.492	26.584	6.693	13.881
89	11.905	7.080	22.094	5.070	10.793
90	8.900	5.042	17.766	3.686	8.040
91	6.323	3.398	13.729	2.554	5.689
92	4.221	2.144	10.112	1.671	3.782
93	2.611	1.247	7.022	1.021	2.329
94	1.468	.656	4.533	.574	1.303
95	.731	.304	2.670	.292	.645
96	.309	.119	1.397	.130	.272
97	.105	.037	.625	.049	.091
98	.025	0.000	.224	.015	.022
99	0.000	0.000	.058	0.000	0.000

PROBABILITY OF LIVING TO AGE 'X' STARTING FROM AGE 8

1989 U. S. POPULATION

	TOTAL POPULATION	WHITE MALE	WHITE FEMALE	BLACK MALE	BLACK FEMALE
LIFE EXPECTANCY TO AGE	68.20	65.50	72.00	58.50	67.10
9	99.982	99.980	99.985	99.972	99.978
10	99.966	99.963	99.972	99.948	99.955
11	99.949	99.946	99.959	99.924	99.930
12	99.927	99.922	99.943	99.890	99.903
13	99.895	99.883	99.921	99.835	99.873
14	99.848	99.824	99.891	99.652	99.840
15	99.785	99.742	99.852	99.537	99.803
16	99.706	99.640	99.804	99.390	99.761
17	99.616	99.519	99.751	99.214	99.713
18	99.517	99.389	99.696	99.008	99.660
19	99.415	99.252	99.644	98.778	99.598
20	99.309	99.111	99.594	98.520	99.528
21	99.200	98.966	99.546	98.235	99.449
22	99.088	98.816	99.499	97.930	99.362
23	98.974	98.665	99.452	97.614	99.267
24	98.858	98.512	99.404	97.294	99.165
25	98.741	98.360	99.354	96.971	99.056
26	98.623	98.206	99.302	96.643	98.939
27	98.502	98.051	99.249	96.305	98.813
28	98.376	97.892	99.193	95.950	98.675
29	98.247	97.729	99.135	95.572	98.526
30	98.111	97.560	99.073	95.170	98.364
31	97.969	97.385	99.008	94.735	98.189
32	97.821	97.204	98.938	94.263	98.001
33	97.665	97.016	98.866	93.779	97.803
34	97.503	96.820	98.791	93.260	97.595
35	97.333	96.616	98.712	92.704	97.375
36	97.153	96.401	98.628	92.112	97.144
37	96.964	96.178	98.538	91.487	96.899
38	96.766	95.945	98.441	90.836	96.636
39	96.555	95.703	98.333	90.164	96.354
40	96.334	95.452	98.215	89.471	96.049
41	96.113	95.188	98.085	88.753	95.723

1989 U. S. POPULATION

	TOTAL POPULATION	WHITE MALE	WHITE FEMALE	BLACK MALE	BLACK FEMALE
42	95.871	94.909	97.942	88.009	95.373
43	95.611	94.612	97.786	87.237	95.001
44	95.331	94.292	97.617	86.431	94.607
45	95.031	93.947	97.432	85.594	94.188
46	94.707	93.573	97.231	84.659	93.742
47	94.356	93.168	97.008	83.806	93.266
48	93.974	92.729	96.762	82.855	92.760
49	93.557	92.255	96.487	81.830	92.219
50	93.103	91.740	96.182	80.741	91.641
51	92.609	91.180	95.844	79.668	91.022
52	92.068	90.567	95.470	78.532	90.358
53	91.476	89.888	95.059	77.338	89.643
54	90.829	89.138	94.606	76.090	88.873
55	90.121	88.310	94.111	74.791	88.046
56	89.355	87.401	93.568	73.441	87.157
57	88.524	86.407	92.975	72.039	86.198
58	87.621	85.323	92.326	70.579	85.153
59	86.640	84.144	91.621	69.054	84.014
60	85.583	82.867	90.852	67.459	82.774
61	84.444	81.489	90.018	65.794	81.435
62	83.220	80.012	89.116	64.060	80.009
63	81.922	78.443	88.144	62.256	78.511
64	80.537	76.781	87.101	60.384	76.953
65	79.072	75.031	85.981	58.445	75.337
66	77.514	73.169	84.949	56.440	73.645
67	75.855	71.194	83.684	54.372	71.876
68	74.095	69.103	82.395	52.242	70.030
69	72.235	66.895	81.011	50.060	68.106
70	70.263	64.569	79.528	47.824	66.105
71	68.184	62.120	77.938	45.545	64.013
72	65.988	59.551	76.231	43.227	61.832
73	63.678	56.865	74.401	40.884	59.564
74	61.259	54.067	72.445	38.517	57.212
75	58.729	51.166	70.358	36.142	54.778
76	56.086	48.171	68.135	33.765	52.242
77	53.332	45.096	65.757	31.375	49.609
78	50.479	41.956	63.225	28.991	46.886
79	47.531	38.769	60.545	26.623	44.085
80	44.503	35.558	57.711	24.287	41.217

1989 U. S. POPULATION

	TOTAL POPULATION	WHITE MALE	WHITE FEMALE	BLACK MALE	BLACK FEMALE
81	41.250	32.221	54.733	21.996	38.143
82	37.789	28.797	51.455	19.656	34.882
83	34.154	25.331	47.884	17.308	31.464
84	30.380	21.877	44.029	14.988	27.928
85	26.528	18.499	39.917	12.721	24.331
86	22.668	15.264	35.594	10.556	20.738
87	18.882	12.240	31.123	8.534	17.228
88	15.264	9.494	26.589	6.695	13.884
89	11.908	7.081	22.098	5.071	10.795
90	8.902	5.043	17.769	3.687	8.042
91	6.324	3.399	13.732	2.555	5.691
92	4.222	2.144	10.113	1.672	3.783
93	2.612	1.247	7.023	1.022	2.329
94	1.469	.657	4.534	.575	1.303
95	.731	.304	2.670	.292	.645
96	.309	.119	1.397	.130	.272
97	.105	.037	.625	.049	.091
98	.025	0.000	.224	.015	.022
99	0.000	0.000	.058	0.000	0.000

PROBABILITY OF LIVING TO AGE 'X' STARTING FROM AGE 9

1989 U. S. POPULATION

	TOTAL POPULATION	WHITE MALE	WHITE FEMALE	BLACK MALE	BLACK FEMALE
LIFE EXPECTANCY TO AGE	67.20	64.50	71.00	57.50	66.10
10	99.984	99.983	99.987	99.976	99.977
11	99.967	99.966	99.974	99.952	99.952
12	99.945	99.942	99.958	99.918	99.925
13	99.913	99.903	99.936	99.863	99.895
14	99.866	99.844	99.906	99.680	99.862
15	99.803	99.762	99.867	99.565	99.825
16	99.724	99.659	99.819	99.418	99.783
17	99.634	99.539	99.766	99.241	99.735
18	99.535	99.408	99.711	99.036	99.681
19	99.432	99.272	99.659	98.805	99.620
20	99.327	99.131	99.609	98.547	99.550
21	99.218	98.986	99.561	98.262	99.471
22	99.106	98.836	99.514	97.958	99.384
23	98.992	98.685	99.467	97.641	99.289
24	98.876	98.532	99.419	97.321	99.187
25	98.759	98.379	99.369	96.998	99.078
26	98.641	98.226	99.317	96.670	98.961
27	98.519	98.071	99.264	96.332	98.834
28	98.394	97.912	99.208	95.976	98.697
29	98.264	97.748	99.149	95.598	98.548
30	98.129	97.579	99.088	95.197	98.385
31	97.986	97.404	99.023	94.762	98.210
32	97.838	97.223	98.953	94.290	98.023
33	97.683	97.036	98.881	93.805	97.825
34	97.521	96.840	98.806	93.286	97.616
35	97.350	96.635	98.727	92.730	97.397
36	97.170	96.421	98.643	92.138	97.166
37	96.981	96.197	98.553	91.512	96.920
38	96.784	95.964	98.456	90.862	96.657
39	96.573	95.722	98.348	90.189	96.375
40	96.352	95.471	98.230	89.496	96.071
41	96.130	95.207	98.100	88.778	95.744
42	95.889	94.928	97.956	88.034	95.394

1989 U. S. POPULATION

	TOTAL POPULATION	WHITE MALE	WHITE FEMALE	BLACK MALE	BLACK FEMALE
43	95.628	94.631	97.801	87.261	95.022
44	95.349	94.311	97.631	86.456	94.628
45	95.048	93.966	97.447	85.618	94.209
46	94.724	93.592	97.245	84.683	93.762
47	94.373	93.187	97.022	83.829	93.287
48	93.990	92.748	96.776	82.878	92.780
49	93.574	92.273	96.501	81.853	92.239
50	93.120	91.758	96.196	80.764	91.661
51	92.626	91.198	95.859	79.690	91.042
52	92.085	90.585	95.485	78.554	90.378
53	91.493	89.906	95.073	77.359	89.663
54	90.845	89.155	94.621	76.111	88.893
55	90.137	88.327	94.125	74.812	88.065
56	89.371	87.418	93.582	73.462	87.177
57	88.540	86.424	92.988	72.060	86.217
58	87.637	85.340	92.340	70.599	85.172
59	86.655	84.161	91.635	69.073	84.032
60	85.598	82.884	90.866	67.478	82.792
61	84.460	81.505	90.032	65.812	81.453
62	83.235	80.028	89.130	64.078	80.027
63	81.937	78.458	88.157	62.274	78.529
64	80.552	76.796	87.114	60.401	76.970
65	79.086	75.046	85.994	58.461	75.354
66	77.528	73.184	84.962	56.455	73.661
67	75.869	71.208	83.696	54.387	71.892
68	74.109	69.117	82.407	52.257	70.045
69	72.248	66.908	81.023	50.074	68.121
70	70.276	64.582	79.540	47.837	66.119
71	68.196	62.133	77.949	45.558	64.027
72	66.000	59.563	76.242	43.240	61.846
73	63.690	56.876	74.412	40.895	59.577
74	61.270	54.078	72.455	38.528	57.224
75	58.739	51.176	70.369	36.152	54.790
76	56.096	48.181	68.145	33.774	52.254
77	53.342	45.105	65.767	31.384	49.620
78	50.488	41.964	63.235	28.999	46.896
79	47.539	38.777	60.554	26.631	44.094
80	44.511	35.565	57.720	24.294	41.226
81	41.257	32.228	54.741	22.002	38.152

1989 U. S. POPULATION

	TOTAL POPULATION	WHITE MALE	WHITE FEMALE	BLACK MALE	BLACK FEMALE
82	37.796	28.803	51.462	19.661	34.890
83	34.160	25.336	47.891	17.313	31.471
84	30.385	21.882	44.036	14.992	27.935
85	26.532	18.503	39.923	12.725	24.336
86	22.672	15.267	35.599	10.559	20.743
87	18.886	12.243	31.128	8.537	17.231
88	15.267	9.496	26.593	6.697	13.887
89	11.910	7.083	22.101	5.073	10.798
90	8.904	5.044	17.771	3.688	8.044
91	6.325	3.400	13.734	2.555	5.692
92	4.223	2.145	10.115	1.672	3.784
93	2.612	1.248	7.024	1.022	2.330
94	1.469	.657	4.535	.575	1.303
95	.731	.304	2.671	.292	.645
96	.310	.119	1.398	.130	.272
97	.105	.037	.625	.049	.091
98	.025	0.000	.224	.015	.022
99	0.000	0.000	.058	0.000	0.000

PROBABILITY OF LIVING TO AGE 'X' STARTING FROM AGE 10

1989 U. S. POPULATION

	TOTAL POPULATION	WHITE MALE	WHITE FEMALE	BLACK MALE	BLACK FEMALE
LIFE EXPECTANCY TO AGE	66.20	63.60	70.00	56.50	65.10
11	99.983	99.983	99.987	99.976	99.975
12	99.961	99.959	99.971	99.942	99.948
13	99.929	99.920	99.949	99.887	99.918
14	99.882	99.861	99.919	99.704	99.885
15	99.819	99.779	99.880	99.589	99.848
16	99.740	99.676	99.832	99.442	99.806
17	99.650	99.556	99.779	99.265	99.758
18	99.551	99.425	99.724	99.060	99.704
19	99.448	99.289	99.671	98.829	99.643
20	99.343	99.148	99.622	98.571	99.573
21	99.234	99.002	99.574	98.286	99.494
22	99.121	98.853	99.527	97.981	99.407
23	99.007	98.702	99.480	97.665	99.312
24	98.892	98.549	99.431	97.345	99.210
25	98.775	98.396	99.382	97.021	99.101
26	98.656	98.242	99.330	96.693	98.984
27	98.535	98.087	99.276	96.355	98.857
28	98.410	97.928	99.221	95.999	98.720
29	98.280	97.765	99.162	95.621	98.571
30	98.144	97.596	99.101	95.220	98.408
31	98.002	97.421	99.035	94.784	98.233
32	97.854	97.240	98.966	94.312	98.045
33	97.699	97.052	98.894	93.828	97.847
34	97.536	96.856	98.819	93.309	97.639
35	97.366	96.652	98.740	92.753	97.419
36	97.186	96.437	98.656	92.160	97.188
37	96.997	96.213	98.566	91.534	96.942
38	96.799	95.981	98.468	90.883	96.680
39	96.588	95.739	98.361	90.211	96.397
40	96.367	95.487	98.243	89.517	96.093
41	96.145	95.223	98.112	88.799	95.766
42	95.904	94.944	97.969	88.055	95.416
43	95.643	94.647	97.813	87.282	95.044

1989 U. S. POPULATION

	TOTAL POPULATION	WHITE MALE	WHITE FEMALE	BLACK MALE	BLACK FEMALE
44	95.364	94.327	97.644	86.476	94.650
45	95.063	93.982	97.460	85.638	94.231
46	94.739	93.608	97.258	84.703	93.784
47	94.388	93.203	97.035	83.849	93.308
48	94.006	92.764	96.789	82.898	92.802
49	93.589	92.289	96.514	81.872	92.261
50	93.135	91.774	96.209	80.783	91.682
51	92.641	91.214	95.871	79.709	91.063
52	92.100	90.600	95.497	78.573	90.399
53	91.507	89.921	95.086	77.378	89.684
54	90.860	89.171	94.633	76.129	88.913
55	90.152	88.342	94.137	74.830	88.085
56	89.385	87.433	93.594	73.480	87.197
57	88.554	86.439	93.001	72.077	86.237
58	87.651	85.354	92.352	70.616	85.191
59	86.669	84.175	91.647	69.090	84.052
60	85.612	82.898	90.878	67.494	82.811
61	84.473	81.519	90.044	65.828	81.472
62	83.248	80.042	89.141	64.093	80.045
63	81.950	78.472	88.169	62.289	78.547
64	80.565	76.810	87.125	60.416	76.988
65	79.098	75.058	86.005	58.475	75.371
66	77.540	73.196	84.973	56.469	73.678
67	75.881	71.221	83.707	54.400	71.908
68	74.120	69.129	82.418	52.269	70.061
69	72.260	66.919	81.033	50.086	68.136
70	70.287	64.593	79.551	47.849	66.135
71	68.207	62.143	77.960	45.568	64.042
72	66.011	59.573	76.252	43.250	61.860
73	63.700	56.886	74.422	40.905	59.591
74	61.280	54.087	72.465	38.537	57.237
75	58.749	51.185	70.378	36.161	54.803
76	56.105	48.189	68.154	33.782	52.266
77	53.350	45.112	65.775	31.391	49.631
78	50.496	41.971	63.243	29.006	46.907
79	47.547	38.784	60.562	26.637	44.104
80	44.518	35.571	57.727	24.300	41.235
81	41.264	32.233	54.749	22.008	38.161
82	37.802	28.808	51.469	19.666	34.898

1989 U. S. POPULATION

	TOTAL POPULATION	WHITE MALE	WHITE FEMALE	BLACK MALE	BLACK FEMALE
83	34.165	25.340	47.897	17.317	31.478
84	30.390	21.885	44.041	14.996	27.941
85	26.537	18.506	39.928	12.728	24.342
86	22.676	15.270	35.604	10.561	20.748
87	18.889	12.245	31.132	8.539	17.235
88	15.270	9.498	26.596	6.698	13.891
89	11.912	7.084	22.104	5.074	10.800
90	8.905	5.045	17.774	3.689	8.046
91	6.326	3.400	13.736	2.556	5.693
92	4.223	2.145	10.116	1.673	3.785
93	2.613	1.248	7.025	1.022	2.330
94	1.469	.657	4.535	.575	1.304
95	.731	.304	2.671	.292	.645
96	.310	.119	1.398	.130	.272
97	.105	.037	.625	.049	.091
98	.025	0.000	.224	.015	.022
99	0.000	0.000	.058	0.000	0.000

PROBABILITY OF LIVING TO AGE 'X' STARTING FROM AGE 11

1989 U. S. POPULATION

	TOTAL POPULATION	WHITE MALE	WHITE FEMALE	BLACK MALE	BLACK FEMALE
LIFE EXPECTANCY TO AGE	65.20	62.60	69.00	55.50	64.10
12	99.978	99.976	99.984	99.966	99.973
13	99.946	99.937	99.962	99.911	99.943
14	99.899	99.878	99.932	99.728	99.910
15	99.836	99.796	99.893	99.612	99.873
16	99.757	99.693	99.845	99.466	99.831
17	99.666	99.573	99.792	99.289	99.783
18	99.568	99.442	99.737	99.083	99.729
19	99.465	99.306	99.684	98.853	99.667
20	99.360	99.165	99.635	98.595	99.598
21	99.250	99.019	99.587	98.310	99.519
22	99.138	98.870	99.540	98.005	99.431
23	99.024	98.718	99.493	97.688	99.337
24	98.908	98.565	99.444	97.368	99.235
25	98.792	98.413	99.395	97.045	99.126
26	98.673	98.259	99.343	96.717	99.009
27	98.552	98.104	99.289	96.378	98.882
28	98.427	97.945	99.234	96.023	98.744
29	98.297	97.781	99.175	95.644	98.595
30	98.161	97.612	99.114	95.242	98.433
31	98.019	97.438	99.048	94.807	98.257
32	97.871	97.256	98.979	94.335	98.070
33	97.715	97.069	98.907	93.850	97.872
34	97.553	96.873	98.832	93.331	97.663
35	97.382	96.668	98.752	92.775	97.443
36	97.202	96.454	98.669	92.182	97.212
37	97.013	96.230	98.579	91.556	96.967
38	96.816	95.997	98.481	90.905	96.704
39	96.605	95.755	98.374	90.233	96.421
40	96.383	95.503	98.256	89.539	96.117
41	96.162	95.240	98.125	88.821	95.790
42	95.920	94.960	97.982	88.076	95.440
43	95.659	94.663	97.826	87.303	95.068
44	95.380	94.343	97.657	86.497	94.673

1989 U. S. POPULATION

	TOTAL POPULATION	WHITE MALE	WHITE FEMALE	BLACK MALE	BLACK FEMALE
45	95.080	93.998	97.472	85.659	94.254
46	94.755	93.624	97.270	84.724	93.807
47	94.404	93.218	97.048	83.870	93.332
48	94.021	92.779	96.801	82.918	92.825
49	93.605	92.304	96.526	81.892	92.284
50	93.151	91.789	96.221	80.803	91.705
51	92.656	91.229	95.884	79.728	91.086
52	92.115	90.615	95.510	78.592	90.421
53	91.523	89.937	95.098	77.397	89.706
54	90.875	89.186	94.645	76.147	88.935
55	90.167	88.357	94.149	74.848	88.107
56	89.401	87.448	93.606	73.497	87.218
57	88.569	86.454	93.013	72.094	86.258
58	87.666	85.369	92.364	70.633	85.213
59	86.684	84.190	91.659	69.107	84.073
60	85.626	82.912	90.890	67.510	82.832
61	84.488	81.533	90.055	65.844	81.492
62	83.262	80.056	89.153	64.108	80.065
63	81.964	78.485	88.180	62.304	78.566
64	80.578	76.823	87.136	60.430	77.007
65	79.112	75.071	86.017	58.489	75.390
66	77.553	73.209	84.984	56.482	73.697
67	75.894	71.233	83.718	54.413	71.926
68	74.133	69.141	82.429	52.282	70.079
69	72.272	66.931	81.044	50.098	68.153
70	70.299	64.604	79.561	47.860	66.151
71	68.218	62.154	77.970	45.579	64.058
72	66.022	59.583	76.262	43.260	61.876
73	63.711	56.895	74.432	40.915	59.606
74	61.290	54.096	72.474	38.547	57.252
75	58.759	51.193	70.387	36.170	54.817
76	56.115	48.197	68.163	33.791	52.279
77	53.359	45.120	65.784	31.399	49.643
78	50.505	41.978	63.251	29.013	46.919
79	47.555	38.790	60.569	26.644	44.116
80	44.526	35.577	57.735	24.305	41.246
81	41.271	32.239	54.756	22.013	38.170
82	37.808	28.813	51.476	19.671	34.907
83	34.171	25.344	47.903	17.321	31.486

1989 U. S. POPULATION

	TOTAL POPULATION	WHITE MALE	WHITE FEMALE	BLACK MALE	BLACK FEMALE
84	30.395	21.889	44.047	14.999	27.948
85	26.541	18.509	39.933	12.731	24.348
86	22.679	15.272	35.608	10.564	20.753
87	18.892	12.247	31.136	8.541	17.240
88	15.272	9.499	26.599	6.700	13.894
89	11.914	7.085	22.107	5.075	10.803
90	8.907	5.046	17.776	3.690	8.048
91	6.327	3.401	13.737	2.557	5.695
92	4.224	2.145	10.118	1.673	3.786
93	2.613	1.248	7.026	1.022	2.331
94	1.469	.657	4.536	.575	1.304
95	.731	.304	2.672	.292	.646
96	.310	.119	1.398	.130	.272
97	.105	.037	.625	.049	.091
98	.025	0.000	.224	.015	.022
99	0.000	0.000	.058	0.000	0.000

PROBABILITY OF LIVING TO AGE 'X' STARTING FROM AGE 12

1989 U. S. POPULATION

	TOTAL POPULATION	WHITE MALE	WHITE FEMALE	BLACK MALE	BLACK FEMALE
LIFE EXPECTANCY TO AGE	64.30	61.60	68.00	54.50	63.10
13	99.968	99.961	99.978	99.945	99.970
14	99.921	99.902	99.948	99.762	99.937
15	99.858	99.820	99.909	99.646	99.900
16	99.779	99.717	99.861	99.500	99.858
17	99.688	99.597	99.808	99.323	99.810
18	99.590	99.466	99.753	99.117	99.756
19	99.487	99.330	99.700	98.886	99.694
20	99.382	99.189	99.651	98.628	99.625
21	99.272	99.043	99.603	98.343	99.546
22	99.160	98.893	99.556	98.038	99.458
23	99.046	98.742	99.509	97.722	99.364
24	98.930	98.589	99.460	97.401	99.261
25	98.813	98.436	99.411	97.078	99.152
26	98.695	98.283	99.359	96.750	99.035
27	98.574	98.127	99.305	96.411	98.909
28	98.448	97.968	99.250	96.055	98.771
29	98.318	97.805	99.191	95.677	98.622
30	98.183	97.636	99.130	95.275	98.459
31	98.040	97.461	99.064	94.839	98.284
32	97.892	97.280	98.995	94.367	98.096
33	97.737	97.092	98.923	93.882	97.898
34	97.574	96.896	98.847	93.363	97.690
35	97.404	96.691	98.768	92.807	97.470
36	97.223	96.477	98.684	92.213	97.239
37	97.035	96.253	98.595	91.587	96.993
38	96.837	96.020	98.497	90.936	96.730
39	96.626	95.778	98.390	90.263	96.447
40	96.405	95.526	98.272	89.569	96.143
41	96.183	95.262	98.141	88.851	95.816
42	95.941	94.983	97.998	88.106	95.466
43	95.680	94.686	97.842	87.333	95.094
44	95.401	94.366	97.672	86.527	94.699
45	95.101	94.021	97.488	85.688	94.280

1989 U. S. POPULATION

	TOTAL POPULATION	WHITE MALE	WHITE FEMALE	BLACK MALE	BLACK FEMALE
46	94.776	93.646	97.286	84.752	93.833
47	94.425	93.241	97.063	83.898	93.357
48	94.042	92.802	96.817	82.946	92.850
49	93.626	92.327	96.542	81.920	92.309
50	93.171	91.811	96.237	80.830	91.730
51	92.677	91.251	95.899	79.755	91.111
52	92.136	90.637	95.525	78.619	90.446
53	91.543	89.958	95.113	77.423	89.730
54	90.895	89.207	94.660	76.173	88.959
55	90.187	88.378	94.164	74.873	88.131
56	89.420	87.469	93.621	73.522	87.242
57	88.589	86.475	93.028	72.119	86.281
58	87.685	85.389	92.379	70.657	85.236
59	86.703	84.210	91.673	69.130	84.095
60	85.645	82.932	90.904	67.533	82.854
61	84.506	81.553	90.070	65.866	81.514
62	83.281	80.075	89.167	64.130	80.087
63	81.982	78.504	88.194	62.325	78.588
64	80.596	76.841	87.150	60.451	77.028
65	79.129	75.089	86.030	58.509	75.410
66	77.570	73.226	84.998	56.502	73.716
67	75.910	71.250	83.731	54.431	71.946
68	74.149	69.157	82.442	52.299	70.097
69	72.288	66.947	81.057	50.115	68.172
70	70.315	64.619	79.574	47.877	66.169
71	68.233	62.169	77.982	45.595	64.075
72	66.036	59.597	76.274	43.275	61.892
73	63.725	56.909	74.444	40.929	59.622
74	61.303	54.109	72.486	38.560	57.267
75	58.772	51.206	70.398	36.182	54.832
76	56.127	48.209	68.174	33.802	52.293
77	53.371	45.131	65.794	31.410	49.657
78	50.516	41.988	63.261	29.023	46.932
79	47.566	38.799	60.579	26.653	44.127
80	44.536	35.585	57.744	24.314	41.257
81	41.280	32.246	54.764	22.020	38.180
82	37.817	28.819	51.484	19.677	34.916
83	34.179	25.350	47.911	17.327	31.494
84	30.402	21.894	44.054	15.004	27.956

1989 U. S. POPULATION

	TOTAL POPULATION	WHITE MALE	WHITE FEMALE	BLACK MALE	BLACK FEMALE
85	26.547	18.514	39.940	12.735	24.355
86	22.684	15.276	35.614	10.568	20.758
87	18.896	12.250	31.141	8.544	17.244
88	15.276	9.501	26.604	6.702	13.898
89	11.917	7.087	22.110	5.077	10.806
90	8.909	5.047	17.779	3.691	8.050
91	6.329	3.402	13.740	2.558	5.696
92	4.225	2.146	10.119	1.674	3.787
93	2.614	1.248	7.027	1.023	2.332
94	1.470	.657	4.536	.575	1.304
95	.731	.305	2.672	.292	.646
96	.310	.119	1.398	.130	.272
97	.105	.037	.625	.049	.091
98	.025	0.000	.224	.015	.022
99	0.000	0.000	.058	0.000	0.000

PROBABILITY OF LIVING TO AGE 'X' STARTING FROM AGE 13

1989 U. S. POPULATION

	TOTAL POPULATION	WHITE MALE	WHITE FEMALE	BLACK MALE	BLACK FEMALE
LIFE EXPECTANCY TO AGE	63.30	60.60	67.00	53.50	62.10
14	99.953	99.941	99.970	99.817	99.967
15	99.890	99.859	99.931	99.701	99.930
16	99.811	99.756	99.883	99.555	99.888
17	99.720	99.635	99.830	99.377	99.840
18	99.622	99.505	99.775	99.172	99.786
19	99.519	99.369	99.722	98.941	99.724
20	99.413	99.228	99.672	98.682	99.655
21	99.304	99.082	99.625	98.397	99.576
22	99.192	98.932	99.578	98.092	99.488
23	99.078	98.781	99.531	97.775	99.394
24	98.962	98.628	99.482	97.455	99.291
25	98.845	98.475	99.432	97.131	99.182
26	98.727	98.321	99.381	96.803	99.065
27	98.605	98.166	99.327	96.464	98.938
28	98.480	98.007	99.271	96.108	98.801
29	98.350	97.843	99.213	95.729	98.651
30	98.214	97.674	99.151	95.327	98.489
31	98.072	97.499	99.086	94.892	98.313
32	97.924	97.318	99.017	94.419	98.126
33	97.768	97.130	98.944	93.934	97.927
34	97.606	96.934	98.869	93.414	97.719
35	97.435	96.729	98.790	92.858	97.499
36	97.255	96.514	98.706	92.264	97.268
37	97.066	96.290	98.616	91.638	97.022
38	96.868	96.057	98.519	90.986	96.759
39	96.657	95.815	98.411	90.313	96.476
40	96.435	95.563	98.293	89.618	96.171
41	96.214	95.300	98.162	88.900	95.844
42	95.972	95.020	98.019	88.155	95.495
43	95.711	94.723	97.863	87.381	95.122
44	95.432	94.403	97.694	86.574	94.727
45	95.131	94.057	97.509	85.735	94.308
46	94.807	93.683	97.307	84.799	93.861

1989 U. S. POPULATION

	TOTAL POPULATION	WHITE MALE	WHITE FEMALE	BLACK MALE	BLACK FEMALE
47	94.455	93.277	97.085	83.944	93.385
48	94.072	92.838	96.838	82.991	92.878
49	93.656	92.363	96.563	81.965	92.336
50	93.201	91.847	96.258	80.875	91.757
51	92.706	91.287	95.920	79.799	91.138
52	92.165	90.673	95.546	78.662	90.473
53	91.572	89.993	95.134	77.466	89.757
54	90.924	89.242	94.681	76.215	88.986
55	90.216	88.413	94.185	74.914	88.158
56	89.449	87.503	93.642	73.563	87.268
57	88.617	86.508	93.048	72.158	86.307
58	87.713	85.423	92.399	70.696	85.261
59	86.731	84.243	91.694	69.168	84.120
60	85.673	82.964	90.924	67.570	82.879
61	84.533	81.584	90.090	65.903	81.539
62	83.307	80.106	89.187	64.165	80.111
63	82.008	78.534	88.214	62.359	78.611
64	80.622	76.871	87.169	60.484	77.051
65	79.155	75.118	86.049	58.541	75.433
66	77.595	73.255	85.017	56.533	73.739
67	75.935	71.278	83.750	54.461	71.967
68	74.173	69.184	82.460	52.328	70.119
69	72.311	66.973	81.075	50.142	68.192
70	70.337	64.644	79.591	47.903	66.189
71	68.255	62.193	77.999	45.620	64.095
72	66.057	59.621	76.291	43.299	61.911
73	63.745	56.931	74.460	40.951	59.640
74	61.323	54.130	72.502	38.581	57.284
75	58.790	51.226	70.414	36.202	54.848
76	56.145	48.227	68.189	33.821	52.309
77	53.388	45.149	65.809	31.427	49.672
78	50.532	42.005	63.275	29.039	46.946
79	47.581	38.815	60.592	26.667	44.141
80	44.550	35.599	57.757	24.327	41.269
81	41.293	32.259	54.776	22.033	38.192
82	37.829	28.831	51.495	19.688	34.927
83	34.190	25.360	47.922	17.337	31.504
84	30.412	21.903	44.064	15.013	27.964
85	26.556	18.521	39.948	12.742	24.362

1989 U. S. POPULATION

	TOTAL POPULATION	WHITE MALE	WHITE FEMALE	BLACK MALE	BLACK FEMALE
86	22.692	15.282	35.622	10.573	20.765
87	18.902	12.255	31.148	8.548	17.250
88	15.281	9.505	26.610	6.706	13.902
89	11.920	7.090	22.115	5.080	10.809
90	8.912	5.049	17.783	3.693	8.052
91	6.331	3.403	13.743	2.559	5.698
92	4.226	2.147	10.121	1.675	3.788
93	2.614	1.249	7.028	1.023	2.332
94	1.470	.657	4.537	.576	1.305
95	.732	.305	2.673	.292	.646
96	.310	.120	1.399	.130	.272
97	.105	.037	.625	.049	.091
98	.025	0.000	.224	.015	.022
99	0.000	0.000	.058	0.000	0.000

PROBABILITY OF LIVING TO AGE 'X' STARTING FROM AGE 14

1989 U. S. POPULATION

	TOTAL POPULATION	WHITE MALE	WHITE FEMALE	BLACK MALE	BLACK FEMALE
LIFE EXPECTANCY TO AGE	62.30	59.60	66.00	52.60	61.20
15	99.937	99.918	99.961	99.884	99.963
16	99.858	99.815	99.913	99.737	99.921
17	99.767	99.694	99.860	99.560	99.873
18	99.668	99.564	99.805	99.354	99.819
19	99.566	99.427	99.752	99.122	99.757
20	99.460	99.286	99.702	98.863	99.687
21	99.351	99.140	99.655	98.578	99.609
22	99.239	98.990	99.608	98.272	99.521
23	99.124	98.839	99.561	97.955	99.426
24	99.008	98.686	99.512	97.633	99.324
25	98.892	98.533	99.462	97.309	99.215
26	98.773	98.379	99.411	96.980	99.098
27	98.651	98.224	99.357	96.641	98.971
28	98.526	98.065	99.301	96.284	98.833
29	98.396	97.901	99.243	95.905	98.684
30	98.260	97.731	99.181	95.502	98.521
31	98.118	97.557	99.116	95.066	98.346
32	97.970	97.375	99.046	94.592	98.158
33	97.814	97.187	98.974	94.106	97.960
34	97.652	96.991	98.899	93.586	97.751
35	97.481	96.786	98.820	93.028	97.531
36	97.300	96.571	98.736	92.433	97.300
37	97.112	96.347	98.646	91.806	97.054
38	96.913	96.114	98.548	91.153	96.791
39	96.702	95.872	98.441	90.478	96.508
40	96.481	95.620	98.323	89.783	96.203
41	96.259	95.356	98.192	89.063	95.876
42	96.017	95.076	98.048	88.316	95.526
43	95.756	94.779	97.893	87.541	95.154
44	95.476	94.458	97.723	86.733	94.759
45	95.176	94.113	97.539	85.892	94.339
46	94.851	93.738	97.337	84.955	93.892
47	94.499	93.332	97.114	84.098	93.416

1989 U. S. POPULATION

	TOTAL POPULATION	WHITE MALE	WHITE FEMALE	BLACK MALE	BLACK FEMALE
48	94.117	92.893	96.867	83.144	92.909
49	93.700	92.417	96.592	82.115	92.367
50	93.245	91.901	96.287	81.023	91.788
51	92.750	91.341	95.949	79.945	91.168
52	92.208	90.726	95.575	78.806	90.503
53	91.615	90.047	95.163	77.608	89.787
54	90.967	89.295	94.710	76.355	89.015
55	90.258	88.465	94.213	75.052	88.187
56	89.491	87.555	93.670	73.698	87.297
57	88.659	86.559	93.076	72.291	86.336
58	87.754	85.473	92.427	70.825	85.289
59	86.772	84.293	91.721	69.295	84.148
60	85.713	83.013	90.951	67.694	82.906
61	84.573	81.633	90.117	66.023	81.566
62	83.347	80.153	89.214	64.283	80.137
63	82.046	78.581	88.240	62.474	78.637
64	80.660	76.916	87.196	60.595	77.076
65	79.192	75.163	86.075	58.649	75.458
66	77.632	73.298	85.042	56.636	73.763
67	75.970	71.320	83.775	54.561	71.991
68	74.208	69.225	82.485	52.424	70.142
69	72.345	67.013	81.099	50.234	68.215
70	70.370	64.683	79.615	47.991	66.211
71	68.287	62.230	78.023	45.704	64.116
72	66.088	59.656	76.314	43.378	61.931
73	63.775	56.965	74.482	41.026	59.660
74	61.352	54.162	72.524	38.652	57.303
75	58.818	51.256	70.435	36.268	54.866
76	56.171	48.256	68.209	33.883	52.326
77	53.413	45.175	65.829	31.484	49.688
78	50.556	42.030	63.294	29.092	46.961
79	47.603	38.837	60.611	26.716	44.155
80	44.571	35.620	57.774	24.372	41.283
81	41.313	32.278	54.793	22.073	38.204
82	37.847	28.848	51.511	19.724	34.938
83	34.206	25.375	47.936	17.368	31.514
84	30.426	21.916	44.077	15.040	27.973
85	26.568	18.532	39.960	12.765	24.370
86	22.702	15.291	35.633	10.593	20.771

1989 U. S. POPULATION

	TOTAL POPULATION	WHITE MALE	WHITE FEMALE	BLACK MALE	BLACK FEMALE
87	18.911	12.262	31.157	8.564	17.255
88	15.288	9.511	26.618	6.718	13.907
89	11.926	7.094	22.122	5.089	10.813
90	8.916	5.052	17.788	3.700	8.055
91	6.334	3.405	13.747	2.564	5.700
92	4.228	2.148	10.124	1.678	3.789
93	2.616	1.250	7.030	1.025	2.333
94	1.471	.658	4.539	.577	1.305
95	.732	.305	2.673	.293	.646
96	.310	.120	1.399	.130	.272
97	.105	.037	.626	.049	.091
98	.025	0.000	.225	.015	.022
99	0.000	0.000	.058	0.000	0.000

PROBABILITY OF LIVING TO AGE 'X' STARTING FROM AGE 15

1989 U. S. POPULATION

	TOTAL POPULATION	WHITE MALE	WHITE FEMALE	BLACK MALE	BLACK FEMALE
LIFE EXPECTANCY TO AGE	61.30	58.60	65.10	51.60	60.20
16	99.921	99.700	99.952	99.853	99.958
17	99.830	99.776	99.899	99.675	99.910
18	99.731	99.645	99.844	99.469	99.856
19	99.629	99.509	99.791	99.237	99.794
20	99.523	99.368	99.741	98.978	99.724
21	99.413	99.222	99.693	98.692	99.646
22	99.301	99.072	99.647	98.386	99.558
23	99.187	98.920	99.600	98.068	99.463
24	99.071	98.767	99.551	97.747	99.361
25	98.954	98.614	99.501	97.422	99.252
26	98.835	98.460	99.449	97.093	99.134
27	98.714	98.304	99.396	96.753	99.007
28	98.588	98.145	99.340	96.396	98.870
29	98.458	97.981	99.281	96.016	98.721
30	98.322	97.812	99.220	95.613	98.558
31	98.180	97.637	99.154	95.176	98.382
32	98.031	97.455	99.085	94.702	98.194
33	97.876	97.267	99.013	94.215	97.996
34	97.713	97.070	98.937	93.694	97.787
35	97.542	96.866	98.858	93.136	97.567
36	97.362	96.651	98.774	92.541	97.336
37	97.173	96.426	98.684	91.912	97.090
38	96.975	96.193	98.587	91.259	96.827
39	96.763	95.951	98.479	90.584	96.544
40	96.542	95.698	98.361	89.887	96.239
41	96.319	95.434	98.230	89.166	95.912
42	96.078	95.154	98.087	88.419	95.562
43	95.816	94.857	97.931	87.643	95.189
44	95.537	94.536	97.761	86.834	94.794
45	95.236	94.190	97.577	85.992	94.374
46	94.911	93.815	97.375	85.053	93.927
47	94.559	93.409	97.152	84.196	93.450
48	94.176	92.969	96.905	83.240	92.943

1989 U. S. POPULATION

	TOTAL POPULATION	WHITE MALE	WHITE FEMALE	BLACK MALE	BLACK FEMALE
49	93.759	92.493	96.630	82.211	92.401
50	93.304	91.977	96.324	81.117	91.822
51	92.808	91.416	95.986	80.038	91.202
52	92.266	90.801	95.612	78.898	90.536
53	91.673	90.120	95.200	77.698	89.820
54	91.024	89.368	94.747	76.444	89.048
55	90.315	88.538	94.250	75.139	88.219
56	89.547	87.627	93.706	73.783	87.329
57	88.715	86.630	93.112	72.375	86.368
58	87.810	85.543	92.463	70.908	85.321
59	86.826	84.362	91.757	69.375	84.179
60	85.767	83.081	90.987	67.773	82.937
61	84.626	81.700	90.152	66.100	81.596
62	83.399	80.219	89.248	64.358	80.167
63	82.098	78.645	88.275	62.546	78.666
64	80.711	76.980	87.230	60.665	77.105
65	79.242	75.224	86.109	58.717	75.486
66	77.681	73.358	85.075	56.702	73.790
67	76.018	71.378	83.808	54.625	72.018
68	74.255	69.282	82.517	52.485	70.168
69	72.391	67.068	81.131	50.293	68.240
70	70.415	64.736	79.646	48.047	66.235
71	68.330	62.281	78.053	45.757	64.140
72	66.130	59.705	76.344	43.429	61.954
73	63.816	57.012	74.512	41.074	59.682
74	61.391	54.207	72.552	38.697	57.324
75	58.855	51.298	70.462	36.311	54.886
76	56.207	48.295	68.236	33.922	52.345
77	53.447	45.212	65.854	31.521	49.706
78	50.588	42.064	63.319	29.126	46.979
79	47.633	38.869	60.634	26.747	44.172
80	44.599	35.649	57.797	24.400	41.298
81	41.339	32.304	54.814	22.099	38.219
82	37.870	28.871	51.531	19.747	34.951
83	34.227	25.396	47.955	17.388	31.526
84	30.445	21.934	44.094	15.058	27.983
85	26.585	18.547	39.976	12.780	24.379
86	22.717	15.303	35.646	10.605	20.779
87	18.923	12.272	31.169	8.574	17.262

1989 U. S. POPULATION

	TOTAL POPULATION	WHITE MALE	WHITE FEMALE	BLACK MALE	BLACK FEMALE
88	15.297	9.519	26.628	6.726	13.912
89	11.933	7.100	22.130	5.095	10.817
90	8.921	5.056	17.795	3.704	8.058
91	6.338	3.408	13.752	2.567	5.702
92	4.231	2.150	10.128	1.680	3.791
93	2.617	1.251	7.033	1.026	2.334
94	1.472	.658	4.541	.577	1.306
95	.732	.305	2.674	.293	.646
96	.310	.120	1.400	.131	.272
97	.105	.037	.626	.049	.092
98	.025	0.000	.225	.015	.022
99	0.000	0.000	.058	0.000	0.000

PROBABILITY OF LIVING TO AGE 'X' STARTING FROM AGE 16

1989 U. S. POPULATION

	TOTAL POPULATION	WHITE MALE	WHITE FEMALE	BLACK MALE	BLACK FEMALE
LIFE EXPECTANCY TO AGE	60.40	57.70	64.10	50.70	59.20
17	99.909	99.879	99.947	99.822	99.952
18	99.810	99.748	99.892	99.615	99.898
19	99.707	99.612	99.839	99.383	99.836
20	99.602	99.470	99.789	99.124	99.766
21	99.492	99.324	99.741	98.837	99.687
22	99.380	99.174	99.694	98.531	99.600
23	99.2659	99.022	99.648	98.213	99.505
24	99.149	98.869	99.599	97.891	99.403
25	99.032	98.715	99.549	97.566	99.293
26	98.913	98.561	99.497	97.236	99.176
27	98.792	98.406	99.443	96.896	99.049
28	98.666	98.246	99.388	96.538	98.911
29	98.536	98.082	99.329	96.158	98.762
30	98.400	97.912	99.268	95.754	98.599
31	98.257	97.737	99.202	95.316	98.424
32	98.109	97.555	99.133	94.841	98.236
33	97.953	97.367	99.060	94.354	98.037
34	97.790	97.170	98.985	93.832	97.828
35	97.619	96.965	98.906	93.273	97.608
36	97.439	96.750	98.822	92.677	97.377
37	97.250	96.526	98.732	92.048	97.131
38	97.051	96.292	98.634	91.393	96.867
39	96.840	96.049	98.526	90.717	96.584
40	96.618	95.797	98.408	90.019	96.279
41	96.396	95.532	98.277	89.297	95.952
42	96.154	95.253	98.134	88.549	95.602
43	95.892	94.954	97.978	87.772	95.229
44	95.612	94.633	97.808	86.961	94.834
45	95.311	94.287	97.623	86.119	94.414
46	94.986	93.912	97.421	85.178	93.966
47	94.634	93.505	97.198	84.320	93.490
48	94.250	93.065	96.951	83.363	92.982
49	93.833	92.588	96.676	82.332	92.440

1989 U. S. POPULATION

	TOTAL POPULATION	WHITE MALE	WHITE FEMALE	BLACK MALE	BLACK FEMALE
50	93.378	92.072	96.371	81.237	91.860
51	92.882	91.510	96.032	80.156	91.240
52	92.339	90.894	95.658	79.014	90.574
53	91.746	90.213	95.245	77.812	89.858
54	91.096	89.460	94.792	76.556	89.086
55	90.386	88.629	94.295	75.249	88.256
56	89.618	87.717	93.751	73.892	87.366
57	88.785	86.720	93.157	72.481	86.404
58	87.879	85.631	92.508	71.012	85.357
59	86.895	84.449	91.801	69.478	84.215
60	85.835	83.167	91.031	67.873	82.972
61	84.693	81.784	90.195	66.197	81.630
62	83.465	80.302	89.291	64.453	80.201
63	82.163	78.726	88.317	62.638	78.699
64	80.775	77.059	87.271	60.755	77.137
65	79.304	75.302	86.150	58.803	75.517
66	77.742	73.434	85.116	56.786	73.821
67	76.078	71.452	83.848	54.705	72.048
68	74.313	69.353	82.557	52.562	70.197
69	72.448	67.137	81.170	50.367	68.269
70	70.470	64.802	79.684	48.117	66.263
71	68.384	62.345	78.091	45.824	64.166
72	66.182	59.766	76.380	43.493	61.980
73	63.866	57.070	74.547	41.134	59.707
74	61.439	54.263	72.587	38.754	57.348
75	58.902	51.351	70.496	36.364	54.909
76	56.251	48.345	68.269	33.972	52.367
77	53.489	45.259	65.886	31.567	49.727
78	50.628	42.107	63.349	29.169	46.998
79	47.671	38.909	60.663	26.787	44.190
80	44.634	35.686	57.824	24.436	41.316
81	41.371	32.338	54.841	22.131	38.235
82	37.900	28.901	51.556	19.776	34.966
83	34.254	25.422	47.978	17.414	31.539
84	30.469	21.957	44.115	15.080	27.995
85	26.606	18.566	39.995	12.799	24.389
86	22.735	15.319	35.664	10.621	20.788
87	18.938	12.285	31.184	8.587	17.269
88	15.309	9.528	26.641	6.736	13.918

| | 1989 U. S. POPULATION | | | | |
	TOTAL POPULATION	WHITE MALE	WHITE FEMALE	BLACK MALE	BLACK FEMALE
89	11.943	7.107	22.141	5.102	10.821
90	8.929	5.062	17.804	3.710	8.061
91	6.343	3.412	13.759	2.570	5.704
92	4.234	2.152	10.133	1.682	3.792
93	2.619	1.252	7.037	1.028	2.335
94	1.473	.659	4.543	.578	1.306
95	.733	.305	2.676	.293	.647
96	.310	.120	1.400	.131	.272
97	.105	.037	.626	.049	.092
98	.025	0.000	.225	.015	.022
99	0.000	0.000	.058	0.000	0.000

PROBABILITY OF LIVING TO AGE 'X' STARTING FROM AGE 17

1989 U. S. POPULATION

	TOTAL POPULATION	WHITE MALE	WHITE FEMALE	BLACK MALE	BLACK FEMALE
LIFE EXPECTANCY TO AGE	59.40	56.80	63.10	49.80	58.20
18	99.901	99.869	99.945	99.793	99.946
19	99.798	99.732	99.892	99.560	99.884
20	99.692	99.591	99.842	99.301	99.814
21	99.583	99.444	99.794	99.014	99.735
22	99.470	99.294	99.747	98.707	99.647
23	99.356	99.142	99.700	98.388	99.553
24	99.239	98.988	99.652	98.065	99.450
25	99.122	98.835	99.602	97.740	99.341
26	99.003	98.681	99.550	97.409	99.224
27	98.882	98.525	99.496	97.068	99.097
28	98.756	98.365	99.440	96.710	98.959
29	98.626	98.201	99.382	96.329	98.809
30	98.490	98.031	99.320	95.925	98.646
31	98.347	97.856	99.255	95.486	98.471
32	98.198	97.674	99.185	95.011	98.283
33	98.042	97.485	99.113	94.522	98.084
34	97.879	97.288	99.037	94.000	97.875
35	97.708	97.083	98.958	93.439	97.655
36	97.527	96.867	98.874	92.842	97.424
37	97.338	96.643	98.784	92.212	97.177
38	97.140	96.409	98.686	91.556	96.914
39	96.928	96.166	98.579	90.879	96.631
40	96.706	95.913	98.460	90.180	96.326
41	96.483	95.648	98.329	89.457	95.998
42	96.241	95.368	98.186	88.707	95.648
43	95.980	95.069	98.030	87.928	95.275
44	95.699	94.748	97.860	87.117	94.879
45	95.398	94.401	97.675	86.272	94.459
46	95.072	94.026	97.473	85.330	94.011
47	94.720	93.618	97.250	84.470	93.535
48	94.336	93.178	97.003	83.511	93.027
49	93.918	92.700	96.727	82.478	92.484
50	93.463	92.183	96.422	81.381	91.904

1989 U. S. POPULATION

	TOTAL POPULATION	WHITE MALE	WHITE FEMALE	BLACK MALE	BLACK FEMALE
51	92.966	91.621	96.083	80.299	91.284
52	92.424	91.004	95.709	79.155	90.618
53	91.829	90.323	95.296	77.951	89.901
54	91.179	89.568	94.842	76.693	89.129
55	90.469	88.736	94.345	75.384	88.299
56	89.700	87.823	93.801	74.024	87.408
57	88.866	86.825	93.206	72.611	86.446
58	87.959	85.735	92.557	71.139	85.398
59	86.974	84.551	91.850	69.601	84.255
60	85.913	83.268	91.079	67.994	83.012
61	84.770	81.883	90.243	66.316	81.669
62	83.541	80.399	89.339	64.567	80.239
63	82.238	78.822	88.364	62.750	78.737
64	80.848	77.152	87.318	60.863	77.174
65	79.377	75.393	86.196	58.908	75.554
66	77.813	73.523	85.161	56.887	73.857
67	76.148	71.538	83.892	54.803	72.083
68	74.381	69.437	82.600	52.656	70.231
69	72.514	67.218	81.213	50.457	68.302
70	70.535	64.881	79.727	48.203	66.295
71	68.447	62.421	78.132	45.906	64.197
72	66.243	59.839	76.421	43.570	62.010
73	63.924	57.140	74.587	41.208	59.736
74	61.495	54.328	72.625	38.823	57.376
75	58.955	51.413	70.534	36.429	54.936
76	56.302	48.404	68.305	34.033	52.392
77	53.538	45.314	65.921	31.624	49.751
78	50.674	42.159	63.383	29.221	47.021
79	47.714	38.957	60.696	26.834	44.211
80	44.675	35.729	57.855	24.479	41.335
81	41.409	32.377	54.870	22.171	38.253
82	37.935	28.936	51.583	19.811	34.983
83	34.286	25.453	48.003	17.445	31.554
84	30.497	21.983	44.139	15.107	28.009
85	26.630	18.589	40.016	12.822	24.401
86	22.755	15.338	35.683	10.640	20.798
87	18.955	12.299	31.201	8.602	17.277
88	15.323	9.540	26.655	6.748	13.924
89	11.954	7.116	22.153	5.111	10.826

1989 U. S. POPULATION

	TOTAL POPULATION	WHITE MALE	WHITE FEMALE	BLACK MALE	BLACK FEMALE
90	8.937	5.068	17.813	3.716	8.065
91	6.349	3.416	13.766	2.575	5.707
92	4.238	2.154	10.139	1.685	3.794
93	2.622	1.253	7.040	1.030	2.336
94	1.474	.660	4.545	.579	1.307
95	.734	.306	2.677	.294	.647
96	.311	.120	1.401	.131	.272
97	.105	.037	.626	.049	.092
98	.025	0.000	.225	.015	.022
99	0.000	0.000	.058	0.000	0.000

PROBABILITY OF LIVING TO AGE 'X' STARTING FROM AGE 18

1989 U. S. POPULATION

	TOTAL POPULATION	WHITE MALE	WHITE FEMALE	BLACK MALE	BLACK FEMALE
LIFE EXPECTANCY TO AGE	58.50	55.80	62.10	48.80	57.30
19	99.897	99.863	99.947	99.767	99.938
20	99.791	99.721	99.897	99.507	99.868
21	99.681	99.575	99.849	99.219	99.789
22	99.569	99.424	99.802	98.911	99.701
23	99.454	99.272	99.755	98.592	99.607
24	99.338	99.118	99.706	98.269	99.504
25	99.221	98.965	99.657	97.942	99.395
26	99.102	98.810	99.605	97.611	99.277
27	98.980	98.654	99.551	97.270	99.150
28	98.854	98.494	99.495	96.911	99.012
29	98.723	98.330	99.436	96.529	98.863
30	98.587	98.160	99.375	96.123	98.700
31	98.444	97.984	99.309	95.684	98.524
32	98.296	97.802	99.240	95.208	98.336
33	98.139	97.613	99.167	94.718	98.137
34	97.976	97.416	99.092	94.195	97.928
35	97.805	97.210	99.013	93.633	97.708
36	97.624	96.994	98.928	93.035	97.476
37	97.435	96.769	98.838	92.403	97.230
38	97.236	96.535	98.741	91.746	96.966
39	97.024	96.292	98.633	91.067	96.683
40	96.802	96.039	98.515	90.367	96.378
41	96.579	95.774	98.384	89.642	96.050
42	96.337	95.493	98.240	88.891	95.699
43	96.075	95.194	98.084	88.110	95.326
44	95.794	94.872	97.914	87.297	94.930
45	95.492	94.525	97.729	86.451	94.510
46	95.167	94.149	97.527	85.507	94.062
47	94.814	93.741	97.303	84.645	93.585
48	94.430	93.300	97.056	83.685	93.077
49	94.011	92.822	96.781	82.649	92.534
50	93.555	92.304	96.475	81.550	91.954
51	93.059	91.741	96.136	80.466	91.333

1989 U. S. POPULATION

	TOTAL POPULATION	WHITE MALE	WHITE FEMALE	BLACK MALE	BLACK FEMALE
52	92.515	91.124	95.761	79.319	90.667
53	91.920	90.441	95.348	78.113	89.949
54	91.269	89.686	94.895	76.852	89.177
55	90.558	88.853	94.397	75.540	88.347
56	89.789	87.938	93.853	74.177	87.455
57	88.954	86.939	93.258	72.761	86.492
58	88.046	85.848	92.608	71.286	85.444
59	87.060	84.662	91.900	69.746	84.301
60	85.998	83.377	91.129	68.135	83.056
61	84.854	81.990	90.292	66.453	81.713
62	83.624	80.505	89.388	64.701	80.283
63	82.319	78.925	88.413	62.880	78.780
64	80.928	77.253	87.366	60.989	77.216
65	79.455	75.492	86.243	59.030	75.594
66	77.890	73.619	85.208	57.005	73.897
67	76.223	71.632	83.939	54.916	72.122
68	74.455	69.528	82.646	52.765	70.269
69	72.586	67.306	81.257	50.561	68.338
70	70.604	64.966	79.770	48.303	66.331
71	68.515	62.502	78.175	46.001	64.232
72	66.308	59.917	76.463	43.660	62.044
73	63.988	57.214	74.628	41.293	59.768
74	61.556	54.400	72.665	38.903	57.407
75	59.014	51.480	70.572	36.504	54.965
76	56.358	48.467	68.342	34.103	52.421
77	53.591	45.373	65.957	31.689	49.778
78	50.724	42.214	63.418	29.282	47.046
79	47.762	39.008	60.729	26.890	44.235
80	44.719	35.776	57.887	24.530	41.358
81	41.450	32.419	54.900	22.217	38.274
82	37.973	28.974	51.611	19.852	35.002
83	34.320	25.487	48.030	17.481	31.571
84	30.527	22.012	44.163	15.138	28.024
85	26.656	18.613	40.038	12.848	24.414
86	22.778	15.358	35.702	10.662	20.809
87	18.974	12.316	31.218	8.620	17.287
88	15.339	9.552	26.670	6.762	13.932
89	11.966	7.125	22.165	5.122	10.832
90	8.945	5.074	17.823	3.724	8.069

	TOTAL POPULATION	1989 U. S. POPULATION WHITE MALE	WHITE FEMALE	BLACK MALE	BLACK FEMALE
91	6.355	3.420	13.774	2.580	5.710
92	4.243	2.157	10.144	1.689	3.796
93	2.624	1.255	7.044	1.032	2.337
94	1.476	.661	4.548	.580	1.308
95	.734	.306	2.679	.295	.647
96	.311	.120	1.402	.131	.273
97	.105	.037	.627	.049	.092
98	.025	0.000	.225	.015	.022
99	0.000	0.000	.058	0.000	0.000

PROBABILITY OF LIVING TO AGE 'X' STARTING FROM AGE 19

1989 U. S. POPULATION

	TOTAL POPULATION	WHITE MALE	WHITE FEMALE	BLACK MALE	BLACK FEMALE
LIFE EXPECTANCY TO AGE	57.50	54.90	61.20	47.90	56.30
20	99.894	99.858	99.950	99.739	99.930
21	99.784	99.711	99.902	99.451	99.851
22	99.671	99.561	99.855	99.142	99.763
23	99.557	99.408	99.808	98.822	99.668
24	99.440	99.254	99.759	98.498	99.566
25	99.323	99.100	99.709	98.171	99.456
26	99.204	98.946	99.658	97.839	99.339
27	99.082	98.789	99.604	97.497	99.212
28	98.956	98.629	99.548	97.137	99.074
29	98.825	98.465	99.489	96.754	98.924
30	98.689	98.294	99.427	96.348	98.761
31	98.546	98.118	99.362	95.908	98.585
32	98.397	97.936	99.292	95.430	98.397
33	98.241	97.747	99.220	94.940	98.198
34	98.077	97.549	99.144	94.415	97.989
35	97.906	97.344	99.065	93.852	97.768
36	97.725	97.128	98.981	93.252	97.537
37	97.535	96.902	98.891	92.619	97.290
38	97.336	96.668	98.793	91.960	97.026
39	97.124	96.424	98.685	91.280	96.743
40	96.902	96.170	98.567	90.578	96.437
41	96.679	95.905	98.436	89.852	96.109
42	96.436	95.624	98.292	89.099	95.759
43	96.174	95.325	98.136	88.316	95.385
44	95.893	95.003	97.966	87.501	94.989
45	95.591	94.655	97.781	86.653	94.569
46	95.265	94.278	97.578	85.707	94.120
47	94.911	93.870	97.355	84.843	93.643
48	94.527	93.428	97.108	83.880	93.135
49	94.108	92.949	96.832	82.842	92.592
50	93.652	92.431	96.526	81.741	92.011
51	93.155	91.867	96.187	80.654	91.390
52	92.611	91.249	95.812	79.504	90.723

1989 U. S. POPULATION

	TOTAL POPULATION	WHITE MALE	WHITE FEMALE	BLACK MALE	BLACK FEMALE
53	92.015	90.565	95.399	78.295	90.005
54	91.364	89.809	94.945	77.031	89.232
55	90.652	88.975	94.447	75.716	88.401
56	89.881	88.059	93.902	74.350	87.509
57	89.045	87.058	93.307	72.931	86.546
58	88.137	85.965	92.657	71.453	85.497
59	87.150	84.778	91.949	69.909	84.353
60	86.087	83.491	91.177	68.294	83.108
61	84.942	82.103	90.340	66.608	81.764
62	83.710	80.615	89.435	64.852	80.332
63	82.404	79.033	88.459	63.027	78.829
64	81.012	77.359	87.412	61.132	77.264
65	79.537	75.596	86.289	59.168	75.641
66	77.970	73.720	85.253	57.138	73.942
67	76.302	71.730	83.983	55.045	72.166
68	74.532	69.624	82.690	52.888	70.312
69	72.661	67.399	81.301	50.679	68.381
70	70.677	65.055	79.813	48.416	66.372
71	68.585	62.588	78.217	46.108	64.272
72	66.377	60.000	76.504	43.762	62.082
73	64.054	57.293	74.667	41.390	59.805
74	61.619	54.474	72.704	38.994	57.443
75	59.075	51.551	70.610	36.590	55.000
76	56.416	48.534	68.379	34.183	52.453
77	53.646	45.435	65.992	31.763	49.809
78	50.776	42.272	63.451	29.350	47.075
79	47.811	39.061	60.761	26.953	44.263
80	44.765	35.825	57.918	24.588	41.383
81	41.493	32.464	54.929	22.268	38.297
82	38.012	29.014	51.639	19.899	35.023
83	34.355	25.522	48.055	17.522	31.591
84	30.559	22.042	44.187	15.173	28.041
85	26.684	18.639	40.060	12.878	24.429
86	22.801	15.379	35.721	10.687	20.822
87	18.994	12.333	31.235	8.640	17.297
88	15.354	9.566	26.684	6.778	13.940
89	11.978	7.135	22.177	5.134	10.839
90	8.955	5.081	17.832	3.733	8.074
91	6.361	3.425	13.781	2.586	5.714

	TOTAL POPULATION	1989 U. S. POPULATION WHITE MALE	WHITE FEMALE	BLACK MALE	BLACK FEMALE
92	4.247	2.160	10.150	1.693	3.798
93	2.627	1.257	7.048	1.034	2.339
94	1.477	.662	4.550	.582	1.308
95	.735	.307	2.680	.295	.648
96	.311	.120	1.402	.132	.273
97	.105	.038	.627	.050	.092
98	.025	0.000	.225	.015	.022
99	0.000	0.000	.058	0.000	0.000

PROBABILITY OF LIVING TO AGE 'X' STARTING FROM AGE 20

1989 U. S. POPULATION

	TOTAL POPULATION	WHITE MALE	WHITE FEMALE	BLACK MALE	BLACK FEMALE
LIFE EXPECTANCY TO AGE	56.60	54.00	60.20	47.10	55.30
21	99.890	99.853	99.952	99.711	99.921
22	99.777	99.702	99.905	99.402	99.833
23	99.662	99.550	99.858	99.081	99.738
24	99.546	99.395	99.809	98.756	99.635
25	99.428	99.241	99.759	98.428	99.526
26	99.309	99.086	99.707	98.095	99.408
27	99.187	98.930	99.654	97.752	99.281
28	99.061	98.770	99.598	97.391	99.143
29	98.930	98.605	99.539	97.008	98.994
30	98.794	98.434	99.477	96.600	98.830
31	98.650	98.258	99.412	96.159	98.654
32	98.501	98.075	99.342	95.680	98.466
33	98.345	97.886	99.269	95.188	98.267
34	98.182	97.688	99.194	94.662	98.058
35	98.010	97.482	99.115	94.097	97.837
36	97.828	97.266	99.030	93.496	97.605
37	97.639	97.040	98.940	92.861	97.358
38	97.439	96.805	98.842	92.201	97.094
39	97.227	96.561	98.735	91.519	96.811
40	97.004	96.307	98.616	90.815	96.505
41	96.781	96.041	98.485	90.087	96.177
42	96.538	95.760	98.341	89.332	95.826
43	96.276	95.460	98.185	88.547	95.452
44	95.995	95.138	98.015	87.730	95.056
45	95.692	94.789	97.830	86.880	94.635
46	95.366	94.412	97.627	85.931	94.186
47	95.012	94.003	97.404	85.065	93.709
48	94.627	93.561	97.156	84.100	93.200
49	94.208	93.082	96.880	83.059	92.656
50	93.751	92.562	96.574	81.955	92.076
51	93.253	91.998	96.235	80.865	91.454
52	92.709	91.378	95.860	79.712	90.786
53	92.113	90.694	95.447	78.500	90.068

1989 U. S. POPULATION

	TOTAL POPULATION	WHITE MALE	WHITE FEMALE	BLACK MALE	BLACK FEMALE
54	91.460	89.937	94.992	77.233	89.295
55	90.748	89.101	94.495	75.914	88.463
56	89.977	88.184	93.949	74.545	87.571
57	89.140	87.182	93.354	73.122	86.607
58	88.231	86.088	92.703	71.640	85.557
59	87.242	84.899	91.995	70.092	84.412
60	86.178	83.610	91.223	68.472	83.166
61	85.032	82.219	90.386	66.783	81.821
62	83.799	80.730	89.480	65.022	80.389
63	82.492	79.146	88.504	63.192	78.884
64	81.098	77.469	87.456	61.292	77.318
65	79.622	75.703	86.332	59.323	75.694
66	78.053	73.825	85.296	57.288	73.994
67	76.383	71.832	84.025	55.189	72.217
68	74.611	69.723	82.731	53.027	70.362
69	72.738	67.494	81.341	50.812	68.429
70	70.752	65.148	79.853	48.543	66.418
71	68.658	62.677	78.256	46.229	64.317
72	66.447	60.085	76.542	43.877	62.126
73	64.121	57.374	74.705	41.498	59.847
74	61.685	54.552	72.740	39.096	57.483
75	59.137	51.624	70.645	36.685	55.038
76	56.476	48.603	68.413	34.272	52.490
77	53.703	45.500	66.025	31.846	49.844
78	50.830	42.332	63.483	29.427	47.108
79	47.862	39.117	60.792	27.023	44.294
80	44.813	35.876	57.946	24.652	41.412
81	41.537	32.510	54.956	22.327	38.324
82	38.052	29.055	51.665	19.951	35.048
83	34.391	25.558	48.079	17.568	31.613
84	30.591	22.074	44.209	15.213	28.061
85	26.712	18.665	40.080	12.912	24.446
86	22.826	15.401	35.739	10.715	20.837
87	19.014	12.350	31.250	8.662	17.309
88	15.371	9.579	26.697	6.796	13.950
89	11.991	7.145	22.188	5.147	10.847
90	8.964	5.088	17.841	3.743	8.080
91	6.368	3.430	13.788	2.593	5.718
92	4.251	2.163	10.155	1.697	3.801

1989 U. S. POPULATION

	TOTAL POPULATION	WHITE MALE	WHITE FEMALE	BLACK MALE	BLACK FEMALE
93	2.630	1.259	7.051	1.037	2.340
94	1.479	.662	4.552	.583	1.309
95	.736	.307	2.681	.296	.648
96	.312	.120	1.403	.132	.273
97	.105	.038	.627	.050	.092
98	.025	0.000	.225	.015	.022
99	0.000	0.000	.058	0.000	0.000

PROBABILITY OF LIVING TO AGE 'X' STARTING FROM AGE 21

1989 U. S. POPULATION

	TOTAL POPULATION	WHITE MALE	WHITE FEMALE	BLACK MALE	BLACK FEMALE
LIFE EXPECTANCY TO AGE	55.60	53.00	59.20	46.20	54.40
22	99.887	99.849	99.953	99.690	99.912
23	99.772	99.696	99.906	99.368	99.817
24	99.655	99.542	99.857	99.042	99.714
25	99.538	99.387	99.807	98.713	99.605
26	99.418	99.232	99.755	98.380	99.487
27	99.296	99.076	99.701	98.035	99.360
28	99.170	98.915	99.646	97.674	99.222
29	99.039	98.750	99.587	97.289	99.072
30	98.902	98.579	99.525	96.880	98.908
31	98.759	98.403	99.459	96.437	98.732
32	98.610	98.220	99.390	95.957	98.544
33	98.453	98.030	99.317	95.464	98.345
34	98.290	97.832	99.242	94.936	98.135
35	98.118	97.626	99.162	94.370	97.914
36	97.936	97.409	99.078	93.767	97.682
37	97.746	97.183	98.988	93.130	97.435
38	97.547	96.948	98.890	92.468	97.171
39	97.334	96.703	98.782	91.784	96.887
40	97.111	96.449	98.663	91.078	96.581
41	96.888	96.183	98.532	90.348	96.253
42	96.645	95.901	98.388	89.591	95.901
43	96.382	95.601	98.232	88.804	95.527
44	96.100	95.278	98.062	87.984	95.131
45	95.798	94.929	97.877	87.132	94.710
46	95.471	94.551	97.674	86.180	94.261
47	95.117	94.142	97.450	85.312	93.783
48	94.732	93.698	97.203	84.343	93.274
49	94.312	93.219	96.927	83.300	92.730
50	93.854	92.698	96.621	82.192	92.148
51	93.356	92.133	96.281	81.099	91.526
52	92.811	91.513	95.906	79.943	90.858
53	92.214	90.828	95.493	78.727	90.140
54	91.561	90.069	95.038	77.457	89.365

1989 U. S. POPULATION

	TOTAL POPULATION	WHITE MALE	WHITE FEMALE	BLACK MALE	BLACK FEMALE
55	90.848	89.232	94.540	76.135	88.533
56	90.076	88.314	93.995	74.761	87.640
57	89.238	87.310	93.399	73.334	86.675
58	88.328	86.214	92.748	71.847	85.625
59	87.339	85.024	92.039	70.295	84.479
60	86.273	83.733	91.267	68.671	83.232
61	85.126	82.341	90.429	66.976	81.886
62	83.891	80.849	89.523	65.211	80.452
63	82.583	79.262	88.546	63.375	78.946
64	81.187	77.583	87.498	61.469	77.379
65	79.709	75.815	86.373	59.495	75.754
66	78.139	73.934	85.337	57.454	74.053
67	76.467	71.938	84.065	55.349	72.274
68	74.693	69.825	82.771	53.181	70.417
69	72.818	67.594	81.380	50.959	68.483
70	70.830	65.243	79.891	48.683	66.471
71	68.734	62.769	78.293	46.363	64.368
72	66.520	60.173	76.579	44.004	62.175
73	64.192	57.459	74.741	41.618	59.894
74	61.753	54.632	72.775	39.209	57.528
75	59.202	51.700	70.679	36.792	55.082
76	56.538	48.674	68.446	34.372	52.531
77	53.762	45.567	66.057	31.939	49.883
78	50.886	42.394	63.514	29.512	47.146
79	47.914	39.174	60.821	27.102	44.329
80	44.862	35.929	57.974	24.723	41.445
81	41.583	32.558	54.983	22.391	38.355
82	38.094	29.098	51.689	20.009	35.076
83	34.429	25.595	48.102	17.619	31.638
84	30.625	22.106	44.230	15.257	28.083
85	26.742	18.693	40.099	12.950	24.466
86	22.851	15.423	35.756	10.746	20.853
87	19.035	12.368	31.265	8.688	17.323
88	15.388	9.593	26.710	6.815	13.961
89	12.004	7.155	22.199	5.162	10.855
90	8.974	5.096	17.850	3.753	8.086
91	6.375	3.435	13.794	2.601	5.722
92	4.256	2.167	10.160	1.702	3.804
93	2.633	1.260	7.055	1.040	2.342

	1989 U. S. POPULATION				
	TOTAL POPULATION	WHITE MALE	WHITE FEMALE	BLACK MALE	BLACK FEMALE
94	1.480	.663	4.555	.585	1.310
95	.737	.308	2.683	.297	.649
96	.312	.121	1.404	.132	.273
97	.106	.038	.628	.050	.092
98	.025	0.000	.225	.015	.022
99	0.000	0.000	.058	0.000	0.000

PROBABILITY OF LIVING TO AGE 'X' STARTING FROM AGE 22

1989 U. S. POPULATION

	TOTAL POPULATION	WHITE MALE	WHITE FEMALE	BLACK MALE	BLACK FEMALE
LIFE EXPECTANCY TO AGE	54.70	52.10	58.30	45.30	53.40
23	99.885	99.847	99.953	99.677	99.905
24	99.768	99.692	99.904	99.350	99.802
25	99.650	99.538	99.854	99.020	99.692
26	99.531	99.382	99.802	98.686	99.575
27	99.408	99.225	99.748	98.340	99.447
28	99.282	99.065	99.692	97.977	99.309
29	99.151	98.899	99.634	97.591	99.159
30	99.014	98.728	99.572	97.181	98.995
31	98.871	98.551	99.506	96.737	98.819
32	98.721	98.368	99.436	96.255	98.630
33	98.564	98.178	99.364	95.761	98.431
34	98.401	97.980	99.288	95.231	98.222
35	98.229	97.773	99.209	94.664	98.001
36	98.047	97.556	99.125	94.059	97.768
37	97.857	97.330	99.034	93.420	97.521
38	97.657	97.094	98.936	92.756	97.257
39	97.444	96.850	98.828	92.069	96.973
40	97.221	96.595	98.710	91.361	96.666
41	96.997	96.328	98.579	90.629	96.338
42	96.754	96.046	98.435	89.869	95.986
43	96.491	95.745	98.278	89.080	95.612
44	96.209	95.422	98.108	88.258	95.215
45	95.906	95.073	97.923	87.403	94.793
46	95.579	94.694	97.720	86.448	94.344
47	95.224	94.284	97.496	85.577	93.865
48	94.839	93.840	97.249	84.606	93.356
49	94.419	93.360	96.972	83.559	92.811
50	93.961	92.839	96.666	82.448	92.230
51	93.462	92.272	96.327	81.351	91.607
52	92.916	91.651	95.951	80.192	90.938
53	92.318	90.965	95.537	78.972	90.219
54	91.665	90.205	95.083	77.698	89.444
55	90.951	89.367	94.584	76.371	88.611

1989 U. S. POPULATION

	TOTAL POPULATION	WHITE MALE	WHITE FEMALE	BLACK MALE	BLACK FEMALE
56	90.178	88.448	94.039	74.994	87.717
57	89.339	87.442	93.443	73.562	86.751
58	88.428	86.345	92.791	72.071	85.700
59	87.437	85.152	92.082	70.513	84.553
60	86.371	83.860	91.310	68.884	83.305
61	85.222	82.465	90.471	67.184	81.958
62	83.986	80.971	89.565	65.413	80.523
63	82.676	79.382	88.588	63.572	79.016
64	81.279	77.701	87.539	61.660	77.447
65	79.799	75.929	86.414	59.680	75.821
66	78.227	74.045	85.377	57.632	74.118
67	76.553	72.047	84.105	55.521	72.338
68	74.777	69.931	82.810	53.346	70.479
69	72.900	67.696	81.419	51.118	68.543
70	70.910	65.342	79.929	48.835	66.529
71	68.811	62.864	78.330	46.507	64.424
72	66.596	60.264	76.615	44.141	62.229
73	64.265	57.546	74.776	41.748	59.947
74	61.823	54.715	72.809	39.331	57.579
75	59.269	51.779	70.712	36.906	55.130
76	56.602	48.748	68.478	34.478	52.578
77	53.823	45.636	66.088	32.038	49.927
78	50.944	42.458	63.544	29.604	47.187
79	47.968	39.234	60.849	27.186	44.368
80	44.913	35.983	58.002	24.800	41.482
81	41.630	32.607	55.009	22.461	38.388
82	38.137	29.142	51.714	20.071	35.107
83	34.468	25.634	48.125	17.674	31.666
84	30.659	22.139	44.251	15.305	28.108
85	26.772	18.721	40.118	12.990	24.487
86	22.877	15.447	35.773	10.779	20.871
87	19.056	12.387	31.280	8.715	17.338
88	15.405	9.608	26.722	6.836	13.973
89	12.017	7.166	22.209	5.178	10.865
90	8.984	5.104	17.858	3.765	8.094
91	6.382	3.440	13.801	2.609	5.727
92	4.261	2.170	10.164	1.707	3.807
93	2.636	1.262	7.058	1.043	2.344
94	1.482	.664	4.557	.587	1.312

| | 1989 U. S. POPULATION | | | | |
	TOTAL POPULATION	WHITE MALE	WHITE FEMALE	BLACK MALE	BLACK FEMALE
95	.737	.308	2.684	.298	.649
96	.312	.121	1.404	.133	.273
97	.106	.038	.628	.050	.092
98	.025	0.000	.225	.015	.022
99	0.000	0.000	.058	0.000	0.000

PROBABILITY OF LIVING TO AGE 'X' STARTING FROM AGE 23

1989 U. S. POPULATION

	TOTAL POPULATION	WHITE MALE	WHITE FEMALE	BLACK MALE	BLACK FEMALE
LIFE EXPECTANCY TO AGE	53.88	51.20	57.30	44.40	52.40
24	99.883	99.845	99.951	99.672	99.897
25	99.765	99.690	99.901	99.341	99.787
26	99.645	99.535	99.849	99.005	99.669
27	99.523	99.377	99.795	98.659	99.542
28	99.396	99.216	99.739	98.295	99.403
29	99.265	99.051	99.680	97.907	99.253
30	99.128	98.879	99.619	97.496	99.090
31	98.985	98.702	99.553	97.051	98.913
32	98.835	98.519	99.483	96.567	98.724
33	98.678	98.329	99.411	96.071	98.525
34	98.514	98.130	99.335	95.540	98.315
35	98.342	97.923	99.256	94.970	98.094
36	98.160	97.706	99.171	94.363	97.861
37	97.969	97.479	99.081	93.723	97.614
38	97.769	97.243	98.983	93.056	97.349
39	97.556	96.998	98.875	92.368	97.065
40	97.333	96.743	98.756	91.657	96.758
41	97.109	96.476	98.625	90.922	96.429
42	96.865	96.193	98.481	90.160	96.077
43	96.602	95.892	98.324	89.369	95.703
44	96.320	95.568	98.154	88.544	95.305
45	96.016	95.218	97.969	87.686	94.883
46	95.689	94.839	97.766	86.728	94.433
47	95.334	94.429	97.542	85.854	93.955
48	94.948	93.984	97.294	84.880	93.444
49	94.527	93.503	97.018	83.830	92.900
50	94.069	92.981	96.711	82.715	92.317
51	93.569	92.414	96.372	81.615	91.694
52	93.023	91.792	95.996	80.452	91.025
53	92.425	91.104	95.582	79.228	90.305
54	91.770	90.344	95.127	77.949	89.529
55	91.055	89.504	94.629	76.619	88.695
56	90.281	88.583	94.083	75.237	87.801

1989 U. S. POPULATION

	TOTAL POPULATION	WHITE MALE	WHITE FEMALE	BLACK MALE	BLACK FEMALE
57	89.442	87.576	93.486	73.800	86.834
58	88.530	86.477	92.835	72.304	85.781
59	87.538	85.283	92.126	70.742	84.634
60	86.470	83.988	91.353	69.108	83.384
61	85.320	82.591	90.514	67.402	82.036
62	84.083	81.095	89.607	65.625	80.600
63	82.771	79.504	88.629	63.778	79.091
64	81.372	77.820	87.580	61.860	77.521
65	79.891	76.046	86.455	59.873	75.893
66	78.317	74.159	85.417	57.819	74.188
67	76.642	72.157	84.145	55.701	72.406
68	74.863	70.038	82.849	53.519	70.546
69	72.984	67.800	81.457	51.283	68.608
70	70.992	65.442	79.966	48.993	66.593
71	68.891	62.961	78.367	46.658	64.486
72	66.672	60.357	76.651	44.284	62.289
73	64.339	57.634	74.811	41.883	60.004
74	61.894	54.798	72.843	39.459	57.634
75	59.338	51.858	70.746	37.026	55.183
76	56.667	48.823	68.510	34.590	52.628
77	53.885	45.706	66.119	32.142	49.975
78	51.002	42.523	63.573	29.700	47.232
79	48.024	39.294	60.878	27.274	44.410
80	44.965	36.039	58.029	24.881	41.521
81	41.678	32.657	55.035	22.534	38.425
82	38.181	29.187	51.738	20.136	35.140
83	34.508	25.673	48.147	17.731	31.696
84	30.695	22.173	44.272	15.354	28.135
85	26.803	18.750	40.137	13.032	24.510
86	22.903	15.470	35.790	10.814	20.891
87	19.078	12.406	31.295	8.743	17.355
88	15.423	9.623	26.735	6.859	13.987
89	12.031	7.177	22.219	5.195	10.875
90	8.995	5.111	17.867	3.777	8.101
91	6.390	3.445	13.807	2.617	5.733
92	4.266	2.173	10.169	1.713	3.811
93	2.639	1.264	7.061	1.047	2.347
94	1.484	.665	4.559	.589	1.313
95	.738	.308	2.685	.299	.650

	1989 U. S. POPULATION				
	TOTAL POPULATION	WHITE MALE	WHITE FEMALE	BLACK MALE	BLACK FEMALE
96	.313	.121	1.405	.133	.274
97	.106	.038	.628	.050	.092
98	.025	0.000	.226	.015	.022
99	0.000	0.000	.058	0.000	0.000

PROBABILITY OF LIVING TO AGE 'X' STARTING FROM AGE 24

1989 U. S. POPULATION

	TOTAL POPULATION	WHITE MALE	WHITE FEMALE	BLACK MALE	BLACK FEMALE
LIFE EXPECTANCY TO AGE	52.80	50.30	56.30	43.60	51.50
25	99.882	99.845	99.950	99.668	99.890
26	99.762	99.689	99.898	99.331	99.772
27	99.639	99.532	99.844	98.983	99.644
28	99.513	99.370	99.788	98.618	99.506
29	99.382	99.205	99.729	98.230	99.356
30	99.244	99.033	99.667	97.817	99.192
31	99.100	98.856	99.602	97.370	99.015
32	98.951	98.672	99.532	96.885	98.826
33	98.794	98.481	99.459	96.387	98.626
34	98.630	98.282	99.384	95.854	98.416
35	98.457	98.075	99.304	95.283	98.195
36	98.275	97.857	99.220	94.674	97.962
37	98.084	97.630	99.130	94.031	97.714
38	97.884	97.394	99.031	93.363	97.450
39	97.671	97.149	98.923	92.672	97.165
40	97.447	96.893	98.805	91.959	96.858
41	97.223	96.626	98.673	91.222	96.529
42	96.979	96.343	98.529	90.457	96.176
43	96.715	96.041	98.373	89.663	95.801
44	96.433	95.716	98.202	88.835	95.404
45	96.129	95.366	98.017	87.975	94.981
46	95.801	94.986	97.814	87.014	94.531
47	95.446	94.575	97.590	86.137	94.052
48	95.059	94.130	97.342	85.159	93.541
49	94.638	93.648	97.066	84.106	92.995
50	94.179	93.125	96.759	82.987	92.412
51	93.679	92.557	96.419	81.883	91.789
52	93.132	91.934	96.043	80.716	91.119
53	92.533	91.246	95.629	79.489	90.398
54	91.878	90.484	95.174	78.206	89.621
55	91.162	89.643	94.675	76.871	88.787
56	90.387	88.721	94.129	75.484	87.891
57	89.547	87.712	93.532	74.043	86.923

1989 U. S. POPULATION

	TOTAL POPULATION	WHITE MALE	WHITE FEMALE	BLACK MALE	BLACK FEMALE
58	88.633	86.611	92.880	72.542	85.870
59	87.641	85.415	92.171	70.975	84.721
60	86.571	84.119	91.397	69.335	83.470
61	85.420	82.720	90.558	67.624	82.121
62	84.181	81.221	89.651	65.841	80.683
63	82.868	79.627	88.673	63.988	79.172
64	81.468	77.941	87.623	62.064	77.601
65	79.985	76.164	86.497	60.070	75.971
66	78.409	74.274	85.459	58.009	74.265
67	76.731	72.269	84.186	55.884	72.481
68	74.951	70.147	82.889	53.695	70.619
69	73.070	67.905	81.497	51.452	68.679
70	71.075	65.544	80.005	49.154	66.661
71	68.971	63.058	78.405	46.812	64.552
72	66.750	60.450	76.688	44.430	62.353
73	64.414	57.723	74.848	42.021	60.066
74	61.966	54.883	72.879	39.589	57.693
75	59.407	51.938	70.780	37.148	55.239
76	56.734	48.898	68.544	34.704	52.682
77	53.948	45.777	66.151	32.248	50.026
78	51.062	42.589	63.605	29.797	47.281
79	48.080	39.355	60.908	27.364	44.456
80	45.017	36.095	58.057	24.962	41.564
81	41.726	32.708	55.062	22.608	38.464
82	38.226	29.232	51.763	20.202	35.176
83	34.548	25.713	48.171	17.789	31.729
84	30.731	22.208	44.293	15.405	28.164
85	26.834	18.779	40.156	13.075	24.536
86	22.930	15.494	35.807	10.850	20.913
87	19.100	12.425	31.310	8.772	17.373
88	15.441	9.637	26.748	6.881	14.001
89	12.045	7.188	22.230	5.212	10.886
90	9.005	5.119	17.875	3.790	8.110
91	6.397	3.451	13.814	2.626	5.738
92	4.271	2.177	10.174	1.718	3.815
93	2.642	1.266	7.065	1.050	2.349
94	1.486	.666	4.561	.591	1.314
95	.739	.309	2.686	.300	.650
96	.313	.121	1.406	.134	.274

| | 1989 U. S. POPULATION | | | | |
	TOTAL POPULATION	WHITE MALE	WHITE FEMALE	BLACK MALE	BLACK FEMALE
97	.106	.038	.629	.050	.092
98	.025	0.000	.226	.015	.022
99	0.000	0.000	.058	0.000	0.000

PROBABILITY OF LIVING TO AGE 'X' STARTING FROM AGE 25

1989 U. S. POPULATION

	TOTAL POPULATION	WHITE MALE	WHITE FEMALE	BLACK MALE	BLACK FEMALE
LIFE EXPECTANCY TO AGE	51.90	49.40	55.30	42.70	50.60
26	99.880	99.844	99.948	99.662	99.882
27	99.757	99.686	99.894	99.313	99.754
28	99.630	99.525	99.838	98.947	99.615
29	99.499	99.359	99.779	98.557	99.465
30	99.362	99.187	99.717	98.143	99.301
31	99.218	99.009	99.652	97.694	99.124
32	99.068	98.825	99.582	97.208	98.935
33	98.910	98.634	99.509	96.708	98.735
34	98.746	98.435	99.433	96.173	98.525
35	98.573	98.227	99.354	95.600	98.303
36	98.391	98.009	99.269	94.989	98.070
37	98.200	97.782	99.179	94.344	97.822
38	98.000	97.545	99.081	93.674	97.557
39	97.786	97.299	98.973	92.980	97.272
40	97.562	97.043	98.854	92.265	96.965
41	97.338	96.776	98.723	91.525	96.635
42	97.093	96.492	98.579	90.758	96.282
43	96.829	96.190	98.422	89.962	95.907
44	96.547	95.865	98.252	89.131	95.509
45	96.242	95.514	98.066	88.268	95.086
46	95.914	95.134	97.863	87.304	94.635
47	95.558	94.722	97.639	86.424	94.155
48	95.171	94.276	97.391	85.443	93.644
49	94.750	93.793	97.114	84.386	93.098
50	94.290	93.270	96.807	83.263	92.514
51	93.790	92.701	96.467	82.156	91.890
52	93.242	92.077	96.091	80.985	91.219
53	92.642	91.387	95.677	79.754	90.497
54	91.986	90.624	95.222	78.466	89.720
55	91.270	89.782	94.723	77.127	88.885
56	90.494	88.858	94.176	75.736	87.988
57	89.652	87.848	93.579	74.290	87.019
58	88.738	86.746	92.927	72.784	85.964

1989 U. S. POPULATION

	TOTAL POPULATION	WHITE MALE	WHITE FEMALE	BLACK MALE	BLACK FEMALE
59	87.744	85.548	92.217	71.211	84.814
60	86.674	84.249	91.443	69.566	83.562
61	85.521	82.848	90.604	67.849	82.211
62	84.281	81.347	89.696	66.061	80.772
63	82.966	79.751	88.717	64.201	79.260
64	81.564	78.062	87.667	62.271	77.686
65	80.079	76.282	86.540	60.270	76.055
66	78.502	74.389	85.502	58.203	74.347
67	76.822	72.382	84.228	56.070	72.561
68	75.040	70.256	82.931	53.874	70.697
69	73.156	68.010	81.538	51.623	68.755
70	71.159	65.646	80.045	49.318	66.735
71	69.053	63.156	78.444	46.967	64.623
72	66.829	60.544	76.727	44.578	62.422
73	64.490	57.813	74.885	42.161	60.132
74	62.040	54.969	72.916	39.720	57.757
75	59.477	52.019	70.816	37.271	55.300
76	56.801	48.974	68.578	34.820	52.740
77	54.012	45.848	66.185	32.355	50.081
78	51.122	42.655	63.636	29.897	47.333
79	48.137	39.416	60.938	27.455	44.505
80	45.070	36.151	58.086	25.046	41.610
81	41.776	32.759	55.089	22.683	38.507
82	38.271	29.277	51.789	20.270	35.215
83	34.589	25.753	48.195	17.849	31.763
84	30.767	22.242	44.315	15.456	28.195
85	26.866	18.808	40.176	13.118	24.563
86	22.957	15.519	35.825	10.886	20.936
87	19.123	12.444	31.326	8.801	17.392
88	15.459	9.652	26.761	6.904	14.017
89	12.060	7.200	22.241	5.230	10.898
90	9.016	5.127	17.884	3.802	8.119
91	6.405	3.456	13.821	2.635	5.745
92	4.276	2.180	10.179	1.724	3.819
93	2.645	1.268	7.068	1.054	2.352
94	1.487	.668	4.563	.593	1.316
95	.740	.309	2.688	.301	.651
96	.313	.121	1.407	.134	.274
97	.106	.038	.629	.050	.092

1989 U. S. POPULATION

	TOTAL POPULATION	WHITE MALE	WHITE FEMALE	BLACK MALE	BLACK FEMALE
98	.026	0.000	.226	.015	.022
99	0.000	0.000	.058	0.000	0.000

PROBABILITY OF LIVING TO AGE 'X' STARTING FROM AGE 26

1989 U. S. POPULATION

LIFE EXPECTANCY TO AGE	TOTAL POPULATION	WHITE MALE	WHITE FEMALE	BLACK MALE	BLACK FEMALE
	50.90	48.40	54.40	41.90	49.60
27	99.877	99.842	99.946	99.650	99.872
28	99.750	99.680	99.890	99.282	99.733
29	99.618	99.514	99.831	98.891	99.583
30	99.481	99.342	99.769	98.476	99.418
31	99.337	99.164	99.703	98.026	99.241
32	99.187	98.979	99.634	97.538	99.052
33	99.029	98.788	99.561	97.036	98.852
34	98.865	98.589	99.485	96.500	98.641
35	98.692	98.381	99.406	95.924	98.419
36	98.509	98.162	99.321	95.312	98.186
37	98.318	97.935	99.231	94.664	97.938
38	98.117	97.698	99.132	93.991	97.672
39	97.904	97.451	99.024	93.296	97.387
40	97.679	97.195	98.906	92.578	97.079
41	97.455	96.927	98.774	91.836	96.749
42	97.210	96.643	98.630	91.066	96.396
43	96.946	96.340	98.473	90.267	96.020
44	96.663	96.015	98.303	89.434	95.622
45	96.358	95.663	98.117	88.567	95.198
46	96.029	95.283	97.914	87.600	94.747
47	95.673	94.870	97.690	86.717	94.266
48	95.286	94.423	97.441	85.733	93.754
49	94.864	93.940	97.165	84.672	93.208
50	94.404	93.416	96.858	83.546	92.623
51	93.902	92.846	96.518	82.435	91.998
52	93.354	92.221	96.141	81.260	91.327
53	92.754	91.530	95.727	80.024	90.604
54	92.097	90.766	95.271	78.732	89.826
55	91.379	89.923	94.772	77.389	88.990
56	90.603	88.997	94.225	75.992	88.092
57	89.760	87.985	93.628	74.542	87.122
58	88.845	86.881	92.975	73.031	86.066
59	87.850	85.681	92.265	71.453	84.914

1989 U. S. POPULATION

	TOTAL POPULATION	WHITE MALE	WHITE FEMALE	BLACK MALE	BLACK FEMALE
60	86.778	84.381	91.491	69.802	83.661
61	85.624	82.977	90.651	68.079	82.308
62	84.382	81.474	89.743	66.285	80.867
63	83.066	79.875	88.763	64.419	79.353
64	81.662	78.184	87.712	62.482	77.778
65	80.176	76.401	86.585	60.475	76.145
66	78.596	74.506	85.546	58.400	74.435
67	76.914	72.495	84.272	56.260	72.647
68	75.130	70.365	82.974	54.056	70.780
69	73.244	68.117	81.580	51.799	68.836
70	71.244	65.748	80.087	49.485	66.814
71	69.136	63.255	78.485	47.127	64.700
72	66.909	60.639	76.766	44.729	62.495
73	64.568	57.903	74.924	42.304	60.203
74	62.114	55.055	72.954	39.855	57.825
75	59.549	52.100	70.853	37.398	55.366
76	56.869	49.051	68.614	34.938	52.802
77	54.077	45.919	66.219	32.465	50.140
78	51.184	42.722	63.670	29.998	47.389
79	48.195	39.477	60.970	27.548	44.557
80	45.125	36.207	58.117	25.131	41.659
81	41.826	32.810	55.118	22.760	38.552
82	38.317	29.323	51.816	20.338	35.256
83	34.631	25.793	48.220	17.909	31.801
84	30.804	22.277	44.338	15.509	28.228
85	26.898	18.837	40.197	13.163	24.592
86	22.984	15.543	35.844	10.923	20.961
87	19.146	12.464	31.342	8.831	17.412
88	15.478	9.668	26.775	6.927	14.033
89	12.074	7.211	22.253	5.247	10.911
90	9.027	5.135	17.894	3.815	8.128
91	6.412	3.461	13.828	2.644	5.752
92	4.281	2.183	10.184	1.730	3.824
93	2.648	1.270	7.072	1.057	2.354
94	1.489	.669	4.566	.595	1.317
95	.741	.310	2.689	.302	.652
96	.314	.122	1.407	.135	.275
97	.106	.038	.629	.051	.092

	1989 U. S. POPULATION				
	TOTAL POPULATION	WHITE MALE	WHITE FEMALE	BLACK MALE	BLACK FEMALE
98	.026	0.000	.226	.015	.022
99	0.000	0.000	.058	0.000	0.000

PROBABILITY OF LIVING TO AGE 'X' STARTING FROM AGE 27

1989 U. S. POPULATION

	TOTAL POPULATION	WHITE MALE	WHITE FEMALE	BLACK MALE	BLACK FEMALE
LIFE EXPECTANCY TO AGE	50.00	47.50	53.40	41.00	48.70
28	99.873	99.838	99.944	99.631	99.861
29	99.741	99.671	99.885	99.238	99.710
30	99.604	99.499	99.823	98.822	99.546
31	99.459	99.321	99.757	98.370	99.368
32	99.309	99.136	99.687	97.880	99.179
33	99.151	98.945	99.615	97.377	98.978
34	98.986	98.745	99.539	96.839	98.768
35	98.813	98.536	99.459	96.261	98.545
36	98.630	98.318	99.375	95.646	98.312
37	98.439	98.090	99.284	94.997	98.063
38	98.238	97.852	99.186	94.321	97.797
39	98.024	97.606	99.078	93.623	97.512
40	97.800	97.349	98.959	92.903	97.204
41	97.575	97.080	98.827	92.158	96.873
42	97.330	96.796	98.683	91.386	96.519
43	97.065	96.493	98.526	90.584	96.143
44	96.782	96.167	98.356	89.748	95.744
45	96.477	95.815	98.170	88.878	95.320
46	96.148	95.433	97.967	87.907	94.868
47	95.791	95.020	97.742	87.021	94.387
48	95.403	94.573	97.494	86.034	93.875
49	94.980	94.088	97.217	84.969	93.327
50	94.520	93.563	96.910	83.839	92.742
51	94.018	92.993	96.570	82.724	92.116
52	93.469	92.367	96.193	81.545	91.444
53	92.868	91.675	95.779	80.305	90.720
54	92.210	90.909	95.323	79.009	89.941
55	91.492	90.065	94.823	77.660	89.104
56	90.714	89.138	94.276	76.259	88.205
57	89.871	88.125	93.678	74.804	87.234
58	88.954	87.019	93.025	73.287	86.176
59	87.958	85.817	92.315	71.704	85.023
60	86.885	84.514	91.540	70.047	83.768

1989 U. S. POPULATION

	TOTAL POPULATION	WHITE MALE	WHITE FEMALE	BLACK MALE	BLACK FEMALE
61	85.729	83.109	90.700	68.318	82.414
62	84.486	81.603	89.791	66.518	80.971
63	83.168	80.002	88.811	64.645	79.455
64	81.762	78.307	87.760	62.701	77.878
65	80.274	76.522	86.632	60.687	76.242
66	78.693	74.623	85.593	58.605	74.530
67	77.009	72.609	84.317	56.458	72.740
68	75.222	70.477	83.019	54.246	70.871
69	73.334	68.224	81.624	51.980	68.924
70	71.332	65.852	80.130	49.659	66.899
71	69.221	63.355	78.528	47.292	64.783
72	66.992	60.735	76.808	44.886	62.575
73	64.647	57.995	74.965	42.452	60.280
74	62.191	55.142	72.993	39.995	57.899
75	59.622	52.183	70.891	37.529	55.437
76	56.939	49.128	68.651	35.060	52.870
77	54.143	45.992	66.255	32.579	50.205
78	51.247	42.790	63.704	30.103	47.449
79	48.254	39.540	61.003	27.645	44.614
80	45.180	36.264	58.148	25.219	41.712
81	41.877	32.862	55.148	22.840	38.602
82	38.364	29.369	51.844	20.410	35.302
83	34.673	25.834	48.246	17.972	31.842
84	30.842	22.312	44.362	15.563	28.264
85	26.931	18.867	40.219	13.209	24.623
86	23.013	15.567	35.863	10.961	20.987
87	19.170	12.484	31.359	8.862	17.435
88	15.497	9.683	26.790	6.952	14.051
89	12.089	7.222	22.265	5.266	10.925
90	9.038	5.144	17.903	3.829	8.139
91	6.420	3.467	13.836	2.653	5.759
92	4.286	2.187	10.190	1.736	3.829
93	2.651	1.272	7.076	1.061	2.357
94	1.491	.670	4.568	.597	1.319
95	.742	.310	2.691	.303	.653
96	.314	.122	1.408	.135	.275
97	.106	.038	.630	.051	.092
98	.026	0.000	.226	.015	.022
99	0.000	0.000	.058	0.000	0.000

PROBABILITY OF LIVING TO AGE 'X' STARTING FROM AGE 28

1989 U. S. POPULATION

	TOTAL POPULATION	WHITE MALE	WHITE FEMALE	BLACK MALE	BLACK FEMALE
LIFE EXPECTANCY TO AGE	49.10	46.60	52.40	40.20	47.70
29	99.868	99.833	99.941	99.606	99.849
30	99.730	99.660	99.879	99.188	99.684
31	99.586	99.482	99.813	98.734	99.507
32	99.435	99.297	99.743	98.243	99.317
33	99.277	99.105	99.670	97.738	99.116
34	99.112	98.905	99.595	97.197	98.905
35	98.939	98.696	99.515	96.618	98.682
36	98.756	98.477	99.430	96.001	98.449
37	98.564	98.249	99.340	95.349	98.200
38	98.363	98.011	99.242	94.671	97.933
39	98.149	97.764	99.133	93.970	97.647
40	97.924	97.507	99.014	93.248	97.339
41	97.699	97.238	98.883	92.500	97.008
42	97.454	96.953	98.738	91.725	96.654
43	97.188	96.649	98.581	90.919	96.277
44	96.905	96.323	98.411	90.080	95.877
45	96.599	95.970	98.225	89.207	95.453
46	96.270	95.588	98.022	88.233	95.000
47	95.913	95.174	97.797	87.344	94.519
48	95.524	94.726	97.549	86.352	94.005
49	95.101	94.241	97.272	85.284	93.457
50	94.640	93.715	96.964	84.150	92.871
51	94.137	93.144	96.624	83.031	92.244
52	93.588	92.517	96.247	81.847	91.571
53	92.986	91.824	95.832	80.603	90.847
54	92.328	91.057	95.376	79.302	90.066
55	91.608	90.211	94.876	77.948	89.228
56	90.830	89.283	94.329	76.542	88.327
57	89.985	88.268	93.731	75.081	87.355
58	89.067	87.160	93.078	73.559	86.296
59	88.070	85.956	92.366	71.969	85.142
60	86.995	84.651	91.591	70.307	83.885
61	85.838	83.244	90.751	68.571	82.528

1989 U. S. POPULATION

	TOTAL POPULATION	WHITE MALE	WHITE FEMALE	BLACK MALE	BLACK FEMALE
62	84.593	81.735	89.841	66.764	81.083
63	83.274	80.132	88.861	64.884	79.566
64	81.866	78.434	87.809	62.933	77.986
65	80.376	76.646	86.681	60.912	76.348
66	78.793	74.745	85.641	58.822	74.634
67	77.107	72.727	84.364	56.667	72.841
68	75.318	70.591	83.065	54.447	70.970
69	73.428	68.335	81.670	52.173	69.020
70	71.423	65.959	80.175	49.843	66.992
71	69.309	63.458	78.572	47.467	64.873
72	67.077	60.833	76.851	45.052	62.662
73	64.729	58.089	75.007	42.610	60.364
74	62.270	55.231	73.034	40.143	57.980
75	59.698	52.267	70.931	37.668	55.514
76	57.012	49.208	68.689	35.190	52.943
77	54.212	46.067	66.292	32.699	50.275
78	51.312	42.859	63.740	30.215	47.516
79	48.315	39.604	61.037	27.747	44.676
80	45.238	36.323	58.181	25.312	41.770
81	41.931	32.915	55.178	22.925	38.655
82	38.413	29.417	51.873	20.485	35.351
83	34.717	25.876	48.273	18.039	31.886
84	30.881	22.348	44.387	15.621	28.303
85	26.965	18.898	40.241	13.258	24.658
86	23.042	15.593	35.883	11.002	21.017
87	19.194	12.504	31.376	8.895	17.459
88	15.516	9.699	26.805	6.978	14.071
89	12.104	7.234	22.277	5.285	10.940
90	9.049	5.152	17.913	3.843	8.150
91	6.429	3.472	13.843	2.663	5.767
92	4.292	2.190	10.196	1.742	3.834
93	2.655	1.274	7.080	1.065	2.361
94	1.493	.671	4.571	.599	1.321
95	.743	.311	2.692	.304	.654
96	.315	.122	1.409	.135	.275
97	.106	.038	.630	.051	.093
98	.026	0.000	.226	.015	.022
99	0.000	0.000	.058	0.000	0.000

PROBABILITY OF LIVING TO AGE 'X' STARTING FROM AGE 29

1989 U. S. POPULATION

	TOTAL POPULATION	WHITE MALE	WHITE FEMALE	BLACK MALE	BLACK FEMALE
LIFE EXPECTANCY TO AGE	48.10	45.70	51.50	39.30	46.80
30	99.862	99.827	99.938	99.580	99.835
31	99.717	99.648	99.872	99.125	99.657
32	99.567	99.463	99.802	98.631	99.467
33	99.408	99.271	99.729	98.124	99.266
34	99.243	99.070	99.653	97.582	99.055
35	99.070	98.861	99.574	97.000	98.832
36	98.886	98.642	99.489	96.380	98.597
37	98.695	98.413	99.399	95.726	98.348
38	98.493	98.175	99.300	95.045	98.082
39	98.278	97.928	99.192	94.342	97.795
40	98.053	97.670	99.073	93.616	97.486
41	97.828	97.400	98.941	92.866	97.155
42	97.582	97.115	98.797	92.087	96.800
43	97.317	96.811	98.640	91.279	96.422
44	97.033	96.484	98.469	90.436	96.022
45	96.727	96.131	98.283	89.560	95.597
46	96.397	95.748	98.079	88.582	95.144
47	96.040	95.334	97.855	87.689	94.661
48	95.651	94.885	97.606	86.694	94.147
49	95.227	94.399	97.329	85.621	93.599
50	94.765	93.872	97.021	84.483	93.012
51	94.262	93.299	96.681	83.359	92.384
52	93.711	92.671	96.304	82.171	91.709
53	93.109	91.977	95.889	80.921	90.984
54	92.450	91.209	95.432	79.615	90.202
55	91.729	90.362	94.932	78.256	89.363
56	90.950	89.432	94.385	76.845	88.461
57	90.104	88.415	93.786	75.378	87.487
58	89.185	87.306	93.132	73.850	86.427
59	88.186	86.100	92.421	72.254	85.270
60	87.110	84.793	91.646	70.585	84.012
61	85.952	83.383	90.804	68.843	82.653
62	84.705	81.872	89.894	67.028	81.206

1989 U. S. POPULATION

	TOTAL POPULATION	WHITE MALE	WHITE FEMALE	BLACK MALE	BLACK FEMALE
63	83.384	80.266	88.914	65.141	79.686
64	81.975	78.566	87.861	63.182	78.104
65	80.483	76.774	86.732	61.153	76.464
66	78.897	74.870	85.691	59.055	74.747
67	77.209	72.849	84.414	56.891	72.951
68	75.418	70.709	83.114	54.663	71.077
69	73.525	68.449	81.718	52.379	69.125
70	71.517	66.069	80.223	50.040	67.094
71	69.400	63.564	78.618	47.655	64.971
72	67.166	60.935	76.896	45.230	62.757
73	64.815	58.186	75.051	42.778	60.455
74	62.352	55.324	73.077	40.302	58.067
75	59.777	52.355	70.972	37.817	55.598
76	57.087	49.291	68.730	35.329	53.024
77	54.284	46.144	66.331	32.829	50.351
78	51.380	42.931	63.777	30.334	47.587
79	48.379	39.670	61.073	27.857	44.744
80	45.297	36.384	58.215	25.412	41.833
81	41.986	32.970	55.211	23.015	38.714
82	38.464	29.466	51.904	20.566	35.404
83	34.763	25.919	48.302	18.110	31.934
84	30.922	22.386	44.413	15.682	28.346
85	27.001	18.929	40.265	13.310	24.695
86	23.072	15.619	35.905	11.045	21.048
87	19.219	12.525	31.395	8.930	17.485
88	15.537	9.715	26.821	7.005	14.092
89	12.120	7.246	22.291	5.306	10.957
90	9.061	5.160	17.924	3.858	8.162
91	6.437	3.478	13.852	2.673	5.776
92	4.297	2.194	10.202	1.749	3.840
93	2.658	1.276	7.084	1.069	2.364
94	1.495	.672	4.573	.601	1.323
95	.744	.311	2.694	.305	.655
96	.315	.122	1.410	.136	.276
97	.107	.038	.630	.051	.093
98	.026	0.000	.226	.015	.022
99	0.000	0.000	.058	0.000	0.000

PROBABILITY OF LIVING TO AGE 'X' STARTING FROM AGE 30

1989 U. S. POPULATION

	TOTAL POPULATION	WHITE MALE	WHITE FEMALE	BLACK MALE	BLACK FEMALE
LIFE EXPECTANCY TO AGE	47.20	44.70	50.50	38.50	45.90
31	99.855	99.821	99.934	99.543	99.822
32	99.704	99.635	99.864	99.047	99.631
33	99.546	99.443	99.791	98.538	99.430
34	99.380	99.242	99.715	97.993	99.218
35	99.207	99.033	99.636	97.409	98.995
36	99.023	98.813	99.551	96.787	98.760
37	98.831	98.584	99.460	96.130	98.511
38	98.629	98.345	99.362	95.446	98.244
39	98.414	98.097	99.253	94.740	97.957
40	98.189	97.839	99.134	94.011	97.647
41	97.963	97.569	99.003	93.257	97.315
42	97.717	97.283	98.858	92.476	96.960
43	97.451	96.979	98.701	91.664	96.582
44	97.167	96.651	98.530	90.818	96.181
45	96.861	96.297	98.344	89.938	95.755
46	96.530	95.914	98.140	88.956	95.301
47	96.172	95.499	97.916	88.059	94.818
48	95.783	95.049	97.667	87.060	94.303
49	95.359	94.562	97.389	85.983	93.753
50	94.896	94.035	97.082	84.839	93.165
51	94.392	93.461	96.741	83.711	92.537
52	93.841	92.832	96.364	82.518	91.861
53	93.237	92.137	95.948	81.263	91.134
54	92.577	91.367	95.492	79.951	90.352
55	91.856	90.519	94.991	78.586	89.510
56	91.075	89.587	94.443	77.169	88.607
57	90.228	88.569	93.844	75.695	87.632
58	89.308	87.457	93.190	74.161	86.570
59	88.308	86.249	92.478	72.559	85.411
60	87.230	84.940	91.702	70.882	84.151
61	86.070	83.527	90.861	69.133	82.790
62	84.822	82.014	89.950	67.311	81.340
63	83.499	80.405	88.969	65.416	79.818

1989 U. S. POPULATION

	TOTAL POPULATION	WHITE MALE	WHITE FEMALE	BLACK MALE	BLACK FEMALE
64	82.088	78.702	87.915	63.449	78.233
65	80.594	76.907	86.786	61.411	76.590
66	79.006	74.999	85.744	59.304	74.870
67	77.315	72.975	84.467	57.131	73.072
68	75.522	70.832	83.166	54.893	71.194
69	73.626	68.568	81.769	52.600	69.239
70	71.616	66.184	80.272	50.251	67.205
71	69.496	63.674	78.667	47.856	65.078
72	67.259	61.041	76.944	45.421	62.861
73	64.905	58.287	75.097	42.959	60.555
74	62.438	55.419	73.122	40.472	58.163
75	59.859	52.446	71.016	37.977	55.690
76	57.166	49.376	68.772	35.478	53.111
77	54.359	46.224	66.372	32.967	50.434
78	51.451	43.005	63.817	30.462	47.666
79	48.446	39.739	61.111	27.975	44.818
80	45.360	36.447	58.251	25.520	41.903
81	42.044	33.027	55.245	23.113	38.778
82	38.517	29.517	51.936	20.653	35.463
83	34.811	25.964	48.332	18.186	31.987
84	30.965	22.425	44.441	15.749	28.393
85	27.038	18.962	40.290	13.367	24.736
86	23.104	15.646	35.927	11.092	21.083
87	19.246	12.547	31.414	8.967	17.514
88	15.558	9.732	26.837	7.035	14.115
89	12.137	7.259	22.304	5.329	10.975
90	9.074	5.169	17.935	3.874	8.176
91	6.446	3.484	13.860	2.684	5.785
92	4.303	2.198	10.208	1.757	3.846
93	2.662	1.279	7.088	1.074	2.368
94	1.497	.673	4.576	.604	1.325
95	.745	.312	2.695	.306	.656
96	.315	.122	1.411	.137	.276
97	.107	.038	.631	.051	.093
98	.026	0.000	.226	.015	.022
99	0.000	0.000	.058	0.000	0.000

PROBABILITY OF LIVING TO AGE 'X' STARTING FROM AGE 31

1989 U. S. POPULATION

	TOTAL POPULATION	WHITE MALE	WHITE FEMALE	BLACK MALE	BLACK FEMALE
LIFE EXPECTANCY TO AGE	46.20	43.80	49.50	37.60	44.90
32	99.849	99.814	99.930	99.502	99.809
33	99.690	99.621	99.857	98.991	99.607
34	99.525	99.420	99.781	98.443	99.395
35	99.351	99.210	99.701	97.856	99.172
36	99.167	98.990	99.617	97.231	98.937
37	98.974	98.760	99.526	96.571	98.686
38	98.772	98.521	99.427	95.884	98.419
39	98.557	98.273	99.319	95.175	98.131
40	98.331	98.015	99.200	94.443	97.821
41	98.105	97.744	99.068	93.685	97.489
42	97.859	97.458	98.923	92.900	97.133
43	97.593	97.153	98.766	92.085	96.754
44	97.308	96.824	98.595	91.235	96.353
45	97.001	96.470	98.409	90.351	95.926
46	96.671	96.086	98.205	89.364	95.471
47	96.312	95.670	97.980	88.463	94.987
48	95.922	95.219	97.731	87.459	94.471
49	95.497	94.732	97.454	86.377	93.920
50	95.034	94.203	97.146	85.229	93.332
51	94.529	93.629	96.805	84.095	92.702
52	93.977	92.999	96.427	82.897	92.025
53	93.373	92.302	96.012	81.636	91.297
54	92.712	91.531	95.555	80.318	90.513
55	91.990	90.681	95.054	78.947	89.670
56	91.208	89.748	94.505	77.523	88.765
57	90.359	88.727	93.906	76.043	87.788
58	89.438	87.614	93.252	74.502	86.724
59	88.436	86.404	92.539	72.892	85.564
60	87.357	85.092	91.763	71.208	84.301
61	86.195	83.677	90.921	69.450	82.938
62	84.945	82.161	90.010	67.620	81.485
63	83.620	80.549	89.028	65.716	79.960
64	82.207	78.843	87.973	63.740	78.373

1989 U. S. POPULATION

	TOTAL POPULATION	WHITE MALE	WHITE FEMALE	BLACK MALE	BLACK FEMALE
65	80.711	77.045	86.843	61.693	76.727
66	79.121	75.134	85.801	59.576	75.004
67	77.428	73.106	84.522	57.393	73.202
68	75.631	70.959	83.221	55.145	71.321
69	73.733	68.691	81.823	52.842	69.362
70	71.720	66.303	80.325	50.482	67.324
71	69.597	63.788	78.719	48.076	65.194
72	67.356	61.150	76.995	45.630	62.973
73	64.999	58.392	75.147	43.156	60.663
74	62.529	55.519	73.171	40.658	58.267
75	59.946	52.540	71.063	38.151	55.789
76	57.249	49.464	68.818	35.641	53.206
77	54.438	46.307	66.416	33.119	50.524
78	51.525	43.082	63.859	30.602	47.751
79	48.516	39.810	61.151	28.103	44.898
80	45.426	36.512	58.289	25.637	41.977
81	42.105	33.086	55.282	23.219	38.847
82	38.573	29.570	51.970	20.748	35.526
83	34.862	26.011	48.364	18.270	32.044
84	31.010	22.465	44.470	15.821	28.444
85	27.078	18.996	40.317	13.428	24.780
86	23.138	15.674	35.951	11.143	21.121
87	19.274	12.569	31.435	9.009	17.545
88	15.581	9.749	26.855	7.067	14.140
89	12.155	7.272	22.319	5.353	10.994
90	9.087	5.179	17.947	3.892	8.190
91	6.455	3.490	13.869	2.697	5.796
92	4.310	2.202	10.215	1.765	3.853
93	2.666	1.281	7.093	1.078	2.372
94	1.499	.674	4.579	.606	1.327
95	.746	.312	2.697	.308	.657
96	.316	.123	1.411	.137	.277
97	.107	.038	.631	.052	.093
98	.026	0.000	.227	.015	.022
99	0.000	0.000	.058	0.000	0.000

PROBABILITY OF LIVING TO AGE 'X' STARTING FROM AGE 32

1989 U. S. POPULATION

	TOTAL POPULATION	WHITE MALE	WHITE FEMALE	BLACK MALE	BLACK FEMALE
LIFE EXPECTANCY TO AGE	45.30	42.90	48.60	36.80	44.00
33	99.841	99.807	99.927	99.486	99.798
34	99.675	99.605	99.851	98.936	99.585
35	99.501	99.395	99.771	98.346	99.361
36	99.317	99.175	99.686	97.718	99.126
37	99.124	98.944	99.596	97.054	98.875
38	98.922	98.705	99.497	96.364	98.607
39	98.706	98.456	99.389	95.651	98.319
40	98.480	98.197	99.269	94.916	98.009
41	98.254	97.926	99.137	94.154	97.675
42	98.007	97.639	98.993	93.365	97.319
43	97.740	97.334	98.835	92.546	96.939
44	97.455	97.005	98.664	91.691	96.537
45	97.148	96.650	98.478	90.803	96.109
46	96.817	96.265	98.274	89.811	95.654
47	96.458	95.848	98.049	88.906	95.169
48	96.067	95.397	97.800	87.897	94.652
49	95.641	94.908	97.522	86.810	94.100
50	95.178	94.379	97.214	85.655	93.510
51	94.672	93.803	96.873	84.516	92.879
52	94.119	93.172	96.495	83.312	92.201
53	93.514	92.474	96.079	82.044	91.472
54	92.852	91.702	95.622	80.720	90.686
55	92.129	90.850	95.121	79.342	89.842
56	91.346	89.915	94.572	77.911	88.935
57	90.496	88.893	93.972	76.424	87.956
58	89.573	87.777	93.317	74.874	86.890
59	88.570	86.565	92.604	73.256	85.727
60	87.489	85.251	91.827	71.564	84.462
61	86.326	83.833	90.984	69.798	83.096
62	85.074	82.314	90.073	67.958	81.641
63	83.747	80.699	89.090	66.045	80.113
64	82.331	78.990	88.035	64.059	78.523
65	80.833	77.189	86.904	62.002	76.874

1989 U. S. POPULATION

	TOTAL POPULATION	WHITE MALE	WHITE FEMALE	BLACK MALE	BLACK FEMALE
66	79.241	75.274	85.861	59.874	75.147
67	77.545	73.242	84.582	57.681	73.342
68	75.746	71.091	83.279	55.421	71.458
69	73.845	68.819	81.880	53.106	69.495
70	71.829	66.426	80.382	50.734	67.453
71	69.703	63.907	78.774	48.316	65.319
72	67.458	61.264	77.049	45.858	63.094
73	65.097	58.500	75.200	43.372	60.779
74	62.623	55.622	73.222	40.861	58.379
75	60.037	52.638	71.113	38.342	55.896
76	57.335	49.557	68.866	35.820	53.308
77	54.520	46.393	66.463	33.284	50.620
78	51.603	43.163	63.904	30.755	47.842
79	48.590	39.884	61.194	28.244	44.984
80	45.495	36.580	58.330	25.765	42.058
81	42.169	33.148	55.320	23.335	38.921
82	38.631	29.625	52.007	20.852	35.594
83	34.915	26.059	48.397	18.361	32.105
84	31.057	22.507	44.501	15.900	28.498
85	27.119	19.031	40.345	13.495	24.827
86	23.173	15.703	35.976	11.198	21.161
87	19.303	12.592	31.457	9.054	17.579
88	15.605	9.767	26.874	7.102	14.167
89	12.173	7.285	22.335	5.380	11.016
90	9.101	5.188	17.959	3.912	8.206
91	6.465	3.497	13.879	2.710	5.807
92	4.316	2.206	10.222	1.774	3.860
93	2.670	1.283	7.098	1.084	2.377
94	1.501	.675	4.583	.610	1.330
95	.747	.313	2.699	.309	.658
96	.316	.123	1.412	.138	.277
97	.107	.038	.632	.052	.093
98	.026	0.000	.227	.015	.022
99	0.000	0.000	.058	0.000	0.000

PROBABILITY OF LIVING TO AGE 'X' STARTING FROM AGE 33

1989 U. S. POPULATION

	TOTAL POPULATION	WHITE MALE	WHITE FEMALE	BLACK MALE	BLACK FEMALE
LIFE EXPECTANCY TO AGE	44.40	42.00	47.60	36.00	43.10
34	99.834	99.798	99.924	99.447	99.787
35	99.659	99.587	99.844	98.854	99.562
36	99.475	99.366	99.759	98.223	99.327
37	99.282	99.136	99.668	97.556	99.075
38	99.079	98.896	99.570	96.862	98.807
39	98.863	98.647	99.461	96.145	98.518
40	98.637	98.387	99.342	95.406	98.207
41	98.410	98.116	99.210	94.641	97.873
42	98.163	97.828	99.065	93.848	97.516
43	97.896	97.522	98.907	93.024	97.135
44	97.610	97.192	98.736	92.165	96.732
45	97.303	96.837	98.550	91.272	96.304
46	96.971	96.451	98.346	90.275	95.847
47	96.611	96.034	98.120	89.365	95.361
48	96.220	95.581	97.871	88.351	94.844
49	95.794	95.092	97.593	87.258	94.291
50	95.329	94.561	97.285	86.098	93.699
51	94.823	93.984	96.943	84.953	93.067
52	94.269	93.352	96.565	83.742	92.388
53	93.663	92.653	96.149	82.468	91.657
54	93.000	91.879	95.691	81.137	90.869
55	92.275	91.026	95.190	79.752	90.023
56	91.491	90.089	94.641	78.313	89.115
57	90.640	89.065	94.041	76.818	88.134
58	89.716	87.947	93.385	75.261	87.066
59	88.711	86.732	92.672	73.635	85.901
60	87.629	85.416	91.894	71.934	84.633
61	86.463	83.995	91.051	70.159	83.264
62	85.209	82.473	90.138	68.309	81.806
63	83.880	80.855	89.155	66.386	80.275
64	82.463	79.143	88.099	64.390	78.682
65	80.962	77.338	86.967	62.322	77.029
66	79.367	75.419	85.924	60.184	75.299

1989 U. S. POPULATION

	TOTAL POPULATION	WHITE MALE	WHITE FEMALE	BLACK MALE	BLACK FEMALE
67	77.668	73.384	84.643	57.979	73.491
68	75.866	71.229	83.340	55.707	71.603
69	73.962	68.952	81.940	53.381	69.636
70	71.943	66.555	80.440	50.997	67.590
71	69.814	64.031	78.832	48.566	65.451
72	67.566	61.383	77.105	46.095	63.221
73	65.201	58.614	75.255	43.596	60.902
74	62.723	55.730	73.275	41.072	58.497
75	60.133	52.739	71.165	38.540	56.009
76	57.427	49.652	68.916	36.005	53.416
77	54.607	46.483	66.511	33.456	50.723
78	51.686	43.246	63.950	30.914	47.939
79	48.667	39.962	61.239	28.390	45.075
80	45.567	36.651	58.373	25.898	42.143
81	42.236	33.212	55.361	23.455	39.000
82	38.692	29.683	52.045	20.960	35.666
83	34.970	26.110	48.433	18.456	32.170
84	31.106	22.550	44.534	15.982	28.556
85	27.162	19.068	40.375	13.565	24.877
86	23.210	15.733	36.002	11.256	21.204
87	19.334	12.617	31.480	9.100	17.615
88	15.629	9.786	26.893	7.139	14.196
89	12.192	7.299	22.351	5.408	11.038
90	9.115	5.198	17.973	3.932	8.223
91	6.475	3.504	13.889	2.724	5.818
92	4.323	2.210	10.229	1.783	3.868
93	2.674	1.286	7.103	1.089	2.382
94	1.504	.677	4.586	.613	1.332
95	.748	.314	2.701	.311	.660
96	.317	.123	1.413	.139	.278
97	.107	.038	.632	.052	.093
98	.026	0.000	.227	.016	.022
99	0.000	0.000	.058	0.000	0.000

PROBABILITY OF LIVING TO AGE 'X' STARTING FROM AGE 34

1989 U. S. POPULATION

	TOTAL POPULATION	WHITE MALE	WHITE FEMALE	BLACK MALE	BLACK FEMALE
LIFE EXPECTANCY TO AGE	43.50	41.00	46.60	35.10	42.20
35	99.825	99.789	99.920	99.404	99.775
36	99.640	99.567	99.835	98.769	99.539
37	99.447	99.336	99.744	98.098	99.287
38	99.244	99.096	99.645	97.401	99.018
39	99.028	98.846	99.537	96.680	98.729
40	98.801	98.586	99.417	95.936	98.417
41	98.574	98.314	99.285	95.167	98.082
42	98.326	98.026	99.140	94.370	97.724
43	98.059	97.719	98.983	93.541	97.343
44	97.773	97.389	98.811	92.678	96.939
45	97.465	97.033	98.625	91.780	96.509
46	97.132	96.646	98.420	90.777	96.052
47	96.772	96.228	98.195	89.862	95.565
48	96.380	95.775	97.946	88.842	95.046
49	95.953	95.284	97.667	87.743	94.492
50	95.488	94.753	97.359	86.576	93.899
51	94.981	94.175	97.017	85.425	93.266
52	94.426	93.541	96.639	84.208	92.585
53	93.819	92.840	96.222	82.927	91.852
54	93.155	92.065	95.764	81.588	91.063
55	92.429	91.210	95.262	80.196	90.216
56	91.643	90.271	94.713	78.749	89.305
57	90.791	89.245	94.112	77.246	88.322
58	89.865	88.125	93.456	75.680	87.252
59	88.858	86.908	92.742	74.044	86.084
60	87.774	85.589	91.964	72.334	84.814
61	86.607	84.165	91.120	70.549	83.442
62	85.351	82.640	90.207	68.689	81.981
63	84.020	81.019	89.223	66.756	80.446
64	82.600	79.303	88.166	64.748	78.850
65	81.096	77.495	87.033	62.668	77.194
66	79.499	75.572	85.989	60.518	75.460
67	77.797	73.532	84.708	58.301	73.647

1989 U. S. POPULATION

	TOTAL POPULATION	WHITE MALE	WHITE FEMALE	BLACK MALE	BLACK FEMALE
68	75.993	71.373	83.403	56.017	71.755
69	74.085	69.092	82.002	53.677	69.784
70	72.063	66.689	80.502	51.280	67.734
71	69.930	64.160	78.891	48.836	65.591
72	67.678	61.507	77.164	46.351	63.356
73	65.309	58.732	75.312	43.838	61.032
74	62.827	55.843	73.331	41.301	58.622
75	60.233	52.846	71.219	38.754	56.128
76	57.522	49.753	68.969	36.205	53.530
77	54.698	46.577	66.562	33.642	50.831
78	51.771	43.334	63.999	31.086	48.042
79	48.748	40.042	61.285	28.547	45.171
80	45.643	36.725	58.417	26.042	42.233
81	42.306	33.279	55.403	23.586	39.083
82	38.757	29.743	52.084	21.076	35.742
83	35.028	26.163	48.470	18.559	32.239
84	31.158	22.596	44.568	16.071	28.617
85	27.207	19.107	40.405	13.640	24.931
86	23.248	15.765	36.029	11.319	21.249
87	19.366	12.642	31.504	9.151	17.652
88	15.655	9.806	26.914	7.179	14.226
89	12.213	7.314	22.368	5.438	11.061
90	9.130	5.209	17.986	3.954	8.240
91	6.486	3.511	13.900	2.739	5.831
92	4.330	2.215	10.237	1.793	3.876
93	2.679	1.288	7.109	1.095	2.387
94	1.506	.678	4.589	.616	1.335
95	.749	.314	2.703	.313	.661
96	.317	.123	1.415	.139	.278
97	.107	.038	.633	.052	.094
98	.026	0.000	.227	.016	.022
99	0.000	0.000	.058	0.000	0.000

PROBABILITY OF LIVING TO AGE 'X' STARTING FROM AGE 35

1989 U. S. POPULATION

	TOTAL POPULATION	WHITE MALE	WHITE FEMALE	BLACK MALE	BLACK FEMALE
LIFE EXPECTANCY TO AGE	42.50	40.10	45.70	34.30	41.30
36	99.815	99.778	99.915	99.361	99.763
37	99.621	99.547	99.824	98.686	99.511
38	99.418	99.306	99.725	97.985	99.241
39	99.201	99.055	99.617	97.260	98.951
40	98.974	98.795	99.497	96.512	98.638
41	98.747	98.522	99.365	95.738	98.303
42	98.499	98.234	99.220	94.935	97.944
43	98.231	97.926	99.062	94.102	97.562
44	97.944	97.595	98.890	93.233	97.157
45	97.635	97.238	98.704	92.330	96.727
46	97.303	96.851	98.499	91.322	96.269
47	96.942	96.431	98.274	90.401	95.780
48	96.549	95.977	98.024	89.375	95.260
49	96.121	95.486	97.746	88.269	94.705
50	95.655	94.953	97.437	87.095	94.111
51	95.147	94.374	97.095	85.937	93.476
52	94.591	93.739	96.716	84.712	92.794
53	93.983	93.037	96.299	83.424	92.060
54	93.318	92.260	95.841	82.078	91.269
55	92.591	91.403	95.339	80.676	90.419
56	91.804	90.462	94.789	79.221	89.507
57	90.950	89.434	94.188	77.709	88.521
58	90.022	88.311	93.531	76.134	87.448
59	89.014	87.092	92.817	74.488	86.278
60	87.928	85.770	92.038	72.768	85.005
61	86.759	84.343	91.193	70.972	83.630
62	85.501	82.815	90.279	69.101	82.166
63	84.167	81.190	89.294	67.156	80.628
64	82.744	79.470	88.237	65.136	79.027
65	81.239	77.659	87.103	63.044	77.368
66	79.638	75.732	86.058	60.881	75.630
67	77.934	73.688	84.776	58.650	73.813
68	76.126	71.524	83.470	56.353	71.917

1989 U. S. POPULATION

	TOTAL POPULATION	WHITE MALE	WHITE FEMALE	BLACK MALE	BLACK FEMALE
69	74.215	69.238	82.068	53.999	69.942
70	72.189	66.830	80.566	51.588	67.887
71	70.052	64.296	78.955	49.129	65.739
72	67.797	61.637	77.226	46.629	63.499
73	65.424	58.856	75.372	44.101	61.170
74	62.938	55.961	73.390	41.548	58.754
75	60.338	52.958	71.276	38.987	56.255
76	57.623	49.858	69.024	36.422	53.650
77	54.794	46.675	66.615	33.844	50.946
78	51.862	43.425	64.050	31.273	48.150
79	48.833	40.127	61.335	28.719	45.273
80	45.723	36.803	58.464	26.198	42.328
81	42.380	33.350	55.447	23.727	39.172
82	38.825	29.806	52.126	21.202	35.823
83	35.090	26.218	48.508	18.670	32.312
84	31.212	22.644	44.604	16.167	28.681
85	27.255	19.147	40.438	13.722	24.987
86	23.289	15.799	36.058	11.387	21.297
87	19.400	12.669	31.529	9.206	17.692
88	15.683	9.827	26.935	7.222	14.259
89	12.234	7.329	22.386	5.470	11.086
90	9.146	5.220	18.001	3.977	8.259
91	6.498	3.518	13.911	2.756	5.844
92	4.338	2.219	10.245	1.803	3.885
93	2.683	1.291	7.114	1.102	2.392
94	1.509	.680	4.593	.620	1.338
95	.751	.315	2.705	.315	.662
96	.318	.124	1.416	.140	.279
97	.108	.039	.633	.053	.094
98	.026	0.000	.227	.016	.022
99	0.000	0.000	.058	0.000	0.000

PROBABILITY OF LIVING TO AGE 'X' STARTING FROM AGE 36

1989 U. S. POPULATION

	TOTAL POPULATION	WHITE MALE	WHITE FEMALE	BLACK MALE	BLACK FEMALE
LIFE EXPECTANCY TO AGE	41.60	39.20	44.70	33.50	40.40
37	99.806	99.768	99.909	99.321	99.747
38	99.602	99.527	99.810	98.615	99.477
39	99.385	99.276	99.701	97.885	99.186
40	99.158	99.015	99.582	97.132	98.873
41	98.930	98.741	99.449	96.353	98.537
42	98.681	98.452	99.304	95.546	98.177
43	98.413	98.144	99.146	94.707	97.794
44	98.126	97.812	98.975	93.833	97.388
45	97.816	97.454	98.788	92.924	96.957
46	97.483	97.066	98.583	91.909	96.497
47	97.121	96.646	98.357	90.982	96.008
48	96.728	96.191	98.107	89.950	95.487
49	96.299	95.698	97.829	88.837	94.930
50	95.832	95.164	97.520	87.656	94.335
51	95.323	94.584	97.177	86.490	93.698
52	94.767	93.947	96.798	85.257	93.014
53	94.157	93.244	96.381	83.961	92.278
54	93.491	92.465	95.922	82.605	91.486
55	92.762	91.606	95.420	81.195	90.634
56	91.974	90.663	94.869	79.731	89.719
57	91.119	89.633	94.268	78.209	88.732
58	90.189	88.508	93.611	76.623	87.656
59	89.179	87.285	92.896	74.967	86.483
60	88.091	85.960	92.116	73.236	85.207
61	86.920	84.531	91.271	71.428	83.829
62	85.659	82.999	90.356	69.545	82.361
63	84.323	81.371	89.370	67.588	80.819
64	82.898	79.647	88.312	65.555	79.215
65	81.389	77.831	87.177	63.450	77.552
66	79.786	75.900	86.131	61.273	75.810
67	78.078	73.852	84.848	59.028	73.989
68	76.267	71.683	83.541	56.716	72.088
69	74.353	69.392	82.138	54.347	70.108

1989 U. S. POPULATION

	TOTAL POPULATION	WHITE MALE	WHITE FEMALE	BLACK MALE	BLACK FEMALE
70	72.323	66.979	80.634	51.919	68.048
71	70.182	64.439	79.022	49.445	65.895
72	67.922	61.774	77.291	46.929	63.650
73	65.545	58.987	75.436	44.385	61.315
74	63.054	56.085	73.452	41.816	58.893
75	60.450	53.076	71.337	39.237	56.389
76	57.730	49.969	69.083	36.656	53.778
77	54.895	46.779	66.672	34.062	51.067
78	51.958	43.522	64.105	31.474	48.264
79	48.924	40.216	61.387	28.903	45.381
80	45.808	36.885	58.514	26.367	42.429
81	42.459	33.424	55.495	23.880	39.265
82	38.897	29.872	52.170	21.339	35.908
83	35.155	26.276	48.550	18.790	32.389
84	31.270	22.694	44.642	16.271	28.749
85	27.305	19.190	40.472	13.810	25.046
86	23.332	15.834	36.089	11.460	21.348
87	19.436	12.697	31.556	9.265	17.734
88	15.712	9.848	26.958	7.268	14.292
89	12.257	7.346	22.405	5.505	11.113
90	9.163	5.232	18.016	4.003	8.278
91	6.510	3.526	13.923	2.774	5.858
92	4.346	2.224	10.254	1.815	3.894
93	2.688	1.294	7.120	1.109	2.398
94	1.512	.681	4.597	.624	1.342
95	.752	.316	2.708	.317	.664
96	.319	.124	1.417	.141	.280
97	.108	.039	.634	.053	.094
98	.026	0.000	.227	.016	.022
99	0.000	0.000	.058	0.000	0.000

PROBABILITY OF LIVING TO AGE 'X' STARTING FROM AGE 37

1989 U. S. POPULATION

	TOTAL POPULATION	WHITE MALE	WHITE FEMALE	BLACK MALE	BLACK FEMALE
LIFE EXPECTANCY TO AGE	40.70	38.30	43.70	32.70	39.50
38	99.796	99.758	99.901	99.289	99.729
39	99.578	99.507	99.792	98.554	99.438
40	99.350	99.245	99.672	97.796	99.124
41	99.122	98.971	99.540	97.012	98.787
42	98.873	98.681	99.394	96.199	98.426
43	98.604	98.372	99.236	95.354	98.042
44	98.316	98.040	99.065	94.474	97.635
45	98.007	97.681	98.878	93.559	97.203
46	97.672	97.292	98.673	92.537	96.742
47	97.310	96.871	98.447	91.604	96.251
48	96.916	96.415	98.197	90.565	95.729
49	96.487	95.921	97.918	89.444	95.171
50	96.019	95.386	97.609	88.255	94.574
51	95.509	94.804	97.266	87.081	93.936
52	94.951	94.166	96.887	85.840	93.250
53	94.340	93.460	96.469	84.535	92.512
54	93.672	92.680	96.010	83.170	91.718
55	92.943	91.819	95.507	81.750	90.864
56	92.153	90.874	94.956	80.276	89.947
57	91.296	89.841	94.354	78.743	88.957
58	90.365	88.713	93.696	77.147	87.878
59	89.352	87.488	92.980	75.480	86.703
60	88.262	86.160	92.200	73.736	85.423
61	87.088	84.727	91.354	71.917	84.042
62	85.826	83.192	90.438	70.021	82.570
63	84.487	81.560	89.452	68.050	81.024
64	83.059	79.833	88.392	66.003	79.416
65	81.547	78.012	87.257	63.883	77.748
66	79.941	76.077	86.210	61.692	76.002
67	78.230	74.024	84.925	59.431	74.176
68	76.415	71.849	83.617	57.103	72.271
69	74.497	69.553	82.212	54.718	70.286
70	72.463	67.135	80.708	52.274	68.221

1989 U. S. POPULATION

	TOTAL POPULATION	WHITE MALE	WHITE FEMALE	BLACK MALE	BLACK FEMALE
71	70.318	64.589	79.094	49.783	66.062
72	68.054	61.918	77.362	47.250	63.811
73	65.672	59.125	75.505	44.688	61.471
74	63.177	56.216	73.519	42.102	59.043
75	60.568	53.199	71.402	39.506	56.532
76	57.842	50.085	69.146	36.907	53.914
77	55.002	46.888	66.732	34.295	51.196
78	52.059	43.623	64.163	31.689	48.387
79	49.019	40.310	61.443	29.101	45.496
80	45.897	36.971	58.567	26.547	42.536
81	42.542	33.502	55.545	24.043	39.364
82	38.972	29.941	52.218	21.485	35.999
83	35.223	26.337	48.594	18.919	32.471
84	31.331	22.747	44.682	16.383	28.822
85	27.358	19.234	40.509	13.905	25.110
86	23.378	15.871	36.122	11.538	21.402
87	19.474	12.727	31.585	9.328	17.779
88	15.742	9.871	26.983	7.318	14.329
89	12.281	7.363	22.426	5.543	11.141
90	9.181	5.244	18.032	4.030	8.299
91	6.522	3.534	13.935	2.793	5.873
92	4.354	2.229	10.263	1.827	3.904
93	2.694	1.297	7.127	1.117	2.404
94	1.515	.683	4.601	.628	1.345
95	.754	.316	2.710	.319	.666
96	.319	.124	1.418	.142	.280
97	.108	.039	.634	.053	.094
98	.026	0.000	.228	.016	.023
99	0.000	0.000	.058	0.000	0.000

PROBABILITY OF LIVING TO AGE 'X' STARTING FROM AGE 38

1989 U. S. POPULATION

	TOTAL POPULATION	WHITE MALE	WHITE FEMALE	BLACK MALE	BLACK FEMALE
LIFE EXPECTANCY TO AGE	39.80	37.40	42.80	32.00	38.60
39	99.782	99.748	99.891	99.260	99.708
40	99.553	99.486	99.771	98.497	99.393
41	99.325	99.211	99.638	97.707	99.055
42	99.075	98.920	99.493	96.888	98.693
43	98.806	98.611	99.335	96.037	98.309
44	98.517	98.277	99.163	95.151	97.901
45	98.207	97.918	98.976	94.229	97.467
46	97.872	97.528	98.771	93.200	97.005
47	97.509	97.106	98.544	92.260	96.513
48	97.114	96.648	98.294	91.213	95.989
49	96.684	96.154	98.015	90.085	95.429
50	96.215	95.617	97.705	88.887	94.831
51	95.704	95.034	97.362	87.705	94.191
52	95.145	94.394	96.983	86.455	93.503
53	94.533	93.687	96.565	85.140	92.764
54	93.864	92.905	96.105	83.766	91.967
55	93.133	92.042	95.601	82.336	91.111
56	92.341	91.095	95.050	80.850	90.191
57	91.482	90.059	94.447	79.307	89.198
58	90.549	88.929	93.789	77.699	88.117
59	89.535	87.701	93.072	76.020	86.938
60	88.443	86.369	92.291	74.264	85.655
61	87.266	84.933	91.444	72.431	84.270
62	86.001	83.394	90.528	70.522	82.794
63	84.659	81.758	89.540	68.537	81.245
64	83.229	80.026	88.480	66.476	79.632
65	81.714	78.202	87.343	64.341	77.960
66	80.104	76.261	86.295	62.133	76.209
67	78.390	74.203	85.009	59.857	74.378
68	76.571	72.024	83.700	57.512	72.467
69	74.649	69.722	82.294	55.110	70.477
70	72.611	67.298	80.788	52.649	68.406
71	70.462	64.746	79.172	50.139	66.242

1989 U. S. POPULATION

	TOTAL POPULATION	WHITE MALE	WHITE FEMALE	BLACK MALE	BLACK FEMALE
72	68.193	62.068	77.438	47.588	63.985
73	65.807	59.268	75.580	45.008	61.638
74	63.306	56.352	73.592	42.403	59.203
75	60.691	53.328	71.473	39.788	56.685
76	57.960	50.207	69.214	37.171	54.061
77	55.114	47.002	66.798	34.540	51.335
78	52.166	43.729	64.227	31.916	48.518
79	49.119	40.408	61.504	29.309	45.619
80	45.990	37.060	58.625	26.737	42.652
81	42.628	33.583	55.600	24.215	39.471
82	39.052	30.014	52.270	21.639	36.097
83	35.295	26.401	48.642	19.054	32.559
84	31.395	22.802	44.726	16.500	28.901
85	27.414	19.281	40.549	14.004	25.178
86	23.425	15.909	36.158	11.621	21.460
87	19.513	12.758	31.616	9.395	17.827
88	15.775	9.895	27.010	7.370	14.368
89	12.306	7.381	22.448	5.583	11.171
90	9.200	5.256	18.050	4.059	8.322
91	6.536	3.543	13.949	2.813	5.889
92	4.363	2.235	10.274	1.841	3.915
93	2.699	1.300	7.134	1.125	2.410
94	1.518	.684	4.606	.633	1.349
95	.755	.317	2.713	.321	.668
96	.320	.124	1.420	.143	.281
97	.108	.039	.635	.054	.095
98	.026	0.000	.228	.016	.023
99	0.000	0.000	.058	0.000	0.000

PROBABILITY OF LIVING TO AGE 'X' STARTING FROM AGE 39

1989 U. S. POPULATION

	TOTAL POPULATION	WHITE MALE	WHITE FEMALE	BLACK MALE	BLACK FEMALE
LIFE EXPECTANCY TO AGE	38.80	36.50	41.80	31.20	37.70
40	99.771	99.737	99.880	99.231	99.684
41	99.542	99.462	99.747	98.435	99.345
42	99.292	99.170	99.602	97.610	98.982
43	99.022	98.860	99.443	96.753	98.596
44	98.732	98.526	99.271	95.860	98.187
45	98.421	98.165	99.084	94.931	97.752
46	98.086	97.774	98.878	93.895	97.289
47	97.722	97.351	98.652	92.948	96.796
48	97.326	96.893	98.401	91.893	96.270
49	96.895	96.396	98.122	90.757	95.709
50	96.425	95.859	97.812	89.549	95.109
51	95.913	95.274	97.469	88.358	94.467
52	95.353	94.633	97.088	87.099	93.777
53	94.740	93.924	96.670	85.775	93.035
54	94.069	93.140	96.210	84.390	92.236
55	93.336	92.274	95.706	82.950	91.377
56	92.543	91.325	95.153	81.453	90.455
57	91.682	90.286	94.550	79.898	89.460
58	90.747	89.153	93.891	78.279	88.375
59	89.731	87.922	93.174	76.587	87.193
60	88.636	86.587	92.392	74.818	85.906
61	87.457	85.148	91.544	72.971	84.517
62	86.189	83.605	90.627	71.048	83.037
63	84.844	81.964	89.638	69.048	81.482
64	83.411	80.228	88.577	66.972	79.865
65	81.893	78.399	87.438	64.821	78.188
66	80.279	76.454	86.389	62.597	76.432
67	78.561	74.391	85.102	60.303	74.596
68	76.739	72.206	83.791	57.941	72.679
69	74.812	69.898	82.384	55.521	70.683
70	72.770	67.468	80.876	53.041	68.606
71	70.616	64.909	79.259	50.513	66.436
72	68.342	62.225	77.523	47.943	64.172

1989 U. S. POPULATION

	TOTAL POPULATION	WHITE MALE	WHITE FEMALE	BLACK MALE	BLACK FEMALE
73	65.950	59.418	75.662	45.344	61.818
74	63.444	56.494	73.672	42.719	59.377
75	60.824	53.463	71.551	40.085	56.851
76	58.087	50.334	69.290	37.448	54.219
77	55.235	47.120	66.871	34.798	51.486
78	52.280	43.839	64.297	32.154	48.660
79	49.227	40.510	61.571	29.528	45.753
80	46.091	37.154	58.689	26.936	42.777
81	42.722	33.668	55.661	24.396	39.587
82	39.137	30.090	52.327	21.800	36.202
83	35.372	26.468	48.695	19.196	32.654
84	31.464	22.860	44.775	16.623	28.985
85	27.474	19.330	40.593	14.109	25.252
86	23.477	15.949	36.197	11.707	21.523
87	19.556	12.790	31.651	9.465	17.880
88	15.809	9.920	27.039	7.425	14.410
89	12.333	7.399	22.472	5.624	11.204
90	9.220	5.270	18.070	4.089	8.346
91	6.550	3.552	13.964	2.833	5.906
92	4.373	2.240	10.285	1.854	3.926
93	2.705	1.303	7.142	1.133	2.418
94	1.521	.686	4.611	.637	1.353
95	.757	.318	2.716	.323	.669
96	.321	.125	1.421	.144	.282
97	.108	.039	.636	.054	.095
98	.026	0.000	.228	.016	.023
99	0.000	0.000	.059	0.000	0.000

PROBABILITY OF LIVING TO AGE 'X' STARTING FROM AGE 40

1989 U. S. POPULATION

	TOTAL POPULATION	WHITE MALE	WHITE FEMALE	BLACK MALE	BLACK FEMALE
LIFE EXPECTANCY TO AGE	37.90	35.60	40.90	30.40	36.80
41	99.770	99.724	99.867	99.198	99.660
42	99.520	99.432	99.721	98.367	99.296
43	99.249	99.121	99.563	97.503	98.909
44	98.959	98.786	99.390	96.603	98.499
45	98.647	98.424	99.203	95.667	98.062
46	98.311	98.032	98.997	94.622	97.597
47	97.946	97.608	98.770	93.669	97.103
48	97.550	97.148	98.520	92.605	96.575
49	97.117	96.651	98.240	91.460	96.012
50	96.646	96.111	97.929	90.243	95.410
51	96.133	95.525	97.586	89.043	94.766
52	95.572	94.882	97.205	87.774	94.074
53	94.957	94.172	96.786	86.439	93.330
54	94.285	93.385	96.325	85.044	92.529
55	93.550	92.518	95.821	83.592	91.667
56	92.755	91.566	95.268	82.084	90.742
57	91.893	90.525	94.664	80.517	89.743
58	90.955	89.388	94.004	78.885	88.655
59	89.937	88.154	93.286	77.181	87.469
60	88.839	86.816	92.503	75.398	86.178
61	87.658	85.372	91.654	73.537	84.785
62	86.387	83.825	90.736	71.599	83.300
63	85.039	82.180	89.746	69.583	81.741
64	83.602	80.440	88.683	67.491	80.118
65	82.080	78.606	87.543	65.323	78.436
66	80.463	76.656	86.493	63.082	76.674
67	78.742	74.587	85.204	60.770	74.832
68	76.915	72.396	83.892	58.390	72.910
69	74.984	70.082	82.483	55.951	70.907
70	72.937	67.646	80.973	53.452	68.824
71	70.778	65.080	79.354	50.905	66.646
72	68.499	62.389	77.616	48.315	64.376
73	66.102	59.574	75.753	45.695	62.014

1989 U. S. POPULATION

	TOTAL POPULATION	WHITE MALE	WHITE FEMALE	BLACK MALE	BLACK FEMALE
74	63.590	56.643	73.761	43.050	59.565
75	60.964	53.604	71.637	40.396	57.031
76	58.220	50.466	69.373	37.739	54.391
77	55.362	47.245	66.952	35.067	51.649
78	52.400	43.955	64.374	32.403	48.815
79	49.340	40.617	61.645	29.757	45.898
80	46.197	37.252	58.760	27.145	42.912
81	42.820	33.757	55.728	24.585	39.712
82	39.227	30.169	52.390	21.969	36.317
83	35.453	26.538	48.754	19.345	32.758
84	31.536	22.920	44.829	16.752	29.077
85	27.537	19.381	40.642	14.218	25.332
86	23.530	15.991	36.240	11.798	21.591
87	19.601	12.824	31.689	9.539	17.936
88	15.845	9.946	27.072	7.483	14.455
89	12.361	7.419	22.499	5.668	11.239
90	9.241	5.284	18.092	4.121	8.373
91	6.565	3.561	13.981	2.855	5.925
92	4.383	2.246	10.297	1.869	3.939
93	2.711	1.307	7.150	1.142	2.425
94	1.524	.688	4.616	.642	1.357
95	.759	.319	2.719	.326	.672
96	.321	.125	1.423	.145	.283
97	.109	.039	.636	.055	.095
98	.026	0.000	.228	.016	.023
99	0.000	0.000	.059	0.000	0.000

PROBABILITY OF LIVING TO AGE 'X' STARTING FROM AGE 41

1989 U. S. POPULATION

	TOTAL POPULATION	WHITE MALE	WHITE FEMALE	BLACK MALE	BLACK FEMALE
LIFE EXPECTANCY TO AGE	37.00	34.70	39.90	29.70	35.90
42	99.749	99.707	99.854	99.162	99.635
43	99.478	99.395	99.695	98.291	99.246
44	99.187	99.059	99.523	97.384	98.835
45	98.875	98.696	99.335	96.440	98.397
46	98.538	98.304	99.129	95.387	97.930
47	98.172	97.878	98.902	94.426	97.434
48	97.774	97.417	98.651	93.354	96.905
49	97.341	96.918	98.371	92.199	96.340
50	96.869	96.377	98.060	90.973	95.736
51	96.355	95.789	97.716	89.763	95.090
52	95.792	95.145	97.335	88.484	94.395
53	95.176	94.432	96.915	87.138	93.649
54	94.502	93.644	96.454	85.732	92.844
55	93.766	92.774	95.948	84.268	91.980
56	92.969	91.819	95.395	82.748	91.052
57	92.105	90.775	94.790	81.168	90.049
58	91.165	89.636	94.129	79.523	88.958
59	90.144	88.398	93.410	77.805	87.768
60	89.044	87.056	92.626	76.007	86.472
61	87.860	85.608	91.776	74.132	85.074
62	86.586	84.057	90.856	72.177	83.584
63	85.235	82.408	89.865	70.146	82.020
64	83.795	80.663	88.801	68.036	80.392
65	82.270	78.823	87.660	65.851	78.703
66	80.649	76.868	86.608	63.592	76.936
67	78.923	74.793	85.318	61.262	75.088
68	77.092	72.596	84.004	58.862	73.159
69	75.157	70.276	82.593	56.403	71.149
70	73.105	67.833	81.081	53.884	69.059
71	70.941	65.261	79.459	51.316	66.874
72	68.657	62.561	77.719	48.705	64.595
73	66.254	59.739	75.854	46.064	62.226
74	63.736	56.800	73.859	43.398	59.768

1989 U. S. POPULATION

	TOTAL POPULATION	WHITE MALE	WHITE FEMALE	BLACK MALE	BLACK FEMALE
75	61.104	53.752	71.732	40.722	57.226
76	58.354	50.606	69.465	38.044	54.576
77	55.489	47.375	67.041	35.351	51.825
78	52.521	44.077	64.460	32.665	48.981
79	49.453	40.729	61.727	29.997	46.054
80	46.303	37.355	58.838	27.365	43.059
81	42.918	33.850	55.802	24.784	39.848
82	39.318	30.253	52.459	22.146	36.441
83	35.535	26.611	48.819	19.501	32.870
84	31.609	22.983	44.889	16.887	29.176
85	27.601	19.434	40.696	14.333	25.418
86	23.585	16.036	36.289	11.894	21.665
87	19.646	12.859	31.731	9.616	17.997
88	15.882	9.974	27.108	7.543	14.505
89	12.389	7.439	22.529	5.714	11.278
90	9.262	5.298	18.116	4.154	8.401
91	6.580	3.571	14.000	2.879	5.945
92	4.393	2.253	10.311	1.884	3.952
93	2.717	1.311	7.160	1.151	2.433
94	1.528	.690	4.622	.647	1.361
95	.760	.320	2.723	.329	.674
96	.322	.125	1.425	.146	.284
97	.109	.039	.637	.055	.095
98	.026	0.000	.229	.016	.023
99	0.000	0.000	.059	0.000	0.000

PROBABILITY OF LIVING TO AGE 'X' STARTING FROM AGE 42

1989 U. S. POPULATION

LIFE EXPECTANCY TO AGE	TOTAL POPULATION	WHITE MALE	WHITE FEMALE	BLACK MALE	BLACK FEMALE
	36.10	33.80	39.00	28.90	35.00
43	99.728	99.687	99.841	99.122	99.610
44	99.437	99.350	99.668	98.207	99.197
45	99.124	98.986	99.480	97.255	98.757
46	98.786	98.592	99.274	96.193	98.289
47	98.419	98.166	99.047	95.224	97.791
48	98.020	97.703	98.795	94.143	97.260
49	97.586	97.203	98.514	92.978	96.693
50	97.113	96.661	98.203	91.742	96.086
51	96.597	96.071	97.858	90.522	95.438
52	96.033	95.424	97.477	89.232	94.741
53	95.416	94.710	97.057	87.875	93.992
54	94.740	93.919	96.595	86.456	93.184
55	94.002	93.046	96.089	84.980	92.317
56	93.203	92.089	95.534	83.447	91.385
57	92.336	91.042	94.928	81.854	90.379
58	91.394	89.899	94.267	80.195	89.284
59	90.371	88.658	93.547	78.462	88.089
60	89.268	87.312	92.762	76.650	86.789
61	88.081	85.860	91.910	74.758	85.386
62	86.804	84.304	90.989	72.787	83.891
63	85.450	82.650	89.997	70.738	82.320
64	84.006	80.900	88.931	68.611	80.686
65	82.477	79.055	87.788	66.408	78.992
66	80.852	77.094	86.735	64.129	77.217
67	79.122	75.013	85.442	61.779	75.363
68	77.286	72.810	84.127	59.359	73.427
69	75.346	70.483	82.713	56.880	71.410
70	73.289	68.032	81.200	54.340	69.312
71	71.120	65.452	79.576	51.750	67.119
72	68.830	62.745	77.833	49.117	64.832
73	66.421	59.915	75.965	46.454	62.454
74	63.897	56.967	73.967	43.765	59.987
75	61.258	53.910	71.837	41.066	57.436

1989 U. S. POPULATION

	TOTAL POPULATION	WHITE MALE	WHITE FEMALE	BLACK MALE	BLACK FEMALE
76	58.501	50.755	69.567	38.365	54.776
77	55.629	47.515	67.139	35.650	52.015
78	52.653	44.206	64.554	32.941	49.161
79	49.578	40.849	61.817	30.251	46.223
80	46.420	37.465	58.924	27.596	43.216
81	43.026	33.949	55.883	24.993	39.994
82	39.416	30.342	52.536	22.334	36.575
83	35.625	26.689	48.890	19.666	32.990
84	31.688	23.051	44.954	17.030	29.283
85	27.670	19.492	40.756	14.454	25.511
86	23.644	16.083	36.342	11.994	21.744
87	19.695	12.897	31.777	9.697	18.063
88	15.922	10.003	27.147	7.607	14.558
89	12.421	7.461	22.562	5.762	11.319
90	9.286	5.314	18.142	4.190	8.432
91	6.597	3.582	14.020	2.903	5.967
92	4.404	2.259	10.326	1.900	3.967
93	2.724	1.314	7.170	1.161	2.442
94	1.532	.692	4.629	.653	1.366
95	.762	.321	2.727	.331	.676
96	.323	.126	1.427	.148	.285
97	.109	.039	.638	.056	.096
98	.026	0.000	.229	.017	.023
99	0.000	0.000	.059	0.000	0.000

PROBABILITY OF LIVING TO AGE 'X' STARTING FROM AGE 43

1989 U. S. POPULATION

	TOTAL POPULATION	WHITE MALE	WHITE FEMALE	BLACK MALE	BLACK FEMALE
LIFE EXPECTANCY TO AGE	35.20	32.90	38.00	28.10	34.10
44	99.708	99.662	99.827	99.077	99.585
45	99.394	99.297	99.638	98.117	99.144
46	99.055	98.902	99.432	97.046	98.674
47	98.687	98.474	99.204	96.067	98.174
48	98.288	98.010	98.952	94.977	97.641
49	97.852	97.508	98.671	93.802	97.071
50	97.378	96.964	98.360	92.554	96.463
51	96.861	96.373	98.014	91.324	95.812
52	96.295	95.724	97.632	90.022	95.112
53	95.676	95.007	97.211	88.653	94.360
54	94.999	94.214	96.749	87.222	93.549
55	94.258	93.338	96.242	85.733	92.678
56	93.457	92.378	95.686	84.187	91.743
57	92.588	91.328	95.080	82.579	90.733
58	91.644	90.182	94.417	80.906	89.633
59	90.617	88.936	93.696	79.157	88.434
60	89.512	87.586	92.909	77.329	87.129
61	88.321	86.130	92.057	75.420	85.720
62	87.041	84.569	91.134	73.432	84.219
63	85.683	82.910	90.140	71.365	82.642
64	84.235	81.154	89.073	69.219	81.002
65	82.702	79.303	87.928	66.996	79.301
66	81.072	77.336	86.873	64.697	77.520
67	79.337	75.248	85.578	62.327	75.658
68	77.497	73.038	84.261	59.885	73.714
69	75.552	70.704	82.845	57.384	71.689
70	73.489	68.246	81.329	54.821	69.583
71	71.314	65.658	79.702	52.208	67.381
72	69.018	62.942	77.957	49.552	65.086
73	66.602	60.103	76.086	46.865	62.698
74	64.071	57.146	74.085	44.153	60.222
75	61.425	54.079	71.951	41.430	57.661
76	58.661	50.914	69.678	38.705	54.991

1989 U. S. POPULATION

	TOTAL POPULATION	WHITE MALE	WHITE FEMALE	BLACK MALE	BLACK FEMALE
77	55.781	47.664	67.246	35.965	52.219
78	52.796	44.345	64.657	33.233	49.353
79	49.713	40.977	61.915	30.519	46.404
80	46.546	37.582	59.018	27.840	43.386
81	43.144	34.056	55.972	25.214	40.150
82	39.524	30.437	52.620	22.531	36.718
83	35.722	26.773	48.968	19.840	33.119
84	31.775	23.123	45.026	17.181	29.398
85	27.746	19.553	40.821	14.582	25.611
86	23.709	16.133	36.400	12.100	21.829
87	19.749	12.937	31.828	9.783	18.134
88	15.965	10.035	27.191	7.674	14.615
89	12.455	7.485	22.598	5.813	11.363
90	9.311	5.330	18.171	4.227	8.465
91	6.615	3.593	14.043	2.929	5.990
92	4.416	2.266	10.342	1.916	3.982
93	2.732	1.318	7.182	1.171	2.452
94	1.536	.694	4.637	.659	1.372
95	.764	.322	2.731	.334	.679
96	.324	.126	1.429	.149	.286
97	.110	.039	.639	.056	.096
98	.026	0.000	.229	.017	.023
99	0.000	0.000	.059	0.000	0.000

PROBABILITY OF LIVING TO AGE 'X' STARTING FROM AGE 44

1989 U. S. POPULATION

	TOTAL POPULATION	WHITE MALE	WHITE FEMALE	BLACK MALE	BLACK FEMALE
LIFE EXPECTANCY TO AGE	34.30	32.00	37.10	27.40	33.30
45	99.685	99.634	99.811	99.031	99.557
46	99.345	99.237	99.604	97.950	99.085
47	98.977	98.808	99.376	96.962	98.583
48	98.576	98.342	99.124	95.862	98.047
49	98.139	97.839	98.842	94.676	97.476
50	97.663	97.293	98.530	93.417	96.865
51	97.144	96.699	98.184	92.174	96.211
52	96.577	96.049	97.801	90.861	95.508
53	95.956	95.329	97.380	89.479	94.753
54	95.277	94.533	96.916	88.035	93.939
55	94.535	93.655	96.408	86.532	93.064
56	93.731	92.691	95.852	84.971	92.125
57	92.859	91.637	95.244	83.349	91.111
58	91.912	90.487	94.581	81.659	90.007
59	90.883	89.238	93.858	79.895	88.803
60	89.774	87.883	93.070	78.049	87.492
61	88.580	86.422	92.216	76.123	86.077
62	87.296	84.856	91.292	74.116	84.570
63	85.934	83.191	90.296	72.030	82.987
64	84.481	81.429	89.227	69.864	81.339
65	82.944	79.572	88.080	67.620	79.631
66	81.310	77.598	87.023	65.300	77.843
67	79.570	75.504	85.727	62.907	75.973
68	77.724	73.286	84.407	60.443	74.021
69	75.773	70.944	82.989	57.918	71.988
70	73.704	68.477	81.470	55.332	69.873
71	71.523	65.881	79.840	52.695	67.662
72	69.220	63.156	78.092	50.014	65.357
73	66.797	60.307	76.218	47.302	62.960
74	64.259	57.340	74.213	44.564	60.473
75	61.605	54.263	72.076	41.816	57.901
76	58.833	51.087	69.798	39.066	55.220
77	55.944	47.825	67.362	36.300	52.436

1989 U. S. POPULATION

	TOTAL POPULATION	WHITE MALE	WHITE FEMALE	BLACK MALE	BLACK FEMALE
78	52.951	44.495	64.769	33.542	49.559
79	49.859	41.116	62.023	30.803	46.598
80	46.683	37.710	59.120	28.100	43.566
81	43.270	34.172	56.069	25.449	40.318
82	39.640	30.540	52.711	22.741	36.871
83	35.826	26.864	49.053	20.025	33.257
84	31.868	23.202	45.104	17.341	29.520
85	27.827	19.619	40.891	14.718	25.718
86	23.778	16.188	36.463	12.213	21.920
87	19.807	12.981	31.883	9.874	18.210
88	16.012	10.069	27.238	7.746	14.676
89	12.491	7.510	22.637	5.867	11.411
90	9.338	5.349	18.203	4.266	8.500
91	6.634	3.605	14.067	2.956	6.015
92	4.429	2.274	10.360	1.934	3.999
93	2.740	1.323	7.194	1.182	2.462
94	1.541	.696	4.645	.665	1.377
95	.767	.323	2.736	.337	.682
96	.325	.127	1.432	.150	.287
97	.110	.039	.640	.057	.097
98	.026	0.000	.230	.017	.023
99	0.000	0.000	.059	0.000	0.000

PROBABILITY OF LIVING TO AGE 'X' STARTING FROM AGE 45

1989 U. S. POPULATION

	TOTAL POPULATION	WHITE MALE	WHITE FEMALE	BLACK MALE	BLACK FEMALE
LIFE EXPECTANCY TO AGE	33.40	31.10	36.10	26.60	32.40
46	99.659	99.602	99.793	98.908	99.526
47	99.289	99.171	99.564	97.911	99.021
48	98.887	98.704	99.312	96.800	98.484
49	98.449	98.198	99.030	95.602	97.910
50	97.972	97.650	98.717	94.331	97.296
51	97.451	97.055	98.370	93.076	96.639
52	96.882	96.401	97.986	91.750	95.933
53	96.259	95.679	97.564	90.354	95.175
54	95.578	94.881	97.100	88.896	94.357
55	94.833	93.999	96.591	87.379	93.479
56	94.027	93.032	96.034	85.802	92.535
57	93.153	91.974	95.425	84.164	91.517
58	92.203	90.820	94.760	82.458	90.407
59	91.170	89.566	94.036	80.676	89.198
60	90.058	88.206	93.247	78.813	87.881
61	88.860	86.739	92.391	76.868	86.460
62	87.571	85.167	91.465	74.841	84.946
63	86.205	83.496	90.467	72.735	83.356
64	84.748	81.728	89.396	70.547	81.701
65	83.206	79.865	88.247	68.282	79.986
66	81.567	77.883	87.188	65.939	78.189
67	79.821	75.781	85.889	63.523	76.311
68	77.969	73.555	84.566	61.035	74.351
69	76.012	71.205	83.146	58.485	72.308
70	73.937	68.729	81.624	55.873	70.184
71	71.749	66.123	79.992	53.210	67.963
72	69.438	63.388	78.240	50.503	65.648
73	67.008	60.528	76.362	47.765	63.240
74	64.462	57.550	74.354	45.000	60.742
75	61.799	54.462	72.212	42.225	58.158
76	59.019	51.274	69.930	39.448	55.466
77	56.121	48.001	67.490	36.656	52.670
78	53.118	44.659	64.892	33.871	49.779

1989 U. S. POPULATION

	TOTAL POPULATION	WHITE MALE	WHITE FEMALE	BLACK MALE	BLACK FEMALE
79	50.016	41.267	62.140	31.104	46.805
80	46.830	37.848	59.232	28.375	43.760
81	43.407	34.297	56.176	25.698	40.497
82	39.765	30.652	52.811	22.964	37.035
83	35.940	26.963	49.146	20.221	33.405
84	31.968	23.287	45.189	17.511	29.652
85	27.915	19.691	40.969	14.862	25.832
86	23.853	16.247	36.532	12.333	22.018
87	19.870	13.029	31.943	9.971	18.291
88	16.063	10.106	27.289	7.822	14.741
89	12.530	7.538	22.680	5.925	11.461
90	9.368	5.368	18.237	4.308	8.538
91	6.655	3.618	14.094	2.985	6.042
92	4.443	2.282	10.380	1.953	4.017
93	2.748	1.328	7.208	1.194	2.473
94	1.545	.699	4.653	.671	1.384
95	.769	.324	2.741	.341	.685
96	.326	.127	1.434	.152	.288
97	.110	.040	.641	.057	.097
98	.027	0.000	.230	.017	.023
99	0.000	0.000	.059	0.000	0.000

PROBABILITY OF LIVING TO AGE 'X' STARTING FROM AGE 46

1989 U. S. POPULATION

	TOTAL POPULATION	WHITE MALE	WHITE FEMALE	BLACK MALE	BLACK FEMALE
LIFE EXPECTANCY TO AGE	32.50	30.20	35.20	25.10	31.50
47	99.629	99.567	99.771	98.992	99.493
48	99.226	99.098	99.518	97.868	98.953
49	98.786	98.591	99.235	96.658	98.376
50	98.307	98.041	98.921	95.372	97.759
51	97.785	97.442	98.574	94.104	97.099
52	97.214	96.787	98.190	92.763	96.390
53	96.589	96.062	97.767	91.352	95.628
54	95.905	95.260	97.301	89.877	94.806
55	95.158	94.375	96.791	88.343	93.924
56	94.349	93.404	96.233	86.750	92.976
57	93.471	92.342	95.623	85.094	91.952
58	92.518	91.183	94.956	83.369	90.838
59	91.482	89.923	94.231	81.567	89.623
60	90.366	88.558	93.440	79.683	88.300
61	89.164	87.086	92.582	77.716	86.872
62	87.871	85.508	91.655	75.668	85.351
63	86.500	83.830	90.655	73.538	83.753
64	85.038	82.055	89.581	71.326	82.091
65	83.491	80.184	88.430	69.035	80.367
66	81.846	78.194	87.369	66.667	78.562
67	80.094	76.084	86.067	64.224	76.675
68	78.236	73.849	84.742	61.708	74.705
69	76.272	71.489	83.318	59.131	72.653
70	74.190	69.003	81.793	56.490	70.518
71	71.994	66.387	80.158	53.798	68.287
72	69.676	63.641	78.402	51.061	65.960
73	67.237	60.770	76.520	48.292	63.541
74	64.682	57.780	74.508	45.497	61.031
75	62.011	54.680	72.362	42.692	58.435
76	59.220	51.479	70.076	39.883	55.730
77	56.313	48.193	67.630	37.060	52.921
78	53.300	44.837	65.026	34.245	50.016
79	50.187	41.432	62.269	31.448	47.028

1989 U. S. POPULATION

	TOTAL POPULATION	WHITE MALE	WHITE FEMALE	BLACK MALE	BLACK FEMALE
80	46.990	38.000	59.355	28.688	43.969
81	43.555	34.434	56.292	25.982	40.690
82	39.901	30.775	52.920	23.217	37.211
83	36.063	27.070	49.248	20.444	33.564
84	32.078	23.380	45.283	17.704	29.793
85	28.010	19.770	41.054	15.026	25.955
86	23.935	16.312	36.608	12.469	22.123
87	19.938	13.081	32.010	10.081	18.378
88	16.118	10.146	27.346	7.908	14.811
89	12.573	7.568	22.727	5.990	11.516
90	9.400	5.390	18.275	4.355	8.579
91	6.678	3.633	14.123	3.018	6.070
92	4.458	2.291	10.401	1.975	4.036
93	2.758	1.333	7.223	1.207	2.485
94	1.551	.702	4.663	.679	1.390
95	.772	.325	2.747	.344	.688
96	.327	.128	1.437	.154	.290
97	.111	.040	.643	.058	.097
98	.027	0.000	.231	.017	.023
99	0.000	0.000	.059	0.000	0.000

PROBABILITY OF LIVING TO AGE 'X' STARTING FROM AGE 47

1989 U. S. POPULATION

	TOTAL POPULATION	WHITE MALE	WHITE FEMALE	BLACK MALE	BLACK FEMALE
LIFE EXPECTANCY TO AGE	31.60	29.30	34.30	25.90	30.70
48	99.595	99.529	99.746	98.865	99.457
49	99.154	99.019	99.463	97.642	98.877
50	98.673	98.467	99.148	96.343	98.257
51	98.149	97.866	98.800	95.062	97.594
52	97.576	97.208	98.415	93.707	96.882
53	96.948	96.480	97.991	92.282	96.115
54	96.262	95.674	97.524	90.793	95.290
55	95.512	94.785	97.013	89.243	94.402
56	94.700	93.810	96.454	87.633	93.450
57	93.820	92.743	95.842	85.960	92.421
58	92.863	91.579	95.174	84.218	91.301
59	91.822	90.315	94.447	82.398	90.079
60	90.702	88.944	93.655	80.494	88.750
61	89.496	87.464	92.795	78.508	87.315
62	88.198	85.880	91.865	76.438	85.786
63	86.822	84.195	90.863	74.286	84.180
64	85.355	82.411	89.787	72.053	82.509
65	83.802	80.532	88.633	69.738	80.776
66	82.151	78.534	87.570	67.346	78.962
67	80.393	76.415	86.265	64.878	77.065
68	78.528	74.170	84.936	62.337	75.085
69	76.557	71.800	83.509	59.733	73.023
70	74.467	69.303	81.981	57.065	70.877
71	72.262	66.675	80.342	54.346	68.635
72	69.935	63.918	78.582	51.580	66.297
73	67.488	61.034	76.696	48.784	63.865
74	64.923	58.032	74.679	45.960	61.342
75	62.242	54.918	72.528	43.126	58.733
76	59.441	51.703	70.236	40.289	56.014
77	56.522	48.403	67.785	37.438	53.190
78	53.498	45.032	65.175	34.593	50.271
79	50.374	41.612	62.412	31.768	47.267
80	47.165	38.165	59.491	28.980	44.193

1989 U. S. POPULATION

	TOTAL POPULATION	WHITE MALE	WHITE FEMALE	BLACK MALE	BLACK FEMALE
81	43.718	34.584	56.421	26.247	40.897
82	40.050	30.909	53.042	23.454	37.401
83	36.197	27.188	49.361	20.652	33.735
84	32.197	23.482	45.387	17.884	29.945
85	28.115	19.856	41.148	15.179	26.088
86	24.024	16.383	36.692	12.596	22.235
87	20.012	13.138	32.083	10.183	18.471
88	16.178	10.190	27.409	7.989	14.887
89	12.620	7.601	22.779	6.051	11.575
90	9.435	5.413	18.317	4.400	8.623
91	6.702	3.648	14.155	3.048	6.101
92	4.475	2.301	10.425	1.995	4.056
93	2.768	1.339	7.239	1.219	2.498
94	1.556	.705	4.674	.686	1.397
95	.774	.327	2.753	.348	.692
96	.328	.128	1.441	.155	.291
97	.111	.040	.644	.058	.098
98	.027	0.000	.231	.017	.023
99	0.000	0.000	.059	0.000	0.000

PROBABILITY OF LIVING TO AGE 'X' STARTING FROM AGE 48

1989 U. S. POPULATION

	TOTAL POPULATION	WHITE MALE	WHITE FEMALE	BLACK MALE	BLACK FEMALE
LIFE EXPECTANCY TO AGE	30.70	28.40	33.40	24.40	29.80
49	99.557	99.488	99.716	98.763	99.417
50	99.074	98.933	99.401	97.449	98.794
51	98.548	98.329	99.052	96.153	98.127
52	97.973	97.668	98.666	94.783	97.410
53	97.343	96.936	98.240	93.342	96.640
54	96.653	96.127	97.773	91.835	95.810
55	95.900	95.234	97.260	90.267	94.918
56	95.085	94.254	96.699	88.639	93.960
57	94.201	93.182	96.086	86.947	92.926
58	93.240	92.013	95.417	85.184	91.799
59	92.196	90.742	94.688	83.344	90.571
60	91.071	89.364	93.893	81.418	89.234
61	89.860	87.878	93.031	79.409	87.791
62	88.557	86.286	92.099	77.316	86.254
63	87.175	84.593	91.094	75.139	84.639
64	85.702	82.801	90.016	72.880	82.959
65	84.142	80.913	88.859	70.539	81.217
66	82.485	78.906	87.793	68.119	79.393
67	80.720	76.776	86.485	65.623	77.486
68	78.847	74.521	85.153	63.052	75.495
69	76.868	72.140	83.722	60.419	73.422
70	74.769	69.631	82.190	57.720	71.264
71	72.556	66.991	80.546	54.969	69.010
72	70.220	64.220	78.782	52.173	66.658
73	67.762	61.323	76.891	49.344	64.213
74	65.187	58.306	74.869	46.488	61.677
75	62.495	55.177	72.713	43.621	59.054
76	59.683	51.948	70.415	40.752	56.320
77	56.752	48.632	67.958	37.868	53.481
78	53.716	45.245	65.341	34.990	50.546
79	50.579	41.809	62.571	32.133	47.525
80	47.357	38.346	59.643	29.313	44.434
81	43.895	34.748	56.565	26.548	41.121

1989 U. S. POPULATION

	TOTAL POPULATION	WHITE MALE	WHITE FEMALE	BLACK MALE	BLACK FEMALE
82	40.212	31.055	53.177	23.723	37.605
83	36.344	27.317	49.486	20.890	33.919
84	32.328	23.593	45.503	18.089	30.108
85	28.229	19.950	41.253	15.353	26.230
86	24.122	16.461	36.785	12.740	22.357
87	20.093	13.200	32.165	10.300	18.572
88	16.243	10.238	27.478	8.080	14.968
89	12.671	7.637	22.837	6.121	11.638
90	9.473	5.439	18.363	4.450	8.670
91	6.730	3.666	14.191	3.083	6.135
92	4.493	2.312	10.452	2.018	4.078
93	2.779	1.345	7.258	1.233	2.511
94	1.563	.708	4.686	.693	1.405
95	.778	.328	2.760	.352	.695
96	.329	.129	1.444	.157	.293
97	.111	.040	.646	.059	.098
98	.027	0.000	.232	.018	.024
99	0.000	0.000	.059	0.000	0.000

PROBABILITY OF LIVING TO AGE 'X' STARTING FROM AGE 49

1989 U. S. POPULATION

	TOTAL POPULATION	WHITE MALE	WHITE FEMALE	BLACK MALE	BLACK FEMALE
LIFE EXPECTANCY TO AGE	29.80	27.50	32.40	23.70	29.00
50	99.515	99.442	99.684	98.670	99.373
51	98.987	98.835	99.334	97.358	98.702
52	98.408	98.170	98.947	95.970	97.982
53	97.776	97.435	98.520	94.511	97.207
54	97.083	96.621	98.051	92.985	96.372
55	96.327	95.724	97.538	91.398	95.474
56	95.508	94.739	96.975	89.749	94.511
57	94.620	93.662	96.360	88.036	93.471
58	93.655	92.486	95.688	86.251	92.338
59	92.606	91.209	94.957	84.387	91.102
60	91.476	89.824	94.161	82.438	89.758
61	90.260	88.331	93.296	80.404	88.306
62	88.951	86.730	92.361	78.284	86.760
63	87.563	85.028	91.354	76.080	85.136
64	86.083	83.227	90.272	73.793	83.446
65	84.517	81.330	89.112	71.422	81.693
66	82.852	79.312	88.043	68.972	79.859
67	81.079	77.171	86.731	66.445	77.940
68	79.198	74.905	85.395	63.842	75.938
69	77.210	72.511	83.961	61.175	73.852
70	75.102	69.990	82.424	58.443	71.682
71	72.879	67.336	80.776	55.658	69.414
72	70.532	64.551	79.007	52.826	67.049
73	68.064	61.639	77.110	49.962	64.590
74	65.477	58.606	75.082	47.070	62.039
75	62.773	55.461	72.920	44.168	59.400
76	59.948	52.215	70.616	41.262	56.650
77	57.005	48.882	68.151	38.342	53.794
78	53.955	45.478	65.527	35.429	50.842
79	50.804	42.024	62.749	32.535	47.804
80	47.568	38.543	59.812	29.680	44.695
81	44.091	34.926	56.726	26.880	41.362
82	40.391	31.215	53.328	24.020	37.826

| | 1989 U. S. POPULATION | | | | |
	TOTAL POPULATION	WHITE MALE	WHITE FEMALE	BLACK MALE	BLACK FEMALE
83	36.506	27.457	49.627	21.151	34.118
84	32.472	23.714	45.632	18.316	30.285
85	28.354	20.052	41.370	15.546	26.384
86	24.229	16.545	36.890	12.900	22.488
87	20.183	13.268	32.256	10.429	18.681
88	16.316	10.291	27.557	8.182	15.056
89	12.728	7.676	22.902	6.197	11.706
90	9.515	5.467	18.416	4.506	8.721
91	6.760	3.685	14.232	3.122	6.171
92	4.513	2.324	10.482	2.043	4.102
93	2.792	1.352	7.278	1.249	2.526
94	1.570	.712	4.699	.702	1.413
95	.781	.330	2.768	.356	.699
96	.331	.129	1.448	.159	.295
97	.112	.040	.648	.060	.099
98	.027	0.000	.232	.018	.024
99	0.000	0.000	.060	0.000	0.000

PROBABILITY OF LIVING TO AGE 'X' STARTING FROM AGE 50

1989 U. S. POPULATION

	TOTAL POPULATION	WHITE MALE	WHITE FEMALE	BLACK MALE	BLACK FEMALE
LIFE EXPECTANCY TO AGE	28.90	26.70	31.50	23.00	28.20
51	99.469	99.390	99.649	98.670	99.325
52	98.888	98.721	99.260	97.264	98.600
53	98.252	97.982	98.833	95.785	97.820
54	97.557	97.164	98.362	94.239	96.980
55	96.797	96.261	97.847	92.630	96.077
56	95.974	95.270	97.282	90.959	95.107
57	95.081	94.187	96.665	89.223	94.060
58	94.112	93.005	95.992	87.414	92.920
59	93.057	91.721	95.258	85.525	91.677
60	91.922	90.328	94.459	83.549	90.324
61	90.700	88.826	93.592	81.487	88.863
62	89.384	87.217	92.654	79.339	87.307
63	87.990	85.505	91.643	77.106	85.673
64	86.503	83.694	90.558	74.787	83.972
65	84.929	81.786	89.394	72.385	82.209
66	83.256	79.757	88.322	69.902	80.362
67	81.474	77.604	87.006	67.340	78.432
68	79.584	75.325	85.666	64.703	76.417
69	77.586	72.918	84.227	62.000	74.318
70	75.468	70.382	82.685	59.231	72.135
71	73.234	67.714	81.032	56.408	69.852
72	70.876	64.913	79.257	53.538	67.472
73	68.395	61.985	77.355	50.635	64.998
74	65.796	58.935	75.320	47.705	62.430
75	63.079	55.773	73.151	44.763	59.775
76	60.240	52.508	70.840	41.819	57.007
77	57.283	49.156	68.367	38.859	54.134
78	54.218	45.733	65.735	35.906	51.163
79	51.052	42.260	62.948	32.974	48.106
80	47.800	38.759	60.002	30.080	44.977
81	44.306	35.122	56.906	27.243	41.623
82	40.588	31.390	53.497	24.344	38.064
83	36.684	27.611	49.785	21.436	34.334

1989 U. S. POPULATION

	TOTAL POPULATION	WHITE MALE	WHITE FEMALE	BLACK MALE	BLACK FEMALE
84	32.630	23.847	45.777	18.563	30.476
85	28.493	20.165	41.501	15.755	26.550
86	24.347	16.638	37.007	13.074	22.630
87	20.281	13.342	32.359	10.570	18.799
88	16.395	10.349	27.644	8.292	15.151
89	12.790	7.719	22.975	6.281	11.780
90	9.562	5.497	18.474	4.567	8.776
91	6.793	3.705	14.277	3.164	6.210
92	4.535	2.337	10.515	2.071	4.128
93	2.805	1.360	7.302	1.265	2.542
94	1.577	.716	4.714	.712	1.422
95	.785	.332	2.776	.361	.704
96	.332	.130	1.453	.161	.296
97	.112	.041	.650	.061	.100
98	.027	0.000	.233	.018	.024
99	0.000	0.000	.060	0.000	0.000

Cases

B

Baulieu v Elliot, 434 P2d 665
(Alaska 1967) §§5.02, 18.01

C

Chesapeake & Ohio RR v Kelly, 241
US 485 (1916) §5.02

H

Higgins v Kinebrew Motors, Inc, 547
F2d 1223 (5th Cir 1977) §14.12

K

Kuczkowski v Bolubasz, 491 Pa 561,
421 A2d 1027 (1980) §5.02

N

Norfolk & Western Ry v Liepelt, 444
US 490, *rehg denied*, 445 US 972
(1980) §15.02

Annotations

Annotation, *Propriety of Considering Future Income Taxes in Awarding Damages Under Federal Tort Claims Act*, 47 ALR Fed 735 (1980) §15.02

Annotation, *Propriety of Taking Income Tax into Consideration in Fixing Damages in Personal Injury or Death Action*, 16 ALR4th 589 (1983) §15.02

Annotation, *Validity and Construction of State Statute or Rule Allowing Changing Rate Prejudgment Interest in Torts Actions*, 40 ALR4th 147 (1985) §2.11

Authorities

L. Bassett, The Use of Economists in Personal Injury Actions (No 2 1984) §17.02

K. Black, Jr & H. Skipper, Jr, Insurance (11th ed 1987) §12.03

W. Boumol & A. Binder, Economics (3d ed 1985) §14.02

Michael L. Brookshire & Stan V. Smith, Economic/Hedonic Damages: The Practice Book for Plaintiff and Defense Attorneys (1990) §11.01

Michael L. Brookshire & Stan V. Smith, Hedonic Damages and Personal Injury: A Conceptual Approach, III, No 1 Forensic Econs (Dec 1989) §11.07

W. Keith Bryant, Cathleen D. Zick & Hyoshin Kim, *Household Work: What's It Worth and Why?*, Cornell Univ Bulletin 322 IB228 (1992) §§2.10, 9.05, 21.03, 21.05, 23.02

Bureau of Labor Statistics, Civilian Labor Force Participation Rate By Sex, Race and Age, Handbook of Labor Statistics, Bulletin 2340, at 25-30 (Aug 1989) §23.02

Chapman, *The Consumer Price Index: A History and Source List*, 13, No 4 Reference Servs Rev 47 (Winter 1985) §4.17

E. Cheit, Injury and Recovery in the Course of Employment (1961) §14.04

Douglass, Kenney & Miller, *Which Estimates of Household Production are Best?*, IV, No 1 Forensics Econs (Winter 1990) §9.04

Duns Marketing Serv, Million Dollar Directory (1987) §7.09

Economic Report of the President (1993) §§2.06, 2.07, 2.08, 4.20, 5.12, 5.15, 5.16, 7.08, 21.03, 21.05

Federal Reserve Bulletin (Apr 1993) §§2.07, 21.03

Fisher, Ann, Lauraine G. Chestnut & Daniel M. Violette, *The Value of*

Reducing Risks of Death: A Note of New Evidence, 8, No 1 Policy Analysis & Mgmt (Winter 89) §11.06

Franz, *Should Income Taxes Be Included When Calculating Lost Earnings*, Trial, Oct 1982, at 53 §14.03

Franz, *Simplified Calculation of Future Lost Earning*, Trial, Aug 1977, at 34 §18.02

Gauger & Walker, *The Dollar Value of Household Work*, 60 Info Bull 11 (New York State College of Human Ecology 1980) §9.03

Gilbert, 4, No 2 Forensic Econs 175 (1991) §14.04

Harju & Adams, 4, No 2 Forensic Econs 65 (1990) §14.04

Harris, *Selecting Income Growth and Discount Rates in Wrongful Death and Injury Cases: Comment*, 44 Noa J Risk & Ins 117 (Mar 1977) §5.17

Health and Human Servs, Social Security Admin, Disability Survey (Apr 1981) §8.08

Ibbotson Assocs, Stock, Bond, Bills and Inflation: 1993 Yearbook Market Results, 1926-1992 (Chicago 1993) §5.19

R. Ibbotson & R. Sinquenfield, Stocks, Bonds, Bills and Inflation: The Past and the Future (Fin Analyst Research Foundation, Univ of Va 1987) §5.17

Industrial Production, Federal Reserve Bulletin (Apr 1993) §2.08

N. Jacob & R. Pettit, Investments (1984) §5.07

R. Kolb, Investments (1986) §5.16

Ted R. Miller, The Plausible Range for the Value of Life—Red Herrings Among the Mackerel, III, No 3 Forensic Econs 17 (Fall 1990) §11.06

Patton & Nelson, 4, No 2 Forensic Econs 233 (1990) §14.04

S. Porter, New Money Book for the 80's (1980) §§2.10, 9.02

G. Reynolds, The Mortality Merchants (1978) §12.02

P. Rose & D. Fraser, Financial Institutions (2d ed 1985) §2.18

Standard & Poor's Register of Corps (McGraw-Hill, Inc 1987) §7.09

Statistical Abstracts of the United States (1992) §§4.16, 7.10, 23.01, 23.02

Stewart & Greenhalgh, *Work History Patterns and the Occupational Attainment of Women*, 94 Econ J 498 (Sept 1984) §9.02

US Department of Commerce, Bureau of the Census, Economics and Statistics Administration (112th ed 1992) §§12.02, 17.04

US Dept of Labor, Bureau of Labor Statistics, Employment Hours and Earnings, United States, 1909-1990, 2 volumes (Washington, DC) §4.15

US Dept of Labor, Bureau of Labor Statistics, Expectation of Life and

Expected Deaths By Race, Sex and Age: 1989 (1992) §12.02

US Dept of Labor, Bureau of Labor Statistics, Special Labor Force Report, Length of Working Life for Men and Women (rev ed 1976) §16.03

US Dept of Labor, Bureau of Labor Statistics, Unemployment Rates by Sex, Race, and Age, Handbook of Labor Statistics, Bulletin 2340 at 136-41 (Aug 1989) §23.02

US Dept of Labor, Bureau of Labor Statistics, Worklife Estimates: Effects of Race and Education, Bulletin 2254 (Feb 1986) §§16.01, 16.03

US Dept of Labor, Revised Equivalency Scale for Urban Families of Different Size, Age and Composition, Derived from the Bureau of Labor Statistics of Consumer Expenditures (1960-61) §14.04

US Dept of Labor, Technical Notes, Current Population Survey (Household Survey), Handbook of Labor Statistics, Bulletin 2217 (June 1985) §§13.02, 13.04

US Govt Printing Office, Standard Indus Classification Tables Manual (Washington, DC ___) §7.09

US National Center for Health Statistics, *Life Expectancy Tables*, Vital Statistics of US (1989) §23.02

J. Viscione & G. Roberts, Contemporary Financial Management (1987) §12.04

R. Vukas, Description of SIC Codes (Washburn Univ 1987) (unpublished manuscript) §7.09

T. Yamane, Statistics, An Introductory Analysis (1964) §17.03

Index

G